PSYCHOSOMATIC DISORDERS

PSYCHOSOMATIC DISORDERS

A Psychophysiological Approach
to Etiology and Treatment

Edited by

Stephen N. Haynes
Linda Gannon

PRAEGER

PRAEGER SPECIAL STUDIES • PRAEGER SCIENTIFIC

Library of Congress Cataloging in Publication Data

Main entry under title:

Psychosomatic disorders.

Includes bibliographies.
Contents: The psychophysiology of psychosomatic dis-
orders / Linda Gannon—The problem of pain / C. Richard
Chapman and Margo Wyckoff—Psychological and physiologi-
cal factors in the development, maintenance, and treat-
ment of menstrual disorders / Linda Gannon—[etc.]
1. Medicine, Psychosomatic. I. Haynes, Stephen N.
II. Gannon, Linda. [DNLM: 1. Psychophysiologic disorders.
WM 90 P974]
RC49.P783   616.08   81-10754
ISBN: 0-03-059458-8   AACR2

Published in 1981 by Praeger Publishers
CBS Educational and Professional Publishing
A Division of CBS, Inc.
521 Fifth Avenue, New York, New York 10175 U.S.A.

© 1981 by Praeger Publishers

123456789   145   987654321

Printed in the United States of America

3·7·90

PREFACE

Psychosomatic disorders have received increasing attention from researchers and clinicians from a variety of disciplines. Psychologists, psychiatrists, social workers, physicians, and other professionals in the fields of mental and medical health have, in recent years, become more aware of the interaction between medical, psychological, and social factors in affecting the incidence, severity, and treatment of numerous organic illnesses. The increasing interdisciplinary research on these disorders reflects the growing recognition that multiple factors interact in the etiology and treatment of these disorders.

Psychosomatic disorders have traditionally included a number of medical problems affecting millions of individuals. The importance of psychosomatic disorders stems not only from their high incidence but also from their frequently severe medical and psychological ramifications. Many psychosomatic disorders are associated with impairment in personal and social functioning and occupational and academic performance and, in some cases, are associated with considerable organic damage or death. There is little doubt that they are a major health problem.

Historically, psychosomatic disorders have been conceptualized within rather narrow medical or psychodynamic models. These theoretical formulations provided some insight into the etiology and treatment of psychosomatic disorders but did not stimulate rigorous empirical investigation. Recent attempts to understand psychosomatic disorders have involved more highly controlled experimental methods with contributions from the fields of medicine, psychology, physiology, pharmacology, and, particularly, psychophysiology. As a result, we have significantly increased our understanding of these disorders and assisted in identifying and testing possible treatments. Advances in our understanding of these disorders has also been facilitated by an increasingly sophisticated measurement technology, such as electrophysiology, telemetry, computer analysis, and physiological feedback.

This book is an attempt to present the recent, experimentally based research on the etiology and treatment of selected psychosomatic disorders. The book emphasizes a psychophysiological approach to psychosomatic disorders, which implies an emphasis on controlled investigation and an integration of research techniques and findings from a number of disciplines. It is hoped that this volume will acquaint the reader with recent developments in the conceptualization, assessment, and treatment of psychosomatic disorders and serve as a stimulus for additional research.

The disorders selected for inclusion in this volume (pain, cardiac dysfunctions, ulcers, sexual dysfunctions, obesity, migraine headache, muscle-contraction headache, asthma, hypertension, and menstrual dysfunctions) represent a variety of medically or organically manifested dysfunctions in which nonmedical factors have been presumed to play a significant role. As will be noted in the individual chapters, the relative degree of influence of medical and nonmedical factors varies considerably among the disorders. It is also evident that there is considerable variability in the methods and quality of research endeavors associated with the various disorders.

In an attempt to integrate the presentation of medical and nonmedical factors in each of the disorders, most chapters are organized in a similar fashion. Presented in each chapter are the physiological bases of the various disorders, research on medical and nonmedical etiologies, assessment and measurement procedures, and issues and research concerned with treatment. Integrated within each chapter is a presentation of issues, methods, and trends within the area. Because much of the research presented involves psychophysiological concepts, methods, and principles, the first chapter presents an overview of the autonomic nervous system and general factors assumed to be associated with psychosomatic disorders.

The book will be of particular interest to psychologists, psychiatrists, internists, social workers, nurses, and others who are interested in psychosomatic disorders from a clinical or research perspective. The book is also suited for graduate and medical courses focusing on psychosomatic disorders.

CONTENTS

LIST OF CONTRIBUTORS

Henry E. Adams, Professor and Chairman, Division of Social and Behavioral Sciences, Department of Psychology, University of Georgia, Athens, Georgia.

A. Barney Alexander, Director, Department of Psychophysiology, National Jewish Hospital/National Asthma Center, Denver, Colorado.

Richard R. Bootzin, Professor, Department of Psychology, Northwestern University, Evanston, Illinois.

Phillip J. Brantley, Assistant Professor, Louisiana State University and Medical School, Baton Rouge, Louisiana.

C. Richard Chapman, Associate Professor, Departments of Anesthesiology, Psychiatry and Behavioral Sciences, and Psychology, University of Washington, Seattle, Washington.

S. Thomas Elder, Professor, Department of Psychology, University of New Orleans, New Orleans, Louisiana.

Linda Gannon, Associate Professor, Department of Psychology, Southern Illinois University, Carbondale, Illinois.

Dolores J. Geoffray, Research Associate, Department of Psychology, University of New Orleans, New Orleans, Louisiana.

John P. Hatch, Research Instructor, Department of Psychiatry, School of Medicine, The University of Texas Health Science Center at San Antonio, San Antonio, Texas.

Stephen N. Haynes, Professor, Department of Psychology, Southern Illinois University, Carbondale, Illinois.

Julia R. Heiman, Research Scientist and Research Assistant Professor, Long Island Research Institute, Department of Psychiatry and Behavioral Science, School of Medicine, Health Sciences Center, State University of New York at Stony Brook, Stony Brook, New York.

D. Balfour Jeffrey, Associate Professor, Department of Psychology, University of Montana, Missoula, Montana.

Maxwell R. Knauss, Clinical Psychologist, Greater Lakes Mental Health Center, Tacoma, Washington.

Robert D. McAfee, Senior Scientist, Veterans Administration Medical Center, New Orleans, Louisiana.

Benjamin H. Natelson, Associate Professor and Research Associate, Department of Neurosciences, College of Medicine and Dentistry of New Jersey, New Jersey Medical School, Veterans Administration Medical Center, East Orange, New Jersey.

Curt A. Sandman, Professor of Psychiatry, Adjunct Professor of Psychology, University of California, Irvine, California and Director of Research, Fairview Hospital, Costa Mesa, California.

Ellie T. Sturgis, Assistant Professor, Department of Psychology, University of North Carolina, Chapel Hill, North Carolina.

Barbara B. Walker, Assistant Professor, University of Michigan, Ann Arbor, Michigan.

Margo Wyckoff, Clinical Lecturer, Department of Anesthesiology and Assistant Director, Pain Clinic, Swedish Hospital Medical Center, Seattle, Washington.

Hildreth D. Youkilis, Assistant Professor, Department of Psychology, Boston University, Boston, Massachusetts.

PSYCHOSOMATIC DISORDERS

1

THE PSYCHOPHYSIOLOGY OF PSYCHOSOMATIC DISORDERS

Linda Gannon

The empirical investigation of the etiology and treatment of psychosomatic disorders is of relatively recent interest to practitioners and researchers. Previously, psychosomatic disorders were primarily viewed in a medical or psychoanalytic context. Etiology was viewed in a broad sense, that is, personality and behavioral characteristics and/or environmental factors were indirectly implicated but were placed within conceptual systems which precluded empirical validation. More recently, however, interest in psychosomatic disorders has spread to other disciplines which are strongly research based, such as psychophysiology, behavioral therapy, and sociology. The medical profession, with the advent of family practice as a speciality, has also demonstrated an increased interest in prevention and research. These factors are at least partially responsible for the recent empirical developments in psychosomatic etiology and treatment.

The task of defining a psychosomatic disorder is difficult and, admittedly, somewhat arbitrary. In the present context, *psychosomatic disorders* are defined as those disorders which are accompanied by observable or self-reported physical change, are exacerbated by psychological states or environmental stress, are chronic, and are commonly, although not exclusively, treated with psychological therapies. Clearly, not all disorders which meet these criteria are included in this book; we have chosen to include only those disorders which have been the topic of sufficient research to make a summary of the relevant literature useful and coherent. With all the disorders included in this volume, it has been traditionally assumed that behavioral and environmental factors account for a "significant" proportion of the variance in occurrence, duration, or intensity. There

The author wishes to thank Stephen N. Haynes for his helpful comments on earlier versions of this chapter.

or psychological etiology for psychosomatic disorders and which view biofeedback as a possible mode of treatment.

Although functional differences between the somatic and autonomic nervous systems are not particularly distinct, the two systems do have clear anatomical differences. At the level of the spinal cord, cell bodies of the efferent fibers of the somatic nervous system lie inside the spinal cord, while the efferent cell bodies of the autonomic system lie outside the spinal cord. The *interneurons* of the somatic system, lying inside the cord, allow for synapses with other cells in the cord. The resulting complex interconnections provide the precision and coordination necessary for normal skeletal muscle activity. For example, stimulation of a flexor reflex involves not only the flexion of the target muscle but also the extension of the antagonistic muscle. Connections within the spinal cord provide this type of coordination, which is necessary for complex muscle activity, such as walking.

The activity of the autonomic nervous system, with synapses outside the spinal cord, is far less precise and coordinated than that of the somatic system. The efferent cells of the ANS are peripheral to the spinal cord, either in ganglia or in isolated, peripheral groups of cells. A more detailed analysis requires dividing the autonomic nervous system into the sympathetic and parasympathetic branches.

Sympathetic and Parasympathetic Nervous Systems

The distinction between the sympathetic and parasympathetic nervous systems is based on the anatomical position of the efferent cells and the section of the spinal cord from which the interneuron leaves. Interneuron axons of the sympathetic nervous system leave from the *thoracic* and *lumbar* regions of the spinal cord; those of the parasympathetic system leave from the *cranial* and *sacral* regions. After these axons leave the spinal cord, they synapse with the cell bodies of the efferent fibers. In the sympathetic system, the efferent cell bodies lie in the *lateral sympathetic chain* — a ganglion close to the spinal cord — or in more distantly situated ganglia. The efferent cell bodies of the parasympathetic nervous system are not in ganglia but, rather, are isolated and lie close to the organ which they innervate. The interneurons are commonly referred to as *preganglionic* fibers, and the efferent neurons as *postganglionic* fibers. In general, the preganglionic fibers of the sympathetic system are short, since they synapse close to the spinal cord, while those of the parasympathetic system are long, since they synapse near the effector organ. The opposite relationship holds for the postganglionic fibers.

The two systems also differ in the chemical substance of neural transmission. In both the sympathetic and parasympathetic systems, *acetylcholine* is the neurotransmitter for the preganglionic cells. The neurotransmitter released by the postganglionic axon to stimulate the effector organ, however, is *norepinephrine* in the sympathetic cells and acetylcholine in the parasympathetic cells. There are two exceptions to this rule: the sympathetic fibers that innervate the sweat glands and those responsible for vasodilation of the blood vessels supplying skeletal muscles are cholinergic. In addition, the adrenal medulla is innervated by sympathetic preganglionic fibers which are cholinergic.

Both the sympathetic and parasympathetic nervous systems tend to produce antagonistic effects on the organs and smooth muscles which they supply. The result is coordinated activity, in which both systems contribute to produce a change. For example, an increase in heart rate can be achieved by increased sympathetic activity, decreased parasympathetic activity, or both. This general rule does not hold in cases where an organ is innervated by only one division. Most salivary glands, the stomach glands, and the pancreas receive only para-sympathetic innervation; the sweat glands, most blood vessels, the uterus, and the adrenal medulla receive only sympathetic innervation. In these instances of single division innervation, provision for bidirectional changes is maintained in one of two ways. In some cases, such as the peripheral arterioles of the skin, sympathetic innervation is solely adrenergic and tonically active. Increases and decreases in activity are achieved by the same fibers − in this case, vasocon-striction and vasodilation are produced by variation in the tonic activity of sympathetic vasoconstrictor fibers. In other cases, the antagonistic activity is provided by two distinctly different types of fibers which have opposing action. For example, in the case of the blood vessels supplying skeletal muscle, sympa-thetic adrenergic nerves produce vasoconstriction, while sympathetic cholinergic nerves produce vasodilation.

The sympathetic nervous system responds to physical or psychological stress and creates conditions for optimal performance of the skeletal muscles. Activation of the sympathetic nervous system may produce such changes as increases in heart rate, blood sugar, sweating, and vasoconstriction of peripheral blood vessels and decreases in gastric motility. The parasympathetic nervous system, on the other hand, tends to maintain a homeostatic state for restoration of cellular functions. Some consequences of parasympathetic activity are decreases in heart rate, increases in gastrointestinal functions, and excretion of waste products.

The degree of integration of the two systems differs considerably. Sympa-thetic activity tends to be general; changes in many bodily functions occur together, and these changes are relatively long lasting. In contrast, parasympa-thetic activity is localized and relatively brief. These differences have both ana-tomical and chemical causes. As stated above, the preganglionic fibers of the sympathetic nervous system synapse in sympathetic ganglia just outside the spinal cord. The ganglia provide the possibility of intercommunication among the cells and simultaneous stimulation of more than one postganglionic fiber, thus producing a diffuse response. The preganglionic fibers of the parasympathetic nervous system, on the other hand, are long, synapse close to the target organ, and allow little opportunity for conduction to more than one site from a single preganglionic fiber.

One effect of sympathetic activation is stimulation of the adrenal medulla, which secretes norepinephrine, the neurotransmitter for sympathetic postganglionic fibers. Thus, increased norepinephrine in the bloodstream from the adrenal medulla serves to potentiate sympathetic activity by directly stimulating the target organs. A further chemical difference between the two systems is in the method of disposal of the neurotransmitters subsequent to release and stimulation. Acetylcholine is inactivated through hydrolysis by acetylcholinesterase, a substance continually present in all body tissues. Norepinephrine, on the other hand, is largely inactivated through reuptake by adrenergic nerve terminals. The reuptake process is slower than hydrolysis, and this time differential contributes to the relatively longer lasting effects of sympathetic activity compared with parasympathetic activity.

Thus, the sympathetic and parasympathetic branches of the autonomic nervous system act in a synergistic manner to provide the body with the metabolic requirements necessary to cope with physical and psychological stress while maintaining a relatively constant internal milieu. Most psychosomatic disorders involving the ANS involve changes consistent with sympathetic arousal. Since the anatomical and chemical characteristics of the sympathetic nervous system are such as to promote a generalized arousal common to all systems, one must ask why an individual develops a disorder in one particular system. This issue is addressed in greater detail in a later section, but, in general, it is presumed that persons exhibit differential responsiveness; that is, an individual responds to stress with his or her particular idiosyncratic pattern of autonomic activity. Furthermore, the system in which an individual exhibits the maximal response may be the system most susceptible to the development of psychosomatic symptomatology. The cause of these individual differences may be at the level of neural and receptor activity and due to genetic, traumatic, or disease factors. On the other hand, the fact that central nervous system structures can influence autonomic activity extends the possible causes to psychological and learning factors.

Central Nervous System Influences on Autonomic Activity

The functional activities of the autonomic nervous system are, for the most part, automatic, but cortical influences can and do influence ANS activity. In general, the complexity of the regulation varies from the simple and direct action of reflexes in the spinal cord to the more complicated emotional manifestations originating in the cortex. In addition to effecting changes in autonomic activity, central structures are also involved in the integration of somatic and autonomic functions.

The lowest central nervous system structures involved with autonomic activity lie in the *brain stem* — specifically in the *medulla, pons,* and *dorsal root nucleus of the vagus*. Here there are nuclei specific to the various systems of the autonomic nervous system. For example, the *vasomotor center* in the medulla regulates sympathetic innervation of the heart and peripheral blood vessels. Neurons are present which, when stimulated, increase heart rate and peripheral vasoconstriction; stimulation of other neurons inhibits heart rate and vaso-constriction. In addition to both the facilitating and inhibiting effects in the vasomotor center, the center for parasympathetic activity lies in the dorsal root nucleus of the vagus. Excitation of neurons in this center decreases heart rate. The antagonistic activity from the medulla is due to excitement and inhibition of tonic sympathetic discharge rather than to increased parasympathetic discharge. Another example of brain stem control originates in the respiratory center and consists of distinct nuclei responsible for inspiration and expiration; together, these nuclei regulate rate and depth of respiration.

These centers in the brain stem receive sporadic input from the hypothalamus and cortex and continuous input from internal structures of the body. Input from the latter completes the loop needed for normal homeostatic functioning. Both the vasomotor center and the dorsal root nucleus of the vagus receive connections from *baroreceptors* of the carotid sinus and aortic regions and from atrioventricular junctions and heart ventricles. Stretch receptors in the bronchioles and receptors in the joints, as well as peripheral chemoreceptors, have afferent fibers to the respiratory center. In addition, both the vasomotor center and the respiratory center are locally sensitive to oxygen and carbon dioxide content of the blood. Hence, the centers in the brain stem receive and coordinate information from the peripheral receptors of the body and from the hypothalamus and send out information to the autonomic ganglia in the spinal cord.

The next level of central nervous system control is in the *hypothalamus*. The hypothalamus regulates body and blood temperature, appetite, and food intake, and it coordinates input from the cortex. Electrical stimulation studies suggest that the posterior parts of the hypothalamus are concerned primarily with parasympathetic activity, while the anterior portion plays a role in sympathetic activation. The hypothalamus is said to be responsible for coordinating the defense reaction, which involves increasing blood flow to muscles, increasing blood pressure and heart rate, and increasing vasoconstriction in the skin and intestine, in response to sensory stimulation. In addition, the hypothalamus sends efferent messages to the cortex, relaying information from internal stimuli which require motor responses, such as sexual behavior and eating behavior. Since this structure is also a center for somatic activity, it is likely that basic integration of somatic and autonomic activities occurs here.

The hypothalamus not only has efferent connections with the centers in the brain stem but also has direct connections to the *pituitary gland* and synthesizes the hormones released by the posterior pituitary. The pituitary gland, in turn, secretes hormones which affect the smooth muscle of the blood vessels and uterus, the kidney (vasopressin and oxytocin), and other glands, such as the thyroid (thyrotrophin) and sex glands (gonadotrophins). The hypothalamus also contains feedback receptors for many hormones in the body, thus making it a major center for the integration of autonomic and endocrinic functions.

The most complex level of autonomic regulation, as well as integration of autonomic and somatic functions, is in the *cerebral cortex*. Anatomical evidence — nerve connections between the cortex and the hypothalamus — and physiological evidence — autonomic responses to anticipation of exercise and to psychological stress, as well as studies demonstrating autonomic responses to electrical stimulation of a wide variety of areas of the cortex — suggest a strong cortical component in the regulation of autonomic activity. Indeed, the cortex may be viewed as the mediator of the effect of environmental stress on the ANS. Furthermore, the shape, duration, and/or occurrence of a peripheral autonomic response is dependent upon the intensity, frequency, and meaningfulness of the sensory stimulation; this suggests that the cortex plays the role of a rather subtle tuning mechanism for autonomic activity.

When one views the autonomic nervous system in total, one is struck by the amazing complexity of the system. Autonomic responses to internal or external stimuli are generally described as occurring in a steady-state resting organism. For example, physical exercise produces increased blood flow to the skeletal muscles, vasoconstriction in the skin and gastrointestinal tract, and increased sweating; hot temperatures produce vasodilation in the skin and increased sweating. But what if these two events occur simultaneously? Not only do the central and peripheral structures of the autonomic nervous system integrate sometimes opposing environmental demands, but they also, at the same time, respond to internal stimuli demanding a return to homeostatic functioning. Although central and peripheral structures participate in determining the level of activity in the autonomic nervous system at any particular point in time, the final common pathway for autonomic regulation is in the centers of the brain stem, such as the vasomotor and respiratory centers. These centers ensure that, regardless of environmental and psychological events, the nutritional requirements of the body will be met.

Although structural or chemical abnormalities in the central nervous system may be involved in the etiology of psychosomatic disorders, the influence of the cerebral cortex on autonomic activity allows etiological theory to include psychological and environmental parameters. Thus, individual differences in autonomic patterns may be a consequence of classical or instrumental conditioning, and psychological stress of sufficient magnitude and duration, coupled with an overreactive system, could result in psychosomatic symptomatology.

Ergotropic and Trophotropic Response Systems

The automatic nervous system is but one system in the body which responds to internal and external stimulation; actual physiological functioning involves other systems as well. Response to a threatening stimulus involves not only autonomic activity, such as an increase in heart rate, but nonspecific cortical arousal and increased skeletal muscle tone as well. Physiological balance is based upon reciprocally inhibiting systems termed the *ergotropic* and *trophotropic* systems; these terms represent hypothetical constructs, rather than structural entities, and derive from the observation that certain responses tend to occur together. This reciprocal organization is evidenced, for the most part, in all systems and at all levels. The ergotropic system is characterized by increased sympathetic activity (such as increased heart rate, blood pressure, and sweat secretion and decreased gastrointestinal activity), a high-frequency/low-amplitude electroencephalogram, increased skeletal muscle tone, release of catabolic hormones, and increased activity and emotionality. The trophotropic system is characterized by increased parasympathetic activity (such as decreased heart rate, blood pressure, and sweat secretion and increased gastrointestinal activity), a low-frequency/high-amplitude electroencephalogram, decreased skeletal muscle tone, release of anabolic hormones, and decreased activity. In general, the ergotropic system alerts the individual for action, while the trophotropic system allows rest and concentration on the nutritional demands of the body.

Both types of responses are well integrated to produce an efficient pattern of physiological activity. It is hypothesized that this integration is achieved through distinct structures, connections, and neurotransmitters for each system. For example, the ergotropic system is presumed to be activated via the posterior hypothalamus, which has connections with the vasomotor center in the brain stem and the sympathetic ganglia of the spinal cord. The sympathetic ganglia directly innervate the adrenal medulla, which releases catecholamines to enhance sympathetic activity. The posterior hypothalamus also has connections with the reward system in the medial forebrain bundle, the reticular activating system, which produces cortical arousal, and the motor areas of the cortex, which effect skeletal changes. Similar but different structures and connections exist and may account for trophotropic responses. Further integration within each system may be effected through chemical neurotransmitters. Norepinephrine and dopamine seem to be common to the structures and neurons of the ergotropic system, while the structures and neurons of the trophotropic system tend to utilize serotonin and acetylcholine. Efficiency is further enhanced by reciprocal inhibition and the presence of tonic neural activity; centers which excite one system also directly inhibit the other system by reducing tonic discharges. This reciprocity and tonicity provide the body with the ability to make dramatic changes in a relatively brief period of time.

The fact that autonomic, skeletal, and cortical functions tend to act in concert suggests further possibilities for psychosomatic etiology. Autonomic dysfunction may represent the unconditioned effects of abnormal cortical or skeletal activity. For example, increased activity of the skeletal musculature requires an increased supply of oxygen and would thus cause elevations in cardiovascular activity. Thus, changes in autonomic activity may be secondary to changes in other systems, and dysfunction may not originate in the ANS.

Conclusions

Most current theoretical conceptualizations concerned with the etiology of psychosomatic symptoms postulate an organic predisposition. It is clear from the above discussion that an organic predisposition may originate in any one of numerous anatomical structures or physiological systems throughout the human body and may be the result of heredity, disease, trauma, and/or learning. Furthermore, the search for specific causation is complicated by the possibility that physiological functioning may alter in response to environmental stress. The latter issue is addressed in the next section.

CONCEPTS RELEVANT TO THE ETIOLOGY OF PSYCHOSOMATIC DISORDERS

As mentioned previously, psychosomatics is a relatively young and immature science characterized by a lack of agreement on etiological issues and methods of inquiry. Early theoreticians viewed psychosomatic disorders as products of a particular personality trait or psychological state. For example, Alexander (1950) postulated particular unconscious emotional conflicts specific to each disorder, while Graham (Grace & Graham, 1952) proposed that particular attitudes are associated with each disorder. More recent formulations, however, have included both a psychological component and an organic component and may be appropriately labeled *diathesis-stress models* (Schwartz, 1977; Sternbach, 1966). According to this model, both a diathesis, or predisposing organic state within the individual, and stress or precipitating events are necessary and, together, sufficient for the development of psychosomatic symptoms. Note that while the early theories considered the psychological component as some characteristic of the individual, the later theories included the possibility that environmental events may contribute to the development of a disorder.

For our purposes, given the lack of sufficient research, it would be premature to select a specific model with which to view psychosomatic disorders. On the other hand, a model which is both theoretical and general would provide a context within which one may develop research hypotheses and treatment programs and attempt to integrate diverse information. A diathesis-stress model meets such a need. In the present discussion, the parameters of this model are broadly defined to provide a very general conceptual paradigm with which to view psychosomatic etiology and treatment.

Factors Influencing Predisposition

Early theories assumed that psychosomatic disorders were solely psychogenic. For example, essential hypertension was frequently defined as elevated blood pressure in the absence of organic etiology (Wolf, Cardon, Shepard, & Wolff, 1955). It must be pointed out that *absence of organic etiology* may mean that either the causes are not organic or the lack of knowledge or techniques prevents the identification of organic causes. On the other hand, any adequate theory must account for the fact that given the same degree of subjective stress, some persons develop psychosomatic symptoms and others do not. Furthermore, the theory must specify why an individual develops one disorder rather than another. Thus, an integral component of the more recent etiological theories is a predisposing organic state which renders an individual susceptible to psychosomatic symptoms in general and/or to a specific symdrome.

The organic component is typically defined as susceptibility of, or over-activity and/or damage to, a particular organ system. It is exemplified by *individual-response (I-R) specificity*, a term coined by Engel (1960) to refer to the tendency of an individual to respond maximally and consistently in one particular physiological system. I-R specificity has been commonly accepted as the primary physiological etiology for the development of psychosomatic disorders; in a particularly stressful environment, a person would be expected to develop the psychosomatic disorder associated with the physiological system in which that person shows the greatest response to stress (Cohen, Rickles, & McArthur, 1978; Engel, 1960; Lacey, Kagan, Lacey, & Moss, 1963; Malmo, Shagass, & Davis, 1950; Safranek, 1978; Sternbach, 1966).

I-R specificity has been experimentally demonstrated in a healthy population by Engel (1960). He presented subjects with five stimuli and measured the response magnitude of eight physiological variables. He found that, regardless of the nature of the arousing situation, an individual responds with his or her particular, idiosyncratic pattern of autonomic activity. Additional empirical support for the existence of I-R specificity in a normal population was provided by Sersen, Clausen, and Lidsky (1978). In a further study employing a psychosomatic sample, Engel and Bickford (1961) repeated the previous procedure with twenty hypertensives and twenty normotensives. The frequency of occurrence of I-R specificity, determined by maximal activation, was not different between the two groups, but the hypertensives showed specificity in systolic blood pressure significantly more often that did normotensives.

The experimental methodology used to assess I-R specificity in the studies described above places strict limits on the utility of this concept in understanding and treating psychosomatic disorders. In order to compare responses from different systems, Engel (1960) and Sersen et al. (1978) transformed response magnitude scores to standard scores and then analyzed the standard scores to determine which system was most active. Thus, *maximal activation*, as used here, does not refer to the actual size of the response but to the size of the response relative to other physiological responses in a given individual. Thus, from the study by Engel and Bickford (1961), one cannot conclude that hypertensives were overreactive in blood pressure, only that their blood pressure response was the largest response of those systems measured. Even this last statement requires further qualification.

The *law of initial values*, formulated by Wilder (1956), states that the magnitude and direction of a physiological response to a stimulus are functions, in part, of the prestimulus level. The relationship between response magnitude and prestimulus level is, in normal ranges, linear and negative, that is, the higher the prestimulus level, the smaller the response. This is intuitively obvious and is a result of natural homeostatic processes. Thus, in order to compare different physiological variables in one subject or to compare the same variable across subjects, some believe it necessary to correct for prestimulus levels by analysis of covariance (Benjamin, 1963). For example, a consequence of covariance techniques is that a heart rate response of 10 bpm at a prestimulus level of 120 bpm would be evaluated as larger than a 10-bpm response at a prestimulus level of 60.

Engel and Bickford (1961) used the recommended analysis of covariance in their study. Since their groups were defined according to prestimulus level (hypertensive 140/90 to 220/140 mm Hg), it is likely that the actual magnitude of the hypertensives' blood pressure response was equal to, or smaller than, the magnitude of response in their other physiological systems or the response among the normotensives, but when corrected for prestimulus levels, it was judged to be larger. Thus, although analysis of covariance may be statistically appropriate, it may not be an accurate reflection of the physiological activity of an individual or a group of individuals, particularly when groups are defined according to basal physiological levels.

At this early stage in the acquisition of an empirical base for psychosomatic theory and treatment, simply describing the physiological response patterns of individuals grouped according to psychosomatic disorder might prove to be the most heuristic approach. An excellent example is one provided by Walker and Sandman (1977), who compared resting levels and responses to stress for a variety of physiological systems and a variety of stressors among groups of ulcer patients, arthritics, and normals. The result was a clear and detailed description of physiological response patterns for these individuals. This kind of basic information is clearly necessary for the development of theoretical conceptualizations and programs for the treatment of psychosomatic disorders.

Resting Levels, Response to Stress, and Recovery from Stress

The research on specificity and most theoretical conceptualizations of psychosomatic disorders postulating specificity as the diathesis component have been concerned primarily with the response magnitude of autonomic functions to discrete stimuli. Clearly, the concept of specificity need not be limited to responses but may also include resting levels and recovery functions of autonomic activity.

That resting levels may be of importance in understanding psychosomatic disorders is evidenced by the fact that some disorders, such as hypertension, are defined according to resting physiological levels. For other disorders, it has been shown that during a resting state, parameters of the relevant system differ between persons with and those without a particular disorder. In a relevant study, Vaughn, Pall, and Haynes (1977) compared the resting levels and responses to stress of frontalis electromyogram (EMG) activity in subjects with high and low frequencies of tension headaches. (Subjects were headache free at the time of testing.) High-frequency headache subjects were found to have significantly higher resting EMG levels than low-frequency headache subjects. In addition, one would expect, following the law of initial values, that the headache subjects, given that their resting levels were high, would show smaller responses to stress than the controls. This is precisely what occurred; nonheadache subjects showed significantly greater EMG responses to stress than headache subjects, and headache subjects did not show a significant increase in EMG to a cognitive stressor. In this study, if emphasis had been placed on response magnitude, and response magnitude had been corrected for prestimulus levels, headache subjects might have been identified as exhibiting larger responses to stress than nonheadache subjects, when, in fact, they did not and would only have seemed to as a result of the specific statistical analyses employed. Thus, in some disorders, such as muscle-tension headache, "rest specificity" may be a more salient feature than response specificity.

An additional parameter of possible relevance to psychosomatic disorders is physiological recovery from stress. Sternbach (1966) suggested that I–R specificity is insufficient to account for the development of a psychosomatic disorder. "If a person with marked response stereotypy is continually exposed to stressful situations, he may nevertheless avoid having psychosomatic symptoms if his autonomic feedback and control mechanisms operate efficiently" (p. 146). Sternbach proposed that persons who develop psychosomatic disorders are those who have inadequate homeostatic restraints; subsequent to stressful stimulation, their physiological activity requires a longer-than-normal period of time to return to prestimulus levels. In the author's laboratory, empirical evidence has been found implicating the importance of recovery functions for migraine headaches. Initial analyses on small samples of subjects suffering from migraine headaches and headache-free subjects suggest that, following termination of stress, control subjects exhibit rebound earlobe vasodilation, while migraine subjects continue to vasoconstrict. The two groups did not differ in their blood volume response to stress, nor was a similar pattern evidenced in other physiological systems (heart rate, frontal and forearm muscle tension).

Further refinement of specificity concepts may be possible by considering the various operational definitions of rest, stress, and recovery. For example, resting levels of electrodermal activity may be measured either as the average conductance for a given period of time or as the number of spontaneous fluctuations in a given period of time. Although it is generally assumed that these measures covary, Gatchel and Proctor (1976) found that the stress experienced in a noncontingent aversive situation produced lowered skin conductance levels and increased spontaneous activity. Similar points can be made for response measurements and recovery rates. For example, the cardiac response may be defined in terms of peak amplitude or average activity during stimulation and may be expressed either as absolute values or as change scores; recovery may be operationalized as the amount of change per unit of time or as the time required to return to basal levels. Thus, differences in autonomic functions between psychosomatic and nonpsychosomatic populations and between populations at risk and those not at risk may be specific to the method of measurement, and delineating those parameters which distinguish the populations may be an important contribution toward understanding psychosomatic etiology.

To summarize, elevated activity in a particular system may increase an individual's vulnerability to develop a psychosomatic disorder in that system. The elevated activity, however, need not be limited to response to stress but may include resting levels and recovery from stress; the concept of individual specificity may be extended to *indvidual-rest specificity* and *individual-recovery specificity* as well as individual-response specificity. Furthermore, within each type of specificity, the method of operationalizing activity should not be viewed as an arbitrary decision, since different definitions may reflect different underlying abnormalities that may be specific to a particular psychosomatic disorder. Furthermore, delineating the particular parameters of specificity that are associated with a particular psychosomatic disorder may have implications for treatment, in that the treatment may be tailored to normalize the specific variable that is aberrant.

The Etiology of Specificity

Although the necessary longitudinal studies with which to establish a causal relationship are lacking, the research to date suggests that, for at least some psychosomatic disorders, symptoms occurring in a particular system are associated with some type of abnormal physiological functioning in that system. In addition, Engel's (1960) original study found that, in a normal population, individuals exhibit idiosyncratic and similar patterns of autonomic activity across stimuli, so that, for example, some people could be appropriately labeled as heart rate responders and others as gastrointestinal responders. In the diathesis-stress model, however, individual specificity must be viewed as a mediator between etiological factors and symptoms. In other words, to address the issue of etiology of psychosomatic disorders, we need to examine the etiology of specificity.

On a theoretical level, we may assume that the abnormal functioning of a particular organ system can originate in the anatomical structure or chemistry of the central or peripheral nervous system and be the result of genetic, traumatic, or disease factors. With the exception of those studies which suggest genetic factors (for example, Lacey, Bateman, & Van Lehn, 1953) but fail to adequately separate the influence of heredity from that of shared environment, the necessary research linking these factors to psychosomatic disorders has not been done.

Given the influence of cortical processes on autonomic activity, the possibility exists that specificity can be a learned response. A considerable body of literature exists (examples of which are cited below) which has reported the use of operant feedback techniques to modify autonomic functions such as heart rate (Lang & Twentyman, 1976), blood pressure (Elder & Eustis, 1975), electrodermal activity (Ikeda & Harai, 1976), vasomotor activity (Lynch, Hama, Kohn, & Miller, 1976), skin temperature (Keefe, 1975), and salivation (White, 1978). Furthermore, autonomic functions which typically covary during sympathetic arousal can be disassociated with the aid of instrumental conditioning techniques (Shapiro, Turskey, & Schwartz, 1970). Thus, an individual may learn the particular pattern of autonomic activity which brings rewards and/or avoids punishments. Whether or not such a process actually occurs and results in a psychosomatic disorder is, at this point, hypothetical.

The research cited as demonstrating the operant conditioning of autonomic functions has been criticized on the grounds that the data do not justify the conclusions. The conditioned response could be a muscular or respiratory one, and the observed autonomic changes could be the unconditioned effects of these responses. Central structures do influence the integration of somatic and autonomic functions, but to what extent and under what conditions integration occurs and disassociation is possible are yet to be determined. The issue raised by this criticism, however, has potential relevance to psychosomatic etiology. Specificity in autonomic activity may not originate in the autonomic nervous system but may be a result or covariate, mediated by either peripheral or central structures, of somatic activity. For example, cardiovascular and skeletal muscle activities are clearly interrelated, since the cardiovascular system is responsible for supplying the oxygen necessary for the metabolic requirements of the musculature. Thus, the predisposing specificity for tachycardia may be a somatic specificity rather than a cardiac specificity.

Differences in autonomic activity between women and men and between blacks and whites suggest the possibility of an organic, possibly genetic, etiology for specificity. Men have been found to have higher basal skin conductance levels and less phasic activity, both elicited and spontaneous, than women (Fisher & Kotses, 1974; Kopacz & Smith, 1971), while women have been found to show faster habituation of the electrodermal orienting response than men (Korn & Moyer, 1968). Using cardiovascular measures, women have been shown to exhibit faster basal heart rates and lower basal blood pressure than men (Master, Garfield, & Walters, 1952). Sex differences have also been found in the patterning of physiological responses. For example, when stimulated with painful electric shock, men exhibited significant changes in systolic blood pressure, while women exhibited such changes in respiration rate (Liberson & Liberson, 1975). The only psychophysiological variable that has consistently been found to differ among races is electrodermal activity. Researchers have found that whites have higher basal skin conductance levels than blacks (Fisher & Kotses, 1973; Lieblich, Kugelmass, & Ben-Shakhar, 1973). In addition, Janes, Hesselbrock, and Stern (1978) report that white children have more nonspecific electrodermal activity than black children. Patterns of physiological activity have been found to differ between races. Janes, Worland, and Stern (1976) found black children to be more responsive in finger blood volume and less responsive in skin potential than white children. Of course, one cannot assume an organic etiology for these differences, since, in our society, the two sexes and the two races differ in their experiences and environments. Thus far, no attempt has been made to relate these autonomic differences to similar differences in the incidence of specific psychosomatic disorders.

Conclusions

Most etiological theories of psychosomatic disorders postulate the necessity of a predisposition or a vulnerability or a susceptibility of the affected organ system; there is, however, a virtual dearth of empirical work investigating the specific predisposing factors and directly relating them to the development and maintenance of psychosomatic disorders. Although individual-response specificity as the predisposing factor in the development of psychosomatic disorders has been so widely accepted as to appear in undergraduate psychopathology texts, there are several factors which serve to mitigate the present importance of this concept:

1. The populations and disorders researched have been limited.
2. Methods of assessment which define I-R specificity as *relative* to a particular subject sample and *relative* to other physiological variables and which rely on complex mathematical procedures are important in a theoretical sense, but more basic research programs are needed.
3. The empirical and theoretical emphasis has been on response magnitude, while the nature of some psychosomatic symptoms suggests that resting levels or recovery rates may be more salient.
4. The research has been descriptive and cross-sectional and so does not necessarily support a causal relationship between I-R specificity and psychosomatic disorders.
5. Investigations concerned with demonstrating the existence of I-R specificity typically have not addressed the issue of the etiology of the specificity.

Factors Influencing Stress

The stress component of the diathesis-stress model is even more elusive in terms of definition than the predisposition component. Certain physical, psychological, and social stimuli are viewed as inherently stressful because, in an experimental situation, they produce cognitive, behavioral, and/or physiological arousal. For example, presenting white noise at an intensity of 100 db or requiring a person to perform a complex mathematical problem in a limited time period is perceived as stressful by most subjects and tends to produce sympathetic arousal and increased somatic activity. Most stimuli cannot be defined as stressful, however, simply on the basis of stimulus properties; the intensity of the stress is subjective and depends not only on the actual threat to the organism but also on how the individual perceives the event and what coping mechanisms are available to him or her.

Stimulus Parameters

In the laboratory, stress is usually defined as sympathetic arousal or decrements in task performance, and this stress response has been shown to be associated with the presentation of particular stimuli. The association between particular autonomic responses and specific stimulus parameters has been labeled *stimulus-response specificity* (Engel, 1960) or *response stereotypy* (Lacey, 1967). Engel found that in a given set of subjects, consistent patterns of responses occurred for three of five of the stimuli he employed. Lacey specified the stimulus parameters relevant to the variation in physiological response and developed a theory based on the attentional requirements of a given stimulus situation; tasks requiring cognitive processing and inattention to environmental stimuli effect heart rate increases and skin conductance increases, while tasks requiring attention to external stimuli effect heart rate decreases and skin conductance increases.

Focusing on different stimulus parameters, Sokolov (1963) and Graham and Clifton (1966) provided a theoretical model which postulates a relationship between physiological responses to discrete stimuli and various properties of the stimuli. The model distinguishes between an orienting response and a defensive response, the former involving increased sensitivity, listening, and watching, and the latter, decreased sensitivity and avoidance. The original model was based primarily on research with simple tones of various intensities (Sokolov, 1963). Low-intensity tones produced heart rate deceleration, peripheral vasoconstriction, and cephalic vasodilation, while high-intensity tones resulted in heart rate acceleration, peripheral vasoconstriction, and cephalic vasoconstriction. The former was labeled an *orienting response*, which habituated with repeated stimulation, and the latter a *defensive response*, which did not habituate.

Subsequent research has refined and expanded the original model, particularly with respect to the orienting response, and has specified additional stimulus parameters which are related to the direction and magnitude of physiological responses. Sokolov (1966) suggested that the degree of uncertainty that the stimulus will occur is the key parameter in determining the size and the presence or absence of an orienting response. If a person holds a high subjective probability

Compared with the 60-cps group, the group expecting 75-cps shocks had a set to perceive the shocks as being more stressful and, indeed, rated the shocks as being of greater intensity.

Harris, Katkin, Lick, and Habberfield (1976) attempted to induce a relaxed state by having subjects breathe deeply and slowly while pacing their respirations to a visual signal. Autonomic indices were measured during shock and anticipation of shock. Subjects who paced their breathing exhibited smaller electrodermal responses to the stressor than did those who simply attended to the visual signals; there were no group differences for heart rate. One interpretation of these data is that this respiration manipulation, which is similar to that used to relax by students of the eastern religions and by women desiring natural childbirth, reduces the autonomic response to stress.

Since laboratory-induced sets have been shown to affect response to stress, it is reasonable to expect that individual differences determined by factors external to the laboratory, such as personality or prior learning, may also affect responses. Of considerable recent interest to researchers of coronary disease are the personality types formulated by Friedman (1969). Type A people are those with high achievement motivation, a persistent sense of time urgency, and poorly modulated hostility, while type B people are noted for the absence of these characteristics. Clinical work by Jenkins (1976) suggests that type A people are more likely to develop coronary heart disease than type B. In addition, laboratory research (Dembroski, MacDougall, & Shields, 1977) found that type A people exhibited larger systolic blood pressure responses during a reaction time task than did type B people..

In a similar vein, Graham proposed that particular attitudes are associated with certain physiological patterns of response and, thus, with specific disorders. He proposed, for example, that people suffering from duodenal ulcer are seeking revenge and wish to injure the person or thing that has injured them, while those with hives feel mistreated and are not retaliatory but are preoccupied with what is happening to them (Grace & Graham, 1952). In analog studies designed to test his theory (Graham, Kabler, & Graham, 1962; Graham, Stern, & Winokur, 1958), normal subjects were hypnotized and given suggestions designed to induce attitudes thought to be specific to hives, Raynaud's disease, or hypertension; these suggestions were associated with increases in skin temperature, decreases in skin temperature, and increases in blood pressure, respectively. Although these early studies offer support for the attitude specificity theory, recent attempts at replication (Peters & Stern, 1971) have not been successful.

Other research suggests that autonomic responses are a function of the interaction between individual traits and the experimental situation. DeGood (1975) investigated the possibility that one's general expectancy of control might interact with the availability of control. He formed two groups — those scoring high or low on Rotter's Internal-External Locus of Control Scale. All subjects were required to perform a matching task in which they were shocked for slow performance. Half the subjects were provided time out to rest at their request, while the other half were given time out at the discretion of the experimenter. Externality interacted with situation control in determining changes in diastolic blood pressure: greater blood pressure changes were exhibited when personality was incongruous with experimental conditions (internal subjects with no control, external subjects with control) than when they were congruous.

Hare (1972, 1973) has shown an interaction between stimulus properties and learned fears. He (1972) grouped subjects according to their heart rate responses to slides of homicide victims. The cephalic vasomotor response of those showing declerative cardiac reactions was dilation and of those showing accelerative reactions was constriction. Hare speculated that an orienting response was evoked in those subjects who found the slides interesting, while a defensive response was elicited in those subjects who felt anxious about or disgusted with the slides. In a later study, Hare (1973) tested this hypothesis by showing slides of spiders to spider phobics and nonphobics. The nonphobics responded with typical orienting responses, and the phobics with typical defensive responses.

In a similar study, Klorman, Weissberg, and Wiesenfeld (1977) showed neutral slides of mutilated bodies to subjects who were either high or low in fear of mutilation. Mutilation slides produced cardiac acceleration in fearful subjects and decreased heart rate in low-fear subjects, while responses to neutral slides did not differentiate the two groups. A further refinement was added by Gang and Teft (1975), who hypothesized that autonomic responses would vary as a function of familiarity with the stressor as well as stress value. The stressor was the sound of a high-speed dental engine. Familiarity was determined by major — dental hygiene students versus liberal arts students — and stress value was assessed by an inventory designed to assess past annoyance with visits to a dentist. Large increases in heart rate were found to be associated with high annoyance and low familiarity, while small increases were associated with low annoyance and high familiarity.

In summary, an individual's personality, experience, and socialization, that is, one's learning history, may instill a set to view specific stimuli as threatening or stressful. In such a case, any variables which influence the self-reported intensity of stress may affect the degree, direction, and patterning of autonomic activity. In turn, a change in degree of autonomic arousal may render a person susceptible to any psychosomatic disorder — the specific disorder being determined by a predisposing physiological vulnerability — while a change in direction or patterning may affect an individual's susceptibility to a specific psychosomatic disorder.

Coping Strategies

The way in which a person deals with stress may affect not only the self-reported intensity of the stress but also the physiological aspects of the response. This can be illustrated with a personal example. For two years the author was a member of a group of Peace Corps volunteers in an underdeveloped country. Because of dietary changes and sanitation conditions, all the volunteers had a continuing bout with dysentery, which made them potential victims of ulcers, ileitis, and colitis. The single, most significant stressor was a rather intense hostility toward the group from the people of the country. The hostility was due to their previous experience with the United States Armed Forces, but this knowledge did not alleviate the stress experienced by a group of idealistic, recent college graduates who had come to save and help and had received for it obscenities and stone throwing. The volunteers tended to respond in one of two ways: either they continued to smile and passively accept the situation, or they translated the obscenities into the native language and returned those as well as the stones. Of those who adopted the passive strategy, many had to return to the United States because of severe gastrointestinal problems. Although these anecdotal recollections are not "hard" data, they do serve to illustrate the potential utility of including coping responses in a model of psychosomatic disorders.

An area of research relevant to this discussion is that concerned with the behavior associated with anger. According to Sternbach (1971), anger is the emotion most likely to be associated with the onset of psychosomatic symptoms, and it has been found to covary with diastolic blood pressure (Ax, 1953; Schill, 1972). The question of interest here is, how does the behavior associated with anger affect physiology? Subjects allowed to directly aggress against a frustrator returned to base line blood pressure levels faster than those allowed to aggress against a nonfrustrator (Gambaro & Rabin, 1969; Hokanson, Burgess, & Cohen, 1963) and than those allowed fantasy aggression or no aggression (Hokanson & Burgess, 1962).

Although aggression and assertion are distinct on a conceptual level, the behavioral manifestations can be quite similar, and a few studies have assessed the treatment effectiveness of assertiveness training for psychosomatic disorders. Increasing assertiveness has been found to covary with improved food intake patterns in obese women (Conoley, 1976) and improvement on a variety of measures in men suffering from duodenal ulcers (Brooks, 1976). Thus, the coping responses available in an individual's repertoire may modify the autonomic activity associated with stress, and in this particular example, they seem to influence the duration of, and/or the recovery from, the stress response.

Work by Barrell and Price (1977) suggested that coping strategies may determine which physiological parameter is most responsive to stress. Pilot work implied that persons may be categorized according to their response orientation in a stressful situation: some attempt to avoid and delay the stress, while others prefer to confront it and get it over with. The researchers categorized subjects into confronters and avoiders according to a questionnaire and then measured heart rate and trapezius muscle tension during shock anticipation. Group differences were found for the physiological variables, with confronters exhibiting higher muscle tension responses and avoiders higher heart rate responses.

Further research implicates the outcome of the coping response with the degree of experienced stress. Weiss (1971), working with rats, employed a design that included three warning signal conditions preceding shock: a single signal, a progressive signal, and no signal. In the first two conditions, a response terminated the signal and allowed the animal to avoid the shock, while in the third condition, a response postponed the shock; in all three conditions, if a response occurred during shock, the shock would terminate, allowing the animal to escape. Under each condition were three groups: an escape-avoidance group, a group yoked to the escape-avoidance group in the sense that they received an equal number of shocks but could not control the shocks, and a nonshock control group. Subjective stress was measured by stomach ulceration. In all three conditions, escape-avoidance animals showed significantly less ulceration than did the yoked animals, and the no-signal condition yielded more ulceration than the two signaled conditions, which were similar. Weiss utilized these results to develop a hypothetical model which relates coping behavior and stress: given a situation where responses do not result in stimuli associated with the absence of shock, ulceration increases with the number of responses; given a situation where responses result in stimuli that are associated with the absence of shock, ulceration will not occur, regardless of the number of responses. In other words, responding may reduce stress if it results in the organism receiving relevant feedback, or it may increase stress if it does not. Thus, individual parameters, such as response or activity level, and situation parameters, such as those which elicit or inhibit responding as well as the availability of feedback, may influence the intensity of the stress reaction. Although it would be inappropriate to relate these data directly to the development of ulcers in humans, the ulceration in the rats may be viewed as an indicator of experienced stress, and the parameters influencing this stress may be relevant to human stressful conditions.

The examples discussed here serve to illustrate the potential relevance of coping strategies to the development and maintenance of psychosomatic disorders. Most would agree from their personal experiences that the coping response utilized in response to stress can ameliorate or exacerbate the subjective intensity of stress. More research is needed, however, to specify the physiological covariates of various coping responses and the role that coping strategies play in the etiology of psychosomatic disorders.

Conclusions and Suggestions for Future Research

In the present discussion, psychosomatic disorders are viewed in the context of a diathesis-stress model. According to this model, psychosomatic symptoms result from a particular organic predisposition occurring in conjunction with precipitating stressful events. Organic predispositions may be manifest in continued physiological arousal, excessive response to stress, and/or delayed recovery from stress. It is suggested that the degree and type of stress experienced by an individual are determined by an interaction among environmental events, an individual's learning history, and the responses available to cope with stress.

Although the diathesis-stress model proposed here has little actual empirical support, it does have face validity and provides a structure within which one can attempt to organize diverse but relevant information. The model should not be viewed, however, as static. It is possible, for example, to view precipitating factors as predisposing factors. Repeated and continual feelings of anger may cause one predisposed to hypertension to develop that disorder, or these feelings may cause a previously normal system to become overactive, resulting in large blood pressure responses to all stressors; in the first instance, anger would be viewed as precipitating, in the second as predisposing. A further example is that attitudes are viewed here as affecting the perceived or subjective intensity of stress. Attitudes could be viewed, instead, as reflecting coping strategies, since their descriptions include the behavioral response (seeking revenge, preoccupied with self). It is also possible that the relative importance of the various factors and whether or not they are predisposing or precipitating depends on the individual.

The goal of this section is not to determine the relative importance of various parameters to the etiology of psychosomatic disorders but to instill an appreciation for the complexities involved, to encourage creative and well-designed research and treatment programs, and to describe the current "state of the art." The present level of sophistication in theoretical and empirical approaches to the etiology of psychosomatic disorders is, to some extent, a reflection of the fact that this is a relatively new area of scientific endeavor. At present, a much larger number of concepts than could ever hopefully be integrated into one general and accepted theory are considered relevant; this is a characteristic of an immature science (Kuhn, 1970) but a necessary phase in the development of a scientific field.

Traditional methodology may not be the most useful for narrowing the focus and obtaining consensus. Researchers need to adapt their methodology to the phenomenon being studied; traditional designs and analyses allow us to recognize which variables have potential relevance, but they do not allow us to determine the relative importance of a particular variable or the relationship among variables. Multivariate approaches are more suited to these purposes than are the traditional, univariate analyses. Discriminate function analysis, for example, considers the relative importance of the various dependent measures in discriminating between groups or between stimuli. Weights are assigned to the dependent variables, which, when linearly combined, provide an equation which maximizes differences and allows the researcher to decide which of the dependent variables are most useful in distinguishing among people or stimuli (Lachin & Schachter, 1974). A potential use for this procedure in the study of psychosomatic disorders would be to determine which of several variables most reliably discriminates a particular psychosomatic sample from a nonsymptomatic sample.

A further problem concerns the rigid adherence to analysis-of-variance (ANOVA) techniques to analyze data. Use of ANOVA requires that independent variables be categorical. Thus, continuous variables are forced into categories by the use of extreme groups or median splits, and this results in the loss of potentially valuable information and the imposition of artificial dichotomies. Multiple regression techniques are preferable, in that they provide the same information as ANOVA but allow independent variables to be continuous and utilize all the available information.

A final comment on methodology relates to determining the importance of a factor in the development of a psychosomatic disorder. Typically, if statistical significance is achieved, the variable of interest is considered relevant or important. One determinant of statistical significance is sample size, however, and with a large enough sample, any size difference between groups or any degree of relationship can be significant. Thus, as a criterion of importance, statistical significance is relatively meaningless. A clear indication of importance is some measure of the proportion of variance accounted for in the dependent measure by the independent variable or by the relationship between two variables. This can be estimated by W^2 (Hays, 1973) when using ANOVA or by R^2 (McNeil, Kelly, & McNeil, 1975) when using multiple regression or correlations.

For example, one may find that the outcome of coping responses accounts for 45% of the variability in heart rate during a noise avoidance task, while degree of predictability of the noise accounts for 3% of the variance. Both variables may yield significant results, but one would infer from these results that the type of outcome is of considerable importance, and the degree of predictability of minimal importance, in determining cardiac activity. In the study of psychosomatic disorders, where a wide variety of variables have been found statistically significant, regular reporting of a measure indicating the proportion of variance accounted for will aid in the elimination of irrelevant variables and in emphasis being placed on important variables in future research.

Finally, the discussion in this section indicates several areas in which researchers concerned with psychosomatic disorders may productively concentrate their resources. First, longitudinal research designs are of obvious importance in determining causal relationships between hypothesized etiological variables and the occurrence of symptoms. Second, physiological response to stress has typically been evaluated in a laboratory setting and has employed such stimuli as shock or aversive noise. Such stimuli allow precise control of parameters, such as intensity and duration; however, they may bear little resemblance to the environmental stressors which have been implicated in psychosomatic etiology. With the advent of telemetric recording procedures, it is possible — and desirable — to assess the physiological covariates of real-life stressors. Third, interest in psychosomatic disorders may be found among a variety of disciplines, including medicine, psychology, and sociology, and, as was noted above, the parameters researched by the various disciplines may best be viewed as interactive rather than additive. Thus, an interdisciplinary approach is clearly appropriate and would allow the knowledge and methodological expertise from a variety of disciplines to be concentrated and productively channeled.

REFERENCES

Alexander, F. *Psychosomatic medicine.* New York: Norton, 1950.

Appenzeller, O. *The autonomic nervous system.* New York: Elsevier, 1970.

Ax, A. F. The physiological differentiation between fear and anger in humans. *Psychosomatic Medicine*, 1953, *15*, 433-442.

Barrell, J. J., & Price, D. D. Two experiential orientations toward a stressful situation and their related somatic and visceral responses. *Psychophysiology*, 1977, *14*, 514-521.

Benjamin, L. S. Statistical treatment of the law of initial values (LIV) in autonomic research: A review and recommendation. *Psychosomatic Medicine*, 1963, *25*, 556-566.

Brodman, K., Erdmann, A. J., Lorge, I., & Wolff, H. G. The Cornell Medical Index — Health Questionnaire VI. The relation of patients' complaints to age, sex, race, and education. *Journal of Gerontology*, 1953, *8*, 339-342.

Brooks, G. R. *Emotional skills training: A treatment program for duodenal ulcer.* Unpublished doctoral dissertation, University of Texas-Austin, 1976.

Cohen, M. J., Rickles, W. H., & McArthur, D. L. Evidence for physiological response stereotype in migraine headache. *Psychosomatic Medicine*, 1978, *40*, 344-354.

Conoley, C. W. *The effects of vicarious reinforcement in assertive training, on assertive behavior, anxiety, and food intake of underassertive obese females.* Unpublished doctoral dissertation, University of Texas-Austin, 1976.

DeGood, D. E. Cognitive control factors in vascular stress responses. *Psychophysiology*, 1975, *12*, 399-401.

Dembroski, T. M., MacDougall, J. M., & Shields, J. L. Physiologic reactions to social challenge in persons evidencing the type A coronary-prone behavior pattern. *Journal of Human Stress*, 1977, *3*, 2-9.

Elder, S. T., & Eustis, N. R. Instrumental blood pressure conditioning in outpatient hypertensives. *Behavior Research and Therapy*, 1975, *13*, 185-188.

Engel, B. T. Stimulus-response and individual-response specificity. *Archives of General Psychiatry*, 1960, *2*, 305-313.

Engel, B. T., & Bickford, A. F. Response specificity: Stimulus-response and individual-response specificity in essential hypertensives. *Archives of General Psychiatry*, 1961, *5*, 478-489.

Fisher, L. E., & Kotses, H. Race differences and experimenter race effect in galvanic skin response. *Psychophysiology*, 1973, *10*, 578-582.

Fisher, L. E., & Kotses, H. Experimenter and subject sex effects in the skin conductance response. *Psychophysiology*, 1974, *11*, 191-196.

Friedman, M. *Pathogenesis of coronary artery disease*. New York: McGraw-Hill, 1969.

Gambaro, A., & Rabin, S. Diastolic blood pressure response following direct and displaced aggression after anger arousal, in high and low guilt subjects. *Journal of Personality and Social Psychology*, 1969, *12*, 87-94.

Gang, M. J., & Teft, L. Individual differences in heart rate responses to affective sound. *Psychophysiology*, 1975, *12*, 423-426.

Gatchel, R. J., & Proctor, J. D. Physiological correlates of learned helplessness in man. *Journal of Abnormal Psychology*, 1976, *85*, 27-34.

Gellhorn, E. *Principles of autonomic-somatic integrations*. Minneapolis: University of Minnesota Press, 1967.

Grace, W. J., & Graham, D. T. Relationship of specific attitudes and emotions to certain bodily diseases. *Psychosomatic Medicine*, 1952, *14*, 243-251.

Graham, D. T., Kabler, J. D., & Graham, F. K. Physiological response to the suggestion of attitudes specific for hives and hypertension. *Psychosomatic Medicine*, 1962, *24*, 159-169.

Graham, D. T., Stern, J. A., & Winokur, G. Experimental investigation of the specificity of attitude hypothesis in psychosomatic disease. *Psychosomatic Medicine*, 1958, *20*, 446-457.

Graham, F. K., & Clifton, R. C. Heart-rate changes as a component of the orienting response. *Psychological Bulletin*, 1966, *65*, 305-320.

Greenfield, N. S., & Sternbach, R. A. (Eds.). *Handbook of psychophysiology*. New York: Holt, Rinehart & Winston, 1972.

Hamilton, M., Pond, D. A., & Ryle, A. Relation of CMI responses to some social and psychological factors. *Journal of Psychosomatic Research*, 1962, *6*, 157-165.

Hare, R. D. Cardiovascular components of orienting and defensive responses. *Psychophysiology*, 1972, *9*, 606-614.

Hare, R. D. Orienting and defensive responses to visual stimuli. *Psychophysiology*, 1973, *10*, 453-464.

Harris, V. A., Katkin, E. S., Lick, J. R., & Habberfield, T. Paced respiration as a technique for the modification of autonomic response to stress. *Psychophysiology*, 1976, *13*, 386-391.

Hays, W. L. *Statistics for the social sciences* (2nd ed.). New York: Holt, Rinehart & Winston, 1973.

Hokanson, J. E., & Burgess, M. Effects of three types of aggression on vascular processes. *Journal of Abnormal and Social Psychology*, 1962, *64*, 446-449.

Hokanson, J. E., Burgess, M., & Cohen, M. F. Effects of displaced aggression on systolic blood pressure. *Journal of Abnormal and Social Psychology*, 1963, *67*, 214-218.

Holmes, T. H., & Rahe, R. H. The social readjustment rating scale. *Journal of Psychosomatic Research*, 1967, *11*, 213-218.

Holmes, T. S., & Holmes, T. H. Short-term intrusions into the life style routine. *Journal of Psychosomatic Research*, 1970, *14*, 121-132.

Ikeda, Y., & Harai, H. Voluntary control of electrodermal activity in relation to imagery and internal perception scores. *Psychophysiology*, 1976, *13*, 330-333.

Janes, C. L., Hesselbrock, V., & Stern, J. A. Parental psychopathology, age, and race as related to electrodermal activity of children. *Psychophysiology*, 1978, *15*, 24-34.

Janes, C. L., Worland, J., & Stern, J. A. Skin potential and vasomotor responsiveness of black and white children. *Psychophysiology*, 1976, *13*, 523-527.

Jenkins, C. C. Recent evidence supporting psychologic and social risk factors for coronary disease. *New England Journal of Medicine*, 1976, *294*, 987-994.

Keefe, F. J., Conditioning changes in differential skin temperature. *Perceptual and Motor Skills*, 1975, *40*, 283-288.

Keele, C. A., & Neil, E. *Samson Wright's applied physiology* (12th ed.). New York: Oxford University Press, 1971.

Klorman, R., Weissberg, R. P., & Wiesenfeld, A. R. Individual differences in fear and autonomic reactions to affective stimulation. *Psychophysiology*, 1977, *14*, 45-51.

Kopacz, F. M., & Smith, B. D. Sex differences in skin conductance measures as a function of shock threat. *Psychophysiology*, 1971, *8*, 293-303.

Korn, J. H., & Moyer, K. E. Effects of set and sex on the electrodermal orienting response. *Psychophysiology*, 1968, *4*, 453-459.

Kuhn, T. S. *The structure of scientific revolutions* (2nd ed.). Chicago: University of Chicago Press, 1970.

Lacey, J. Somatic response patterning and stress: Some revisions of activation theory. In M. Appley & R. Trumbell (Eds.), *Psychological stress: Issues in research*. New York: Appleton-Century-Crofts, 1967.

Lacey, J. I., Bateman, D. E., & VanLehn, R. Autonomic response specificity: An experimental study. *Psychosomatic Medicine*, 1953, *15*, 8-21.

Lacey, J. I., Kagan, J., Lacey, B. C., & Moss, H. A. The visceral level: Situational determinants and behavioral correlates of autonomic response patterns. In P. Knapp (Ed.), *Expression of the emotions in man*. New York: International Universities Press, 1963.

Lachin, J. M., & Schachter, J. On stepwise discriminant analyses applied to physiologic data. *Psychophysiology*, 1974, *11*, 703-709.

Lang, P. J., & Twentyman, C. T. Learning to control heart rate: Effects of varying incentive and criterion of success on task performance. *Psychophysiology*, 1976, *13*, 378-385.

Liberson, C. W., & Liberson, W. T. Sex differences in autonomic responses to electric shock. *Psychophysiology*, 1975, *12*, 182-186.

Lieblich, I., Kugelmass, S., & Ben-Shakhar, G. Psychophysiological baselines as a function of race and ethnic origin. *Psychophysiology*, 1973, *10*, 426-430.

Lynch, W. C., Hama, H., Kohn, S., & Miller, N. E. Instrumental control of peripheral vasomotor responses in children. *Psychophysiology*, 1976, *13*, 219-221.

Malmo, R. B., Shagass, C., & Davis, F. H. Symptom specificity and bodily reactions during psychiatric interview. *Psychosomatic Medicine*, 1950, *12*, 362-376.

Master, A. M., Garfield, C. I., & Walters, M. B. *Normal blood pressure and hypertension*. Philadelphia: Lea & Febiger, 1952.

McNeil, K. A., Kelly, F. J., & McNeil, J. T. *Testing research hypotheses using multiple linear regression*. Carbondale: Southern Illinois University Press, 1975.

Peters, J. E., & Stern, R. M. Specificity of attitude hypothesis in psychosomatic medicine: A re-examination. *Journal of Psychosomatic Research*, 1971, *15*, 129-135.

Rahe, R. H., & Lind, E. Psychosocial factors and sudden cardiac death: A pilot study. *Journal of Psychosomatic Research*, 1971, *15*, 19-24.

Safranek, R. *Response specificity in people with migraine headache*. Unpublished master's thesis, Southern Illinois University-Carbondale, 1978.

Schill, T. R. Aggression and blood pressure responses of high- and low-guilt subjects following frustration. *Journal of Consulting and Clinical Psychology*, 1972, *38*, 461-465.

Schwab, J. J., Fennell, E. B., & Warheit, G. J. The epidemiology of psychosomatic disorders. *Psychosomatics*, 1974, *15*, 88-93.

Schwartz, G. E. Psychosomatic disorders and biofeedback: A psychobiological model of disregulation. In J. D. Maser & M. E. P. Selisman (Eds.), *Psychopathology: Experimental models*. San Francisco: W. H. Freeman, 1977.

Sersen, E. A., Clausen, J., & Lidsky, A. Autonomic specificity and stereotypy revisited. *Psychophysiology*, 1978, *15*, 60-67.

Shapiro, D., Turskey, B., & Schwartz, G. E. Differentiation of heart rate and systolic blood pressure in man by operant conditioning. *Psychosomatic Medicine*, 1970, *32*, 417-423.

Sokolov, E. *Perception and the conditioned reflex*. New York: Macmillan, 1963.

Sokolov, Y. H. Orienting reflex as information regulator. In A. Leontyer, A. Luria, & A. Smirnov (Eds.), *Psychological research in the USSR* (Vol. 1). Moscow: Progress Publishers, 1966.

Sternbach, R. A. Autonomic responsivity and the concept of sets. In N. S. Greenfield & W. C. Lewis (Eds.), *Psychoanalysis and current biological thought*. Madison: University of Wisconsin Press, 1965.

Sternbach, R. A. *Principles of psychophysiology*. New York: Academic Press, 1966.

Sternbach, R. A. Psychosomatic diseases. In G. D. Shean (Ed.), *Studies in abnormal behavior*. Chicago: Rand McNally, 1971.

Vaughn, R., Pall, M. L., & Haynes, S. N. Frontalis EMG response to stress in subjects with frequent muscle-contraction headaches. *Headache*, 1977, *16*, 313-317.

Walker, B. B., & Sandman, C. A. Physiological response patterns in ulcer patients: Phasic and tonic components of the electrogastrogram. *Psychophysiology*, 1977, *14*, 393-400.

Weiss, J. M. Effects of coping behavior in different warning signal conditions on stress pathology in rats. *Journal of Comparative and Physiological Psychology*, 1971, *77*, 1-13.

White, K. D. Salivation: The significance of imagery in its voluntary control. *Psychophysiology*, 1978, *15*, 196-203.

Wilder, J. The law of initial values in neurology and psychiatry. Facts and problems. *Journal of Nervous and Mental Disease*, 1956, *125*, 73-86.

Wold, D. A. *The adjustment of siblings to childhood leukemia.* Unpublished medical thesis, University of Washington-Seattle, 1968.

Wolf, S., Cardon, P., Shepard, E., & Wolff, H. *Life stress and essential hypertension.* Baltimore: Williams & Wilkins, 1955.

2

THE PROBLEM OF PAIN:
A PSYCHOBIOLOGICAL PERSPECTIVE

C. Richard Chapman

Margo Wyckoff

INTRODUCTION

The control of pain is one of the oldest needs of mankind. Despite the enormous achievements of medical science in the twentieth century, this need is still largely unmet. Victims of accidental injury, burn trauma, war, and painful disease still suffer significantly, as do patients recovering from surgery and child-birth. More importantly, pain sometimes persists for months or years, imposing severe physical, emotional, social, and economic stresses on its victims, their families, and society as a whole. Such problems are so remarkably resistant to conventional medical therapies that chronic pain is the most frequent cause of disability in the United States today.

This chapter is intended to provide an overview of the field of pain and an introduction to the major issues in this area. The focus of the discussion is primarily clinical and concerned with real-world, rather than laboratory, pain phenomena. Nevertheless, basic information about the fundamental physiology and sensory psychology of pain has been included to give the reader some appreciation of the physiological bases of the behavior patterns of patients experiencing pain or pain relief. The first sections of the chapter introduce pain as an area of scientific inquiry and discuss issues of definition, pain as a clinical problem, approaches to measurement, and the physiological and psychological dimensions of pain. Next, medical and psychological approaches to pain therapy are presented and examined. Finally, current and developing trends in the field of pain are discussed.

Preparation of this chapter was supported, in part, by a research grant (DE04004) from the National Institute of Dental Health.

PROBLEMS OF DEFINITION AND COMMUNICATION

Finding a General Definition

A conceptual block that continually frustrates investigators is that pain seems to elude adequate definition. In common English parlance, a variety of different subjective experiences are identified as pain. The word may refer to an unpleasant body sensation, a mental anguish associated with purely psychological injury, a general experience of suffering, an annoyance, or even a threat.

As has the general public, investigators and clinicians have come to describe various complex and loosely related phenomena by this single term (Liebeskind & Paul, 1977). Scientists have generated a legion of operational definitions for pain in the laboratory, while clinicians have labeled a myriad of organic and psychological syndromes as pain problems. The impact of this verbal potpourri upon medical science has been the production of a subtle, but unrelenting, confusion in thinking. Indeed, many health-science professionals in the pain field wrestle with the disquieting conviction that numerous and seemingly unrelated biological and psychological phenomena labeled as pain must have a hidden commonality.

Psychiatrists have been among those most concerned with the problems of defining pain. A general definition offered by Merskey and Spear (1967) has come to dominate thinking in the pain field. They termed *pain* "an unpleasant experience which we primarily associate with tissue damage or describe in terms of tissue damage or both" (p. 21). Bond (1979) recently defined pain in a similar, but more detailed, way. "Pain is a subjective experience arising from activity within the brain in response to damage to body tissues, to changes in the function of the brain itself either as a result of damage due to injury or disease, or to changes of a more subtle nature perhaps depending upon biochemical changes which also appear to play a role in mental illness" (p. 1). These attempts at definition represent significant progress in the problem of clarifying the concept of pain, but the scientific and clinical fields remain divided in their conceptualizations of pain phenomena.

Scientific Definitions

Scientists find it necessary to simplify the semantic complexity of pain in order to study its phenomena under controlled conditions. They do this by operationalizing pain, using neural or behavioral language, and developing laboratory models that use animal or human subjects. In the laboratory, pain commonly takes a wide variety of operational definitions, such as rodent tail-flick, primate avoidance response, depolarization of a peripheral nerve fiber, or brain-evoked potential (Chapman, Dong, & Chen, in press).

While there is no obvious relationship between the rat tail-flick and the complaints of patients in pain clinics, heuristic and perhaps clinically meaningful parallels can be drawn between experimental laboratory preparations and clinical manifestations of certain pathological states. For example, the literature on learned helplessness shows that animals exposed to uncontrollable aversive stimuli behave in ways that resemble some forms of depression in man (Seligman, 1975). To the extent that the dynamics of some cancer pain are similar to the operations that produce helplessness in animals, it is not surprising that cancer patients feel and behave as if helpless or depressed (Chapman, 1979).

The multiple models and operational definitions for pain are scientifically useful and, indeed, necessary, but the evident lack of relationship and perspective among the models reflects a scientific enterprise that is, as yet, characterized by immaturity. Recent trends in pain research have emphasized the importance of ongoing interchange between researchers and clinicians and cross-disciplinary interaction among investigators. Such experiences serve to remind the scientist that clinical pain problems are complex and that their solutions will eventually emerge, not from a single laboratory paradigm, but from multidisciplinary teamwork.

Clinical Definitions

The problem of word meaning becomes even more frustrating in the clinical encounter of the physician with the patient when the issue is pain. While most patients express pain in a straightforward way, some who complain of persistent pain may be trying to communicate loneliness, depression, preoccupation with bodily symptoms, or even grief at the loss of a loved one. For the physician, the word has a narrow meaning, and, sometimes inappropriately, the physician understands the patient as saying that there are noxious sensations arising from bodily tissues that may signal systemic disease, injury, or neurologic disorder. Disparity between the connotative meanings of *pain* in the general society and medicine's restricted definitions leads both patient and physician to frustration in the clinical interchange.

Another dimension of the problem is that the complaint of pain (and hence the definition of the patient's problem as pain) has a significant social impact. Pain is almost always heard as a plea for help arising from a disturbed biological process, but it is often uttered to express moods and emotions or simply to evoke nurturance from others. In some cases, it can be used as an act of aggression to punish or blame others or even to accuse a therapist of failure. The encounter of patients suffering from chronic pain with their doctors can sometimes be usefully described in the game language of transactional analysis (Sternbach, 1974). Semantically, patients may use the word *pain* in any connotative or symbolic way that they choose, but physicians are expected to respond in terms of medical definitions and to provide only medical therapies.

Fordyce (1976) pointed out that the classical clinical definition of *pain* is based on a "disease model"; that is, the conceptualization implies that an underlying organic or psychiatric disease gives rise to pain complaints and pain behaviors. Alternatively, a behavioral model can be adapted, so that pain is seen as a class of behaviors that can, by virtue of selective reinforcements, come under the control of the patient's social environment. The use of the word *pain* by a complaining patient may reflect the secondary gains accessible to the patient through pain behavior rather than, or in addition to, neurologic signals from damaged bodily tissues. The incorporation of the behavioral definition of pain into the language of the clinician can considerably enhance communication in the clinical encounter and in the exchanges between physicians dealing with problem patients.

Conclusions

To recapitulate, the problem of defining pain is a complex one. The various scientists and clinicians, both biomedically and behaviorally oriented, are much like the mythical blind men who examined the elephant. Each found and reported a different thing. The problem is not so much one of proving who is right and who is wrong as it is of assembling and integrating information to arrive at the whole picture. But the problem is even more complicated than this analogy suggests. Investigators differ from one another in focus; that is, some view pain from a macroscopic perspective (such as illness behavior) at one extreme, while others see it from a microscopic perspective (such as sensory neurophysiology) at the other extreme. Perhaps the elephant is not yet seen as a whole greater than the sum of its parts because each of its parts is still being examined at different qualitative levels of analysis. As research progresses, bridges in understanding will emerge, and the various conceptualizations of pain may well begin to fit together like pieces of a puzzle.

AN OVERVIEW OF CLINICAL PAIN

Acute Pain

Pain with an abrupt onset that is generated by traumatic injury or disease is termed *acute pain*. Familiar examples include postoperative pain, pain associated with appendicitis, the hurt of intravenous injection or endoscopy, and a painful athletic or accidental injury. Most acute pain problems can be adequately controlled by drugs, inhalation of anesthetics, nerve blocks, or other treatments, and the pain disappears with time as healing progresses.

A major psychological complication associated with acute pain is that of situational anxiety, and often it is necessary either to counsel patients, explain the situation to them in detail, and give reassurance or medicate psychotropically so that major anxiety does not occur. Demonstrations of natural childbirth after counseling, psychological preparation for surgery, and recent work on the control of postoperative pain without medication illustrate that acute pain can come under cortical control, given the right conditions.

Examples of Acute Pain

Postoperative pain varies in accordance with the type of surgery performed, the anesthesia used, and the relationship of the surgical wound to normal vital functions, such as breathing. Like other forms of acute pain, it can be more than a source of intense suffering and misery. When pain is sufficiently severe, it can threaten life by provoking reflex responses that block respiration and alter cardiovascular function. Fortunately, however, patients are generally able to modulate their own pain levels. Those who receive no postoperative medication experience more initial pain and anxiety on the first day of recovery, but these experiences are greatly reduced by the second day, so that these patients appear to be recovering more comfortably and rapidly than those who were medicated (Chapman & Cox, 1977).

The pain associated with burn trauma is one of the frontiers in the control of acute pain. Patients suffer burns suddenly (with the exception of sunburn), and industrial accidents generate severe burns of all sizes and degrees. In many instances, the receptor structures in the skin are totally destroyed, and pain is most evident in the burn margins. Typically, the patient reports either no pain or a very short period of pain at the time of injury. After hospitalization, however, pain becomes a major problem. Debridement of the burned area may be done one or more times each day, with each experience being exquisitely painful.

Management of anxiety is a major concern with most acute pain problems, and anticipatory anxiety is especially troublesome in situations in which patients know in advance that they will encounter severe pain. The basic fear is compounded for many who worry that they may lose control during extreme pain and, in so doing, lose personal dignity.

Chronic Pain

Any painful disorder that does not respond to conventional medical therapy and that lasts for six months or longer is considered chronic pain. There are many types of chronic pain syndromes, the most common involving the lower back, the abdomen, various joints and connective tissue, and the neck.

Categories of Chronic Pain

It is useful to divide chronic pain problems into two types: *benign* and *malignant*. Benign problems are those in which the symptom of pain is related to an organic problem that is not progressive and life threatening. Lower back pain, for example, often occurs in the absence of any clearly identifiable physical pathology. In other cases, the pain symptom becomes a major problem when pathology is minimal, and, in such circumstances, there is a disparity between the organic disease evident and the impact of the pain in the patient's life. Most benign pain problems are static, in that they do not represent progressive physiological deterioration. While the examples of clearly organic disorders, such as arthritis, are often contrasted to pain problems in which no physical pathology is evident on examination, most pain problems seen in typical pain clinics have symptomatology reflecting both organic disorders and psychological stresses.

Malignant chronic pain is that associated with potentially terminal disease, cancer being the most common example. In such cases, pain signals the progressive deterioration of the patient's health. While its onset can be diagnostically valuable to physicians as an indicator of the metastatic process, it has no other apparent value to the patient. Psychologically, it becomes a symbol of suffering and hopelessness, and pain complaints are often expressions of the patients' despair and fear as well as of their bodily sensations.

CHRONIC PAIN AS A SOCIAL PROBLEM

While acute pain is a matter of concern in day-to-day medical practice, chronic pain is a major problem of epidemic proportions. Until recent years, this problem has remained hidden, and the lack of publicity has allowed even physicians to be completely naive in terms of the extent of chronic pain in our society. The problem emerges subtly in most instances, when acute pain problems related to trauma or disease fail to respond to conventional medical therapies. Often the injury or disease giving rise to the pain symptomatology heals, leaving only scars and an elaborate pattern of pain behaviors that cannot be clearly linked to organic causes.

Costs to Society

Pain and Disability

It is unfortunate that clear statistics are not yet available for the large variety of chronic pain syndromes in the United States. Among those under study, however, is back pain. It is impressive to consider that approximately 1.25 million U.S. residents sustain back injuries annually. Of these, approximately 56,000 experience some degree of permanent disability. Therefore, in the United States, there are currently about 2.5 million people with chronic back pain (Beals & Hickman, 1972). A large proportion of these are treated surgically without success. In a study of 170 patients (Aitken, 1959), it was observed that only 13% obtained complete pain relief following surgery so that they could return to their normal work. The follow-up on these patients after two or more years showed that 35% of those who had had clear organic diagnoses at the time of operation were still 100% disabled and that 52% of those showing no organic signs were still receiving total disability payments.

Loeser (in press) reviewed the incidence of lower back pain by looking at studies of hospitalization data as well as records of workmen's compensation. One source estimated that, in 1974, 721,000 hospitalizations due to lower back pain occurred in the United States, representing 6,482,340 patient days. Some 27% of these patients were treated surgically, which Loeser interpreted as a national estimate of 200,000 operations per year for lower back pain. The hospital costs alone for this group of patients in 1974 amounted to approximately $1 billion (Pheasant, 1977). Another study in New England showed that the average patient with lower back pain missed 14 days of work with every episode of pain (Ward, Knowelden, & Sharrard, 1968).

Compensation and Litigation

In a review of the workmen's compensation records of the state of Washington, Loeser (in press) noted that, in 1977, lower back pain patients received $63.5 million in compensation, or 36% of the state compensation payments. Over 75% of such patients typically do not show physical findings with their pain complaints. Since these individuals represent 36% of the total state compensation payments, and since a large variety of other chronic pain disorders (such as neck pain, knee pain, shoulder pain, hip pain, and abdominal pain, to name just a few) are related to workmen's compensation, it seems clear that an enormous amount of money is being spent in each state in compensation for chronic pain disorders.

Yet another cost incurred by society is that caused by the pain patient who is successful in litigation in the courts. Every therapist working in a pain clinic is familiar with the problem of treating a patient with pending litigation. Such patients almost invariably fail to respond to any form of therapy, and their visits to doctors often reflect a need to legitimize their pain problems rather than a search for relief. The vested interest of the patient in such situations is best served by the maintaining of pain rather than its cure.

Statistics are not available about the number of pain-based litigations related to traffic and other accidental injuries and on-the-job injuries. In examining the workmen's compensation records for the state of Washington, however, Loeser (in press) noted that 25% of the injured workmen had hired an attorney. It is clear that society supports chronic pain problems related to certain kinds of injuries, so that for many individuals, the onset of pain may be a mixed curse and blessing. Physicians who assume the role of would-be healer are sometimes expected by their patients to do no more than produce legally viable statements that can serve as legitimizations for the organic nature of pain complaints.

Chronic Pain Consequential to Cancer

Incidence of Pain

Persistent pain is one of the most dreaded aspects of progressive malignant disease. The data from several surveys of small groups of patients have suggested that moderate to severe pain is experienced by about one-third of those with intermediate stages of cancer and by about 60% to 80% of those with advanced cancer (Twycross, 1974; Wilkes, 1974). Foley (1979) surveyed 540 cancer patients and observed that pain was experienced by 85% of those with primary bone tumors, 80% of those with cancer of the oral cavity, 75% of males and 70% of females with cancer of the genitourinary system, 52% of patients with breast cancer, 45% of patients with carcinoma of the lungs, 20% of patients with lymphoma, and 5% of those suffering with leukemia. In a subsequent survey of 397 patients, it was observed that about 38% had pain related to cancer. Among those terminally ill, the figure rose to 60%. In a British study (Cartwright, Hockey, & Anderson, 1973), 87% of patients who died from cancer were observed to have pain prior to death. It is clear from these and other studies that pain is a major problem in the management of the cancer patient. The incidence of pain varies with the type of cancer and with the stage of disease progression.

Effects of Pain

The emotional and physiological impact of pain due to advanced cancer is, in most instances, a greater burden for the patient than is the impact of benign chronic pain. Such patients have more problems with sleep disturbance, appetite loss, and nausea and vomiting in relation to their pain. Moreover, in many instances, it seems that their pain tolerance decreases so that they become hypersensitive. Feelings of hopelessness and despair are evoked by repeated bouts of pain, and these, like sleeplessness, spiral to greater proportions if patients are subjected to surgical operations, chemotherapy, radiation therapy, or other anticancer treatments. Many patients become increasingly preoccupied with pain and gradually lose interest in social activities, so that pain becomes the central focus of their lives.

Chronic pain from both benign and malignant problems typically has a major impact on the patient's social environment. In some instances, we have seen that benign chronic pain becomes the theme around which family life is organized. The patient adopts a stable, invalid role, and the spouse and children adopt reciprocal roles of care giving and nurturance. While these are not productive or healthy situations, they are often emotionally stable and satisfying to all involved. Clinical experience has demonstrated that therapists attempting to rehabilitate the patient sometimes meet with severe resistance from all concerned because such rehabilitation means a breakdown of family structure and security.

Quite the opposite is true in most situations involving cancer pain. Patients with pain tend to develop interpersonal problems within their families, among friends, and with neighbors as well as professional associates. Loss of ability to work is an emotional stress, and patients suffer with feelings of dependency and uselessness. Family members frequently feel helpless and distressed by the physical appearance and behavior of the deteriorating patient, and they sometimes react defensively by becoming cold, distant, and objective. Unrealistic attitudes of optimism, confidence in therapy, and supposed unconcern often continue into terminal stages of the patient's disease, when intimacy and nurturance are very much needed. Some patients with severe, intractable pain become so discouraged and desperate that they contemplate suicide.

Problems in Medical Management

Benign Pain

In an attempt to find relief, many patients suffering with benign chronic pain go to a large number of doctors and clinics. This behavior pattern, sometimes described as *doctor shopping*, is not only expensive but dangerous. Well-meaning physicians, hoping to alleviate pain problems that they are unable to satisfactorily diagnose, prescribe drugs for their patients. Through repeated visits to different doctors, patients collect long lists of prescription drugs, often taking many different things at one time. Intake of multiple pharmacologic agents is dangerous, and patients commonly ingest strange combinations of analgesics, psychotropics, and other drugs.

In many instances, drug abuse produces peculiar problems in terms of mental function and bowel function as well as biological rhythm disturbance. All too often, physicians, unaware of the patient's history of doctor shopping, prescribe yet other drugs to correct such symptoms. At the University of Washington Pain Center, patients are seen who are taking as many as 25 different major drugs daily. Others show severe problems of addiction to one drug or to a combination of several drugs. It is necessary to detoxify problem drug users before carrying out a diagnostic workup, because such patients are poor historians when mentation is severely clouded.

A second problem associatied with benign chronic pain may be termed *polysurgical addiction*. The doctor-shopping habits of patients lead them to undergo multiple diagnostic examinations. Indeed, some seem to find invasive diagnostic procedures especially satisfying. Patients with abdominal pain are particularly prone to find physicians who feel it necessary to do exploratory abdominal surgery, but such exploratory operations are a problem with many chronic pain syndromes. After several surgeries, exploratory and therapeutic, patients often begin to develop iatrogenic (therapy-caused) problems, such as impingement .of scar tissue on nerve roots, neurogenic bladder, or paresthesia of limbs. It is common at the University of Washington Pain Center to see patients with as many as ten operations (Black, 1975), and, in one instance, the patient's record revealed 47 operations for chronic pain. While it is important to emphasize that this patient population consists of the nation's extreme, problematic cases, our observations do point to a serious problem in medical management of benign chronic pain.

Cancer Pain

Management of malignant chronic pain has also been less than satisfactory for different reasons than those surrounding benign pain. As Marks and Sachar (1973) emphasized, it is common for physicians to prescribe inadequate amounts of analgesics for terminal patients with cancer pain, with most patients actually receiving only about 20% to 25% of the amount initially prescribed. Moreover, nurses managing such patients on the wards are often concerned that too much analgesic drug may lead to addiction, and they are hesitant to dispense as much as the physician may specify. Consequently, in some patients, noteworthy pain persists after narcotic therapy begins. Parkes (1978) surveyed 276 patients with cancer pain and found that over 50% of those hospitalized had moderate to severe pain that continued to be unrelieved, even during the terminal stages of the disease. Of 65 cancer patients managed at home, 20% had moderate pain and 65% had severe to very severe pain that persisted during the terminal phase of the cancer. These findings seem to suggest that the technology now available for the control of pain is not being satisfactorily applied to the management of chronic malignant pain.

THE MEASUREMENT OF PAIN

Scaling

Measurement is a process of assigning numbers to an object, an event, or a phenomenon in such a way that the numbers are isomorphically aligned with some salient characteristic of the thing being measured. In the case of measuring pain, the investigator seeks to attach numbers to the unobservable experience of pain and to do so in such a way that the progression of the numbers on the numerical scale lines up in a one-to-one fashion with some dimension of the pain, such as its intensity or its aversiveness.

Certain characteristics of pain, such as its duration, can be scaled efficiently and with minimal inaccuracy; that is, with proper historical documentation, most investigators can accurately assign time units to measure the duration of a pain problem. Unfortunately, such variables as intensity or aversiveness are much more difficult to scale. The experience is entirely private, and a myriad of variables contributes to the pain report given by the patient or the experimental subject, as indicated in Figure 2.1. Because complaints of pain have an impact on the social environment, they are rarely cold, objective, factual

FIGURE 2.1
Factors Contributing to the Report or Complaint of Pain. In some
instances, neurologic signals play only a small role in the generation
of pain verbalization.

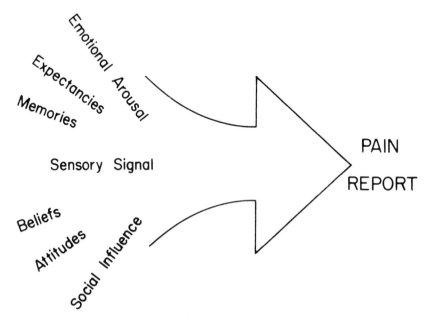

statements about a sensory experience. While researchers can measure and
perhaps quantify the pain complaint, it is indeed difficult to make the assumption that they are quantifying the pain per se. This problem remains a confounding one for investigators dealing with clinical pain phenomena.

Quantification of Human Pain in the Laboratory

The laboratory environment is attractive to the would-be researcher partly
because it provides a clean, simple, and well-controlled situation for investigation. The problem can be operationally defined, simplified, and tightly controlled
in a laboratory, where human verbal reports provide much higher validity and
reliability than they do in the clinic.

The research of pain in the laboratory represents an attempt at intentional
oversimplification on the part of the investigators that undertake it. The most
classical methodology is that of psychophysics. Investigators have long sought to
observe changes in pain threshold, the range of pain sensitivity, and pain tolerance. Even these measures are susceptible to distortion by uncontrolled factors
influencing the pain report, however, and early work on the pain threshold to
radiant heat was soundly criticized by Beecher (1959) and other authorities

in the field. Indeed, early investigators had difficulty demonstrating that morphine and other powerful analgesic agents, in contrast to placebos, can reliably raise the threshold (Beecher, Keats, Mosteller, & Lasagna, 1953). Retrospective reviews of the literature have shown that placebos are more reliable than morphine in raising pain thresholds. This frustrating outcome reflects the influence of psychological factors on the pain report, even in a well-controlled laboratory context.

Sensory decision theory has recently emerged as an alternative method of scaling pain in the laboratory (Chapman, 1977; Clark, 1974; Lloyd & Appel, 1976). This methodology yields two measures: a measure of perceptual capability, or ability to discriminate among various levels of stimuli, and a measure of criterion location, which reflects the strategic biases used by the subject in giving a pain report. While this methodology is time-consuming and demanding, it is helpful, both in principle and in actual scaling procedure, in separating measures of performance ability in a psychophysical task from those of attitudes or beliefs that tend to confound measures of performance abilities.

More recently, measures of reactivity of the central nervous system have entered the pain field (Chapman, Chen, & Harkins, 1979). The cerebral evoked potential to painful stimulation can be measured conveniently from the human scalp in the laboratory. Electrical stimulation of tooth pulp (Chatrian, Canfield, Knauss, & Lettich, 1975; Harkins & Chapman, 1978), laser stimulation of the skin (Mor & Carmon, 1975), and painful electrical cutaneous shocks (Stowell, 1977) all give rise to a roughly similar, late-occurring evoked potential between 60 and 500 milliseconds. The amplitude of this evoked potential appears to correlate with the intensity of the stimulation delivered (Harkins & Chapman, 1978). The stronger the painful stimulus, the greater the amplitude of the response, even though the latencies of the peaks from the evoked potential remain invariant. Recent work has shown that the early components of the evoked-potential waveform correlate with the intensity of the stimulation delivered, while the later components correlate with the subjective judgments of pain (Chen, Chapman, & Harkins, 1979). This promises to be a fruitful and progressive area for further research in pain studies in the laboratory.

Methods of Quantifying Clinical Pain

One of the simplest ways to measure clinical pain is by using rating scales. The visual analog scale is perhaps the best known (Ohnhaus & Adler, 1975; Scott & Huskisson, 1976). Here, patients are presented with a ten-centimeter line labeled at one end as "no pain" and at the other end as "unbearable pain." Patients are asked to make a mark along the ten-centimeter line to indicate the intensity of their personal experience. These rating scales are easy to score, generally not difficult to communicate to patients, and tend to be reasonably reliable. Unfortunately, when only a single dimension is used to represent a complex experience, the validity of the scaling is in question.

Validity is a term that refers to whether a scale truly measures what it purports to measure. In one circumstance, the patient may judge the apparent intensity of a pain that he or she feels as harmless and not threatening. In another circumstance, the same patient may assign numbers to what seem to him or her the most prominent characteristic of a pain, namely, its emotional threat. Thus, under two circumstances, and unbeknown to the investigator, the same patient may assign numbers, using the same visual analog scale, to two different dimensions of the pain experience. This is a common problem that has been almost entirely overlooked in scaling work in research on clinical pain.

The McGill Pain Questionnaire (Melzack, 1975) is the most sophisticated attempt at pain scaling to date. This questionnaire, introduced by Melzack and Torgerson (1971), presents a long list of word descriptors for pain. These descriptors include three classes of pain experience: sensory, affective, and evaluative. The words may be used by patients to specify and describe their experiences of pain. Although the words used are qualitatively different, the questionnaire provides quantitative measures of clinical pain that can be treated statistically. Three major measurements can be made: a pain-rating index derived from the assignment of numerical values to each word descriptor, the number of words chosen by the patient, and the present pain intensity based on a one-to-five-point intensity scale.

Most forms of the questionnaire also ask patients to indicate the location of their pain by shading or marking in on a profile sketch of the human body. The development of this questionnaire has clearly been a significant step forward in pain-scaling procedures, and it represents a departure from the constricting assumptions made by earlier investigators that pain must be scaled unidimensionally.

In spite of its many advantages, the McGill Pain Questionnaire also has its limitations. The problem is simply that this and other questionnaires quantify what the patient *says*, but they reveal nothing about what the patient *does*. For this reason, direct measures of behavior are equally important, and self-report questionnaires must always be regarded as incomplete evaluations of pain problems.

Illness behaviors can be evaluated in a variety of ways in pain patients. The first of these is to require of the patient a diary of daily activities (Fordyce, 1976). Patients may be asked to complete daily schedules, on which they indicate the activities undertaken in half-hour blocks throughout the day. This permits the investigator to measure "up time" and "down time" in order to derive an activity index for an individual patient. Other ways of assessing pain behavior are to score medication intake (since the need for analgesic drugs should be directly proportional to the amount of pain being experienced) and use of other symptomatic therapy, such as hot packs, transcutaneous electrical stimulation, topical ointments, or massage. Finally, it is useful to list and score, at least crudely, the activities of the patient's normal daily life that are limited or prevented by the experience of pain. These data, taken in combination with subjective report information, provide a comprehensive view of the patient's pain problem.

Conclusions

Measurement is one of the major problems in pain research. The laboratory provides a good environment for developing methods for pain quantification, but there is a tendency to lose sight of the real phenomenon. Too often, laboratory researchers achieve precision at the cost of gross distortion and over-simplification. In contrast, clinical researchers often address complex issues with scaling techniques that are imprecise and insensitive. In recent years, progress in these areas has been promising, but measurement remains one of the frontiers in the pain field.

THE PHYSIOLOGY OF PAIN AND ANALGESIA

Nociception

The sensory transduction and neural transmission of noxious events, termed *nociception*, occur when a stimulus from the environment damages body tissues. It may also happen when noxious mechanical or chemical stimuli activate injury-sensitive receptors (nociceptors) deep within body tissues. This process has been described by Bonica (1977). High-threshold nociceptors may be found in skin, blood vessels, subcutaneous tissue, fasciae, periostea, viscera, joints, and other structures. When activated, these structures, like other receptors, convert stimulus energy into impulses that are transmitted along peripheral fibers to the central nervous system. Certain specific characteristics differentiate nociceptors from other somatosensory receptors: small receptive fields, high response thresholds, relatively persistent discharges to a suprathreshold stimulus without rapid adaptation, and location at the endings of small afferent fibers. Like other somatosensory afferents, nociceptors vary in myelination and size. Since speed of neural transmission is closely related to the size and myelination of the fibers involved, there is variability in the conduction speed of different types of nociceptors. Small, unmyelinated fibers conduct slowly, while the larger, myelinated afferents transmit impulses more rapidly.

Afferent fibers have been classified into three major groups: A, B, and C. In class A, all fibers are myelinated and are larger in diameter than those in classes B and C. The subdivision of A fibers into alpha, beta, gamma, and delta subgroups allows further specifications. Roughly 10% to 25% of the A-delta fibers, which are thinly myelinated, carry noxious impulses caused only by very strong stimuli that are potentially or frankly damaging to tissues. Other types of A fibers do not appear to carry nociceptive information, nor do class B fibers, which are comprised of the myelinated, preganglionic fibers of the autonomic nervous system. Fibers in class C are slow conducting and unmyelinated. About 20% to 50% of these respond to innocuous stimulation, while the remaining react to noxious stimuli.

Nociceptive transmission is thus limited to subclasses of A-delta and C nociceptive fibers. These afferents have cell bodies located in the spinal ganglia. They enter the dorsal horn posteriorly and terminate by making synaptic contact with the cells of laminae I, IV, V, and perhaps VI in the dorsal horn of the spinal cord. From the dorsal horn, nociceptive impulses are transmitted to different parts of the neuraxis. Some stimulate somatic motor neurons in the anterior horn, while others stimulate preganglionic neurons of the autonomic nervous system in the anterolateral horn. The information contributing to consciousness comes from impulses that are transmitted along ascending afferent systems in the spinal cord and is sent to various parts of the brain from the thalamus.

Spinal Cord Pathways

The *spinothalamic system* is now known to consist of two different parts: the *neospinothalamic tract* and the *paleospinothalamic tract*. Other information, in addition to pain, is transmitted through these pathways, and, conversely, other sensory tracts also contribute to pain. The neospinothalamic tract is composed of long fibers that connect directly to the ventrolateral and posterior thalamus, where they synapse with a third relay of fibers that projects to the primary somatosensory cortex. Information delivered through this pathway arrives rapidly and permits perception of the site, intensity, and duration of the injuring stimulus. Simply speaking, the neospinothalamic tract delivers impulses that give rise to the perception of sharp, well-localized pain, and it delivers a warning of possible progressive injury.

The paleospinothalamic tract, which is older, is composed of both long and short fibers projecting to the reticular formation, the medulla, the midbrain, the periaqueductal grey, the hypothalamus, and, finally, the medial thalamus. Impulses arriving through the paleospinothalamic pathways then synapse with neurons that reach the limbic forebrain structures and profusely project to many other parts of the brain. Such impulses may provoke suprasegmental reflex responses, which modulate ventilation, endocrine function, and circulation. In simple terms, the paleospinothalamic pathway appears to carry information that gives rise to motivational and emotional dimensions of the pain experience, and it makes possible the perception of burning, aching, dull, and poorly localized pain sensations.

Endogenous Pain Control

It is highly probable that multiple systems of pain modulation exist within the central nervous system. At least one has recently been clearly defined — that related to the action of opiate drugs.

The stage was set for the discovery of a system of pain modulation with the introduction of *gate-control theory* (Melzack & Wall, 1965). Melzack and Wall asserted that pain is generated by the small fibers when tissue damage occurs and that simultaneous activity in adjacent large fibers could modulate small-fiber information by activating inhibitory cells in the substantia gelatinosa of the spinal cord. This mechanism was described as a gate. Melzack and Wall postulated that central control systems in the brain further modulate pain by means of antidromic fibers that carry signals from the brain to the gate in the spinal cord to inhibit the transmission of nociception.

The early central control postulates of gate-control theory are being crystallized by recent research. It has been shown that electrical stimulation of periaqueductal grey areas of the mammalian brain (Mayer, Wolfle, Akil, Carder, & Liebeskind, 1971) and the human brain (Adams, 1976; Richardson & Akil, 1977) results in profound analgesia. This analgesia occurs because cortiocofugal pathways in the dorsolateral funiculus of the spinal cord carry signals that inhibit nociception at the first synapse. The neurotransmitters serotonin and dopamine are necessary in order for this type of analgesia to occur, while norepinephrine depresses such an analgesic effect. Interestingly, morphine analgesia also depends on serotonin, and it is known that electrical stimulation of certain raphae nuclei enhances the action of morphine (Akil & Liebeskind, 1975). The narcotic antagonist naloxone reverses the analgesic effect of both electrical stimulation of the deep brain and opiate drugs.

Opiate analgesia and stimulation-induced analgesia thus appear to share a common mechanism, and this is further supported by the recent observation that opiate receptors exist throughout the brain and in heavy concentration in periaqueductal grey matter (Barchas, Akil, Elliott, Holman, & Watson, 1978). When drugs are given, analgesia occurs because opiate molecules bind to the specific receptor structures. Presumably, this phenomenon is a coincidence, since the structures appear to exist in order to bind to naturally produced substances that happen to be chemically similar to opiate drugs in certain structural respects.

It is now clear that the brain produces a variety of morphinelike substances, termed *endorphins* (Barchas et al., 1978). A certain subset of these substances is called *enkephalins*. One type of enkephalin is located in interneurons of the substantia gelatinosa. It is thought that the binding of this enkephalin to specific receptors inhibits the release of an excitatory peptide, substance P, that is necessary for the transmission of noxious impulses from the periphery to the higher centers of the brain. Thus, morphinelike substances act both within the brain and at the spinal cord to inhibit transmission of noxious input.

Because this area of research is new, the system of pain modulation is not yet fully defined. Furthermore, data available suggest that substance P may be involved in other, descending-pain, inhibitory systems, about which little is currently known.

The relationship between consciousness, cortical functioning, and the release of morphinelike substances in centers in the deep brain has yet to be specified. Nevertheless, current information suggests that people's capacity to control their own pain experience is far greater than previously imagined (Benedetti, 1979). The link between this area of research and such clinical phenomena as painfree natural childbirth, acupuncture anesthesia, and hypnotic control of pain promises to be an exciting development. Other spontaneously observed phenomena also seem related. Analgesia is often observed in association with trauma, for example, with the victim evidencing no pain immediately after a seemingly painful experience, such as a severe burn or a bone fracture in an automobile accident or athletic event. Moreover, chronic pain must be considered in this context, since it may well reflect a depletion of critical neurotransmitters or morphinelike substances that leaves the patient unable to cope with minor, normal, noxious sensory input. Such a hypothesis would, indeed, account for many of the behavior patterns displayed by patients whose pain seems inappropriate for the amount of tissue damage evident.

Nociception versus Pain

This brief overview of nociception and modulating systems would be incomplete without an emphasis on the distinction between nociception and pain. The term *nociception* refers to a neurologic process of information transmission that is *necessary* for pain to occur but *not sufficient* to explain pain as it is seen clinically. It is the integration of nociceptive information with other sensory input and the interpretation of this entire package of sensory data (with regard to memory, expectations, sociocultural context, emotional state, and motivational state) that gives rise to the human experience of pain.

THE PSYCHOLOGY OF PAIN

The psychology of pain is a broad field characterized by several different paradigms that have little in common with one another. The sensory psychologist, for example, sees pain as a sense modality and is concerned with its basic physiology, processes of detection and discrimination, and cross-species comparisons of sensory function. At the other extreme, the clinical psychologist is concerned with patterns of illness behavior, personality characteristics related to pain complaint, and the relationship of emotional and mood disorders to pain behavior. A bridge between the extreme perspectives evident in psychological approaches to pain is difficult to achieve, but a beginning can be made if one adopts a conceptualization of pain as a complete perception that originates with a sensory phenomenon but is shaped in its formation by a host of emotional, motivational, personality, social, and cultural variables (Chapman, 1978).

Pain as a Perception

Components of Pain Perception

A rough model for the pain experience is shown in Figure 2.2. The fundamental building block of pain in this model is the centripetal transmission of noxious sensory information from the periphery, where tissues are damaged or stressed. In addition, motivational and emotional responses occur concomitantly. Thinking human beings are continually evaluating their circumstances, the meaning of sensations they experience, and the impact of any injuries on their future well-being and the well-being of others who are important to them. Patients' social and cultural backgrounds have determined their learning history, socialization, social identity, and cultural predispositions to behave in certain ways in particular circumstances. Indeed, the sociocultural context in which the

FIGURE 2.2
A Multidimensional Conceptualization of the Human Pain Experience.
The bidirectional arrows indicate that each factor tends to influence
the other factors.

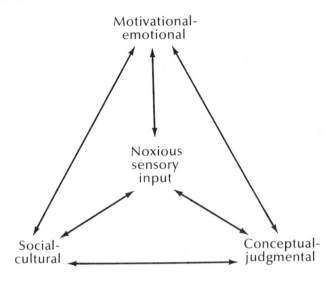

pain experience occurs is very determining — not only for the behavior emitted
by patients but for the formation of their perceptual experience. Patients'
interpretation of a sensation may be very much a function of the social context
in which an injury takes place. The apparent insensitivity of young people in
primitive societies to mutilating right-of-passage rituals is a familiar example
of this.

In Figure 2.2, the arrows have been made bidirectional to illustrate that
every component of the pain process is constantly and dynamically modulating
other components. Consider, for example, the case of the patient who suffers
angina pectoris, the pain associated with heart attack. Angina occurs in response
to myocardial ischemia, the product of insufficient blood flow to cardiac tissues.
Chronic occlusion of an artery, temporary constriction of an arterial vessel, or
a combination of both may cause a section of the heart to undergo oxygen
deprivation, thus provoking noxious sensations. The patient perceives a crushing
retrosternal pain, which may or may not radiate into the throat, the shoulder,
or the left hand and arm. Concomitantly, as the patient recognizes this to be a
noxious signal associated with heart disease, there occurs also a subjective arousal
or drive state that impels him or her to reduce the sensation and a sense of fear
with ruminations about whether or not this may be a fatal heart attack.

As the victim becomes fearful, the sympathetic nervous system becomes
increasingly activated, and this leads to tachycardia. The heavier work load on
the heart causes additional ischemia, and noxious sensory input becomes even

more intense. Thus, it is evident that a series of vicious cycles occur and that this form of pain tends to be a self-perpetuating phenomenon.

All pain experiences are greatly shaped by the social context in which they occur. If the patient is on a tennis court with friends, the pain will be experienced differently than if he or she were undergoing a treadmill test in a "safe" hospital environment, with the pain being purposely evoked. Patients may well express themselves very differently in the company of people whom they socially dominate and whose respect they wish to maintain than in the company of those they perceive as givers of care, sympathy, affection, and nurturance. As Preston (1977) emphasized, the patient's reaction to noxious cardiogenic sensations is determined by the situational context, and it is this interaction that forms the symptoms and the pain behavior or, conversely, the denial of symptoms and refusal to engage in pain behaviors, as described by Olin and Hackett (1964) in their study of "deniers."

Because pain in a person is a complex perception, its occurrence depends on the integration of memory and thinking processes with sensory signals. This is illustrated by the behavior of a nine-year-old boy observed by one of the authors just after an operation in which the child's kidney was removed. As soon as he recovered from the anesthetic, the boy was transferred to his room. He was given no drugs for postoperative pain, in accordance with his surgeon's normal practice. As he lay in bed with his hands outside the bed covers, the surgeon and his associates came to visit. They told him that he could not drink water for the entire day, and they gave him special instructions. Since no drugs had been given, they repeatedly asked whether he felt any pain in his belly. He reliably said, "No, it doesn't hurt." After the surgical team went away, the boy talked more casually with the others in the room. When asked whether there was anything he feared, he began to cry. He confessed that he was frightened of the forthcoming operation that would remove his kidney. His surprised nurse tried to reassure him that the surgery had been done, that it was all over, and that there was nothing to worry about. He refused to believe her. "But don't you remember?" she contended. "That's why they put you to sleep this morning — so they could do the operation." The little boy looked very threatened. "It's not true!" he shouted. "It's not true! I haven't got any bandages." He was asked to feel his belly, since his hands were outside of the bedclothes. When he did, an expression of astonishment came over his face, and he broke into tears, screaming, "It hurts! It hurts!"

This story, like many other similar instances commonly seen in medical settings, illustrates that pain is a complex perception and not simply an alarm signal sent to the brain by special nerve endings. Perception is incomplete unless the emotional state and the thinking mind are coordinated with the pain signals from the injury.

Social Factors in Pain Perception

It is well-known that pain may vary as a function of social context or social influences. Indeed, hypnosis may be interpreted as a social manipulation.

Influences of social modeling on pain expression and pain perception have been studied extensively by Craig and his associates (Craig, 1975, 1978; Craig & Neidermayer, 1974). Individuals undergoing or about to undergo a painful experience often study the behaviors of others in similar circumstances. Laboratory subjects will model their behaviors on those of other laboratory subjects undergoing similar testing. Craig and his associates have demonstrated that performance in a variety of pain-related laboratory tests can be dramatically altered by the behavior of a person who appears to be a fellow subject but who, in reality, is a confederate of the experimenter. Stoical confederate models tend to increase the pain tolerance of laboratory subjects and decrease their pain sensitivity as well. Querulous confederates, who serve as negative models for laboratory subjects, tend to make the subjects less tolerant of pain and apparently more sensitive to painful stimulation. Craig and Coren (1975) even demonstrated an alteration of the d′ (sensory sensitivity index) of sensory decision theory with manipulations of the behavior of social models.

In clinical and real-life situations in which pain or sickness is involved, the suffering behavior of the individual is often a function of early learning experiences and modeling in the primary family situation as well as of learning in the immediate social context. Mechanic (1966) discussed the concept of illness behavior and emphasized that individuals perceive, evaluate, and act or fail to act on symptomatology in different ways, depending on cultural and social conditioning, coping skills, and possible immediate or long-term gain from the illness experience.

An investigation of illness behavior, as assessed by questionnaire, was carried out by Pilowsky, Chapman, and Bonica (1977), who compared chronic pain sufferers in a referral clinic with patients in a family-medicine clinic who presented without pain complaints. The questionnaire assessed hypochondriasis, disease conviction, somatic versus psychological focus of concern, affective inhibition, affective disturbance, denial of psychosocial problems, and irritability. It was observed that patients with chronic pain had a significantly stronger conviction of serious organic disease than did family-medicine patients. They also had an intense somatic, rather than psychological, focus of concern for their illness. Interestingly, the pain patients were characterized by a tendency to deny life problems and stresses not related to physical illness, while family-medicine patients were not. Differences among pain patients in terms of measures of illness behavior were observed when pain patients in the referral clinic were compared with those seen in a private-practice setting (Chapman, Sola, & Bonica, 1979). The patients who had received multiple referrals were significantly more extreme than the others in terms of hypochondriasis, disease conviction, somatic focus, and affective disturbance. These studies indicate that the complex of beliefs and attitudes held by patients with persistent pain sets them apart from other patients commonly seen in medical settings, and they suggest that social learning is an important determinant of the chronic syndrome. The role of secondary gains and social reinforcements and the learning of patterns of pain behavior has been emphasized by Fordyce (1976).

Illness Behavior versus the Disease Model

A useful framework for considering pain behavior in the medical context has been offered by Kleinman (1977) in the context of medical anthropology. Here a distinction is made between disease and illness, with both factors considered to be interrelated dimensions of sickness. Disease refers to the malfunction of a biological or psychological process, while illness is the personal, interpersonal, and cultural reaction to disease. The behavior of a patient in a medical or other social context, when that patient has adopted the sick role, can be termed *illness behavior*, and it is considered to be a function of both the organic disease and the psychosocial impact of that disease.

It is generally accepted in the medical community that illness behaviors exhibited by patients reflect underlying organic pathology, but the literature previously described makes it clear that illness behavior is determined by a multitude of social variables. Clinical experience reveals that most chronic pain problems begin with a disease process, but often the disease largely heals, and the habit pattern of illness behavior remains. This can occur when illness behaviors are reinforced by attention, nurturance, financial compensation, and other secondary gains (Fordyce, 1976). The result is that the patient may continue presenting to physicians with an elaborate sick role (including elegant descriptions of suffering, a history of unsuccessful surgeries, and drug abuse), even though there is an absence or virtual absence of organic pathology.

Repeated attempts at medical therapy cannot succeed in such a case, because the problem is one of habit patterns rather than of organic disease. In such instances, a combination of insight therapy and social learning is necessary for the rehabilitation of the patient.

One of the difficulties in the psychological management of pain patients stems from a failure to recognize the processes by which pain behaviors become relatively autonomous and persist well beyond the point at which the organic disease has healed. The traditional medical model holds that pain is a symptom that will disappear when underlying pathology is corrected. The traditional psychoanalytic approach holds a parallel line of thought; that is, it assumes a form of *disease model*. Treatment is directed toward recall and resolution of those early childhood experiences that are felt to be the determinants of adult pain behavior. It is assumed that when the underlying emotional pathology is treated, the symptoms will disappear. In general, this model has been a failure in the therapy of chronic pain patients. It has been criticized by Mischel (1968), Ullmann and Krasner (1965), and Neuringer and Michael (1970), all of whom reported empirical data challenging the use of the disease model as a basis for psychological treatment.

The emerging illness-behavior paradigm for the study and management of chronic pain presently takes on many forms, ranging from Kleinman's (1977) anthropologic perspective to Fordyce's (1976) operant-therapy conceptualizations. Description of pain patients' manipulative activities as "the pain game"

(Sternbach, 1974), in the language of transactional analysis, and an emphasis on pain as a form of communication and as a search for validation of the sick role (Szasz, 1968) can also be described as variations of the theme of illness behavior. It would seem that new directions in the psychological conceptualization of chronic pain will involve moving away from the traditional psychoanalytic models and exploring new explanatory schemes based on social learning and related frameworks.

Culture and Pain Expression

A number of studies have examined, in both clinical and laboratory settings, the relationship between patients' cultural background and their perception of pain. A representative collection of these papers has been provided by Weisenberg (1975), and Wolff and Langley (1968) have presented a comprehensive review of the literature prior to the last decade.

One of the classic studies was done by Zborowski (1952), who investigated a hospitalized group of male veterans of World War II. He observed that Jewish and Italian-American patients expressed pain in an emotive fashion and tended to exaggerate pain experiences, whereas Irish-American patients engaged in pain denial and "Old Americans" were quiet and stoical. Tursky and Sternbach (1967) made cross-cultural comparisons roughly similar to those of Zborowski, examining psychophysical and autonomic responses to painful, electrical cutaneous shock. The "Yankees" showed the fastest rate of adaptation to the electrical shocks in terms of diphasic palmar skin potentials. The Irish consistently showed lower palmar skin resistance, while the Italians were characterized by a positive correlation between upper pain threshold and heart rate. Jewish subjects showed a negative correlation between these variables.

Cultural differences in pain expression are far from inevitable, however. Winsberg and Greenlick (1967) examined pain behavior in black and white obstetrical patients. When black women and white women were matched in social class and in cooperation, there were no differences in pain response or estimated degree of pain. Differences were observed, however, with respect to age and parity. This finding suggests that differences observed across cultural groups in the laboratory may reflect responsiveness to the laboratory situation and to the novelty of laboratory stimulation as well as to the pain itself. While cultural differences undoubtedly exist, they have not yet been clearly defined in the nonclinical situation, and more work is needed in this area.

Summary

Difficulties in definition and communication have been ongoing problems in the field of pain research as well as in the clinical management of pain. Pain is a complex, perceptual experience even in its simplest forms, and clinical pain phenomena involve a host of intrapersonal, interpersonal, and cultural variables. It is useful to divide pain problems into acute and chronic forms. Acute pain is that brought about by abrupt traumatic injury or disease onset, and its control is a serious problem in medicine. Acute pain is the basis for a considerable amount of human suffering, in spite of the many developments in pharmacologic and other types of pain control. The problems of anxiety associated with acute pain are also serious concerns for those managing patients.

When pain persists for more than six months, it is said to be a chronic problem. The incidence of chronic pain is epidemic, and the costs to society are enormous. Chronic pain problems may be divided into benign and malignant types. Benign chronic pain is that associated with conditions that are not life threatening, and, indeed, benign chronic pain may appear in some patients in the absence of any significant organic pathology. Malignant chronic pain is that associated with terminal disease, such as cancer. Persistent and significant pain is experienced by a large number of patients with advanced cancer, in spite of medication, radiation, and other therapies.

The critical step necessary for progress in the pain field is the development of measurement techniques. Because pain is a subjective experience, quantification is extremely difficult. Laboratory researchers have made substantial inroads in psychophysical work and in the study of the response of the central nervous system to painful stimulation, but this progress has contributed little to the quantification of clinical pain. Recent introduction of the McGill Pain Questionnaire has helped in the development of techniques for assessing clinical pain, and, in addition, recent emphasis on records of activity levels, illness behaviors, and drug use has helped to clarify the clinical pain problems.

Substantial progress has been made in understanding the physiology of pain. It is now known that certain selective sensory structures respond to tissue damage or stress and that their associated neurons synapse with relatively specific pathways in the spinal cord. Modulation of impulses can occur at various levels of the neuraxis. Correspondingly, there are antidromic pathways descending from the midbrain to various levels of the spinal cord, and these exhibit an inhibitory influence on ascending noxious impulses. Endogenously occurring, opiatelike substances produced by the pituitary gland appear to control the pain inhibitory system, and the receptors that bind these substances also seem to subserve the analgesic effects of exogenous opiate drugs, such as morphine.

Progress in the psychology of pain includes new developments in methods for quantifying the pain experience, a broadened perspective on the nature of pain, and the development of models for illness behavior. It is now recognized that pain consists not only of a sensory message about tissue damage but also of emotional, motivational, and thinking responses to the delivery of such sensory messages at higher centers. When pain is chronic, psychological factors often play a major role in the persistence of the condition. Pain complaints and invalidism, like other forms of behavior, can come under the control of the environment when they are selectively reinforced by consequences that are satisfying to the individual.

THERAPIES FOR CHRONIC PAIN

Medical Treatments

Because pain can be generated by a wide variety of injuries and diseases, a myriad of biological therapies can alter pain symptomatology. Abdominal pain can be caused by appendicitis, for example, and removal of the inflamed appendix puts an end to the pain symptoms. Nevertheless, it is possible to describe several general approaches to the control of pain problems. Medical therapies include chemical blockade of pain pathways, neurosurgery, and drug analgesia. Psychological methods of pain control include operant conditioning, biofeedback, hypnosis, and general psychological preparation.

Nerve Blocks

Chemical interruption of the neurologic pathways involved in the transmission of nociceptive information from the receptors in the periphery to the central nervous system can often be used to control pain (Bonica, 1974). Anesthetic blocks — that is, the injection of chemical substances, such as lidocaine, that block the activity of nerves — may be used effectively at several points in the neuraxis. These are commonly applied to provide temporary relief from painful stimulation, such as that experienced during surgery, but they are occasionally used for chronic pain therapy as well. Furthermore, such procedures involving alcohol or phenol may be used to chemically destroy a neuropathway in order to abolish pain permanently or semipermanently.

The simplest form of nerve block is that used when the pain can be clearly linked to a signal originating in the periphery. A common example is that of the maxillary or mandibular nerve block used by dentists to achieve pain control for patients undergoing dental work. This treatment is also used for nerve-entrapment neuropathies, for certain kinds of facial pain, and as an anesthetic for minor surgical procedures in the extremities.

Another approach to controlling pain with nerve block involves the injection of a local anesthetic at the spinal nerve root, the point at which neurologic signals giving rise to pain enter the spinal cord (Swerdlow, 1974). Such blocks generally involve both sensory and motor nerves, and substantial side effects are seen in some cases, including retention of urine, rectal disability, and headaches. Peculiar perceptual disorders also have been seen in a few cases, in which patients have experienced kinesthetic sensations normally associated with severe contortion of limbs. Many patients having this hallucinationlike experience find it extremely disturbing. In spite of these problems, spinal blockade is a powerful technique for controlling pain in many instances. Black and Bonica (1973) reported a series of cases for which spinal block provided good relief in greater than 50% of the patients with chronic pain that were treated, and the duration of relief averaged three months. It is a highly reliable method for controlling pain associated with surgical procedures, and it can often be used to provide help for patients with intractable pain due to cancer.

An alternative approach to controlling pain with nerve block is the blockade of the sympathetic nervous system (Bonica, 1974). The relationship of the autonomic nervous system to emotional states is well-known, and control of sympathetic pathways can be effectively used in therapy for certain pain problems. The stellate ganglion, the celiac plexus, and the lumbar sympathetic chain are all targets for local anesthetic injection. Sympathetic blocks can be used to control certain referred-pain problems, reflex sympathetic dystrophies (such as causalgia) and certain types of cancer pain. Procacci, Francini, Zoppi, and Maresca (1975) demonstrated that the cutaneous pain threshold to radiant heat can be altered by blockade of sympathetic ganglia. They suggested that the pain threshold for deeper tissues is similarly modified by sympathetic block.

Techniques of nerve blockade can be used diagnostically as well as therapeutically by physicians. When chronic pain syndromes elude diagnosis, anesthetic agents characterized by varying durations of efficacy can be used in addition to normal saline (a placebo) in a series of injections. It is possible for the physician to predict both the duration and the course of pain relief on the basis of the concentration of the agent used. By including a placebo, the physician can evaluate the placebo-response tendency of the patient, and other central components of the pain problem may be inferred if the pain fails to yield to certain types of spinal blocks. There are cases in which patients with pain report that it persists even though the spinal block produced total anesthesia below the segmental level of injection. Other patients simply have difficulty identifying pain relief. For example, one of the authors recently interviewed a 37-year-old woman who had had abdominal pain for five years for which she had undergone a total hysterectomy that provided no relief. When given a spinal block by an anesthetist to the level of T2, the level typically used for abdominal surgery, she reported that she could not tell whether she had pain or not. She emphasized that she had forgotten the physical feeling of the absence of pain. One of the advantages of this kind of diagnostic workup is that it helps to forecast the success or failure of possible surgical interventions.

Neurologic Treatments

When pain is chronic, and the problem can be construed as that of a sensory message transmitted along specific pathways, the neurosurgeon can destroy a part of the neurologic structure subserving the pain. These techniques are applicable for fewer problems than patients generally suppose, because pain is an extremely complex experience. Nonetheless, there are certain cases in which neurosurgery is the procedure of choice.

Cutting the posterior sensory divisions of the spinal nerve roots, termed *posterior rhizotomy*, is one of the more common neurosurgical operations. The cordotomy, sometimes called *spinothalamotractotomy*, may also be performed at the spinal cord or the brain stem. This can be done using a number of different surgical or chemical lesion techniques. These operations are costly to patients, in that they produce a permanent numbness, and, if there are complications, other serious neurologic disorders may occur. One of the fundamental problems is that, with time, the analgesia produced by the surgery tends to fade, so that after a period of months or years the pain returns. In some cases, this is probably due to the regeneration of fibers, but, as White and Sweet (1969) emphasized, it would seem that other fibers in the spinal cord take over the transmission of pain. The long-term success of neurosurgical procedures, then, is less than most laymen generally suppose.

Intractable pain may also be treated by certain types of brain surgery. The so-called psychosurgery (such as frontal leucotomy, a resection of the prefrontal cortex) tends to reduce the suffering and reactive expression associated with pain, even though patients report that they can still feel the sensations clearly (Freeman & Watts, 1950; Scarff, 1950). For ethical reasons, such surgery is becoming infrequent, but it is interesting that the most disturbed patients have tended to exhibit the best response to this type of operation. A unique and unfortunate characteristic of this procedure is that patients generally become sloppy, insolent, and uninterested in their world. When psychosurgery is used, the relief of suffering associated with pain is often accomplished only at the cost of patients' psychological integrity.

More recently, other brain operations have been carried out in deeper structures. Thalamotomy is effective for the control of certain kinds of cancer pain, but sometimes it produces a general loss in all somatosensory modalities. Furthermore, as with cordotomy, the pain tends to return. Injection of the pituitary body with alcohol — chemical hypophysectomy — is receiving increasing attention as a method of controlling the pain associated with cancer (Moricca, 1974). Just why this operation works to control pain is not yet understood, but, in recent years, positive reports have been generated by different groups of physicians throughout the world. Another recently developed technique is the electrical stimulation of the periaqueductal grey tissues (Adams, 1976). This treatment can produce long-lasting periods of relief in patients with severe pain, and this developing procedure promises to yield a useful approach to pain control in patients with severe malignant disease.

Analgesic Medication

The most common method for controlling both acute and chronic pain is the administration of analgesic agents. In most cases, these act on the central nervous system to diminish both the effect of responses to nociceptive stimulation and the individual's ability to detect such responses (Halpern, 1973; Stephen, 1973). In addition, drugs, such as aspirin, that block prostaglandins and other antiinflammatory or antipyretic agents may be used to control pain, since they interfere with the chemical substances involved in the generation of pain. In general, three major classes of drugs have been used to control pain and the suffering associated with it: narcotics, sedatives, and antidepressant agents.

Acute pain associated with significant injury is generally treated with narcotics or other moderate to strong analgesics. As discussed above, narcotic drugs bind to specific receptor sites in the periaqueductal grey area of the brain. In so doing, they trigger activity in a system of pain inhibition and reduce the amount of information transmitted to the brain from nociceptors. The effect of such drugs is complicated, however. Receptor sites that bind narcotic substances also exist throughout the limbic system, in other grain structures, and in multiple sites throughout the body, including the intestinal tract. Thus, the administration of a narcotic agent may have multiple effects on the patient, including sedation, analgesia, and a host of side effects that may be desirable or undesirable.

As Foldes (1974) emphasized, narcotic substances may cause significant side effects, such as respiratory and circulatory depression, nausea, constipation, urinary retention, dysphoria, or euphoria. The physician must always weigh the payoff of analgesia against the complications and dangers associated with the side effects, particularly respiratory depression. With repeated administration of the drug, tolerance begins to develop, so that greater and greater dosages are needed to control pain. The consequences of the side effects become increasingly important the longer the drug is used, so that opiates become more dangerous with prolonged use. The situation is further complicated because cross-tolerance may occur when one drug is used for a period of time and another of equal or nearly equal potency is introduced to replace it. The use of one narcotic drug thus increases the need for greater dosages of others. Since it is now known that there is cross-tolerance between the endorphins and narcotic drugs, there is reason to believe that prolonged use of narcotics affects patients' responsiveness to their own pain-modulating biochemical processes, but documentation of this is not yet available.

Yet another problem associated with the use of narcotic drugs is that of addiction. It is this concern that has led both physicians and nurses on hospital wards to be highly conservative in the use of narcotic agents for problems of persistent pain. Perhaps the best example of this problem is that of terminal cancer patients who suffer extreme pain. In many instances, such patients are undermedicated, and they spend their last weeks or days of life in significant pain in spite of the medication they receive (Marks & Sachar, 1973). Problems of addiction are not a realistic concern in this population of patients, but providers of health care are often sensitive to the problems of extreme medication usage. When heavy medication is given, patients typically become unresponsive to their environment, and meaningful interaction with family members in the last days of life is impossible. Efforts to develop procedural guidelines for physicians managing dying patients in pain have been made in recent years (Saunders, 1979; Twycross, 1974).

Sedative agents, particularly psychotropic drugs (such as diazepam), are commonly used for the control of the emotional dimension of acute pain. Beecher (1959) argued that sedation is often more effective in reducing the pain complaint than is analgesia, particularly in the management of postoperative pain. For certain kinds of patients, psychotropic medication seems highly effective. The emotional, excitable patient who tends to act out when experiencing pain is quieted by the administration of a sedative. Such therapy perhaps benefits the caregivers and family more than the patient, but there are clearly situations in which such drugs can be used efficaciously. In contrast, stoic patients who rarely complain when experiencing pain tend to become disinhibited when given psychotropic drugs, and for these patients the drug may have the opposite effect — that of making the quiet and unexpressive patient a complainer. Such drugs must thus be used judiciously by physicians. While it is known that narcotic analgesics have the side effect of sedation, there is no evidence that psychotropic agents, in general, have analgesic qualities. An exception to this statement is hydroxyzine, which has recently proved effective in the control of postoperative pain (Beaver & Feise, 1976).

Tricyclic antidepressants are also used for the control of pain, but their use is limited to chronic pain problems. It has often been emphasized that depression is a major problem for patients with chronic pain (Fordyce, 1976; Sternbach, 1974). Because complaints of chronic pain sometimes stem from chronic masked depression, tricyclic antidepressants have been introduced to control pain that is related to mood disorders. Most tricyclic agents take as much as one month before their effects on depression can be observed, but they have immediate side effects of increased sleep and sedation. While thorough documentation is still needed, there is evidence that such drugs are effective in relieving the suffering and pain of patients afflicted with chronic pain problems (Chapman & Butler, 1978).

The following case provides an example from the experience of one of the authors. Mrs. C. presented to the pain clinic with abdominal pain that had begun after a colostomy was performed. She was ingesting large amount of Percodan, a narcotic analgesic, and she complained of interrupted sleep patterns and depression. Mrs. C. was detoxified and given 150 milligrams of imipramine. Notable improvements were seen within five days, and in three weeks she reported no pain, a full night of sleep, and mood elevation.

While the efficacy of tricyclic agents for patients suffering from chronic pain seems clear, the reasons for the drugs' beneficial effects remain uncertain. Recent studies have shown that patients with severe chronic pain problems are, on the whole, only mildly depressed rather than moderately or severely depressed (Chapman, Sola, & Bonica, 1979; Pilowsky et al., 1977; Wyckoff, 1978). Furthermore, tricyclic drugs benefit patients in as quickly as one or two weeks after administration is begun, rather than after four or more weeks (Chapman & Butler, 1978). Moreover, Chapman and Butler have shown that these drugs have no analgesic properties when tested in the laboratory. Their findings suggest that tricyclic antidepressant drugs are beneficial for patients suffering from chronic pain because they restore disturbed biorhythms, particularly sleep patterns, and because they are administered with instructions that tend to maximize the placebo component of the treatment effect. Since the relief of depression occurs only after the drug has begun to show good responses, it would seem that the relief of depression is not the basic mechanism of tricyclic efficacy.

One of the major problems seen in the chronic-pain referral clinic is that of abuse of prescription drugs. Intent on relieving the suffering of patients, doctors tend to prescribe analgesic or sedative drugs when they are at a loss to suggest other therapies. Such drugs are rarely helpful for chronic pain problems, and patients often shop around from doctor to doctor in an attempt to find some meaningful solution. In so doing, they collect multiple prescriptions and eventually take several different drugs simultaneously, in a combination that no single physician would ever prescribe. These combinations of powerful analgesic and sedative agents may have major effects on patients' mentation, biorhythms, and general health. Peculiar combinations of side effects are often seen, and patients seek help for bowel disorders, respiratory problems, or other physiological malfunctions seemingly unrelated to pain. This leads to yet more prescriptions and more unhealthy combinations of drugs.

Problems of drug abuse often reflect family history, and sometimes a patient's chronic pain may lead other family members to take medications. Wyckoff (1978) gave the following case example.

Mr. B., accompanied by his wife, presented with chronic shoulder pain at the pain clinic. During the interview, it was learned that Mr. B.'s father had also experienced upper body pain and that he had abused alcohol in an effort to "ease the pain." Mr. B. did not use alcohol but relied heavily on Valium (40 milligrams per day) and Percodan (six to eight tablets per day). Mrs. B.'s mother had ingested tranquilizers for headache due to the "tension." Mrs. B. also utilized tranquilizers and, at the time of presentation, was quite reliant on pills as a mechanism for "time-out" from the efforts of caring for her husband.

A further frustration often encountered with patients suffering from chronic pain who abuse drugs is that they are poor historians and present with a variety of confusing symptoms. Proper diagnosis can be carried out in such patients only after they have been detoxified, a difficult and delicate task that may take from one to several weeks. Unless detoxification is carried out, neither the pain complaints nor the diagnostic tests done by the physician can be meaningfully interpreted. In some instances, detoxified patients report that their pain spontaneously disappears. This is most likely to occur in patients who have abused drugs for many years.

It is clear that, while drugs may be an excellent way of controlling many problems of acute pain and some chronic pain disorders, particularly those associated with cancer, serious problems of drug abuse can and do occur when drugs are prescribed for benign chronic pain.

Psychological Treatments

A primary contribution of the psychologist in most multidisciplinary pain clinics is diagnostic. This is because psychological evaluation points out what physicians should not do for the patient. In many instances, patients who come to referral clinics have been repeatedly operated upon and will not benefit from another surgical procedure, no matter how technically sound the surgical intervention may be, nor will they respond to medication therapies or nerve blocks. The psychologist is thus able to "head off" invasive and potentially dangerous therapeutic attempts that will not improve a behavior pattern that is rooted in the patient's life-style and psychological makeup. In addition to performing valuable diagnostic functions, however, psychological therapists are able to contribute in other ways to the management of pain patients. These contributions include behavioral therapies (such as operant conditioning), the use of hypnosis, biofeedback treatments, and general psychological counseling.

Operant Conditioning

While pain is generally construed to be a sensory phenomenon and chronic pain a type of sensory malfunction, behavioral therapists are quick to point out that pain can be operationally defined as a pattern of behavior. Indeed, the physician encountering the patient with persistent pain cannot see the pain itself, for it is an entirely private experience. The physician's encounter is with verbal complaints of pain and various postural and other behavior patterns that imply the presence of pain. In addition, reports from family members or information from the patient's employer may be obtained about limitations of normal daily life allegedly brought about by the presence of pain.

Thus, in many instances, it is convenient and desirable to look on pain as a behavioral phenomenon. Once seen in this light, it is apparent that pain is vulnerable to influence by the host of factors that control all behaviors. Moreover, the emission of pain behaviors may influence the interpersonal environment of the patient, and it may have more widespread social consequences that lead to monetary payoffs, such as compensation payments or the winning of litigation.

As Skinner (1953) emphasized, ongoing behavior is altered and controlled by the selective administration of rewards. When pain behavior seems to be maintained and supported by reinforcement from the patient's social environment, behavioral therapy is indicated.

The developer and primary advocate of the operant-conditioning approach to therapy is Fordyce (1976). He pointed out that certain pain states may be exacerbated or prolonged by selective reinforcement of pain behaviors; that is, if a patient carries out an action associated with pain, such as a postural change or grimace, that action is more likely to recur if it has been followed by attention and sympathy than if it has been ignored. Thus, the patient who suffers in the presence of an attentive and nurturing family may have serious stumbling blocks to recovery. If life before injury or disease was unsatisfactory and lonely, the patient may find that pain brings new success at manipulating family members, friends, and employers and in gaining attention and nurturance from others; time-out from behaviors in which he or she would rather not engage (such as work); and a well-defined and organized life-style that may have been lacking in the past.

It is critical to note that, in many instances, patients have such poor repertoires of healthy behaviors that there is no payoff for recovery from pain. For such a patient, a life of suffering may be more satisfying than the one known as a "healthy" individual. Fordyce (1973, 1976) and his associates (Fordyce, Fowler, Lehmann, DeLateur, Sand, & Trieschmann, 1973) have emphasized that management of such patients requires, first, the identification and prevention of factors that serve as positive reinforcers for pain behaviors, second, increments in the level of physical activity, and, third, withdrawal from drugs. In order to achieve these goals, a structured hospital environment is necessary, since no one can be allowed to reward or acknowledge expressions of suffering or pleas for sympathy on the part of patients. Volunteers enter into such a therapeutic program, which typically takes weeks or months, with full understanding of the process and the reasons for the behavior of the hospital staff that they will encounter. During treatment, patients gradually increase their activity level according to a schedule, with rest being used as a reward to achieving new levels of accomplishment. Pain complaints are ignored, while healthy behaviors and conversations about topics other than physical illness and pain are encouraged and supported with attention and appreciation. Upon release, patients return to a family environment modified by counseling and education in operant conditioning.

For most patients, it becomes possible to live with the noxious sensations that were previously crippling and overwhelming, and these remain as minor annoyances that do not merit attention. For a few, the pain spontaneously remits. This therapy achieves its success partly by altering the attentional focus of the parient, thereby allowing attention to be directed toward the environment and things other than somatic complaints. This therapy also depends on a rehabilitation process, which helps the patient achieve successful patterns of healthy behavior that are viable alternatives to being in pain. Many untreated patients enter and remain, more or less voluntarily, in invalid patterns because they do not have the social skills to succeed as "healthy" individuals.

Biofeedback Therapy

Biofeedback treatment, a variation of operant conditioning that involves the physiological monitoring of some bodily process, consists of a continuous presentation of that monitoring to the patient, who uses it in learning to modify that bodily process. Fundamentally, biofeedback therapists assume that the pathophysiology of pain can be identified and voluntarily (consciously) controlled. This assumption is rather limiting for most kinds of pain problems. Hence, the bulk of the work on biofeedback therapy is related to pain originating in muscle tension, such as tension headache, or to that related to vasodilation, such as migraine headache. When pain is treated by biofeedback technology, two principal methods are generally used: temperature feedback, and muscle-tension feedback.

Work on temperature feedback began when Sargent, Green, and Walters (1973a) serendipitously observed that an increase in hand temperature in a laboratory subject spontaneously led to recovery from a migraine attack. Using biofeedback methods, they taught hand-warming exercises to migraine victims. A device monitored simultaneously the temperatures of the subject's forehead and right index finger, and feedback was based on the differential temperature between the two points. Relaxation instructions were given to help subjects develop hand-warming techniques. After extended daily practice, subjects were able to produce subjective feelings of warmth in the hands and a change in the temperature-training device. Some 63% of the subjects with migraine problems improved, while 33% of the patients with tension headaches showed positive results. In a later study, these authors (1973b) investigated the responses of 150 patients and studied 75 of them extensively in follow-up. Significant improvement was evident in 81%.

This phenomenon has been further investigated in numerous studies, including that of Blanchard and Young (1975), who seriously criticized the original report. They contended that the treatment was not clearly defined, that adequate controls were not used, and that the statistical analysis of data was weak. A variety of other reports, which do not warrant review in detail here, point to the complexity of this area of investigation, and findings are, as yet, inconclusive.

Recently, Sovak, Kunzel, Sternbach, and Dalessio (in press) observed that, when hand temperature was increased by volition, there was digital arterial dilation that coincided with vasoconstriction in the supraorbital and superficial temporal arterial beds. In migraine patients who improved clinically with such training, feedback on finger temperature seemed to result, not in the conditioning of a single autonomic response (such as digital vasodilation), but in a general decrease of sympathetic tonic outflow. Sovak et al. described a conditioned vasomotor reflex, termed the *relaxation reflex*, which is the antithesis of the orienting reflex. They postulated that this reflex can be learned through biofeedback and that it is a central requirement for successful training for migraine.

Tension headaches, unlike migraine attacks, appear to originate with sustained contraction of the musculature in the neck and possibly in the scalp (Wolff, 1963). Using electromyography to evaluate the tension in frontalis and other muscles, investigators have been able to develop biofeedback techniques for tension-headache therapy. Budzynski, Stoyva, Adler, and Mullaney (1973) reported successful reduction in headache, using techniques of muscle relaxation based on electromyogram (EMG) biofeedback. Electrodes were applied over the frontalis muscles of the subject, and a tone was delivered with a frequency proportional to the muscle tension. The subject was instructed to keep the tone at a low level, and shaping was used so that the task became increasingly more difficult due to a controlled reduction in gain of the feedback circuit. Thus, as the gain was adjusted, the subject was required to progressively alter EMG activity to perform the task. Controls receiving pseudobiofeedback and other controls receiving no treatment were included in the study. Significant reductions in muscle-contraction headaches were found in the biofeedback groups, but the pseudobiofeedback controls and no-treatment controls showed no reductions. After three months, a follow-up questionnaire interview indicated that treated subjects had greatly decreased their use of medication. As few as three to six, 20-minute feedback sessions were necessary for new patients with tension headaches to learn to reduce forehead muscle-tension levels by 50% to 70%.

Of course, the distinction between biofeedback therapy and general relaxation is an important one for this area of work, and several studies have investigated whether biofeedback therapy is more effective than simple relaxation training. Haynes, Griffin, Mooney, and Parise (1975), for example, compared subjects undergoing EMG biofeedback therapy with others receiving relaxation training and found no significant differences between these two effective treatments. Moreover, tension headaches not only may originate in frontalis muscles but may reflect a variety of patterns of muscle tension throughout the head, neck, and shoulders.

The data available to date suggest that biofeedback therapy for tension headache is effective — but not necessarily any more effective than general relaxation training. Considerable refinements in technology need to be explored, together with individual differences in responsiveness of headache patients, before any firm conclusions can be reached about the specific benefits of biofeedback for tension headache. In addition, other muscle-tension pain syndromes throughout the body need to be investigated with biofeedback therapy.

Hypnosis

The control of pain has been frequently used by both professionals and laymen as evidence for hypnotic trance. Unfortunately, the potentials of hypnosis for pain control are more limited than is generally assumed. When the problem is acute pain, hypnosis can be effectively utilized in some patients to prevent the pain reactions associated with tissue trauma. For example, Lassner (1967) reported that hypnosis can prevent pain responses in patients undergoing surgery, and Erickson (1967) indicated that it can be employed to ameliorate pain of pathological origin. Numerous studies (such as Orne, 1974) indicate that hypnotic techniques can modify pain in the laboratory. While the issue is somewhat moot, the present consensus is that hypnosis can be used with confidence for only certain suggestible individuals (Hilgard & Hilgard, 1975) and that it can be expected to work reliably only in limited circumstances. For example, hypnotic analgesia is inadequate for surgical cases in which profound muscle relaxation is required (Lassner, 1967).

Hypnosis has not been used extensively for the management of benign chronic pain. Barber (1963) conducted an extensive review of both clinical and experimental literature and concluded that pain is at times reduced, but rarely abolished, in situations in which noxious stimulation continually occurs. Merskey (1974) contended that hypnosis is not worthwhile in patients whose pain is generated by a clear-cut physical disorder, and he has found it seldom useful for other problems. It is sometimes employed in therapy for patients with malignant chronic pain, because it can be used to displace the pain, bring about a reinterpretation of the pain experience, create a time distortion, or control the emotional reaction to persistent pain (Hilgard & Hilgard, 1975).

The problems associated with hypnotherapy for chronic pain are illustrated by a patient seen by one of the authors. Mr. G. presented with long-standing, intractable pain in the area of a surgical scar on his abdomen. He was unable to work because of the pain, which would not yield to either infiltration of local anesthetic in the scar or spinal nerve block. The patient, also complaining of insomnia, underwent hypnosis in an exploratory session to determine whether hypnotic techniques could be used to control the pain and sleep problems. During trance, the patient was told that he would awaken feeling as though he had experienced a refreshing sleep and with an absence of pain and that this relief was to last for a trial period of three hours. Upon waking, the patient appeared refreshed, euphoric, and very thankful. He later recounted that he had left the hospital and had enjoyed his hours of pain relief, returning home just at the end of his trial period. As he opened his door, pain returned suddenly and with such vicious intensity that he fell to the floor of his apartment and was unable to rise for some hours. He recounted that his brief episode of pain relief seemingly had caused the pain to return with a punishing vengeance, and he refused any further participation in hypnotic sessions.

Subsequent interviews revealed that the patient had been a serious alcoholic prior to the operation that gave rise to the pain problem. Following surgery, the patient was able to give up alcoholism by replacing it with pain. The sick role associated with being a pain invalid sheltered the patient from social pressures that had once led him to drink, and it kept him in a close relationship with a very nurturing, motherly, older woman. The hypnotic experience was a confrontation with the possibility that his pain could be controlled, and, hence, it threatened an end to his sick role and dependence. To the patient, the loss of pain meant an inevitable return to despair and alcoholism, a fate he feared far more than his ongoing pain.

Despite an extensive literature on hypnosis and hypnotic analgesia, the nature of the phenomenon is not yet clear. Recent work by Hilgard and his associates (Hilgard, 1971; Hilgard & Hilgard, 1975; Hilgard, Ruch, Lange, Lenox, Morgan, & Sachs, 1974; Knox, Morgan, & Hilgard, 1974) provides evidence that hypnotic analgesia involves the controlled dissociation of conscious experience, rather than an actual loss in sensory function. When hypnotic analgesia is induced, blood pressure remains elevated, as it does in pain states, even though the patient denies the pain experience. This suggests that the patient has pain at some level of awareness. Hypnotic subjects who engage in automatic writing or other forms of dissociation procedures while undergoing a cold pressor test (ice water immersion) may assert verbally that they are quite comfortable, while writing with the dissociated hand, "It hurts!" This phenomenon suggests that there are multiple levels of awareness existing simultaneously, even though only one is dominant, and that the pain can exist as an experience, linked to physiological reaction, on a nondominant level of awareness. These observations have led Hilgard and Hilgard (1975) to distinguish between *overt* and *covert* pain experiences.

It has been previously emphasized in this chapter that pain is an extremely complex experience involving far more than the simple transmission of sensory information about tissue damage. Work by Hilgard et al. (1974) provided some clues on how hypnotic analgesia may work. These authors investigated the pain response to ice water immersion in the laboratory and examined changes in heart rate that occurred during hypnosis and suggestion of analgesia. They concluded that hypnosis had little influence on the sensory information transmission of nociceptive signals provoked by the ice water. Rather, there seemed to be reductions in the motivational and emotional aspects of the pain experience and in the suffering behaviors that would tend to accentuate physiological arousal. Implications of these and other findings are that hypnosis appears to modify the perceptual experience but that it does so by affecting the organization and interpretation of sensory input, rather than by blocking out the input itself.

Prophylactic Control of Acute Pain

There is evidence that psychological manipulation before the experience of acute pain may reduce the associated subjective suffering. Such psychological interventions have involved providing information about the nature of the painful stimulation and counseling about the sensations to be experienced. Much of the literature concerned with psychological pain control is focused on the surgical context. The control of intraoperative pain, such as the pain of endoscopy, and of postoperative pain is a major problem in medicine. In general, studies indicate that the suffering surrounding the surgical experience can be greatly reduced by preoperative counseling and psychological preparation. Indeed, such variables as medication usage and length of hospital stay have been reduced by preoperative psychological manipulation.

A large literature has recently developed in this field that cannot be reviewed in detail here. A few of the representative studies merit attention, however. Johnson (1972) investigated patients about to undergo gastrointestinal endoscopy. She studied one group of patients who received description of the sensations people typically experience during endoscopy, another group who received descriptions of the exact procedures followed during endoscopic examination, and a control group. Those who received preparation differed significantly from the controls in the amount of medication needed, but they did not differ from one another, except that those receiving instructions about sensations were less restless during the endoscopy. Johnson, Morrissey, and Leventhal (1973) confirmed and extended these findings, showing that those patients who were properly prepared psychologically showed less restlessness and lower heart rates while the endoscopy was taking place.

Some patients are made anxious by being put in situations in which they perceive themselves as helpless. For these individuals, information about how to cope may make a major difference. Observations by a U.S. study team, including one of the authors of this chapter, in the People's Republic of China (AAASG, 1976) led to the suggestion that Chinese acupuncture patients cope with intraoperative pain partly on the basis of careful preoperative preparation and intraoperative coaching aimed at showing the patient how to actively work on controlling pain during the operation.

The effects of psychological preparation on pain in the medical context may well depend on variables involving patient personality. Andrew (1970) divided surgical patients into avoiders, sensitizers, and neutrals on the basis of their coping styles. Patients either heard a tape containing information on their condition or were given a control condition. For subjects in the neutral group, the giving of information was associated with reduced hospital stay and reduced analgesic intake. Avoiders required more analgesics as a result of the information, but it made no difference to the sensitizers. Auerbach, Kendall, Cuttler, and Levitt (1976) compared patients on the basis of locus of control and observed that internal-control patients adjusted better to dental surgery when given specific information as opposed to marginally relevant, rather broad information. In contrast, externals responded more favorably to the broader, less relevant information than to the highly specific information.

The literature available thus far suggests that there are no simple answers about optimal procedures for psychological prophylaxis in the medical context. Variables in patient personality appear to be important, as do the nature of the medical experience generating pain and the meaning of that experience for the patient. It should be expected that patients suffering from advanced cancer, who are preoccupied with concerns of death, disfiguration, and uncontrollable pain, will respond differently to such treatments than will patients who enter the hospital for prostate surgery, appendectomy, or cholecystectomy.

Clearly, the role of anxiety during intraoperative procedures or postoperative recuperation is a major one, and the issue of patients' coping responses has emerged as a prominent concern in this area of literature.

SUMMARY

Pain as a clinical problem can be treated both medically and psychologically. Medical therapies include drug treatments and procedures that block or destroy pain pathways. Nerve blocks are chemical interruptions of the neurologic pathways that subserve pain. There are a variety of techniques for chemical denervation that may be applied to pain problems that originate with clearly defined organic pathology. Local injection of anesthetic agents to parts of the sympathetic nervous system can also help to control certain kinds of painful disorders.

Techniques of nerve blockade have been used diagnostically to determine the extent to which chronic pain problems are under the control of organic factors as opposed to emotional or environmental factors. Neurosurgical treatments are carried out using much the same principle as that involved in nerve-block therapy, except that destruction of neurologic pathways tends to be relatively permanent when neurosurgery is employed. In recent years, several brain operations have been developed that are effective in controlling severe pain problems associated with cancer.

Analgesic drugs are commonly used to control both acute and chronic pain problems, but drug therapies for pain are full of potential pitfalls. Particularly when pain is chronic, drug treatments may lead to severe complications, such as addiction, disruptive side effects, and clouding of mentation. Some chronic pain problems are helped by administration of tricyclic antidepressants, but the mechanism of action of these drugs is not yet clear. Drug abuse among patients suffering with chronic pain is currently a major problem.

There are several approaches to psychological therapy for pain. One of the best developed is that of operant conditioning. When pain is construed to be a behavioral phenomenon that has come under the control of the patient's social environment, it can be modified by a program of selective reinforcement. Operant therapy, combined with family and personal counseling, has proven to be a powerful procedure for the rehabilitation of patients with chronic pain problems.

Biofeedback, a variation of operant conditioning, is an attempt to put patients in control of their own bodily processes. Certain forms of pain are related to muscle tension or circulatory disorders, and biofeedback methods can be used to help patients with such disorders develop control over critical body processes that give rise to pain.

Hypnosis has long been known as a psychological method of controlling pain, and it continues to be used. While there are severe limitations on the applications of hypnosis for pain control, it is useful for certain kinds of acute pain problems and for selected application and therapy for patients with malignant chronic pain. It can be used to displace pain, bring about a reinterpretation of the pain experience, induce a distortion of time, or control emotional responses to pain.

Because pain is a complex perception that involves the understanding, memory, and expectations of the patient, it can be prevented, to a large extent, by prophylactic preparation. Patients about to undergo a painful experience, such as surgery, can benefit substantially by proper psychological preparation involving counseling about the nature of the sensations to be experienced and the procedures to be carried out. Preparatory psychological exercises designed to reduce the anticipatory anxiety of patients and to clarify the patients' understanding of the situation have proven to be significant for the control of pain behavior in medical situations.

CURRENT STATUS OF THE PAIN FIELD

Immediate Problems

The management of pain in clinical settings has been and continues to be a major concern in medicine. Examples of particular difficulties are control of the pain associated with burn trauma (including that related to debridement), the diagnosis and therapy of benign chronic pain, and the control of pain related to advanced cancer. Bonica and Butler (1978) pointed out the lack of progress in recent decades in the pain field and attributed this shortcoming to three primary factors: a fundamental lack of knowledge, inadequate application of the knowledge currently available, and problems of communication. These merit elaboration.

Lack of Knowledge

The mechanisms and basic physiology of pain are still incompletely understood. It has been only during the last two decades that major information has become available about basic pain mechanisms, and great voids of knowledge remain in this field. There has been insufficient time to incorporate this understanding into clinical pain management and to develop adequate new technology for pain control. Research scientists have characteristically worked within the isolation of a laboratory environment and have had little or no first-hand experience with clinical pain. Indeed, until recently, most have been unaware of the seriousness of the problems in pain management. As a result, there have been fragmented research efforts, involving artificially induced pain, that have never been integrated with clinical observations or concerns. Thus, in spite of substantial progress in the definition of sensory pain mechanisms, exact causes of such pain syndromes as headache, arthritis, causalgia, and phantom-limb pain, for example, are not yet understood.

The inability to measure pain is yet another substantial problem in the pain field. Shortcomings of attempts at measurement of clinical pain have been due, in part, to the consistent oversimplification of the problem by clinicians who have tried to adopt some of the techniques used in laboratory research. Until clinical pain problems can be properly quantified, it will be difficult to make significant progress with development of technologies for controlling these problems.

The frustrations of working in a field in which measurement is difficult have contributed to the critical lack of sufficient, scientifically trained personnel and the funds needed for research and research training in this area. There exists a vicious cycle in which inadequate scientific manpower leads to inadequate numbers of grant applications submitted, which in turn leads to inadequate amounts of funds budgeted for pain research and training, which causes discouragement among scientists who would otherwise investigate this area, and which finally completes the circle by promoting inadequate scientific manpower.

Inadequate Application of Current Knowledge

There have been progressive trends toward specialization in medicine. This, associated with the lack of organized teaching of medical students and other health-science professionals who manage patients with chronic pain, has contributed to an inadequate application of the current knowledge in the clinical setting. A fundamental problem is that many medical and dental students are not taught the distinction between acute and chronic pain. Consequently, when confronting a patient suffering from chronic pain, they attempt to use the pain as a diagnostic tool and to treat it as though it were an acute pain. The result is failure in diagnosis, drug toxicity, unsuccessful operations that sometimes lead to serious complications, and other iatrogenic disorders.

Communication Problems

The final reason for contemporary problems in pain management is, in Bonica and Butler's (1978) view, one of communication difficulties. Specifically, there has traditionally been poor − or total lack of − communication among research scientists, who tend to work within narrow cliques, and between laboratory investigators as a whole and clinicians. For this reason, dissemination of new information has been slow, and progress made in one area that could contribute to progress in another is often not communicated. Moreover, research scientists all too often carry out their work with no appreciation of the nature and extent of clinical pain problems. While there is no need for a reorientation of basic scientists to applied work, basic clinical understanding is important for the research scientist who is developing new laboratory models for pain. Eventual convergence of laboratory research and clinical efforts can occur only if there is some communication between individuals in these two fields.

New Trends

It has been encouraging to see, in recent years, important new developments that rectify some of the shortcomings of the past. In the last decade, for example, numerous multidisciplinary pain clinics have emerged and developed throughout the world. Such clinics foster communication among different clinical professionals, and many have made a point of building bridges to research laboratories in order to maintain an active interchange with scientific colleagues. International symposia and meetings have attempted to include broader groups of participants rather than bring together a small and exclusive group of individuals with a narrow interest.

Formation of the International Association for the Study of Pain (IASP) in 1974 was a major step forward in terms of improving communication among professionals, disseminating awareness and concern for the problems of pain management within medicine, promoting the development of new technologies for the control of pain, and encouraging effective application of current technologies. This organization has a membership of more than 1,500 individuals representing 55 countries and more than 80 different professional disciplines. IASP has held two world congresses on pain and has fostered or sponsored numerous smaller meetings on such topics as trigeminal pain and pain related to advanced cancer. International symposia have brought together investigators from numerous countries who would otherwise never have an opportunity to interact. Publication of the journal *Pain* by IASP has provided a forum for communication and interchange among investigators from varying backgrounds in the world community.

Conclusion

Pain is one of the frontiers of both physiologically and behaviorally oriented medical research. Numerous serious medical and social problems related to pain merit attention, and a fruitful area for scientific investigation is still largely unexplored. Recent trends of growth in clinical consciousness, communication, and research endeavors are encouraging, and it appears that pain will be one of the active and exciting research areas in the concluding decades of the twentieth century.

REFERENCES

Adams, J. E. Naloxone reversal of analgesia produced by brain stimulation in the human. *Pain*, 1976, *2*, 161-166.

Aitken, A. J. The present status of invertebrae disc surgery. *Michigan State Medical Society*, 1959, *58*, 1121-1127.

Akil, H., & Liebeskind, J. C. Monoaminergic mechanisms of stimulation-produced analgesia. *Brain Research*, 1975, *94*, 279-296.

American Acupuncture Anesthesia Study Group. *Acupuncture anesthesia in the People's Republic of China*. Washington, D.C.: National Academy of Sciences, 1976. (A trip report)

Andrew, J. M. Recoveries from surgery, with and without preparatory instructions, for three coping styles. *Journal of Personality and Social Psychology*, 1970, *15*, 223-226.

Auerbach, S. M., Kendall, P. C., Cuttler, H. F., & Levitt, N. R. Anxiety, locus of control type of preparatory information, and adjustment to dental surgery. *Journal of Counseling and Clinical Psychology*, 1976, *44*, 809-818.

Barber, T. X. The effects of hypnosis on pain: A critical review of experimental and clinical findings. *Psychosomatic Medicine*, 1963, *25*, 303-333.

Barchas, J. D., Akil, H., Elliott, G. R., Holman, R. B., & Watson, S. J. Behavioral neurochemistry: Neuroregulation and behavioral states. *Science*, 1978, *200*, 964-973.

Beals, R. K., & Hickman, N. Industrial injuries of the back and extremities. *Journal of Bone and Joint Surgery*, 1972, *54-A*, 1593-1611.

Beaver, W. J., & Feise, G. Comparison of the analgesic effects of morphine, hydroxyzine, and their combination in patients with postoperative pain. In J. J. Bonica & D. Albe-Fessard (Eds.), *Advances in pain research and therapy* (Vol. 1). New York: Raven Press, 1976.

Beecher, H. K. *Measurement of subjective responses: Quantitative effects of drugs*. London: Oxford University Press, 1959.

Beecher, H. K., Keats, A. S., Mosteller, F., & Lasagna, L. The effectiveness of oral analgesics (morphine, codeine, acetylsalicylic acid) and the problem of placebo "reactors" and "non-reactors." *Journal of Pharmacology and Experimental Therapeutics*, 1953, *109*, 393-400.

Benedetti, C. Neuroanatomy and biochemistry of antinociception. In J. J. Bonica & V. Ventafridda (Eds.), *Advances in pain research and therapy* (Vol. 2). New York: Raven Press, 1979.

Black, R. G. The chronic pain syndrome. *Clinical Medicine*, 1975, *82*(5), 17-20.

Black, R. G., & Bonica, J. J. Analgesic blocks. *Postgraduate Medicine*, 1973, *53*, 105-110.

Blanchard, E. B., & Young, L. D. Clinical applications of biofeedback training: A review of evidence. In L. V. DiCara, T. X. Barber, J. Kamiya, N. E. Miller, D. Shapiro, & J. Stoyva (Eds.), *Biofeedback and self-control*. Chicago: Aldine, 1975.

Bond, M. R. *Pain: Its nature, analysis, and treatment*. Edinburgh: Churchill Livingstone, 1979.

Bonica, J. J. Current role of nerve blocks in diagnosis and therapy of pain. In J. J. Bonica (Ed.), *Advances in neurology* (Vol. 4). New York: Raven Press, 1974.

Bonica, J. J. Neurophysiologic and pathologic aspects of acute and chronic pain. *Archives of Surgery*, 1977, *112*, 750-761.

Bonica, J. J., & Butler, S. H. The management and functions of pain centres. In M. Swerdlow (Ed.), *Relief of intractable pain: Monographs in anaesthesiology* (2nd ed., Vol. 1). Amsterdam: Elsevier/North Holland, 1978.

Budzynski, T. H., Stoyva, J. M., Adler, C. S., & Mullaney, D. J. EMG biofeedback in tension headache: A controlled outcome study. *Psychosomatic Medicine*, 1973, *35*, 484-496.

Cartwright, A., Hockey, L., & Anderson, A. B. M. Treatment of pain in patients with advanced cancer. In J. Gybels, H. Andriaesen, & P. Cosyns (Eds.), *Life before death*. London: Routledge & Kegan Paul, 1973.

Chapman, C. R. Sensory decision theory methods in pain research: A reply to Rollman. *Pain*, 1977, *3*, 295-305.

Chapman, C. R. Pain: The perception of noxious events. In R. A. Sternbach (Ed.), *The psychology of pain*. New York: Raven Press, 1978.

Chapman, C. R. Psychologic and behavioral aspects of cancer pain. In J. J. Bonica & V. Ventafridda (Eds.), *Advances in pain research and therapy* (Vol. 2). New York: Raven Press, 1979.

Chapman, C. R., & Butler, S. H. Effects of doxepin on perception of laboratory-induced pain in man. *Pain*, 1978, *5*, 253-262.

Chapman, C. R., Chen, A. C. N., & Harkins, S. W. Brain evoked potentials as correlates of laboratory pain: A review and perspective. In J. J. Bonica, J. C. Liebeskind, & D. Albe-Fessard (Eds.), *Advances in pain research and therapy* (Vol. 3). New York: Raven Press, 1979.

Chapman, C. R., & Cox, G. B. Anxiety, pain, and depression surrounding elective surgery: A multivariate comparison of abdominal surgery patients with kidney donors and recipients. *Journal of Psychosomatic Research*, 1977, *21*, 7-15.

Chapman, C. R., Dong, W. K., & Chen, A. C. N. Algometry: Clinical and experimental. *Polish Journal of Anesthesiology*, in press.

Chapman, C. R., Sola, A. E., & Bonica, J. J. Illness behavior and depression compared in pain center and private practice patients. *Pain*, 1979, *6*, 1-7.

Chatrian, G. E., Canfield, R. C., Knauss, J., & Lettich, E. Cerebral responses to electrical tooth pulp stimulation in man. *Neurology*, 1975, *25*, 745-757.

Chen, A. C. N., Chapman, C. R., & Harkins, S. W. Brain evoked potentials are functional correlates of induced pain in man. *Pain*, 1979, *6*, 365-374.

Clark, W. C. Pain sensitivity and the report of pain: An introduction to sensory decision theory. *Anesthesiology*, 1974, *40*, 272-287.

Craig, K. D. Social modelling determinants of pain processes. *Pain*, 1975, *1*, 375-378.

Craig, K. D. Social modelling influences on pain. In R. A. Sternbach (Ed.), *The psychology of pain*. New York: Raven Press, 1978.

Craig, K. D., & Coren, S. Signal detection analyses of social modelling influences on pain expressions. *Journal of Psychosomatic Research*, 1975, *19*, 105-112.

Craig, K. D., & Neidermayer, H. Autonomic correlates of pain thresholds influenced by social modelling. *Journal of Personality and Social Psychology*, 1974, *29*, 246-252.

Erickson, M. H. An introduction to the study and application of hypnosis for pain control. In J. Lassner (Ed.), *Hypnosis and psychosomatic medicine: Proceedings from the International Congress for Hypnosis and Psychosomatic Medicine*. Berlin: Springer-Verlag, 1967.

Foldes, F. F. The role of drugs in the management of intractable pain. In M. Swerdlow (Ed.), *Relief of intractable pain: Monographs in Anesthesiology* (Vol. 1). Amsterdam: Excerpta Medica, 1974.

Foley, K. M. Pain syndromes in patients with cancer. In J. J. Bonica & V. Ventafridda (Eds.), *Advances in pain research and therapy* (Vol. 2). New York: Raven Press, 1979.

Fordyce, W. E. An operant conditioning method for managing chronic pain. *Postgraduate Medicine*, 1973, *53*, 123-128.

Fordyce, W. E. *Behavioral methods for chronic pain and illness*. St. Louis: C. V. Mosby, 1976.

Fordyce, W. E., Fowler, R. S., Lehmann, J. F., DeLateur, B. J., Sand, P. L., & Trieschmann, R. B. Operant conditioning in the treatment of chronic pain. *Archives of Physical Medicine and Rehabilitation*, 1973, *54*, 399-408.

Freeman, W., & Watts, J. W. *Psychosurgery* (2nd ed.). Springfield, Ill.: Charles C. Thomas, 1950.

Halpern, L. M. Analgesics and other drugs for relief of pain. *Postgraduate Medicine*, 1973, *53*, 91-100.

Harkins, S. W., & Chapman, C. R. Cerebral evoked potentials to noxious dental stimulation: Relationship to subjective pain report. *Psychophysiology*, 1978, *15*(3), 248-252.

Haynes, S. N., Griffin, P., Mooney, D., & Parise, M. Electromyographic biofeedback and relaxation instructions in the treatment of muscle contraction headaches. *Behavior Therapy*, 1975, *6*, 672-678.

Hilgard, E. R. Hypnotic phenomena: The struggle for scientific acceptance. *American Scientist*, 1971, *59*(5), 567-577.

Hilgard, E. R., & Hilgard, J. R. *Hypnosis in the relief of pain*. Los Altos, Calif.: William Kaufmann, 1975.

Hilgard, E. R., Ruch, J. C., Lange, A. F., Lenox, J. R., Morgan, A. H., & Sachs, R. B. The psychophysics of cold pressor pain and its modification through hypnotic suggestion. *American Journal of Psychology*, 1974, *87*(1-2), 17-31.

Johnson, J. E. Effects of structuring patients' expectations on their reactions to threatening events. *Nursing Research*, 1972, *21*, 499-504.

Johnson, J. E., Morrissey, J. F., & Leventhal, H. Psychological preparation for an endoscopic examination. *Gastrointestinal Endoscopy*, 1973, *19*, 180-182.

Kleinman, A. Depression, somatization, and the new cross-cultural psychiatry. *Social Science and Medicine*, 1977, *11*, 3-10.

Knox, V. J., Morgan, A. H., & Hilgard, E. R. Pain and suffering in ischemia. *Archives of General Psychiatry*, 1974, *30*, 840-847.

Lassner, J. (Ed.). *Hypnosis and psychosomatic medicine: Proceedings from the International Congress for Hypnosis and Psychosomatic Medicine*. Berlin: Springer-Verlag, 1967.

Liebeskind, J. C., & Paul, L. A. Psychological and physiological mechanisms of pain. *Annual Review of Psychology*, 1977, *28*, 41-60.

Lloyd, M. A., & Appel, J. B. Signal detection theory and the psychophysics of pain: An introduction and review. *Psychosomatic Medicine*, 1976, *38*, 79-94.

Loeser, J. D. Low back pain. *Research Publications of the Association for Research in Nervous and Mental Disease*, in press.

Marks, B. M., & Sachar, E. J. Under treatment of medical inpatients with narcotic analgesics. *Annals of Internal Medicine*, 1973, *78*, 173-181.

Mayer, D. J., Wolfle, T. L., Akil, H., Carder, B., & Liebeskind, J. C. Analgesia from electrical stimulation in the brainstem of the rat. *Science*, 1971, *174*, 1351-1354.

Mechanic, D. Response factors in illness: The study of illness behavior. *Social Psychiatry*, 1966, *1*, 11-20.

Melzack, R. The McGill Pain Questionnaire: Major properties and scoring methods. *Pain*, 1975, *1*, 277-299.

Melzack, R., & Torgerson, W. S. On the language of pain. *Anesthesiology*, 1971, *34*, 50-59.

Melzack, R., & Wall, P. D. Pain mechanisms: A new theory. *Science*, 1965, *150*, 971-979.

Merskey, H. Psychological aspects of pain relief, hypnotherapy, and psychotropic drugs. In M. Swerdlow (Ed.), *Relief of intractable pain: Monographs in anesthesiology* (Vol. 1). Amsterdam: Excerpta Medica, 1974.

Merskey, H., & Spear, F. G. *Pain: Psychological and psychiatric aspects.* London: Balliere, Tindall & Cassel, 1967.

Mischel, W. *Personality and assessment.* New York: Wiley, 1968.

Mor, J., & Carmon, A. Laser emitted radiant heat for pain research. *Pain*, 1975, *1*, 233-237.

Moricca, G. Chemical hypophysectomy for cancer pain. In J. J. Bonica (Ed.), *Advances in neurology* (Vol. 4). New York: Raven Press, 1974.

Neuringer, C., & Michael, J. *Behavior modification in clinical psychology.* New York: Appleton-Century-Crofts, 1970.

Ohnhaus, E. E., & Adler, R. Methodological problems in the measurement of pain: A comparison between the verbal rating scale and the visual analogue scale. *Pain*, 1975, *1*, 379-385.

Olin, H. S., & Hackett, T. P. The denial of chest pain in 32 patients with acute myocardial infarction. *Journal of the American Medical Association*, 1964, *190*(11), 977-981.

Orne, M. T. Pain suppression by hypnosis and related phenomena. In J. J. Bonica (Ed.), *Advances in neurology*. New York: Raven Press, 1974.

Parkes, C. M. Home or hospital? Terminal care as seen by surviving spouse. *Journal of the Royal College of General Practitioners*, 1978, *28*, 19-30.

Pheasant, H. C. Backache — Its nature, incidence, and cost. *Western Journal of Medicine*, 1977, *126*, 330-332.

Pilowsky, I., Chapman, C. R., & Bonica, J. J. Pain, depression, and illness behavior in a pain clinic population. *Pain*, 1977, *4*, 183-192.

Preston, T. A. *Coronary artery surgery: A critical review.* New York: Raven Press, 1977.

Procacci, P., Francini, F., Zoppi, M., & Maresca, M. Cutaneous pain threshol changes after sympathetic block in reflex dystrophies. *Pain*, 1975, *1*, 167-173.

Richardson, D. E., & Akil, H. Pain reduction by electrical brain stimulation in man. *Journal of Neurosurgery*, 1977, *47*, 178-183.

Sargent, J. D., Green, E. E., & Walters, E. D. Preliminary report on the use of autogenic feedback training and treatment of migraine and tension headaches. *Psychosomatic Medicine*, 1973, *35*, 129-135. (a)

Sargent, J. D., Walters, E. D., & Green, E. E. Psychosomatic self-regulation of migraine headaches. *Seminars in Psychiatry*, 1973, *5*, 415-428. (b)

Saunders, D. The nature and management of terminal pain and the hospice. In J. J. Bonica & V. Ventafridda (Eds.), *Advances in pain research and therapy* (Vol. 2). New York: Raven Press, 1979.

Scarff, J. E. Unilateral prefrontal lobotomy for the relief of intractable pain. Report of 58 cases with special consideration of failures. *Journal of Neurosurgery*, 1950, *7*, 330-336.

Scott, J., & Huskisson, E. C. Graphic representation of pain. *Pain*, 1976, *2*, 175-184.

Seligman, M. E. P. *Helplessness: On depression, development, and death*. San Francisco: W. H. Freeman, 1975.

Skinner, B. F. *Science and human behavior*. New York: Macmillan, 1953.

Sovak, M., Kunzel, M., Sternbach, R. A., & Dalessio, D. J. Current investigations in headache. *Research Publications of the Association for Research in Nervous and Mental Disease*, in press.

Stephen, C. R. Drug management of the patient with pain: Pharmacologic considerations. *Southern Medical Journal*, 1973, *66*, 1421-1425.

Sternbach, R. A. *Pain patients – Traits and treatment*. New York: Academic Press, 1974.

Stowell, H. Cerebral slow waves related to the perception of pain in man. *Brain Research Bulletin*, 1977, *2*, 23-30.

Swerdlow, M. (Ed.). *Relief of intractable pain*. Amsterdam: Excerpta Medica, 1974.

Szasz, T. W. The psychology of persistent pain. A portrait of l'homme douloureux. In A. Soulairac, J. Cahn, & J. Charpentier (Eds.), *Pain*. London: Academic Press, 1968.

Tursky, B., & Sternbach, R. A. Further physiological correlates of ethnic differences in response to shock. *Psychophysiology*, 1967, *4*, 67-74. Reprinted in M. Weisenberg (Ed.), *Pain: Clinical and experimental perspectives*. St. Louis: C. V. Mosby, 1975.

Twycross, R. G. Clinical experience with diamorphine in advanced malignant disease. *International Journal of Clinical Pharmacology*, 1974, *93*, 184-198.

Ullmann, L., & Krasner, L. *Case studies in behavior modification*. New York: Holt, Rinehart & Winston, 1965.

Ward, T., Knowelden, J., & Sharrard, W. J. W. Low back pain. *Journal of the Royal College of General Practice*, 1968, *15*, 128-136.

Weisenberg, M. (Ed.). *Pain: Clinical and experimental perspectives*. St. Louis: C. V. Mosby, 1975.

White, J. E., & Sweet, W. H. *Pain and the neurosurgeon*. Springfield, Ill.: Charles C. Thomas, 1969.

Wilkes, E. Some problems in cancer management. *Proceedings of the Royal Society of Medicine*, 1974, *67*, 23-27.

Winsberg, B., & Greenlick, M. Pain response in Negro and white obstetrical patients. *Journal of Health and Social Behavior*, 1967, *8*, 222-227. Reprinted in M. Weisenberg (Ed.), *Pain: Clinical and experimental perspectives*. St. Louis: C. V. Mosby, 1975.

Wolff, B. B., & Langley, S. Cultural factors and the response to pain: A review. *American Anthropologist*, 1968, *70*, 494-501. Reprinted in M. Weisenberg (Ed.), *Pain: Clinical and experimental perspectives*. St. Louis: C. V. Mosby, 1975.

Wolff, H. B. *Headache and other head pain* (2nd ed.). New York: Oxford University Press, 1963.

Wyckoff, M. G. *The relationship of maladaptive illness behavior to chronic pain*. Unpublished doctoral dissertation, Union Graduate School, 1978.

Zborowski, M. Cultural components in responses to pain. *Journal of Social Issues*, 1952, *8*, 16-30.

3

PSYCHOLOGICAL AND PHYSIOLOGICAL FACTORS IN THE DEVELOPMENT, MAINTENANCE, AND TREATMENT OF MENSTRUAL DISORDERS

Linda Gannon

INTRODUCTION

Although a variety of disorders can be included in a chapter on menstrual disorders, the present emphasis is on dysmenorrhea and premenstrual syndrome. In addition to being the most common menstrual disorders, they have also generated the most interest in the scientific community. These disorders are generally considered "psychosomatic," because the symptomatology includes both psychological and physical components, and because, on a theoretical level, both psychological and organic etiologies are logically justifiable. Psychological theories have viewed the development of menstrual disorders as due to a manifestation of general neurotic tendencies, a rejection of femininity or the woman's role, and/or a consequence of the negative attitude which society conveys concerning menstruation. On the other hand, both dysmenorrhea and premenstrual syndrome are temporally related to distinct hormonal changes which have potentially pervasive effects on physiological functioning.

In addition to the usual problems associated with theoretical conceptualizations and empirical research in the area of psychosomatic medicine — namely, the difficulty of either separating or integrating physiological and psychological factors — the study of menstrual disorders has the added burden of having both social and political implications. Women who seek treatment for menstrual disorders are no longer content with ineffective analgesics and advice to stay in bed a few days each month; they are demanding more effective treatment which will enable them to lead economically independent lives and hold positions of responsibility and influence. These demands, coupled with improved techniques of hormonal assay and a general interest in biorhythms, have precipitated a surge of interest in recent years in the etiology and treatment of menstrual disorders.

THE MENSTRUAL CYCLE

Normal menstrual cycle activity relies on activity of the *hypothalamus*, the *anterior pituitary*, and the *ovaries*. Using menstruation as an arbitrary starting point, the hypothalamus secretes *follicle-stimulating hormone releasing factor* and *luteinizing hormone releasing factor*. These act on the anterior pituitary and cause it to secrete *follicle-stimulating hormone* (FSH) and *luteinizing hormone* (LH). (Figure 3.1 graphically depicts the hormonal changes which occur during the menstrual cycle.) FSH causes one of the many follicles in the ovary to develop and begin to secrete *estrogen*. The increase in circulating estrogens is responsible for the proliferation of the *endometrium* (the lining of the uterus), which occurs prior to ovulation. When estrogen reaches a certain level, the pituitary is inhibited in its production of FSH. Falling FSH levels reduce stimulation of the ovaries so that estrogen levels begin to fall, and this stimulates the pituitary to produce a surge of LH. LH causes the mature follicle to rupture through the wall of the ovary and to develop into a secretory organ known as the *corpus luteum*. This preovulatory phase is variously referred to as the *follicular* or *proliferative* phase.

In the postovulatory phase, the source of most hormones is the corpus luteum. The corpus luteum secretes some estrogen, causing estrogen to again rise, but the primary secretion of the corpus luteum is *progesterone*, which,

FIGURE 3.1
Hormonal Changes in the Normal Menstrual Cycle

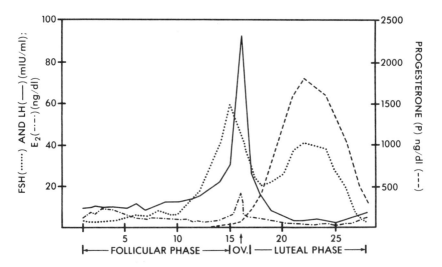

Reprinted, by permission, from R. Kolodny, W. Masters, V. Johnson, and M. Briggs (eds.), *Textbook of Human Sexuality for Nurses* (Boston: Little, Brown) 1979.

ir to ovulation, was secreted by the adrenal cortex in only small quantities. gesterone acts to differentiate the proliferated endometrium into a secretory i in preparation for implantation and to inhibit secretions from the hypo- .amus which, in turn, inhibits the anterior pituitary from secreting the iadotropins FSH and LH. The resulting decrease in LH causes the corpus iuteum to fail if fertilization does not occur, and without the corpus luteum, levels of progesterone and estrogen decline. Since maintenance of the endometrium requires estrogen and progesterone, this structure then degenerates and menstruation occurs. Without the inhibiting influence of progesterone and estrogen, the hypothalamic hormones resume activation of the anterior pituitary, and the resultant release of FSH and LH begins the repetition of the cycle. This phase is called the *postovulatory*, *luteal*, or *secretory* phase. The *premenstrual* phase refers to the latter part, including from three to ten days prior to the onset of menstruation.

The hormones responsible for the continuing cycle associated with female reproduction, particularly estrogen and progesterone, have more diverse effects than those described above. Various research has implicated these hormones as causative agents in a variety of physiological, endocrinological, psychological, and behavioral changes that have been found to covary with the menstrual cycle. Central to this research is the temporal relationship of various dependent variables to the menstrual cycle. A common research procedure is to divide the menstrual cycle into several phases and compare these phases on some criterion measure of interest, such as depression or reaction time. Inherent in this procedure are several problems. Since the length of the menstrual cycle varies considerably among different women and within the same woman, a particular phase will vary in the length of time it represents. A common solution to this problem is to designate the phases of primary interest as fixed and the phase of least interest as variable. For example, Dalton (1968) labeled the four days preceding menses as the premenstrual phase, the four days following onset as the menstrual phase and the remainder of the cycle the intermenstrual phase. Unfortunately, no standard procedure exists for phase differentiation and definition; the consequence is a tremendous amount of procedural variability in the research on menstruation. According to Sommer (1973), who presented an extensive tabulation of the idiosyncratic research procedures, the number of differentiated phases varies from one to seven. In addition, the definition of the same phase varies from study to study; for example, the premenstrual phase has been designated as two days (Pierson & Lockhart, 1963), four days (Dalton, 1968), five days (Dalton, 1960b), and seven days (Sommer, 1972) prior to menstruation. Clearly, this procedural variability makes comparisons among studies difficult.

Much research is theoretically based on the assumed fluctuations in circulating levels of estrogen and progesterone during the menstrual cycle. Since the levels of these hormones are time locked to ovulation, and since hormonal assays are expensive and time-consuming, researchers characteristically employ some indirect method to determine the time of ovulation and then assume that, prior to this time, estrogen levels are high and progesterone levels minimal and that, subsequent to this time, levels of both estrogen and progesterone are high. In ovulatory cycles, these assumptions are appropriate; however, methods for determining the time of ovulation vary in their accuracy. The most common method utilizes the date of the last menses, the normal length of the cycle, and the predicted date of the next menses; ovulation is assumed to occur approximately fourteen days prior to the onset of menses. This procedure is based on the widespread belief that the length of the menstrual cycle varies directly with the preovulatory phase, while the postovulatory phase is an invariant fourteen days. Marshall (1963) ascertained the time of ovulation by basal temperature fluctuations and found that only 67% of 155 women exhibited a postovulatory phase between eleven and fourteen days. In a later study, Abplanalp, Livingston, Rose, and Sandwisch (1977) measured estrogen and progesterone concentrations and concluded that pinpointing ovulation on the basis of the dates of past and expected periods was successful in 50% of the cases. Thus, the self-report method of determining the time of ovulation has questionable validity.

A more objective method is that of recording basal temperature on a daily basis. It is believed that basal temperature increases slightly but noticeably at the time of ovulation and remains elevated until menses. Although this method is widely used not only by researchers but by women who wish to avoid or facilitate pregnancy, Sommer (1973) noted that only 25% of all women exhibit a clear temperature change at ovulation. Furthermore, Southam and Gonzaga (1965) compared dates of ovulation determined by endometrial and ovarian histology and basal temperature and reported as much as a four-day discrepancy between the two procedures.

The contradictions and inconsistencies which characterize the research concerned with investigating menstrual disorders and menstrual cycle covariates is at least partially due to the lack of standardized procedures for defining cycle phases and to the use of less than adequate methods for pinpointing the time of ovulation. The reader is requested to keep these limitations in mind when considering the research presented below.

THE MEASUREMENT OF MENSTRUAL SYMPTOMS

The majority of research studies concerned with menstrual symptoms do not employ standardized instruments to assess symptomatology associated with the menstrual cycle but, rather, use unvalidated questionnaires or unstructured interviews to obtain data. These idiosyncratic techniques are discussed with individual studies. Two instruments have been developed, however, in the attempt to provide a reliable and valid assessment of symptoms: the Menstrual Distress Questionnaire and the Menstrual Symptom Questionnaire.

Moos (1968, 1977) developed the *Menstrual Distress Questionnaire* (MDQ), which was designed to evaluate menstruation-related symptoms during the premenstrual, menstrual, and intermenstrual phases of the cycle. The questionnaire consists of forty-seven symptoms, which were initially obtained from interviews with women and previous research in the area of menstrual cycle symptomatology. In addition, symptoms not typically associated with the menstrual cycle, such as buzzing or ringing in the ears and feelings of suffocation, were included in order to obtain a measure of general complaining. Of the forty-seven symptoms, four are positive — affection, excitement, feelings of well-being, and bursts of energy or activity. A six-point scale, which rates severity from "no experience of symptom" to "acute or partially disabling," accompanies each symptom.

In the initial sample of 839 wives of graduate students, each subject completed four questionnaires rating symptoms for the menstrual (during flow), premenstrual (the week prior to flow), and intermenstrual (the rest of the cycle) phases of her most recent menstrual cycle and of her worst menstrual cycle. Data from each phase were factor analyzed separately and resulted in eight symptom groups. All items, except change in eating habits, loaded consistently on a factor. Moos labeled the scales as follows: pain, water retention, concentration, negative affect, behavior change, arousal, autonomic reactions, and control. All the positive items loaded on the arousal scale. Pain, concentration, behavior change, and autonomic reactions were higher during the menstrual than the premenstrual phase, while the reverse was true for water retention and negative affect; all these scales were lowest during the intermenstrual phase. The arousal and control scales did not show cyclic variation. Unfortunately, Moos did not report statistics for these cyclic effects, so it is difficult to determine the reliability of these phase differences.

Other reasearch which employed the MDQ to measure differences in menstrual symptomatology among different phases have yielded mixed results. Golub (1976a) found negative affect, concentration, and behavior change to be significantly higher premenstrually than intermenstrually. Gruba and Rohrbaugh (1975) found significant differences between all pairs of menstrual, premenstrual, and intermenstrual comparisons for all scales except arousal. On the other hand, none of the eight scales showed significant variability over the menstrual cycle in a study by Favreau (1974). Others have used Form T of the MDQ, which is modified to assess symptoms on a daily basis ("indicate how you feel *today*"). With this form, a study by Wilcoxen, Schrader, and Sherif (1976) showed that four of the eight scales differed significantly among phases. Markum (1976) found no significant phase effects; Silbergeld, Brast, and Noble (1971) analyzed each item and each scale for phase effects and found one scale and three items to vary significantly — approximately what one would expect by chance.

Moos (1977) provided intercorrelations for the eight scales for each phase; all were positive, with a range of .18 to .63, indicating that women who scored high on one scale also scored high on other scales, including the control scale.

He also intercorrelated the three cycle phases for each scale; again, all the correlation coefficients were positive, ranging from .17 to .77, an indication that women tended to endorse the same symptoms for all three phases. Parlee (1974) pointed out that these interscale and interphase correlations suggest that a response bias may be operating, that is, the questionnaire may be measuring a tendency to respond high or low, regardless of the content of the item. This suggestion receives further support when one considers that Moos, Kopell, Melges, Yalom, Lunde, Clayton, and Hamburg (1969) reported a small but positive correlation between arousal, which consists of positive items, and all other scales, which consist of negative items.

An important consideration for any assessment procedure is reliability. Markum (1976) assessed split-half reliability for each scale of the MDQ and for each phase; all were significant, with all but one correlation coefficient being above .80. She also analyzed both forms of the MDQ for intercycle stability for all scales and for the three phases. All correlations were high (.41-.96), except for the total score and the arousal scale on the daily form for the menstrual phase, which were .26 and .20, respectively. Moos et al. (1969) studied fifteen women for two cycles on twenty-four of the items and found generally high correlations (.39-.95). These studies suggest that the MDQ is a fairly reliable instrument.

Several researchers have questioned the validity of the original form of the MDQ, Form A, on the basis that it is a retrospective questionnaire and relies on memory. A possible test for the adequacy of retrospective data is to administer both Form A and Form T to the same women and compare the responses from the two forms. Moos et al. (1969) selected two groups of women — one high on premenstrual tension, the other low on premenstrual tension — on the basis of their responses to Form A. They then administered Form T to these women for two consecutive cycles. Nine of the fifteen women showed consistency between Form A and Form T. Rouse (1978) reported significant differences between the two forms on the pain, water retention, and negative affect scales. Although it is not clear from the information published, it appears that women overrated their symptoms on Form A. In a final study, Brockway (1975) administered Form A and, on the basis of these data, formed three groups which were low, moderate, and high on premenstrual symptoms. The subjects then completed Form T daily for two cycles. Brockway analyzed the water retention, pain, and negative affect scales and found significant differences between Forms A and T for all groups and all scales, except the low symptom group on water retention. The results of these studies clearly raise doubt as to the validity of the retrospective form of the MDQ to assess menstrual cycle symptoms.

Parlee (1974) suggested that retrospective questionnaires, such as the MDQ, are more a measure of stereotypic beliefs or expectations than of actual symptomatology. She administered the MDQ to twenty-five women and thirty-four men, with instructions to complete one questionnaire for each of the three phases according to their experience with, or knowledge of, these symptoms.

The data from both groups showed significant phase effects for most scales. In all but one of the twenty-four instances (eight scales, three phases), men gave greater severity ratings than women; these differences were statistically significant in eleven cases. Parlee concluded that the stereotypic beliefs act to exaggerate actual, experienced symptomatology when reported on retrospective questionnaires.

Further evidence for this view comes from a study by Ruble (1977), unique for its creative design. Women subjects were told that it is now scientifically possible to predict the date of their next period. Subjects were given fake brain wave tests; then a third of the subjects were told that their period was not expected for seven to ten days, a third that their period was due in one or two days, and a third were given no information. (All subjects were actually tested about one week prior to their period.) They were then asked to fill out the MDQ on the basis of symptoms they had experienced in the last day or two. Ruble analyzed three of the eight scales. The water retention, pain, and negative affect scales were higher for those women who believed they were premenstrual than for those who believed they were intermenstrual; differences in the first two scales reached statistical significance. Ruble suggests that learned associations or beliefs may result in women exaggerating their actual experience.

In summary, the MDQ, particularly Form A, may not be appropriate for use in research where the goal is to assess menstrual cycle symptoms in samples of normal women. It does not consistently differentiate between cycle phases, although this probably reflects a lack of cyclic variability in the normal population. Furthermore, the MDQ appears to be somewhat sensitive to response biases, demand characteristics, and belief systems. These criticisms, however, do not negate the potential utility of this instrument, particularly Form T, as a screening device when it is desirable to obtain a sample of women who experience particular symptoms or as an assessment device in a clinical setting.

A second instrument, the *Menstrual Symptom Questionnaire* (MSQ), was developed by Chesney and Tasto (1975a) and was theoretically derived from Dalton's (1964) distinction between spasmodic symptoms — spasms of pain which begin on the first day of menstruation — and congestive symptoms — dull, aching pain accompanied by lethargy and depression prior to menstruation. According to Dalton, the former is due to an excess of progesterone, the latter to insufficient progesterone; thus, it is unlikely that an individual would experience both.

The purpose of the MSQ was to distinguish between these two types of symptoms. Fifty-one items were obtained from the literature; each was rated on a five-point scale, which reflected the degree to which the symptom was present. Their first sample consisted of fifty-six women who stated that they experienced menstrual discomfort. A factor analysis resulted in two factors on which twenty-five of the items loaded. These two factors conformed somewhat to the definitions of spasmodic and congestive dysmenorrhea. Data from a second sample of forty-eight subjects essentially replicated those of the first group.

Since these authors assumed that the two types of symptoms did not occur in the same woman, they developed a scoring procedure which reversed the scoring for spasmodic items, resulting in high scores being indicative of a spasmodic disorder and low scores of a congestive disorder. In other words, women received high scores if they endorsed spasmodic items and not congestive items and low scores if they endorsed congestive items and not spasmodic items. This scoring procedure does not distinguish between women who experience neither group of symptoms and women who experience both. Chesney and Tasto (1975a) reported a test-retest reliability coefficient of .87, and Cox (1977) reported similar results. In addition, Chesney and Tasto (1975b) found differential treatment effectiveness for the two types of symptoms using behavior modification techniques. Cox (1977) and Cox and Meyer (1978), however, found behavioral therapy to be equally effective for spasmodic and congestive disorders.

Criticism of the MSQ has come from several sources. Data from Cox (1977) lead one to question if the MSQ is an adequate instrument to assess symptoms. He found that the mean scores of a group of women who complained of menstrual distress were almost identical to those of a group who claimed to experience no distress; these results raised doubts concerning the discriminative validity of the instrument. Probably the most serious criticism of the MSQ came from Webster, Martin, Uchalik, and Gannon (1979). Claiming that Chesney and Tasto's sample was too small for their statistical techniques, they performed an hypothesis-testing factor analysis on data from 275 subjects. Ten of the twelve spasmodic items correlated significantly with the spasmodic factor, and four of the twelve congestive items correlated with the congestive factor. Thus, ten of the twenty-four items did not load as predicted, and the original factors were not supported. Furthermore, if Dalton (1964) was correct, and the two disorders are mutually exclusive, then spasmodic and congestive scores should be inversely related. The correlation coefficient between the two scores was .56, indicating that not only is it possible for the two disorders to occur together, but it is likely that they will. The results of these studies not only raise doubts as to the validity of the MSQ but question the soundness of the theoretical base as well.

Neither of the standardized instruments described above completely meets the need of researchers for a reliable and valid assessment procedure for menstruation-related symptoms. Of the two, the MDQ seems preferable, in that it has at least face validity. In addition to the problems discussed above, a further criticism of both instruments is their concentration on negative symptoms. Israel (1953) pointed out that women frequently report increased energy and feelings of well-being in relation to the menstrual cycle. In research where the goal is to investigate physical, psychological, and behavioral changes which covary with the menstrual cycle, the emphasis on negative events seems unjustified and a practice which may act to perpetuate stereotypic beliefs concerning women.

SYMPTOMS ASSOCIATED WITH THE MENSTRUAL CYCLE IN NORMAL POPULATIONS

Disagreement exists as to the incidence and even the existence of the two most common menstruation-related disorders — dysmenorrhea and premenstrual syndrome (Parlee, 1973). Viewed as a unit, the research concerned with menstrual symptoms is frequently contradictory and rarely replicable. A possible cause for this apparent confusion is subject selection. Some researchers have chosen to assess symptoms associated with the menstrual cycle in a normal population; others have chosen to employ samples of women who complain of, or who have been diagnosed as suffering from, a menstrual disorder. Contradictory conclusions may well result from attempting to integrate the research without regard to subject selection. Thus, for heuristic reasons, research assessing symptomatology in normal populations will be reviewed prior to a discussion of etiology and treatment of the disorders.

Physical Symptoms

Pain is a component of both dysmenorrhea and premenstrual syndrome. The pain in the former is generally described as spasms in the abdominal region, possibly spreading to the thighs or back. In premenstrual syndrome, the pain is typically associated with swelling in the breasts or extremities and is described as dull or aching. Several studies have investigated fluctuations in pain associated with the menstrual cycle in normal populations. Moos (1968) named one of his scales "pain," which consisted of muscle stiffness, headache, cramps, backache, fatigue, and general aches and pains. For his original sample of 839 women, he reported this scale was higher menstrually than premenstrually and higher premenstrually than intermenstrually, although he did not say if these differences were statistically significant. Gruba and Rohrbaugh (1975) and Wilcoxon et al. (1976) found significant phase effects for the pain scale of the MDQ. On the other hand, Favreau (1974), Markum (1976), Zimmerman and Parlee (1973), and Janowsky, Berens, and Davis (1973) failed to find significant phase effects for this scale.

Other physical symptoms include swelling and weight gain, which tend to contribute to the discomfort experienced by women who complain of premenstrual tension. Studies of variables assumed to be associated with these symptoms have yielded contradictory, usually negative findings when subjects were drawn from a normal population. One of the scales on the MDQ is water retention, which consists of weight gain, skin disorders, painful breasts, and swelling. Moos (1968) found these items to be highest during the premenstruum. Gruba and Rohrbaugh (1975) and Wilcoxon et al. (1976) found significant phase effects for water retention as measured with the MDQ.

Studies using objective measures of water retention, however, have generally failed to find similar results. Janowsky et al. (1973) found weight and potassium-sodium ratio to vary with the phase of the menstrual cycle (statistics unspecified), with both ratios increasing premenstrually, while Gray, Strausfeld, Watanabe, Sims, and Solomon (1968) found no phase effects for potassium-sodium ratio. Andersch, Hahn, Andersson, and Isaksson (1978) did not find weight to vary with the menstrual cycle but did note a slight variation in total body water. Abramson and Torghele (1961) reported that peaks in weight occurred on days 3-6, 13-15, and 24-26; they viewed these weight fluctuations as significant but did not present statistics. An average weight fluctuation of .7 pounds was reported for sixty-nine subjects by Golub, Menduke, and Conly (1965), and the subjects differed as to where in the cycle they weighed the most. Wong, Freedman, Levan, Hyman, and Quilligan (1972) measured the capillary filtration coefficient as an index of the flow of fluid from the intravascular to the extravascular compartment and reported no cyclic variation in normal subjects.

In summary, research assessing menstrual cycle variation of physical variables associated with common menstrual complaints of pain and swelling or weight gain has yielded inconsistent results. The fact that self-report measures typically yield stronger results than objective measures suggests either that women are reporting their expectations rather than their experiences or that the relevant objective variables are not those being assessed. Consistent use and reporting of statistics would certainly aid interpretation; however, the research to date suggests that physical variables show minimal fluctuations with the menstrual cycle in samples of normal women.

Psychological Symptoms

That a woman's psychological state fluctuates with her menstrual cycle is a commonly held belief, although the soundness of the scientific evidence for these fluctuations has been questioned (Parlee, 1973). Clinical reports have suggested that negative psychological states are a major complaint of women with menstrual disorders, particularly premenstrual syndrome (Israel, 1967). According to Moos's (1968) factor analysis of the MDQ, negative affect was one of the eight coherent factors. This scale consists of crying, loneliness, anxiety, restlessness, irritability, mood swings, depression, and tension. In the original sample, negative affect was higher during the premenstruum and menses than during the intermenstruum. Not only were statistical tests of these differences not reported, but the problems with retrospective questionnaires have already been discussed.

Fifteen studies investigating the relationship between the menstrual cycle and psychological symptoms (not assessed retrospectively) are summarized in Table 3.1. It should be pointed out that many of these studies included other measures and/or other groups. Only psychological measures in normal, unmedicated women are reported in the table. Most of the instruments are

TABLE 3.1
Studies Relating Psychological Variables to the Menstrual Cycle

Study	Number of Subjects	Measures	Results
Altmann, Knowles, and Bull (1941)	10	Daily interviews were rated for negative psychological symptoms for 5 cycles	Tension, irritability, and depression peaked at premenstruum. No statistics reported.
Beaumont, Richards, and Gelder (1975)	25	Symptom check list daily for 1 cycle. Scored for negative mood.	Significant cyclic variation in mood. Higher negative mood premenstrually and menstrually than intermenstrually.
Marinari, Leshner, and Doyle (1976)	60	Rated depressed, confused, embarrassed, confident, cheerful, anxious, excitable, apathetic after stressor either premenstrually or midcycle.	No significant differences.
Silbergeld, Brast, and Noble (1971)	8	MDQ (Form T), Mood Adjective Check List, half-hour unstructured interview. 9 times during 1 cycle.	Analyzed 138 variables in separate analyses. 8 showed significant phase effects (expect 7 by chance).
Wilcoxon, Schrader, and Sherif (1976)	11	Pleasant Activities Schedule, MDQ (Form T), Mood Adjective Check List, Personal Stress Inventory. Daily for 1 cycle.	Assessed negative affect, impaired concentration, and number of stressful events. All 3 variables showed significant cycle effects peaking during premenstruum.
Patkai, Johannson, and Post (1974)	6	Verbal attitudes toward words *I*, *man*, *woman*, and *sex*. Scored for brisk, tense, concentrated, apprehensive, irritable, efficient, gloomy, restless. Tested 5 days/week for 1-2 cycles.	Apprehensive and restless showed significant cycle effects. Peak restlessness was premenstrual, peak apprehension was postmenstrual.

(continued)

Table 3.1, continued

Study	Number of Subjects	Measures	Results
Little and Zahn (1974)	12	Nowlis Mood Adjective Check List. 6 days/week for 1 cycle.	No phase effects for negative mood scale scores.
Gottschalk, Kaplan, Gleser, and Winget (1962)	5	G-GFAT* scored for anxiety and three measures of hostility. Tested 5-7 times/week for 1-3 cycles.	Analyzed data for individual subjects. Of the 20 analyses, 5 were significant. Of these 5, 3 peaked during premenstruum.
Halbreich and Kas (1977)	22	Taylor Manifest Anxiety Scale. 4 times in 1 cycle.	No phase effects.
Ivey and Bardwick (1968)	26	G-GFAT* scored for anxiety. Tested at ovulation and premenstruum for cycles.	Premenstrual anxiety significantly higher than ovulatory
Abplanalp, Livingston, Rose, and Sandwisch (1977)	21	State-Trait Anxiety Inventory. Half Ss tested during menses, half during midcycle.	No significant differences.
Abramson and Torghele (1961)	34	Anxiety, fear, depression, irritability. Rated daily for 3 cycles.	They described 3 peaks during cycle which they "considered significant," but no statistics were reported.
Zimmerman and Parlee (1973)	14	Same measures as Abramson and Torghele. Daily for 1 cycle.	No significant phase effects.
Paige (1971)	38	G-GFAT* scored for hostility and anxiety. Combined for total negative affect. Tested on days 4, 10, 16, and 26 of 1 cycle.	Significant decrease in all three measures between days 4 to 16. Significant increase in total negative affect and hostility between days 16 and 26.

90

| Golub (1976b) | 50 | Depression Adjective Check List, MDQ, State-Trait Anxiety Inventory. Tested 4 days prior to menses and 2 weeks after menses. | Significant cycle effects for depression and state anxiety with premenstruum higher than midcycle. |

*Gottschalk-Gleser Free Association Test.

Source: Compiled by the author.

self-explanatory, with the exception of the G-GFAT, which refers to the Gottschalk-Gleser Free Association Test. In this test, subjects are requested to speak for five minutes about any memorable experience in their lives. The verbal content of the speech is then analyzed for death anxiety, mutilation anxiety, separation anxiety, guilt anxiety, shame anxiety, diffuse anxiety, total anxiety, hostility outwards-overt, hostility outwards-covert, hostility inwards, ambivalent hostility, and total hostility.

Of the fifteen studies listed, two did not report statistics; one involved numerous analyses, and the number of significant results approximated what one would expect by chance; two reported equivocal results in the sense that significance was achieved, but the differences were not consistently in the hypothesized direction; five failed to find phase effects; and five reported statistically significant phase effects. Two of the latter group require additional comment. Golub (1976b), who found elevated depression and anxiety scores during the premenstruum, compared these elevated scores to the scores of subjects in other research studies. Although one can only speculate when comparing data from independent studies, she noted that the premenstrual depression scores were lower than those reported by psychiatric patients, similar to those of pregnant women in the first trimester, and higher than those of female students. The premenstrual state anxiety scores were lower than those of students undergoing the mild stress of freshman orientation or an examination. Golub concluded that, although the phase effects were statistically significant, they were probably not clinically significant.

The fifth study in Table 3.1 (Wilcoxon et al., 1976) had subjects record stressful events in their daily lives, as well as symptoms and moods. A further analysis revealed that the negative affect variables and impaired concentration were associated to a significantly greater extent with stressful events than with phase of menstrual cycle. This result diminishes the importance of menstrual cycle phase as a determinant of mood but leaves one trying to explain the increase in stressful events occurring in the premenstruum. One possible explanation is that during the premenstruum, a woman may evaluate events as more stressful or react more to stressful events than during other times. Little and Zahn (1974) presented data which suggest cyclic variation in autonomic responsivity, but the peak of responsivity occurs around ovulation rather than premenstrually. Another possible explanation is that women are more physically active during the premenstruum and, therefore, experience more of any type of event at that time than during other phases. This hypothesis is discussed in more detail in the next section.

Suicide is usually assumed to be associated with a negative psychological state, so the research on suicide and the menstrual cycle is included in this section. Three studies (Dalton, 1959b; Mandell & Mandell, 1967; Wetzel, Reich, & McClure, 1971) have reported a greater number of suicide attempts during menstruation than during other times in the cycle. A serious criticism of these studies is that they relied on retrospective reporting to determine the phase of the cycle, and women unable to remember when their last period began were usually eliminated from the samples. This procedure would clearly bias the results in the sense that women who were menstruating would be more likely to remember when their period began than women who were not menstruating, and, thus, menstruating women would be more likely to be included in the studies. On the other hand, Tonks, Rack, and Rose (1968) found the highest rate of suicide attempts to be in the premenstruum, but again, they relied on retrospective reporting of phase. A similar study is reported by Birtchnell and Floyd (1974), who did not find significant phase effects for suicide attempts.

One study not relying on retrospective reporting of cycle phase (Mac-Kinnon, MacKinnon, & Thomson, 1959) determined the phase of the menstrual cycle by postmortem examination of the uterus. They determined the frequency of deaths occurring in various phases in 102 women who died from suicide, disease, or accident. Sixty deaths occurred in the midluteal phase (six to thirteen days prior to menstruation). Although they did not report separate statistics for the different causes of death, their graphs suggest that the phase differences were marked for death due to suicide and disease but not accident. Thus, the research on suicide and the menstrual cycle has not consistently placed high suicide rates in any one particular phase. The study least subject to criticism on methodological grounds reported the highest rate to be in the midluteal phase, and these results applied to death by disease as well as death by suicide.

In summary, the widespread belief that a woman's psychological state varies with her menstrual cycle seems to be just that — a belief. Future research, free of the methodological difficulties discussed here, may provide scientific support for this belief, but, at this point, the evidence is weak. The most that can be said is that there may be a slight trend for a woman to experience an increase in negative affect in the week prior to her period and that six to thirteen days prior to her period, there may be an increased probability that she will die of suicide or disease. The extreme statements that appear in the literature, such as that the premenstruum is ". . . a time of regression, of an increased libido, poorly controlled by a weakened ego, and of a recurrence of neuroses originally established at the time of puberty" (Tuch, 1975, p. 388) do not have empirical support and do not belong in the scientific literature.

Behavioral Changes

Along with the assumption that a woman experiences negative affect prior to or during her period is the belief that a woman's behavioral changes and/or her performance deteriorates during the *paramenstruum* (premenstrual plus menstrual phases). If it is true that psychological variables, such as anxiety and depression, are elevated, it seems reasonable to conclude that these may interfere with performance and affect behavior. Although the evidence for phase-related negative affect is slight, the assessment of negative affect relies almost exclusively on self-report, and the validity of self-report measures can be questioned on the grounds that they are influenced by response bias, demand characteristics, and belief systems. Task performance and behavior are common and relatively objective measures of negative psychological states. For example, learned helplessness, the laboratory analog of depression, is typically assessed by performance on cognitive and instrumental tasks (Seligman, 1975).

Table 3.2 presents a summary of fifteen studies which investigated various aspects of behavior in relation to the menstrual cycle in normal women. The first study did not report statistics, but a description of the data is included. Of the remaining fourteen studies, four provided at least some support for the notion that women experience negative behavioral changes during the paramenstruum. There is evidence for less arm-hand steadiness, a greater likelihood of taking one's child to a doctor, a greater likelihood of committing crimes of theft and prostitution, and a greater likelihood of being involved in an accident during the paramenstruum than during other phases. The last result, that of Dalton (1960b), was true for both active and passive accidents, the latter being those where another person was responsible and where greater judgment on the part of the injured would have not prevented the accident. Two studies reported results opposite of that hypothesized: reaction time and math performance were found to be superior in the luteal phase and to peak premenstrually, and women were found to perform better on a practical mechanical test during the paramenstruum than during the intermenstruum. This last result was one of many analyses done and could have been significant by chance. Also, estimated time intervals were found to be longest in the premenstruum, but since accuracy was not assessed, it is difficult to interpret these data.

Seven studies in Table 3.2 which investigated a wide variety of behaviors, including reaction time, class examinations, job absences, and activity, and a wide variety of intellectual and mechanical tests showed no variation with phase of the menstrual cycle. Thus, there is little evidence in support of performance decrements being related to menstrual cycle phase and considerable evidence to suggest a lack of relationship. In an extensive review of this area, Sommer (1973) reached a similar conclusion.

A possible, although at this point speculative, explanation for the few results that do support the popular view is that women do increase their activity level during the paramenstruum. Altmann, Knowles, and Bull (1941) and Weiner and Elmadjian (1962) observed an increase in physical activity prior to menses; neither study reported statistics, however. Others have noted increased autonomic and cortical arousal. Wineman (1971) found low autonomic lability scores, reflecting relative sympathetic dominance, during the luteal phase, and others suggest that women may have less EEG alpha (Lamb, Ulett, Masters, & Robinson, 1953) and a greater number of EEG driving responses to photic stimulation (Vogel, Broverman, & Klaiber, 1971) during the premenstrual phase than during the follicular phase. Morris and Udry (1970) measured activity in twenty-five women who wore pedometers for three cycles. Motor activity

TABLE 3.2
Studies Relating Behavioral Variables to the Menstrual Cycle

Study	Number of Subjects	Measures	Results
Dalton (1960a)	217 high school students	Weekly school grades for 1 term.	Falling marks compared to previous week occurred in premenstrual week for 27%, menstrual week for 25%, postmenstrual for 10%, intermenstrual for 22%. Rising marks occurred in premenstrual week for 17%, menstrual for 21%, postmenstrual for 30%, intermenstrual for 24%. No statistics reported.
Bernstein (1977)	126	8 course exams during 1 semester.	Compared paramenstrual to intermenstrual. No significant differences.
Golub (1976a)	50	Cognitive battery tapping sensory-perceptual factors, memory, problem solving, induction, concept formation, creativity. Tested in premenstruum and midcycle.	No significant differences.
Dor-Shav (1976)	155	Embedded-figures test and human figure drawing.	Both studies found superior performance in 3rd week (days 14-21). Other weeks similar to one another. No significant results in either study.

(continued)

TABLE 3.2, continued

Study	Number of subjects	Measures	Results
Wickham (1958)	Group A: 1,525 taking exam to change job. Group B: 1,000 taking exam to obtain job.	Progressive matrices, mechanical comprehension, arithmetic, squares test, spelling, comprehension, practical mechanics, and verbal. Tested once.	Compared paramenstruum to rest of cycle. Only indication of cycle effect was better performance in paramenstruum on the practical mechanical test for group B.
Sommer (1972) Study 1	11 replication=79	Watson-Glaser Critical Thinking Appraisal. Tested during premenstrual, menstrual, follicular, and luteal phases.	No significant phase effects.
Sommer (1972) Study 2	207	Multiple-choice class exams during 1 semester.	No significant phase effects.
Wuttke, Arnold, Becker, Creutzfeldt, Langenstein, and Tirsch (1975)	16	Reaction time, visual orientation, math tasks, memory. Tested every other day for 1 cycle.	Reaction time and math significantly better in luteal than follicular phase with peak 2-4 days prior to menses.
Zimmerman and Parlee (1973)	14	Arm-hand steadiness, GSR to auditory stimuli, reaction time, time estimation, digit-symbol subset of WAIS. Tested during menstrual, follicular, luteal, and premenstrual phases.	Significant differences for arm-hand steadiness: greatest during luteal, lowest during premenstrual. No other significant phase effects.
Pierson and Lockhart (1963)	25	Reaction time. Tested days 2, 8, 18, and 26.	No significant phase effects.

Study	N	Measure	Findings
Kopell, Lunde, Clayton, and Moos (1969)	8	2-flash threshold, reaction time, time estimation, skin potential. Tested days 3, 14, 24, 26, and 28 for 2 cycles.	Time estimated to be significantly longer in premenstruum than intermenstruum. No other significant phase effects.
Tuch (1975)	140	Length of child's sickness, severity of child's sickness. Cycle phase of mother when she brought child to doctor.	Mothers significantly more likely to bring children to doctor during paramenstruum than during intermenstruum.
Dalton (1960b)	84	Cycle phase of woman when involved in accident requiring hospitalization.	52% of accidents occurred when women were in paramenstruum. Phase effects significant. True for both active and passive accidents.
Dalton (1961)	156 prisoners	Cycle phase of woman when crime was committed.	Nearly half the crimes were committed during paramenstruum. Phase effects significant. (Crimes were theft and prostitution.)
Smith (1950)	38, 29, 41 (3 factories)	Activity level and absences of factory workers rated by foremen. Assessed during 41 working days.	No significant differences for either. If split up groups for absences: 2nd shift was high postmenstrual, low premenstrual; age 29-38, high postmenstrual, low menstrual; age 39-50, high premenstrual, low menstrual. Differences for these subgroups were significant.

Source: Compiled by the author.

showed significant peaks on days 2, 15-16 and 27. A simple increase in physical activity and arousal could account for several rather paradoxical results: (1) Dalton (1960b) found that *both* passive and active accidents were highest in the paramenstruum; (2) the highest number of stressful events were reported in the paramenstruum (Wilcoxon et al., 1976); (3) the premenstruum seems to be a high point for both negative events and positive events (Kashiwagi, McClure, & Wetzel, 1976; Moos, 1968). In addition, the increased number of crimes and the greater probability of taking a child to the doctor, both of which have been shown to occur premenstrually, could simply be due to an increase in activity; if activity increases, the probability increases that one would engage in any type of activity or have any type of experience.

Considering the minimal support for psychological fluctuations and the lack of any real support for behavioral fluctuations occurring in conjunction with the menstrual cycle, one must ask why the stereotypic beliefs are perpetuated. Several answers have been offered. Parlee (1973) suggested that authors cite past research without attending to the quality of the cited research. The example she provided is the frequently cited study which claims an association between crashes of women pilots and phase of the menstrual cycle. The reference is to Whitehead (1934), which ". . . consisted of reports of three airplane crashes over a period of eight months in which the women pilots were said to be menstruating at the time of the crash" (p. 455). Further examples come from two frequently cited studies by Dalton. The first (1960c) investigated the relationship between behavioral offenses committed by school girls and their menstrual cycle phase; there was a total of 272 offenses in one term, most occurring during menstruation. The second (1968) studied examination scores in high school girls, which were lowest during the paramenstruum. In both studies, Dalton concluded that the phase of the menstrual cycle was an important determinant of behavior. In both studies, however, the number of data points from each subject was greater than one, and the number varied among subjects, so the data are not independent and cannot be interpreted. In addition, Dalton (1960a), summarized in Table 3.2, did not report statistical tests for weekly school grades varying with the menstrual cycle, so we do not know the probability of these results occurring by chance. Yet, later authors frequently make general statements referring to these three studies by Dalton as support for deteriorating behavior and performance during the paramenstruum. Thus, one reason for the continued support of unfounded beliefs is the uncritical acceptance of the conclusions from studies which are methodologically unsound.

Sommer (1973) suggested that the stereotypic beliefs continue because of an editorial bias of favoring the publication of studies which find positive results. "While the demand for positive results is appropriate when the null hypothesis is assumed, in the case of issues with social implications, often the null hypothesis is not assumed and therefore support may be as important as rejection" (p. 531). The published research could, therefore, reflect only a small portion of the actual research and be biased in such a way as to perpetuate societal attitudes.

The section above presents a review of the literature concerned with physical, psychological, and behavioral variables in relationship to the menstrual cycle in samples of women drawn from a normal population. From the studies reviewed, one must conclude that there is little support for the concept that the menstrual cycle exerts a significant influence on the lives of most women. The practice of studying menstrual disorders in a normal population maximizes the portion of the variability of the criterion measures due to individual differences. Advantageous utilization of statistical techniques requires that one minimize this source of variability, and one way of accomplishing this is to study samples of women who exhibit a common symptomatology.

The assumption that all women experience menstrual dysfunction not only influences research design but may also affect attitudes. Women sufferers and clinicians who view menstrual disorders as synonymous with being a woman diminish the seriousness with which menstrual disorders are viewed; that is, since it is a natural part of being a woman, nothing can or should be done to treat the disorders. The effect of such an attitude is exemplified by Weideger (1976). In a discussion with an endocrinologist as to the benefits of hormone analysis treatment for premenstrual syndrome, the physician responded that ". . . if every woman with premenstrual syndrome went to see an endocrinologist, the physicians would be swamped and unable to offer treatment to anyone else" (p. 54). The research reviewed in this section suggests that such a statement is not in accord with reality.

DYSMENORRHEA AND PREMENSTRUAL SYNDROME

Dysmenorrhea and premenstrual syndrome (PMS) are the two most prevalent menstrual disorders, although there is a tremendous range in incidence estimates — from 3% (Bickers, 1954) to 100% (Moos, 1968). Both are usually considered psychosomatic disorders, although it has been argued that their respective etiologies are strictly physiological (Dalton, 1964) or strictly psychological (Gregory, 1957). The various statuses derive from several sources: there are both psychological and organic components in the symptomatology; the disorders seem to be exacerbated by stress, which suggests a psychological etiology, yet they covary with distinct hormonal changes, which implies organic causation; and treatment based on both organic and psychological causation have been effective to varying degrees. In general, psychological factors tend to be emphasized to a greater degree in theories accounting for PMS than in those accounting for dysmenorrhea. This is undoubtedly due to the fact that "psychological" symptoms, such as depression, comprise the major symptoms of PMS, while "physical" symptoms, such as abdominal pain, are diagnostic of dysmenorrhea. It is possible that the term *psychosomatic disorder*, as applied to PMS, is being used as a wastebasket category and reflects the confusion and contradictions apparent in the literature. On the other hand, in the case of dysmenorrhea, recent medical discoveries have turned attention away from psychological interpretations and toward a purely physiological explanation.

Symptoms associated with PMS are primarily depression, irritability, lethargy and water retention, although other symptoms, such as indecisiveness, dizziness, irrationality, constipation, skin disorders, migraine headaches, and graying of hair, have also been mentioned in relation to PMS. Diagnosis generally depends on the idiosyncratic definitions of individual clinicians or researchers, and the presence and severity of symptoms are usually determined by various self-report methods. Structural variables that have been found to be associated with an increased incidence and severity of PMS are age (Dalton, 1964; Moos. 1968), marriage (Coppen & Kessel, 1963), and childbearing (Greene & Dalton, 1953). Individual differences in terms of most salient symptoms, severity of symptoms, and response to treatment are considerable and have led to the speculation that there is more than one distinct disorder under the heading of PMS (Moos, 1969).

The term *dysmenorrhea* is derived from Greek and directly translates as painful monthly flow. The present day medical meaning is painful menstruation, consisting, in general, of cramping and/or pain accompanying the menstrual flow. The discomfort is most intense over the abdomen but may radiate to the thighs and back. Systemic symptoms which infrequently occur include nausea, vomiting, diarrhea, headache, fatigue, nervousness, and dizziness (Ylikorkala & Dawood, 1978). Although there is considerable individual variability, dysmenorrhea is normally distinguishable from premenstrual syndrome by the type of symptoms and the temporal relationship with the menstrual cycle. The former coincides with the onset of menses and lasts from one to five days, while the latter occurs one to five days prior to, and terminates with, menses. In contrast to PMS, dysmenorrhea tends to decrease with age and parity (Moos, 1968) and is unaffected by marriage (Coppen & Kessel, 1963).

Psychological Factors

The psychological aspects of PMS and dysmenorrhea will be considered separately, as there are distinct bodies of research literature for each. The literature concerned with psychological factors, however, tends either to not distinguish between the symptoms associated with the two disorders or to combine women with premenstrual symptoms and women with dysmenorrheic symptoms into a single, "distressed" group. In addition, the general issues, criticisms, and problems relevant to the psychological literature are similar for both disorders.

The assumption that personality characteristics, transitory or permanent psychological states, and femininity or acceptance of the woman's role cause, contribute to, or exacerbate symptoms of menstrual disorders is apparent in the literature. This assumption is evidenced by such statements as:

> A consideration of the main syndromes of menstrual disturbance is inseparable from that of the question of the relationship between disturbance and neurosis (Gregory, 1957, p. 65).

> Many patients present gynecological symptoms without being sick. Their illness represents a psychic conflict sailing under a gynecological flag . . . (Rogers, 1950, p. 322).

> If . . . a successful effort is made to modify her attitudes towards the acceptance of and pride in her womanly status, then the intolerable aspect of her dysmenorrhea, that which brought her to the doctor, can be overcome by simple analgesics (Sturgis, 1970, p. 150).

The validity of such statements is diminished when one considers the research.

Bloom, Shelton, and Michaels (1978) administered the MSQ to 200 women and chose groups which they labeled spasmodic, congestive, and symptom free. These groups completed the Minnesota Multiphasic Personality Inventory (MMPI), the Personality Research Form, and the Tennessee Self-Concept Scale. In comparison to the symptom-free group, those with spasmodic or congestive disorders scored higher on the depression, psychasthenia, and social introversion scales of the MMPI; on other tests, they scored in the direction of being less autonomous, less prone to play and amusement, less satisfied with themselves, and less positive about their physical and social selves. The authors concluded that, although there were personality differences among the groups, all groups were well within normal limits, and the scores were not indicative of pathology.

Gruba and Rohrbaugh (1975) administered the MDQ and the MMPI to sixty women. Premenstrual pain correlated significantly with four MMPI scales (Hs, Hy, Pd, and Sc), and premenstrual negative affect with two (Pt and Sc). The MDQ behavior change scale for symptoms occurring during menses significantly correlated with the Hy and Hs scales of the MMPI. There are two difficulties with this research, which makes interpretation difficult. First, while pain is characteristic of dysmenorrhea, it is not typical of PMS; thus, women who complain of premenstrual pain cannot be classified according to traditional distinctions. Second, the authors did not report whether or not the MMPI scale scores were within normal limits, so the range of covarying personality characteristics is unknown.

Research frequently cited in support of an association between menstrual symptoms and neuroticism is that by Coppen and Kessel (1963). A sample of 465 women completed a "menstrual symptom questionnaire" and the Maudsley Personality Inventory. While dysmenorrhea and neuroticism were not significantly correlated, significant correlations were found between PMS and neuroticism; however, the correlation coefficients ranged from .190 to .297, meaning that this relationship accounted for, at most, 9% of the variance.

In a large sample of normal college women, Levitt and Lubin (1967) investigated the relationship between frequency and severity of menstrual symptoms and scores on a menstrual attitude survey, the Edwards Personal Preference Schedule, and the Guilford-Zimmerman Temperament Survey. Of seventy-five correlations, fourteen were significant and were interpreted to mean that an increased number of menstrual complaints was associated with neurotic and paranoid tendencies and "a set to look at the surface of human behavior." These conclusions seem to be somewhat of an overstatement, since the variance accounted for in one variable by knowledge of the other ranged from 3% to 16%, and the means of the personality variables were in the normal range.

Several studies have reported small positive correlations between degree of irregularity and number of symptoms (Moos, 1977; Sheldrake & Cormack, 1976; Wickham, 1958). Hain, Linton, Eber, and Chapman (1970) found low but significant correlations between irregularity and some MMPI scales, and comparisons between extreme groups of irregular and regular women on MMPI scores yielded significant differences on five of the thirteen scales. The conclusion of the authors that ". . . regularity of menstrual cycle . . . is associated with the occurrence of specific and general premenstrual and menstrual symptoms and with personality maladjustment" (p. 86) seems unwarranted, however, considering that both groups of women scored within normal ranges on the MMPI.

Several researchers have focused on anxiety rather than global psychological traits. Women suffering from PMS scored higher and exhibited more cyclic variability on the Taylor Manifest Anxiety Scale than did women who were symptom free (Halbreich & Kas, 1977); pain and cramps during menstruation, while not related to neuroticism, were found to be related to anxiety (Hirt, Kurtz, & Ross, 1967). Paige (1973) tested the hypothesis that anxiety is related to amount of bleeding during menses. She compared anxiety levels, assessed four times a month by the Gottschalk-Gleser technique, of women whose flow was reduced due to oral contraceptives and those whose flow remained heavy; women with heavy flow were significantly more anxious than women with light flow.

The studies just described suggest that the frequency and severity of menstrual symptoms and various traits related to neuroticism share some small variance. A difficulty in the interpretation of these data stems from the fact that similar questions are asked in order to assess both symptomatology and neuroticism. For example, an item on the Maudsley Personality Inventory asks, "Does your mood often go up and down?" Another asks, "Are you sometimes bubbling over with energy and sometimes very sluggish?" A few items which appear on the MMPI are, "Often I can't understand why I have been so cross and grouchy," and "I have periods of such great restlessness that I cannot sit long in a chair." It seems likely that women who would check such items as fatigue, restlessness, irritability, or bursts of energy or activity on the MDQ would also answer the above questions in the affirmative. Any statistical association noted between menstrual questionnaires and personality scales could be due simply to the similarity in items rather than to any real association between menstrual disorders and psychopathology.

A further psychological variable which has been postulated as being etiological to menstrual symptoms is femininity or acceptance of one's role as a woman, the hypothesis being that a woman low on either would resent being a woman and, thus, would be susceptible to menstrual disorders. Levitt and Lubin (1967) reported that frequency and severity of menstrual complaints were correlated with a negative attitude toward menstruation and, although their statistics precluded inferences of causality, concluded that "this appears to support the gynecologists' contention that an unwholesome attitude toward menstruation may be involved in the etiology of menstrual complaints" (p. 269). A later study (May, 1976) compared women suffering from PMS with women suffering from dysmenorrhea and found the former to feel more resentment over traditional role expectations (such as, that women be nice and well behaved and passively attractive) and more negative about menstruation than the latter group. Berry and McQuire (1972) found a significant association (accounting for 9% of the variance) between the pain, concentration, autonomic reaction, and control scales of the MDQ and low role acceptance. They appropriately pointed out that correlative data cannot dictate causality and that ". . . it would be logical to assume that most women would be unhappy with a role which required such discomfort for much of their lives" (p. 86).

In contradiction to the results above, Gough (1975) reported small but significant correlations (.15-.20) between the femininity scale on the California Psychological Inventory and scores on the MDQ, indicating that women who report many menstrual complaints are more nurturant and deferent and less likely to initiate activity and make decisions than women with few menstrual complaints. Paige (1973) divided her sample according to religious affiliation and noted an association between family and motherhood orientation and menstrual complaints for only the Catholic women; they were most likely to report symptoms if they believed in motherhood and had no career ambitions.

Thus, the data from these studies are somewhat contradictory, and it is difficult to draw any definite conclusions. Furthermore, in postulating role acceptance or femininity as a psychological cause of menstrual disorders, one needs to define one end of the continuum as psychologically healthy. Although most authors state their biases when interpreting data, one could logically argue either way, that is, that psychological health is adjusting to one's role, even though it requires being passive and accepting the more dominant social role of men, or psychological health is rebelling against the inferior role of women in our society.

Given the rather extensive research interest in psychological correlates and etiologies of menstrual disorders, there is surprisingly little research investigating the effectiveness of psychological treatment for these disorders. Psychotherapy as treatment of menstrual disorders was found to be unsuccessful in a study by Rees (1953). Behavior modification techniques have resulted in some success, however. A series of studies was done comparing the effectiveness of relaxation in conjunction with menstrual imagery on symptoms of spasmodic and congestive dysmenorrhea, as measured by the MSQ. With these techniques, Chesney and Tasto (1975b) were successful in the treatment of spasmodic symptoms but not congestive symptoms, while Cox (1977) and Cox and Meyer (1978) were able to demonstrate symptom reduction in women suffering from both types of distress. Only the first study utilized attention-placebo control groups, and all three confounded the effects of relaxation training and menstrual imagery.

Considering the evidence for abnormally high muscle activity in women suffering from dysmenorrhea (see discussion below), it is likely that the active element is muscle relaxation. Treatment effectiveness does not provide conclusive evidence for etiology; nevertheless, the practical implications are that behavioral therapy has potential utility in the treatment of menstrual symptoms.

In general, research investigating a possible psychological etiology for menstrual disorders is correlational, and, therefore, causality cannot be inferred. Much research can be criticized for at least implying a cause-and-effect relationship from correlational data. A significant association between neuroticism and menstrual symptomatology could mean that neuroticism causes symptoms, symptoms cause neuroticism, or a third variable causes both. This is a particularly salient point when common logic supports either direction of causality, as is the case here. It is equally logical to suppose that because a woman suffers from regular episodes of pain and depression which she attributed to menstruation, she resents being a woman, she has a negative attitude toward menstruation, or the situation has an effect on her psychological health as it is to suppose the reverse. On a theoretical level, one can argue a psychological etiology, especially if one considers the historical attitudes that societies had in the past and the current attitudes they still have toward menstruation. Primitive societies would not allow women to touch food or associate with men while they were menstruating, and present society advertises sanitary napkins with "your secret is safe" and "nothing will show" slogans. The theory has not been adequately tested, however, and empirical evidence which would support or refute the theory is lacking.

Although theoretically defensible, a psychological etiology for menstruation-related disorders has yet to be demonstrated. In general, the correlations which support an association between menstrual symptomatology and psychological ill health have been small and account for a small amount of the variance of either variable. Furthermore, women suffering from menstrual disorders typically score within the normal limits of psychological and personality tests. The continued emphasis on psychogenic theories, in spite of a lack of empirical evidence, encourages a "blame the victim" view of these disorders and diverts attention away from demands for improved medical solutions. Lennane and Lennane (1973) commented with reference to several disorders, including dysmenorrhea, that "despite the well documented presence of organic etiological factors, the therapeutic literature is characterized by an unscientific recourse to psychogenics and a correspondingly inadequate, even derisory, approach to their management" (p. 288).

Research by Paulson and Wood (1966) implied that scientists' beliefs in psychological theories may be more dependent upon their education and training than on empirical evidence. They developed a 180-item questionnaire consisting of common experiences and feelings and asked eight psychiatrists and eight gynecologists to complete the questionnaire by rating the degree of importance of each item in terms of contributing to a better understanding of dysmenorrhea. Psychiatrists emphasized psychological conflict, early experiences of menstruation, and attitudes toward feminity and womanhood, while the gynecologists viewed the etiology of dysmenorrhea as primarily organic. The results of this study make salient a remark by Kaplan (1964): "It comes as no particular surprise to discover that a scientist formulates problems in a way which requires for their solution just those techniques in which he himself is especially skilled" (p. 31). Rather than allowing the didactic aspects of their education and societal stereotypes to determine their approach to illness, scientists and practitioners need to utilize those facets of their training dealing with methods of inquiry and inference in order to evaluate research and base their theories and treatment on the most sound evidence available.

Physiological Factors in PMS

Because PMS occurs at a time in the menstrual cycle when progesterone is at its peak, most theories which posit a physiological etiology for PMS attribute the symptoms, either directly or indirectly via a mediating mechanism, to progesterone. Some suggest that women suffering from PMS produce too much progesterone, others say too little progesterone, others imply that the estrogen-progesterone ratio is too high or too low, and still others suggest that although the absolute quantities of progesterone and estrogen may be normal, women who suffer from PMS have an abnormal physiological response to one or both of the hormones.

The most common theoretical orientation among researchers and clinicians concerned with PMS assumes that this disorder is caused by an insufficiency of progesterone or an insufficiency of progesterone relative to estrogen, that is, a high estrogen-progesterone ratio. Such theories were originally derived from speculation based on clinical observation. For example, Dalton (1964) noted that women who suffer from PMS either have a worsening of symptoms or a complete relief of symptoms during pregnancy, which she attributes, respectively, to a lower-than-normal or normal production of progesterone from the placenta. Others (for example, Hackmann, Wirz-Justice, & Lichtsteiner, 1973) have noted the similarity of symptoms occurring during the premenstruum, postpartum, and menopause — all of which are accompanied by a rapid decline in progesterone. These similarities have led others to suspect that the common factor may be genetically determined abnormalities in progesterone metabolism (Hamburg, 1966).

Considering the prevalence of the assumption that PMS results from abnormal hormone levels, there is surprisingly little direct data to offer as support. Morton (1950) measured hormone levels in twenty-nine psychiatric patients who complained of premenstrual symptoms; twenty-six had a relative excess of estrogen, but the author did not compare these levels with those of a symptom-free group. Smith (1975) compared hormone levels of women suffering from premenstrual depression with those of women who were symptom free. Mean levels of plasma progesterone were lower for patients than for controls, while estrogen levels and estrogen-progesterone ratios did not differ between groups. The relationship between hormone levels and symptoms in a group of women suffering from slight to moderate PMS was studied by Backstrom and Mattsson (1975). High intercorrelation coefficients, ranging from .453 to .720, were reported for estrogen levels, estrogen-progesterone ratios, and feelings of anxiety, irritability, and depression; progesterone levels did not correlate highly with symptoms.

The dearth of published research investigating the theories of absolute or relative deficiencies of progesterone or estrogen in women with PMS may result from researchers failing to find significant differences in hormone levels; indeed, the editorial policies of most professional journals would typically operate to prevent publication of these results. Another possibility is that researchers have concentrated their efforts on the hypothesized mechanisms which mediate between abnormal hormone production and symptoms. These mechanisms include increased production of prolactin and/or aldosterone, which results from abnormally low levels of progesterone and causes the symptoms associated with water retention; decreased blood sugar levels, a result of abnormal hormone levels producing reduced levels of growth hormone and/or cortisol and causing symptoms commonly associated with hypoglycemia; and elevated monoamine oxidase activity, which results from insufficient estrogen or low estrogen-progesterone ratios and causes premenstrual depression. Research related to these mechanisms will be discussed individually.

Water Retention

Common complaints of women suffering from PMS are weight gain, swelling, and a bloated feeling. This cluster of symptoms has been studied in relation to the effects of progesterone on fluid and electrolyte metabolism, which can occur in at least three ways:

1. Progesterone tends to inhibit the secretion of prolactin (Halbreich, Ben-David, Assael, & Bornstein, 1976), and prolactin facilitates the retention of sodium, potassium, and water (Andersch et al., 1978). Thus, lower-than-normal levels of progesterone could act to increase prolactin and, thus, increase fluid and electrolyte retention.

2. A direct action of progesterone is to promote diuresis through sodium excretion; the decreased sodium levels then stimulate an increased production of renin and angiotensin II, which in turn stimulates the adrenal cortex to release aldosterone, a sodium-retaining mineralocorticoid (Katz & Romfh, 1972). Thus, water retention can result from an aldosterone-favored imbalance between the diuretic effects of progesterone and the antidiuretic effects of aldosterone or from an exaggerated aldosterone response to the progesterone-induced diuresis.

3. Since estrogen has sodium-retaining properties, a high estrogen-progesterone ratio could produce an overall effect of electrolyte and fluid retention.

Although no studies have demonstrated dramatic weight fluctuations during the menstrual cycle in women who suffer from PMS, several studies have reported phasic variation in certain variables which are associated with fluid and electrolyte balance. Andersch et al. (1978) measured total body water, total potassium, and weight in women suffering from PMS and women who were symptom free. PMS women experienced more variability in body water and had more body water per mol of body potassium in the luteal phase than did the controls; however, body water was not higher during the luteal phase than during the follicular phase. Although the results were somewhat inconsistent, the authors concluded that PMS symptoms are accompanied by changes in fluid retention, and, since weight did not vary, the authors suggested that these changes are a function of a redistribution of fluid rather than an absolute increase. Further evidence comes from Wong et al. (1972), who measured capillary filtration coefficient (CFC) as an index of the integrity of the vessel wall to water. Women with symptoms of PMS showed clear cyclic fluctuation, with CFC increasing throughout the cycle and peaking just prior to menstruation, while control women without PMS showed a relatively constant CFC throughout the cycle. Janowsky et al. (1973) measured weight, urinary potassium-sodium ratio, and mood in normal women. All three measures increased premenstrually and dropped on the first day of menses, and the three measures were significantly intercorrelated. These data, however, must be interpreted with caution, since the authors did not report statistics to support the observed variation with phase of cycle. In summary, the research to date supports the idea that PMS is associated with changes in fluid retention or distribution, but further research is certainly necessary in order to clarify the inconsistencies in the data.

Prolactin as the link between progesterone and fluid and electrolyte changes was investigated by Halbreich et al. (1976), who measured serum prolactin levels during the menstrual cycle in women with and without PMS. Throughout the cycle, women suffering from PMS had significantly higher levels of prolactin and greater increases during the premenstruum than the controls. This suggests that increased prolactin could be etiological in producing symptoms; however, Mason (1975) pointed out that increases in prolactin may result from psychological stress, so the direction of causality in the relationship between prolactin and symptoms in women with PMS is not obvious.

Bromocriptine, a long-acting dopaminergic agonist, suppresses the production of prolactin and has been studied as a treatment for PMS. Research to date has shown that bromocriptine does not affect body weight or total body water (Andersch et al., 1978) and is no more effective than a placebo in reducing subjective symptoms (Ghose & Coppen, 1977), with the exception of premenstrual mastodynia, which significantly improved with treatment (Andersen, Larsen, Steenstrup, Svendstrup, & Nielsen, 1977). The latter study also validated bromocriptine as a prolactin suppressant by measuring prolactin levels, which were significantly reduced during treatment. On the other hand, Benedek-Jaszmann and Hearn-Sturtevant (1976) compared bromocriptine and a placebo in a double-blind crossover study. When treated with the drug, women experienced significant improvement in breast symptoms, edema, weight gain, and mood; the placebo effected no similar improvement. The only obvious explanation for the discrepant results is the length of treatment: in the latter study, women were treated for eighteen days prior to menses, while in the other three studies, treatment varied between ten and fourteen days. Therefore, bromocriptine seems to be a potentially useful treatment if begun early in the cycle, although nine of the twenty-one subjects in the study by Andersen et al. (1977) experienced side effects which, in four of them, were serious enough to require discontinuation of treatment.

The renin-angiotensin-aldosterone system is advocated by several researchers as the mediator of fluid and electrolyte changes in women with PMS. Studies assessing levels of these substances during the menstrual cycle have yielded the following results:

1. Three of four subjects showed phasic changes in plasma renin activity and plasma aldosterone, although the phase of peak activity varied among the subjects (Katz & Romfh, 1972).
2. In six subjects, the average level of plasma renin and plasma aldosterone was twice as high in the luteal phase than in the follicular phase, with peak activity occurring around days 22-25 (Michelakis, Yoshida, & Dormois, 1975).
3. Aldosterone was significantly higher during the second half of the cycle than during the first half of the cycle (Schwartz & Abraham, 1975; Brown, Davies, Lever, & Robertson, 1964).
4. Plasma renin and renin concentration significantly increased during the luteal phase in six subjects (Skinner, Lumbers, & Symonds, 1969).
5. Plasma angiotensin II and aldosterone increased from the early follicular phase to the late luteal phase (Sundsfjord & Aakvaag, 1970).

Only one study looked at these variables in women suffering from PMS. Gray et al. (1968) studied aldosterone secretion rates in thirteen women complaining of PMS and found a significant increase in the luteal phase. This increase in aldosterone, however, was not accompanied by changes in the sodium-potassium ratio. Sundsfjord and Aakvaag (1970) suggested that progesterone and aldosterone levels vary inversely to maintain a constant ratio.

Although this research has provided useful information about the endocrinology of the menstrual cycle, it has contributed little to a theory of etiology for PMS. Research investigating the differences on these and related variables between women who suffer from PMS and those who are symptom free should certainly be a first concern. Thus far, the theory which hypothesizes that the renin-angiotensin-aldosterone system is responsible for fluid and electrolyte retention and the related symptoms lacks empirical support. There are no reports of these mechanisms operating differently or deficiently in women who suffer from PMS than in symptom-free women.

If water retention is an etiological factor in producing symptoms associated with PMS, then diuretics should be effective as treatment. Appleby (1960) treated women suffering from PMS with chlorothiazide, and approximately one-third of the thirty patients reported total or marked relief of symptoms. Ammonium chloride was found to be effective in preventing swelling but did not always relieve tension, irritability, depression, or anxiety (Rees, 1953). Singer, Cheng, and Schou (1974) tested the effectiveness of lithium, a treatment based on the diuretic action of lithium in addition to its known effects on periodic psychiatric disorders. Patients improved with both lithium and placebo, and although lithium was better at relieving symptoms, the differences were not significant. Lithium, chlorthalidone, and a placebo were compared on treatment effectiveness for PMS in a study by Mattsson and Schoultz (1974). Both drugs and the placebo effected improvement in symptoms, and the placebo was preferred by most patients. Those who responded well to lithium had pronounced premenstrual weight increases prior to treatment but not during treatment.

The treatment effectiveness of diuretics is variable, although there is some support for their use, especially for women whose primary symptoms are those of swelling, heaviness, weight increase, and bloating. Treatment outcome research could provide more useful information than that described above if all symptoms associated with PMS were not considered as a unit but separated into meaningful categories. It is possible that there are several syndromes which occur in the premenstruum, each with separate etiologies and preferred treatments.

Hypoglycemia

Hypoglycemia, or low blood sugar, is characterized by a variety of symptoms similar to those described by women who suffer from PMS, such as fatigue, anxiety, excitation, and depression. Dalton (1964) included hypoglycemia as one of many premenstrual symptoms; however, if carbohydrate metabolism or glucose tolerance is altered in such a way as to produce low blood sugar during the premenstruum, the mechanism by which this occurs has not been clarified. Dalton and others proposed the elusive estrogen-progesterone imbalance as etiological. One possible hypothesis is based on research that suggests growth hormone decreases during the luteal phase, presumably as an action of progesterone (Genazzani, Lemarchand-Beraud, Aubert, & Felber, 1975). Growth hormone tends to have antiinsulin effects (Bacchus, 1976); thus, a decrease in growth hormone could lower blood sugar levels.

A second mechanism was offered by Weideger (1976). She speculated that under normal conditions, progesterone levels are maintained by secretions of the corpus luteum. When insufficient amounts of progesterone are produced for normal cyclic functioning, the reproductive system appropriates progesterone from the adrenal cortex, which produces progesterone as a precursor in the synthesis of corticosteroids. According to this theory, if the adrenal cortex secretes progesterone in response to the body's need, fewer corticosteroids are manufactured. A primary corticosteroid is cortisol, which acts to increase the production of glucose and raise or maintain blood sugar levels. Thus, if synthesis of cortisol is decreased due to a lack of progesterone, lowered blood sugar levels may result.

Morton (1950) examined twenty psychiatric patients who reported premenstrual symptoms. Sixteen of them showed signs of hypoglycemia, as measured by a glucose tolerance test, and the timing of the hypoglycemia corresponded to self-report of symptoms. A later study by Morton, Additon, Addison, Hunt, and Sullivan (1965) studied PMS in a group of 249 women prisoners, who were given a combined treatment of a diuretic, an antispasmodic, a mild stimulant, vitamin B, and a supplementary protein diet. Twelve PMS subjects were given a glucose tolerance test, which revealed a pronounced hypoglycemic reaction. Posttreatment tests showed these subjects exhibiting less reaction, but they still had a lower-than-normal blood sugar. In neither study were statistics reported or control groups included, and the latter study was not designed to separate the effects of various treatments.

The evidence that hypoglycemia occurring during the premenstruum is the cause of premenstrual psychological symptoms and the result of hormone imbalance is minimal and indirect. Considering the striking similarity between the symptoms of hypoglycemia and the symptoms common to PMS, however, and considering the ease of treatment for mild hypoglycemia, such as simple dietary changes, this area deserves considerably more research attention than it has received in the past.

Monoamine Oxidase Activity

Increased monoamine oxidase (MAO) activity has been suggested as the mediator between estrogen-progesterone levels and the depressive affect frequently encountered in women suffering from PMS. MAO is an enzyme located in the mitochondria of the nerve cell, and its function is to metabolize a portion of reabsorbed norepinephrine subsequent to neural firing. This is the basis of one theoretical explanation of endogenous depression; that is, that an excess of MAO reduces available norepinephrine, resulting in slowed or reduced central neural activity. Evidence for this theory is primarily indirect and stems from the ability of MAO inhibitors to effect clinical improvement in depression.

Several studies have found higher levels of MAO in the secretory endometrium than in the proliferative endometrium (Grant & Pryse-Davies, 1968; Southgate, Grant, Pollard, Pryse-Davies, & Sandler, 1968). Gilmore, Robinson, Nies, Sylwester, and Ravaris (1971) failed to find phasic effects in plasma or platelet MAO and concluded that the previously found fluctuations were local to specific organs rather than systemic. On the other hand, significant increases in plasma MAO from the follicular to the luteal phase were reported by Klaiber, Kobayashi, Broverman, and Hall (1971). A later study (Klaiber, Broverman, Vogel, Kobayashi, & Moriarity, 1972) comparing normal and endogenously depressed women showed depressed women having significantly higher levels of plasma MAO than normal women. Both groups exhibited higher MAO levels during the luteal phase than the follicular phase; this difference was significant for the normals but not for the depressed women. These investigators also assessed the EEG driving response to photic stimulation, which is assumed to reflect, via the reticular activating system, the arousal threshold to environmental stimuli; that is, when central adrenergic functioning is enhanced, EEG driving is diminished. The driving response results paralleled those of MAO activity for the depressed and nondepressed women. A separate study (Vogel et al., 1971) replicated these findings for normal women, who showed significantly more driving responses premenstrually than during the preovulatory phase.

Since estrogen is high in both the follicular and the luteal phases, and progesterone is present in quantity only in the luteal phase, one might logically speculate that progesterone is, in some way, implicated in the differential MAO levels. Nevertheless, the available research suggests that a lack of estrogen or a low estrogen-progesterone ratio is etiological. Exogenous estrogen has been found to reduce elevated MAO levels (Klaiber et al., 1971) and decrease driving responses (Vogel et al., 1971) in amenorrheic women and to reduce both MAO levels and driving responses in endogenously depressed women (Klaiber et al., 1972). In addition, Grant and Pryse-Davies (1968) followed 797 women who were taking various oral contraceptives and noted lower levels of endometrial MAO and a lower incidence of depression for women taking strongly estrogenic tablets than for those taking strongly progesteronic contraceptives. They concluded that progesterone acts to increase MAO levels but that high estrogen levels protect against an extreme elevation. Neither these measures nor the treatment effectiveness of estrogen has been directly tested in women suffering from PMS.

The MAO hypothesis of PMS has been criticized primarily on the grounds that it lacks concrete support and requires too many unverified assumptions. Parlee (1973) presented an excellent critique; two of her most salient points were (1) that the psychological effects of the pharmacologic doses of exogenous estrogen used in birth control pills and as treatment may not be similar to the psychological effects of physiological levels and (2) that endometrial and/or systemic MAO levels do not necessarily reflect levels in the central nervous system. Furthermore, if MAO levels do, indeed, act as causal agents in PMS, they could reasonably explain only premenstrual depression and lethargy, leaving other symptoms unexplained.

Hormone Therapy

Several studies have assessed the treatment effectiveness of exogenous progesterone on PMS. Dalton (1964) viewed PMS essentially as a disorder resulting from lower-than-normal levels of progesterone and claimed overwhelming success in alleviating symptoms with progersterone therapy. In a clinical report of seventy-eight patients (Greene & Dalton, 1953), women suffering from severe PMS were treated with either intramuscular progesterone injections or implants; 83.5% became symptom free from injections, 6.6% were improved, and 6.6% reported no relief. Women suffering from mild or moderate PMS were treated with ethisterone, a synthetic progesterone that may be taken orally; 47.9% reported complete relief, and 17.4% partial relief. Of the fourteen patients who were not improved, nine experienced complete relief with progesterone injections.

Aware of the inconvenience and expense of regular injections, Dalton (1959a) tested the effects of three oral progestogens on PMS symptoms in fifty-eight patients who had experienced complete relief of symptoms from progesterone injections. Good or moderate relief was reported by 59% who received ethisterone, 37% who received dimesthisterone, and 59% who received norethisterone. Similar results were reported by Rees (1953), who treated thirty patients suffering from severe PMS; intramuscular injections of progesterone were effective in relieving PMS in the five patients thus treated. All patients were treated with ethisterone for some cycles, and in 85% of the trials, "significant" (no statistics were reported) relief was obtained. No relief was noted during cycles in which placebo tablets were administered. Dalton (1964) speculated that while both forms (oral and injected) of treatment affect the endometrium in a similar way, only injected progesterone provides a sodium-dissipating action, which accounts for its greater treatment effectiveness.

In a group of thirty women with moderate or severe PMS, Appleby (1960) compared the treatment effectiveness of meprobamate (a tranquilizer), chlorothiazide (a diuretic), and oral progesterone and noted total or marked relief of symptoms in one-half, one-third, and one-fifth of the patients, respectively. The author commented that rarely did a patient respond to more than one form of treatment, suggesting multiple etiologies and optimal treatments for PMS.

The widespread use of oral contraceptives in the last fifteen years has provided an available population of women who have artificially altered hormone levels. Kutner and Brown (1972) studied psychological symptoms in women who had never used oral contraceptives, in those who were past users, and in current users. Current users reported significantly less premenstrual moodiness and irritability, with users of combination-type pills reporting less of both symptoms than sequential-type users. Within the group of combination-pill users, those who were taking pills with a high progesterone content experienced less depression than those taking pills with little progesterone. Similar results were reported by Paige (1971), whose subjects taking combination-type oral contraceptives experienced less phasic fluctuation in anxiety and hostility than subjects not taking medication. Similar improvement was not effected through use of sequential-type pills. These studies offer indirect evidence for reduced symptomatology resulting from increased progesterone.

In contrast, Grant and Pryse-Davies (1968), in a large sample studied longitudinally, compared the incidence of depression and endometrial MAO levels among women taking a wide variety of oral contraceptives. Their data suggested that the use of strongly progestogenic, combination-type pills is associated with elevated levels of endometrial MAO and a high (28%) incidence of depression, while strongly estrogenic, sequential-type pills are associated with lowered levels of MAO and a low (7%) incidence of depression. These results are in agreement with those of Klaiber et al. (1972), reported above, who found that exogenous estrogen decreased plasma MAO and improved mood in endogenously depressed women.

The contradictions apparent in the research are obvious but may be at least partially explained by the confounding of a general psychological state and transitory psychological distress occurring during the premenstruum. Only in the study by Kutner and Brown (1972) were symptoms specific to the premenstrual period assessed. It is certainly possible that the exacerbation or alleviation of symptoms occurring premenstrually and the reduction or elevation of general affect could be influenced via different mechanisms. Cullberg (1972) tested three types of oral contraceptives — high, moderate, and low progesterone content with estrogen content constant. Approximately one-third of each group suffered adverse mental changes in response to the medication. Further analyses were done by breaking down the groups into those with and those without a history of premenstrual irritability; subjects who reacted negatively to high progestogenic compounds were mainly those who did not previously suffer from premenstrual irritability, while those subjects who reacted negatively to high estrogenic compounds were mainly those with a history of premenstrual irritability. These results agree with Dalton's research and support the "low progesterone" or "high unopposed estrogen" theory of PMS. These results also serve to emphasize the necessity of studying PMS in women who experience PMS rather than in the general population.

Conclusions

Research and clinical reports concerned with the physiological etiology of PMS have yielded contradictory results and left many questions unanswered. Perhaps studies which employ a variety of methods to determine the phase of the menstrual cycle, numerous methods of dividing the cycle into phases for purposes of comparisons, and idiosyncratic procedures for assessing biochemical, endocrinological, and psychological variables cannot be expected to yield consistent results. On the other hand, the confusion apparent in the published literature could be a reflection of the enormous complexity of the problem; reductionism may provide simple answers, but we are left with a number of simple answers that cannot be integrated in any meaningful manner.

There are several issues related to the physiological etiology of PMS which have not received sufficient attention:

1. The most popular theory views reduced progesterone or a high estrogen-progesterone ratio as etiologically related to PMS. The advocates of this theory, however, do not address the issue that during the preovulatory phase, there are high levels of estrogen, minimal progesterone, and no symptoms.

2. The mechanism of interest is typically treated as if it were not part of an integrated organism, and possible interactions among systems are ignored. Several examples will serve to illustrate. Both MAO levels and hypoglycemia have been implicated in the development of premenstrual depression, but MAO inhibitors have been shown to induce hypoglycemia; norepinephrine, which is assumed to vary inversely with MAO, tends to inhibit insulin release; and aldosterone effects both fluid retention and carbohydrate metabolism (Hall, Anderson, Smart, & Besser, 1974). Thus, restricting one's attention to the association between premenstrual symptoms and one's favorite dependent variable is likely to provide an incomplete view of the actual relationships.

3. The vast majority of the studies are descriptive or correlational in the sense that independent variables are not manipulated, that is, women with and without PMS are compared, or symptoms and physiological variables are correlated. This type of design is clearly the most practical (and ethical) and can lend support to a particular theory, but causality cannot be determined. This is a particularly relevant problem in PMS research, since most of the hypothesized physiological mechanisms are influenced by environmental events. Psychological trauma or stress can elevate serum prolactin levels (Mason, 1975), increase the formation of glucocorticoids which, in turn, effect changes in blood sugar level (Navratil, 1975), deplete norepinephrine (Miller & Weiss, 1969), and lower gonadotropin production to the point of inducing amenorrhea (Check, 1978). Therefore, the considerable individual differences typically found could be partially due to external events influencing the physiological variables.

4. The only reason for combining symptoms, such as depression, irritability, sluggishness, restlessness, and swelling, under the title *PMS* is because of their temporal relationship to the menstrual cycle. At other times or in other contexts, one would not logically expect such divergent symptoms to occur together. Indeed, it is possible that they do not occur simultaneously and that the various symptoms are caused by different mechanisms. For example, premenstrual water retention may be due to elevated prolactin, while premenstrual depression may result from increased MAO activity. If this is the case, contradictory or negative results are likely to ensue if prolactin suppressants are studied as treatment for premenstrual water retention in a group of women in which only some suffer from that symptom. Improved assessment of symptomatology, along with the recognition that PMS may consist of several distinct syndromes, could improve the quality and utility of the research.

5. Finally, the necessity of studying women who clearly suffer from PMS must again be stressed. The physiological manifestations of artificially increasing progesterone may be very different in normal women than in women who suffer from PMS, and the cyclic fluctuations of aldosterone in normal women do

not necessarily tell us anything about aldosterone activity in PMS women. One cannot legitimately generalize from one population to the other.

Physiological Factors in Dysmenorrhea

There is ample documentation that the direct cause of menstrual cramping and pain is abnormal contractility of the myometrium (the uterine muscle). Although the published literature typically does not report standard statistics and significance levels, research over the past thirty-five years is amazingly consistent in describing the myometrial contractile patterns associated with dysmenorrhea. Contractility during the normal, nonpainful menstrual cycle is characterized by low-amplitude, high-frequency, and somewhat tetanic muscle activity during the follicular phase; during the luteal phase, there is a change to high-amplitude, low-frequency contractions with reduced tetany; and menses is characterized by similar high-amplitude contractions with an absence of tetany. Women suffering from dysmenorrhea show similar activity during follicular and luteal phases, but menses is marked by high-amplitude, irregular or uncoordinated contractions superimposed on a high degree of tetany (Bickers, 1941; Garrioch, 1978).

A further difference in myometrial activity between normal and dysmenorrheic women pertains to the differing contractility patterns within the uterus. In the luteal phase, there is a gradient of tonicity between a hypotonic *fundus* and a hypertonic *isthmus*, which facilitates retention and implantation of the zygote, should fertilization occur. Immediately prior to menstruation, this gradient is reversed, and the relaxed lower segment allows expulsion of the menstrual product. In painful menstruation, this gradient is frequently such that the isthmus continues to be hypertonic, requiring increased force to expel the uterine lining and blood (Bickers, 1954; Sturgis, 1970).

Recordings of myometrial activity during the time when pain is experienced point, once again, to abnormal contractility as the cause of pain. Continuous recordings in dysmenorrhic women demonstrated that periods of high tetany were accompanied by complaints of pain, while pain dissipated when activity returned to base line between contractions, and that medication which reduced tone also reduced complaints of pain (Filler & Hall, 1970). Akerlund, Andersson, and Ingemarsson (1976) described the pain experienced by their patients as a continuous, dull ache with colicky exacerbations; the continuous component was accompanied by elevated tone, while the colicky component was reported during contractions of high amplitude. Although there is no direct experimental evidence, it is generally believed that this type of muscular activity is painful because the continuously elevated tone produces hypoxia of the uterine muscle (Israel, 1967; Ylikorkala & Dawood, 1978).

Although a variety of theories exist to account for dysmenorrhea, and a variety of treatments have been relatively effective, this discussion will be limited to the etiologies and treatments which relate to prostaglandins and to progesterone and estrogen.

Prostaglandins

There has recently been considerable interest in the role of prostaglandins in dysmenorrhea. Prostaglandins are unsaturated fatty acids that have actions similar to hormones but are synthesized in tissues rather than glands. Originally discovered in human seminal fluid, they have since been found to be widely distributed in mammalian tissue, particularly in the lung, kidney, and uterus, and released by such mechanical stimuli as stretching, squeezing, and compression (Fuchs, 1977). The effect of prostaglandin release on the uterus is one of increased myometrial motility (Karim & Hillier, 1973), and it has been suggested that the uterus contains receptors specific to prostaglandins (Kirton, 1973).

The specific prostaglandins thought to be relevant to uterine contractility are PGE_1 and PGF_{2a}. Endometrial content of these prostaglandins is relatively low during proliferative and early luteal phases; an increase is seen during the late luteal phase, and a dramatic increase from late luteal to menstrual phase (Singh, Baccarini, & Zuspan, 1975; Willman, Collins, & Clayton, 1976). The latter study found the menstrual levels to be approximately eight times higher than the follicular levels. Pulkkinen, Henzl, and Csapo (1978) studied prostaglandin levels from uterine jet-washings in both normal and dysmenorrheic women; the postovulatory increase was greater in dysmenorrheic women than in symptom-free women. Plasma levels of prostaglandins have also been reported to fluctuate in a similar manner. According to a study by Lundstrom and Green (1978), plasma levels in normal women varied between 20 and 33 picograms per milliliter (pg/ml), while those in dysmenorrheic women varied between 32 and 105 pg/ml. These differences occurred during the menstrual phase; premenstrual differences were not significantly different.

Further evidence for the hypothesized relationship between prostaglandins and dysmenorrhea comes from research studying the effects of exogenous administrations of prostaglandins. Fuchs and Fuchs (1973) reported that the uterine activity resulting from exogenous prostaglandin stimulation is characterized by uncoordinated contractions and an elevation of tone, both of which are properties of uterine activity during painful menstruation. Lundstrom, Green, and Wiqvist (1976) successfully treated patients with a prostaglandin synthesis inhibitor and then gave one patient an intravenous infusion of PGF_{2a}, which induced severe cramps, a rise in uterine tone, and spastic contractions. Finally, the similarity between the symptoms of dysmenorrhea (flushing, abdominal cramping, nausea, and diarrhea) and the side effects produced by administering prostaglandins to induce abortion and labor has been pointed out by Halbert, Demers, Fontana, and Jones (1975).

The research clearly supports a covarying relationship between the degree of pain accompanying menstruation and endometrial and plasma levels of particular prostaglandins. The cause of this relationship has not been clarified, however. Several authors (Downie, Poyser, & Wunderlich, 1974; Halbert et al., 1975; Karim & Hillier, 1973; Schwartz, Zor, Lindner, & Naor, 1974) have suggested that the prostaglandins present in the menstrual fluid originate in the disintegrating endometrium and that, in addition to locally stimulating uterine contractility, they may also be absorbed into the circulation, thereby causing systemic symptoms. Thus, according to this theory, dysmenorrheic women have an excessive release of prostaglandins or an excessive sensitivity to their presence. Others (Filler & Hall, 1970; Lundstrum & Green, 1978; Ylikorkala & Dawood, 1978) have interpreted the elevated prostaglandin level to be a consequence, rather than a cause, of painful contractions. Cervical obstruction to either a small cervical exit or large fragments of endometrium may increase the contractility required to expel the menstrual product; since prostaglandins are released in response to stretching, the increased muscle contractions may result in increased levels of prostaglandins. Furthermore, a delayed discharge could increase the absorption of prostaglandins.

A further hypothesis concerns the possible role of oxytocin. Oxytocin is a hormone secreted by the posterior pituitary. Exogenous oxytocin is frequently administered to induce labor or to cause contraction of the uterus after delivery of the placenta. Oxytocin is the most potent and specific activator of the myometrium known, and because of this property, it has been implicated in the etiology of painful contractility associated with dysmenorrhea. Fuchs (1977) noted that oxytocin seemed to stimulate uterine production of prostaglandins and suggested that prostaglandins mediate the oxytocic reaction. Csapo and Csapo (1974) tested uterine reactivity subsequent to naproxen, a prostaglandin synthesis inhibitor; PGF_{2a} but not oxytocin restored excitability, which further supports the idea that prostaglandin production is a necessary step in the uterine response to oxytocin. Mechanical dilation of the uterus, cervix, or vagina reflexively stimulates oxytocin release (Hall et al., 1974), suggesting the possibility that cervical obstruction or large endometrial fragments may set off a sequence involving oxytocin and prostaglandin production. In addition, alcohol, which inhibits the release of oxytocin, has been found to inhibit uterine activity in threatened premature labor (Fuchs, Fuchs, Poblete, & Risk, 1967) and to reduce myometrial tone in normally menstruating women, with the most marked depression occurring during menses (Fuchs, Coutinho, Xavier, Bates, & Fuchs, 1968). One might note that a shot of brandy is an old home remedy for menstrual cramps.

On the other hand, there is no direct evidence that dysmenorrheic women, compared with symptom-free women, have higher levels of oxytocin, greater oxytocin responses, or greater sensitivity to oxytocin. Furthermore, the reactivity of the nonpregnant uterus to oxytocin is questionable. Coutinho and Lopes (1968) observed a positive response to oxytocin in eighty-nine women only during the premenstruum and menses, while Hendricks (1966), testing only two subjects, found essentially no response to oxytocin. The involvement of prostaglandins in the oxytocic reaction certainly does not preclude the production of prostaglandins independent of oxytocin. With present knowledge, the role of oxytocin in the development of dysmenorrhea can only be speculative.

A predictable consequence of the research described above has been the attempt to treat dysmenorrhea with prostaglandin synthesis inhibitors. Indomethacin has been found to totally eliminate spontaneous activity in isolated strips of myometrium (Garrioch, 1978). Lundstrom et al. (1976) treated five dysmenorrheic women with indomethacin. Prior to treatment, all exhibited uterine activity characterized by spastic contractions and elevated tone. During the treated cycle, all subjects were symptom free, myometrial contractions became synchronized, tone decreased, and plasma $PGF_{2\alpha}$ levels were reduced by 85-90%. Flufenamic acid not only inhibits production of prostaglandins but also neutralizes preformed prostaglandins. Schwartz et al. (1974) compared this compound with analgesics, spasmolytics, tranquilizers, and vitamin pills in sixteen women who reported severe dysmenorrhea. Substances other than flufenamic acid afforded no "significant" (no statistics reported) relief, while the cycles treated with flufenamic acid were symptom free for all but two subjects; symptoms returned when treatment was withheld. The authors pointed out that aspirin also inhibits prostaglandin production but is only partially effective in the treatment of dysmenorrhea, possibly because it does not neutralize preformed prostaglandins.

A final prostaglandin synthesis inhibitor that has been used to treat dysmenorrhea is naproxen (or its sodium salt). The direct effect of naproxen has been demonstrated by Csapo and Csapo (1974), who reported that naproxen eliminated spontaneous activity and electrical excitability in rabbit uteri, in vitro, and that administration of exogenous prostaglandin restored electric excitability. Csapo, Pulkkinen, and Henzl (1977) administered placebos and naproxen-sodium to ten women while monitoring intrauterine pressure. Pretreatment uterine motlity showed high tone and high-frequency contractions; the placebo had no effect, while the drug reduced the parameters of both contractility and reported pain. In two independent samples of dysmenorrheic women, Henzl, Buttram, Segre, and Bessler (1977) found naproxen-sodium to be significantly more effective than a placebo in relieving symptoms. A final study, reported by Pulkkinen et al. (1978), found naproxen-sodium to be more effective than a placebo in reducing prostaglandin levels and reducing pain in six women who had been suffering from dysmenorrhea for at least one year. Thus, regardless of the causal mechanisms relating prostaglandins and dysmenorrhea, prostaglandin synthesis inhibitors appear to provide effective treatment.

Estrogen and Progesterone

Although there is no direct evidence, there is a general belief apparent in the literature that dysmenorrhea is the result of an excess of progesterone or a high progesterone-estrogen ratio in the late luteal phase of the menstrual cycle. Ylikorkala and Dawood (1978) suggested that, since dysmenorrhea occurs only in ovulatory cycles, a secretory endometrium and progesterone are necessary prerequisites for dysmenorrhea and that the progesterone effect is possibly mediated by prostaglandins, because concentrations of prostaglandins in menstrual fluid are higher during ovulatory than anovulatory cycles. The empirical support for this theory is indirect:

1. Patients suffering from PMS who receive too much progesterone for treatment may experience dysmenorrhea (Dalton, 1964).
2. If ovulation is prevented by the use of estrogen, and progesterone is administered at the onset of withdrawal bleeding, cramps will ensue (Sturgis, 1970).
3. Exogenous estrogen produces a uterine motility pattern characteristic of the proliferative phase; when progesterone is added, motility becomes labor-like (Moawad & Bengtsson, 1968).
4. Under estrogen influence, the uterus responds with few contractions to PGE_1, but if there is pretreatment with progesterone, the responses are greatly enhanced and prolonged (Fuchs, 1977).

Not only is this research rather tangential to the central theory, but, as Israel (1967) points out, an estrogen-progesterone imbalance has not been demonstrated in the blood or urine of women with dysmenorrhea.

Oral contraceptives have been used effectively to treat dysmenorrhea, and women who take oral contraceptives to prevent pregnancy report a reduction in the symptoms associated with dysmenorrhea (Israel, 1967). The uterine motility during anovulatory cycles is characterized by hypotonia, and labor-like patterns are absent (Sturgis, 1970). It is assumed that this reduced uterine motility results from the absence of a progesterone-producing corpus luteum. Cullberg (1972), however, studied the effects on dysmenorrhea of a variety of oral contraceptives containing various amounts of progesterone; dysmenorrhea was relieved by progesterone-dominated compounds in a dose-related response. It is difficult to integrate these findings with the general belief that excess progesterone causes dysmenorrhea, although oral progestins do not necessarily have the same action as endogenous progesterones (Dalton, 1959a).

Conclusions

Although the research investigating the etiology of dysmenorrhea has yielded some contradictory results, the data is fairly consistent in terms of describing certain covariates of painful menstruation, such as contractility patterns and prostaglandin levels. That the physiological research on dysmenorrhea seems more consistent and focused than that on PMS is probably due to several factors:

1. There is one primary and distinct symptom diagnostic of dysmenorrhea — pain during menses — as opposed to the various vague and diffuse symptoms of PMS. Thus, a sample of dysmenorrheic women is more likely to be homogeneous

in symptomatology than is a sample of PMS women; this would tend to reduce individual variability and increase the power of statistical tests.

2.   Since dysmenorrhea typically coincides with the onset of menses, the symptom is readily associated with menstruation; on the other hand, symptoms of PMS, because of their temporal relationship to the menstrual cycle and because of the nature of the symptoms, may be viewed by the sufferer as a reaction to environmental events or an exacerbation of neurotic tendencies. In addition, dysmenorrhea, compared with PMS, is more likely to be incapacitating in terms of preventing afflicted women from carrying out their normal daily activities. Both factors would magnify the likelihood that a woman would seek professional help to alleviate the symptoms of dysmenorrhea, which could act to sensitize clinicians to the problem and generate interest in research.

3.   Prostaglandins have generated much interest in the scientific community, not only in relation to dysmenorrhea, but also for other purposes, such as the use of synthesized prostaglandins to induce abortion and labor. The result is that there is sufficient basic research on prostaglandins, which is useful in generating theories of dysmenorrhea.

Although much of the recent research on dysmenorrhea is encouraging and practical, the question of etiology remains unanswered. Why do some women and not others have abnormal uterine contractility during menses? Why do women who experience dysmenorrhea have elevated levels of certain prostaglandins? These are a few of the questions which need to be addressed prior to formulating testable conceptualizations of etiology.

Thus far, research indicates that effective treatment is available for women suffering from dysmenorrhea. Prostaglandin synthesis inhibitors appear to alleviate the symptoms without major side effects, and behavior modification techniques, particularly relaxation training, may prove to be useful. Of interest to women suffering from mild forms of dysmenorrhea is the research which indirectly offers validation for common home remedies. Alcohol has been found to relax uterine muscle, and, if menstrual pain is a consequence of myometrial ischemia, as has been suggested, the effectiveness of hot baths and heating pads may be due to the vasodilating properties of heat, since vasodilation would act to increase the supply of oxygen.

FUTURE DIRECTIONS

In the present chapter, the psychological and physiological research investigating the etiology and treatment of dysmenorrhea and PMS was critically reviewed. Clearly, an integration of the two areas of research, culminating in a comprehensive theory, would be desirable. Unfortunately, the quantity and quality of the available research allows nothing more than wild speculation.

Although no attempts have been made to provide evidence for an integrated model of menstrual dysfunction, evidence does exist which recommends the potential usefulness of such a model. PMS has been associated with elevated prolactin levels, lowered blood sugar levels, and increased MAO levels, all of which are influenced by both physiological and psychological events. Dysmenorrhea has been linked to hypercontractility of the uterine muscle; this could be a result of local biochemical agents or a manifestation of general muscle activity brought about by anxiety and tension. The possibility exists that both disorders have multiple etiologies and that any event — physiological or psychological — which activates a mediating mechanism can produce the disorder.

The treatment research presents an even more imposing task in terms of integration. All the present medical treatments of both dysmenorrhea and PMS are symptomatic — that is, the goal is to relieve symptoms rather than to alter underlying abnormalities — and since causes are not altered, medication must be taken on a continuous basis. Moreover, studies which evaluate the effectiveness of such treatment do not contribute, on a theoretical level, to the understanding of etiology. Psychological treatment generally attempts to cure, but there is simply too little of this research to allow adequate evaluation. A further issue relates to the treatment of PMS. Studies have typically found a particular treatment to be effective for some women and not others. For example, diuretics may be found to alleviate symptoms for only a third of a particular sample and are, therefore, dismissed as ineffective. Diuretics may be effective, however, for those women whose primary symptom is water retention and not for those whose primary symptom is depression. For future research, logic dictates the use of samples which are homogeneous in symptomatology. This view concurs with that of previous authors, who have concluded that PMS most likely consists of several disorders with distinct etiologies, symptoms, and preferred treatments.

As with most psychosomatic disorders, research on menstrual disorders is directed by a variety of individuals who represent a diversity of levels and types of training. Most of the literature on menstrual disorders may be classified into two general categories. One type of research, which tends to be most common in studies employing psychological variables, involves the use of appropriate control groups in a standard experimental design and employs sophisticated statistical analyses but fails to employ adequate methods for determining cycle phase or hormone levels. The other type of research, typical of studies employing physiological variables, may be commended for careful hormone analyses and valid methods for determining time of ovulation, but it is clearly lacking in appropriate experimental design and statistical analyses; frequently, phenomena are observed and reported with no indication as to the likelihood of these observations occurring by chance.

A solution would be to relax the barriers separating the various disciplines and to encourage collaboration among researchers with various specializations. Hopefully, this would not only generate studies free from the above criticisms but facilitate an appreciation for the interaction among environmental, psychological, and physiological causes and a willingness to accept that the understanding and treatment of menstrual disorders requires complex, rather than simple, solutions.

REFERENCES

Abplanalp, J. M., Livingston, L., Rose, R. M., & Sandwisch, D. Cortisol and growth hormone responses to psychological stress during the menstrual cycle. *Psychosomatic Medicine*, 1977, *39*, 158-177.

Abramson, M., & Torghele, J. R. Weight, temperature changes and psychosomatic symptomatology in relation to the menstrual cycle. *American Journal of Obstetrics and Gynecology*, 1961, *81*, 223-232.

Akerlund, M., Andersson, K. E., & Ingemarsson, I. Effects of terbutaline on myometrial activity, uterine blood flow, and lower abdominal pain in women with primary dysmenorrhea. *British Journal of Obstetrics and Gynecology*, 1976, *83*, 673-678.

Altmann, M., Knowles, E., & Bull, H. D. A psychosomatic study of the sex cycle in women. *Psychosomatic Medicine*, 1941, *3*, 199-225.

Andersch, B., Hahn, L., Andersson, M., & Isaksson, B. Body water and weight in patients with premenstrual tension. *British Journal of Obstetrics and Gynecology*, 1978, *85*, 546-550.

Andersen, A. N., Larsen, J. F., Steenstrup, O. R., Svendstrup, B., & Nielsen, J. Effect of bromocriptine on the premenstrual syndrome. A double-blind clinical trial. *British Journal of Obstetrics and Gynecology*, 1977, *84*, 370-374.

Appleby, B. P. A study of premenstrual tension in general practice. *British Medical Journal*, February 1960, pp. 391-393.

Bacchus, H. *Essentials of metabolic diseases and endocrinology*. Baltimore: University Park Press, 1976.

Backstrom, T., & Mattsson, B. Correlation of symptoms in premenstrual tension to oestrogen and progesterone concentrations in blood plasma. *Neuropsychobiology*, 1975, *1*, 80-86.

Beaumont, P. J. V., Richards, D. H., & Gelder, M. G. A study of minor psychiatric and physical symptoms during the menstrual cycle. *British Journal of Psychiatry*, 1975, *126*, 431-434.

Benedek-Jaszmann, L. J., & Hearn-Sturtevant, M. D. Premenstrual tension and functional infertility. *Lancet*, May 1976, pp. 1095-1098.

Bernstein, B. E. Effect of menstruation on academic performance among college women. *Archives of Sexual Behavior*, 1977, *6*, 289-296.

Berry, C., & McQuire, F. L. Menstrual distress and acceptance of sexual role. *American Journal of Obstetrics and Gynecology*, 1972, *114*, 83-87.

Bickers, W. Uterine contractions in dysmenorrhea. *American Journal of Obstetrics and Gynecology*, 1941, *42*, 1023-1030.

Bickers, W. B. *Menorrhalgia – Menstrual distress*. Springfield, Ill.: Charles C. Thomas, 1954.

Birtchnell, J., & Floyd, S. Attempted suicide and the menstrual cycle – A negative conclusion. *Journal of Psychosomatic Research*, 1974, *18*, 361-369.

Bloom, L. J., Shelton, J. L., & Michaels, A. C. Dysmenorrhea and personality. *Journal of Personality Assessment*, 1978, *42*, 272-276.

Brockway, J. *Prediction of premenstrual symptomatology using the Moos Menstrual Distress Questionnaire*. Unpublished dissertation, University of Iowa, 1975.

Brown, J. J., Davies, D. L., Lever, A. F., & Robertson, J. I. S. Variations in plasma renin during the menstrual cycle. *British Medical Journal*, October 1964, pp. 1114-1115.

Check, J. H. Emotional aspects of menstrual dysfunction. *Psychosomatics*, 1978, *19*, 178-184.

Chesney, M. A., & Tasto, D. L. The development of the menstrual symptom questionnaire. *Behaviour Research and Therapy*, 1975, *13*, 237-244. (a)

Chesney, M. A., & Tasto, D. L. The effectiveness of behavior modification with spasmodic and congestive dysmenorrhea. *Behaviour Research and Therapy*, 1975, *13*, 245-253. (b)

Coppen, A., & Kessel, N. Menstruation and personality. *British Journal of Psychiatry*, 1963, *109*, 711-721.

Coutinho, E. M., & Lopes, A. C. V. Response of the nonpregnant uterus to vasopressin as an index of ovarian function. *American Journal of Obstetrics and Gynecology*, 1968, *102*, 479-489.

Cox, D. J. Menstrual symptom questionnaire; further psychometric evaluation. *Behaviour Research and Therapy*, 1977, *15*, 506-508.

Cox, D. J., & Meyer, R. G. Behavioral treatment parameters with primary dysmenorrhea. *Journal of Behavioral Medicine*, 1978, *1*, 297-310.

Csapo, A. I., & Csapo, E. E. The "prostaglandin step," a bottleneck in the activation of the uterus. *Life Sciences*, 1974, *14*, 719-724.

Csapo, A. I., Pulkkinen, M. O., & Henzl, M. R. The effect of naproxen sodium on the intrauterine pressure and menstrual pain of dysmenorrheic patients. *Prostaglandins*, 1977, *13*, 193-199.

Cullberg, J. Mood changes and menstrual symptoms with different gestation/ estrogen combinations. *Acta Psychiatrica Scandinavica*, 1972, *suppl. 236*, pp. 1-86.

Dalton, K. Comparative trials of new oral progestogenic compounds in treatment of premenstrual syndrome. *British Medical Journal*, December 1959, pp. 1307-1309. (a)

Dalton, K. Menstruation and acute psychiatric illness. *British Medical Journal*, January 1959, pp. 148-149. (b)

Dalton, K. Effect of menstruation on schoolgirls' weekly work. *British Medical Journal*, January 1960, pp. 326-328. (a)

Dalton, K. Menstruation and accidents. *British Medical Journal*, November 1960, pp. 1425-1426. (b)

Dalton, K. Schoolgirls' behaviour and menstruation. *British Medical Journal*, December 1960, pp. 1647-1649. (c)

Dalton, K. Menstruation and crime. *British Medical Journal*, December 1961, pp. 1752-1753.

Dalton, K. *The premenstrual syndrome*. Springfield, Ill.: Charles C. Thomas, 1964.

Dalton, K. Menstruation and examinations. *Lancet*, December 1968, pp. 1386-1388.

Dor-shav, N. K. In search of pre-menstrual tension: Note on sex differences in psychological differentiation as a function of cyclical physiological changes. *Perception and Motor Skills*, 1976, *42*, 1139-1142.

Downie, S., Poyser, N. L., & Wunderlich, M. Levels of prostaglandin in human endometrium during the normal menstrual cycle. *Journal of Physiology*, 1974, *236*, 465-472.

Favreau, O. *Menstrual cycles and sex differences*. Unpublished manuscript. University of Montreal, 1974.

Filler, W. W., & Hall, W. C. Dysmenorrhea and its therapy: A uterine contractility study. *American Journal of Obstetrics and Gynecology*, 1970, *106*, 104-109.

Fuchs, A. Prostaglandins. In F. Fuchs & A. Klopper (Eds.), *Endocrinology of pregnancy* (2nd ed.). New York: Harper and Row, 1977.

Fuchs, A., Coutinho, E. M., Xavier, R., Bates, P. E., & Fuchs, F. Effect of ethanol on the activity of the nonpregnant human uterus and its reactivity to neurohypophyseal hormones. *American Journal of Obstetrics and Gynecology*, 1968, *101*, 997-1000.

Fuchs, A. R., & Fuchs, F. Possbile mechanisms of the inhibition of labor by ethanol. In J. B. Josimovich (Ed.), *Uterine contraction: Side effects of steroidal contraceptives*. New York: Wiley, 1973.

Fuchs, F., Fuchs, A., Poblete, V., & Risk, A. Effect of alcohol on threatened premature labor. *American Journal of Obstetrics and Gynecology*, 1967, *99*, 627-637.

Garrioch, D. B. The effect of indomethacin on spontaneous activity in the isolated human myometrium and on the response to oxytocin and prostaglandin. *British Journal of Obstetrics and Gynecology*, 1978, *85*, 47-52.

Genazzani, A. R., Lemarchand-Beraud, Th., Aubert, M. L., & Felber, J. P. Pattern of plasma ACTH, hGH, and cortisol during menstrual cycle. *Journal of Clinical Endocrinology and Metabolism*, 1975, *41*, 431-437.

Ghose, K., & Coppen, A. Bromocriptine and premenstrual syndrome: Controlled study. *British Medical Journal*, January 1977, pp. 147-148.

Gilmore, N. J., Robinson, D. S., Nies, A., Sylwester, D., & Ravaris, C. L. Blood monoamine oxidase levels in pregnancy and during the menstrual cycle. *Journal of Psychosomatic Research*, 1971, *15*, 215-220.

Golub, L. J., Menduke, H., & Conly, S. S. Weight changes in college women during the menstrual cycle. *American Journal of Obstetrics and Gynecology*, 1965, *91*, 89-94.

Golub, S. The effect of premenstrual anxiety and depression on cognitive function. *Journal of Personality and Social Psychology*, 1976, *34*, 99-104. (a)

Golub, S. The magnitude of premenstrual anxiety and depression. *Psychosomatic Medicine*, 1976, *38*, 4-12. (b)

Gottschalk, L. A., Kaplan, S. M., Gleser, G. C., & Winget, C. M. Variations in magnitude of emotion: A method applied to anxiety and hostility during phases of the menstrual cycle. *Psychosomatic Medicine*, 1962, *24*, 300-311.

Gough, H. G. Personality factors related to reported severity of menstrual distress. *Journal of Abnormal Psychology*, 1975, *84*, 59-65.

Grant, E. C. G., & Pryse-Davies, J. Effect of oral contraceptives on depressive mood changes and on endometrial monamine oxidase and phosphates. *British Medical Journal*, 1968, *3*, 777-780.

Gray, M. J., Strausfeld, K. S., Watanabe, M., Sims, E. A. H., & Solomon, S. Aldosterone secretory rates in the normal menstruating cycle. *Journal of Clinical Endocrinology and Metabolism*, 1968, *28*, 1269-1275.

Greene, R., & Dalton, K. The premenstrual syndrome. *British Medical Journal*, May 1953, pp. 1007-1014.

Gregory, B. A. J. C. The menstrual cycle and its disorders in psychiatric patients: Review of the literature. *Journal of Psychosomatic Research*, 1957, *2*, 61-79.

Gruba, G. H., & Rohrbaugh, M. MMPI correlates of menstrual distress. *Psychosomatic Medicine*, 1975, *37*, 265-273.

Hackmann, E., Wirz-Justice, A., & Lichtsteiner, M. The uptake of dopamine and serotonin in rat brain during progesterone decline. *Psychopharmacology*, 1973, *32*, 183-191.

Hain, J. D., Linton, P. H., Eber, H. W., & Chapman, M. M. Menstrual irregularity, symptoms and personality. *Journal of Psychosomatic Research*, 1970, *14*, 81-87.

Halbert, D. R., Demers, L. M., Fontana, J., & Jones, D. E. D. Prostaglandin levels in endometrial jet wash specimens in patients with dysmenorrhea before and after indomethacin therapy. *Prostaglandins*, 1975, *10*, 1047-1056.

Halbreich, U., Ben-David, M., Assael, M., & Bornstein, R. Serum-prolactin in women with premenstrual syndrome. *Lancet*, September 1976, pp. 654-656.

Halbreich, U., & Kas, D. Variations in the Taylor MAS of women with premenstrual syndrome. *Journal of Psychosomatic Research*, 1977, *21*, 391-393.

Hall, R., Anderson, J., Smart, G. A., & Besser, M. *Fundamentals of clinical endocrinology* (2nd ed.). London: Pitman Medical, 1974.

Hamburg, D. A. Effects of progesterone on behavior. In R. Levine (Ed.), *Endocrines and the central nervous system*. Baltimore: Williams & Wilkins, 1966.

Hendricks, C. H. Characteristics of the nonpregnant human uterus. *American Journal of Obstetrics and Gynecology*, 1966, *96*, 824-843.

Henzl, M. R., Buttram, V., Segre, E. J., & Bessler, S. The treatment of dysmenorrhea with naproxen sodium: A report on two independent double-blind trials. *American Journal of Obstetrics and Gynecology*, 1977, *127*, 818-823.

Hirt, M., Kurtz, R., & Ross, W. D. The relationship between dysmenorrhea and selected personality variables. *Psychosomatics*, 1967, *8*, 350-353.

Israel, S. The clinical pattern and etiology of premenstrual tension. *International Record of Medicine*, 1953, *166*, 469-474.

Israel, S. L. *Diagnosis and treatment of menstrual disorders and sterility*. New York: Harper and Row, 1967.

Ivey, M. E., & Bardwick, J. M. Patterns of affective fluctuation in the menstrual cycle. *Psychosomatic Medicine*, 1968, *30*, 336-345.

Janowsky, D. S., Berens, S. C., & Davis, J. M. Correlations between mood, weight, and electrolytes during the menstrual cycle: A renin-angiotensin-aldosterone hypothesis of premenstrual tension. *Psychosomatic Medicine*, 1973, *35*, 143-154.

Kaplan, A. *The conduct of inquiry*. San Francisco: Chandler, 1964.

Karim, S. M., & Hillier, K. The role of prostaglandins in myometrial contraction. In J. B. Josimovich (Ed.), *Uterine contraction – Side effects of steroidal contraceptives*. New York: Wiley, 1973.

Kashiwagi, T., McClure, J. N., & Wetzel, R. D. Premenstrual affective syndrome and psychiatric disorder. *Diseases of the Nervous System*, 1976, *37*, 116-119.

Katz, F. H., & Romfh, P. Plasma aldosterone and renin activity during the menstrual cycle. *Journal of Clinical Endocrinology and Metabolism*, 1972, *34*, 819-821.

Kirton, K. T. Biochemical effects of prostaglandins as they might relate to uterine contraction. In J. B. Josimovich (Ed.), *Uterine contraction – Side effects of steroidal contraceptives*. New York: Wiley, 1973.

Klaiber, E. L., Broverman, D. M., Vogel, W., Kobayashi, Y., & Moriarity, D. Effects of estrogen therapy on plasma MAO activity and EEG driving response of depressed women. *American Journal of Psychiatry*, 1972, *128*, 1492-1498.

Klaiber, E. L., Kobayashi, Y., Broverman, D. M., & Hall, F. Plasma monoamine oxidase activity in regularly menstruating women and in amenorrheic women receiving cyclic treatment with estrogens and a progestin. *Journal of Clinical Endocrinology and Metabolism*, 1971, *33*, 630-638.

Kopell, B. S., Lunde, D. T., Clayton, R. B., & Moos, R. H. Variations in some measures of arousal during the menstrual cycle. *Journal of Nervous and Mental Diseases*, 1969, *148*, 180-187.

Kutner, S. J., & Brown, W. L. Types of oral contraceptives, depression, and premenstrual symptoms. *Journal of Nervous and Mental Diseases*, 1972, *155*, 153-162.

Lamb, W. M., Ulett, G. A., Masters, W. H., & Robinson, D. W. Premenstrual tension: EEG, hormonal, and psychiatric evaluation. *American Journal of Psychiatry*, 1953, *109*, 840-848.

Lennane, K. J., & Lennane, R. J. Alleged psychogenic disorders in women – A possible manifestation of sexual prejudice. *New England Journal of Medicine*, 1973, *288*, 288-292.

Levitt, E. E., & Lubin, B. Some personality factors associated with menstrual complaints and menstrual attitude. *Journal of Psychosomatic Research*, 1967, *11*, 267-270.

Little, B. C., & Zahn, T. P. Changes in mood and autonomic functioning during the menstrual cycle. *Psychophysiology*, 1974, *11*, 579-590.

Lundstrom, V., & Green, K. Endogenous levels of prostaglandin $F_{2\alpha}$ and its main metabolites in plasma and endometrium of normal and dysmenorrheic women. *American Journal of Obstetrics and Gynecology*, 1978, *130*, 640-646.

Lundstrom, V., Green, K., & Wiqvist, N. Prostaglandins, indomethacin and dysmenorrhea. *Prostaglandins*, 1976, *11*, 893-904.

MacKinnon, I. L., MacKinnon, P. C. D., & Thomson, A. D. Lethal hazards of the luteal phase of the menstrual cycle. *British Medical Journal*, April 1959, pp. 1015-1016.

Mandell, A. J., & Mandell, M. P. Suicide and the menstrual cycle. *Journal of the American Medical Association*, 1967, *200*, 792-793.

Marinari, K., Leshner, A. I., & Doyle, M. P. Menstrual cycle status and adrenocortical reactivity to psychological stress. *Psychoneuroendocrinology*, 1976, *1*, 213-218.

Markum, R. A. Assessment of reliability of and the effect of neutral instructions on the symptom ratings on the Moos Menstrual Distress Questionnaire. *Psychosomatic Medicine*, 1976, *38*, 163-172.

Marshall, J. Thermal changes in the normal menstrual cycle. *British Medical Journal*, January 1963, pp. 102-104.

Mason, J. W. Psychologic stress and endocrine function. In E. J. Sackar (Ed.), *Topics in psychoendocrinology*. New York: Grune & Stratton, 1975.

Mattsson, B., & Schoultz, B. A comparison between lithium, placebo, and a diuretic in premenstrual tension. *Acta Psychiatrica Scandanavica*, 1974, *suppl. 255*, 75-84.

May, R. R. Mood shifts and the menstrual cycle. *Journal of Psychosomatic Research*, 1976, *20*, 125-130.

Michelakis, A. M., Yoshida, H., & Dormois, J. C. Plasma renin activity and plasma adolsterone during the normal menstrual cycle. *American Journal of Obstetrics and Gynecology*, 1975, *123*, 724-726.

Miller, N. E., & Weiss, J. M. Effects of somatic or visceral responses to punishment. In B. A. Campbell & R. M. Church (Eds.), *Punishment and aversive behavior*. New York: Appleton-Century-Crofts, 1969.

Moawad, A. H., & Bengtsson, L. P. In vivo studies of the motility pattern of the nonpregnant human uterus: III. The effect of anovulatory pills. *American Journal of Obstetrics and Gynecology*, 1968, *101*, 473-478.

Moos, R. H. The development of a Menstrual Distress Questionnaire. *Psychosomatic Medicine*, 1968, *30*, 853.

Moos, R. H. Typology of menstrual cycle symptoms. *American Journal of Obstetrics and Gynecology*, 1969, *103*, 390-402.

Moos, R. H. *Menstrual Distress Questionnaire Manual*. Palo Alto, Cal.: Social Ecology, 1977.

Moos, R. H., Kopell, B. S., Melges, F. T., Yalom, I. D., Lunde, D. T., Clayton, R. B., & Hamburg, D. A. Fluctuations in symptoms and moods during the menstrual cycle. *Journal of Psychosomatic Research*, 1969, *13*, 27-44.

Morris, N. M., & Udry, J. R. Variations in pedometer activity during the menstrual cycle. *Obstetrics and Gynecology*, 1970, *35*, 199-201.

Morton, J. H. Premenstrual tension. *American Journal of Obstetrics and Gynecology*, 1950, *60*, 343-352.

Morton, J. H., Additon, H., Addison, R. G., Hunt, L., & Sullivan, J. J. A clinical study of premenstrual tension. *American Journal of Obstetrics and Gynecology*, 1965, *65*, 1182-1191.

Navratil, J. The pathogenesis of premenstrual tension. *Activitas Nervosa Superior*, 1975, *17*, 304-305.

Paige, K. E. Effects of oral contraceptives on affective fluctuations associated with the menstrual cycle. *Psychosomatic Medicine*, 1971, *33*, 515-537.

Paige, K. E. Women learn to sing the menstrual blues. *Psychology Today*, September 1973, pp. 41-46.

Parlee, M. B. The premenstrual syndrome. *Psychological Bulletin*, 1973, *80*, 454-465.

Parlee, M. B. Stereotypic beliefs about menstruation: A methodological note on the Moos Menstrual Distress Questionnaire and some new data. *Psychosomatic Medicine*, 1974, *36*, 229-240.

Patkai, P., Johannson, G., & Post, B. Mood alertness and sympathetic adrenal medullary activity during the menstrual cycle. *Psychosomatic Medicine*, 1974, *36*, 503-512.

Paulson, J. M., & Wood, K. R. Perceptions of the emotional correlates of dysmenorrhea. *American Journal of Obstetrics and Gynecology*, 1966, *95*, 991-996.

Pierson, W. R., & Lockhart, A. Effect of menstruation on simple reaction and movement time. *British Medical Journal*, March 1963, pp. 796-797.

Pulkkinen, M. O., Henzl, M. R., & Csapo, A. I. The effect of naproxen-sodium on the prostaglandin concentrations of menstrual blood and uterine "jet-washings" in dysmenorrheic women. *Prostaglandins*, 1978, *15*, 543-550.

Rees, L. The premenstrual tension syndrome and its treatment. *British Medical Journal*, May 1953, pp. 1014-1016.

Rogers, F. S. Emotional factors in gynecology. *American Journal of Obstetrics and Gynecology*, 1950, *59*, 321-327.

Rouse, P. Premenstrual tension: A study using the Moos Menstrual Questionnaire. *Journal of Psychosomatic Research*, 1978, *22*, 215-222.

Ruble, D. N. Premenstrual symptoms: A reinterpretation. *Science*, 1977, *197*, 291-292.

Schwartz, A., Zor, U., Lindner, H. R., & Naor, S. Primary dysmenorrhea: Alleviation by an inhibitor of prostaglandin synthesis and action. *British Journal of Obstetrics and Gynecology*, 1974, *44*, 709-712.

Schwartz, U. D., & Abraham, G. E. Corticosterone and aldosterone levels during the menstrual cycle. *Obstetrics and Gynecology*, 1975, *45*, 339-342.

Seligman, M. E. P. *Helplessness*. San Francisco: W. H. Freeman, 1975.

Sheldrake, P., & Cormack, M. Variations in menstrual cycle symptom reporting. *Journal of Psychosomatic Research*, 1976, *20*, 169-177.

Silbergeld, S., Brast, N., & Noble, E. P. The menstrual cycle: A double-blind study of symptoms, mood and behavior, and biochemical variables using Enovid and placebo. *Psychosomatic Medicine*, 1971, *33*, 411-428.

Singer, K., Cheng, R., & Schou, M. A controlled evaluation of lithium in the premenstrual tension syndrome. *British Journal of Psychiatry*, 1974, *124*, 50-51.

Singh, E. J., Baccarini, I. M., & Zuspan, F. P. Levels of prostaglandins $F_{2\alpha}$ and E_2 in human endometrium during the menstrual cycle. *American Journal of Obstetrics and Gynecology*, 1975, *121*, 1003-1006.

Skinner, S. L., Lumbers, E. R., & Symonds, E. M. Alteration by oral contraceptives of normal menstrual changes in plasma renin activity, concentration and substrate. *Clinical Science*, 1969, *36*, 67-76.

Smith, A. J. Menstruation and industrial efficiency. I. Absenteeism and activity level. *Journal of Applied Psychology*, 1950, *34*, 1-5.

Smith, S. L. Mood and the menstrual cycle. In E. J. Sachar (Ed.), *Topics in psychoendocrinology*. New York: Grune & Stratton, 1975.

Sommer, B. Menstrual cycle changes and intellectual performance. *Psychosomatic Medicine*, 1972, *34*, 263-269.

Sommer, B. The effect of menstruation on cognitive and perceptual-motor behavior: A review. *Psychosomatic Medicine*, 1973, *35*, 515-534.

Southam, A. L., & Gonzaga, F. P. Systemic changes during the menstrual cycle. *American Journal of Obstetrics and Gynecology*, 1965, *91*, 142-165.

Southgate, J., Grant, E. C. G., Pollard, W., Pryse-Davies, J., & Sandler, M. Cyclical variations in endometrial monoamine oxidase: Correlation of histochemical and quantitative biochemical assays. *Biochemical Pharmacology*, 1968, *17*, 721-726.

Sturgis, S. H. Primary dysmenorrhea: Etiology and management. In S. H. Sturgis & M. L. Taymor (Eds.), *Progress in gynecology* (Vol. V). New York: Grune & Stratton, 1970.

Sundsfjord, J. A., & Aakvaag, S. Plasma angiotensin II and aldosterone excretion during the menstrual cycle. *Acta Endocrinologia*, 1970, *64*, 452-458.

Tonks, C. M., Rack, P. H., & Rose, M. J. Attempted suicide and the menstrual cycle. *Journal of Psychosomatic Research*, 1968, *11*, 319-323.

Tuch, R. H. The relationship between a mother's menstrual status and her response to illness in her child. *Psychosomatic Medicine*, 1975, *37*, 388-394.

Vogel, W., Broverman, D. M., & Klaiber, E. L. EEG responses in regularly menstruating women and in amenorrheic women treated with ovarian hormones. *Science*, 1971, *172*, 388-391.

Webster, S. K., Martin, H. J., Uchalik, D., & Gannon, L. The menstrual symptom questionnaire and spasmodic/congestive dysmenorrhea: Measurement of an invalid construct. *Journal of Behavioral Medicine*, 1979, *2*, 1-19.

Weideger, P. *Menstruation and menopause*. New York: Knopf, 1976.

Weiner, J. S., & Elmadjian, F. Excretion of epinephrine and norepinephrine in premenstrual tension. *Federation Proceedings*, 1962, *21*, 184.

Wetzel, R. D., Reich, T., & McClure, J. N. Phase of menstrual cycle and self-referrals to a suicide prevention center. *British Journal of Psychiatry*, 1971, *119*, 523-524.

Whitehead, R. E. Women pilots. *Journal of Aviation Medicine*, 1934, *5*, 47-49. Cited by M. B. Parlee, The premenstrual syndrome. *Psychological Bulletin*, 1973, *80*, 454-465.

Wickham, M. The effects of the menstrual cycle on test performance. *British Journal of Psychology*, 1958, *49*, 34-41.

Wilcoxon, L. A., Schrader, S. L., & Sherif, C. W. Daily self-report on activities, life events, moods, and somatic changes during the menstrual cycle. *Psychosomatic Medicine*, 1976, *38*, 399-417.

Willman, E. A., Collins, W. P., & Clayton, S. G. Studies in the involvement of prostaglandins in uterine symptomatology and pathology. *British Journal of Obstetrics and Gynecology*, 1976, *83*, 337-341.

Wineman, E. W. Autonomic balance changes during the human menstrual cycle. *Psychophysiology*, 1971, *8*, 1-6.

Wong, W. H., Freedman, R. I., Levan, N. E., Hyman, C., & Quilligan, E. J. Changes in the capillary filtration coefficient of cutaneous vessels in women with premenstrual tension. *American Journal of Obstetrics and Gynecology*, 1972, *114*, 950-953.

Wuttke, W., Arnold, P., Becker, D., Creutzfeldt, O., Langenstein, S., & Tirsch, W. Circulating hormones, EEG, and performance in psychological tests of women with and without oral contraceptives. *Psychoneuroendocrinology*, 1975, *1*, 141-151.

Ylikorkala, O., & Dawood, M. Y. New concepts in dysmenorrhea. *American Journal of Obstetrics and Gynecology*, 1978, *130*, 833-847.

Zimmerman, E., & Parlee, M. B. Behavioral changes associated with the menstrual cycle. *Journal of Applied Social Psychology*, 1973, *3*, 335-344.

4

DISREGULATION OF THE
GASTROINTESTINAL SYSTEM

Barbara B. Walker
Curt A. Sandman

INTRODUCTION

It is a curious fact that the gastrointestinal tract, a system hidden deep within the human body, is actually one of the few systems that maintains direct contact with the environment. Like the simple cell membrane of the protozoan, this system is responsible for extracting all our nutritional needs from the environment. Given the wide variety of substances we ingest, this is truly a remarkable accomplishment. It is the result of a highly integrated system, with regulatory mechanisms distributed at every level of the organism.

At times, the gastrointestinal system becomes disregulated, leading to various gastrointestinal and behavioral disorders. These disorders are among the most common of all afflictions; half our population suffers from acute gastrointestinal illnesses every year. More than 10% have chronic diseases of the digestive tract, and these diseases are a major cause of absenteeism from work (Hill & Kern, 1977). In view of this, it is surprising that there is such a paucity of psychophysiological research focusing on gastrointestinal activity. Perhaps one reason for this is that investigators conceptualize the gastrointestinal tract as a system that is unresponsive to psychological events. Another reason may be the widespread misbelief that adequate techniques are not available for studying gastrointestinal psychophysiology.

In this chapter, we shall review evidence indicating not only that psychological events elicit profound changes in the gastrointestinal system but also that changes in gastrointestinal activity influence the brain and behavior. Several

The authors wish to thank William E. Whitehead for his comments on an earlier version of this chapter.

models are proposed to illustrate different views regarding the etiology and treatment of various gastrointestinal disorders. We shall begin, however, by introducing the gastrointestinal system and the various methods of investigating gastrointestinal responsivity.

THE DIGESTIVE TRACT

The human digestive tract is basically a tube that receives, digests, and absorbs nutrients. The tube is equipped with accessory glands which secrete the chemicals that are necessary for digestion. The major components of the digestive tract are the mouth, pharynx, esophagus, stomach, small intestine duodenum, jejunum, and ileum), and large intestine. The major accessory glands are the salivary glands, pancreas, and liver (see Figure 4.1).

Digestion begins when food enters the mouth and the salivary glands begin secreting enzymes. After the food is swallowed, it passes through the esophagus into the stomach. Enzymes are secreted by glands in the stomach to break down the food, while the motor activity of the stomach pushes the food into the small intestine. In the small intestine, nutrients are absorbed into the bloodstream for distribution throughout the body, and the remaining substances are moved into the large intestine, which temporarily stores waste products, absorbs water, and acts as an incubator for various types of bacteria until the desired materials are excreted.

The chemical reactions involved in digestion are basically the same in all animals. As food passes through the tract, different enzymes act to catalyze different chemical portions of the digestive tract. It is important to note, however, that while each portion of the digestive tract is specialized to perform specific functions, food is continually being processed by many enzymes and moved through the digestive tract in a highly coordinated manner. Digestion is a complex process that is regulated at many levels by the combined efforts of hormonal and nervous system activity.

In the following section, the gastrointestinal system has been divided into discrete segments, in order that the structure, function, and disorders associated with each portion of the tract might be introduced. It must be emphasized, however, that the salivary glands, esophagus, stomach, and intestines are best conceptualized as small portions of a highly integrated system rather than as separate entities. Following this introduction and a discussion of techniques for studying gastrointestinal activity, we shall focus on the integrative activity of the gastrointestinal system, which, as will become apparent, is highly dependent upon continuous interactions between the organism and the environment.

The Salivary Glands

There are three major glands pouring fluid, known as saliva, into the mouth. The largest is the *parotid* gland, which lies below and in front of the ear. Its

FIGURE 4.1
Major Organs of the Digestive System

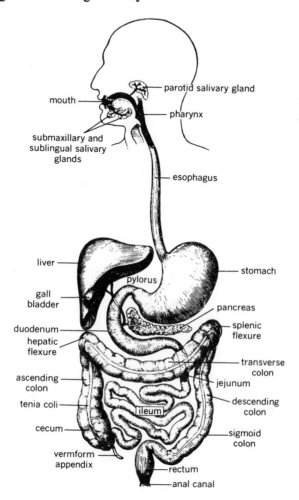

duct, the parotid (or Stensen's) duct, opens onto the inner surface of the cheek. The *sublingual* and *submaxillary* glands lie under the jaw, with the submaxillary (or Wharton's) duct, along with ducts from the sublingual gland, opening into the floor of the mouth. The three glands differ in the proportion of serous cells (which produce a thin, watery substance) and mucous cells (which secrete a thick substance). The parotid gland, for example, possesses only serous cells, whereas the sublingual gland consists primarily of mucous cells. The submaxillary gland contains both types. The consistency of the saliva depends upon the relative contribution of the three glands.

Although saliva is 98% water, several ions are also present. In fact, most ions present in blood plasma are also present in saliva. These ion concentrations change as a function of secretion. For example, the concentration of sodium increases as the rate of secretion increases, and the concentration of potassium decreases as the rate of secretion increases. Saliva also contains the important enzyme *ptyalin*, which catalyzes the digestion of carbohydrates.

The control of the salivary glands, unlike that of other glands in the digestive system, is exclusively neural. Although the salivary glands are innervated by both branches of the autonomic nervous system, primary control of secretion appears to be parasympathetic. Stimulation of these fibers induces changes in blood flow to the glands as well as in the composition and quantity of the saliva. The role of the sympathetic nervous system is unclear; stimulation of these nerves leads to vasoconstriction and salivary secretions that are not well maintained. It seems certain that, unlike other organ systems, the sympathetic and parasympathetic branches of the nervous system do not function as two balanced systems in controlling salivation (Hendrix, 1974).

Salivation can be induced in many ways. While the most common stimuli are those related to digestion, mechanical stimulation and various types of learning can also lead to salivation. Early demonstrations by Pavlov (1927), showing that salivation can be classically conditioned, are among the most well-known experiments in the history of psychology. Interestingly, the quantity and composition of saliva are related to the nature of the agent that stimulates secretion, and this relationship seems to be unrelated to learning. Edible substances, for example, produce saliva that is rich in mucin and enzymes, whereas inedible substances produce a more watery secretion.

The most commonly known function of saliva is to secrete ptyalin, an enzyme that initiates carbohydrate digestion, but saliva also performs other functions that are extremely important. Taste buds, for example, can be stimulated only by substances in solution. If salt were placed on a dry tongue, there would be no sensation of taste. As the salt began to dissolve in saliva, however, taste sensations would occur. Saliva also facilitates the swallowing reflex. If one reduces the amount of saliva in the mouth by swallowing repeatedly, it becomes extremely difficult, if not impossible, to swallow. Even when there is no food in the mouth, salivation occurs to aid in speaking and to prevent the mucous membranes from drying. This drying of the mucous membranes also plays a role in the sensation of thirst. Saliva has an important protective function as well. If strong acids or bases are introduced into the mouth, the organs are protected by saliva, which acts quickly to neutralize these noxious substances. Microorganisms are constantly introduced into the system with food, and saliva kills the bacteria that are not beneficial.

White (1977) pointed out in a recent review that salivation has generally been ignored when compared with psychophysiological studies of other autonomic indices. This is surprising, since salivation is associated with several important developments in psychology (Cannon, 1915; Pavlov, 1927; Rosenzweig, 1959), and it is an indicator of psychiatric disorders (Bolwig & Rafaelsen, 1972; Davies & Gurland, 1961; Peck, 1959), personality differences (Corcoran,

1964; Wardell, 1974), and hormone activity (Dawes, 1972; Palmai & Blackwell, 1965). White (1977) suggested that one reason for the lack of interest in salivation may be that salivation has not been related to any specific disorders. Malhotra (1978), however, recently presented evidence to suggest that the pathogenesis of peptic ulcers may be related to the protective action of saliva. He has found that when certain foods (such as, yogurt, vegetable fibers, and fermented milk products) are well masticated, there is an increase in the amount of salivary mucus swallowed with the food, and this mucus serves as a protective mechanism against ulceration. Thus, salivation may play a much more important role in various gastrointestinal disorders than previous evidence has indicated.

The Esophagus

The esophagus is a unique section of the gastrointestinal system, in that it serves only a motor function. It is essentially a hollow, muscular tube extending from the pharynx to the stomach, with a sphincter, the *cricopharyngeous*, at the upper end, and another sphincter, the *lower esophageal sphincter*, at the lower end. The propulsive rhythm of the esophagus and the changes in pressure in the two sphincters are responsible for the safe passage of food from the mouth to the stomach and the prevention of reflux of harmful gastric contents into the esophagus.

The esophagus is innervated by both parasympathetic and sympathetic nerves containing fibers that convey impulses to and from the blood vessels, glands, and muscles associated with the esophagus. The extrinsic nerves are essential for coordinated esophageal function to occur, but there is also a network of intrinsic esophageal nerves, which is probably responsible for peristaltic movements in isolated portions of the esophagus. Several hormones, such as *gastrin, secretin,* and *cholecystokinin,* also influence esophageal function. Gastrin stimulates postganglionic nerves to release *acetylcholine,* leading to an increase in lower esophageal sphincter tone. On the other hand, secretin and cholecystokinin inhibit the effects of gastrin and lead to a decrease in pressure in the lower esophageal sphincter.

Coordinated esophageal function is critical in the process of swallowing. Primary esophageal peristalsis, initiated by a swallow, is a contraction of considerable force (50-100 mm Hg), moving from the upper to the lower end and lasting approximately eight seconds. Pressure in the lower esophageal sphincter is usually higher than esophageal pressure above it or gastric pressure below it, but it decreases after swallowing and remains low until the peristaltic wave arrives. Contraction of this sphincter completes the contraction.

If the bolus is such that the first primary wave does not succeed in moving it, the mechanical distention produced will initiate a secondary peristaltic contraction. Secondary peristalsis proceeds caudally from the site of stimulation, and the afferent nerves traveling with the vagus are related to this process.

Secondary peristalsis plays an important protective role, ridding the esophagus of substances not moved into the stomach after primary peristalsis and any substances regurgitated by the stomach.

The reflux of gastric contents into the esophagus is inhibited by increased pressure in the lower esophageal sphincter. While the precise mechanisms governing the integrity of the lower esophageal sphincter are unknown, both neural and humoral factors have been implicated (see Cohen, 1976). It is clear, for example, that this sphincter is particularly responsive to gastrin, suggesting a complex interplay between gastric activity and esophageal function. When large quantities of acid are present in the stomach, gastrin levels and sphincter pressure decrease, leading to enhanced reflux of acid. If the pH of the gastric contents is raised by antacids, the gastrin level and sphincter pressure increase. Both cigarette smoking and caffeine contribute to diminished competence of the lower esophageal sphincter and thus may lead to reflux of acid into the esophagus, creating heartburn.

The most common disorders of the esophagus are related to motor activity, and the most common of these is *achalasia*. Achalasia is characterized by failure of esophageal peristalsis, increased resting pressure in the lower esophageal sphincter, and failure of the sphincter to relax after a swallow. It is a chronic disease associated with tremendous difficulties in swallowing. In advanced cases, the esophagus may retain a meal and empty into the stomach by gravity alone. Complications arise when the patient lies down and the esophageal contents are free to flow into the pharynx. Another complication may result from the stagnation of food in any portion of the gastrointestinal system, which may lead to pain and ulceration. At present, effective medical treatment of achalasia involves either severing the muscle fibers of the lower esophageal sphincter to enhance drainage by gravity or inflating a balloon in the sphincter to stretch it.

Another common disorder of the esophagus is associated with *gastroesophageal reflux*. As mentioned earlier, when the lower esophageal sphincter fails, gastric contents are free to flow into the esophagus, leading to a disorder called *esophagitis*, or inflammation of the esophagus. Esophagitis causes symptoms of heartburn and ulceration. One widely used antacid, Gavison, produces a foamy layer on the surface of the stomach contents, which acts as a barrier to reflux. Elevating the head and trunk during sleep is also standard therapy. Changing the pH of the gastric contents is also therapeutic, since gastrin levels and sphincter pressure increase as the pH increases.

The Stomach and the Duodenum

The functions of the stomach are complex, since it is concerned not only with storing and transporting food but also with modifying the food so that it is in a form capable of being delivered to the small intestine, where absorption takes place. The stomach must adjust the temperature, pH, consistency, and osmolarity of the food as well as begin protein digestion. To perform these functions, it is equipped with an exquisite network of motor and secretory equipment, which is subject to an elaborate set of neural and hormonal controls.

The stomach is basically a reservoir where food is soaked in gastric juice containing enzymes and hydrochloric acid and then released by peristalsis into the duodenum. The esophagus meets the stomach at a point known as the *cardiac*, or *fundus*, of the stomach. The stomach then curves downward and to the right, incorporating what has been termed the *body* of the stomach. The distal portion leading to the duodenum has been termed the *antrum*. Both openings to the stomach are guarded by sphincters.

There are several types of cells in the gastric mucosa; the most notable are the *chief cells*, which secrete *pepsinogen* (the precursor to *pepsin*), and the *parietal cells*, which secrete *hydrochloric acid*. Hydrochloric acid appears in such high concentrations that gastric juice has a pH ranging between 1 and 5, and it has been estimated that at least 1,500 calories are necessary to produce one liter of juice with this acidity (Langley, 1971). This degree of acidity is critical for digestion, since pepsin, the enzyme necessary for protein digestion, requires an acid environment. If acidity is less than normal, protein digestion will be impaired. Mucus is secreted in large quantities to buffer the acid and to serve as a protective barrier between the contents of the stomach and the stomach wall. The mucosa of the duodenum continually monitors the chemical and physical properties of the material coming from the stomach and helps maintain hormonal and neural regulation of gastric activity.

The mechanisms involved in the neural and hormonal regulation of gastric activity are complex and highly interdependent. For this reason, most investigators prefer to discuss these mechanisms as they relate to various phases of gastric secretion. The *interdigestive* or *basal* period, refers to secretions that occur in the absence of any known stimuli. Only a small amount of secretion is apparent, and it is probably stimulated by both vagal and hormonal mechanisms.

The *cephalic* phase refers to the secretory response to stimuli acting on the brain, such as the sight of food. These may be either conditioned or unconditioned responses and are completely eliminated by vagotomy, indicating that this phase is entirely neurogenic.

In the *gastric* phase, gastric activity is stimulated by both neural and hormonal activity in the stomach. In this phase, mechanical and chemical stimuli elicit the release of gastrin from the antrum, which stimulates hydrochoric acid secretion.

In contrast to the other phases, the *intestinal* phase is thought to be exclusively hormonal and occurs when food is delivered to the intestine. During this phase, *enterogastrones* are released, which inhibits gastric activity.

The primary neural and hormonal mechanisms for controlling gastric activity are shown in Figures 4.2 and 4.3. Figure 4.2 illustrates that the cortex, thalamus, hypothalamus, and brain stem have been implicated in the regulation

FIGURE 4.2
Neural Mechanisms for Controlling Gastric Activity

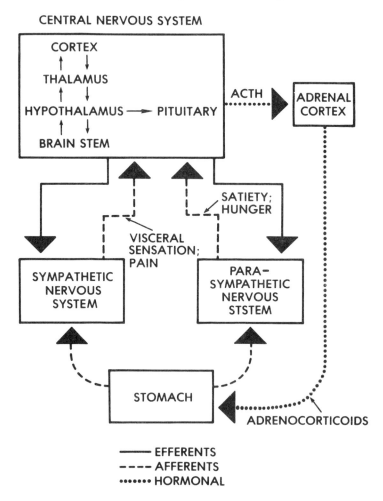

of gastric activity. Although autonomic innervation is primarily parasympathetic, sympathetic activity does play a distinct role in regulation. Vagal stimulation and the release of *adrenocorticotropic hormones* (ACTH) stimulate gastric activity, whereas sympathetic stimulation inhibits activity. The sensation of pain is related to the sympathetic afferent fibers, whereas sensations of hunger and satiety are associated with the vagal afferent fibers.

Figure 4.3 illustrates the interrelationships among different systems and the importance of feedback in controlling gastric activity. Neural activity (that is, vagal stimulation), chemical activity (secretagogues), and mechanical activity (distention of the stomach) are capable of stimulating the pyloric glands in the

FIGURE 4.3
Integration of Neural, Chemical and Mechanical
Activity for Regulating Gastric Activity

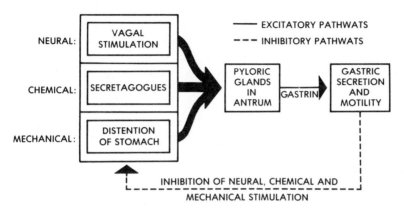

antrum of the stomach to secrete gastrin. In the normal process of digestion, all three of these stimuli are present. Gastrin is a potent stimulator of gastric secretion and motility. As food is digested and moved into the duodenum, enterogastrones are released, the mechanical and neural stimuli are removed, and gastric activity is inhibited.

Almost every type of ulcerating lesion in the gastrointestinal system has been termed *peptic ulcer* at one time or another, and it has generally been assumed that peptic ulcers are a result of excess secretion of hydrochloric acid (Greenberger & Winship, 1976). It is clear, however, that not all ulcers are alike; there are fundamental differences among ulcers occurring in different portions of the gastrointestinal system. Our understanding of ulcers has suffered greatly from efforts to attribute a common etiology and pathogenesis to all types of ulcers.

The most common ulcers (80% of all peptic ulcers) occur in the duodenum, and sufficient evidence has accumulated to support the notion that duodenal ulcers are related to excess hydrochloric acid secretion. Epigastric pains experienced by the duodenal ulcer patient are rhythmic and usually occur when the stomach is empty. The pains generally subside after the ingestion of food or an antacid, providing support for the concept that it is the acid content of the stomach that is the inciting factor. Unlike duodenal ulcers, however, gastric ulcers usually occur in the antral portion of the stomach and are more related to the integrity of the mucosa than to increases in hydrochloric acid. In fact, the mean secretory rate in patients with chronic gastric ulcers is *less* than that of normal subjects (Greenberger & Winship, 1976). It has been suggested that the mucosal membrane in these patients is incapable of secreting an adequate layer of mucus to provide protection. While the pain associated with gastric ulcers is similar to that associated with duodenal ulcers, it lacks the periodicity observed in duodenal ulcer patients, and food and antacids do not provide as much relief to gastric ulcer patients.

A number of drugs damage the gastric mucosa and are therefore thought to be ulcerogenic. Corticosterioids, for example, have been used to treat rheumatoid arthritics and frequently lead to gastric ulcers by causing irritations in the mucosal barrier. Salicylates (aspirin) can cause severe damage to the mucosal barrier and lead to inflammation, erosion, and bleeding (Woodbury, 1970). Smoking also may play a role in the pathogenesis of ulcers, since nicotine leads to decreases in pancreatic secretion, which can result in inadequate neutralization of gastric acid.

A disorder for which massive gastric hypersecretion is clearly responsible is the *Zollinger-Ellison syndrome*. In this syndrome, a gastrin-producing tumor continuously stimulates parietal cells to secrete hydrochloric acid. This marked acid secretion can total five to six liters in twelve hours, completely overwhelming all neutralizing mechanisms. These patients often have multiple ulcerations of the esophagus, stomach, duodenum, and small intestine.

The Small Intestine

As food is propelled through the duodenum, it enters the *jejunum* and then the *ileum*, the narrowest part of the small intestine. The ileum joins the large intestine at a right angle, and the *ileocecal valve* prevents the return of material from the large into the small intestine. The primary function of the small intestine is absorption, and its structure is remarkably suitable for this function. The circular folds of the intestine and the villi, projections from the surface of the intestinal membrane, increase the absorptive surface area of the intestine from about 2,000 cm^2 (the length of the tube) to more than 2 million cm^2.

The entry of *chyme* into the duodenum initiates a variety of responses necessary for digestion and absorption. The mucosa, for example, is stimulated to secrete cholecystokinin, secretin, and other polypeptide hormones. Secretin stimulates the pancreas and the liver to produce a neutralizing substance, and cholecystokinin stimulates the pancreas to secrete digestive enzymes and the gall bladder to empty bile into the duodenum. The vagus can also stimulate the pancreas and gall bladder, but its effect is minor compared with the influence of the hormones.

We shall not focus on malabsorption disorders in this chapter, since absorption is primarily under hormonal control, and the relative inaccessibility of the small intestine has led to a paucity of psychophysiological data. Freedman (1954) reported the appearance of a "malabsorption pattern" in subjects under stress, but this appears to be the only such study in the literature. Symptoms of malabsorption syndromes include diarrhea, weight loss, abdominal cramps, and anorexia. Simple changes in diet can lead to marked improvement. The interested reader is referred to Greenberger and Winship (1976) and Hill and Kern (1977) for more detail.

The Large Intestine

The last five feet of the alimentary tract is the large intestine. The *ascending colon* on the right side joins the *transverse colon*, which is situated below the umbilicus. The *descending colon* meets the *sigmoid colon* on the left side and pursues an S-shaped course ending in the *rectum*. The autonomically innervated internal, and somatically innervated external, sphincters are the only sphincters in the anal canal. Both are in a tonic state of contraction, and it has traditionally been thought that the external sphincter is under voluntary control, whereas the internal sphincter is not. Recent evidence (Engel, Nikoomanesh, & Schuster, 1974) suggests, however, that they both may be brought under voluntary control. This evidence will be discussed in more detail later in the chapter.

Like the stomach, the large intestine is intermittently active. Digestion in the small intestine is so efficient that practically no usable food reaches the large intestine. The main functions of the large intestine are to conserve water, act as an incubator for bacteria, and propel waste products to the rectum. Activity occurs in the colon even after neural connections are severed, but both parasympathetic and sympathetic innervation are necessary for coordinated propulsive activity. Interestingly, different types of motor activity in the colon are related to different types of colonic dysfunction. Exaggeration of the nonpropulsive, drying activity of the colon, for example, is related to a form of constipation, whereas the motor activity associated with propulsion is associated with diarrhea (Kantor, 1924, 1925). This is somewhat controversial, however, and studies are currently being conducted which may help clarify these relationships (Whitehead, unpublished).

Irritable bowel symdrome and *ulcerative colitis* are the most common disorders of the large intestine. Patients with irritable bowel syndrome often experience pain in the lower abdomen, which is often associated with increased peristaltic activity in the small intestine and colon. These patients generally suffer from defecatory distress, ranging from extreme constipation to severe diarrhea. Ulcerative colitis is an inflammation of the large intestine, characterized by bloody diarrhea. There is a striking abnormality of motor function as well. The cause of this disorder is, as yet, unclear, but immunological factors (Hill & Kern, 1977) and psychological factors have been implicated. Engel (1955), for example, has found that patients with ulcerative colitis are obsessive-compulsive, immature, and dependent. This will be discussed in greater detail later in the chapter.

To summarize, the gastrointestinal tract is basically a tube consisting of the mouth, pharynx, esophagus, stomach, and intestines, with accessory glands, such as salivary glands, pancreas, and liver. The function of the system is to adjust the temperature, pH, consistency, and osmolarity of food, so that nutrients that are critical for survival can be absorbed into the blood. The adjustments are accomplished as a result of processes related to secretion, motility, and absorption. Methods of investigating these processes are discussed in the following section.

METHODS OF INVESTIGATION

In view of the important role the gastrointestinal system has played in the development of psychological principles (Cannon, 1915; Miller, 1969; Pavlov, 1927) and the increasing prevalence of gastrointestinal disorders, it is surprising that there is such a paucity of psychophysiological studies focusing on gastrointestinal activity. As mentioned earlier, this may be due, in part, to the widespread misbelief that reliable techniques for studying the gastrointestinal system are not available. In fact, there are several methods currently available for studying gastrointestinal changes. For ease of discussion, they have been segregated into categories according to the physiological activity they have been designed to measure.

Secretion

The traditional methods for collecting salivary secretions included chewing dry food and measuring the increase in weight (Tuczek, 1916) and inserting cannulae into either Stensen's or Wharton's duct (Clark & Carter, 1927; Enfors, 1962; Kerr, 1961). Both these methods were quite limited, since an increase in weight after chewing food is directly related to the bolus, and cannulation can be extremely painful. More accurate measurement of salivary secretions was facilitated by the development of a collection disc held to the inner cheek by a vacuum, with the inner chamber positioned over Stensen's duct (Lashley, 1916). Similar capsules have been devised for measuring secretion from both the sublingual and submandibular glands (Schneyer, 1955; Truelove, Bixler, & Merritt, 1967).

While these techniques achieve maximum precision, they are quite unnatural and require special equipment. As a result, other methods have been employed, such as allowing the saliva to accumulate in the mouth and then measuring what is voided (Kerr, 1961) and absorbing saliva with cotton swabs (Poth, 1933; Razran, 1955). In a recent review of techniques for assessing salivation, White (1977) presented evidence that the capsule, whole mouth, and cotton swab techniques are highly correlated.

Methods of assessing gastric secretion are somewhat more complex than those required for assessing salivary secretions. One method consists of putting a tube through the subject's mouth or nose into the stomach and withdrawing samples of secretions by aspiration. Palmer (1957) pointed out that aspiration is an unreliable sampling technique, since fluid in the stomach is not homogeneous, and different portions are reached by the aspirating tube. Although Welgan (1974, 1977) overcame this limitation by demonstrating the ability to position an aspirating tube in the antrum of the stomach using fluoroscopic control, fluids may be contaminated while being drawn up from the stomach and being analyzed. Whitehead, Renault, and Goldiamond (1975) overcame this difficulty by devising a technique for measuring intragastric pH, but there seems to be no possible resolution to the more serious objection to using tubes. This objection stems from the fact that inserting a tube into the stomach may stimulate secretion.

Another method of measuring gastric secretion involves the use of fistulous subjects. These are individuals who, due to accident or disease, are unable to pass food by mouth and have been forced to live with their stomachs open and connected directly to the surface of their bodies. Studies of these individuals (Beaumont, 1833; Richet, 1878; Wolf & Wolff, 1947) are classics in psychophysiology, since fistulous subjects are rare, and conditions are ideal for directly observing gastric secretion, blood flow, and motility in a variety of situations. In fact, the study of the fistulous subject Tom (Wolf & Wolff, 1947) was among the first to show a clear relationship between emotions and visceral activity; decreases in gastric activity were related to depression and fear, whereas increases in gastric activity were related to anger and resentment.

Absorption

Absorption is a critical process in digestion, and studies of this process have generally relied on introducing a material to be studied along with a "marker" substance. After a certain period of time, the material being studied is withdrawn and corrected for loss by the amount of "marker" substance lost to the pylorus. This method is quite reliable, but it has been suggested (Wolf & Welsh, 1972) that it is of little interest to the psychophysiologist, since absorption is primarily under hormonal control. In view of the fact that the digestive process involves complex interactions between neural and hormonal activity, however, absorption may actually prove to be an interesting measure for psychophysiologists in the future.

Blood Flow

Jacobson (1967) has reviewed the difficulties in measuring blood flow in the gastrointestinal tract and has indicated that there are no methods for studying blood flow in the intact human. In their classic study of the fistulous subject Tom, Wolf and Wolff (1947) were able to use changes in color as an indicator of blood flow: a bright red color suggested increases in blood flow, whereas a deeper shade of red suggested stagnation and an increase in blood volume. It was difficult to quantify these measures, however, and color photography has served as the only method of presenting and describing these changes. It is unfortunate that there are no methods for studying blood flow in the intact human, since blood flow in the gastrointestinal system appears to be highly related to emotional events.

Rate of Travel through the Gastrointestinal Tract

The rate at which food passes through the tract has been related to the type of food, environmental conditions, and the emotional state of the individual. As a result, there are large inter- and intraindividual differences. Since there is a mixing of the contents of the intestine, substances excreted represent material that has been eaten over a period of several days. These factors contribute to making this measure another one that has been largely ignored by psychophysiologists, and one that may be useful to those who are willing to institute the necessary controls for the data to be meaningful.

Motility

As indicated earlier, different portions of the digestive tract are associated with different patterns of motility. The esophagus, stomach, small intestine, and large intestine each evidence different patterns of motility and are monitored using slightly different techniques. Truelove (1966) demonstrated that different methods can be used to record intraluminal pressures, and differences in these methods make some more suitable for certain parts of the gastrointestinal tract than others.

One method involves having the subject swallow balloons that are then filled with water or gas and connected to a system designed to measure contractile activity. This method is the simplest, but as with collection tubes, the balloon itself may induce motility. In addition, it is difficult to know the precise location of the balloon, and pressure recordings are related to the shape of the segment of the balloon where the balloon is lodged. Another method utilizes open-end tubes or catheters filled with water or air and connected outside the body to pressure-sensing units. This technique records changes in intraluminal pressure and not necessarily changes in motor activity.

In an attempt to minimize the effects due to introducing objects into the gut, two methods have been developed. Davis, Garafolo, and Gault (1957) asked their subjects to swallow a ¼-inch bearing and then traced its movements using a modified mine detector. This method shows only gross indications of the amplitude of contraction but is probably an ". . . accurate indicator of the occurrence of contraction and its frequency" (Wenger, Engel, Clemens, & Cullen, 1961). The second method makes use of radiotelemetering capsules, which are small radio transmitters swallowed by the subjects, the signal from which can be monitored by an external receiving set. Connell and Rowlands (1960) pointed out that this method provides recording from only a single point, and since the capsule is free to move within the tract, localization is difficult.

Electrical Activity

All the techniques reviewed thus far have been invasive. As a result, they are stressful for the subject and influence the same physiological processes they are employed to measure. When techniques were developed for electrophysiological recordings, the possibility arose that the gastrointestinal tract might also be studied using electrical potentials. Several electrophysiological studies have focused on intraluminal recordings of electrical activity in animals (Bozler, 1945; Carlson, Code, & Nelson, 1966), and a technique using surface electrodes to record electrical activity in humans has also been developed and described (Russell & Stern, 1967; Stern, Ray, & Davis, 1980). Since the validity of the measures has been demonstrated (Stevens & Worrall, 1974), and the procedure is used clinically in other countries (Krasil'nikov & Fishzon-Ryss, 1963; Sobakin, Smirnov, & Mishin, 1962), it is surprising that this technique, the electrogastrogram (EGG), has been virtually ignored in the United States.

The EGG is a useful technique, because it is probably the only noninvasive and relatively inexpensive method currently available for studying gastrointestinal psychophysiology. Figure 4.4 illustrates a typical polygraph recording of the EGG. It is recorded using two stable, nonpolarized electrodes, with the active electrode attached to any one of the four abdominal quadrants and the reference electrode attached to an inactive site on the arm or leg. Stern, Ray, and Davis (1980) suggested placing the active electrode on the skin at the intersection of the midline and epigastric line. As shown in the figure, the typical EGG recording consists of waves that occur approximately every twenty seconds (the phasic component) superimposed upon a changing baseline (the tonic component). The figure also illustrates several methods that have been used to quantify changes in the two components. The tonic component, for example, has been described in terms of basal resting levels and measures of displacement

FIGURE 4.4
Electrode Placements and Methods of Quantifying the Electrogastrogram (EGG)

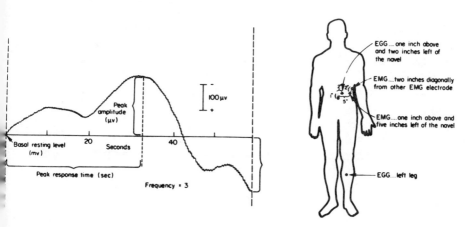

(changes from the baseline). Measures of frequency and amplitude have also been presented by Lilie (1974) and Walker and Sandman (1977), among others, to describe phasic activity.

To establish that the EGG is a measure of motility, Davis, Garafolo, and Kveim (1959) recorded simultaneously from surface electrodes and from an intragastric balloon and found a close correspondence between the two. In a more sophisticated experiment, Stevens and Worrall (1974) demonstrated that the electrogastric activity recorded from cats correlated significantly with measures of stomach contractions obtained using a strain gauge. Thus, it seems clear that the phasic component is related to gastric motility. The processes underlying the tonic components, however, have yet to be elucidated. Results of studies using intraluminal electrodes (Goodman, Colcher, Katz, & Dangler, 1955; Martin & Morton, 1952) suggest that the tonic component may actually reflect ionic, mucosal, and secretory changes. Differences in both the phasic and tonic components of the EGG have been reported in individuals with various gastrointestinal disorders, using both intraluminal (Nelson & Kohatsu, 1968) and surface (Nelson & Kohatsu, 1968; Stern & Davis, 1977; Walker & Sandman, 1977) electrodes. Elucidation of the various processes underlying the tonic and phasic activity of the gastrointestinal system promises significant theoretical and clinical advances.

As discussed earlier, digestion is a highly regulated process which, at times, becomes disregulated. Before examining the processes involved in disregulation, however, it is necessary to review some relatively recent changes in the conceptualization of regulation.

REGULATION

The survival of any organism depends upon its ability to regulate itself. Walter B. Cannon's notion of the "emergency reaction" (1939) and Hans Selye's formulation of a "general adaptation syndrome" (1946) have provided the basis for classical views regarding regulation. Although Cannon focused on autonomic changes that occur in response to stress, and Selye was concerned primarily with biochemical changes, both scientists held similar views of the relationship between the environment and the organism. This view emphasizes that the brain is the sole dictator of all bodily responses to environmental stimulation. The body passively responds to orders from the brain.

This view gave rise to a conceptualization of psychosomatic disorders as diseases that result from emotional disturbances. Dunbar (1935) suggested that personality patterns may be associated with different psychosomatic disorders, and later, Alexander (1950) suggested that specific emotional states might give rise to specific types of pathology. Regardless of the etiology, however, the treatment of psychosomatic disorders focused on the emotional reactions of the individual. The mind was the focus of attention, since the mind was thought to control bodily functions. Most often, this took the form of psychoanalysis.

In the past twenty years, it has become clear that the relationship between bodily processes and environmental events is more complex than Cannon and Selye initially described. The body does not merely execute commands from the brain; there are afferent fibers which complete visceral feedback systems with the central nervous system and influence psychological as well as physiological processes. This has given rise to an alternative model of regulation, which emphasizes that the brain constantly receives information from the body and that this information is one factor in providing a context for all environmental stimulation. Cognitive activity, personality factors, heredity, and learning also play a role in determining this context. It is this context that determines both the physiological and psychological impact of environmental stimulation. As a result, perception is an active process, involving both physiological and psychological processes. This idea dates back to William James (1890), and several lines of evidence have now accumulated to support this model. For ease of discussion, they are divided into two categories in the following section: the role of efferent activity and the role of afferent activity in regulation.

The Role of Efferent Activity in Regulation

Whereas Cannon (1939) believed that the same physiological responses occur in pain, hunger, fear, and rage, experimental evidence does not support this. Ax (1953), for example, demonstrated that the patterns of responses associated with fear could be clearly differentiated from those associated with anger. Other investigators (Davis, Buchwald, & Frankmann, 1955; Lacey, 1959) have also described the different physiological reactions that occur in response to a variety of stimuli. Further evidence suggests that individuals exhibit different patterns of autonomic responses to stress (Engel, 1960; Engel & Bickford, 1961; Lacey, 1959). Lacey demonstrated that, regardless of the stressor, some individuals respond maximally, with changes in the same physiological system. Furthermore, patients with specific disorders respond to stress maximally, with changes in the symptomatic system (Malmo & Shagass, 1949; Moos & Engel, 1962; Walker & Sandman, 1977).

The evidence cited above indicates that different stressors elicit different patterns of responses, and different individuals show idiosyncratic patterns of physiological responses. As such, cognitive factors, heredity, learning, and personality factors are important considerations when conceptualizing the interactions among the brain, the viscera, and the environment. Schachter, for example, proposed that emotional states are actually the interaction of cognitive factors and a state of "physiological arousal." He found that emotional states can be manipulated by changing the cognitive set or the physiological reactions of subjects (Schachter & Singer, 1962). Similarly, Lazarus (1967) emphasized the overriding importance of appraisal and cognitive factors in emotion. He and his colleagues (Lazarus, Speisman, Mordkoff, & Davison, 1962) demonstrated that physiological responses and emotional states can be influenced by changing the instructional sets that are given to subjects. Furthermore, it has long been known that certain individuals are genetically predisposed to various disorders (Gardner, 1972) and that autonomic activity is subject to principles of learning (Pavlov, 1927; Miller, 1969). In fact, much theorizing and research about psychosomatic disorders has recently focused on attitudes (Graham, 1972) and learning (Miller, 1969; Miller & Dworkin, 1977).

The Role of Afferent Activity in Regulation

Although most investigations have been related to the role of the brain in regulating autonomic activity, a substantial amount of evidence has accumulated to indicate that visceral afferent activity affects a variety of perceptual and cognitive processes. Most of the research regarding the behavioral significance of visceral activity has focused on the cardiovascular system and is a direct result of inferences stemming from a series of studies carried out by Lacey (1967) and Lacey, Kagan, Lacey, and Moss (1963). Lacey et al. found that both heart rate and blood pressure differentiate tasks that require attention to input (such as, the detection of flashes) from those in which attention to the environment is detrimental to the performance of the tasks (such as, mental arithmetic). These authors suggested that "mental concentration" is accompanied by transient hypertensive states, whereas attention to the environment is accompanied by brief hypotensive states. Experiments demonstrating that faster reaction times are associated with slower heart rate (Coquery & Lacey, 1966; Lacey & Lacey, 1970; Obrist, Webb, & Sutterer, 1969) provided initial support for this speculation, and the relationship between heart rate and behavior has since been demonstrated in a variety of paradigms, such as complex problem solving (Kaiser & Sandman, 1975), visual search (Coles, 1972), auditory threshold (Saxon & Dahle, 1971), and response to stressful stimuli (Hare, 1973; Sandman, 1975; Walker & Sandman, 1977).

The relationship between heart rate and behavior has also been demonstrated in two studies using operant conditioning paradigms to change heart rate. In one study, subjects perceived tachistoscopic stimuli more accurately during conditioned cardiodeceleration than during cardioacceleration (McCanne & Sandman, 1974). In another, subjects were able to generate more counterarguments to persuasive messages (indicating facilitated cognitive processing) during cardiac acceleration than during deceleration (Cacioppo, Sandman, & Walker, 1978). Furthermore, recent data indicate that spontaneous changes in heart rate are related to perception (Sandman, McCanne, Kaiser, & Diamond, 1977) and electrocortical activity (Walker & Sandman, 1979). These data, when taken together, indicate that decreases in heart rate facilitate attention to the environment, whereas increases in heart rate enhance cognitive activity.

Although studies of the influence of afferent autonomic activity on the brain and behavior have dealt primarily with cardiovascular changes and attention, there is little reason to doubt that afferent activity is equally important in the regulation of other physiological and behavioral processes. Kukorelli and Juhasz (1976), for example, demonstrated that intestinal stimulation induces electrocortical changes and changes in the wakefulness-sleep balance in cats (see Adam, 1978). Inflating a balloon in the duodenum of dogs and humans leads to desynchronization of electrocortical activity (Adam, Heffler, Kovacs, Nagy, & Szigeti, 1965; Preisich & Adam, 1964), and individuals can be taught to perceive visceral stimulation that they were unable to perceive prior to conditioning (see Adam, 1978). Thus, it seems clear that visceral afferent impulses associated with systems other than the cardiovascular sytem also exert extra-homeostatic influences on the brain and behavior. The role of these afferent impulses in maintaining states of behavioral and physiological regulation has only begun to be explored.

It should be apparent that afferent and efferent activities constantly work together to maintain regulation. They rely upon feedback systems to communicate, and a lack of appropriate feedback or the inability to interpret feedback often leads to disregulation (Schwartz, 1977).

DISREGULATION

How does disregulation occur in the gastrointestinal system? As with studies of regulation, most investigations have focused on efferent activity. Typically, these investigations have been attempts to examine the changes in the gastrointestinal system that occur as a result of stress. Jacobson (1927) and Faulkner (1941), for example, observed spastic esophageal contractions during emotional stress and a lessening of the contractions during a period of recovery. Wolf and Almy (1949) reported dysrhythmic esophageal motor activity in healthy subjects who were experiencing headaches caused by wearing a steel headband and in students undergoing examinations in school. These authors also induced delays in esophageal emptying in patients with achalasia by engaging them in stressful interviews. In four fistulous subjects with colostomies, Grace, Wolf, and Wolff (1951) found that three distinct patterns of colonic activity were associated with different emotions. Transport activity (peristalsis on the right side with shortening and narrowing on the left) was associated with sudden fright and often resulted in diarrhea. Desiccating activity (nonpropulsive segmental contractions), often associated with constipation, was related to depression in these patients. Hypotonia (inactivity of the colon), the third type of activity, was associated primarily with depression and pronounced psychomotor retardation.

Probably the most well-known experiments demonstrating a relationship between stress and gastrointestinal activity, however, have focused on changes in the stomach. Brady and his colleagues (Brady, 1958; Porter, Brady, Conrad, Mason, Galambos, & Rioch, 1958), demonstrated that they could induce ulcers in a monkey that had to press a lever at least once every twenty seconds to prevent a shock to itself and to a control monkey. They called the former the "executive monkey," and the phenomenon gained considerable attention in both basic research and applied clinical settings. The studies seemed to provide experimental evidence for the fact that ulcers are related to decision making; that is, the individual responsible for making decisions is the most likely to develop an ulcer.

There are several problems with the interpretation of these findings, however, that deserve to be pointed out. First, the only schedule that induced ulcers was one involving six hours of rest and six hours of lever pressing. Other schedules did not lead to chronic ulcers (see Natelson, 1977). Second, rather than selecting the animals randomly, monkeys that showed the most initiative in pressing the lever were chosen as "executive monkeys," and the more passive monkeys served as controls. Furthermore, the "executive monkeys" did not merely develop ulcers; they died while in the apparatus, and the ulcers were determined at autopsy. Subsequent studies involving the use of fistulas revealed that increases in gastric acid occur during the rest period rather than during performance of an avoidance task (Brady, 1963; Polish, Brady, Mason, Thack, & Niemack, 1962). All these factors contribute to the fact that several studies have failed to replicate the "executive monkey" phenomenon (Foltz & Millett, 1964; Natelson, 1977).

Weiss (1977) presented findings that are in direct opposition to those of the "executive monkey" study, and he developed a model which apprears to reconcile the two sets of results. These data and the model provide interesting evidence to support the notion that feedback systems play a critical role in disregulation. The model suggests that gastric lesions are a function of the amount of relevant feedback available as well as the number of responses that are made. Gastric lesions decrease as the amount of relevant feedback increases, but they increase as the number of responses increases. The model is a pyramid, with one edge of the base representing the number of responses made and another edge representing the amount of relevant feedback. The amount of ulceration can be determined by finding the intersection of these two points and measuring the height of the pyramid above that point. If, for example, many responses are made and the amount of feedback is low, the intersection occurs below a high point in the pyramid, and severe ulceration can be predicted. On the other hand, if few responses are made and the amount of feedback is large, the points intersect below the lowest point in the pyramid, and ulceration will be minimal.

One implication of this model is that feedback systems elicit organized patterns of behavior which serve as coping responses and lessen the impact of a stressor. Weiss's studies, for example, demonstrated that animals given the opportunity to avoid shock develop less severe gastric lesions than those without the opportunity (see Weiss, 1977). Furthermore, fighting can be induced in rats by shocking their tails, and animals allowed to fight show less severe gastric ulceration (Weiss, Pohorecky, Salmon, & Gruenthal, 1976) and lower levels of ACTH (Conner, Levine, & Vernikos-Danellis, 1970) than animals who are alone and therefore unable to fight. Even rats that are merely allowed to make aggressive responses toward each other without physical contact (because of a plexiglas grid between them) show a reduction in gastric lesions (Weiss et al., 1976).

Whereas organized behavior patterns serve as coping responses and diminish physiological responses to stress in lower animals, it appears as if cognitive activity can serve a similar function in humans (Lazarus, 1967). In view of this, it is interesting that ulcer patients have been described as being "oral-aggressive" (Alexander, 1950) and as having the attitude of one who "has been deprived of what he is due and wants revenge" (Grace & Graham, 1952). Like the rats that are prevented from fighting and develop gastric lesions, ulcer patients may have developed coping styles which prevent them from adequately expressing aggressive impulses. Lazarus (1966, 1968) found that physiological responses to stress change dramatically when coping responses are manipulated, and perhaps changes in coping style would lead to physiological changes that are therapeutically beneficial for ulcer patients. The situation is complicated, however, since change in physiological activity can also lead to changes in coping responses.

Regardless of the relationship between coping processes and physiological activity, it seems clear that ulcer patients display dramatically different physiological responses to stress than do other individuals. In one study in the authors' laboratory, duodenal ulcer patients, rheumatoid arthritics, and healthy subjects were exposed to mildly stressful cognitive and affective stimuli while a variety of physiological measures were recorded (Walker & Sandman, 1977). The ulcer patients were consistently the least responsive physiologically. With the exception of increased skin responses while solving arithmetic problems, the ulcer patients were responsive only during affective stimuli, when they showed increases in gastric activity as well as skin responses. Furthermore, while the other groups responded to each set of stimuli with changes in heart rate, heart rates of ulcer patients remained remarkably stable throughout the experimental session. As mentioned earlier, physiological responses to stress are part of a complex feedback system devoted to maintaining both physiological and psychological regulation. The diminished and atypical physiological responses to stress in ulcer patients suggest a disruption of regulatory processes.

All the studies discussed above focus on physiological changes that occur as a response to stressful environmental events. As emphasized earlier, however, afferent as well as efferent pathways are critical for maintaining regulation. Perhaps nowhere in the gastrointestinal system is the importance of afferent activity more obvious than in the regulation of food intake itself.

Although the importance of the hypothalamus in this process was emphasized in previous years (Anand, 1961; Brobeck, 1946), there has recently been a surge of interest in the role of peripheral factors and environmental and social variables in maintaining regulation (Rodin, 1977). Gibbs and his colleagues, for example, have found that injections of the hormone cholecystokinin elicits the complete behavioral sequence of satiety in rats (Antin, Gibbs, Holt, Young, & Smith, 1975; Gibbs, Young, & Smith, 1973). Other findings suggest that glucoreceptors in the liver transmit messages about changes in nutritional state to the brain via the vagus nerve (Novin, VanderWeele, & Rezek, 1973). Injections of estrogen, growth hormone, and insulin also alter food intake (Woods, Decke, & Vasselli, 1974).

In addition to internal feedback mechanisms, feedback systems linking the organism to the environment also appear to be critical for regulating food intake. Rodin (1976, 1977) and Schachter (Schachter & Rodin, 1974) emphasized that responsiveness to external stimuli plays an important role in the regulation of food intake, and a considerable amount of data has accumulated to indicate that obese subjects are more responsive to external events than are healthy subjects (Rodin, Herman, & Schachter, 1974; Schachter, Goldman, & Gordon, 1968). Stunkard and Koch (1964) found that gastric motility is highly related to reports of "hunger" in nonobese subjects but not in obese subjects. When obese subjects receive feedback about gastric motility, however, their ability to identify gastric contractions improves (Griggs & Stunkard, 1964). These data, taken together, illustrate the importance of both afferent and efferent systems in insuring our nutritional needs and maintaining gastrointestinal regulation.

By now, it should be apparent that no single cause can be identified for any specific gastrointestinal disorder. Disregulation is multifaceted, and therefore, developing treatments for disorders is a complicated task. The most common approach is the medical approach, although psychological and psychobiological treatments have also been developed.

THE MEDICAL APPROACH TO TREATMENT

The medical approach assumes that there is an identifiable physiological cause for a patient's symptoms and that it is this cause that needs to be discovered and treated. Therefore, if a patient complains of gastrointestinal disturbances, the physician begins to search the gastrointestinal tract for the cause of the symptoms. Once the cause is thought to be identified, the physician attempts to repair the damage. In the cast of the gastrointestinal system, this generally entails surgery, drugs, or a change in diet.

Surgery

Surgical intervention for achalasia involves severing the lower esophageal sphincter, permanently removing the barrier provided by the unrelaxed sphincter. Since there are no drugs to restore normal peristalsis to the esophagus of patients with this disorder, this surgery is often recommended. Unfortunately, there is still a lack of peristalsis following surgery; the esophagus empties by gravity through the incompetent sphincter.

Approximately 20% of all ulcer patients also undergo surgery. One surgical intervention, *vagotomy*, involves severing the two large vagal trunks that innervate the stomach. This surgery decreases secretion but also inhibits peristalsis, creating an inability of the stomach to empty. As a result, the surgeon may then perform a *gastrojejunostomy* to widen the pylorus and assist in emptying. This combination of a vagotomy and a drainage procedure is the simplest operation for peptic ulcer; unfortunately, there is a 10-15% recurrence rate. If the surgeon chooses to do so, an *antrectomy* also may be performed, which removes the portion of the stomach that secretes gastrin. This increases the effectiveness of the surgery, since two major stimuli for parietal cell secretion are removed, and parietal cell mass is reduced.

Surgical intervention is used frequently for ulcerative colitis. Various portions of the large intestine can be removed, depending upon the individual case. Although this type of surgery necessitates some very basic changes in lifestyle, most patients prefer it to the pain and discomfort they suffered previously. Unfortunately, the recurrence rate after surgery has been estimated to be as high as 50%, and the surgery itself often leads to chronic difficulties with absorption (Dworkin, 1974).

Chronic complications of gastrointestinal surgery are of considerable importance. Regardless of the type of surgery, patients may begin to lose weight and strength. Unusual patterns of gastric motility may develop and lead to pain, diarrhea, or constipation. Vagotomized patients often suffer from either gastric retention or an inability of the stomach to retain its contents. Both these situations are associated with extreme discomfort. These complications, coupled with the relatively high recurrence rate, emphasize that surgery is not a "cure" for any gastrointestinal disorder. Unfortunately, however, there is often no alternative.

Pharmacologic Agents

Since duodenal ulcers have typically been associated with increases in acid secretion, it seems reasonable to suspect that *antacids* may be effective in treating this type of ulcer. The initial uncontrolled studies and clinical experience suggested that they are effective, but more recent evidence has cast doubts. In a double-blind, well-controlled study, Sturdevant, Isenberg, Secrist, and Ansfield (1977) found no differences between antacid and placebo in the time to onset, the degree, or the duration of pain relief in duodenal ulcer patients. Other studies have also reported nonsignificant differences between antacids and placebo (Butler & Gersh, 1975; Hollander & Harlan, 1973). Sturdevant et al. (1977) suggested that the expectation of relief may play a critical role in modifying a patient's affective response to pain. Since relief of duodenal ulcer pain by antacids is regularly reported by patients and is supported by some early studies (Bonney & Pickering, 1946; Lawrence, 1952; Palmer, 1927), it is premature to conclude that antacids have no effect on ulcer pain. These new data, however, suggest that factors other than gastric acid neutralization play a role in the pain associated with duodenal ulcers.

Since the major stimuli inducing gastric acid secretion are gastrin and vagal stimulation, *anticholinergics* have traditionally been used to block stimulation of the parietal cells. These drugs reduce basal, nocturnal, and stimulated acid secretion (Fordtran, Morawski, & Richardson, 1973), but because of extreme variation among individuals, the dosage is difficult to determine. Unfortunately, the dosage must be increased until side effects (such as, dry mouth and blurred vision) are noted and then reduced one step. Since all anticholinergics produce side effects, double-blind controlled studies of their effectiveness in the treatment of ulcers have been impossible. In spite of this problem, some studies have attempted to determine whether these drugs are superior to placebo (Hunt & Wales, 1966; Sun & Ryan, 1970; Walan, 1970); the majority have found that they are not (see MacGregor, 1977).

Recently, several new agents that appear to be effective in healing peptic ulcers have become available (Jeejeebhoy, 1978). *Carbenoxolone sodium* increases gastric mucosal resistance and has been shown to accelerate healing in both gastric and duodenal ulcers (Brown, Salmon, & Thien-Htut, 1972; Horwich & Galloway, 1965). Unfortunately, the main effects of the drug are related to sodium retention, which causes edema, weight gain, and congestive heart failure. *Cimetidine*, another new pharmacologic agent, blocks histamine (H_2) receptors and thus inhibits the stimulating effect of histamine on gastric secretion (Burland & Simkins, 1977). It has been found to significantly increase the rate of healing of duodenal ulcers (Gillespie, Gray, & Smith, 1977) and may even be useful in preventing recurrence (Jeejeebhoy, 1978). *Metoclopramide* is a new drug that hastens gastric emptying and reduces the flow of bile into the duodenum. It also increases the tone of the gastroesophageal sphincter (Heitmann & Moller, 1970) and helps control reflux esophagitis and ulcerations of the esophagus (Johnson, 1971). In addition, it seems to have a positive effect on gastric ulceration and gastritis (Jeejeebhoy, 1978). The side effects of metoclopramide, however, are depression, lethargy, and parkinsonism, which may limit its usefulness. Currently, carbenoxolone sodium is the drug of choice for gastric ulcer, whereas cimetidine is the drug of choice for duodenal ulcer.

Diet

A bland diet which includes milk, cottage cheese, and white meat has traditionally been recommended as part of ulcer therapy, but there is no evidence that this diet has any effect on ulcer pain or the healing of ulcers (MacGregor,

1977). Doll, Friedlander, and Pygott (1956) found that gastric ulcers are unaffected by bland diets, and other investigators (Lennard-Jones & Babouris, 1965) showed that milk and cream not only do not decrease gastric acid secretion but may actually increase it. In fact, Ippoliti, Maxwell, and Isenberg (1976) recently showed that the calcium in milk can be a potent stimulator of gastric acid secretion.

The three major forms of medical intervention — surgery, drugs, and diet — which focus on the gastrointestinal system also exert powerful influences on other systems. The significance of this fact can be seen more clearly if viewed in terms of the model emphasized throughout this chapter. Figure 4.5 illustrates the model as it pertains to the development and medical treatment of duodenal ulcers. It can be seen in the figure that medical treatments focus on the gastrointestinal system itself: anticholinergic drugs and vagotomies interrupt vagal stimulation, cimetidine inhibits secretion by blocking histamine receptors, and dietary changes directly alter the substances introduced to the stomach and duodenum. The model emphasizes, however, that these treatments can have profound effects on other processes as well. The precise outcome of vagotomy, for example, may represent more than the mere loss of parasympathetic stimulation

FIGURE 4.5
Medical Treatment of the Gastrointestinal System

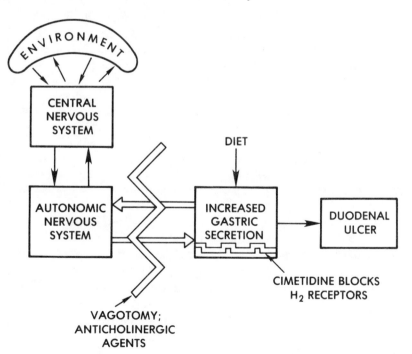

of gastric secretion. Studies of gastric mucosal cells after vagotomy show changes in sympathetic nerve terminals. In addition, afferent as well as efferent impulses are severed during vagotomy, and, as discussed above, these impulses are critical for regulating other physiological and behavioral processes. Although cimetidine does inhibit gastric secretion, there are reports of side effects, such as breast changes in males (Hall, 1976) and mental confusion (Delaney & Ravey, 1977; Nelson, 1977), emphasizing that both afferent and efferent systems are involved and that caution should be taken when prescribing these new substances (Castell, 1978). As seen in the figure, these treatments may, in fact, perpetuate disregulation rather than reinstate regulatory processes.

PSYCHOLOGICAL APPROACHES TO TREATMENT

It is interesting that psychoanalysis, which is the prevailing psychological approach to the treatment of physical disorders, is a direct outgrowth of the medical approach. Like the medical approach, psychoanalysis focuses on underlying causes rather than on the symptoms of the disorder. Whereas the physician searches the gastrointestinal tract for the cause, the psychoanalyst focuses on intrapsychic events. One assumption of this approach is that physical symptoms result from disturbances of mental events; as soon as intrapsychic conflicts are resolved, bodily processes will resume normal functioning. Alexander and Flagg (1965) stated the position clearly: ". . . psychotherapy is the only treatment which can alter the patients' psychic conflict, which constitutes the primary disturbance in the chain of events causing the ulcer" (p. 874).

According to psychoanalytic thought (Alexander, 1950), the critical factor in the development of ulcers is the frustration associated with the wish to receive love. When this wish is rejected, it is converted into a wish to be fed. This, in turn, leads to chronic gastric hyperfunction and, ultimately, an ulcer. Similarly, ulcerative colitis has been related to disturbances of the mother-child relationship, leading to helplessness and despair (Engel, 1955).

There are data from both clinical and psychophysiological studies that provide evidence for a relationship between conflicts and gastrointestinal disorders. Several clinical investigators, for example, have confirmed oral-dependent tendencies in ulcer patients (Garma, 1958; Streitfeld, 1954; Weisman, 1956) as well as frustration associated with demands for love (Taboroff & Brown, 1954). Fear (Mahl, 1949) and anxiety (Heller, Levine, & Sohler, 1953) have been found to cause increases in gastric secretion, whereas depression has been related to changes in the vascularity and mucosa of the large intestine and to ulcerative colitis (Engel, 1954). Karush, Hiatt, and Daniels (1955) measured secretion of the parotid glands, activity of the peripheral vasculature, and activity of the distal colon in six patients with ulcerative colitis and found that fear was associated with segmental colon contractions and a marked inhibition of salivary secretions.

These data suggest that emotions and subconscious processes are related to gastrointestinal disturbances, but evidence regarding the benefits of psychotherapy is sparse. Most of the studies designed to assess the efficacy of psychotherapy have been uncontrolled, and the data are equivocal (see Brautigan & VonRad, 1977). Traditional forms of psychotherapy seem to contribute to physical and emotional improvements in some iindividuals but not in others.

The fact that traditional psychotherapy is helpful only in "carefully chosen" cases (Alexander & Flagg, 1965) has led to the development of other psychological approaches to the treatment of physical ailments. The most notable among these is the behavioral approach, which focuses on learned responses to environmental events rather than on intrapsychic activity. The behavioral therapist attempts to determine the factors in the environment that control symptomatic behavior and then applies concepts from learning theory to alter the response.

Stunkard (1972) pointed out that some of the most consistent evidence of the effectiveness of behavioral techniques comes from the treatment of eating disorders. He reviewed several well-controlled studies on obese subjects, which demonstrated the superiority of behavioral methods over no treatment (Harris, 1969), nonspecific therapy and social pressure (Wollersheim, 1970), and group therapy (Penick, Filion, & Fox, 1971). Behavioral techniques are also successful in helping anorexic patients to gain weight (Bachrach, Erwin, & Mohr, 1965; Blinder, Freeman, & Stunkard, 1970; Hallsten, 1965). As with the medical approach, however, there is a high recurrence rate, which has led some investigators (such as Bruch, 1974) to suggest that the behavioral approach to eating disorders may actually be deleterious.

It is curious that, except in rare cases, both psychoanalysis and behavioral methods ignore physiological activity. In response to this, a psychobiological approach has emerged, which attempts to integrate psychological and psychophysiological principles in devising treatment plans for patients with physical ailments.

THE PSYCHOBIOLOGICAL APPROACH

According to the psychobiological approach, disregulation occurs when feedback systems are disrupted (see Schwartz, 1977). Therefore, the goal of treatment is to reinstate regulatory processes. Figure 4.6 illustrates how feedback can be provided to a patient in an attempt to modify dysfunctional feedback systems. The figure also emphasizes the holistic view of the psychobiological approach. Providing people with feedback contingent upon actual physiological changes has been termed *biofeedback*, which, in conjunction with strict operant conditioning techniques, is being explored as a treatment for many gastrointestinal disorders.

A study recently completed in the author's laboratory illustrates how the biofeedback paradigm can be used to teach individuals to control gastrointestinal

FIGURE 4.6
Model of the Psychobiological Approach to Treatment

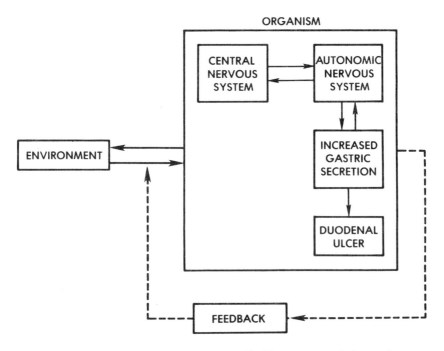

activity (Walker, Lawton, & Sandman, 1978). The purpose of the study was to examine the possibility that individuals can modify electrogastric activity as it is reflected by the tonic component of the EGG. This was of considerable interest, since the tonic component differentiates healthy subjects from those with duodenal ulcers (Walker & Sandman, 1977). It is conceivable that specific control of tonic EGG activity can be of therapeutic benefit to duodenal ulcer patients.

Eight fasting male subjects participated in two sessions on two consecutive mornings. Transducers were attached to enable monitoring of EGG, respiration, heart rate, abdominal EMG, and digital blood flow. Half the subjects were instructed that when a light was illuminated, they were to try to move the needle on a meter in front of them to the right, indicating a negative deflection of the EGG, without changing respiration or tensing any muscles. They were also informed that the electrical activity of their stomach would control the meter during each trial. During the second session, they were asked to try to move the needle on the meter to the left, indicating a positive deflection of the EGG. This order was reversed for the other half of the subjects. The experimental procedure is illustrated in Figure 4.7.

The results of the study indicated that individuals can modify tonic EGG activity. Changes in the negative direction were more easily obtained than changes in the positive direction. Consistent with investigations of the gastrointestinal

FIGURE 4.7
Experimental Procedure for Biofeedback

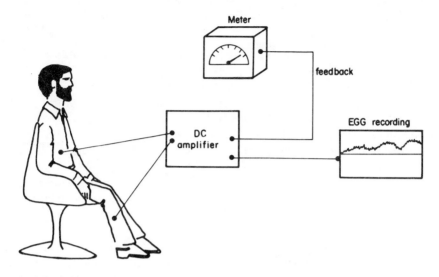

(Whitehead et al., 1975) and other systems (Walker, Sandman, & Cacioppo, in preparation), some subjects evidenced discriminative control, while others did not. Those who showed the least amount of abdominal EMG activity and reported being the most relaxed and "indifferent" were the ones who evidenced discriminative control.

Weiss (1977) speculated that increases in skeletal muscle activity may be related to the vulnerability of an individual to gastric ulceration, and it seems possible that muscle activity plays an important role in the feedback system related to the regulation of gastrointestinal activity. There are data to suggest that EMG biofeedback and relaxation training may be effective in treating duodenal ulcers (Aleo & Nicassio, 1978; Beaty, 1976) and functional colitis (Weinstock, 1976).

Several other experiments have demonstrated that the biofeedback paradigm can be used to teach healthy individuals to modify other gastrointestinal activity. Moore and Schenkenberg (1974), for example, found that a subject could increase and decrease gastric acid secretion when provided with feedback but could not do so when the feedback was removed. These authors used a nasogastric tube to collect gastric contents and provided the subject with feedback of his success approximately every ten minutes. Other investigators (Gorman & Kaniya, 1972; Whitehead et al., 1975) have found that healthy subjects can learn to control gastric acid secretion when gastric pH is recorded using a pH electrode located within the stomach. Schuster, Nikoomanesh, and Wells (1973) found that healthy individuals can control pressure in the lower esophageal sphincter when feedback is provided.

These data, in conjunction with data from studies with animals, have led to attempts to apply biofeedback techniques to the treatment of various gastrointestinal disorders. As Whitehead (1978) indicated in a recent review, the focus of these studies has been on clinical syndromes, such as ruminative vomiting, disorders of the esophagus, peptic ulcers, and disorders of the large intestine.

Ruminative Vomiting

The first report of the application of operant conditioning procedures to the treatment of vomiting was by White and Taylor (1967). These authors applied electric shock to two mentally retarded patients whenever throat, eye, or coughing gestures signaled rumination, and they observed significant improvements after one week of treatment. Similarly, Lang and Melamed (1969) demonstrated the efficacy of aversive conditioning in reversing the vomiting of an infant whose life was in danger. They applied shocks to the leg whenever EMG activity indicated that vomiting was about to occur and found that vomiting was eliminated within only six sessions. Furthermore, the effect generalized to the home environment, and the infant resumed eating and gained weight. Other studies using aversive stimuli — such as electric shock (Cunningham & Linscheid, 1976; Linscheid & Cunningham, 1977; Toister, Colin, Worley, & Arthur, 1975) and lemon juice in the patient's mouth (Becker, Turner, & Sajwaj, 1978; Sajwaj, Libet, & Agras, 1974) — have also been published, and all indicate that operant techniques are effective in treating vomiting.

Disorders of the Esophagus

As mentioned earlier, the lower esophageal sphincter is innervated exclusively by the autonomic nervous system. Since reflux disorders and achalasia are associated with imparied contractions of this sphincter, the demonstration that healthy individuals can modify their esophageal sphincter pressure has been of considerable interest.

Schuster et al. (1973) described a method for measuring pressure in the sphincter. Three perfused, open-tipped catheters were positioned so that the distal tip was in the stomach, the middle tip in the sphincter, and the proximal tip in the esophagus. The pressure from the middle tip was recorded and displayed to the subject, using a meter in much the same way that EGG is displayed in Figure 4.7. The subject was asked to try to move the needle on the meter without using abdominal muscles or altering respiration. These authors demonstrated that normal subjects and subjects with esophageal reflux can increase resting sphincter pressure, provided they receive feedback. Some patients increased pressure as much as 100%, although in reflux patients, this is still below the normal range. It is too early to say whether this technique will be useful in the treatment of reflux esophagitis, esophageal spasm, or achalasia (Schuster, 1977).

Ulcers

Although the etiology of gastric and duodenal ulcers has not been firmly established, it seems clear that excess hydrochloric acid plays a primary role in duodenal ulcers, whereas diminished mucosal resistance plays a primary role in gastric ulcers. Since it is difficult to measure mucosal activity in intact humans, feedback studies have focused on the control of gastric secretion in duodenal ulcer patients.

Welgan (1974) asked duodenal ulcer patients to decrease gastric acid secretion while receiving feedback provided by continuous aspiration of gastric contents. Although the concentration of acid decreased from the baseline period, no differences were observed between subsequent periods of feedback and no feedback. Later studies (Welgan, 1977) suggested that pH feedback results in changes in the volume of secretions rather than in acid concentration. Welgan (1977) pointed out the many technical difficulties with these measurements, and it is apparent that resolution must await technical advances.

Disorders of the Large Intestine

Irritable bowel syndrome, one of the most common disorders of the gastrointestinal system, is characterized by abdominal pain, altered bowel habits, and the occurrence of spastic contractions of the colon (Wangel & Deller, 1965). Bueno-Mirada, Cerulli, and Schuster (1976) used balloons inserted into the sigmoid colon to stimulate spasmodic contractions and to provide biofeedback to patients suffering from irritable bowel syndrome. Two-thirds of the twenty-one patients were able to inhibit these spasmodic contractions. Studies eight weeks later illustrated that improvements were maintained.

Balloons can also be used to record pressure changes in the internal and external sphincters, structures that are responsible for various forms of incontinence. When the rectosigmoid colon is stimulated, there is reflex relaxation of the internal sphincter and a brief contraction of the external sphincter (Schuster, 1977). In cases of fecal incontinence, the contraction of the external sphincter is severely impaired or absent. Thus, the response that must be learned is not merely external sphincter contraction, but external sphincter contraction in synchrony with internal sphincter relaxation.

Engel, Nikoomanesh, and Schuster (1974) used balloons to stimulate internal sphincter relaxation and contraction and to record pressure changes in the sphincters. Feedback was provided by allowing the patients to watch the polygraph pens as the recordings were made. Patients were able to increase their awareness of rectal distention and to contract the external sphincter after sensing relaxation of the internal sphincter. Schuster (1977) reported that 70% of the patients who received this treatment developed good reflexes, and, of this group, half achieved complete control with no further indication of incontinence.

It appears that only three or four training sessions over a period of a few months are sufficient to produce these dramatic effects.

SUMMARY

The gastrointestinal tract is basically a tube which functions to adjust various properties of food so that nutrients can be absorbed into the blood. These adjustments are accomplished as a result of processes related to secretion, motility, and absorption. In this chapter, we have discussed these processes and their role in various gastrointestinal disorders. Methods of investigating gastro-intestinal activity have also been reviewed.

Evidence has been presented to indicate that the gastrointestinal system does not merely respond to commands from the brain. There are complex feed-back systems between the central and autonomic nervous systems, which serve to regulate both physiological and behavioral processes. Both afferent and efferent activities constantly work together to maintain regulation, and when communication is disrupted, disregulation occurs.

Since disregulation is multifaceted, and no single cause can be identified for any specific gastrointestinal disorder, developing treatments is a complicated task. Medical, psychological, and psychobiological approaches to treatment have been developed. The medical approach searches the gastrointestinal tract for the cause of disregulation and attempts to remedy the cause by surgery, drugs, or changes in diet. Although this approach has the advantage of providing some immediate relief, the treatments often lead to other forms of disregulation (see Figure 4.5).

The psychoanalytic approach also searches for underlying causes but assumes them to be intrapsychic events. Unfortunately, there is little evidence to support the contention that resolving mental conflicts is therapeutically beneficial for patients with gastrointestinal disorders. In contrast, the behavioral approach, which focuses on learned responses to environmental events, has been extremely successful in the treatment of patients suffering from eating disorders. Unfortunately, there is little evidence to suggest that the approach is effective in treating other common types of gastrointestinal disorders, such as ulcers or colitis.

The psychobiological approach emphasizes the interaction of the entire organism with the environment and attempts to reinstate regulatory processes by altering the feedback related to specific physiological changes. Although this approach is in its infancy, and it is still too early to assess its usefulness, the evidence to date appears to promise significant theoretical and clinical advances.

REFERENCES

Adam, G. Visceroception, awareness, and behavior. In G. E. Schwartz & D. Shapiro (Eds.), *Consciousness and self-regulation* (Vol. 2). New York: Plenum Press, 1978.

Adam, G., Heffler, J., Kovacs, A., Nagy, A., & Szigeti, A. Electrographic test for the discrimination of intestinal stimuli. *Acta Physiologica Academiae Scientarum Hungaricae*, 1965, *27*, 145-157.

Aleo, S., & Nicassio, P. *Auto-regulation of duodenal ulcer disease: A preliminary report of four cases.* Paper presented at the ninth annual meeting of the Biofeedback Society of America, Albuquerque, 1978.

Alexander, F. *Psychosomatic medicine: Its principles and applications.* New York: Norton, 1950.

Alexander, F., & Flagg, G. W. The psychosomatic approach. In B. B. Wolman (Ed.), *Handbook of clinical psychology*. New York: McGraw-Hill, 1965.

Anand, B. K. Nervous regulation of food intake. *Physiology Reviews*, 1961, *41*, 677-708.

Antin, J., Gibbs, J., Holt, J., Young, R. C., & Smith, G. Cholecystokinin elicits the complete behavioral sequence of satiety in rats. *Journal of Comparative and Physiological Psychology*, 1975, *89*, 784-790.

Ax, A. F. The physiological differentiation between fear and anger in humans. *Psychosomatic Medicine*, 1953, *14*, 433-442.

Bachrach, A. J., Erwin, W., & Mohr, J. P. The control of eating behavior in an anorexic by operant conditioning techniques. In L. P. Ullman & L. Krasner (Eds.), *Case studies in behavior modification*. New York: Holt, Rinehart & Winston, 1965.

Beaty, E. T. Feedback assisted relaxation training as a treatment for peptic ulcers. *Biofeedback and Self-Regulation*, 1976, *1*, 323-324. (Abstract)

Beaumont, W. Experiments and observations on the gastric juice and the physiology of digestion. Plattsburg, N. Y.: F. P. Allen, 1833.

Becker, J., Turner, W., & Sajwaj, T. E. Multiple behavioral effects of the use of lemon juice with a ruminating toddler-age child. *Behavior Modification*, 1978, *2*, 267-278.

Blinder, B. J., Freeman, D. M. A., & Stunkard, A. J. Behavior therapy of anorexia nervosa: Effectiveness of activity as a reinforcer of weight gain. *American Journal of Psychiatry*, 1970, *126*, 1093-1098.

Bolwig, T. G., & Rafaelsen, O. J. Salivation in affective disorders. *Psychosomatic Medicine*, 1972, *2*, 232-238.

Bonney, G. L. W., & Pickering, G. W. Observations on the mechanism of pain in ulcers of the stomach and duodenum. *Clinical Science*, 1946, *6*, 63-89.

Bozler, E. The action potentials of the stomach. *American Journal of Physiology*, 1945, *144*, 693-700.

Brady, J. V. Ulcers in "executive monkeys." *Scientific American*, October, 1958, pp. 95-100.

Brady, J. V. Further comments on the gastrointestinal system and avoidance behavior. *Psychology Reports*, 1963, *12*, 742.

Brautigan, W., & VonRad, M. Toward a theory of psychosomatic disorders. *Psychotherapy and Psychosomatics*, 1977, *28*, 285-343.

Brobeck, J. R. Mechanisms of the development of obesity in animals with hypothalamic lesions. *Physiology Reviews*, 1946, *26*, 541-559.

Brown, P., Salmon, P., & Thien-Htut, A. F. Double-blind trial of carbenoxolone sodium capsules in duodenal ulcer therapy, based on endoscopic diagnosis and follow-up. *British Medical Journal*, 1972, *3*, 661-664.

Bruch, H. Perils of behavior modification in treatment of anorexia nervosa. *Journal of the American Medical Association*, 1974, *230*, 1419-1422.

Bueno-Mirada, F., Cerulli, M., & Schuster, M. M. Operant conditioning of colonic motility in irritable bowel syndrome. *Gastroenterology*, 1976, *70*, 867.

Burland, W. L., & Simkins, M. A. (Eds.). *Cimetidine*. Proceedings of the second international symposium on histamine H_2 receptor antagonists. Oxford: Excerpta Medica, 1977.

Butler, M. L., & Gersh, H. Antacid vs. placebo in hospitalized gastric ulcer patients: A controlled therapeutic study. *American Journal of Digestive Disorders*, 1975, *20*, 803-807.

Cacioppo, J. T., Sandman, C. A., & Walker, B. B. The effects of operant heart rate conditioning on cognitive elaboration and attitude change. *Psychophysiology*, 1978, *15*, 330-338.

Cannon, W. B. *Bodily changes in pain, hunger, fear and rage*. New York: Appleton, 1915.

Cannon, W. B. *The wisdom of the body*. New York: Norton, 1939.

Carlson, H. C., Code, C. F., & Nelson, R. A. Motor action of the canine gastroduodenal junction: A cireradiographic pressure and electric study. *American Journal of Digestive Disorders*, 1966, *11*, 155-172.

Castell, D. Sense with Cimetidine. *Journal of the American Medical Association*, 1978, *240*, 564.

Clark, G. W., & Carter, K. L. Factors involved in the reaction changes of human saliva. *Journal of Biological Chemistry*, 1927, *73*, 391-404.

Cohen, S. The diagnosis and management of gastroesophageal reflux. *Advances in Internal Medicine*, 1976, *21*, 47-75.

Coles, M. G. Cardiac and respiratory activity during visual search. *Journal of Experimental Psychology*, 1972, *96*, 371-379.

Connell, A. M., & Rowlands, E. N. Wireless telemetering from the digestive tract. *Gut*, 1960, *1*, 266-272.

Conner, R. L., Levine, S., & Vernikos-Danellis, J. Shock-induced fighting and pituitary adrenal activity. *Proceedings of the 78th Annual Convention of the American Psychological Association*, 1970, *5*, 201-202.

Coquery, J., & Lacey, J. I. *The effect of foreperiod duration on the components of the cardiac response during the foreperiod of a reaction time experiment.* Paper delivered at the annual meeting of the Society for Psychophysiological Research, Denver, October 1966.

Corcoran, D. W. J. The relationship between introversion and salivation. *American Journal of Psychology*, 1964, *77*, 298-300.

Cunningham, C. E., & Linscheid, T. R. Elimination of chronic ruminating by electric shock. *Behavior Therapy*, 1976, *7*, 231-235.

Davies, B. M., & Gurland, J. B. Salivary secretion in depressive illness. *Journal of Psychosomatic Research*, 1961, *5*, 269-271.

Davis, R. C., Buchwald, A. M., & Frankmann, R. W. Autonomic and muscular responses and their relation to simple stimuli. *Psychology Monographs*, 1955, *69* (20), 1-71.

Davis, R. C., Garafolo, L., & Gault, F. An exploration of abdominal potentials. *Journal of Comparative and Physiological Psychology*, 1957, *50*, 519-523.

Davis, R. C., Garafolo, L., & Kveim, K. Conditions associated with gastrointestinal activity. *Journal of Comparative and Physiological Psychology*, 1959, *52*, 466-475.

Dawes, C. Circadian rhythms in human salivary flow rate and composition. *Journal of Physiology*, 1972, *220*, 529-545.

Delaney, J. C., & Ravey, M. Cimetidine and mental confusion. *Lancet*, 1977, *2*, 512.

Doll, R., Friedlander, P., & Pygott, F. Dietetic treatment of peptic ulcer. *Lancet*, 1956, *1*, 5-9.

Dunbar, H. *Emotions and bodily changes*. New York: Columbia University Press, 1935.

Dworkin, H. J. *The alimentary tract*. Philadelphia: Saunders, 1974.

Enfors, B. The parotid and submandibular secretion in man. *Acta Otolaryngologica*, 1962, *suppl. 162*, 1-67.

Engel, B. T. Stimulus-response and individual-response specificity. *Archives of General Psychiatry*, 1960, *2*, 305-313.

Engel, B. T., & Bickford, A. F. Response specificity: Stimulus-response and individual-response specificity in essential hypertensives. *Archives of General Psychiatry*, 1961, *5*, 478-489.

Engel, B. T., Nikoomanesh, P., & Schuster, M. M. Operant conditioning of rectosphincteric responses in the treatment of fecal incontinence. *New England Journal of Medicine*, 1974, *290*, 646-649.

Engel, G. L. Studies of ulcerative colitis. II. The nature of the somatic processes and the adequacy of the psychosomatic hypotheses. *American Journal of Medicine*, 1954, *16*, 416-433.

Engel, G. L. Studies of ulcerative colitis. III. The nature of the psychological process. *American Journal of Medicine*, 1955, *19*, 231-256.

Faulkner, W. B. Effect of emotions upon diaphragmatic functions: Observations in 5 patients. *Psychosomatic Medicine*, 1941, *3*, 187-189.

Foltz, E. L., & Millett, F. E. Experimental psychosomatic disease states in monkeys. I. Peptic ulcer — "Executive monkeys." *Journal of Surgical Research*, 1964, *4*, 445-453.

Fordtran, J. C., Morawski, S. G., & Richardson, C. T. In vivo and in vitro evaluation of liquid antacids. *New England Journal of Medicine*, 1973, *288*, 923-928.

Fordtran, J. S. Reduction of acidity by dot antacids and anticholinergic agents. In M. Sleisenger & J. Fordtran (Eds.), *Gastrointestinal disease*. Philadelphia: Saunders, 1973.

Freedman, J. Roentgen studies of the effects on the small intestine from emotional disturbances. *American Journal of Roentgenology*, 1954, *22*, 367-379.

Gardner, E. J. *Principles of genetics*. New York: Wiley, 1972.

Garma, A. *Peptic ulcer and psychoanalysis*. Baltimore: Williams & Wilkins, 1958.

Gibbs, J., Young, R. C., & Smith, G. P. Cholecystokinin elicits satiety in rats with open fistulas. *Nature*, 1973, *245*, 323-325.

Gillespie, G., Gray, G., & Smith, I. Short-term and maintenance cimetidine treatment in severe duodenal ulceration. In W. L. Burland & M. A. Simkins (Eds.), *Cimetidine*. Oxford: Excerpta Medica, 1977.

Goodman, E. N., Colcher, H., Katz, G. M., & Dangler, C. L. The clinical significance of the electrogastrogram. *Gastroenterology*, 1955, *29*, 598-607.

Gorman, P. J. & Kamiya, J. Biofeedback training of stomach pH. Paper presented to the Western Psychological Association, San Francisco, 1972.

Grace, W. J., & Graham, D. T. Relationship of specific attitudes and emotions to certain bodily diseases. *Psychosomatic Medicine*, 1952, *14*, 243-251.

Grace, W. J., Wolf, S., & Wolff, H. G. *The human colon: An experimental study based on direct observation of four fistulous subjects*. New York: Hoeber, 1951.

Graham, D. T. Psychosomatic medicine. In N. Greenfield & R. Sternbach (Eds.), *Handbook of psychophysiology*. New York: Holt, Rinehart & Winston, 1972.

Greenberger, N. J., & Winship, D. H. *Gastrointestinal disorders: A pathophysiological approach*. Chicago: Year Book Medical Publisher, 1976.

Griggs, R. C., & Stunkard, A. J. The interpretation of gastric motility: Sensitivity and bias in the perception of gastric motility. *Archives of General Psychiatry*, 1964, *11*, 82-89.

Hall, W. H. Breast changes in males on cimetidine. *New England Journal of Medicine*, 1976, *295*, 841.

Hallsten, E. A. Adolescent anorexia nervosa treated by desensitization. *Behavior Research Therapy*, 1965, *3*, 87-91.

Hare, R. D. Orientating and defensive responses to visual stimuli. *Psychophysiology*, 1973, *10*, 453-464.

Harris, M. B. Self-directed program for weight control: A pilot study. *Journal of Abnormal Psychology*, 1969, *74*, 263-270.

Heitmann, P., & Moller, N. The effect of metoclopramide on the gastroesophageal junctional zone and the distal esophagus in man. *Scandinavian Journal of Gastroenterology*, 1970, *5*, 620-626.

Heller, M. H., Levine, J., & Sohler, T. P. Gastric acidity and normally produced anxiety. *Psychosomatic Medicine*, 1953, *15*, 509-512.

Hendrix, T. R. The secretory function of the alimentary canal. In V. B. Mountcastle (Ed.), *Medical physiology*. St. Louis: C. V. Mosby, 1974.

Hill, R. B., & Kern, F. *The gastrointestinal tract*. Baltimore: Williams & Wilkins, 1977.

Hollander, D., & Harlan, J. Antacids vs. placebo in peptic ulcer therapy: A controlled double-blind investigation. *Journal of the American Medical Association*, 1973, *226*, 1181-1185.

Horwich, L., & Galloway, R. Treatment of gastric ulceration with carbenoxolone sodium: Clinical and radiological evaluation. *British Medical Journal*, 1965, *2*, 1274-1277.

Hunt, J. N., & Wales, R. C. Progress in patients with peptic ulceration treated for more than five years with polidine including a double-blind trial. *British Medical Journal*, 1966, *3*, 13-16.

Ippoliti, A. F., Maxwell, V., & Isenberg, J. I. The effect of various forms of milk on gastric acid secretion. *Annals of Internal Medicine*, 1976, *84*, 286-289.

Jacobson, E. D. Spastic esophagus and mucous colitis: Etiology and treatment by progressive relaxation. *Archives of Internal Medicine*, 1927, *39*, 433-445.

Jacobson, E. D. Recent advances in the gastrointestinal circulation and related areas: Comments on a symposium on gastrointestinal circulation. *Gastroenterology*, 1967, *52*, 332-337.

James, W. *The principles of psychology*. New York: Holt, Rinehart & Winston, 1890.

Jeejeebhoy, K. N. Symposium on peptic ulcer disease: Medical treatment of peptic ulcer. *Canadian Journal of Surgery*, 1978, *21*, 17-18.

Johnson, A. G. Controlled trial of metoclopramide in the treatment of flatulant dyspepsia. *British Medical Journal*, 1971, *2*, 25-26.

Kaiser, D. N., & Sandman, C. A. Physiological patterns accompanying complex problem solving during warning and nonwarning conditions. *Journal of Comparative and Physiological Psychology*, 1975, *89*, 356-363.

Kantor, J. L. A clinical study of some common anatomical abnormalities of the colon: I. Redundant colon. *American Journal of Roentgenology*, 1924, *12*, 414-430.

Kantor, J. L. A clinical study of some common anatomical abnormalities of the colon: II. The low cecum. *American Journal of Roentgenology*, 1925, *14*, 207-215.

Karush, A., Hiatt, R. B., & Daniels, G. E. Psychophysiological correlation in ulcerative colitis. *Psychosomatic Medicine*, 1955, *17*, 35-56.

Kerr, A. C. *The physiological regulation of salivary secretions in man*. New York: Pergamon Press, 1961.

Krasil'nikov, L. G., & Fishzon-Ryss, Y. Interpretation of electrogastrogram and its variants in healthy persons during digestion. *Terapeuticheskii Arkhiv*, 1963, *35*, 56-59.

Kukorelli, T., & Juhasz, G. Electroencephalographic synchronization induced by stimulation of small intestine and splanchnic nerve in cats. *Electroencephalography and Clinical Neurophysiology*, 1976, *41*, 491-500.

Lacey, J. I. Psychophysiological approaches to the evaluation of psychotherapeutic process and outcome. In E. A. Rubinstein & M. B. Parloff (Eds.), *Research in psychotherapy*. Washington, D.C.: American Psychological Assn., 1959.

Lacey, J. I. Somatic response patterning and stress: Some revisions of activation theory. In M. H. Appley & R. Trumbull (Eds.), *Psychological stress: Issues in research*. New York: Appleton-Century-Crofts, 1967.

Lacey, J. I., Kagan, J., Lacey, B. C., & Moss, H. The visceral level: Situational determinants and behavioral correlates of autonomic response patterns. In P. H. Knapp (Ed.), *Expression of the emotions in man*. New York: International Universities Press, 1963.

Lacey, J. I., & Lacey, B. C. Some autonomic-central nervous system interrelationships. In P. Black (Ed.), *Physiological correlates of emotion*. New York: Academic Press, 1970.

Lang, P. J., & Melamed, B. G. Case report: Avoidance conditioning therapy of an infant with chronic ruminative vomiting. *Journal of Abnormal Psychology*, 1969, *74*, 1-8.

Langley, L. L. *Physiology of man*. New York: Van Nostrand Reinhold, 1971.

Lashley, K. S. The human salivary reflex and its use in psychology. *Psychology Review*, 1916, *23*, 446-464.

Lawrence, J. S. Dietetic and other methods in the treatment of peptic ulcer. *Lancet*, 1952, *1*, 482-485.

Lazarus, R. S. *Psychological stress and coping process*. New York: McGraw-Hill, 1966.

Lazarus, R. S. Cognitive and personality factors underlying threat and coping. In M. H. Appley & R. Trumbull (Eds.), *Psychological stress: Issues in research*. New York: Appleton-Century-Crofts, 1967.

Lazarus, R. S. Emotions and adaptation: Conceptual and empirical relations. *Nebraska Symposium on Motivation*, 1968, pp. 175-270.

Lazarus, R. S., Speisman, J. C., Mordkoff, A. M., & Davison, L. A. A laboratory study of psychological stress produced by a motion picture film. *Psychological Monographs*, 1962, *76* (Whole No. 553).

Lennard-Jones, J. B., & Babouris, N. Effect of different foods on the acidioms of the gastric contents in patients with duodenal ulcer. *Gut*, 1965, *6*, 113-117.

Lilie, D. The electrogastrogram. In R. F. Thompson & M. M. Patterson (Eds.), *Bioelectric recording techniques* (Part C). New York: Academic Press, 1974.

Linscheid, T. R., & Cunningham, C. E. A controlled demonstration of the effectiveness of electric shock in the elimination of chronic infant rumination. *Journal of Applied Behavior Analysis*, 1977, *10*, 500.

MacGregor, I. L. The treatment of peptic ulcer. *New Zealand Journal of Medicine*, 1977, *86*, 86-88.

Mahl, G. F. Effect of chronic fear on the gastric secretion of HCL in dogs. *Psychosomatic Medicine*, 1949, *11*, 30-44.

Malhotra, S. L. New approaches to the pathogenesis of peptic ulcer based on the protective action of saliva with special reference to roughage, vegetable fibre and fermented milk products. *Medical Hypotheses*, 1978, *4*, 1-14.

Malmo, R. B., & Shagass, C. Physiologic study of symptom mechanisms on psychiatric patients under stress. *Psychosomatic Medicine*, 1949, *11*, 25-29.

Martin, W., & Morton, W. Clinical studies with the electrogastrogram. *AMA Archives of Surgery*, 1952, *65*, 382-397.

McCanne, T. R., & Sandman, C. A. Instrumental heart rate responses and visual perceptions: A preliminary study. *Psychophysiology*, 1974, *11*, 283-287.

Miller, N. E., & Dworkin, B. R. Effects of learning on visceral functions: Biofeedback. *New England Journal of Medicine*, 1977, *296*, 1274-1278.

Miller, W. E. Learning of visceral and glandular responses. *Science*, 1969, *163*, 434-445.

Moore, J. G., & Schenkenberg, T. Psychic control of gastric acid: Response to anticipated feeding and biofeedback training in man. *Gastroenterology*, 1974, *66*, 954-959.

Moos, R. H., & Engel, B. T. Psychophysiological reactions in hypertensive and arthritic patients. *Journal of Psychosomatic Research*, 1962, *6*, 227-241.

Natelson, B. The "executive" monkey revisited. In F. P. Brooks & P. W. Evens (Eds.), *Nerves and the gut*. Philadelphia: C. B. Slack, 1977.

Nelson, P. G. Cimetidine and mental confusion. *Lancet*, 1977, *2*, 928.

Nelson, T. S., & Kohatsu, S. Clinical electrogastrography and its relationship to gastric surgery. *American Journal of Surgery*, 1968, *116*, 215-222.

Novin, D., VanderWeele, D. A., & Rezek, M. Infusion of 2-deoxy-D-glucose into the hepatic portal system causes eating: Evidence for peripheral glucoreceptors. *Science*, 1973, *181*, 858-860.

Obrist, P. A., Webb, R. A., & Sutterer, J. R. Heart rate and somatic changes during aversive conditioning and a simple reaction time task. *Psychophysiology*, 1969, *5*, 696-723.

Palmai, G., & Blackwell, B. The diurnal pattern of salivary flow in normal and depressed patients. *British Journal of Psychiatry*, 1965, *111*, 334-338.

Palmer, E. D. *Clinical gastroenterology*. New York: Hoeber-Harper, 1957.

Palmer, W. L. The "acid test" in gastric and duodenal ulcer. *Journal of the American Medical Association*, 1927, *88*, 1778-1780.

Pavlov, I. P. [*Conditioned reflexes*] (G. V. Anrep, Ed. and trans.). London: Oxford University Press, 1927.

Peck, R. E. The SHP test — An aid in the detection and measurement of depression. *Archives of General Psychiatry*, 1959, *1*, 35-40.

Penick, S. B., Filion, R., & Fox, S. Behavior modification in the treatment of obesity. *Psychosomatic Medicine*, 1971, *33*, 49-55.

Polish, E., Brady, J. V., Mason, J. W., Thack, J. S., & Niemack, W. Gastric contents and the occurrence of duodenal lesions in the rhesus monkey during avoidance behavior. *Gastroenterology*, 1962, *43*, 193-201.

Porter, R. W., Brady, J. V., Conrad, D., Mason, J. W., Galambos, R., & Rioch, D. Some experimental observations on gastrointestinal lesions in behaviorally conditioned monkeys. *Psychosomatic Medicine*, 1958, *20*, 379-394.

Poth, E. J. A simplified technique for quantitative collection of salivary secretions of man. *Proceedings of the Society for Experimental Biology and Medicine*, 1933, *30*, 977-978.

Preisich, P., & Adam, G. La discrimination nonconsciente des stimuli duodenaux: Le test de differentiation d'habituation electroencephalographique. *Acta Gastro-Enterologica Belgica*, 1964, *27*, 625-629.

Razran, G. Conditioning and Perception. *Psychology Reivew*, 1955, *62*, 83-94.

Richet, C. Des proprietes cliniques et physiologiques du suc gastrique chez l'homme et les animaux. *App. A.J. d'Anatomie et Physiologie*, 1878, *14*, 170-333.

Rodin, J. The relationship between external responsiveness and the development and maintenance of obesity. In D. Novin, W. Wyrwicka, & G. A. Bray (Eds.), *Hunger: Basic mechanisms and clinical implications*. New York: Raven Press, 1976.

Rodin, J. Bidirectional influences of emotionality, stimulus responsivity and metabolic events in obesity. In J. Maser & M. Seligman (Eds.), *Psychopathology: Experimental models*. San Francisco: W. H. Freeman, 1977.

Rodin, J., Herman, C. P., & Schachter, S. Obesity and various tests of external sensitivity. In S. Schachter & J. Rodin (Eds.), *Obese humans and rats*. Washington, D. C.: Erlbaum/Wiley, 1974.

Rosenzweig, M. R. Salivary conditioning before Pavlov. *American Journal of Psychology*, 1959, *72*, 628-633.

Russell, R. W., & Stern, R. M. Gastric motility: The electrogastrogram. In P. Venables & I. Martin (Eds.), *A manual of psychophysiological methods*. Amsterdam: North Holland Publishing, 1967.

Sajwaj, T., Libet, J., & Agras, S. Lemon-juice therapy: The control of life-threatening rumination in a six-month-old infant. *Journal of Applied Behavior Analysis*, 1974, *7*, 557-563.

Sandman, C. A. Physiological responses during escape and non-escape from stress in field independent and field dependent subjects. *Biological Psychology*, 1975, *2*, 205-216.

Sandman, C. A., McCanne, T. R., Kaiser, D. N., & Diamond, B. Heart rate and cardiac phase influences on visual perception. *Journal of Comparative and Physiological Psychology*, 1977, *91*, 189-202.

Saxon, S., & Dahle, A. Auditory threshold variations during periods of induced high and low heart rates. *Psychophysiology*, 1971, *8*, 23-29.

Schachter, S., Goldman, R., & Gordon, J. A. Effects of fear, food deprivation and obesity on eating. *Journal of Personality and Social Psychology*, 1968, *10*, 91-97.

Schachter, S., & Rodin, J. (Eds.), *Obese humans and rats*. Washington, D. C.: Erlbaum/Wiley, 1974.

Schachter, S., & Singer, J. E. Cognitive, social and psychological determinants of emotional state. *Psychology Review*, 1962, *69*, 379-399.

Schneyer, L. H. Method for the collection of separate submaxillary and sublingual salivas in man. *Journal of Dental Research*, 1955, *34*, 257-261.

Schuster, M. M. Biofeedback treatment of gastrointestinal disorders. *Medical Clinics of North America*, 1977, *61*, 907-912.

Schuster, M. M., Nikoomanesh, P., & Wells, D. Biofeedback control of lower esophageal sphincter contraction in men. *Proceedings of the IV International Symposium on Gastrointestinal Motility*, 1973, pp. 138-144.

Schwartz, G. E. Psychosomatic disorders and biofeedback: A psychobiological model of disregulation. In J. D. Maser & M. P. Seligman (Eds.), *Psychopathology: Experimental models*. San Francisco: W. H. Freeman, 1977.

Selye, H. The general adaptation syndrome and the diseases of adaptation. *Journal of Clinical Endocrinology*, 1946, *6*, 117-128.

Sobakin, M. A., Smirnov, I. P., & Mishin, L. N. Electrogastrography. *Transactions on Biomedical Electronics*, 1962, pp. 129-132.

Stern, R. M., & Davis, C. M. *Electrogastrograms of subjects with subtotal gastric resections*. Paper presented to the Society for Psychophysiological Research, Philadelphia, 1977.

Stern, R. M., Ray, W. J., & Davis, C. M. *Psychophysiological recording*. New York: Oxford University Press, 1980.

Stevens, J. K., & Worrall, N. External recording of gastric activity: The electrogastrogram. *Physiological Psychology*, 1974, *2*, 175-180.

Streitfeld, H. S. The specificity of peptic ulcer to intense oral conflict. *Psychosomatic Medicine*, 1954, *16*, 315-326.

Stunkard, A. New therapies for the eating disorders. *Archives of General Psychiatry*, 1972, *26*, 391-398.

Stunkard, A. J., & Koch, C. The interpretation of gastric motility: I. Apparent bias in the reports of hunger by obese persons. *Archives of General Psychiatry*, 1964, *11*, 74-82.

Sturdevant, R., Isenberg, J., Secrist, D., & Ansfield, J. Antacid and placebo produced similar pain relief in duodenal ulcer patients. *Gastroenterology*, 1977, *72*, 1-5.

Sun, D. C., & Ryan, M. L. A controlled study on the use of propantheline and amylopectin sulphate (SM-263) for recurrences of duodenal ulcer. *Gastroenterology*, 1970, *58*, 756-761.

Taboroff, L. H., & Brown, W. H. Study of the personality patterns of children and adolescents with a peptic ulcer syndrome. *American Journal of Orthopsychiatry*, 1954, *24*, 602-610.

Toister, R. P., Colin, J., Worley, L. M., & Arthur, D. Faradic therapy of chronic vomiting in infancy: A case study. *Journal of Behavior Therapy and Experimental Psychiatry*, 1975, *6*, 55-59.

Truelove, E. L., Bixler, D., & Merritt, A. D. Simplified method of collection of pure submandibular saliva in large volumes. *Journal of Dental Research*, 1967, *46*, 1400-1403.

Truelove, S. C. Movements of the large intestine. *Physiology Reviews*, 1966, *46*, 457-512.

Tuczek, F. Cited in K. S. Lashley, The human salivary reflex and its use in psychology. *Psychological Review*, 1916, *23*, 446-464.

Walan, A. Studies on peptide ulcer disease with special reference to the effect of L-hyoscyamine. *Acta Medica Scandinavica*, 1970, *516* (Suppl.), 1-57.

Walker, B. B., Lawton, C. A., & Sandman, C. A. Voluntary control of electrogastric activity. *Psychosomatic Medicine*, 1978, *40*, 610-619.

Walker, B. B., & Sandman, C. A. Physiological response patterns in ulcer patients: Phasic and tonic components of the electrogastrogram. *Psychophysiology*, 1977, *14*, 393-400.

Walker, B. B., & Sandman, C. A. Human visual evoked responses are related to heart rate. *Journal of Comparative and Physiological Psychology*, 1979, *93*, 717-729.

Walker, B. B., & Sandman, C. A., & Cacioppo, J. T. Individual differences in the physiological concomitants of human operant heart rate conditioning. In preparation.

Wangel, A. G., & Deller, D. J. Intestinal motility in man. III. Mechanisms of constipation and diarrhea with particular reference to the irritable colon syndrome. *Gastroenterology*, 1965, *48*, 69-84.

Wardell, D. Stimulus intensity and introversion-extraversion. *British Journal of Social and Clinical Psychology*, 1974, *13*, 425-426.

Weinstock, S. A. The reestablishment of intestinal control in functional colitis. *Biofeedback and Self-Regulation*, 1976, *1*, 324-325. (Abstract)

Weisman, A. D. A study of psychodynamics of duodenal ulcer exacerbations with special reference to treatment and the problem of specificity. *Psychosomatic Medicine*, 1956, *28*, 2-42.

Weiss, J. M. Ulcers. In J. Maser & M. Seligman (Eds.), *Psychopathology: Experimental models*. San Francisco: W. H. Freeman, 1977.

Weiss, J. M. Pohorecky, L. A., Salmon, S., & Gruenthal, M. Attenuation of gastric lesions by psychological aspects of aggression in rats. *Journal of Comparative and Physiological Psychology*, 1976, *90*, 252-259.

Welgan, P. R. Learned control of gastric acid secretion in ulcer patients. *Psychosomatic Medicine*, 1974, *36*, 411-419.

Welgan, P. R. Biofeedback control of stomach acid secretions and gastrointestinal reactions. In J. Beatty and J. Legewie (Eds.), *Biofeedback and behavior*. New York: Plenum Press, 1977.

Wenger, M. A., Engel, B. T., Clemens, T. L., & Cullen, T. D. Stomach motility in man recorded by the magnetometer method. *Gastroenterology*, 1961, *41*, 479-485.

White, J. D., & Taylor, D. Noxious conditioning as a treatment for rumination. *Mental Retardation*, 1967, *5*, 30-33.

White, K. D. Salivation: A review and experimental investigation of major techniques. *Psychophysiology*, 1977, *14*, 203-212.

Whitehead, W. E. *Gastrointestinal biofeedback*. Unpublished report of the Biofeedback Society of America Task Force, 1978.

Whitehead, W. E., Renault, P. F., & Goldiamond, I. Modification of human gastric acid secretion with operant-conditioning procedures. *Journal of Applied Behavior Analysis*, 1975, *8*, 147-156.

Wolf, S., & Almy, T. P. Experimental observations on cardiospasm in man. *Gastroenterology*, 1949, *13*, 401-421.

Wolf, S., & Welsh, J. D. The gastrointestinal tract as a responsive system. In N. Greenfield and R. Sternbach (Eds.), *Handbook of psychophysiology*. New York: Holt, Rinehart & Winston, 1972.

Wolf, S., & Wolff, H. G. *Human gastric function*. New York: Oxford University Press, 1947.

Wollersheim, J. P. The effectiveness of group therapy based upon learning principles in the treatment of overweight women. *Journal of Abnormal Psychology*, 1970, *76*, 462-474.

Woodbury, D. M. Analgesic-antipyretics, anti-inflammatory agents and inhibitors of uric acid synthesis. In L. Goodman and A. Gilman (Eds.), *The pharmacological basis of therapeutics*. London: Macmillan, 1970.

Woods, S. C., Decke, E., & Vasselli, T. R. Metabolic hormones and regulation of body weight. *Psychological Review*, 1974, *81*, 26-43.

5

A PSYCHOPHYSIOLOGICAL PERSPECTIVE ON THE ETIOLOGY AND TREATMENT OF INSOMNIA

Hildreth D. Youkilis

Richard R. Bootzin

INTRODUCTION

Insomnia refers to a heterogeneous set of problems reflecting a disturbance of the sleep process. Sleep may be disrupted in various ways; these include difficulty in falling asleep, frequent or prolonged awakenings, premature awakening in the morning, or the subjective impression of an unsatisfactory quantity or quality of overall sleep. Although objective assessments are available, which may or may not corroborate a person's reported difficulty in sleeping, many researchers and clinicians contend that the subjective criteria ultimately outweigh the objective signs in importance (Kleitman, 1963).

Enormous individual differences exist in sleep requirements. For example, of two individuals who experience relatively long sleep onset latencies (that is, more than thirty minutes), one may describe himself or herself as an insomniac, while the other may not. Similar differences may be observed among people who awaken during the night and/or generally obtain less than seven to eight hours of sleep. Thus, a definitional or diagnostic question of insomnia arises when an individual reports sleeping for relatively short amounts nightly but exhibits no appreciable negative effects during the day. There appears to be general agreement among clinicians that if a person sleeps for less than seven to eight hours, which is the average for healthy adults, but experiences no energy loss or increased irritability the next day, he or she is getting an adequate amount of sleep. Reports have been made, in fact, of individuals who regularly sleep as little as two or three hours per night over a number of years. They were found to be in good health, showed no detrimental effects, and expressed no complaints (Jones & Oswald, 1968; Meddis, Pearson, & Langford, 1973).

Although the variability in sleep patterns of those with sleep complaints makes it difficult to define insomnia, researchers at sleep laboratories typically operationalize insomnia as (1) a sleep onset latency in excess of thirty minutes, (2) a total of thirty minutes or more spent awake during the night, and (3) less than six and one-half hours of overall sleep (Dement & Guilleminault, 1973). Although these criteria provide useful normative discriminations, they do not constitute a functional and/or clinical definition of insomnia, since they do not include assessment of fatigue, irritability, and performance decrements the next day. In addition, chronic insomniacs show considerable night-to-night variability on sleep indices, making single-night criteria for insomnia rather inefficient and potentially invalid as standards for identifying insomniacs (Karacan, 1971).

Several epidemiologic studies have been conducted in order to more accurately determine the incidence of insomnia within the general population (Karacan, Warheit, Thornby, & Schwab, 1973). Using a survey sampling approach, Kales, Bixler, Leo, Healey, and Slye (1974) canvassed one thousand households in metropolitan Los Angeles and found that 32.2% of the respondents reported having one or more symptoms of insomnia. In addition, sleep disturbances were found to increase linearly with age. Overall, females reported greater difficulty sleeping and greater use of hypnotic drugs than males. A sample of 2,336 subjects sampled in Scotland (McGhie & Russell, 1962) showed similar trends for both age and sex of the respondents. Karacan and his colleagues (Karacan, Thornby, Anch, Holzer, Warheit, Schwab, & Williams, 1976) sampled 1,645 subjects in an urban Florida county in order to find the distribution and severity of sleep disturbances in this population. Results of this survey indicated that 35% of the respondents reported having trouble sleeping at least some of the time, with 13% of those on a chronic basis. In general, trouble falling asleep was the major complaint (68.5%), while staying asleep (19%), insufficient amount of sleep (8.1%), and early awakening (3.9%) followed in order of difficulty. (In contrast, Kales et al. [1974] found that frequent awakening was a more frequent sleep complaint than trouble falling asleep.) Type of sleeping difficulty was found to interact with age. Individuals in the twenty-thirty-nine-year-old bracket, for example, reported that inadequate amount of sleep was most troublesome, while those in the forty-forty-nine-year-old age group reported greater difficulty with awakening too early. These differences may reflect natural developmental trends as well as differences in life-style, pressures, and economic or interpersonal demands. While this survey reported sex differences in the same direction as previous surveys, those differences did not appear until after the age of twenty-nine. Reporting the greatest sleeping difficulties were older, nonsingle women of lower socioeconomic status. Although exact percentages of the number of individuals suffering from sleep disturbances shift among investigations, regional and seasonal differences as well as variations in survey instruments may account for some of this variation.

Objective measures (that is, behavioral observations and electrophysiological polygraph recordings, such as electromyogram [EMG], electrooculogram [EOG], and electroencephalogram [EEG]) have been applied during all-night sleep laboratory studies in order to validate verbal complaints of insomnia. Dement (1972) noted that approximately half the patients seen at the Stanford Sleep Clinic showed no relationship between the reported severity of the problem and the amount of sleep they obtained in the sleep laboratory. The other half of these patients had their subjective sleeping difficulties confirmed through EEG records. On the basis of the degree of correspondence between subjective and objective reports, those who showed high agreement were classified as *idiopathic insomniacs*; those who demonstrated poor or no agreement Dement labeled *pseudoinsomniacs*. This differential diagnosis may prove to be an important one, not only for investigating etiology, but also for tailoring treatment to the specific needs of the individual. Without sleep laboratory data, however, it is not possible to make this differential diagnosis. Measures used in current epidemiologic studies, therefore, are not adequate for determining what percentages of the general population fit these respective categories.

A number of laboratory investigations have confirmed Dement's (1972) observations of the discrepancy often found between subjective measures of insomnia and electrophysiological measures (Bixler, Kales, Leo, & Slye, 1974; Borkovec & Weerts, 1976; Carskadon, Dement, Mitler, Guilleminault, Zarconi, & Spiegel, 1976; Dement & Guilleminault, 1973; Karacan, Salis, & Williams, 1973). In these studies, subjects consistently reported that they took longer to fall asleep than indicated by EEG criteria. Some general comments are in order, at this point, regarding the interpretation and judgment of such discrepancies in assessment. Webb (1975) pointed out that EEG measures serve many critical needs for accurate, reliable measurement, in that they are continuous, widely applicable, stable, and sensitive. Although this is an easily defensible position, this measurement modality should not be considered sacrosanct. In particular, sleep and sleep onset represent states which can be operationalized in multiple ways. Each evaluation mode represents one particular version of the reality of the situation. Thus, in addition to EEG measures, it has been found that the type and quantity of mental activity, the observations made of sleep-related behavior, and the changes in particular physiological states provide more comprehensive criteria for determining whether or not a person is asleep.

Significant discrepancies between any two or more of these modalities merit careful interpretation. Where electrophysiological measures of brain activity differ from subjective impressions of time of sleep onset, the sleep problem has been labeled *pseudoinsomnia*. In the past, as reflected by this label, discrepancies between EEG and verbal report have been interpreted routinely as indicating that the verbal report is wrong and the EEG measure is the "real" measure of sleeping difficulty. It is just as likely, however, that the pseudoinsomniac has severe sleeping difficulties to which EEG measures are not sensitive. Thus, EEG and verbal report measures provide convergent, but somewhat independent, information about sleep. Both may be required to obtain a complete picture.

A CONSIDERATION OF THE ROLE OF SLEEP

An evaluation of the nature of insomnia would not be complete without raising these questions: "What is the purpose of sleep?" and "What happens if a person is deprived of sleep?" These two questions have particular relevance for the understanding of both natural and disturbed sleep patterns and their subsequent effects on waking behavior.

Hartmann (1973) provided an excellent review of current theories of the function of sleep. Among those theories, many of which have been tested extensively, are those which propose that the primary function of sleep is restorative, in that it prevents fatigue and balances the demands of wakefulness (Claparède, 1908). Pavlov (1952) conceptualized sleep as a protective mechanism, the onset of which is prompted by either insufficient or excessive stimulation. He viewed this protective inhibition or hindrance as therapeutic. In some senses, then, this function suggests a homeostasis in the brain between excitement and inhibition. Ephron and Carrington (1966) extended this position to examine the differential functions of rapid eye movement (REM) versus non-REM sleep. Within their formulation, non-REM sleep is a period of relative sensory deprivation, which is necessary within a limited period; REM sleep is important in that it serves to restore the homeostasis by introducing cortical excitement or stimulation.

Several theories of the function of sleep emphasize its role in learning and memory. Jackson (1932) suggested that the function of sleep is related to memory in a two-fold manner. During sleep, irrelevant information memories can be erased, while more critical daily input is organized and synthesized. Similarly, Greenberg and Pearlman (1974) extended this position by proposing an information-processing and -integrating model of sleep. On the other hand, Lewin and Glaubman (1975) demonstrated that the mental activity observed during REM sleep is not necessarily integrative in nature. Rather, they found it to be divergent, creative, and exploratory. Glaubman, Orbach, Aviram, Frieder, Frieman, Pelled, and Glaubman (1978) confirmed this position by replicating and extending the Lewin and Glaubman (1975) study. According to the latter results, REM sleep, more than non-REM sleep, appears to be instrumental in an individual's ability to adapt to novel situations.

THE CONSEQUENCES OF SLEEP DEPRIVATION

Many of the above noted theories have been tested by means of experimentally induced sleep deprivation. This involves either prohibiting an individual from sleeping altogether or selectively depriving him or her of sleep during various sleep stages. Any changes in behavior noted as a result of this process may be construed as a consequence of the sleep loss. There is a substantial body of literature on sleep deprivation, dating back to the middle of the nineteenth century (Patrick & Gilbert, 1896). Reviews of this literature (see Horne, 1978; Naitoh, 1976; Wilkinson, 1965) have reported that, in general, there is little evidence that total sleep deprivation produces any significant biochemical or psychophysiological effects on the subject. Neurologic evaluations, however, are able to detect signs of distress following sixty hours of sleep deprivation (Sassin, 1970). These include nystagmus, neck muscle weakness, tremors in the hands, and swaying or rhythmic body movements. As noted by Webb and Cartwright (1978), psychological distortions, such as hallucinations and illusions, tend to be rare and tend not to occur with less than sixty hours of sleep deprivation. The appearance of a number of other psychological disturbances has been reported with progressive sleep deprivation of up to ninety hours. In addition to visual misperception, these include temporal and cognitive disorientation and occasional examples of incoherent speech. Within one or two nights of recovery sleep, however, all these symptoms disappear. Various indices of performance decrements have been noted as well, but they tend to be task specific. A number of studies, however, have reported no psychological effects resulting from total sleep deprivation, and, paradoxically, for certain psychopathological disorders, such as depression, sleep deprivation has therapeutic effects.

Among the methodological considerations which arise in sleep deprivation experimentation are the ability to generalize between imposed and naturally occurring sleep deprivation, variations in deprivation time among investigations, individual differences in subjects' natural sleep patterns (such as sleep deprivation in normal versus insomniac populations), and individual differences in physiological responsiveness to sleep deprivation. All these issues need to be considered when determining whether or not sleep deprivation has an impact on various aspects of human functioning.

Traditional methods for keeping subjects awake involve providing constant stimulation while minimizing physical exertion. The excessive mental stimulation to which subjects are exposed may account for much of the observed impairment in intellectual functioning. This possibility should be considered as one explanation for observed decrements instead of, or in addition to, any effects derived directly from sleep loss. Investigations vary the length of sleep deprivation that subjects encounter. While there may be no evidence of physical or psychological change during a twenty-four hour period, alterations may be observed over longer periods. In addition, subjects vary among themselves in the amount of sleep they usually obtain. Thus, more detrimental effects may be observed in individuals who generally sleep for long periods and are experimentally prevented from sleeping, while such profound differences may be unnoticed in individuals who regularly demand less sleep. These differences, as well as other individual variations, need to be taken into consideration.

Furthermore, for a variety of practical and ethical reasons, most of the sleep deprivation studies have included healthy, young, male subjects. Although adverse consequences of sleep deprivation appear to be minimal in this population, it may not be the case for dissimilar populations. To the extent that it is feasible, it is important to determine the degree to which this population is representative of the general population. Finally, since it is well known that individuals differ considerably in autonomic responsiveness, group means may obfuscate differences within individuals in physiological responses to sleep deprivation. Replicated single-case designs may be desirable methods for considering both clinical and experimental changes which may arise.

PROCEDURES AND ISSUES IN THE ASSESSMENT OF INSOMNIA

The normal sleep process is comprised of various stages which cyclically alternate throughout the entire course of the night. Because of these natural changes in sleep, which have been noted both prior to and subsequent to the use of sophisticated electrophysiological equipment, agreement on the meaning of sleep and sleeplessness has varied among clinicians, researchers, and sleepers. In particular, some have regarded the percentage of time spent in particular sleep stages (as determined through electrophysiological measurement or the amount of physical movement) as the best criterion of a good night's sleep. Others, however, have relied on the subjective daily reports of individuals whose sleep is being evaluated. Those who favor the latter method have maintained that these data provide more critical determinants of both the quality and quantity of sleep obtained.

A number of other, indirect indices of sleep and sleep disturbances, such as reports by roommates and spouses, subjective accounts of daytime efficiency, and pupillography, have been included by some researchers. While some clinicians and researchers have expressed a strong preference for one method over another, there is obvious value in incorporating several forms of evaluation. In particular, multiple measurement enhances the understanding of the multifaceted nature of insomnia. The convergent validity among measures unfortunately, has not always been high.

The Nature of Sleep and Its Measurement

Sleep stages have been discerned through tracings made from electrophysiological instrumentation (Aserinsky & Kleitman, 1953, 1955; Loomis, Harvey, & Hobart, 1937). All-night sleep recordings of brain activity have demonstrated that, rather than "falling" into a state of sleep, normal, healthy adults progress gradually through regularly occurring sequences of sleep stages. These stages rhythmically alternate throughout the night. Rechtschaffen and Kales (1968) provided scoring procedures for differentiating various stages of sleep, which have been accepted as standards.

In brief, electroencephalographic (EEG) patterns indicate that wakefulness is characterized by both *alpha waves* (8-12 cps) and low-voltage activity of mixed frequency. During sleep onset, alpha rhythm is gradually terminated as stage 1 appears. *Stage 1* is the lightest stage of sleep. It is illustrated by low-voltage (4-6 cps) and regular and irregular activity. Stage 1 lasts for only a few minutes and is followed by the onset of stage 2. *Stage 2* is characterized by the appearance of *sleep spindles* (brief bursts of waves at 12-14 cps) and *K complexes* (a high amplitude negative wave followed by a positive wave). After several more minutes, high-voltage (at least 75 μv) slow waves (1-4 cps) emerge, which are called *delta waves*. This stage (*stage 3*) lasts for approximately 10 minutes. This is followed by *stage 4*, the deepest level of sleep. During this stage, delta waves predominate (in excess of 50%). The sleeper experiences the soundest sleep of the night during these periods.

Sleep spindles may also be observed in both stages 3 and 4, usually in response to auditory stimulation. Individuals in this deep, stage 4 sleep are very difficult to arouse. Children, in particular, may take several minutes to become aware of their environment when awakened while in this sleep stage. Night terrors, somnambulism, and bed-wetting, all seemingly active disturbances in children, surprisingly appear during this deepest period of sleep.

The initial progression through sleep stages 1 through 4 takes approximately thirty to forty minutes. At this time, an individual begins to regress back through each of these stages. This entire progression-regression period lasts approximately seventy to ninety minutes. When the stage 1 sleep pattern reappears, there is a notable difference in that, along with the mixed frequency EEG pattern, saw-toothed waves now appear. Furthermore, rapid eye movements begin, as recorded in the electrooculogram (EOG) tracings, coupled with a decrease in submental muscle activity, as measured by electromyogram (EMG) activity. These combined indices reflect a very different sleep state than noted during the earlier stage 1 period. This active stage has several labels: it is most commonly referred to as *REM sleep* but has also been called *desynchronous*, *paradoxical*, and *active* sleep. The period which precedes REM sleep is referred to as *NREM* (non-REM) *sleep*, alternatively known as *synchronous, orthodox*, or *quiet* sleep.

A number of sleep laboratories have demonstrated empirically that NREM and REM sleep cycles persist throughout the night. The duration from one REM episode to the next averages approximately ninety minutes. The frequency and duration of particular sleep stages, however, vary over the course of the night (Dement, 1972; Feinberg, 1974). For example, the earlier part of the night typically consists predominantly of NREM, slow wave sleep (stages 3 and 4), with a short REM period averaging ten minutes in length. As the night wears on, subsequent sleep cycles show a shift toward progressively shorter NREM periods and longer REM intervals. The time spent in REM sleep, in fact, can last up to sixty minutes toward morning.

Even prior to EEG measurement, a variety of physiological changes had been noted to accompany changes in sleep states (MacWilliam, 1923). During NREM sleep, respiration becomes slow and regular, pulse rate slow and steady, and blood pressure and body temperature lowered. The reverse holds for REM sleep (Snyder, Hobson, Morrison, & Goldfrank, 1964; Williams & Cartwright, 1969). Changes have also been noted in muscle tension. While relaxation of the gross muscles is seen during NREM periods, in contrast with waking periods, these muscles become functionally immobilized during REM sleep (Jacobson, Kales, Lehman, & Hoedemacher, 1964; Jouvet, 1962). Small muscles may be observed to twitch from time to time during this period, however. Other physiological changes noted during REM sleep are penile erections in the male, irrespective of dream content (Fisher, Gross, & Zuch, 1965; Karacan, Goodenough, Shapiro, & Starker, 1966); increased cerebral blood flow (Reivich, Isaacs, Evarts, & Kety, 1968); and elevated brain temperature (Kawamura & Sawyer, 1965).

Arousability is another variable which has been examined during sleep. Arousal thresholds appear to be highest during both stage 4 sleep and REM sleep. While it is consistent to expect this relationship during stage 4, the sleep stage associated with the deepest sleep, it is counterintuitive with REM sleep, which is marked by EEG criteria for light sleep (Williams, Hammack, Daly, Dement, & Lubin, 1964).

Ontogenetic and phylogenetic studies have been conducted in order to understand both the degree to which human sleep is similar or dissimilar to other species and the degree to which human sleep varies throughout one's lifetime. Sleep, as we define it, does not occur to species lower than amphibians on the phylogenetic scale. Periods of quiescence versus activity can be discerned in amphibians and some fish. Most reptiles, however, appear to experience a sleep state similar to NREM but show no evidence of full REM periods (Tauber, Rojas-Ramirez, & Hernandez-Peon, 1968). Most mammals, even the more primitive varieties, demonstrate differentiable periods of REM and NREM sleep (see Freemon, 1972; Hartmann, 1967; Snyder, 1964). There is tremendous variance among mammalian species in the amount of sleep obtained per day. The sloth, for example, sleeps as much as twenty hours, while the elephant sleeps only four. Similarly, the REM-to-REM cycles vary across species, with the mouse taking approximately four minutes to complete the cycle, the adult human ninety minutes, and the elephant over one hundred minutes (Hartmann, 1967).

Ontogenetic differences have also been noted by sleep researchers. It is particularly noteworthy that the amount of REM in the mammalian neonate is remarkably large. The newborn sleeps approximately sixteen to eighteen hours per day, with at least 50% of this time in REM. Premature infants have been shown to spend as much as 75% of sleep time in a REM state, which has caused researchers to speculate that REM time in utero may be even greater than in the newborn (Astic & Jouvet-Monnier, 1970). With age, the overall amount of sleep declines to approximately seven to eight hours per night in adulthood and six hours in the elderly. While the greatest amounts of both REM sleep and stage 4 sleep are found in infancy, a gradual decline is observed in these stages as one reaches young adulthood. Typically, a young adult spends 50% of sleep time in stage 2, 25% in REM, 10% in stage 3, 10% in stage 4, and 5% in stage 1

(Mendelson, Gillin, & Wyatt, 1977). These changes may be even more profound in the elderly, who show continued decreases in stages 3 and 4 and increases in stage 1 and wakefulness. The nature of the changes in sleeping patterns which occur throughout one's lifetime suggests a "natural" progression toward "insomnia," which can serve as a standard by which to compare "problematical" insomnia. This natural shift in sleeping patterns, both across and within species, has served to stimulate researchers to understand the basic functions that sleep and its component stages serve. Understanding the natural course of sleep in normal individuals aids in defining and understanding deviations from these patterns.

The Evaluation of Insomnia

Electrophysiological Measures

An initial screening for the evaluation of insomnia should begin with data derived from a general medical examination. In order to accurately assess the nature and intensity of an individual's sleep problem, it is crucial to know his or her current physical health status and to obtain a list of all medications recently used. In the absence of detectable medical problems or drug influences, additional evaluation is warranted which specifically focuses on the patient's sleep patterns and factors which may influence those patterns.

Electrophysiological recordings of sleep are currently being used more routinely for evaluating insomnia. These measures include an electroencephalogram (EEG) to evaluate changes in brain activity, electrooculogram (EOG) to determine the amount and frequency of eye movement, and an electromyogram (EMG) to indicate changes in muscle tension. Measurement is taken through continuous, all-night monitoring in a sleep laboratory. Webb (1975) maintained that EEG measures, in particular, represent the best and most efficient modality for evaluating and discriminating sleep disturbances. There is a lack of universal agreement, however, that this is the best measure of an individual's sleeping difficulty. Since electrophysiological measures are taken within a laboratory setting, a person's sleeping ability may be influenced by this novel setting. In addition, latency of sleep onset and the number of awakenings during the night may be affected by emotional factors related to being subjected to an evaluation procedure of this nature, thereby threatening the reliability of the sleep stage information obtained.

Several investigations have used EEG data to compare insomniacs with non-sleep-disturbed control subjects. The findings from these studies have been equivocal. For example, while some investigations have demonstrated that insomniacs have diminished slow wave sleep (e.g., Coursey, Buchsbaum, & Frankel, 1975; Kales, 1969), others have reported no differences (e.g., Monroe, 1967). Similar disagreement between studies has been reported for the amount of REM sleep obtained between groups. Gaillard (1976) demonstrated that insomniacs showed either excessive or deficient amounts of REM in contrast to control subjects. A number of investigations, however, did not replicate these differences (Kales, 1969). Between-investigation variability may be due to a lack of standardization on measures between laboratories as well as the night in-residence measures were collected. Since insomniacs have been shown to have greater night-to-night variability on a number of measures (Hartmann, 1973), it is necessary to establish a meaningful baseline.

Most recently, researchers have employed all-night sleep recording measures collected in the home of the patient (Coates, Rosekind, & Thoresen, 1978). The merits of this method remain to be compared with sleep laboratory methods. The more obvious benefits are that the patient does not have to leave his or her natural environment and adapt to a sleep laboratory. Rather, a familiar object, such as the telephone, can be used to transmit information to a computer located at the sleep laboratory, while the subject sleeps in his or her own bed.

Other physiological measures are important to collect when evaluating the nature of an individual's insomnia problem. While physiological changes can be important indices of sleep disturbances, they are not included routinely. The fortuitous finding of respiratory irregularity and its role in sleep apnea illustrates the importance of looking at other physiological systems when assessing the source of the sleep disturbance. Since galvanic skin response (GSR), body temperature, heart rate, and respiration are some of the more consistently used measures of arousal, they could prove beneficial in determining the degree to which they play a role in an individual's insomnia. Unfortunately, this data must be collected within a sleep laboratory and may not be practical to collect on a wide scale basis.

Subjective Measures

Subjective reports of sleeping difficulties are perhaps the most widely used source of evaluation. After all, it is the patient's complaint of insomnia that most often induces physicians, psychiatrists, and psychologists to design treatments for coping with this problem. Almost any treatment of insomnia relies on the patient's subjective evaluation as a variable in determining treatment effectiveness. Self-report measures, however, vary considerably. These include global interview questions, such as, "How upsetting is it to you if you are unable to sleep?" or "Are you sleeping better?". An effort to collect more reliable self-report data is represented by more specific assignments to the patient to keep a diary of self-observed, sleep-related information on a daily basis. These data include the patient's phenomenological impressions and are a rich source of information.

For both clinicians and researchers, however, these measures are not without their problems. In particular, subjective impressions are often biased. Insomniacs have been found to overestimate their difficulties in falling asleep and remaining asleep (Borkovec & Weerts, 1976; Carskadon et al., 1976). Discrepancies between perceived and actual sleeping abilities may also arise during the course of treatment. In some cases, subjects may want to appear as cooperative or "good" patients. In that event, their estimates of improvement may be exaggerated in the positive direction. Other patients may believe that there may be undesirable consequences from eliminating their sleeping problem. Thus, they may either inadvertently or intentionally exaggerate the distress they are experiencing.

One way to reduce the bias of global, subjective reports is to use more reliable measurement. Objective questionnaires may suit this need by requiring a patient to record specific information in a structured format such as, the amount of time slept the previous night, bedtime habits, the time of awakening, and the number of awakenings. Daily entries of this type of information are more likely to be reliable than are retrospective accounts made at less frequent intervals. General self-reports have been shown to be less sensitive to treatment effectiveness than are daily recordings of this nature (Nicassio & Bootzin, 1974). Behavioral researchers, in particular, have relied heavily on daily self-observations in both process and outcome evaluations of treatment effectiveness (Borkovec & Fowles, 1973; Nicassion & Bootzin, 1974). Self-observation measures have also been useful for making a functional analysis of sleep disturbances; that is, patients may be able to specify antecedents and consequences of poor sleep.

Independent Observations

To either complement or replace self-observations, various investigators have relied on other individuals' observations of the patient's sleeping behavior. This method was used in an early study of the sleeping behavior of children in an orphanage (Boynton & Goodenough, 1930). Periodic observations made by spouses or roommates of patients in treatment have been found to be a beneficial adjunct for validating other sleep measures. In a study by Tokarz and Lawrence (1974), roommates of students with sleeping problems were trained to make systematic behavioral observations. When these reports were compared with similar measures completed by the insomniacs, the percentage of agreement was remarkably high. Thus, the authors concluded that insomniacs' self-reports are reliable. Other researchers have reported similar interrater agreement (Nicassio & Bootzin, 1974; Nicassio, Boylan, & McCabe, 1976). One cannot minimize the importance of training subjects to make accurate self-observations, if these measures are to be used.

An evaluation of insomnia would not be complete without determining the importance of stressful, situational, or other external factors on the problem. For example, a new baby, job changes and/or demands, a move to a new home, family problems — all may affect the way people sleep.

Sources of Insomnia

A great deal of effort has been directed toward uncovering the etiology of disordered sleep patterns. On a gross level, clinicians and researchers have attempted to evaluate whether or not the complaint of insomnia is accompanied by a more profound physical or psychological disturbance. In those cases where sleeping difficulties cannot be related to other remarkable signs or symptoms of pathology, the distinction *primary insomnia* is made. In contrast, insomnia which appears to result from other clinical problems is considered *secondary insomnia*. A number of researchers have stressed the importance of making a differential diagnosis of primary or secondary insomnia (Greenberg, 1977; Hauri, 1975; Pai, 1969; Williams & Karacan, 1973). According to a number of researchers, diagnostic differences may be particularly important for treatment planning (Dement, 1972; Kales & Kales, 1973). The validity of dichotomizing insomnia on the basis of presumed causal mechanisms, however, remains to be demonstrated.

The multitude of suggested causes of insomnia can be subsumed into the following general categories: gross or microscopic physiological disturbances, physical pathology, drug effects, dream and mental activity, personality style and psychopathology, situational or environmental influences, and behavioral effects or contingencies for sleeplessness. These problem areas should not be considered to be entirely independent of one another. Rather, in chronic sleep disorders, they are found in various, interactive combinations.

Physiological Disturbances

At the gross level, disturbances in respiration, sensations, and muscle activity have been linked to sleeping difficulty. Sleep *apnea* (Gastaut, Duron, Tassinari, Lyagoubi, & Saier, 1969; Guilleminault, Eldridge, & Dement, 1972) is a disorder in which the sufferer stops breathing at the time of sleep onset. In these patients, it appears that the diaphragm and intercostal muscles become paralyzed for fifteen to thirty seconds after sleep begins. This is followed by a collapse of the throat, which obstructs air from passing to the lungs. Although the diaphragm and intercostal muscles regain their activity, the patient is still unable to breathe due to the throat remaining collapsed. After a period lasting up to as much as one minute, the patient regains the ability to take in air. The air intake frequently takes on the sounds of snoring at this point. The patient, in turn, generally is awakened. Sleep laboratory recordings have shown that patients suffering from this disturbance may awaken as much as five hundred times during the night (Dement, 1972). There appear to be no accurate, current estimates of the occurrence of this disorder in the general population. Only in recent years have basic research efforts focused on the importance of respiratory activity during sleep (Phillipson, 1978). Therefore, the malfunctioning respiratory adaptation to sleep found in insomniacs who also exhibit sleep apnea and/or other related problems may be more prevalent than previously considered.

Disturbing sensations felt in the legs and occasionally in the arms during sleep may contribute to sleeping difficulties. *Restless legs syndrome* develops in response to the dysesthesia which the patient experiences during rest. The leg movements appear to be posturing responses which ease or avoid those disturbing feelings (Ekbom, 1960; Frankel, Patten, & Gillin, 1974). Laboratory studies have documented this syndrome and described the ensuing sleep disruption from the perspective of EEG, other physiological recordings, and direct observations. In addition, more profound leg movements have been observed in certain patients who are unable to remain asleep. *Nocturnal myoclonus* is a disorder in which the muscles of the lower legs jerk during sleep. These jerking movements have been found to correlate positively with arousal in both self-reported measures and EEG recordings.

In addition to physical disturbances occurring at a gross level, physiological difficulties at more basic levels have been suggested as causal factors in insomnia. Data obtained from basic research in neuroendocrinology, for example, have established that there are relationships between naturally occurring secretions of anterior-pituitary-regulated hormones and various aspects of sleep. The presence of particular hormones is associated with the onset of particular sleep stages and varies under certain environmental changes or sleep deprivation. Thus, it is possible that these hormones may be involved in both sleep regulation and disregulation. For example, Johns, Gay, Masterson, and Bruce (1971) reported that insomniacs have higher levels of adrenocortical hormones than controls. This finding suggests that the presence of these hormones may elevate the arousal level, thereby disrupting sleep or restfulness. A more recent study by Frankel, Buchbinder, Coursey, and Snyder (1973), however, was unable to find a consistent relationship between adrenocortical level and insomnia. While hormones play a role in sleep, it is obviously a complex one, and future research directed toward evaluating the hormonal and biochemical differences both between individuals and within a particular individual during periods of sleeping difficulty is needed.

Physical Pathology

Insomnia often accompanies various physical illnesses. Sleep disturbances may arise from the discomfort associated with an illness as well as from other aspects of the disease process. Pain and discomfort make sleep difficult, if not impossible, for many people. Temporary aches and pains in the muscles, irritations, itching or burning sensations of the skin, nasal congestion, fevers, and many other symptoms impair sleep. More chronic diseases, such as duodenal ulcers (Armstrong, Burnap, Jacobson, Kales, Ward, & Golden, 1965; Dragstedt, 1959), renal insufficiency and hypothyroidism (Williams & Karacan, 1973), nocturnal angina and cardiac insufficiency (Nowlin, Troyer, Collins, Silverman,

Nichols, McIntosh, Estes, & Bogdonoff, 1965), arthritis, cancer, and other similar conditions, have insomnia as a complicating feature.

Reduced sleep time has also been noted in disorders more directly related to central nervous system problems. For example, in comparison with age-matched controls, mentally deficient children as well as elderly patients with organic brain syndrome were observed to have shorter overall sleep times (Feinberg, 1968). Qualitative differences have also been described in patients with aphasia (Greenberg & Dewan, 1969), encephalitis (Torda, 1969) and prefrontal lobotomy (Hartmann, 1973), although in the latter case this was a clinical impression.

Drug Effects

Drug use has been shown to be responsible for insomnia. Easily obtainable, central nervous system (CNS) stimulants, such as caffeine, can produce sleeping difficulties for sensitive individuals. Because it is often hidden in such substances as chocolate, tea, and carbonated beverages, many people are unaware of the degree to which caffeine intake is responsible for maintaining their insomnia. Karacan, Booth, and Thornby (1973) reported that individuals without sleeping difficulties could significantly increase the number of awakenings they experienced nightly by consuming an equivalent to four cups of coffee prior to going to bed.

Although CNS stimulants have been shown to disrupt sleep, CNS depressants, paradoxically, may show similar disturbing effects. For example, a number of people rely on alcohol as a means to relax and facilitate falling asleep quickly. Studies evaluating the effects of alcohol on sleep patterns have included the immediate effects in normal subjects, the sleep patterns in chronic alcoholics, and the effects of alcohol withdrawal in sleeping patterns. Williams and Salamy (1972) reviewed the effects of alcohol consumption on normal sleep. In general, the findings suggested that sleep onset latency is decreased, REM time shortened, and overall sleeping time relatively unchanged. Chronic, heavy drinking, however, produces sleeping patterns in which individuals experience frequent awakenings similar to those of the aged (Smith, Johnson, & Burdick, 1971). Alcohol withdrawal following chronic administration to normal subjects produces a gradual return to REM sleep. In some cases, this may be coupled with an initial REM rebound (Knowles, Laverty, & Kuechler, 1968), although this does not always occur (Williams & Salamy, 1972). Initial effects of alcohol withdrawal in chronic alcoholics, on the other hand, may lead to an oscillation between REM rebound periods and REM deprivation (Allen, Wagman, Faillace, & McIntosh, 1971). Slow wave sleep reduction has also been noted as a consequence of abstinence. This decrease has been observed for up to two years. Thus, sleep disturbances may result from chronic alcohol use and withdrawal.

Similar sleep-disrupting effects may be the consequence of chronic use of hypnotics or other prescribed pharmacologic agents. Contrary to expectations, chronic use of medications taken for the purpose of alleviating sleeping difficulties may produce *drug withdrawal insomnia*. Consistent use of such drugs results in their becoming virtually ineffective after a period of about two weeks, with flurazepam lasting about twice as long (Kales & Kales, 1973). Psychological and physical dependency may also develop, resulting in individuals seeking larger and larger doses in order to regain the original drug effects. Aside from the factors above, noted sleeping medications may have other significant, undesirable or harmful effects. Abrupt withdrawal of hypnotics, especially after chronic use, produces markedly deteriorated sleeping patterns. In a recent study by Kales, Scharf, and Kales (1978), remarkably similar sleep disruptions were found to occur with abrupt withdrawal following brief periods of drug use. These data suggest that a new clinical entity has appeared as a result of the development of worsening insomnia following discontinuation of short-term drug treatment. Kales and his colleagues have coined this syndrome *rebound insomnia*. The importance of this finding is that even a brief reliance on hypnotics can no longer be considered benign. Rather, it is important to remember that particular patients may have greater difficulty in physiologically and psychologically compensating for the withdrawal of the drugs. The critical factors may be in the abruptness of the withdrawal as well as in the physiological influences of the drugs themselves.

Dreams and Mental Activity

Both falling asleep and staying asleep can be influenced by cognitive or mental activity. Although dreaming occurs throughout the night, it appears to differ qualitatively and quantitatively between NREM and REM periods. NREM dreams have the quality of looser associations and contain less visual imagery. Conversely, dreams which occur during REM periods have a more integrative quality. They have been described as movie-like in character. Because of the more realistic nature of dreams which occur during REM periods, and because of the heightened physiological state of the dreamer, spontaneous awakenings have been observed during REM periods (Greenberg, 1967). Falling back to sleep after a dream has been interrupted is not easily accomplished, especially when the dream has a nightmarish quality.

A more severely disturbing condition is that of night terrors. While vivid dreaming or nightmares are associated with REM state, night terrors occur during stage 4 sleep. Children tend to experience stage 4 disturbances, such as night terrors (pava nocturnis), sleepwalking (somnambulism), and bed-wetting (enuresis). They frequently occur without the child being aware they are happening. For example, in night terrors, a child experiences panic and a desire to escape from the terrifying dream, which actually lasts only about five minutes. He or she may scream out in horror, bringing a family member to the rescue. If the child is awakened at this time, there is usually no recall of what has happened. These childhood sleep disturbances are usually outgrown. They have been found, however, to run in families, which suggests that there may be an hereditary component.

Mental activity in bed has a disruptive influence for a number of people. Worries and concerns may continue to preoccupy the thoughts of an individual trying to fall asleep at bedtime. These cognitive intrusions may recur throughout the night, and with the ensuing awakenings, it may become more and more difficult to fall back to sleep. These worries are often accompanied by emotional upset, yet they also may appear in the absence of excessive physiological arousal (Starker & Hasenfeld, 1976). The content of the insomniac's concerns may shift from the general pressures of current and future problems to persevering worries regarding the inability to fall asleep or to get enough sleep during the night (Hauri, 1975). Continued sleep disturbances seem to increase an individual's sense of inability to handle his or her problems. A negative self-attitude may result, along with feelings of incompetence or depression (Coursey et al., 1975). An additional possibility is that both are related to other single or multiple variables not yet specified.

Personality Style and Psychopathology

There has been a long history of speculation about the relationship between emotional disturbances and sleep disturbances. Many psychological variables have been deemed responsible for precipitating and/or maintaining sleeping difficulties. The chronic worry and ruminative activity previously mentioned, for example, appear to be related to a perfectionistic personality style (cf. Coursey et al., 1975). Insomniacs report setting very high standards for themselves and are quick to be self-critical when they fall short of their goals. Other personality measures have depicted an insomniac to be introverted (Costello & Smith, 1963), anxious (Coursey et al., 1975; Fodor, 1945; Haynes, Follingstad, & McGowan, 1974; Wexberg, 1949), neurotic (Frankel, Coursey, Buchbinder, & Snyder, 1976), and ectomorphic in body build (Sheldon, 1942). Most predominantly noted has been depression (e.g., Coursey et al., 1975; Gresham, Agnew, & Williams, 1965; Hawkins & Mendels, 1966; Kupfer, 1976; Kupfer & Foster, 1973; Nicassio et al., 1976). Kales, Caldwell, Preston, Healey, and Kales (1976) reported that up to 85% of patients who seek treatment for insomnia show elevated depression scale scores on the Minnesota Multiphasic Personality Inventory (MMPI).

The earliest laboratory investigation of the sleep patterns of depressed patients was conducted by Diaz-Guerrero, Gottlieb, and Knott (1946). EEG recordings were made on six manic-depressive patients who were in a depressed state. The authors observed that these patients had a difficult time falling asleep, experienced frequent awakenings during the night, and had a higher proportion of "light" sleep. Frequent oscillations between sleep stages were also reported. Since these data were collected prior to the discovery of REM sleep, direct comparisons with later studies is not possible. This investigation, however, presented findings which have been replicated in a number of other investigations using depressed patients.

While there appear to be generally consistent findings that the sleep of depressed patients is disturbed, the nature of the disturbance is by no means in a single direction. Indeed, much of the variability noticed in depressed patients may be due to the multidimensional aspects of this clinical disorder. Detre, Himmelhock, Schwartzburg, Anderson, Byck, and Kupfer (1972), for example, reported that unipolar depressed patients experience insomnia, while bipolar depressed patients report hypersomnia. Pursuing this line of investigation, Kupfer and Foster (1975) suggested that the differences in sleep quantity observed in depressed patients may be due to the degree to which they are agitated. Thus, agitated depression may result in shortened sleep, while more withdrawn depression may produce excessive sleep periods. It remains to be seen why, in contrast with controls, certain depressed patients sleep more, while others sleep less, and still others show no differences (Hauri & Hawkins, 1973). Any observed sleep differences may be due to changes in diet, exercise, environment, or drug treatment effects. In many studies, it is difficult to determine confidently that sleep changes are valid indices of psychological disturbance if medication, electric convulsive therapy (ECT), and other variables are not controlled.

A number of studies have examined the nature of EEG sleep stages in depressives. Nearly all studies have found that slow wave, delta sleep is reduced in depressives (Mendleson et al., 1977). Reliable changes in REM sleep, however, have not been shown (Williams & Karacan, 1973). Many researchers have observed decreases in REM time during periods when depressive symptoms are most pronounced. As symptoms improve, however, REM time progressively increases (Snyder, 1969). Other sleep researchers have noted no differences between depressed patients with florid symptoms and controls. Use of sleep or antidepressant medication, however, may confound interpretation of EEG data in the same way it does in evaluating overall sleep time.

It has also been suggested that shortened REM latency is symptomatic of depression (Hartmann, 1968; Snyder, 1966). These findings are not unequivocal, since other investigators have reported the presence of both very long and very short latencies (Mendels & Hawkins, 1971). Since depressed patients exhibit such heterogeneity in total sleep time, REM time, and REM latency, it may be efficacious to consider subclassifications of this diagnostic category in order to determine consistent patterns of sleep disturbances. Kupfer (1976) noted sleep pattern differences in primary versus secondary depressed patients, with primary depressives showing the greater sleep loss. For those who argue that efforts are well spent in trying to determine whether insomnia is primary or secondary to depression, this may begin to become a chicken-and-egg phenomenon, especially when treatment planning is in question. Kales and Kales (1970) suggested that when depression underlies insomnia, the treatment of choice is antidepressant medication, since it is presumed that if the depression is reduced, the sleep problem will follow suit. If a further delineation of primary and secondary depression is attempted, it is possible that medication recommendations may be qualified on the basis of this dimension. One of the obvious problems in the search for causal mechanisms is that they become so complex, particularly over time, that it may be virtually impossible to determine exactly the degree to which the depression is influencing the insomnia, or vice versa.

Interestingly enough, treatments of depression which involve total sleep deprivation or selective REM sleep deprivation have been implemented with generally good results (Bhanji & Roy, 1975; Pflug, 1972; Vogel, Thompson, Thurmond, Giesler, & Barrowclough, 1972). Vogel et al. (1972) reported that REM deprivation significantly improved depressive symptoms for endogenous but not reactive depressives. The mechanism by which partial or total sleep deprivation works remains to be determined. It is unclear, for example, whether biochemical changes which occur during sleep deprivation are responsible for alterations in depressive symptomatology. Alternatively, the psychological effects of imposing a treatment which places the patient in the feared situation (that is, staying awake) may be similar to a flooding procedure. Thus, the effectiveness of this practice for both depressive symptoms and subsequent sleep may be via anxiety reduction. In addition, because sleep deprivation treatments have been shown to ameliorate the symptoms rather than exacerbate them, it is not possible to conclude that going without sleep is solely responsible for depression. On the other hand, because sleep reduction may accompany depression, it may serve an important function in the natural process if the disorder is allowed to run its course. Snyder (1966) suggested an REM debt theory, which endorsed the belief that sleep loss is necessary prior to clinical improvement. The intricate relationship between sleep, depression, and various expressions of emotional disturbance remains to be understood.

In summary, a number of personality and psychopathological variables have been suggested to underlie insomnia. The constructs which have been suggested as causal in sleep disturbances, however, consist of heterogeneous symptoms (such as, anxiety and depression). Thus, any one, or a combination, of biochemical, cognitive, and behavioral alterations observed in individuals given these clinical diagnoses may be responsible for concomitant sleep changes. Since the type and severity of a sleep pattern disturbance may vary within diagnostic category, it is critical to determine what subcomponent of emotional disturbance is responsible for the sleep problem, if such a problem develops. In cases where insomnia is considered secondary to depression or anxiety, it remains to be systematically demonstrated that curing the primary disorder reliably eliminates the secondary symptom. In particular, although the insomnia may have originally developed from these psychological factors, it may be maintained by a new set of factors (Bootzin & Nicassio, 1978). Finally, treatments which successfully reduce or eliminate insomnia may not significantly alter the symptoms of depression or anxiety (Nicassio & Bootzin, 1974). Paradoxically, sleep deprivation may prove to be more effective than sleep restoration in remedying depression.

Situational or Environmental Influences on Sleep

A number of situational or external variables may be responsible for making it more difficult to fall asleep and remain asleep. Situations which impose extraordinary or particularly meaningful sensory input may be insomnia inducing. For example, loud or otherwise irritating noises during the night (such as, thunder, noisy neighbors, or traffic) may be responsible for an individual's awakening (Hartley, 1977; Kramer, Roth, & Trindar, 1971). New mothers often report being sensitized to even minor sounds during the night, even though they may have been very sound sleepers prior to the birth of the baby. A large number of patients interviewed for an insomnia project at Boston University reported to the first author that their chronic insomnia began as a consequence of nightly concern developing from listening for their infants or elderly relatives. To the extent that their nightly vigilance was maintained long after it was useful (for over twenty years, in some cases), this speaks to the functional autonomy of their current nightly awakenings. Thus, in many instances, etiological and maintenance factors can be quite different. Researchers have been able to demonstrate that individuals can be taught to become sensitized to a variety of auditory stimuli within the laboratory. Oswald, Taylor, and Treisman (1960), for example, demonstrated that subjects could selectively attend to the environment while they were sleeping. In this study, sleepers were told to awaken whenever they heard a particular name. Oswald and his colleagues demonstrated that subjects were able to awaken when these names were presented, even when they were embedded within the context of other names.

Being jarred or bumped during the night is sleep disturbing for many people. This type of sensitivity may account for Monroe's (1969) finding that couples who sleep in the same bed obtain less slow wave sleep that when they sleep in separate beds. The motion or movement created by cars, buses, or other forms of transportation decreases the likelihood of sleep for some, while increasing it for others. Other sensory disturbances, such as bright lights or unusual, aversive, or even pleasant odors, may have the effect of prematurely awakening people. Lukas (1972) suggested that the elderly are more susceptible to disturbances from various sensory stimuli than are younger individuals, although there are wide individual differences noted among younger persons as well.

Certain occupations may impose changes in sleeping schedules, thereby reducing sleeping time. Medical interns and residents, for example, often operate under erratic work-sleep schedules, which may influence their ability to function well on subsequent days (Poulton, Hunt, Carpenter, & Edwards, 1978). Other occupations place similar requirements for people to change work shifts periodically. Some may involve either transcontinental or transoceanic travel, in which case jet lag may develop and last for as much as several days (Nicholson, 1970). These sleep disturbances represent a disruption of an internal clock or circadian rhythm of the sleep-wakefulness cycle.

Various stressful situations, either current or anticipated, may be important causal factors in insomnia. Sleep loss observed during hospitalization may be associated with fears of aversive medical procedures as well as with critical illness (Broughton, 1978; Murphy, 1977). Obviously, a number of variables may be operating to produce the altered sleep patterns in these and other individuals under similar physical and psychological stress.

Deprived or isolated environments also appear occasionally to produce lessened sleep times. Tagney (1972) reported that rats raised in isolated environments slept significantly less than those raised in an enriched environment. Similar reports of reduced sleep time for humans placed in experimental conditions of stimulus deprivation confirm the adverse effects of this type of environment. These studies may have both practical and theoretical value in remediating sleep difficulties. A deprived environment may be instrumental in producing both sleep difficulties and depression (see Lewinsohn, 1974).

Another possible source of sleeping difficulties is the development of poor sleeping habits. One part of this problem may be that the person never allows him or herself to acquire a consistent sleep rhythm. This may occur as the result of an inconsistent time of going to bed and/or arising in the morning. Hauri (1975) noted that insomniacs who fall into the habit of sleeping late in the morning or taking naps whenever fatigue overwhelms them are likely to develop circadian rhythm disturbances. Insomniacs may inadvertently disrupt many bodily cycles which require twenty-four-hour synchronization. If these circadian cycles become desynchronized, an optimal time for sleeping may never exist. Following this logic, daytime napping has been frequently suggested as a poor practice. There is little empirical evidence evaluating the effects of daytime naps, however, and some reports have suggested that naps may have no deleterious effect on nighttime sleep (Taub, 1977; Youkilis & Savage, unpublished).

In addition to possible circadian rhythm disturbances, insomniacs may engage in activities at bedtime which are incompatible with falling asleep (Bootzin, 1972, 1976, 1977; Bootzin & Nicassio, 1978). Insomniacs may, for example, use their bedrooms for reading, talking on the telephone, watching television, snacking, listening to music, and, probably most disturbing, worrying. The result is that the bed is no longer just a cue for sleeping; it is also a cue for many other activities. Such activities may be well-established habits begun long before the onset of the sleeping difficulties, or they may be activities engaged in to distract the insomniac from his or her primary concern, being unable to sleep. Under these conditions, bed and bedtime may become cues for arousal rather than cues for sleep.

Another source of arousal for the insomniac is that the bedroom can become a cue for the anxiety and frustration associated with *trying* to fall asleep. Insomniacs often can sleep in any place other than their own bed. They might fall asleep in an easy chair or on a couch, and they often have no trouble sleeping when away from home. In contrast, people who have no difficulty falling asleep in their own bed often have difficulty in strange surroundings.

For them, there are strong cues for sleep associated with their bed, and it is only when these cues are not available that they have difficulty.

From the preceding analysis, a stimulus control treatment for insomnia was developed (Bootzin, 1972, 1976, 1977) to strengthen the cues for falling asleep and separate them from the cues for other activities. Evaluation of stimulus control instructions will be discussed in a later section. Although this treatment has been effective in reducing sleep onset insomnia, that does not mean that sleep onset insomnia is caused by poor sleep habits. In fact, comparison of bedtime habits between good and poor sleepers has produced mixed results. Arand, Kramer, Czaya, and Roth (1972) and Haynes, Follingstad, and McGowan (1974) failed to find significant differences in the bedtime habits of insomniacs and noninsomniacs. Kazarian, Howe, and Csapo (1979), however, found that insomniacs were more likely to read, eat, smoke, and have negative thoughts at bedtime than were noninsomniacs.

In summary, pinpointing a single source of an individual's insomnia is extremely difficult. Sleep patterns may be altered by various pathological conditions (physical and/or psychological), excessive cognitive activity, environmental pressures, poor sleep habits, and ingestion of particular foods and drugs. In cases of chronic insomnia, the causal variables may no longer be present, and other factors may serve to maintain the problem. For example, insomniacs may receive reinforcing consequences from their malady. Family, friends, and others may show great concern for a person who looks as though he or she has not gotten enough sleep. Complaints of poor sleep, an appearance of exhaustion, or dark circles under the eyes may elicit extra attention from others. In some situations, insomniacs may be given reduced responsibilities out of the desire not to overburden them. Unfortunately, all of this interest and concern, when differentially focused on symptoms related to poor sleep, may inadvertently lead to their recurrence. This operant model has been applied to other psychosomatic disorders as well. Thus, while identifying the source of the insomnia may be desirable, it may not be sufficient for indicating the mode of treatment; a current, functional analysis of conditions maintaining the problem is also necessary. Efforts to subclassify insomniacs on the basis of etiological factors and current conditions should prove fruitful for treatment planning.

CURRENT TREATMENTS FOR INSOMNIA

Since the problem of insomnia is so pervasive, numerous self-generated and professionally designed treatments have been developed to aid sufferers in obtaining a good night's sleep. Popular folk remedies include counting sheep, drinking a glass of warm milk before retiring, taking a warm bath, or drinking soothing herbal teas. Other solutions have a more superstitious flavor to them; for example, some people feel they can sleep only when using one particular pillow or blanket, sleeping on one side of the bed versus another, or following nightly prayers. Because these efforts represent but a small fraction of ways insomniacs try to avoid or deal with sleeplessness, it is small wonder that the sleep industry has witnessed such remarkable growth.

Pharmacologic Treatments

Turning to external agents for relief from sleeplessness is not a new phenomenon. The early Egyptians and other ancient civilizations relied on various herbs, roots, and other natural remedies to help promote sleep, calm the nerves, and promote relaxation. Advances in pharmaceutical processing have led to the development of a number of synthetic compounds for sleep induction. Over a century ago, Liebreich (1869) noted that one such synthetic compound, chloral hydrate, had soporific properties. At the turn of the century, with the introduction of barbital, the way was paved for the mushrooming of numerous barbiturate derivatives. As new medications were developed, and production methods increased in efficiency, "sleeping pills" became readily available at relatively low cost to the consumer.

Currently, patients who complain of symptoms of insomnia most frequently are given a prescription for one of a number of sleeping medications. If the physician is sidestepped, the insomniac may obtain an over-the-counter preparation which boasts of providing symptomatic relief. Fourteen years ago, Sharpless (1965) reported that approximately 800,000 pounds of sleeping pills were dispensed annually. If one were to add to this alarming figure the minor tranquilizers, alcohol, and other prescription and nonprescription medication people use to cope with their insomnia, the figures would become overwhelming. Results of an epidemiologic survey conducted in Florida by Karacan and his colleagues (Karacan et al., 1973) indicated that 26% of those sampled rely on sleeping medication to help them fall asleep. Recent reports have shown that on prescription medication alone, Americans spent over $60 million annually. With the magnitude of the reliance on drug treatment for insomnia, it is imperative to examine the benefits and risks involved with their use.

Hypnotics

Barbiturates frequently are used and abused. In particular, they have been shown to be the most frequently found chemical in drug overdose deaths. Several investigators have evaluated the effects of barbiturates on various aspects of sleep (such as, ability to fall asleep, ability to remain asleep, day-after effects, and sleep stage disturbance). Because experimental methods vary considerably, results tend to differ among studies. Lasagna (1956) found that fifty-nine patients with chronic illnesses complicated by insomnia reported drug hangover from the use of phenobarbital, secobarbital, and pentobarbital. Despite this unpleasant side effect, improvements were noted on a variety of sleep-related dimensions, including sleep latency, total amount of sleep, and intermittent awakening. Oswald and Priest (1965) noted REM rebound upon abrupt withdrawal of amylobarbitone. (The administration of chlorpromazine, however, has been found to block the REM rebound effect.) Kales and Kales (1973) reported that both secobarbital and pentobarbital produced marked disturbances in REM sleep during both drug administration and withdrawal.

In summary, the general impressions gathered from a number of investigations of acute and longitudinal administration of barbiturates have indicated that barbiturates decrease the percentage of REM sleep, that REM percentage increases back toward normal levels with consistent use, but that REM rebound is produced following drug withdrawal after chronic use. One interpretation of this sequence of effects (REM suppression-REM return-REM rebound upon withdrawal) is that consistent use of the medication leads to a tolerance which is a function of the brain's homeostatic mechanisms. REM percentages are reestablished during the period this tolerance is developed, and abrupt withdrawal of the medication produces REM rebound as the "result of the now unopposed compensatory process" (Feinberg & Evarts, 1969).

Perhaps the most widely investigated hypnotic is flurazepam, a *nonbarbiturate*. Consistent findings (with the exception of an investigation by Bignotti, Bocci, & Luzi, 1972) indicate that flurazepam both increases total amount of sleep and decreases sleep onset latency. Kales and Kales (1974) reported that following a two-week administration of flurazepam, sleep induction and sleep maintenance persisted. They also noted that this drug did not significantly alter REM sleep. In a subsequent study, Kales, Kales, Bixler, and Scharf (1975) evaluated a number of hypnotic medications over an extended, rather than brief, period. They noted that, while all other sleep medications tested became ineffective after a two-week period, flurazepam retained its potency for up to four weeks. Many of the other hypnotics have similar aversive properties to the barbiturates, in that they disturb REM sleep and have disturbing withdrawal effects. Recently, Kales et al. (1978) reported that intense rebound insomnia may occur following even brief use of certain benzodiazepine hypnotics (that is, triazolam, flunitrazepam, and nitrazepam). Thus, sustained use of certain hypnotic medications can produce sleep disturbances not only during both use and withdrawal after chronic use but also following abbreviated periods of use.

Alcohol

One of the most common, self-prescribed, as well as professionally suggested, treatments for insomnia is to drink a bit of alcohol before retiring. As noted previously, alcohol consumption disturbs sleep stages, may disrupt the metabolism of certain biogenetic amines which naturally function to regulate sleep, and, after chronic use, may produce profound effects upon withdrawal (Mendelson et al., 1977). One study which evaluated the effects of ethanol on sleep patterns of nonalcoholic subjects included two dosage levels as the independent variable (Knowles et al., 1968). A single subject was monitored over several nights following the consumption of either 3.5 oz. or 6 oz. of alcohol. On the lower dosage level, no changes in REM sleep for the night as a whole were observed from baseline recordings. When the night was divided into two segments, however, REM sleep was significantly decreased over baseline during the first segment and significantly increased during the latter half of the night. With the higher dosage, REM suppression was observed throughout the night. The authors also noted a rebound effect following withdrawal of the higher dose of alcohol. This study illustrates two important methodological considerations in evaluating drug effects within the context of insomnia research. First, this study considered the overall sleep period both as a whole and within particular segments, and second, it included two dosage levels of the drug being evaluated. This is important, in that dose-related effects may account for much of the between-study variability noted in this literature.

The generally consistent REM suppression effects of alcohol observed in normal subjects appear to *decrease* with more chronic ingestion. Thus, REM sleep eventually returns to baseline averages or slightly above (Williams & Salamy, 1972). Feinberg and Carlson (1968) examined the sleep of chronic alcoholics and observed that their sleep patterns are disturbed. In particular, they reported that alcoholics have more frequent alterations of the sleep stages, increased percentage of REM, and frequent awakenings. Mello and Mendelson (1970) found that chronic alcoholics display fragmented sleep time and disruption of circadian sleep rhythm. Frequent day and night napping was observed during alcohol withdrawal. Since daytime naps have been associated with increased percentages of REM, this may be a common link with delirium tremens experienced by some alcoholics.

Over-the-Counter Medications

The reliance on sleeping medication to achieve a desirable night's rest is not restricted to prescription treatment by a physician. On the contrary, many people follow the advice of advertisements or friends and self-medicate, using any one of the variety of easily accessible, nonprescription drugs sold to ameliorate sleeplessness. The active ingredient of most of these over-the-counter medications is some form of an antihistamine. The primary purpose of these drugs is to counteract the effects of histamine (that is, reduce inflammation and vasodilation) when it is released in the body. A frequently reported side effect of antihistamine is drowsiness. Because of this, many people assume this medication will be effective in inducing sleep.

There is no reliable data to support this supposition, however, particularly in an insomniac population. Using all-night EEG recordings, Kales, Tan, Swearingen, and Kales (1971) investigated the sedative effects of the popular nonprescription drug Sominex in contrast to a placebo. The results of this investigation indicated that neither substance is effective in improving sleep. In addition to the failure of these medications in reducing the sleep disturbances of insomniacs, undesirable side effects may be present. Scopolamine, which is contained in many of the over-the-counter medications, has been shown to produce blurred vision, increased intraocular pressure, and urinary tract problems. Thus, self-medication not only may not lead to an effective solution to sleeping problems but may produce a number of new, hardly-bargained-for difficulties.

Compounds Which Modify Neurotransmitters

L-tryptophan is a precursor of the neurotransmitter serotonin and is found naturally in many high-protein foods. Although its effect on REM sleep is equivocal, there are consistent findings from experimental studies that L-tryptophan increases slow wave sleep as well as overall sleep time. Hartmann, Cravens, and List (1974) noted that the amount of L-tryptophan found in approximately .5 kg of meat significantly reduces sleep onset latencies. One study reported that the sedative effects of L-tryptophan may be relatively short-lived (Wyatt, 1970); it was observed that its positive effects on slow wave sleep decline over a ten-day period of administration. Thus, there is some question of tolerance for this substance during repeated dosages. Another point which must be considered when evaluating the administration of L-tryptophan on sleep is the current diet of the subject. Since this amino acid is found freely in various foods, it is important to determine whether subjects differ with respect to diet.

Since insomnia is frequently accompanied by depression, many people will receive prescriptions for the tricyclic antidepressant medication. Thus, it is necessary to observe the subsequent effects of these medications on the sleep patterns of insomniacs. The mechanism of action of tricyclic antidepressants is to increase serotonergic activity by blocking the reuptake of serotonin. Several studies have been conducted to determine the effects of antidepressant medications on sleep patterns (e.g., Hartmann, 1969; Zung, 1969). In general, these and other studies have suggested that tricyclic drugs (especially imipramine, desipramine and chlorimipramine) suppress REM sleep, have a rebound effect upon withdrawal, and may increase wakefulness and restlessness. In some cases, REM suppression does not diminish during repeated administrations. Future studies focusing on the relationship between depression and insomnia must consider the role these medications play.

Methodological Considerations in Drug Evaluation Studies

One of the disconcerting aspects of assessing the effects of various medications on sleeping patterns is the between-studies variability. A number of investigations contain methodological flaws which reduce the reliability of the conclusions. The following list contains some of the criteria which must be addressed in these studies.

1. *First-night effects* should be avoided by taking measures after a period of accommodation.

2. *Napping*, either daytime or evening, must be controlled.

3. *Other medications, drugs, and diet* should be controlled, especially when insomnia is secondary to a disorder which is under medication.

4. *Type of subject population* is important. When evaluating the effects of alcohol on sleep, differences may be observed based on whether the subject is a normal control, an alcoholic, or an insomniac.

5. *Double-blind* studies are important to reduce experimenter bias.

6. *Temporal evaluation of physiological data* must be considered; that is, average of all-night EEG records versus averages of subsets of the night.

7. *Multiple drug dosage levels* are preferable over single dosages.

8. Comparisons should be made of *drug effects measured acutely, chronically, and after withdrawal.*

9. *Drug metabolism* is subject to individual variation; thus, drug blood levels should be monitored where possible.

10. *Concurrent measures*, such as subjective reports, should be taken to corroborate existing measures.

Since investigations vary among themselves on the above variables, it is difficult to generalize across them. Hopefully, future studies will realize their importance and control for them as much as possible. Greater methodological consistency enhances the possibilities of replications and between-studies comparisons.

Electrosleep

Electrosleep was first described in the early part of the twentieth century in Moscow. The logic behind this procedure, which passes low doses of direct current through the brain in order to achieve normal sleep, is derived from Pavlovian concepts of protective inhibition (Pavlov, 1952). Pavlov contended that protective inhibition occurs in response to overwhelming or exhausting stimulation to the organism. This protective response is considered normal sleep when it occurs in its fullest state. Drowsiness, hypnosis, and other states were thought to be less complete sleep. Sleep was viewed as a therapeutic process. Drug-induced sleep, with its undesirable side effects, was deemed less advantageous than electrosleep procedures, which do not show these effects. This early monograph described the electrosleep process, beginning with the placement of electrodes on the eyelids and mastoid areas. The patient was placed in a supine position in a quiet, dimly lit room. Next, a low frequency current was passed, producing sensations of sleepiness or dizziness. Upon completion of this procedure, many patients reported feeling better, even if they had not actually experienced sleep. Clinical improvement was reported in a number of patients who presented with various physical and psychological disturbances. The exact mechanism of action of this procedure, however, was a mystery.

Numerous investigations of electrosleep have been conducted since this early report. Forster (1963) conducted the first electrosleep studies in the United States. Twenty-three subjects (six normal medical students and seventeen patients with neuromuscular disorders) were given a total of eighty-seven exposures; 50% of the exposures produced immediate sleep, but this occurred exclusively in the patients. Almost all subjects experienced calmness and a sense of tranquility, irrespective of whether or not they slept. No negative side effects were reported by any subject.

More recently, two well-designed studies reported contradictory findings for electrosleep procedures on the sleep patterns of insomniacs. While Weiss (1973) found significant decreases in sleep onset latency, Frankel et al. (1973) found no significant changes in sleep behavior. Demand characteristics of the electrosleep therapy situation may play an important role in treatment effects. In particular, resting in a quiet, dimly lit room with eyes closed may enhance the subjective feelings of well-being and relaxation reported by most of the subjects. More carefully controlled studies using electrosleep sham are needed to evaluate the effectiveness of this procedure (Williams & Webb, 1966).

Relaxation Training

The most frequently recommended psychological intervention for insomnia is some type of relaxation training. This includes a variety of procedures, such as progressive relaxation, autogenic training, transcendental meditation, yoga, and hypnosis. As treatments for insomnia, all these procedures are based on the same premise: if people can learn to be relaxed at bedtime, they will fall asleep faster. (The reader is referred to Bootzin and Nicassio [1978] for a more detailed review of relaxation training procedures.)

Progressive relaxation, developed by Edmund Jacobson (1938, 1964), has been the most thoroughly evaluated relaxation method for treating insomnia. A number of studies have provided evidence for the superior effectiveness of progressive relaxation when compared to placebo control and no-treatment conditions. Progressive relaxation produces substantial improvement for both moderately impaired college student populations (e.g., Borkovec, Kaloupek, & Slama, 1975; Steinmark & Borkovec, 1974) and severe, chronic adult populations (e.g., Nicassio & Bootzin, 1974; Lick & Heffler, 1977). This improvement has been documented in daily sleep diaries (e.g., Nicassio & Bootzin, 1974; Borkovec et al., 1975) and during EEG laboratory assessments (e.g., Borkovec, Grayson, O'Brien, & Weerts, 1979; Borkovec & Weerts, 1976; Freedman & Papsdorf, 1976; Haynes, Sides, & Lockwood, 1977).

In addition to progressive relaxation, which focuses on muscle tension, relaxation can also be induced through cognitive activities, such as meditation, self-suggestion, and imagery. Cognitive relaxation procedures, such as autogenic training (Schultz & Luthe, 1959) and meditation, have been found to be as effective as progressive relaxation (e.g., Nicassio & Bootzin, 1974; Woolfolk, Carr-Kaffashan, McNulty, & Lehrer, 1976).

Although various relaxation procedures have been shown to be effective, the absolute amount of improvement has not been dramatic. The average percentage of improvement, from pretest to posttest, in sleep onset latency as a result of training in relaxation is less than 50% (Bootzin & Nicassio, 1978). Thus, chronic insomniacs receiving progressive relaxation in Nicassio and Bootzin (1974) were still taking about an hour to fall asleep at posttest, even though they had improved 44% in sleep latency.

Despite the modest results, relaxation training is likely to remain an important component of psychological treatment programs for insomnia. As mentioned earlier, many insomniacs are highly aroused and anxious. For them, relaxation training may provide a double benefit — first, as a means of helping to induce sleep, and second, as a general coping skill to be used to deal more adequately with the stresses of the day (Bootzin, 1977).

Biofeedback

Biofeedback training has made promising advances in the treatment of many psychophysiological disorders, as indicated in many chapters in this book. Only recently have biofeedback investigators turned their attention to the treatment of insomnia.

Most investigators have evaluated the efficacy of biofeedback-assisted relaxation by using frontalis EMG biofeedback coupled with home relaxation practice. In three evaluations comparing frontalis EMG biofeedback with progressive relaxation and control conditions, both biofeedback and progressive relaxation produced more improvement than control conditions but were not significantly different from one another (Freedman & Papsdorf, 1976; Haynes et al., 1977; Nicassio et al., 1976).

EMG biofeedback is not the only biofeedback procedure that has been investigated as a treatment for insomnia. Another procedure involves the detection and amplification of an 11-14 Hz rhythm from the sensory motor cortex. Sensory motor rhythm (SMR) biofeedback, unlike EMG biofeedback, does not attempt to produce a low arousal state but attempts, instead, to directly fortify certain components of the sleep circuitry. SMR biofeedback was first suggested as a possible treatment for insomnia after it was observed that increasing the frequency of SMR in cats while they are awake produces longer epochs of undisturbed sleep and more sleep spindles (Sterman, Howe, & MacDonald, 1970).

In a comparison of SMR and frontalis EMG biofeedback, Hauri (1978) found that both are more effective than a control condition but that they do not differ significantly from one another. Subjects who received EMG or SMR biofeedback were further classified as receiving appropriate or inappropriate treatment on the basis of information from their initial assessments. EMG training was presumed to be the appropriate treatment for tense, anxious insomniacs, whereas SMR training was presumed to be appropriate for insomniacs having poor sleep patterns and disrupted sleep. When the results were reanalyzed using this classification, only appropriately treated subjects improved. Subjects receiving the "inappropriate" treatment did not improve. Thus, it may be possible in the future to match treatment to client, but considerably more research along these lines is required.

In summary, both frontalis EMG biofeedback-assisted relaxation and SMR biofeedback have been found to be effective treatments for insomnia. There is no evidence, however, that frontalis EMG biofeedback is superior to other relaxation procedures. No comparable comparisons have been made between SMR biofeedback and relaxation. As with the results from relaxation training, biofeedback training produces only moderate improvement. Likewise, the average reduction in sleep onset latency is less than 50% (Bootzin & Nicassio, 1978).

Stimulus Control Instructions

As mentioned earlier, a set of instructions to strengthen the cues for falling asleep and to separate them from the cues for other activities has been developed. The following rules (Bootzin, 1973, 1976) constitute the stimulus control instructions:

1. Lie down intending to go to sleep *only* when you are sleepy.
2. Do not use your bed for anything except sleep; that is, do not read, watch television, eat, or worry in bed. Sexual activity is the only exception to this rule. On such occasions, the instructions are to be followed afterward, when you intend to go to sleep.
3. If you find yourself unable to fall asleep, get up and go into another room. Stay up as long as you wish, and then return to the bedroom to sleep. Although we do not want you to watch the clock, we want you to get out of bed if you do not fall asleep immediately. Remember the goal is to associate your bed with falling asleep *quickly*! If you are in bed more than about ten minutes without falling asleep and have not gotten up, you are not following this instruction.
4. If you still cannot fall asleep, repeat step 3. Do this as often as is necessary throughout the night.
5. Set your alarm and get up at the same time every morning, regardless of how much sleep you got during the night. This will help your body acquire a consistent sleep rhythm.
6. Do not nap during the day.

Six controlled evaluations of stimulus control instructions from five different laboratories have indicated that substantial improvement in sleep onset latencies can be produced with these instructions. The average improvement in sleep onset latency from the six studies is 71% (see Bootzin & Nicassio, 1978, for a more detailed description of the evidence). In the three studies that compared progressive relaxation training and stimulus control instructions, stimulus control was found to be superior in two studies (Bootzin, 1975; Lawrence & Tokarz, 1976), and there was no significant difference between the two treatments in the third (Turner & Ascher, 1979). No evaluation of stimulus control instructions using convergent EEG assessment has yet been conducted. This is an important remaining step for documenting the superior effectiveness of stimulus control instructions over other psychological interventions.

SUMMARY

The multifocused data presented in this chapter, when considered collectively, underscore the complexity of the problem of insomnia. In particular, there are heterogeneous patterns of disturbed sleep found among insomniacs. Thus, while some individuals complain of difficulty falling asleep, others may experience a problem in remaining asleep. Still others appear to get what is consensually agreed upon as a respectable amount of sleep, yet they feel insufficiently restored and refreshed. Because the subjective component bears an equal weight with the more objective and behavioral indices of insomnia, a simplistic definition, without regard to individual variation, is not feasible.

Recent efforts in evaluation reflect the need for examining the patient's sleep problem within the context of multiple measurement modalities. Global subjective reports of the patient have been replaced by more reliable and systematic accounts of various aspects of the sleeping problem. In some cases, these reports are verified by independent observations and/or electrophysiological measurement. Obviously, more extensive measurement not only yields a more comprehensive picture of the patient's problem but also is indispensable in matching subsequent treatments.

People who chronically experience sleep disturbances have turned to self-medication and folk remedies to help them cope with their problem. Until recently, most professional treatment was restricted exclusively to chemotherapy. Sleeping medication has been dispensed liberally, however, and many of these same medications have unwittingly led to an exacerbation of the insomniac's condition, producing such effects as REM rebound, nightmares, addiction, and death by drug overdose. It is small wonder that there is a growing interest in searching for alternative strategies for working with this population.

A number of psychological tests, personality profiles, and self-reports of insomniacs point to the fact that some insomniacs also experience anxiety, depression, and other signs of psychological disturbance. Although some researchers argue that insomnia is merely a symptom of other underlying pathology, others suggest that psychological distress results from an individual's inability to acquire an adequate amount of sleep. To date, there are no systematic data which demonstrate that one condition always precedes the other. In fact, both insomnia and psychological distress may be attributable to another, unspecified variable or set of variables.

In addition, to the extent that disturbed sleep patterns have been present for a substantial period of time, the causes of the initial sleeping difficulty may no longer be the same as the factors which serve to maintain it. Thus, it may be more cost-effective for patients to work with their sleep disturbances conjointly with their primary psychological and/or physical pathology (Youkilis, 1979). If a patient is under treatment for chronic pain, depression, or an ulcerative condition, for example, and also manifests insomnia, it may prove worthwhile to assess carefully the patient's current stresses and coping capacity, both cognitive and behavioral. Where deficits become apparent, treatments which instruct patients in such procedures as relaxation methods, positive imagery use, attitude shifts, and/or environmental engineering may be matched accordingly. These procedures have shown well-documented success for a variety of anxiety management and self-management problems.

In order for these procedures to be recommended confidently as alternatives to drug treatments, additional studies are needed to document their efficacy on clinical populations. It is important that longitudinal studies be conducted with adult subjects from the community (rather than with college students), comparing those who receive interventions aimed at increasing their own coping capacity with those whose treatments rely on some external agent, such as drugs, to solve their problems. In addition, in order to better understand both the treatment process and the outcome, multiple evaluation methods, including electrophysiological measures, must be used. Hopefully, with both the increased concern for the need of the individual insomniac and the multivariate analysis of his or her behavioral change, investigators of the future will be better equipped to understand the complex, interactive process which mediates change in sleep patterns.

REFERENCES

Allen, R. P., Wagman, A., Faillace, L. A., & McIntosh, M. Electroencephalographic (EEG) sleep recovery following prolonged alcohol intoxification in alcoholics. *Journal of Nervous and Mental Disease*, 1971, *153*, 424-433.

Arand, D., Kramer, M., Czaya, J., & Roth, T. Attitudes toward sleep and dreams in good versus poor sleepers. *Sleep Research*, 1972, *1*, 130.

Armstrong, R. H., Burnap, D., Jacobson, A., Kales, A., Ward, S., & Golden, J. Dreams and gastric secretions in duodenal ulcer patients. *New Physician*, 1965, *14*, 241-243.

Aserinsky, E., & Kleitman, N. Regularly occurring periods of eye motility, and concomitant phenomena during sleep. *Science*, 1953, *118*, 273-274.

Aserinsky, E., & Kleitman, N. Two types of ocular motility occurring in sleep. *Journal of Applied Physiology*, 1955, *8*, 1-10.

Astic, L., & Jouvet-Monnier, D. Etude in utero des etats de veille et de sommeil chez le cogaye. *Journal of Physiology*, 1970, *62*, 115-116.

Bhanji, S., & Roy, G. A. The treatment of psychotic depression by sleep deprivation: A replication study. *British Journal of Psychiatry*, 1975, *127*, 222-226.

Bignotti, N., Bocci, U., & Luzi, T. Il flurazepam da mg 30 nil frattamento dill insomnia. *Rivista Sperimentale di Freniatria*, 1972, *96*, 1543-1577.

Bixler, E. O., Kales, A., Leo, L. A., & Slye, T. A comparison of subjective estimates and objective sleep laboratory findings in insomniac patients. *Sleep Research*, 1974, *4*, 143.

Bootzin, R. R. A stimulus control treatment for insomnia. *Proceedings of the American Psychological Association*, 1972, pp. 395-396.

Bootzin, R. R. *Stimulus control of insomnia*. Paper presented at the meeting of the American Psychological Association, Montreal, 1973.

Bootzin, R. R. *A comparison of stimulus control instructions and progressive relaxation training in the treatment of sleep-onset insomnia*. Unpublished manuscript, Northwestern University, 1975.

Bootzin, R. R. Self-help techniques for controlling insomnia. *Behavior therapy: Techniques, principles, and patient aids*. New York: Biomonitoring Application, 1976.

Bootzin, R. R. Effects of self-control procedures for insomnia. *Behavioral self-management: Strategies and outcomes*. New York: Brunner-Mazel, 1977.

Bootzin, R., & Nicassio, P. Behavioral treatments of insomnia. In M. Hersen, R. Eisler, & P. Miller (Eds.), *Progress in behavior modification* (Vol. 4). New York: Academic Press, 1978.

Borkovec, T. D., & Fowles, D. C. A controlled investigation of the effects of progressive and hypnotic relaxation in insomnia. *Journal of Abnormal Psychology*, 1973, *82*, 153-158.

Borkovec, T. D., Grayson, J. B., O'Brien, G. T., & Weerts, T. C. Treatment of pseudo-insomnia and idiopathic insomnia via progressive relaxation with and without muscle tension-release: An electroencephalographic evaluation. *Journal of Applied Behavior Analysis*, 1979, *12*, 37-54.

Borkovec, T. D., Kaloupek, D., & Slama, K. The facilitative effect of muscle tension in the relaxation treatment of sleep disturbance. *Behavior Therapy*, 1975, *6*, 301-309.

Borkovec, T. D., & Weerts, T. C. Effects of progressive relaxation on sleep disturbance: An electroencephalographic evaluation, *Psychosomatic Medicine*, 1976, *38*, 173-180.

Boynton, M. A., & Goodenough, F. L. The posture of nursery school children during sleep. *American Journal of Psychology*, 1930, *42*, 270-278.

Broughton, R. Sleep patterns in the intensive care unit and on the ward after acute myocardial infarction. *Electroencelphalography and Clinical Neurophysiology*, 1978, *45*, 348-360.

Carskasdon, M. A., Dement, W. C., Mitler, M. M., Guilleminault, C., Zarconi, V. P., & Spiegel, R. Self-reports vs. sleep laboratory findings in 122 drug-free subjects with complaints of chronic insomnia. *American Journal of Psychiatry*, 1976, *133*, 1382-1388.

Claparede, E. La fonchon du sommeil. *Rivista di Scienza*, 1908, *2*, 141-158.

Coates, T. J., Rosekind, M. R., & Thoresen, C. E. All night sleep recording in clients' homes by telephone. *Journal of Behavior Therapy and Experimental Psychiatry*, 1978, *9*, 157-162.

Costello, C. G., & Smith, C. M. The relationships between personality, sleep, and the effect of sedatives. *British Journal of Psychiatry*, 1963, *109*, 568-571.

Coursey, R. D., Buchsbaum, M., & Frankel, B. L. Personality measures and evoked responses in chronic insomniacs. *Journal of Abnormal Psychology*, 1975, *84*, 239-249.

Dement, W. C. *Some must watch, while some must sleep*. Stanford: Stanford Alumni Assn., 1972.

Dement, W. C., & Guilleminault, C. Sleep disorders: The state of the art. *Hospital Practice*, 1973, *8*, 57-71.

Detre, T., Himmelhock, J., Schwartzburg, M., Anderson, D. M., Byck, R., & Kupfer, D. J. Hypersomnia and manic-depressive disease. *American Journal of Psychiatry*, 1972, *128*, 1303-1305.

Diaz-Guerrero, R., Gottlieb, J. S., & Knott, J. R. The sleep of patients with maniac depression. *British Journal of Psychiatry*, 1946, *112*, 1263-1267.

Dragstedt, L. L. Causes of peptic ulcer. *Journal of the American Medical Association*, 1959, *169*, 203-209.

Ekbom, K. A. Restless legs syndrome. *Neurology*, 1960, *10*, 868-873.

Ephron, H. S., & Carrington, P. Rapid eye movement sleep and cortical homeostasis. *Psychological Review*, 1966, *73*, 500-526.

Feinberg, I. The ontogenesis of human sleep and the relationship of sleep variables to intellectual function. *Comprehensive Psychiatry*, 1968, *9*, 138-147.

Feinberg, I. Changes in sleep cycle patterns with age. *Journal of Psychiatric Research*, 1974, *10*, 283-306.

Feinberg, I., & Carlson, V. R. Sleep variables as a function of age in man. *Archives of General Psychiatry*, 1968, *18*, 239-250.

Feinberg, I., & Evarts, F. Some implications of sleep research for psychiatry. *Neurobiological aspects of psychopathology*, Proceedings of the American Psychopathology Association, 1969, *58*, 334-393.

Fisher, C., Gross, J., & Zuch, J. Cycle of penile erection synchronous with dreaming (REM) sleep, a preliminary report. *Archives of General Psychiatry*, 1965, *12*, 29-45.

Fodor, N. Motives of insomnia. *Journal of Clinical Psychopathology*, 1945, *7*, 395-406.

Forster, S. Preliminary Observations on Electrosleep. *Archives of Physical Medicine and Rehabilitation*, 1963, *44*, 481-489.

Frankel, B., Coursey, R., Buchbinder, R., & Snyder, F. Recorded and reported sleep in chronic primary insomnia. *Archives of General Psychiatry*, 1976, *33*, 615-623.

Frankel, B. L., Buchbinder, R., Coursey, R., & Snyder, F. Sleep patterns and psychological test characteristics of chronic primary insomniacs. *Sleep Research*, 1973, *2*, 149.

Frankel, B. L., Patten, B. M., & Gillin, J. C. Restless legs syndrome. Sleep electroencephalographic and neurologic findings. *Journal of the American Medical Association*, 1974, *230*, 1302-1303.

Freedman, R., & Papsdorf, J. Biofeedback and progressive relaxation treatment of insomnia: A controlled, all-night investigation. *Biofeedback and Self-Regulation*, 1976, *1*, 253-271.

Freemon, F. R. *Sleep research*. Springfield, Ill.: Charles C. Thomas, 1972.

Gaillard, J. M. Is insomnia a disease of slow-wave sleep? *European Neurology*, 1976, *14*, 473-484.

Gastaut, H., Duron, B., Tassinari, C., Lyagoubi, S., & Saier, J. Mechanisms of the respiratory pauses accompanying slumber in the Pickwickian syndrome. *Activitas Nervosa Superior*, 1969, *11*, 209-215.

Glaubman, H., Orbach, I., Aviram, O., Frieder, I., Frieman, M., Pelled, O., & Glaubman, K. REM Deprivation and divergent thinking. *Psychophysiology*, 1978, *15*, 75-79.

Greenberg, R. Dream interruption insomnia. *Journal of Nervous and Mental Disease*, 1967, *144*, 18-21.

Greenberg, R. On understanding sleep disorders and their psychopathology. *McLean Hospital Journal*, 1977, *3*, 139-146.

Greenberg, R., & Dewan, E. M. Aphasia and rapid eye movement sleep. *Nature*, 1969, *223*, 183-184.

Greenberg, R., & Pearlman, C. Cutting the REM nerve: An approach to the adaptive role of REM sleep. *Perspectives in Biology and Medicine*, 1974, *17*, 513-521.

Gresham, S. C., Agnew, W. F., Jr., & Williams, R. L. The sleep of depressed patients. *Archives of General Psychiatry*, 1965, *13*, 503-507.

Guilleminault, C., Eldridge, F., & Dement, W. C. Insomnia, narcolepsy, and sleep apneas. *Bulletin de Physio-Pathologie Respiratoire*, 1972, *8*, 1127-1138.

Hartley, L. Sleep loss, noise and decisions. *Ergonomics*, 1977, *20*, 481-489.

Hartmann, E. *The biology of dreaming*. Springfield, Ill.: Charles C. Thomas, 1967.

Hartmann, E. Longitudinal studies of sleep and dream patterns in manic-depressive patients. *Archives of General Psychiatry*, 1968, *19*, 312-329.

Hartmann, E. Antidepressants and sleep: Clinical and theoretical implications. In A. Kales (Ed.), *Sleep physiology and pathology, a symposium*. Philadelphia: Lippincott, 1969.

Hartmann, E. *The functions of sleep*. New Haven: Yale University Press, 1973.

Hartmann, E., Cravens, J., & List, S. Hypnotic effects of L-tryptophan. *Archives of General Psychiatry*, 1974, *13*, 394-397.

Hauri, P. *Psychology of sleep disorders: Their diagnosis and treatment.* Paper presented at the 83rd annual convention of the American Psychological Association, Chicago, August 1975.

Hauri, P. Biofeedback techniques in the treatment of chronic insomnia. In R. L. Williams & I. Karacan (Eds.), *Sleep disorders: Diagnosis and treatment.* New York: Wiley, 1978.

Hauri, P., & Hawkins, D. R. Individual differences in the sleep of depression. In U. J. Jovanovic (Ed.), *The nature of sleep.* Stuttgart: Gustar Fischer Verlag, 1973.

Hawkins, D. R., & Mendels, J. Sleep disturbance in depressive syndromes. *American Journal of Psychiatry*, 1966, *123*, 682-690.

Haynes, S., Follingstad, D., & McGowan, W. Insomnia: Sleep patterns and anxiety level. *Journal of Psychosomatic Research*, 1974, *18*, 69-74.

Haynes, S. N., Sides, H., & Lockwood, G. Relaxation instructions and frontalis electromyographic feedback intervention with sleep onset insomnia. *Behavior Therapy*, 1977, *8*, 644-652.

Horne, J. A. A review of the biological effects of total sleep deprivation in man. *Biological Psychology*, 1978, *7*, 55-102.

Jackson, J. H. *Selected writing of John Hughlings Jackson* (J. Taylor, Ed.). London: Hodder & Stoughton, 1932.

Jacobson, A., Kales, A., Lehman, D., & Hoedemacher, F. Muscle tonus in human subjects during sleep and dreaming. *Experimental Neurology*, 1964, *10*, 418-424.

Jacobson, E. *Progressive relaxation.* Chicago: University of Chicago Press, 1938.

Jacobson, E. *Anxiety and tension control.* Philadelphia: Lippincott, 1964.

Johns, M., Gay, T., Masterson, J., & Bruce, D. Relationship between sleep habits, adrenocortical activity and personality. *Psychosomatic Medicine*, 1971, *33*, 499-508.

Jones, H. S., & Oswald, I. Two cases of healthy insomnia. *Electroencephalography and Clinical Neurophysiology*, 1968, *24*, 378-380.

Jouvet, M. Récherches sur les structures neveuses et les mecanismes responsables des differentes phases du sommeil physiologique. *Archives Italiennes de Biologie*, 1962, *100*, 125-206.

Kales, A. Psychophysiological studies of insomnia. *Clinical Neurophysiology*, 1969, *71*, 625-629.

Kales, A., Bixler, E. D., Leo, L. A., Healey, S., & Slye, E. *Incidence of insomnia in Los Angeles metropolitan area*. Paper presented at the annual meeting of the Association for the Psychophysiological Study of Sleep, Jackson Hole, Wyoming, 1974.

Kales, A., Caldwell, A. B., Preston, T. A., Healey, S., & Kales, J. D. Personality patterns in insomnia: Theoretical implications. *Archives of General Psychiatry*, 1976, *33*, 1128-1134.

Kales, A., & Kales, J. Evaluation, diagnosis, and treatment of clinical conditions related to sleep. *Journal of American Medical Association*, 1970, *213*, 2229-2235.

Kales, A., & Kales, J. Recent advances in the diagnosis and treatment of sleep disorders. In G. Usdin (Ed.), *Sleep research and clinical practice*. New York: Brunner-Mazel, 1973.

Kales, A., & Kales, J. D. Sleep disorders: Recent findings in the diagnosis and treatment of disturbed sleep. *New England Journal of Medicine*, 1974, *290*, 487-499.

Kales, A., Kales, J. D., Bixler, E. O., & Scharf, M. B. Methodology of sleep laboratory drug evaluations: Further considerations. *Hypnotics: Methods of development and evaluation*. New York: Spectrum, 1975.

Kales, A., Scharf, M. B., & Kales, J. D. Rebound insomnia: A new clinical syndrome. *Science*, 1978, *201*, 1039-1040.

Kales, J., Tan, T. L., Swearingen, C., & Kales, A. Are over-the-counter sleep medications effective? Allnight EEG studies. *Current Therapeutic Research*, 1971, *13*, 143-151.

Karacan, I. *Insomnia: All nights are not the same*. Paper presented at the Fifth World Congress of Psychiatry, Mexico City, November 1971.

Karacan, I., Booth, G. H., & Thornby, J. I. *The effect of caffeinated and decaffeinated coffee of nocturnal sleep in young adult males*. Paper presented at annual meeting of the Association for the Psychophysiological Study of Sleep, San Diego, 1973.

Karacan, I., Goodenough, D., Shapiro, A., & Starker, S. Erection cycle during sleep in relation to dream anxiety. *Archives of General Psychiatry*, 1966, *15*, 183-189.

Karacan, I., Salis, P. J., & Williams, R. L. Clinical disorders of sleep. *Psychosomatics*, 1973, *14*, 77-88.

Karacan, I., Thornby, J. I., Anch, M., Holzer, C. E., Warheit, G. J., Schwab, J. J., & Williams, R. L. Prevalence of sleep disturbance in a preliminary urban Florida county. *Social Science and Medicine*, 1976, *10*, 239-244.

Karacan, I., Warheit, J., Thornby, J., & Schwab, J. Prevalence of sleep disturbance in the general population. *Sleep Research*, 1973, *2*, 158.

Kawamura, H., & Sawyer, C. H. Elevation in brain temperature during paradoxical sleep. *Science*, 1965, *150*, 912-913.

Kazarian, S. S., Howe, M. G., & Csapo, K. G. Development of the sleep behavior self-rating scale. *Behavior Therapy*, 1979, *10*, 412-417.

Kleitman, N. *Sleep and wakefulness*. Chicago: University of Chicago Press, 1963.

Knowles, J. B., Laverty, S. G., & Kuechler, H. A. The effects of alcohol on REM sleep. *Quarterly Journal of Studies on Alcohol*, 1968, *29*, 342-349.

Kramer, M. Roth, T., & Trindar, J. Noise disturbance and sleep (Report No. FAA-NO-70-16). Washington: *Department of Transportation*, 1971.

Kupfer, D. J. REM latency: A psychobiologic marker for primary depressive disease. *Biological Psychiatry II*, 1976, pp. 159-174.

Kupfer, D. J., & Foster, F. G. Sleep and activity in a psychotic depression. *Journal of Nervous and Mental Disease*, 1973, *156*, 341-348.

Kupfer, D. J., & Foster, F. G. The sleep of psychotic patients: Does it all look alike? In D. X. Freedman, (Ed.), *The biology of the major psychosis: A comparative analysis*. New York: Raven Press, 1975.

Lasagna, L. A study of hypnotic drugs in patients with chronic diseases. Comparative efficacy of placebo; methyprylon (Noludar); meprobamate (Miltown, Equanil); pentobarbital; phenobarbital; secobarbital. *Journal of Chronic Diseases*, 1956, *3*, 122-133.

Lawrence, P. S., & Tokarz, T. *A comparison of relaxation training and stimulus control*. Paper presented at the meeting of the Association for the Advancement of Behavior Therapy, New York, 1976.

Lewin, I., & Glaubman, H. The effect of REM deprivation: Is it detrimental, beneficial, or neutral? *Psychophysiology*, 1975, *12*, 349-353.

Lewinsohn, P. M. A behavioral approach to depression. In R. M. Friedman, & M. M. Katz (Eds.), *The psychology of depression: Contemporary theory and research*. New York: Wiley, 1974.

Lick, J. R., & Heffler, D. Relaxation training and attention placebo in the treatment of severe insomnia. *Journal of Consulting and Clinical Psychology*, 1977, *45*, 153-161.

Liebreich, O. Das Chloral-ein neues Hypnoticum und Anästheticum. *Berliner Klinische Wochenschrift*, 1869, *6*, 325-327.

Loomis, A. L., Harvey, E. N., & Hobart, G. A. Cerebral states during sleep, as studied by human brain potentials. *Journal of Experimental Psychology*, 1937, *21*, 127-144.

Lukas, J. S. Awakening effects of simulated sonic booms and aircraft noise on men and women. *Journal of Sound and Vibration*, 1972, *20*, 457-466.

MacWilliam, J. A. Some applications of physiology to medicine: III. Blood pressure and heart action in sleep and dreams. *British Medical Journal*, 1923, *2*, 1196-1200.

McGhie, A., & Russell, S. M. The subjective assessment of normal sleep patterns. *Journal of Mental Science*, 1962, *108*, 642-654.

Meddis, R., Pearson, A., & Langford, G. An extreme of healthy insomnia. *Electroencephalography and Clinical Neurophysiology*, 1973, *35*, 213-214.

Mello, N. K., & Mendelson, J. H. Behavioral studies of sleep patterns in alcoholics during intoxification and withdrawal. *Journal of Pharmacology and Experimental Therapeutics*, 1970, *175*, 94-112.

Mendels, J., & Hawkins, D. R. Sleep and depression I. V. Longitudinal studies. *Journal of Nervous and Mental Disease*, 1971, *153*, 251-272.

Mendelson, W. B., Gillin, J. C., & Wyatt, R. J. *Human sleep and its disorders*. National Institute of Mental Health, Bethesda, Maryland. New York: Plenum Press, 1977.

Monroe, L. J. Psychological and physiological differences between good and poor sleepers. *Journal of Abnormal Psychology*, 1967, *72*, 255-264.

Monroe, L. J. Transient changes in EEG sleep patterns of married good sleepers: The effects of altering sleep arrangement. *Psychophysiology*, 1969, *6*, 330-337.

Murphy, F. Sleep deprivation in patients undergoing operation: A factor in the stress of surgery. *British Medical Journal*, 1977, *2*, 1521-1522.

Naitoh, P. Sleep deprivation in human subjects: A reappraisal. *Waking and Sleeping*, 1976, *1*, 53-60.

Nicassio, P., & Bootzin, R. A comparison of progressive relaxation and autogenic training as treatments of insomnia. *Journal of Abnormal Psychology*, 1974, *83*, 253-260.

Nicassio, P., Boylan, M., & McCabe, T. *Progressive relaxation, EMG biofeedback, and biofeedback placebo in the treatment of insomnia.* Paper presented at the XVI meeting of the Inter-American Society of Psychology, Miami, 1976.

Nicholson, A. N. Sleep patterns of an airline pilot operating world-wide east-west routes. *Aerospace Medicine*, 1970, *41*, 626-632.

Nowlin, J. B., Troyer, W. G., Collins, W. S., Silverman, G., Nichols, C. R., McIntosh, H. D., Estes, E. H., Jr., & Bogdonoff, M. D. The association of nocturnal angina pectoris with dreaming. *Annual of Internal Medicine*, 1965, *63*, 1040-1046.

Oswald, I., & Priest, R. G. Five weeks to escape the sleeping pill habit. *British Medical Journal*, 1965, *2*, 1093-1095.

Oswald, I., Taylor, A. M., & Treisman, M. Discriminative responses to stimulation during human sleep. *Brain*, 1960, *83*, 440-453.

Pai, N. I. *Searchlight on sleep disorders.* London: Literary Service, 1969.

Patrick, G. T. W., & Gilbert, J. A. On the effects of loss of sleep. *Psychological Review*, 1896, *3*, 469-483.

Pavlov, I. P. [The sleep problem.] *Fel'd sher' Akusherka*, 1952, *8*, 3-7; *9*, 3-7; *10*, 3-5.

Pflug, B. Uben den schlafentzug in der ambulanten endogenen depression. *Nervenarzt*, 1972, *43*, 614-622.

Phillipson, E. A. Respiratory adaptations in sleep. *Annual Review of Physiology*, 1978, *40*, 133-156.

Poulton, E. C., Hunt, G. M., Carpenter, A., & Edwards, R. S. The performance of junior hospital doctors following reduced sleep and long hours of work. *Ergonomics*, 1978, *21*, 279-296.

Rechtschaffen, A., & Kales, A. (Eds.), *The manual of standardized terminology, techniques and scoring system for sleep stages of human subjects* Pub. No. 204. Bethesda, Md.: *National Institutes of Health*, 1968.

Reivich, M., Isaacs, G., Evarts, E., & Kety, S. The effect of slow wave sleep and REM sleep on regional cerebral blood flow in cats. *Journal of Neurochemistry*, 1968, *15*, 301-306.

Sassin, J. F. Neurological findings following short-term sleep deprivation. *Archives of Neurology*, 1970, *22*, 54-56.

Schultz, J. H., & Luthe, W. *Autogenic training*. New York: Grune & Stratton, 1959.

Sharpless, S. K. Hypnotics and sedatives. In L. S. Goodman, & A. Gilman (Eds.), *The pharmacological basis of therapeutics*. New York: Macmillan, 1965.

Sheldon, W. H. *Varieties of temperament*. New York: Harper, 1942.

Smith, J. W., Johnson, L. C., & Burdick, J. A. Sleep, psychological and clinical changes during alcohol withdrawal in NAD-treated alcoholics. *Quarterly Journal of Studies on Alcohol*, 1971, *32*, 982-994.

Snyder, F. *The REM state in a living fossil*. Report to the Association for the Psychophysiological Study of Sleep, Palo Alto, Cal., March 1964.

Snyder, F. Toward an evolutionary theory of dreaming. *American Journal of Psychiatry*, 1966, *123*, 121-136.

Snyder, F. Dynamic aspects of sleep disturbances in relation to mental illness. *Biological Psychiatry*, 1969, *1*, 119-130.

Snyder, F., Hobson, J., Morrison, D., & Goldfrank, F. Changes in respiration, heartrate and systolic blood pressure in relation to electroencephalographic patterns of human sleep. *Journal of Applied Physiology*, 1964, *19*, 417-422.

Starker, S., & Hasenfeld, R. Daydream styles and sleep disturbance. *Journal of Nervous and Mental Disease*, 1976, *163*, 391-400.

Steinmark, S., & Borkovec, T. Active and placebo treatment effects on moderate insomnia under counterdemand and positive demand instructions. *Journal of Abnormal Psychology*, 1974, *83*, 157-163.

Sterman, M., Howe, R., & MacDonald, L. Facilitation of spindle-burst sleep by conditioning of electroencephalographic activity while awake. *Science*, 1970, *167*, 1146-1148.

Tagney, J. Rearing in an enriched or isolated environment: Sleep patterns in the rat. *Sleep Research*, 1972, *1*, 121.

Taub, J. M. Effects of afternoon naps. *Biological Psychology*, 1977, *5*, 191-210.

Tauber, E. S., Rojas-Ramirez, J., & Hernandez-Peon, R. Electrophysiological and behavioral correlates of wakefulness and sleep in the lizard, Ctenosaura pectinata. *Electroencephalography and Clinical Neurophysiology*, 1968, *27*, 605-606.

Tokarz, T., & Lawrence, P. *An analysis of temporal and stimulus factors in the treatment of insomnia.* Paper presented at the 8th annual meeting of the Association for the Advancement of Behavior Therapy, Chicago, 1974.

Torda, C. Dreams of subjects with loss of memory for recent events. *Psychophysiology*, 1969, *6*, 352-365.

Turner, R. M., & Ascher, L. M. Controlled comparison of progressive relaxation, stimulus control and paradoxical intention therapies for insomnia. *Journal of Consulting and Clinical Psychology*, 1979, *47*, 500-508.

Vogel, G. W., Thompson, F. C., Jr., Thurmond, A., Giesler, D., & Barrowclough, B. The effect of REM deprivation on depressive syndromes. *Sleep Research*, 1972, *1*, 167.

Webb, W. B. *Sleep: The gentle tyrant.* Englewood Cliffs, N. J.: Spectrum, 1975.

Webb, W. B., & Cartwright, R. D. Sleep and dreams. *Annual Review of Psychology*, 1978, *29*, 223-252.

Weiss, M. F. The treatment of insomnia through the use of electrosleep: An EEG study. *Sleep Research*, 1973, *2*, 174.

Wexburg, L. D. Insomnia as related to anxiety and ambition. *Journal of Clinical Psychopathology*, 1949, *10*, 373-375.

Wilkinson, R. T. Sleep deprivation. In O. G. Edholm & A. L. Bocharach (Eds.), *The physiology of human survival.* New York: Academic Press, 1965.

Williams, D. H., & Cartwright, R. D. Blood pressure changes during EEG-monitored sleep. *Archives of General Psychiatry*, 1969, *20*, 307-314.

Williams, H. L., Hammack, J. T., Daly, R. L., Dement, W. C., & Lubin, A. Responses to auditory stimulation, sleep loss, and EEG stages of sleep. *Electroencephalography and Clinical Neurophysiology*, 1964, *16*, 269-279.

Williams, H. L., & Salamy, A. Alcohol and sleep. In B. Kissin & H. Begleiter (Eds.), *The biology of alcoholism.* New York: Plenum Press, 1972.

Williams, R., & Karacan, I. Clinical disorders of sleep. In G. Usdin (Ed.), *Sleep research and clinical practice.* New York: Brunner-Mazel, 1973.

Williams, R. L., & Webb, W. B. *Sleep Therapy.* New York: Charles C. Thomas, 1966.

Woolfolk, R., Carr-Kaffashan, L., McNulty, T., & Lehrer, P. Meditation training as a treatment for insomnia. *Behavior Therapy*, 1976, *7*, 359-365.

Wyatt, R. J. The effects of L-tryptophan (a natural sedative) on human sleep. *Lancet*, 1970, *2*, 842-846.

Youkilis, H. D. *Cognitive-behavioral interventions for insomnia within rehabilitative medicine programs*. Paper presented at the meeting of the American Psychological Association, New York, 1979.

Youkilis, H. D., & Savage, G. S. *Daytime napping as an adjunct for stimulus control treatment for insomnia*. Unpublished manuscript, Boston University, 1979.

Zung, W. W. K. Antidepressant drugs and sleep. *Experimental Medicine and Surgery*, 1969, *27*, 124-137.

6

CONCEPTUAL AND THERAPEUTIC CONTRIBUTIONS OF PSYCHOPHYSIOLOGY TO SEXUAL DYSFUNCTION

Julia R. Heiman
John P. Hatch

INTRODUCTION

Only recently have sexual dysfunctions been connected with the terms *psychosomatics* and *psychophysiology*. There have been allusions to such a connection within the literature of sex therapy (Kaplan, 1974), but not in the form of illuminating conceptualizations of etiology and treatment. Psychophysiology has been used to analyze components of functional and dysfunctional sexual response but, until recently, rarely as more than a descriptive tool (Bancroft, in press; Kaplan, 1974).

In discussing sexual dysfunctions from a psychophysiological perspective, our purposes are to review current information on etiology and treatment and to focus on the interaction of physical and psychological factors. Psychophysiology is not just a methodology; it is also a means of integrating cognitions, behavior, and physiology. Thus, while emphasis is placed on empirical data, an essential theme is the search for constructs borrowed in part from psychophysiology and psychosomatics that might explain how sexual patterns become dysfunctional and how dysfunctional patterns change.

OVERVIEW: INCIDENCE, SIGNIFICANCE, CLASSIFICATION

Within contemporary U.S. marriages, the incidence of sexual dysfunction and dissatisfaction has been reported to be 14% (Rainwater, 1966) and 77%

Preparation of this chapter was supported, in part, by a research grant (5 R01 MH 26631) and a postdoctoral training grant (5 T32 MH14621-03) from the National Institute of Mental Health.

(Frank, Anderson, & Rubenstein, 1978), with the majority of estimates hovering around 50% (Davis, 1929; Frank et al., 1978). Unfortunately, a substantial demographic study looking at frequencies of sexual problems in a cross section of the population has yet to be reported in the literature. The Kinsey work did not ask specific questions about dysfunction (Kinsey, Pomeroy, & Martin, 1948; Kinsey, Pomeroy, Martin, & Gebhard, 1953). The recent Frank et al. (1978) study found that specific sexual dysfunctions (erectile, arousal, or orgasmic problems) were reported by 63% of the women and 40% of the men. Additionally, sexual difficulties, such as loss of interest or inability to relax, were reported by 77% of the women and 50% of the men.

Sexual dysfunctions can have a negative effect on marital happiness and have been documented as a factor in divorce rates (Davis, 1929; Gebhard, 1966; Hamilton, 1929; Locke, 1951; Terman, 1938). Clinicians and researchers have found evidence that increased sexual conflicts may be associated with marital conflict, divorce, and even child abuse (Anthony, 1970; Kaplan, 1974; Rosenbaum, 1979; Wolff, 1961). The direct relationship between sexual and marital satisfaction, however, has not been clearly demonstrated. For instance, in spite of the high incidence of sexual dysfunction reported in the previously mentioned Frank et al. (1978) sample, sex was reported to be a specific complaint in marriage by only 21% of the women and 33% of the men. Further evidence for a lack of powerful relationship between sexual and marital happiness comes from an examination of the Locke-Wallace Marital Inventory (Kimmel & van der Veen, 1974; Locke, 1951), a highly reliable, standardized, and frequently used paper-and-pencil instrument for the evaluation of marital happiness. Out of approximately 138 possible points ($M = 110.22$, $SD = 16.32$, for males; $M = 108.40$, $SD = 16.32$, for females), a total of approximately 11 points, less than one standard deviation, can be lost if sex is or has been a problem in the relationship.

What emerges from looking at the interaction between sexual and marital satisfaction is a complex picture. First, unhappiness in sex and unhappiness in marriage often do go together, although the causal sequence or the factors relating the two are unclear. Second, sexual problems and marital problems can exist independently within a relationship. Third, overall marital satisfaction is not necessarily heavily weighted by sexual satisfaction, although we must keep in mind that this evidence comes from nonclinical populations. And, finally, sex and marriage may be related to each other differentially, depending upon whether one is male or female. Thus, while married women might indicate more sexual problems than their spouses, women less frequently report sex as a complaint within the marriage (Frank et al., 1978).

Sexual problems also have been reported, primarily by clinicians, to be associated with personal distress. Low self-esteem, anxiety, fears of rejection, depression, and poor self-image are several of the numerous correlates of sexually dysfunctional individuals (for example, see Kaplan, 1974; LoPiccolo, 1977a; Masters & Johnson, 1970). The pervasiveness and intensity of personal distress are speculative at this point but seem to be related to sociocultural and individual factors, the overall quality of the relationship, educational level, gender, and the importance of sexuality to the individual as well as his or her current partner.

Before discussing the classification of sexual dysfunction, two related problems deserve mention. One is that, more than in most psychosomatic problems, sociocultural values are heavily infused in the process of defining a sexual dysfunction. The impact of the historical period and the individual investigator's beliefs have been visible and dramatic in the sexual area (LoPiccolo & Heiman, 1978; Robinson, 1976). Clitoral stimulation, for instance, was considered "immature" by Freud (1962), normal by Kinsey (Kinsey et al., 1953), and healthy and desirable by Masters and Johnson (1970).

A related problem in defining sexual dysfunction is that the current classification systems present difficulties for researchers and clinicians. Several of the categories are broad or overlapping, so as to obfuscate the treatment recommendations, outcome research, or etiology (see LoPiccolo & Hogan, 1980). Such classification problems are not unlike those in other clinical areas (Bandura, 1968; Hempel, 1965). It is possible that the nature of typologies themselves prevents any practical system of diagnosis that accounts for complex patterns of behavior.

The classification system currently in use is the one that is the most clinically comprehensive. It was developed from a physiological and biological definition of adequate sex, in that the ability to have coitus was, and still is, in most cases, the most basic definition of adequate sex (Kaplan, 1974; Masters & Johnson, 1970). Kaplan is primarily responsible for the present classification system (Kaplan, 1974, 1977), which has been somewhat modified for the current American Psychiatric Association's *Diagnostic and Statistical Manual of Mental Disorders* – III (Spitzer, Sheehy, & Endicott, 1977).

Kaplan divided sexual dysfunction into three phases: desire, excitement, and orgasm. The first phase, *sexual desire*, includes too little (hypoactive) and too much (hyperactive) desire. The second phase, *sexual excitement*, consists of female *general sexual dysfunction* (lack of arousal, vasocongestion) and male *erectile dysfunction* (erections insufficient for intercourse). *Orgasm* is the third phase, including *premature ejaculation* (no control over ejaculating reflex, ejaculating too quickly) and *retarded ejaculation* (inhibition of the ejaculatory reflex) in males and *orgasmic dysfunction* in females.

All dysfunctions are divided along a temporal dimension (primary/secondary) and a situational dimension (absolute/situational). *Primary* refers to a dysfunction that has always been present since puberty. *Secondary* means that at one time the individual was functional. *Absolute* dysfunctions occur in all situations, and *situational* dysfunctions occur only in certain settings or under certain conditions.

Kaplan did not include certain other dysfunctions in the above system. However, *vaginismus* (involuntary contractions of the vaginal introitus muscles) and *dyspareunia* (painful intercourse) can be considered special cases of inhibition in the excitement phase. Similarly, *retrograde ejaculation* (ejaculation into the bladder) is a problem in the orgasmic phase.

As has been discussed elsewhere (Hogan, 1978; LoPiccolo & Hogan, 1980), an even more multidimensional classification system would help discriminate relevant differentiating characteristics within each dysfunction. Promising, clinically relevant variables include quality of communication, health, partner's sexual functioning, marital satisfaction, and quality and quantity of past nonsexual and sexual relationships with the opposite sex. Attempts to classify subtypes of premature ejaculation and situational orgasmic dysfunction have already appeared in the literature (Ansari, 1975; Cooper, 1968a, 1968b, 1968c, 1969a, 1969b, 1970; Masters & Johnson, 1970). Further research on relevant variables is needed, since the practice of basing outcome statistics on broad categories may obscure important individual differences.

ETIOLOGY

A variety of factors has been suggested as important in the development of sexual dysfunction. Almost all the etiological concepts, however, are based on clinical observations and collected on individuals in treatment for sexual dysfunctions. Research in this area — particularly research that compares dysfunctional individuals with appropriate control groups — is almost nonexistent. The exceptions to this statement are rare and, to date, have been restricted to the consideration of a small number of hypothesized etiological factors (Ansari, 1975; Cooper, 1968a, 1968b, 1969c, 1970).

Information on etiological factors of sexual dysfunction comes from three sources: clinical inference based on the evaluation and treatment of sexually dysfunctional individuals, research on nonclinical populations, and comparisons of sexually functional and dysfunctional samples. The overwhelming majority of etiological factors is derived from observations of clinical samples (for example, Freud, 1962; Kaplan, 1974, 1977; Masters & Johnson, 1970). Correlational research has generally been sociological (Dickinson & Beam, 1931; Frank et al., 1978; Gebhard, 1966; Hamilton, 1929; Hunt, 1974; Kinsey et al., 1948, 1953; Terman, 1938). Most lacking, and limited to the study of a few variables, have been comparisons of sexually dysfunctional clients with appropriate control groups (Ansari, 1975; Cooper, 1968a, 1968b). Until this latter category receives more attention through research on a broad scale, it will remain uncertain which factors are differentially associated with sexual dysfunctions. With this reservation in mind, the following review of etiological factors is presented with an emphasis on current status and clinical utility.

A General Multifactoral Model

While emphases differ, it is generally agreed that sexual dysfunction is the result of psychological, physiological, environmental, and relationship factors.

Disagreement does exist as to what the primary causal agents are and whether they can even be identified. Kaplan (1974), for instance, presented a loosely woven, multicausal model that identifies potential factors and hypothesizes their interactions. In this sense, Kaplan has modified the more linear causal model of Masters and Johnson (1970). The addition of a systems-theory approach to understanding sexual and marital problems (for example, Sager & Kaplan, 1972) has both enriched and complicated the issue of etiology. Hogan (1978) proposed a synthesis of classical systems theory (von Bertalanffy, 1968) with psychodynamic and behavioral approaches (Ellis, 1962, 1971; Kaplan, 1974; Lazarus, 1971; Masters & Johnson, 1970; Wolpe, 1958, 1969), in an attempt to underscore the importance of cyclical patterns in maintaining sexual problems.

Still missing in current classification frameworks are ways to analyze the various factors, weigh their relative importance to therapy, and measure their change when exposed to therapeutic intervention. Given the relatively short-term therapeutic structure of sex therapy, the maintaining variables, rather than the etiological variables, tend to be the more crucial to evaluate. A focus on current interactional patterns that take past histories into account seems to be the more promising, but as yet undifferentiated and understudied, classification strategy for inducing change.

Specific Factors Involved in Etiology

Separate etiological factors have not been identified with specific sexual dysfunctions. Therefore, broad etiological categories will be presented, with remarks on the maintaining factors important to the different dysfunctions.

Anatomical and Physiological Factors in Sexual Dysfunction

Although it is generally agreed that the vast majority of sexual dysfunctions are primarily of psychological etiology, various physiological factors are also directly or indirectly responsible for a clinically significant proportion of sexual problems. Furthermore, the primary symptomatology of sexual dysfunction is indeed physiological, even when etiology is psychological. Therefore, the interaction of psychological and physiological factors must be considered for a complete conceptualization of the dysfunction. In this section, a discussion of some of the most common physiological factors contributing to sexual dysfunction will be presented.

Illness can inhibit sexual desire and response, inasmuch as fatigue, pain, poor nourishment, or general discomfort may be present (Kaplan, 1974; Masters & Johnson, 1970). Aging seems to slow the cycle of sexual response of men, particularly the duration of *arousal to orgasm*, and often decreases the firmness of erections. For postmenopausal women, the decreased circulating levels of estrogen can result in thinning of the vaginal mucosa, resulting in some difficulty in lubrication (Masters & Johnson, 1970). Kinsey et al. (1948, 1953) also noted decreased sexual frequency and desire associated with advancing age. Those data were cross-sectionally sampled, however, and more recent developmental results from the Duke University study of aging show a consistency of sexual frequency and interest in most individuals (George & Weiler, 1979).

Congenital abnormalities and trauma to the genitals, such as hypospadias, episiotomy scars, or prolapsed uterus, are relatively rare and present few diagnostic problems. Systemic disease is also detected through standard medical procedures and can often be readily treated. If therapy for these conditions is successful, sexual function can often be expected to return. Trauma due to surgical procedures can also affect sexual function. One such operation is radical perineal prostatectomy performed for cancer of the prostate. Even surgical exposure of the prostate for biopsy has been reported to result in reduced potency in many men (Dahlen & Goodwin, 1957).

Vascular Abnormalities. Since penile erection depends upon an increase in blood flow into the organ, any condition that retards arterial inflow may interfere with erection. Stenosis or occlusion of the aortic bifurcation or of subsequent branches, including the dorsal artery or deep artery of the penis, may prevent or interfere with the maintenance of an erection. These conditions may be diagnosed by palpation of the femoral or penile pulse, the recording of penile blood pressure (Abelson, 1975), the examination of penile-pulse amplitude and contour with strain-gauge plethysmography (Britt, Kemmerer, & Robinson, 1971), or by penile thermography (Tordjman, 1977). Valvular incontinence in the venous system has also been associated with erectile disorders. Soft-tissue radiological techniques (Fitzpatrick, 1974, 1975; Fitzpatrick & Cooper, 1975) may be useful in diagnosing this disorder. Wagner and Ebbehøj (1978) recently reported that a small percentage of cases of erectile failure are caused by abnormal venous outflow from the corpora cavernosa directly into the glans during erection.

Another vascular disease that may result in impotence is priapism, a condition of continuously sustained erection. If the condition is not relieved promptly, ischemia and fibrosis of the vessels may cause permanent damage to the erectile mechanism. Priapism is confined to the corpora cavernosa, with the corpus spongiosum and glans typically uninvolved. Since the venous drainage of the spongiosum and glans is through the superficial dorsal vein, which is above Buck's fascia, this vessel remains patent.

Drugs. Alcohol, which depresses parasympathetic function, is well-known for its detrimental effects on male potency. Masters and Johnson (1970) identified it as a chief cause of male secondary impotence. Furthermore, a laboratory study of normal men (Briddell & Wilson, 1976) and a separate study of alcoholic men (Wilson, Lawson, & Abrams, 1978) showed a negative linear relation between alcohol dosage and penile tumescence during the viewing of an erotic film. A similar experiment performed on female subjects also showed a significant, negative linear relation between alcohol dosage and vaginal pulse amplitude (Wilson & Lawson, 1976).

Anticholinergics, such as atropine, may inhibit erection due to their parasympatholytic action. Chlorpromazine, haloperidol, reserpine and other rauwolfia alkaloids, and methyldopa are thought to impair erectile responding due to their effect on central dopamine receptors (Tordjman, 1977). In addition, barbiturates, morphine, heroine, cocaine, amphetamines, monoamine oxidase inhibitors, tricyclic antidepressants, digitalis, guanethidine, and methantheline have been associated with erectile dysfunction (Belt, 1973; Reckless & Geiger, 1975).

Sympatholytic drugs may produce alpha-adrenergic blockade, which can interfere with contractions of the seminal vesicle, ampulla, and ductus deferens (Kedia & Markland, 1975). Therefore, these chemicals can abolish the seminal emission phase of orgasm in men without affecting the sensory experience associated with striated muscle contractions.

Neurologic Disease and Injury. The neurologic pathways responsible for mediating the sexual response can be disrupted by surgery or trauma as well as by infectious, degenerative, or neoplastic disease. Temporal-lobe epilepsy has been associated with decreased libido as well as with erectile and ejaculatory problems in men and with anorgasmia in women (Lundberg, 1977).

It has been reported that male patients with tumors of the hypthalamo-pituitary region suffered decreased libido and potency, and females suffered decreased libido (Lundberg, 1977). Multiple sclerosis, amyotrophic lateral sclerosis, Parkinson's disease, and tabes dorsalis can produce a wide variety of sexual problems in men and women. In a study of multiple sclerosis patients, Lundberg (1977) reported erectile and ejaculatory failure in males and anorgasmia and reduced vaginal lubrication in females. Loss of genital sensation was also a problem with some of these patients.

Peripheral nerve injury (due to trauma or surgery) or peripheral neuropathy can cause sexual dysfunction if the somatic or autonomic nerves to the pelvis are involved. Rhizopathy of S2 or S3 generally results in reduced sensation in the genitals of both males and females. Erectile problems, ejaculatory failure, or anorgasmia usually do not occur, however, unless there is bilateral involvement (Lundberg, 1977). Polyneuropathy due to alcoholism, nutritional deficiency, or diabetes mellitus can have similar effects.

Lesions of the spinal cord seem to have a variable and unpredictable effect in sexual functioning. The research in this area is difficult to evaluate, since data are collected posttrauma and the diagnosis of injury is inferred from a functional, rather than physical, examination. Nevertheless, the data on lesions in males show that erectile capability is retained by between 48.2% (Jochheim & Wahle, 1970) and 91.7% (Fitzpatrick, 1974), and ejaculatory capability remains in between 2% (Jochheim & Wahle, 1970) and 16% (Hohmann, 1966). Few studies have included females with injuries of the spinal cord, but research that exists indicates that these women experience orgasm. Higgins (1978) carefully reviewed this literature and suggested that psychophysiological monitoring of genital and extragenital response would contribute valuable information on the relationship between genitopelvic and cerebrospinal eroticism. To date, such research has not been reported in the literature.

Endocrinological Disease. Hypogonadism in women does not appear to be highly detrimental to sexual arousability or orgasmic ability. Women who are ovariectomized after puberty do not generally suffer a decrement in their sexual response, apart from the fact that the vaginal mucosa may not lubricate properly without some exogenous estrogen therapy (Bancroft, in press). In fact, it has been suggested that estrogens in oral contraceptives may even have an inhibitory effect on female sexuality (Bancroft & Skakkeback, 1979). In males, it is generally agreed that postpubertal hypogonadism is frequently associated with erectile failure; however, this is not inevitable (Bancroft, in press).

Another endocrinological disease commonly associated with sexual dysfunction is diabetes mellitus. Approximately 30% to 60% of male diabetics develop erectile failure (Cooper, 1972; Ellenberg, 1971). These problems are thought to be due to neurologic damage, not directly to the endocrinological manifestations of the disease itself. Ellenberg (1971) reported clinical evidence of neuropathy in 88% of the impotent diabetics he examined, but only 12% of the sexually functional diabetics showed such symptoms. These neuropathies may cause reduced sensation in the genitals or weaken muscles involved in the sexual response. A frequent complaint among the diabetics who had remained sexually functional was that the sensory experiences of sex were changed. Angiopathy of the small penile blood vessels may also interfere with erection, and, if the internal bladder sphincter is involved, retrograde ejaculation may occur.

Psychological (Intrapersonal) and Relationship (Interpersonal) Factors

Much of the evidence for psychological factors in sexual dysfunction is derived from clinical history-taking, theory, and speculation. This is not surprising, since therapeutic intervention is centered on psychological, rather than direct physiological, intervention. Psychological factors frequently cited in this literature are depression (Kaplan, 1974), low self-esteem (Barbach, 1974; LoPiccolo, 1977a), anger or hostility (Cooper, 1968b; Kaplan, 1974), guilt (Masters & Johnson, 1970), unrealistic expectations (Ellis, 1971), negative attitudes toward sex from past experience or religious orientation (Masters & Johnson, 1970), and anxiety (Kaplan, 1974).

Two problems become readily apparent in attempting to make sense of the research and clinical literature dealing with psychological factors related to sexual dysfunction. First, the data are correlational, thus confusing whether psychological signs are the consequential or precipitating variables in the appearance of a sexual problem (Cooper, 1968a, 1968b). Second, the majority of psychological variables implicated in dysfunctions are intrinsic to the interpersonal relationship. Thus, anxiety and hostility often seem to be related more to the quality of a couple's interaction than to an individual's isolated psychological condition. Separating inter- and intrapersonal factors is, in some ways, artificial, but this division does reflect past and current thinking and research on sexuality.

We turn now to a review of three of the more frequently noted psychological variables, with attention to the interpersonal quality implied in each case.

Anxiety. Anxiety has been directly implicated as a major problem in most sexual dysfunctions. In psychoanalytic theory, all psychoneurotic responses, including sexual problems, were believed to be based on anxiety and its avoidance (Freud, 1926; Hendrik, 1958). Kaplan (1974), combining a behavioral and analytic orientation to treatment, remarked that anxiety is the root of all sexual dysfunction, in that it physiologically and psychologically interferes with the cycle of sexual response. In Cooper's (1969a) study of erectile failure and premature ejaculation in 49 clients, he found that 94% experienced some degree of self-reported anxiety during coitus. Similarly, using the Neuroticism Scale Questionnaire (Scheier & Cattell, 1961), Cooper (1969b) found that women with vaginismus or sexual aversion had anxiety scores that were above normal.

More important than the existence of anxiety per se are the developmental conditions responsible for the anxiety. For individuals with sexual problems, sexual interactions often become surrounded with worries and fears that may or may not have been present at the onset of the dysfunction. In Cooper's (1968a) work, for instance, there was evidence that, for erectile failure having acute onset, anxiety was prominently associated with initial failure and seemed causally related to the impotence. Further attempts at coitus only exacerbated anxiety for this group. Cooper noted that anxiety was also present in the group of cases of insidious onset of erectile failure, but it was more likely to be a consequence, rather than a cause, of the erectile failure. Members of the group with insidious onset tended to show anxiety *in reaction to* their female partners' critical and castigating complaints about the males' sexual inadequacy. Men with premature ejaculation in Cooper's study were more likely to show signs of somatic anxiety, such as tachycardia, dry mouth, tremulousness, and shakiness, suggesting an overactive autonomic nervous system. Premature ejaculators also scored higher in anxiety, but they were within the normal range on the Neuroticism Scale Questionnaire (Scheier & Cattell, 1961). Thus, Cooper's (1968a, 1968b) work with males (and later support from Ansari, 1975) suggested that the presence of anxiety in sexual dysfunctions may be less important than the circumstances surrounding the anxiety.

The typical cases in which anxiety seem to be closely linked with the onset of the dysfunction include premature ejaculation, dyspareunia, vaginismus, some cases of primary inorgasmic dysfunction, and cases of acute onset of erectile failure (Cooper, 1968a, 1968b, 1969a, 1969b; Kaplan, 1974; Masters & Johnson, 1970). In cases of premature ejaculation, it has been suggested that anxiety occurring under conditions of high arousal may precipitate fast ejaculation due to activation of peripheral autonomic (adrenergic) mechanisms involved in ejaculation (Bancroft, in press). Thus, the ejaculatory threshold is lowered.

Anxiety that is linked to the initial stages of arousal seems to be related to cognitive mediation, whether pervasive to the relationship or specific to the sexual quality of the interaction. Thus, Fisher's (1973) finding that nonorgasmic women were less likely to have learned to depend on or trust men might be seen as fitting into the idea that anxiety may interfere with ease of sexual response. In this case, anxiety may be a more generalized response to the relationship. More specific fears of intercourse, pregnancy, or pain can also reduce arousal or inhibit orgasm for both partners. Masters and Johnson (1970) acknowledged the distracting or blocking effect of anxiety. Although this idea has not been widely researched, Heiman and Morokoff (1977) presented psychophysiological data showing that nonorgasmic women experienced self-reported anxiety, rather than self-reported sexual arousal, in response to erotic materials.

Anxiety that is consequential to dysfunctions is more likely to occur in certain cases of secondary inorgasmic dysfunction, insidious onset or recurrent erectile failure, delayed ejaculation, and low sexual interest or drive. Here, the relationship between cognitive and relationship factors and anxiety is complex and often circular. For instance, Cooper's (1969a) study pointed out that in cases of insidious onset, erectile problems tend to be associated with fear of failure (in 56% of cases), fear of being seen as sexually inferior by the wife (43% of cases), fear of ridicule by the wife (40%), fear of pregnancy (24%), anxiety over genital size (15%), fear of physical disease (15%), pervasive anxiety (11%), and fear of detection (7%).

These results coincide with Masters and Johnson's (1970) concept of "performance anxiety"; that is, worrying about sexual performance (orgasm, erections) during a sexual interaction will diminish sexual response. For those individuals whose anxiety over performance continues, the result can sometimes be avoidance of the anxiety-producing situation, with concomitant loss of frequency and eventual loss of interest in sexual contact.

To acknowledge differences in the point of onset of the anxiety can have important consequences for treatment. It is particularly important that the circumstances under which anxiety is aroused also be carefully analyzed. One obvious distinction to explore in evaluating the role of anxiety in sexual dysfunction is the degree to which anxiety is intra- or interpersonal. On one dimension are people who feel generally fearful of all sexual encounters. On the other, perhaps overlapping, dimension are individuals for whom sex itself is not anxiety provoking but their partner's real or imagined response is.

One theory as to why anxiety interferes with sexual arousal is reflected in Wolpe's (1958) hypothesis of reciprocal inhibition, which posits that sexual arousal and anxiety are neurophysiologically and mutually inhibiting responses. Recently, Burgess and Krop (1977) supported Wolpe's theory by finding a significant, negative relationship between trait anxiety, as measured by the Taylor Manifest Anxiety Scale (Taylor, 1953), and sexual arousal, as measured by the

Sexual Arousal Inventory (SAI) developed by Hoon, Hoon, and Wincze (1976). Yet, there is contradictory evidence on this point (Hoon, Wincze, & Hoon, 1977). For instance, it assumes a competitive effect of parasympathetic (sexual arousal) and sympathetic (anxiety) systems, a view that has been shown to be oversimplified (Sternbach, 1966).

There is other evidence that anxiety and sexual arousal may not be antagonistic emotional conditions. It has been postulated that anxiety is both involved in the inhibition of erection, arousal, and orgasm and responsible for rapid orgasm (for example, Bancroft, in press). Furthermore, a study by Hoon et al. (1977) measured changes in vaginal blood volume in women who were exposed to anxiety-arousing, sexually arousing, and neutral videotapes. When women were sexually aroused by preexposure to erotic stimuli, there was more rapid diminution of sexual arousal during the subsequent anxiety condition than during the subsequent attention-control stimulus condition. Hoon et al. (1977) used these data as support for Wolpe's theory of reciprocal inhibition. They also found, however, that anxiety preexposure increased sexual arousal to a subsequent erotic stimulus more rapidly than did neutral preexposure. While these results suggest an activation effect of anxiety, they must be considered with caution, since the authors used physiological dependent measures (heart rate, vaginal blood volume) but did not include any self-report measures. Thus, it is not clear whether sexual arousal and/or anxiety was being perceived on a subjective level.

Bancroft (1974) also noted cases in which anxiety and sexual arousal were positively correlated. Bancroft looked at the effects of aversive conditioning on sexual response, using an electric shock to the arm when subjects responded to an erotic stimulus. Two subjects showed significant negative correlations, in that shock anticipation reduced penile response latency. The other eight subjects showed no correlations.

With regard to anxiety, therefore, it is clear that it has some negative effect on sexual arousal. However, the onset of anxiety, the context in which it occurs, relationship variables, and the mechanisms of interaction between sex and anxiety are complicated and, as yet, undetermined.

Anger and Hostility. Similar difficulties occur in evaluating the effect of anger and hostility on sexual responses. Clinically, it is not uncommon to see couples express a great deal of anger over their sexual and nonsexual relationships. Cooper's work with sexually dysfunctional females (1970) and males (1968a, 1968b) showed high hostility ratings in both groups that were above normal. Winokur and Gaston (cited in Bancroft, in press), however, found no association between self-reported intercourse frequency and angry episodes in 20 normal couples over a two-week period.

Anger has also been hypothesized to facilitate sexual arousal, at least physiologically (Barclay, 1969; Kinsey et al., 1953). This speculation may be related to an earlier statement by Ax (1953) that, in comparing fear and anger psychophysiologically, anger was a more "integrated" response, since there were consistently larger correlations among physiological variables (heart rate, blood pressure, muscle tension, galvanic skin resistance, and respiration) for anger than for fear. While Ax used these data to oppose a general activation theory, the possibility that anger is more likely than anxiety to increase subsequent sexual arousal remains an open experimental question. It could be worthwhile to examine the conditions under which anger might provide a psychophysiological "warm up" for sexual arousal, should a sexual situation immediately follow an anger-producing one.

As with anxiety, it seems impossible to adequately evaluate the role of anger in sexual dysfunction without a more functional analysis of the context in which anger and hostility occur. For instance, for some couples, expressed anger is a way of bonding, since it permits strong feelings to be expressed in an intensely involved exchange (Heiman, LoPiccolo, & LoPiccolo, 1981). For other couples, anger and hostility help them to avoid sex or inhibit arousal and orgasm (Kaplan, 1974). The onset, conditions, and consequences of angry interactions need to be evaluated before extending a theoretical role of anger in sexual responsiveness.

Boredom. Another personal and interpersonal variable that is implied, but rarely mentioned, in the etiology of sexual dysfunction might be called sexual boredom. This term denotes a general disinterest in sexual responses or interactions. Most recently, this sexual withdrawal has been associated with "low sexual desire," "low sexual drive," or "low sexual interest," a subtype of which consists of individuals who are completely sexually functional in terms of orgasms and arousal but for whom sex is a low-priority, and thus low-frequency, activity (L. LoPiccolo, 1980; Zilbergeld & Rinkleib, 1980). Clinicians have pointed out that apparent sexual disinterest may only be a mask for sexual aversion, inhibition, anxiety, and/or anger (Kaplan, 1977). Nevertheless, for the group of people who simply do not seem interested in sexual interactions, it is important to note that this lack of emotional involvement with sex is as potentially inhibiting to sexual frequency as is anxiety or anger. Alternatively, it is possible that emotional states that show some type of involvement with the partner, rather than withdrawal from the partner, are more facilitative of subsequent sexual interest and responsiveness (Heiman & Morokoff, 1977).

Physiologically, there has been limited evidence that increased sexual interest is correlated with higher levels of testosterone (Bancroft & Skakkeback, 1979; Davidson, 1977). Thus, it seems possible that the etiological factors of sexual disinterest may include a psychological-physiological feedback loop, where interest and frequency affect hormone levels, which, in turn, affect interest and frequency, so that the existing pattern of sexual frequency can be psychologically and physically self-perpetuating.

Other Intrapersonal and Interpersonal Factors. Several general relationship factors, in addition to the ones described above, have been implicated in etiology. Overall marital happiness has been found to be a strong correlate of women's orgasmic consistency in a variety of survey-interview studies (Chesser, 1956; Gebhard, 1966; Terman, 1938, 1951). Distant or negative emotional relationships with parents or peers have been suggested as influential in the development of sexual dysfunction (Kaplan, 1974; Masters & Johnson, 1970), as have poor quality of premarital sexual experience (Kinsey et al., 1953) and past history of sexual trauma (Kaplan, 1974). Lack of sexual information and communication skills interferes with a couple's ability to provide each other with satisfying stimulation (Kaplan, 1974; LoPiccolo, 1977a).

Restricted religious upbringing has been cited as a factor of major import by Masters and Johnson (1970), a view that is not substantiated by other research (Chesser, 1956; Fisher, 1973; Hunt, 1974; Kinsey et al., 1948, 1953). There is some evidence that devout Catholic women have lower rates of coital orgasm than "inactive" Catholics (Hamblin & Blood, 1956). On the other hand, Chesser (1956) found that orgasm was more consistent in females who were regular church attenders than in those who were not. The guilt allegedly associated with religious upbringing, strict parental codes, and personality has been suggested as an inhibitor of sexual behavior in sexually functional samples (for example, Mosher, 1971, 1973).

None of the above relationship and background factors has been shown to separate dysfunctional from nondysfunctional samples. It is unlikely that any one or two factors alone are responsible for dysfunctional patterns. What is likely is that dysfunction depends on a complex of interacting personal and interpersonal factors, both historical and current.

Patterns of Physiological and Psychological Integration

If the preceding sections seem contradictory and underresearched, then the current status of the etiology of sexual dysfunction has been accurately reflected. We turn now to a consideration of several issues in an attempt to integrate psychological and physiological factors. The question, broadly stated, is: Can psychophysiology and psychosomatics illuminate etiological concepts of sexual dysfunction?

Examples of the Interaction of Physiological and Psychological Factors

First, it is worthwhile to note examples in which the interaction of psychological and physiological etiological factors is important but frequently overlooked. Biological illness can cause both psychological and physiological stress, which impedes normal sexual expression. A biological illness may also function as a complicating factor in the treatment of a psychogenic sexual dysfunction. Furthermore, the sexual dysfunction itself can cause emotional reactions that directly interfere with the physiology required for the normal expression of sexual response.

As mentioned previously, a normal biological process, such as aging, can have profound effects upon sexuality not only due to physiological factors, such as hormonal changes and reduced physical strength or stamina, but also due to psychological factors associated with changes in economics, family role, or societal attitudes. Another normal biological condition that can affect sexual function is pregnancy. Pregnancy involves anatomical, physiological, hormonal, and psychological changes of great magnitude. These changes can generate problems ranging from physical discomfort during sex to feelings of unattractiveness and anxiety.

Various forms of biological pathology also interact with psychological factors to jointly determine sexual function. Some common instances will be provided as examples. In people with cardiovascular disease, fear of heart attack, stroke, or even death can significantly inhibit sexual expression not only in the patient but in his or her sexual partner as well. In the neurologically impaired person, urinary incontinence, spasticity, paralysis, and anesthesias may not only detract from sensate pleasure but also reduce sexual pleasure, as a result of the frustration, embarrassment, or guilt they generate. Psychological stress due to the economic burden of a catastrophic illness, such as chronic renal failure, and psychological reaction to being dependent upon mechanical means of life support can adversely affect sexual behavior. It should be remembered that hostility, anxiety, and depression, which are secondary to any serious illness, are likely to affect sexual function and thereby complicate sex therapy.

Social factors concomitant with biological illness can also affect sexual function. For example, when De-Nour (1978) compared male hemodialysis patients who had become impotent with those who had not become impotent, he found that the former had wives who tended to be more negative and that the impotent men were more likely to have lost their dominant role in the family. Wise (1977) also reported several case studies in which social pressures due to physical problems impeded normal sexual functioning. Even when the physical illness is not a direct cause of sexual dysfunction, it can create psychological problems that, in turn, are reflected in sexual behavior.

Finally, it should be noted that the social interaction between a client and therapist may actually cause sexual dysfunction in some patients. Walker (1978) reported that, in some cases, the urologic or gynecologic workup performed in a fertility clinic seemed to generate sexual dysfunctions in patients who had previously not experienced sexual problems. It was noted that dysfunction may be a direct result of certain types of routine diagnostic tests and treatments, especially if the therapist fails to respect cultural, religious, or legal proscriptions concerning sexual behavior. The clinician must also consider the effect of giving patients information regarding their disease. For example, a physician who routinely tells male diabetics that they have a 30% to 60% chance of becoming impotent could possibly be unwittingly contributing to an even further increase in this statistic. This is a complicated issue, however, since a lack of such information may be equally problematic to the individual and his or her partner.

Psychophysiology: Mind-Body Concepts and Research Implications

As mentioned earlier, use of the terms *psychological, physiological,* and even *psychophysiological* relates to the mind-body problem. It shows that our language is shot through with dualistic metaphor and that we essentially have no other way to describe a nonbifurcated process. While the depth of this issue is better discussed elsewhere (for example, Globus, Maxwell, & Savodnik, 1976), its significance to sexual dysfunction deserves mention.

Of interest, in terms of the body-mind problem, is the degree of independence, or *the nature of the relationship* (that is, causal, parallel, sequential), between bodily processes and mental processes. Psychophysiological research — compartmentalizing sex into cognitive, physiological, and behavioral components, to paraphrase Lang (1968, 1971) — aids the empirical analysis of emotional behaviors. Each component is considered a significant part of the emotion being studied. It is expected that there will not always be one-to-one correspondence between components but that there are "constructs that will integrate behavioral and physiological observations" (Lang, Rice, & Sternbach, 1972, p. 624). Thus, neither measures of the body nor of the mind constitute the ultimate reference point or the only dependent variable; the relationship between them is the area of study.

The correlation between subjective measures of sexual arousal and physiological measures of genital response shows evidence of both independence and concordance. In women, Geer, Morokoff, and Greenwood (1974) and Wincze, Hoon, and Hoon (1976) found nonsignificant or inconsistent correlations between self-reported and genital measures of sexual arousal to erotic stimuli. Henson, Rubin, Henson, and Williams (1977) found significant, positive correlations between genital vasocongestion and subjectively measured sexual arousal. Wincze, Hoon, and Hoon (1977) found that a continuous self-report rating of sexual arousal during the erotic stimulus (rather than ratings given after the stimulus) showed significant correlations with a vaginal vasocongestive measure in five out of six women. Erotic passages depicting more socially acceptable sexual behavior, however, were self-rated as being more arousing but physiologically were less arousing than were less socially acceptable erotic passages (Wincze et al., 1977).

Males have shown somewhat different patterns than have females on the subjective-physiological relationship. Heiman (1977) found rather high correlations between amplitude of genital pulse and genital blood volume for males in response to erotic tapes. Subjective response was significantly correlated with pulse amplitude. For females, amplitude of genital pulse correlated significantly with subjective arousal. However, of the women showing the greatest change in blood volume, 42% said they were experiencing no sexual arousal. Later work with female subjects showed a lack of correlation with the measure of pulse amplitude in a sexually dysfunctional sample, a significantly positive subjective-physiological correlation in a sexually functional, nonmarried sample, and a negative correlation in a sexually functional, married sample (Heiman, 1980; Morokoff & Heiman, 1980). In looking at the effects of alcohol on sexual response, Wilson and Lawson (1976) found that, with increasing dosages of alcohol, women reported more arousal, while their vaginal response showed less arousal, a pattern that Briddell and Wilson (1976) did not replicate with males.

The above studies suggest that body and mind do not always correspond in sexual arousal. This lack of correspondence may be related to a variety of variables. It may be that self-report and genital measures are tapping different unrelated variables (Ambroso & Brown, 1973). It may be that the measured levels of physiological arousal are too low to be subjectively perceived (Heiman, 1978a). There may be sex differences that relate to the fact that men have a visual source of feedback, the penis. Moreover, physical arousal may be mislabeled or overlooked because of competing emotions, such as anxiety. Other variables, such as general physiological condition, marital status, personality, adequacy of sexual functioning, and sexual satisfaction, may influence arousal levels and the ability and willingness to perceive those levels (Bancroft, in press; Byrne & Sheffield, 1965; Heiman, 1980; Morokoff & Heiman, 1980). At this point, it is clear that both measures are valuable, not as checks on one another, but as different ways to describe sexual response. It is also apparent that a better understanding of sexual responsiveness will come from a clarification of the affective-emotional context that enhances or diminishes sexual arousal. The importance of perceived genital feelings to the ease of sexual response also needs to be clarified.

The development of scales that differentiate cognitive and somatic self-reported sexual arousal, perhaps modeled after similar multidimensional approaches to other emotional states (Barratt, 1972; Buss, 1962; Davidson & Schwartz, 1976; Schwartz, Davidson, & Goleman, 1978), may be important to future research on the conceptualization of sexual dysfunction. Ansari (1975) attempted this with a measure of male coital anxiety, with some limited, but positive, results in discriminating different clinical subtypes.

Work on biofeedback and sexual response is also relevant to the relationship between psychological and physiological variables. Sexually functional males have been shown to be able to use biofeedback to suppress erections (Rosen, 1973) and facilitate erections (Price, 1973; Rosen, Shapiro, & Schwartz, 1975), although the advantages of feedback were limited. In Csillag's (1976) comparison of six functional and six dysfunctional (erectile-failure) males, there was no difference between feedback and no-feedback conditions, although clinical subjects showed increasing erections to erotic slides across testing sessions, while normal males showed decreasing erections across sessions.

For women, there is less evidence that feedback is of any practical utility. Hoon et al. (1977) showed slight, but confounded, evidence for feedback enhancement of arousal in one of two subjects. Zingheim and Sandman (1978) used nonerotic stimuli (a red and a green slide), to which subjects showed statistically significant vasodilation but no vasoconstriction. The vasodilation was only a 4.7% increase, however, which makes the practical relevance questionable. More importantly, the authors stated that, while subjects did not use erotic fantasies, they did use some unmentioned cognitive strategies. Such strategies would be important in the application to clinical problems, although these authors claimed that only vasomotor conditioning was responsible for the change. Recently, Hoon (1978) presented data on a group of 23 women. She tested the effects of auditory and visual feedback on their ability to increase and decrease arousal. There was a significant feedback effect, with visual and no feedback being more effective than auditory feedback. There was no evidence, however, that visual feedback was in any way superior to no feedback. This result fits well with Cerny's (1978) feedback study of women who watched an erotic videotape. Subjects were able to suppress arousal below baseline but were unable to significantly enhance arousal. The no-feedback group, however, showed more vasocongestion during arousal instructions than did either of the two feedback groups.

An investigation comparing the effect of different states of awareness on sexual arousal would seem to be very worthwhile. One such study with relevance to sexual dysfunction is that of Duvall and Wickland (1973), who posited a dichotomy of awareness states, with one state based on preoccupied critical self-evaluation (concerned about performance and self-preservation) and the other state based on attention directed outward (unconcerned about self and more responsive to environmental and sensory input). These categories fall nicely into place with the hypotheses of performance anxiety, spectatoring, and sensate focus used in sex therapy (Masters & Johnson, 1970).

At this point, the use of biofeedback may be better directed toward the effects of focused effort to increase or decrease arousal, rather than on the clinical utility of biofeedback. Studies so far have shown minor and, in the case of women, sometimes negative effects (Cerny, 1978) on arousability. The studies, except that of Hoon (1978), have generally ignored the subjective-physiological progression of arousal as well as possible cognitive strategies that produce increases and decreases in arousal.* Hence, we would call for greater efforts to be made to clarify the nature of the connection between measures of mind and body.

Sex as a Psychosomatic Symptom of a Troubled Relationship

If we go from the more individualistic to the more interactional framework, it means examining the psychosomatic element of sexual dysfunction in a broader context. Minuchin, Rosman, and Baker (1978) have used the term

---

*It should be noted that other emotional reactions also seem to fade under evaluate observation. In studies of humor, for instance, subjects who are instructed to observe their reactions show less positive feelings than subjects told merely to react to the stimuli (Cupchik & Leventhal, 1974).

psychosomatic families to point out the role that a serious physical complaint can play in the overall family structure and how that role is one that can be stabilized and fostered by interactions among the target individual and the family.

Similarly, sexual problems can serve a variety of functions in a relationship. They can be a sign of emotions that may be too difficult, too frightening, or too hidden to be easily expressed. Thus, lack of arousal or orgasm can signal lack of trust, hostility, anxiety, or disinterest toward the partner. Lack of response or premature response can similarly be expressions of broader control and dependency issues or dissatisfaction over other affectionate aspects of the relationship. Some individuals are more easily able to admit to a sexual problem than to face the threatening possibility that their relationship is in trouble. They can, in effect, blame the problematic relationship on something out of their control – their physical response.

Furthermore, there are roles that accompany certain sexual dysfunctions that also serve the needs of individuals involved. A typical example is female dyspareunia. Women who experience painful intercourse often have mixed feelings about being sexual, are afraid of or are inhibited about sexual expression, have fears about their partner's sexuality, or simply dislike sex. The women, however, cannot admit these conflicts to themselves or their partners. Pain then becomes the less difficult mode of expression of conflict. It is important to acknowledge that the pain is real, while at the same time analyzing the function that the pain serves in the total sexual relationship.

In this section, we have examined the current status of etiology of sexual dysfunction. General theories show etiology to be broadly conceptualized in a multitheoretical framework, thus suggesting general (rather than specific) and correlative (rather than causative) factors. Psychological and physiological factors were examined separately. The integration of psychic and somatic factors into a psychophysiological framework revealed the importance of examining the relationship between these categories.

TREATMENT OF SEXUAL DYSFUNCTIONS

Overview of Current Treatment

Since the 1950s, approaches involving behavioral therapy have dominated the field of sex therapy. Before that time, psychodynamic therapy was the mainstay of both etiology and treatment. While several behavioral techniques were developed before 1970 (for example, Semans, 1956; Wolpe, 1958), it was Masters and Johnson's (1970) behavioral treatment paradigm that significantly changed the field of sex therapy (see LoPiccolo & Hogan, 1980, for a thorough review).

Integrated with this behavioral orientation, however, have been general systems theory and psychodynamic theory as well as Gestalt, rational-emotional, and client-centered therapy. Thus, in discussing various components of sex therapy, a variety of therapeutic and theoretical orientations will be included.

When drawing conclusions from empirical research on sex therapy, one must be cautious. The effectiveness of sex therapy has been inadequately researched, and there are few controlled studies of treatment approaches. Furthermore, active ingredients within the various approaches are ambiguous (J. LoPiccolo, in press). Thus, as in the area of etiology, much of the research to be presented is correlational in nature. Nevertheless, some initial speculations can be made.

While the present review looks first at physically focused and then at psychologically focused treatment, it should be obvious that this dimension is only one of relative emphasis. Even the most delimited physical intervention has psychological impact on the individual. As mentioned earlier, sex therapy works upon the connection between the cognitive, behavioral, and interpersonal aspects of the sexual problem.

Physically Focused Therapeutic Approaches

In cases of vascular damage, surgical repair has been reported to improve arterial pelvic blood flow (May, Deweese, & Rob, 1969). Similarly, Wagner and Ebbehøj (1978) successfully treated abnormal venous outflow with a surgical technique performed under local anesthesia. Another vascular disease, priapism, has been treated by aspiration of the penis and surgical formation of a cavernosum-spongiosum shunt. It has been reported that the return of sexual function is correlated with improved venous drainage following the operation.

In cases in which medicines or drugs interfere with sexual function, the dosage can be reduced, or an alternative compound not having the undesirable side effect can sometimes be substituted. The choice to take either of these steps, however, depends largely on the circumstances under which the drug is taken and on the expected ramifications to other aspects of the patient's life.

When neurologic disease is present, a variety of interventions have been used. In temporal-lobe epilepsy, anticonvulsive drugs are generally not effective in restoring sexual functioning in men and women, but carbamazepine or benzodiazepines sometimes produce good results (Lundberg, 1977). Most patients with hypothalamic-pituitary region tumors respond favorably (with increased libido and erections for males and increased libido for females) to replacement therapy with gonadal steroids. Some do not show sexual improvement, however, even when plasma steroid levels return to normal (Lundberg, 1977). This suggests a possible direct neural effect on sexual behavior, due to basal hypothalamic damage.

Other, neurally based sexual problems are less amenable to physiological treatment. There is no specific treatment for sexual dysfunctions of patients suffering from multiple sclerosis, other than counseling or providing instructions that allow some patients to continue some forms of sexual behavior.

Nonphysiological intervention, such as counseling and instruction, has also been helpful to patients with injuries to the spinal cord, although statistics on improvement are not available (Higgins, 1978).

Hormone treatments of exogenous androgen replacement have been suggested for sexual dysfunction associated with postpubertal hypogonadism. There is also evidence that reduction of plasma androgen levels in females may interfere with sexual function (Schon & Sutherland, 1960) and that exogenous testosterone administration may have beneficial effects for sexually unresponsive women (Carney, Bancroft, & Mathews, 1978). There is no clear consensus in the literature, however, that supplemental hormone therapy reliably produces any beneficial effect on the sexual performance of men or women whose serum titers of gonadal hormones are within normal limits. Additionally, the long-term effects of even low doses of exogenous testosterone have not been adequately evaluated.

Stabilization of the endocrinological manifestations of diabetes does not generally lead to improved sexual performance. Yet, the clinician should not be too quick to conclude that such cases are due to irreversible neuropathy, since diabetics experience at least as many, and possibly more, psychological problems as do nondiabetics. Counseling in the use of noncoital sexual techniques may be helpful in some cases.

For males with erectile failure, two types of penile prostheses, both of which are surgically implanted, are currently in use. One type, commercially known as the Small Carion device, consists of a semirigid plastic rod that is inserted into the body of the penis. The device leaves the penis rigid enough to permit vaginal penetration but not so rigid as to interfere with normal urination. The other device, the Bradley-Scott device, is a hydraulic system in which the man uses a hand pump housed in the scrotum to pump fluid from a collection reservoir into an inflatable chamber implanted within the penis. The advantage of the hydraulic system is that the erection produced is temporary but can be maintained for as long as the user desires. Both prosthetic devices can restore some degree of sexual function, but their use should be generally limited to cases in which erectile failure is clearly due to biological factors that are irreversible or to those in which sexual counseling has been tried and has failed (see Renshaw, 1978). Since the erectile tissues of the penis are destroyed during the operation, the man will certainly be left impotent if, for some reason, the device must be subsequently removed. Candidates for the operation should receive clear counseling on this point as well as on the fact that any ejaculatory problem or sensory deficit will not necessarily improve following the surgery.

Surgical treatment of orgasmic difficulties in women has also been attempted. Clitoral circumcision is an operation designed to prevent retraction of the organ beneath its hood during high sexual arousal. It thereby allows the woman to receive more direct and continuous penile stimulation throughout the cycle of sexual response. More radical surgical reconstruction of the perineum to realign and tighten the vagina has also been used in an attempt to allow the clitoris to receive more direct stimulation during intercourse (Burt & Burt, 1975). The therapeutic efficacy of either of these procedures, however, remains to be properly demonstrated, and, in the case of the vaginal reconstruction, the possibility of serious postsurgical gynecologic or obstetric complications needs to be examined.

A technique relying upon isometric exercise to improve the tone of the musculature adjacent to the vagina is also used occasionally as an adjunct to sexual counseling, and some data have been reported that suggest a relationship between perineal muscle function and orgasmic capacity (Kline-Graber & Graber, 1978).

One other form of biological treatment that should be noted is medicinal therapy. Tranquilizers and ethanol have been used in an attempt to retard orgasm in men who are suffering from premature ejaculation or whose anxiety is thought to be interfering with sexual arousal. The results have been largely negative. In addition, despite extensive use of exogenous testosterone in the treatment of male erectile problems, the experimental literature has failed to provide convincing support for its effectiveness (Bancroft, in press). Carney et al. (1978), however, recently reported the interesting finding that, when drug therapy was combined with sexual counseling, testosterone (given at a dosage low enough not to produce virilizing side effects) was significantly more effective than the tranquilizer diazepam in restoring sexual function in a group of sexually unresponsive women. However, drug adaptation and long-term effects remain in question.

Psychologically Focused Therapeutic Approaches

To put the various components of sex therapy into perspective, we will first describe its overall structure. Generally, therapy is directed at changing the couple's sexual interactions by assigning them homework, which includes massage, sexual and nonsexual communication, and sexual behavior. Therapy assignments usually begin with a period of sensual exploration, which does not include orgasms, intercourse, or other typical sexual activities. The purpose of this phase is to decrease the anxiety, hostility, or other negative feelings that have come to be associated with sex. It is also intended to develop pleasurable physical interactions that are not genitally focused and to help the couple begin building a more generally satisfying sexual interaction. Gradually, more and more sexual elements are added to the homework assignments, as a means of exploring activities of mutual pleasure and learning to solve problems when disagreements arise. Both sexual and nonsexual communications are intrinsic to the progress of homework assignments. The therapist's role is initially very directive and sometimes involves education and skills training, although some therapists incorporate approaches involving psychodynamics and systems theory for conceptualization and intervention. Gradually, the therapist encourages the clients to take more responsibility for the sexual changes and the homework assignments.

Within this general framework, a variety of techniques is used to improve sexual functioning. The following section critically summarizes these techniques and, when possible, evaluates their effectiveness. The purpose here is to illuminate issues that are relevant to psychic and somatic interactions. A more detailed review can be found in Hogan (1978), LoPiccolo (1977a), and Reynolds (1977).

Anxiety Reduction

A technique often used to decrease anxiety in a sexual relationship is *desensitization*. Desensitization is based on Wolpe's (1958) conceptualization of *reciprocal inhibition*, in which a graded hierarchy of increasingly anxiety-producing steps is developed and systematically paired with an antagonistically relaxing stimulus. The structure of sex therapy itself, beginning with low-anxiety homework assignments and gradually including more anxiety-associated exercises, is an implicit desensitization hierarchy (Dengrove, 1971; Laughren & Kass, 1975). Formal systematic desensitization has been shown to be effective with arousal and orgasmic problems in men and women (for example, Annon, 1976; Dengrove, 1971; Ince, 1973; Lazarus, 1961, 1965, 1968; Rachman, 1959; Wincze, 1971; Wolpe, 1958).

Kockott, Dittmar, and Nusselt (1975) did a noteworthy study, in that they used a control-group design and took three types of outcome measures — subjective, behavioral, and psychophysiological. In comparing a desensitization group to "routine-therapy" (medication plus advice) group and to a waiting-list control, they found that ratings of clinical outcome for the three groups did not differ. Physiological data were analyzed for only ten subjects, and no differences were evident. Self-ratings did show an increase in erections for the desensitization group over the other two groups. They subsequently treated 12 of their failures with a modified Masters-and-Johnson procedure, to which eight patients responded favorably. These results suggest that desensitization may work well with "pure" anxiety symptoms but will be enhanced if combined with implicit or explicit skills training (for example, Husted, 1972; Mathews, Bancroft, Whitehead, Hackman, Julier, Bancroft, Gath, & Shaw, 1976; Wincze & Caird, 1976).

In sex therapy, in vivo desensitization is the most commonly used technique for the reduction of anxiety. In the LoPiccolo and Lobitz (1972) program, which develops a woman's orgasmic ability through masturbation, the woman is gradually led from exercises that simply involve viewing and touching her genitals to exercises that include masturbation. What is interesting about the approach of in vivo desensitization in sex therapy is that it alternates between using relaxation and sexual arousal as the anxiety-inhibiting responses (Annon, 1976; Kaplan, 1974; Masters & Johnson, 1970; Wolpe & Lazarus, 1966). Therapy is often supplemented with films or videotapes, which are supposed to aid in anxiety reduction and help in skill training. Therapy that includes in vivo and imaginal exposure to scenes has also been combined with progressive relaxation (Wolpe, 1958, 1969), hypnotic relaxation (for example, Dittborn, 1957; Fuchs, Hoch, Abramovici, Timor-Tritsch, & Kleinhaus, 1975; Fuchs, Hoch, Paldi, Abramovici, Brandes, Timor-Tritsch, & Kleinhaus, 1973; Lazarus, 1973; Lazarus & Rachman, 1960; Leckie, 1964), and various chemical relaxants (Brady, 1966, 1971; Kraft & Al-Issa, 1968).

Whether anxiety is best reduced in vivo, in imagination, or through films and tapes has not been determined (compare Husted, 1972; Wincze & Caird, 1976). Hogan (1978), in reviewing this literature, suggested that it depends on level of anxiety, level of skill, knowledge, and partner availability and cooperation.

One very effective desensitization procedure is the use of fingers, or progressively larger dilators, in cases of vaginismus (Kaplan, 1974; Masters & Johnson, 1970). The procedure has been very successful. Fuchs et al. (1973) reported that six out of nine patients were "cured," and Masters and Johnson (1970) reported that all their 29 cases were successful.

Two other, less frequently used anxiety-reducing techniques are implosion and guided imagery. Implosion is rarely reported in the literature, although Frankel (1970) used it successfully with a primary inorgasmic woman. Guided imagery, which is thought to work through extinction rather than counterconditioning, has been used to successfully treat arousal problems, vaginismus, and dyspareunia (Dittborn, 1957; Hussain, 1964; Leckie, 1964; Wolpin, 1969).

Sexual Enhancement through Cognitive Techniques

A variety of techniques involve the use of cognitive strategies to enhance positive feelings about sex, reduce negative associations, or directly facilitate sexual arousal. One is to direct clients to focus attention on physical enjoyment of arousal and to avoid thinking about aversive, anxious, or other nonsexual interfering thoughts. Such techniques are also used in conjunction with "sensate focus" exercises, in which clients are instructed to be aware of physical sensations.

Another series of techniques involves *rational-emotive therapy* (Ellis, 1962, 1971), which teaches clients to challenge their own irrational thoughts about performance demands and unrealistic expectations. Ellis claimed, without supporting data, to have succeeded in more than 75% of the erectile failure and female arousal-orgasmic cases he saw (Ellis, 1971).

Fantasy has been used in cases of sexual dysfunction to increase arousal and help keep clients in a sexual mood (Kaplan, 1974; LoPiccolo & Lobitz, 1972). As has been shown earlier, sexual arousal during fantasy has been demonstrated in a variety of psychophysiological studies (for example, Heiman, 1977; Hoon, 1978; Hoon et al., 1977). Arousal during self-generated fantasy has been shown to be lower than arousal to erotic materials, although this depends on the subject (Heiman, 1977), and recent work suggests that fantasy-induced physiological arousal may show lower correlations with subjective reporting than does erotica-induced physiological arousal in women (Heiman & Morokoff, 1977; Hoon, 1978).

Heiman and Morokoff (1977) reported a tendency, after completion of therapy, for formerly nonorgasmic women to increase their ability to become physiologically aroused during fantasy in a psychophysiological experimental setting. This finding was tentative, however, since the relationship between laboratory arousal during fantasy and behavioral change outside the laboratory was not evaluated. At this point, then, the value of fantasy training, while widely held to be therapeutically useful, has not been empirically tested.

Occasionally, therapists teach clients to relabel physical sensations. This has been shown to be of use only in the case of female dysfunction in which sexual arousal was mislabeled as anxiety or tension (Lobitz, LoPiccolo, Lobitz, & Brockway, 1974; LoPiccolo, 1977a). Psychophysiological work with women has also emphasized the process of mislabeling or nonlabeling of physical sensations (Heiman, 1976, 1977).

General educational information, correction of clients' misconceptions, or skill training can also aid clients in feeling more sexually comfortable and self-confident. Skill training, a cognitive-behavioral technique, is also used in treating communication problems (Kaplan, 1974; LoPiccolo, 1977a; Masters & Johnson, 1970; Prochaska & Marzilli, 1973), in assertiveness training (Dengrove, 1971; Fodor, 1974; Lazarus, 1971; Salter, 1961), and in developing specific sexual skills (LoPiccolo, 1977a; Masters & Johnson, 1970; Semans, 1956). The only experimental study evaluating the effectiveness of communication training, however, found no differences, in terms of coital frequency and enjoyment, sexual anxiety, and coital and noncoital orgasmic frequency, between patients receiving communication training and those not receiving it (Husted, 1972).

Relationship Enhancement and Partner Involvement

Therapists have observed that the sexual problem and its resolution are embedded in the overall relationship (for example, Kaplan, 1974; LoPiccolo, 1977a; Masters & Johnson, 1970). The empirical evidence on this view is conflicting. Barbach (1974) and Schneidman and McGuire (1976) reported success in treating nonorgasmic women in a group therapy format. Husted's (1972) study of nonorgasmic women, who were treated with either in vivo or systematic desensitization, compared the effect of conjoint treatment to individual therapy and found no differences in frequency of orgasm, anxiety reduction, or coital satisfaction and frequency. Cooper's (1969c) work with dysfunctional male clients complaining of erectile and ejaculatory problems indicated that therapy was more successful if the wife was "cooperative." These results are difficult to interpret, since it is unclear whether the type of problem (primary orgasmic dysfunction versus erectile failure) or the characteristics within a given dysfunction (anxiety, skill deficits), selection procedure (screening out for marital problems), or type of treatment (desensitization, Masters and Johnson) are affecting differences.

Marital therapy is often incorporated into sex therapy and has been shown to improve sexual functioning (Dengrove, 1971; McGovern, Stewart, & LoPiccolo, 1975). Communication training, which has already been discussed, is the major technique used in marital therapy. Marital therapy in this context generally includes issues concerning sex roles, problem solving, trust issues, and the expression of affection and caring outside of sexual interactions.

The value of dealing with relationship issues in combination with sexual issues is obvious to some therapists, although research on this issue is lacking. Therapists' attitudes seem to determine how much they are willing to deal with relationship factors. Some therapists choose to first refer clients for marital counseling, while others accept most degrees of marital distress and use sex as the "symptom" with which to make marital changes (for example, LoPiccolo, 1977a; Masters & Johnson, 1970).

Therapeutic Effectiveness

In one study directed at an evaluation of psychoanalytically oriented therapy, O'Conner and Stern (1972) reported retrospective results of outcome on 35 male and 61 female patients receiving either long-term psychoanalysis or relatively short-term therapy that was also psychoanalytically oriented. Individuals in psychoanalysis were seen four times per week for at least two years. Psychotherapy patients were seen semiweekly for no longer than two years. The authors reported overall success rates of 77% and 46%, respectively, for both men and women. There is some indication, however, that patients in the psychoanalytic group "evidenced less illness" at the onset of treatment than the psychotherapy group. Moreover, improvement rates may be based on differences in number of sessions.

Masters and Johnson's overall outcome results of success varied between 80% and 85%, as of 1970, for couples treated with two weeks of brief therapy at five-year follow-up.* No control groups were used, and selection criteria were selective in favor of high-income, highly educated clients. Furthermore, treatment success varied, depending on the dysfunction, a typical finding in most outcome evaluations.

Careful reviews of the methodological problems as well as the outcome results of sex therapy can be found elsewhere (Hogan, 1978; LoPiccolo, 1977a; and for male dysfunctions, Cooper, 1971; Reynolds, 1977). The following list

---

*Masters and Johnson (1970) reported their outcome results in terms of failure rate rather than success rate. In order that their results be comparable with other research results presented in this chapter, their 15% to 20% failure rate has been converted here to a success percentage.

summarizes the relative effectiveness of sex therapy, across different therapeutic modalities and orientations, with a focus on brief intervention, (that is, less than one year and often approximately 20 sessions). The disorders are listed in approximate order of reported success.

1. *Premature ejaculation.* The pause (Semans, 1956) and squeeze (Masters & Johnson, 1970) techniques seem to be successful at teaching 90% to 98% of males to delay their ejaculations.

2. *Vaginismus.* This dysfunction is the most successfully treated disorder with success rates ranging between 88% and 100% (Fuchs et al., 1973; Masters & Johnson, 1970).

3. *Primary inorgasmic dysfunction.* While the success rate for teaching women to have masturbatory orgasms is high (85% to 95%), reaching orgasm in coitus (but with additional stimulation) shows lower success rates (Kohlenberg, 1974; LoPiccolo & Lobitz, 1972; Masters & Johnson, 1970). This difference may partly reflect the change in attitude to which many therapists currently adhere regarding the importance of coital orgasm. Since most sexually functional women are reported to not experience orgasm coitally (Kinsey et al., 1953), many therapists do not necessarily focus on this aspect of change, although orgasm through other forms of partner stimulation is considered central to therapy.

4. *Secondary inorgasmic dysfunction.* This is a heterogeneous diagnosis that includes women who have rarely had orgasm in any way as well as women who were orgasmic until some time before entering therapy. Some of these women have never masturbated, while others have one pattern of masturbation that is the only source of orgasm. Thus, the effectiveness of treatment varies tremendously, particularly if the outcome measure is only frequency of orgasm. Masters and Johnson (1970) reported a success rate that varies between 63% and 91%, depending on the type of secondary pattern. On a small sample, McGovern et al. (1975) pointed out that while a group of secondary inorgasmic women did not increase their orgasmic ability, significant gains were made in the sexual compatibility of couples.

5. *Erectile failure.* Primary erectile failure cases are rather uncommon in this country, and their success rate is estimated at about 40% (Masters & Johnson, 1970). Secondary erectile failure cases fare somewhat better, averaging 60% to 80% (Cooper, 1969b; Masters & Johnson, 1970).

6. *Ejaculatory incompetence.* This is the least frequently treated male disorder, with success rates between 50% (Tuthill, 1955) and 83% (Masters & Johnson, 1970).

7. *Low sex drive/desire.* Outcome data are not yet available on this group (see L. LoPiccolo, 1980; Zilbergeld & Rinkleib, 1980).

Issues in Therapy and Psychophysiological Conceptualization

As should be clear from the preceding review, there have been few attempts to integrate psychophysiological conceptualizations and procedures with sex therapy. There are two areas that are relevant to sex therapy in which psychophysiology has begun to be involved: assessment and biofeedback. Since biofeedback has already been discussed, we will mention only selected aspects of that research. The focus here is on assessment.

Assessment issues seem to be a major stumbling block in attempting to understand the etiology of sexual dysfunction and to evaluate the effectiveness of treatment. The outcome data presented earlier reflect part of this problem. Change was measured differently across studies. What has been, and might be, the place of psychophysiology in the assessment of sexual functioning?

General Measurement Issues

The measurement of human sexual function and dysfunction is fraught with problems that have perpetually challenged the ingenuity of clinician and researcher alike. It is indeed difficult to imagine any other human behavior that is less open to observation and measurement. Sex is one of the most private and sensitive areas of human life, and clinicians and researchers are often as loath to broach the topic as clients and subjects are to respond to their questions. Consequently, relatively few techniques appropriate for obtaining sexual information have been conceived, and those techniques that are available are undoubtedly affected, to various degrees, by such factors as anxiety, embarrassment, desire to appear socially acceptable, or intentional deception. The situation is further complicated by the fact that human sexuality is an extremely complex psychosocial event that cannot be meaningfully measured in any single dimension. Therefore, the most informative sexual research or the most helpful sex therapy will demonstrate an appreciation of this multidimensional nature.

By far, the most popular method used by therapists for gaining information about a client's sexual functioning is the unstructured clinical interview, which, in some instances, includes taking an extensive "sexual history." Based on information uncovered during the interview, the therapist makes subjective judgments about the client. Such interviews undoubtedly reveal a great deal of information, yet they suffer from the problems of all such clinical interviews, namely, they are largely nonstandardized, subjective, and highly dependent on the particular questions asked by the interviewer. Therefore, it is difficult to assess the accuracy of information elicited in this manner. Although information gathered in this manner is considered clinically useful, there is a lack of evidence showing that the actual conduct of therapy follows from this information. Information gathered from both sexual partners can be used to check on reliability and to detect differing perceptions of the same events. Knowledge about differences in perception can be useful for choosing among therapeutic strategies.

Greater objectivity and some quantification of data can be obtained by having people maintain a formal record of their sexual behavior. By making periodic entries in a diary or some other record form, clients can provide information about such things as frequency and duration of sexual encounters, latency to orgasm, type of sexual behaviors that occur, and any positive or negative effects of contextual elements. A significant advantage of personal record keeping is that it does not rely so heavily on the individual's memory of events as does the interview technique. It also can be used to identify cyclic relationships between cognition and behavior. Yet, personal record keeping can be useful only to the extent that people are able and willing to carefully record the information. Once again, if it is possible to secure information from both sexual partners so that a reliability check can be made, this should be done.

Direct personal observation of sexually interacting couples has also been attempted for both therapeutic (Hartman & Fithian, 1972) and research purposes (Masters & Johnson, 1966). Therapist observation of videotaped sexual interactions has also been used (Serber, 1974). Another form of direct personal observation is the so-called sexological exam (Hartman & Fithian, 1972), in which various erogenous areas of the client's body are stimulated for the purpose of eliciting and evaluating the sexual response. Although an accurate measurement of some aspects of sexual behavior can undoubtedly be made through direct observation, such methods are not acceptable to all people. Furthermore, the obtrusiveness of observers in the same room is likely to so drastically alter the interpersonal dimension of the context for some couples that they would be unable to respond in their typical way. Although videotaping may be somewhat less obtrusive, having sexual relations "on camera" would undoubtedly have a similar effect.

Standardized psychometric instruments for measuring various aspects of sexual behavior are also notably lacking. Currently available, however, are three such instruments that have proven somewhat useful. The SAI (Hoon, Hoon, & Wincze, 1976) requires the female respondent to rate the degree of sexual arousal she typically experiences during various sexual acts. Harbison, Graham, Quinn, McAllister, and Woodward (1974) developed a scale, which can be used with both men and women, for assessing the degree of sexual interest in erotic activities. This scale had high reliability and internal consistency when evaluated on a British sample. Another psychometric scale is the Sexual Interaction Inventory (SII) (LoPiccolo & Steger, 1974). This test, which is administered separately to the man and the woman, inquires about the frequency of occurrence of, as well as the pleasure derived from, a series of heterosexual behaviors. The test yields scores on 11 scales, which have been shown to have good reliability and are able to detect therapeutic gain during sexual counseling.

Until recently, there was no direct means of measuring the physiological component of sexual function or dysfunction, and therapists and researchers had to rely primarily on people's unsubstantiated, subjective reports concerning the physiological changes they experienced during sexual behaviors. However, the development of instruments capable of recording physiological changes in the genital organs has made this dimension of sexuality amenable to reliable measurement.

In men, two basic methods have been used to measure genital changes during sexual arousal: measures of volume and measures of circumference. Some investigators have determined that measures of volume changes are more sensitive than are measures of circumference (Freund, Langevin, & Barlow, 1974; McConaghy, 1974). Moreover, it has been argued that three-dimensional changes in volume more completely describe the penile response than do two-dimensional changes in circumference at a single point, since penile circumference does not expand equally at all points during erection (McConaghy, 1974). Yet, in spite of these advantages, most investigators have opted for the circumferential measures because of advantages they offer in terms of simplicity of operation, inexpensiveness, and subject comfort.

Measurement is accomplished by surrounding the penile shaft with a highly elastic latex tube filled with a column of mercury and containing an electrode in each end (Bancroft, 1974). An electric current is then imposed between the electrodes and is conducted by the mercury column. As erection occurs, the tubing is stretched, causing a lengthening and narrowing of the mercury column. Since the electrical resistance of a conductor depends on its length and cross-sectional area, measuring the changes in this resistance provides a useful metric of penile diameter. In most applications, the mercury strain gauge forms one leg of a Wheatstone bridge, with the output recorded on a polygraph. Another method utilizes an electromechanical strain gauge mounted on a flexible, metal restraining ring, which partially surrounds the penile shaft (Barlow, Becker, Leitenberg, & Agras, 1970). Mechanical deformations produce changes in the electrical resistance of the strain gauge, which are recorded in a manner similar to that used with the mercury device. (For a more thorough coverage of the issues involved in penile recording, see Rosen and Keefe, 1978.)

In women, changes in vaginal vasocongestion during sexual arousal can be measured by means of a vaginal photoplethysmograph (Hoon, Wincze, & Hoon, 1976; Sintchak & Geer, 1975). These devices consist of a light source and some sort of photosensitive transducer, which are mounted on an intravaginal probe. The light source illuminates the vaginal tissues, and the photosensor responds to the fraction of the incident light that is backscattered from the vaginal wall and the blood circulating within it. Since the opacity of the tissue, and hence the amount of light backscattered, is largely dependent upon the volume of blood within it, the vaginal photoplethysmograph provides a measure of vasocongestion. Two components of variation are simultaneously recordable from a single vaginal device. Slowly developing changes in vaginal blood volume due to blood pooling have been shown to yield a valid measure of sexual arousal, as have periodic oscillations in amplitude of vaginal pulse due to the intermittent arrival of the pulse wave at the observation point, (Geer et al., 1974). (For a more comprehensive analysis of methodological issues pertinent to vaginal photoplethysmography, see Hatch, 1979.)

Although the vaginal photoplethysmograph remains the most popular genital measure of sexual arousal in women, experimentation with alternative measurement techniques has recently begun. Henson, Rubin, and Henson (1978) tested a thermistor, which was clipped to a labium minora, and recorded increases in labial temperature when subjects were shown an erotic film. These responses were reliable across stimulus presentations and were positively correlated with subjects' subjective reports of sexual arousal. Bohlen and Held (1979) recently developed a device capable of recording either vaginal or anal muscle contractions during sexual arousal. They showed that vaginal and anal contractions occurring during orgasm correspond temporally with changes in blood volume and pulse of blood volume. Such methodological innovations show promise of becoming useful physiological measures of sexual arousal. However, since they have not yet been utilized in clinical research, the following discussion will include only studies utilizing vaginal photoplethysmography techniques.

Clinical Psychophysiological Research

The results of four studies on clinical populations of women, using sexually functional controls (Heiman, 1978a, 1978b; Heiman & Morokoff, 1977; Wincze et al., 1976), in some ways are contradictory. Wincze et al (1976) found that six women who had arousal and orgasmic difficulties showed less physiological arousal to an erotic videotape than did six sexually functional women. Furthermore, these researchers found significant positive correlations between vaginal engorgement and self-report measures of awareness of physiological changes during arousal, arousing sexual experiences, the frequency of intercourse, and physiological arousal to erotic stimulation (Wincze et al., 1976). Wincze, Hoon, and Hoon (1978) later extended this study to a pretherapy-posttherapy design but did not employ a normal control group. Following sex therapy, ratings of sexual arousability (SAI scores), behavioral measures, and physiological measures showed no clinically significant changes, although interviews with the clients indicated that they were more easily aroused and had better sexual communication.

A preliminary report by Heiman (1978a) confirmed the physiological findings of the Wincze et al. (1976) study, with six sexually dysfunctional women (with arousal and orgasmic difficulties) showing less physiological arousal during an erotic tape and film and fantasy conditions than did 16 functional women.

Morokoff and Heiman (1980), however, later matched women for age and years married and found, with the same design ($n = 11$ per group), that there were no differences in vaginal response (vaginal pulse amplitude) between the two groups. Significant differences did occur in the subjective ratings of arousal, with the clinical sample reporting less arousal to all erotic conditions than the nonclinical sample. There were no significant correlations between vaginal arousal and subjective arousal, although the clinical sample showed a significant positive correlation between vaginal pulse amplitude and reported anxiety. Furthermore, except for subjective-physiological correlations during one fantasy, in the dysfunctional sample no significant physiological or subjective arousal changes occurred following sex therapy, although ease of orgasm and sexual satisfaction increased. Using the same design, Heiman (1980) also reported on a group of 55 sexually functional women and found that high levels of vaginal response in the laboratory were negatively correlated with reports of orgasmic regularity in foreplay and intercourse, frequency of intercourse, and arousal during foreplay and intercourse; however, they were positively related to orgasm in masturbation.

The Wincze et al. (1976, 1978) and Morokoff and Heiman (1980) studies examined both laboratory and nonlaboratory responses. Additionally, the Wincze et al. design traced the arousal curve, which was controlled for sexual experience and menstrual cycle variables, and used a criterion-relevant subjective measure (the SAI) as a correlate. The Morokoff and Heiman work, however, controlled for age and years married between samples, used standard outcome measures for sexual change (the SII), and included subjective reports for correlation during the experimental session. These differences between studies may account for their contradictory results.

Several clinical studies on male sexual response have also been reported. Kockott (1978) evaluated 24 sexually functional men and men who complained of diabetic erectile failure ($n = 10$), primary erectile failure ($n = 8$), secondary erectile failure ($n = 8$), and premature ejaculation ($n = 16$). He reported psychological, psychophysiological, and endocrinological results. The diabetic group showed less penile reaction to erotic material than did the other clinical groups and the control groups but similar reactions in terms of systolic blood pressure and skin conductance. Physiologically, the diabetic group was more akin to the patients with secondary erectile failure, while a different pattern occurred for the primary, premature ejaculation and normal samples. Psychological tests showed the diabetic group to be generally less anxious than the other clinical groups, although more anxious than the normal group. Blood samples, taken at 15-minute intervals for three hours, showed that plasma testosterone, unbound testosterone, and luteinizing hormone were within normal limits in all groups.

Kockott's work is valuable for its sampling of different physiological and psychological components and for its contribution toward the development of a *psychophysiological profile*. He was the first researcher to attempt to use psychophysiology to differentiate clinical categories on several dimensions. His method shows promise for classification and treatment of dysfunctions. It would be useful to see a subjective-affective profile accompany experimentation with female-centered dysfunctions as well.

Speiss (1977) reported a psychophysiological study of men who were functional as opposed to men who were premature ejaculators. Using a psychophysical scaling procedure, Speiss reported no differences on a variety of subjective and physiological responses to erotica between the two groups. Sexual questionnaire data, however, revealed a significant difference in sexual frequency, with the clinical sample having sex less frequently than the nonclinical sample.

One area in which this physiological measurement capability has found application is the differential diagnosis of psychogenic as opposed to biogenic etiology in erectile dysfunction. It is now known that periods of rapid eye movement (REM) sleep are frequently accompanied by penile erection. These periods of nocturnal penile tumescence appear to be universally present in normal males of all ages and are consistently demonstrated in individual subjects from night to night. Karacan, Williams, Thornby, and Salis (1975) tested 125 subjects ranging in age from three to 79 years and reported that all showed erections during sleep.*

While the mechanism and function of the phenomenon of nocturnal penile tumescence remain obscure, it does appear that it can serve as a useful behavioral indicant of organic pathology, and attempts have been made to classify men as organically or psychogenically impotent based upon laboratory measurements of nocturnal erections in sleeping subjects. It was originally hypothesized that men showing a complete absence of nocturnal erections suffer from organic impotence, while those who show nocturnal erections suffer from psychogenic impotence (Karacan, 1970). In a sample of impotent diabetics, it was reported that potency was restored in those who demonstrated nocturnal erections following dietary regulation and psychotherapy (Karacan, 1970).

More recently, Karacan et al. (1975) reported results on 55 impotent men, all of whom were candidates for penile prosthesis implant. Two-thirds of the patients showed abnormal patterns of nocturnal tumescence and subsequently received prosthetic penile implants. The patients who showed normal sleeping erectile responses were usually referred for psychological treatment. Outcome statistics on this group were, unfortunately, not reported.

Another group of investigators (Fisher, Schiavi, Lear, Edwards, Davis, & Witkin, 1975) reported a study involving case histories of nine impotent men, using nocturnal penile tumescence as a measure. Three of the men had been previously diagnosed as being psychogenically impotent, and the remaining six men had been diagnosed as impotent due to organic causes. The variable that best discriminated between the organic and psychogenic subjects was the degree of discrepancy between a man's erectile *potential* observed during REM sleep and his waking erectile *performance*, rather than the fact of whether or not an erection was completely present or absent during sleep. The organic subjects exhibited similarly reduced degrees of erection during both REM sleep and waking sexual activity. The psychogenic men, on the other hand, showed a large discrepancy between the erections they produced during sleep and waking, with waking capacity showing the greater impairment.

The importance of gauging each man's nocturnal erectile capacity in relation to his own waking capacity, rather than in relation to external norms, was

---

*An analogous response is thought to occur in women during REM sleep, but its clinical potential has yet to be explored (Cohen & Shapiro, 1970; Karacan, Rosenbloom, & Williams, 1970).

emphasized in the case of a man whose erections were quite large when compared to those of other men studied but which were still not fully erect or rigid (Fisher et al., 1975). Although the correlation between circumference and rigidity is generally considered good, the above case clearly shows the need for individualized assessment. For this reason, Karacan (1978) recently recommended measuring rigidity, as well as circumference, of the penis. The procedure involves awakening the man and applying a device that measures the buckling pressure of the penis. A buckling pressure of approximately 100 millimeters of mercury is generally considered to be sufficient for vaginal penetration (Karacan, 1978).

So far, the few attempts to utilize psychophysiological measurement techniques in the evaluation of sexual dysfunction have not produced very impressive results, and certainly their clinical validity remains to be properly demonstrated. Yet, it bears repeating that the psychophysiological nature of sexual function and dysfunction demands that this component be embraced by measurement procedures.

CONCLUSION: GENERAL DIRECTIONS FOR FUTURE RESEARCH

Given the insufficiently controlled research on therapy outcome and components, several directions for future research seem worth pursuing.

First, there is a need for multidimensional conceptualization and assessment of sexual dysfunction. A psychophysiological framework reminds us of the necessity of considering physiological, subjective-affective, and behavioral factors from both an intra- and interpersonal perspective. This is a massive task. Additionally, the current level of instrumentation development does not adequately deal with some of these categories.

A second direction that seems needed is the tracing of the process of therapeutic change at a more specific level. One possibility is to assess different change categories at specific points during the course of therapy, along the line of a time series analysis. This would be particularly interesting, in terms of laboratory psychophysiology, in cases of primary orgasmic dysfunction and premature ejaculation, since clinical changes along a physiological path do occur. In addition, tracing the affective correlates of sexual arousal might better help us to understand the total emotional nature of sexual response. Multiple case studies may be a useful beginning in the evaluation of the change process.

Research focused on the interactional and interpersonal components of sexual response has been lacking. Sexual problems are, to some extent, maintained by two people. Etiologically and clinically, it would be useful to obtain the historical and current factors from each person in a sexual relationship, factors that, when brought together, would predispose or maintain particular sexual dysfunctions.

Sexuality, although conceptualized here from a psychophysiological framework, is not limited to a psychophysiological methodology. Etiology and treatment of sexual dysfunction, as well as better understanding of the meaning of sexuality to functional and satisfied people, would benefit from sociological and social psychological models, cognitive psychology, information-processing paradigms, neurobiology, neuroendocrinology, and philosophical inquiry. A process of analysis and synthesis would enrich our understanding of the unique and complex place that sex occupies in individual, relationship, and sociocultural patterns of life.

REFERENCES

Abelson, D. Diagnostic value of the penile pulse and blood pressure: A Doppler study of impotence in diabetics. *Journal of Urology*, 1975, *113*, 636-639.

Ambroso, D., & Brown, M. Problems in studying the effects of erotic material. *Journal of Sex Research*, 1973, *9*, 187-195.

American Psychiatric Association. *Third Diagnostic and Statistical Manual of the American Psychiatric Association*. Washington, D.C.: Author, 1968.

Annon, J. *The behavioral treatment of sexual problems: Intensive therapy* Vol. II. Honolulu: Kapiolani Health Services, 1976.

Ansari, J. M. A. A study of 65 impotent males. *British Journal of Psychiatry*, 1975, *127*, 37-41.

Anthony, E. J. The behavior disorders of children. In P. H. Mussen (Ed.), *Carmichael's manual of child psychology* (Vol. 2). New York: Wiley, 1970.

Ax, A. F. The physiological differentiation between fear and anger in humans. *Psychosomatic Medicine*, 1953, *15*, 433-442.

Bancroft, J. *Deviant sexual behavior: Modification and assessment*. Oxford: Clarendon Press, 1974.

Bancroft, J. Psychophysiology of sexual dysfunction. In H. van Praag, M. Lader, O. Rafaelsen, & E. Sachar (Eds.), *Handbook of biological psychiatry*. New York: Marcel Dekker, in press.

Bancroft, J., & Skakkeback, N. Androgens and human sexual behavior. In CIBA Foundation Symposium. *Sex, Hormones, and Behavior*. Amsterdam: Excerpta Medica, 1979.

Bandura, A. *Principles of behavior modification*. New York: Holt, Rinehart & Winston, 1968.

Barbach, L. G. Group treatment of preorgasmic women. *Journal of Sex and Marital Therapy*, 1974, *1*, 139-145.

Barclay, A. M. The effect of hostility on physiological and fantasy responses. *Journal of Personality*, 1969, *37*, 651-657.

Barlow, D. H., Becker, R., Leitenberg, H., & Agras, W. S. A mechanical strain gauge for recording penile circumference change. *Journal of Applied Behavior Analysis*, 1970, *3*, 73-76.

Barratt, E. S. Anxiety and impulsiveness: Toward a neuropsychological model. In C. D. Spielberger (Ed.), *Anxiety: Current trends in theory and research* (Vol. 1). New York: Academic Press, 1972.

Belt, B. G. Some organic causes of impotence. *Medical Aspects of Human Sexuality*, January 1973, pp. 152-161.

Bohlen, J. G., & Held, J. P. An anal probe for monitoring vascular and muscular events during sexual response. *Psychophysiology*, 1979, *16*, 318-323.

Brady, J. P. Brevital-relaxation treatment of frigidity. *Behavior Research and Therapy*, 1966, *4*, 71-77.

Brady, J. P. Brevital-aided systematic desensitization. In R. D. Rubin, H. Fensterheim, A. A. Lazarus, & C. M. Franks (Eds.), *Advances in behavior therapy: Proceedings of the third conference of the Association for the Advancement of Behavior Therapy*. New York: Academic Press, 1971.

Briddell, D. W., & Wilson, G. T. Effects of alcohol and expectancy set on male sexual arousal. *Journal of Abnormal Psychology*, 1976, *85*, 225-234.

Britt, D. B., Kemmerer, W. T., & Robison, J. R. Penile blood flow determination by mercury strain gauge plethysmography. *Investigative Urology*, 1971, *8*, 673-678.

Burgess, D., & Krop, H. The relationship between sexual arousability, heterosexual attitudes, sexual anxiety, and general sexual anxiety in women. Unpublished manuscript, University of Florida, 1977.

Burt, J. E., & Burt, J. C. *The surgery of love*. New York: Carlton Press, 1975.

Buss, A. H. Two anxiety factors in psychiatric patients. *Journal of Abnormal and Social Psychology*, 1962, *65*, 426-427.

Byrne, D., & Sheffield, J. Response to sexually arousing stimuli as a function of repressing and sensitizing defenses. *Journal of Abnormal Psychology*, 1965, *70*, 114-118.

Carney, A., Bancroft, J., & Mathews, A. Combination of hormonal and psychological treatment for female sexual unresponsiveness: A comparative study. *British Journal of Psychiatry*, 1978, *132*, 339-346.

Cerny, J. Biofeedback and the voluntary control of sexual arousal in women. *Behavior Therapy*, 1978, *9*, 847-855.

Chesser, E. *The sexual marital and family relationships of the English woman*. London: Hutchinson's Medical, 1956.

Cohen, H. D., & Shapiro, A. Vaginal blood flow during sleep. *Psychophysiology*, 1970, *7*, 338. (Abstract)

Cooper, A. J. A factual study of male potency disorders. *British Journal of Psychiatry*, 1968, *114*, 719-731. (a)

Cooper, A. J. Hostility and male potency disorders. *Comprehensive Psychiatry*, 1968, *9*, 621-626. (b)

Cooper, A. J. "Neurosis" and disorders of sexual potency in the male. *Journal of Psychosomatic Research*, 1968, *12*, 141-144. (c)

Cooper, A. J. Clinical and therapeutic studies in premature ejaculation. *Comprehensive Psychiatry*, 1969, *10*, 285-295. (a)

Cooper, A. J. A clinical study of "coital anxiety" in male potency disorders. *Journal of Psychosomatic Research*, 1969, *13*, 143-147. (b)

Cooper, A. J. Disorders of sexual potency in the male: A clinical and statistical study of some factors related to short-term prognosis. *British Journal of Psychiatry*, 1969, *115*, 709-719. (c)

Cooper, A. J. Frigidity, treatment, and short-term prognosis. *Journal of Psychosomatic Research*, 1970, *14*, 133-147.

Cooper, A. J. Treatment of male potency disorders: The present status. *Psychosomatics*, 1971, *12*, 235-244.

Cooper, A. J. Diagnosis and management of "endocrine impotence." *British Medical Journal*, 1972, *2*, 34-36.

Csillag, E. R. Modification of penile erection response. *Behavior Therapy and Experimental Psychiatry*, 1976, *7*, 27-29.

Cupchik, G., & Leventhal, H. Consistency between expressive behavior and the evaluation of humorous stimuli: The role of sex and self-observation. *Journal of Personality and Social Psychology*, 1974, *30*, 429-442.

Dahlen, C. P., & Goodwin, W. E. Sexual potency after perineal biopsy. *Journal of Urology*, 1957, *77*, 660-669.

Davidson, J. M. Neurohormonal bases of male sexual behavior. *International Review of Physiology, Reproductive Physiology II* (Vol. 13). Baltimore: University Park Press, 1977.

Davidson, R. J., & Schwartz, G. E. The psychobiology of relaxation and related status: A multi-process theory. In D. Mostofsky (Ed.), *Behavior control and modification of physiological activity*. Englewood Cliffs, N. J.: Prentice-Hall, 1976.

Davis, K. B. *Factors in the sex life of twenty-two hundred women*. New York: Harper, 1929.

Dengrove, E. Behavior therapy of impotence. *Journal of Sex Research*, 1971, *7*, 177-183.

De-Nour, A. K. Hemodialysis: Sexual functioning. *Psychosomatics*, 1978, *19*, 229-235.

Dickinson, R. L., & Beam, L. *A thousand marriages: A medical study of sexual adjustment*. Baltimore, Md.: Williams & Wilkins, 1931.

Dittborn, J. Hypnotherapy of sexual impotence. *International Journal of Clinical and Experimental Hypnosis*, 1957, *5*, 181-192.

Duvall, S., & Wickland, R. *Theory of objective self-awareness*. New York: Academic Press, 1973.

Ellenberg, M. Impotence in diabetics: The neurologic factor. *Annals of Internal Medicine*, 1971, *75*, 213-219.

Ellis, A. *Reason and emotion in psychotherapy*. New York: Lyle Stuart, 1962.

Ellis, A. Rational-emotive treatment of impotence, frigidity, and other sexual problems. *Professional Psychology*, 1971, *2*, 246-349.

Fisher, C., Schiavi, R., Lear, H., Edwards, A., Davis, D. M., & Witkin, A. P. The assessment of nocturnal REM erection in the differential diagnosis of sexual impotence. *Journal of Sex and Marital Therapy*, 1975, *1*, 277-289.

Fisher, S. *The female orgasm*. New York: Basic Books, 1973.

Fitzpatrick, T. J. Venography of the deep dorsal venous and valvular systems. *Journal of Urology*, 1974, *111*, 518-520.

Fitzpatrick, T. J. The corpus cavernosum intercommunicating venous drainage system. *Journal of Urology*, 1975, *113*, 494-496.

Fitzpatrick, T. J., & Cooper, J. F. A cavernosogram study on the valvular competence of the human deep dorsal vein. *Journal of Urology*, 1975, *113*, 497-499.

Fodor, I. Sex role conflict and symptom formation in women: Can behavior therapy help? *Psychotherapy: Theory, Research, and Practice*, 1974, *11*, 22-29.

Frank, E., Anderson, A., & Rubenstein, D. Frequency of sexual dysfunction in "normal" couples. *New England Journal of Medicine*, 1978, *299*, 111-115.

Frankel, A. S. Treatment of multisymptomatic phobia by a self-directed, self-reinforced technique. *Journal of Abnormal Psychology*, 1970, *76*, 496-499.

Freud, S. *Three essays on the theory of female sexuality*. New York: Avon, 1962. (Originally published, 1905.)

Freud, S. [*The problem of anxiety*], New York: Psychoanalytic Press/Norton, 1926.

Freund, K., Langevin, R., & Barlow, D. Comparison of two penile measures of erotic arousal. *Behavior Research and Therapy*, 1974, *12*, 335-359.

Fuchs, K., Hoch, Z., Abramovici, H., Timor-Tritsch, I., & Kleinhaus, M. Vaginismus — The hypnotherapeutic approach. *Journal of Sex Research*, 1975, *11*, 39-45.

Fuchs, K., Hoch, Z., Paldi, E., Abramovici, H., Brandes, J. M., Timor-Tritsch, I., & Kleinhaus, M. Hypno-desensitization therapy of vaginismus: Part I. "In vitro" method. Part II. "In vivo" method. *International Journal of Clinical and Experimental Hypnosis*, 1973, *21*, 144-156.

Gebhard, P. Factors in marital orgasm. *Journal of Social Issues*, 1966, *22*, 88-96.

Geer, J. H., Morokoff, P. J., & Greenwood, P. Sexual arousal in women: The development of a measurement device for vaginal blood volume. *Archives of Sexual Behavior*, 1974, *3*, 559-564.

George, L. K., & Weiler, S. *Aging and sexual behavior: The myth of declining sexuality*. Manuscript submitted for publication, 1979.

Globus, G., Maxwell, G., & Savodnik, I. (Eds.). *Consciousness and the brain: A scientific and philosophical inquiry*. New York: Plenum Press, 1976.

Hamblin, R. L., & Blood, R. O. Premarital experience and the wife's sexual adjustment. *Social Problems*, 1956, *4*, 122-130.

Hamilton, G. V. *A research in marriage*. New York: A. & C. Boni, 1929.

Harbison, J., Graham, P., Quinn, J., McAllister, H., & Woodward, R. A questionnaire measure of sexual interest. *Archives of Sexual Behavior*, 1974, *3*, 357-365.

Hartman, W. E., & Fithian, M. A. *The treatment of sexual dysfunction*. Long Beach, Cal.: Center for Marital & Sexual Studies, 1972.

Hatch, J. P. Vaginal photoplethysmography: Methodological considerations. *Archives of Sexual Behavior*, 1979, *8*, 357-374.

Heiman, J. Issues in the use of psychophysiology to assess female sexual dysfunction. *Journal of Sex and Marital Therapy*, 1976, *2*, 197-204.

Heiman, J. A psychophysiological exploration of sexual arousal patterns in females and males. *Psychophysiology*, 1977, *14*, 266-274.

Heiman, J. Uses of psychophysiology in the assessment and treatment of sexual dysfunction. In J. LoPiccolo & L. LoPiccolo (Eds.), *Handbook of sex therapy*. New York: Plenum Press, 1978. (a)

Heiman, J. *Sexual arousal patterns in women: Psychophysiological data and theory*. Paper presented at the Third International Congress of Medical Sexology, Rome, 1978. (b)

Heiman, J. Female sexual response patterns: Interactions of physiological, affective, and contextual cues. *Archives of General Psychiatry*, 1980, *37*, 1311-1316.

Heiman, J., LoPiccolo, L., & LoPiccolo, J. The treatment of sexual dysfunction. In A. S. Gurman & D. P. Kniskern (Eds.), *Handbook of family therapy*. New York: Brunner/Mazel, 1981.

Heiman, J.,& Morokoff, P. *Female sexual arousal and experience as correlates of sexual malaise*. Paper presented at American Psychological Association Meetings, San Francisco, Sept. 1977.

Hempel, C. G. Fundamentals of taxonomy. In C. G. Hempel (Ed.), *Aspects of scientific explanation and other essays in the philosophy of science*. New York: Free Press, 1965.

Hendrik, I. *Facts and theories of psychoanalysis*. New York: Dell, 1958. (Originally published, 1934).

Henson, D. E., Rubin, H. B., Henson, C., & Williams, J. Temperature change of the labia minora as an objective measure of human female eroticism. *Journal of Behavior Therapy and Experimental Psychiatry*, 1977, *8*, 401-410.

Henson, D. E., Rubin, H. B., & Henson, C. Consistency of labial temperature change measure of human female eroticism. *Behavior Research and Therapy*, 1978, *16*, 125-129.

Higgins, G. E. Aspects of sexual response in adults with spinal-cord injury: A review of the literature. In J. LoPiccolo & L. LoPiccolo (Eds.), *Handbook of sex therapy*. New York: Plenum Press, 1978.

Hogan, D. The effectiveness of sex therapy. In J. LoPiccolo & L. LoPiccolo (Eds.), *Handbook of sex therapy*. New York: Plenum Press, 1978.

Hohmann, G. W. Some effects of spinal cord lesions on experienced emotional feelings. *Psychophysiology*, 1966, *3*, 143-156.

Hoon, E. F. *Biofeedback assisted sexual arousal in women: A comparison of visual and auditory modalities.* Paper presented at the third annual southeastern regional conference of the American Association of Sex Educators, Counselors, and Therapists, Asheville, N. C., 1978.

Hoon, E. F., Hoon, P., & Wincze, J. An inventory for the measurement of female sexual arousability. *Archives of Sexual Behavior*, 1976, *5*, 291-300.

Hoon, P. W., Wincze, J., & Hoon, E. F. Physiological assessment of sexual arousal in women. *Psychophysiology*, 1976, *13*, 196-204.

Hoon, P., Wincze, J., & Hoon, E. F. A test of reciprocal inhibition: Are anxiety and sexual arousal mutually inhibitory? *Journal of Abnormal Psychology*, 1977, *86*, 65-74.

Hunt, M. *Sexual behavior in the 70's.* Chicago: Playboy Press, 1974.

Hussain, A. Behavior therapy using hypnosis. In J. Wolpe, A. Salter, & L. Reyna (Eds.), *The conditioning therapies: The challenge in psychotherapy*. New York: Holt, Rinehart & Winston, 1964.

Husted, J. R. Effect of method of systematic desensitization and presence of sexual communication in the treatment of sexual anxiety by counterconditioning. *Proceedings of the 80th Annual Convention of the American Psychological Association*, 1972, *7*, 325-326.

Ince, L. P. Behavior modification of sexual disorders. *American Journal of Psychotherapy*, 1973, *27*, 446-451.

Jochheim, K. A., & Wahle, H. A study on sexual function in 56 male patients with complete irreversible lesions of the spinal cord and cauda equina. *Paraplegia*, 1970, *8*, 166-172.

Kaplan, H. S. *The new sex therapy.* New York: Brunner/Mazel, 1974.

Kaplan, H. S. Hypoactive sexual desire. *Journal of Sex and Marital Therapy*, 1977, *3*, 3-9.

Karacan, I. Clinical value of nocturnal erection in the prognosis and diagnosis of impotence. *Medical Aspects of Human Sexuality*, April 1970, pp. 27-34.

Karacan, I. Advances in the psychophysiological evaluation of male erectile impotence. In J. LoPiccolo & L. LoPiccolo (Eds.), *Handbook of sex therapy*. New York: Plenum Press, 1978.

Karacan, I., Rosenbloom, A. L., & Williams, R. L. The clitoral erection cycle during sleep. *Psychophysiology*, 1970, *7*, 338. (Abstract)

Karacan, I., Williams, R. L., Thornby, J. I., & Salis, P. J. Sleep-related penile tumescence as a function of age. *American Journal of Psychiatry*, 1975, *132*, 932-936.

Kedia, K., & Markland, C. The effect of pharmacological agents on ejaculation. *Journal of Urology*, 1975, *114*, 569-573.

Kimmel, P., & van der Veen, F. Factors of marital adjustment in Locke's Marital Adjustment Test. *Journal of Marriage and the Family*, 1974, *2*, 57-63.

Kinsey, A. C., Pomeroy, W. B., & Martin, C. E. *Sexual behavior in the human male*. Philadelphia: Saunders, 1948.

Kinsey, A. C., Pomeroy, W. B., Martin C. E., & Gebhard, P. H. *Sexual behavior in the human female*. Philadelphia: Saunders, 1953.

Kline-Graber, G., & Graber, B. Diagnosis and treatment procedures of pubococcygeal deficiencies in women. In J. LoPiccolo & L. LoPiccolo (Eds.), *Handbook of sex therapy*. New York: Plenum Press, 1978.

Kockott, G. *Symptomatology, psychological and physiological aspects of premature ejaculation, diabetogenic, and psychogenic erectile impotence: Results of an experimental study*. Paper presented at the Third International Congress of Medical Sexology, Rome, 1978.

Kockott, G., Dittmar, F., & Nusselt, L. Systematic desensitization of erectile impotence: A controlled study. *Archives of Sexual Behavior*, 1975, *4*, 493-500.

Kohlenberg, R. J. Directed masturbation and the treatment of primary orgasmic dysfunction. *Archives of Sexual Behavior*, 1974, *3*, 349-356.

Kraft, T., & Al-Issa, I. The use of methohexitone sodium in the systematic desensitization of premature ejaculation. *British Journal of Psychiatry*, 1968, *114*, 351-352. (Abstract)

Lang, P. J. Fear reduction and fear behavior: Problems in treating a construct. In J. M. Shilien (Ed.), *Research in psychotherapy* (Vol. 3). Washington, D. C.: American Psychological Association, 1968.

Lang, P. J. The application of psychophysiological methods to the study of psychotherapy and behavior modification. In A. E. Bergin and S. L. Garfield (Eds.), *Handbook of psychotherapy and behavior change*. New York: Wiley, 1971.

Lang, P. J., Rice, D. C., & Sternbach, R. A. The psychophysiology of emotion. In N. S. Greenfield & R. A. Sternbach (Eds.), *Handbook of psychophysiology*. New York: Holt, Rinehart & Winston, 1972.

Laughren, T. P., & Kass, D. J. Desensitization of sexual dysfunction: The present status. In A. S. Gurman & D. G. Rice (Eds.), *Couples in conflict: New directions in marital therapy*. New York: Aronson, 1975.

Lazarus, A. A. Group therapy in phobic disorders by systematic desensitization. *Journal of Abnormal and Social Psychology*, 1961, *63*, 504-510.

Lazarus, A. A. The treatment of a sexually inadequate man. In L. P. Ullman & L. Krasner (Eds.), *Case studies in behavior modification*. New York: Holt, Rinehart & Winston, 1965.

Lazarus, A. A. Behavior therapy in groups. In G. M. Gazda (Ed.), *Basic approaches to group psychotherapy and group counseling*. Springfield, Ill.: Charles C. Thomas, 1968.

Lazarus, A. A. Behavior therapy of sexual problems. *Professional Psychology*, 1971, *2*, 349-353.

Lazarus, A. A. "Hypnosis" as a facilitator in behavior therapy. *International Journal of Clinical and Experimental Hypnosis*, 1973, *21*, 25-31.

Lazarus, A. A., & Rachman, S. The use of systematic desensitization in psychotherapy. In H. J. Eysenck (Ed.), *Behavior therapy and the neuroses: Readings in modern methods of treatment derived from learning theory*. New York: Pergamon Press, 1960.

Leckie, F. H. Hypnotherapy in gynecological disorders. *International Journal of Clinical and Experimental Hypnosis*, 1964, *12*, 121-146.

Lobitz, W. C., LoPiccolo, J., Lobitz, G., & Brockway, J. A closer look at simplistic behavior therapy for sexual dysfunction: Two case studies. In H. J. Eysenck (Ed.), *Case studies in behavior therapy*. London: Routledge & Kegan Paul, 1974.

Locke, H. J. *Predicting adjustment in marriage: A comparison of a divorced and happily married group*. New York: Henry Holt, 1951.

LoPiccolo, J. Direct treatment of sexual dysfunction in the couple. *Handbook of sexology*. Amsterdam: Elsevier/North Holland, 1977. (a)

LoPiccolo, J. Methodological issues in research and treatment of sexual dysfunction. In R. Green & J. Winer (Eds.), *Methodological issues in sex research*. Washington, D. C.: U. S. Government Printing Office, in press.

LoPiccolo, J., & Heiman, J. The role of cultural values in the prevention and treatment of sexual problems. In B. Qualls, J. Wincze, & D. Barlow (Eds.), *The prevention of sexual disorders: Issues and approaches*. New York: Plenum Press, 1978.

LoPiccolo, J., & Hogan, D. Multidimensional behavioral treatment of sexual dysfunction. In O. Pomerleau & J. P. Brady (Eds.), *Behavioral medicine: Theory and practice*. Baltimore: Williams & Wilkins, 1980.

LoPiccolo, J., & Lobitz, W. C. The role of masturbation in the treatment of orgasmic dysfunction. *Archives of Sexual Behavior*, 1972, *2*, 163-172.

LoPiccolo, J., & Steger, J. C. The Sexual Interaction Inventory: A new instrument for assessment of sexual dysfunction. *Archives of Sexual Behavior*, 1974, *3*, 585-595.

LoPiccolo, L. Low sexual desire. In L. Pervin & S. Lieblum (Eds.), *Casebook of sex therapy*. New York: Guilford Press, 1980.

Lundberg, P. O. Sexual dysfunction in patients with neurological disorders. In R. Gemme & C. C. Wheeler (Eds.), *Progress in sexology*. New York: Plenum Press, 1977.

Masters, W., & Johnson, V. *Human sexual response*. Boston: Little, Brown, 1966.

Masters, W., & Johnson, V. *Human sexual inadequacy*. Boston: Little, Brown, 1970.

Mathews, A., Bancroft, J., Whitehead, A., Hackman, A., Julier, D., Bancroft, J., Gath, D., & Shaw, P. The behavioral treatment of sexual inadequacy: A comparative study. *Behavior Research and Therapy*, 1976, *14*, 427-436.

May, A., DeWeese, J., & Rob, C. Changes in sexual function following operation on the abdominal aorta. *Surgery*, 1969, *65*, 41-47.

McConaghy, N. Measurements of change in penile dimensions. *Archives of Sexual Behavior*, 1974, *4*, 381-388.

McGovern, K., Stewart, R., & LoPiccolo, J. Secondary orgasmic dysfunction I. Analysis and strategies for treatment. *Archives of Sexual Behavior*, 1975, *4*, 165-175.

Minuchin, S., Rosman, B. L., & Baker, L. *Psychosomatic families. Anorexia nervosa in context*. Cambridge: Harvard University Press, 1978.

Morokoff, P., & Heiman, J. Effects of erotic stimuli on sexually functional and dysfunctional women: Multiple measures before and after sex therapy. *Behavior Research and Therapy*, 1980, *18*, 127-137.

Mosher, D. L. Psychological reactions to pornographic films. In *Technical report of the Commission on Obscenity and Pornography*, (Vol. 8). Washington, D. C.: U.S. Government Printing Office, 1971.

Mosher, D. L. Sex differences, sex experience, sex guilt, and explicitly sexual films. *Journal of Social Issues*, 1973, *29*, 95-112.

O'Conner, J. F., & Stern, L. O. Results of treatment in functional sexual disorders. *New York State Journal of Medicine*, 1972, *72*, 1927-1934.

Price, K. P. *Feedback effects of penile tumescence*. Paper presented at meeting of the Eastern Psychological Association, Washington, D.C., 1973.

Prochaska, J. O., & Marzilli, R. Modifications of the Masters and Johnson approach to sexual problems. *Psychotherapy: Theory, Research, and Practice*, 1973, *10*, 294-296.

Rachman, S. The treatment of anxiety and phobic reactions by systematic desensitization psychotherapy. *Journal of Abnormal and Social Psychology*, 1959, *58*, 259-263.

Rainwater, L. Some aspects of lower class sexual behavior. *Journal of Social Issues*, 1966, *22*, 96-109.

Reckless, J., & Geiger, N. Impotence as a practical problem. In H. F. Dowling (Ed.), *Disease-a-Month*. Chicago: Year Book Medical Publishers, 1975.

Renshaw, D. C. Impotence in diabetics. In J. LoPiccolo & L. LoPiccolo (Eds.), *Handbook of sex therapy*. New York: Plenum Press, 1978.

Reynolds, B. S. Psychological treatment models and outcome results for erectile dysfunction: A critical review. *Psychological Bulletin*, 1977, *84*, 1218-1238.

Robinson, P. *The modernization of sex*. New York: Harper & Row, 1976.

Rosen, R. Suppression of penile tumescence by instrumental conditioning. *Psychosomatic Medicine*, 1973, *35*, 509-514.

Rosen, R. C., & Keefe, F. J. The measurement of human penile tumescence. *Psychophysiology*, 1978, *15*, 366-376.

Rosen, R. C., Shapiro, D., & Schwartz, G. E. Voluntary control of penile tumescence. *Psychosomatic Medicine*, 1975, *37*, 479-483.

Rosenbaum, A. Personal communication, 1979.

Sager, C. J., & Kaplan, H. S. (Eds.), *Progress in group and family therapy*. New York: Brunner/Mazel, 1972.

Salter, A. *Conditional reflex therapy, the direct approach to the reconstruction of personality* (2nd ed.). New York: Creative Press, 1961.

Scheier, I., & Cattell, R. *Handbook for the Neuroticism Scale Questionnaire*. Champaign, Ill.: Institute for Personality & Ability Testing, 1961.

Schneidman, B., & McGuire, L. Group therapy for nonorgasmic women: Two age levels. *Archives of Sexual Behavior*, 1976, *5*, 239-247.

Schon, M., & Sutherland, A. M. The role of hormones in human behavior. III. Changes in female sexuality after hypophysectomy. *Journal of Clinical Endocrinology and Metabolism*, 1960, *20*, 833-841.

Schwartz, G. E., Davidson, R. J., & Goleman, D. J. Patterning of cognitive and somatic processes in the self-regulation of anxiety: Effects of meditation versus exercise. *Psychosomatic Medicine*, 1978, *40*, 321-328.

Semans, J. H. Premature ejaculation: A new approach. *Southern Medical Journal*, 1956, *49*, 353-357.

Serber, M. Videotape feedback in the treatment of couples with sexual dysfunction. *Archives of Sexual Behavior*, 1974, *3*, 377-380.

Sintchak, G., & Geer, J. H. A vaginal plethysmograph system. *Psychophysiology*, 1975, *12*, 113-115.

Speiss, W. F. J. *The psycho-physiology of premature ejaculation: Some factors related to ejaculatory latency*. Doctoral dissertation, State University of New York at Stony Brook, 1977.

Spitzer, R. L., Sheehy, M., & Endicott, J. DSM-III: Guiding Principles. In V. M. Rakoff, H. C. Stancer, & H. B. Kedward (Eds.), *Psychiatric diagnosis*. New York: Brunner/Mazel, 1977.

Sternbach, R. A. *Principles of psychophysiology*. New York: Academic Press, 1966.

Taylor, J. A personality scale of manifest anxiety. *Journal of Abnormal and Social Psychology*, 1953, *48*, 285-290.

Terman, L. M. *Psychological factors in marital happiness.* New York: McGraw-Hill, 1938.

Terman, L. M. Correlates of orgasm adequacy in 556 wives. *Journal of Psychology,* 1951, *32,* 115-172.

Tordjman, G. Male erectile impotence. In R. Gemme & C. C. Wheeler (Eds.), *Progress in sexology.* New York: Plenum Press, 1977.

Tuthill, J. F. Impotence. *Lancet,* 1955, *1,* 124-128.

Von Bertalanffy, L. *General systems theory: Foundations, developments, applications.* New York: George Braziller, 1968.

Wagner, G., & Ebbehøj, J. *Erectile dysfunction caused by abnormal outflow from the corpus cavernosum.* Paper presented at the Third International Congress of Medical Sexology, Rome, 1978.

Walker, H. F. Sexual problems and fertility. *Psychosomatics,* 1978, *19,* 477-484.

Wilson, G. T., & Lawson, D. M. Effects of alcohol on sexual arousal in women. *Journal of Abnormal Psychology,* 1976, *85,* 489-497.

Wilson, G. T., Lawson, D., & Abrams, D. B. Effects of alcohol on sexual arousal in male alcoholics. *Journal of Abnormal Psychology,* 1978, *87,* 609-616.

Wincze, J. P. A comparison of systematic desensitization and "vicarious extinction" in a case of frigidity. *Journal of Behavior Therapy and Experimental Psychiatry,* 1971, *1,* 285-289.

Wincze, J. P., & Caird, W. K. The effects of systematic desensitization and video desensitization in the treatment of essential sexual dysfunction in women. *Behavior Therapy,* 1976, *7,* 335-342.

Wincze, J., Hoon, E. F., & Hoon, P. W. Physiological responsivity of normal and sexually dysfunctional women during erotic stimulus exposure. *Journal of Psychosomatic Research,* 1976, *20,* 445-451.

Wincze, J. P., Hoon, E. F., & Hoon, P. W. Multiple measure analysis of women experiencing low sexual arousal. *Behavior Research and Therapy,* 1978, *16,* 43-49.

Wincze, J. P., Hoon, P. W., & Hoon, E. F. Sexual arousal in women: A comparison of cognitive and physiological responses by continuous measurement. *Archives of Sexual Behavior,* 1977, *6,* 121-133.

Wise, T. N. Sexual difficulties with concurrent physical problems. *Psychosomatics,* 1977, *18,* 56-64.

Wolff, S. Symptomatology and outcomes of pre-school children with behavior disorders attending a child guidance clinic. *Journal of Child Psychology and Psychiatry*, 1961, *2*, 260-268.

Wolpe, J. *Psychotherapy and reciprocal inhibition.* Stanford: Stanford University Press, 1958.

Wolpe, J. *The practice of behavior therapy* (1st ed.). New York: Pergamon Press, 1969.

Wolpe, J., & Lazarus, A. A. *Behavior therapy techniques.* New York: Pergamon Press, 1966.

Wolpin, M. Guided imagining to reduce avoidance behavior. *Psychotherapy: Theory, Research, and Practice*, 1969, *6*, 122-124.

Zilbergeld, B., & Rinkleib, C. E. Desire discrepancies and arousal problems in sex therapy. In S. Leiblum & L. Pervin (Eds.), *Casebook of sex therapy.* New York: Guilford Press, 1980.

Zingheim, P. K., & Sandman, C. A. Discriminative control of the vaginal vasomotor response. *Biofeedback and Self-Regulation*, 1978, *3*, 29-41.

7

THE ETIOLOGIES, TREATMENTS, AND ASSESSMENTS OF OBESITY

D. Balfour Jeffrey

Maxwell R. Knauss

INTRODUCTION

Obesity can be defined as excess stored body fat resulting from caloric intake that is greater than the caloric expenditure required for physical activity, somatic maintenance, and growth. An important distinction must be made between *obesity* and *overweight*. According to Bray (1970), the obese person has an unusually high proportion of adipose tissue in relation to lean body mass. Overweight, in comparison, is defined with reference to statistical height-weight tables that have been developed by insurance companies. An overweight person is one whose weight is above an arbitrarily established normal range for people of similar height, age, and body build. While most obese people are overweight, not all overweight people are obese. Bray concluded, however, that when weight exceeds the ideal level by 30% in nonathletic persons, the overweight is almost inevitably due to excess adipose tissue.

It has been estimated that 25% to 45% of the U.S. population over 30 years of age is more than 20% overweight (U.S. Public Health Service, undated). In addition, with childhood obesity defined as 40% above the median weight for a given height, 2% to 15% of U.S. children are obese (U.S. Public Health Service, undated). Of these obese children, 80% grow up to become obese adults (Mauro & Feins, 1977).

Portions of the research for this chapter were supported by the Science and Education Administration of the U.S. Department of Agriculture, under Grant No. 5901-0410-8-0070-0 from the Competitive Research Grants Office to D. Balfour Jeffrey, principal investigator. Thanks are extended to Linda Richtmyer for her typing of the manuscript and to Patricia MacInnes for assistance with the references.

Obesity is regarded as a principal health problem because research has correlated excess weight with increased pathologies in almost every body function (Mayer, 1968). It has been identified as a major risk factor for cardiovascular diseases (Cooper, 1977; Gordon & Kannel, 1973). There is an increase of 30% in susceptibility to these diseases for every 10% above ideal weight.

Obese individuals have less exercise tolerance, greater difficulty in normal breathing, and a higher incidence of respiratory infections than do people of normal weight. The accumulation of excess adipose tissue changes blood lipid metabolism, damages glucose tolerance, and increases blood pressure and cardiac work load (Gordon & Kannel, 1973). Overweight people also have frequent muscular and skeletal problems, resulting in such complications as arthritis, lower back pain, and hip, knee, and ankle difficulties (Jeffrey & Katz, 1977). Besides the increased incidence of medical problems, obese individuals often have psychological problems, such as extreme self-consciousness, poor self-image, depression, and poor interpersonal relationships (Bruch, 1973; Collipp, 1975; Monello & Mayer, 1963).

In addition, there are tremendous economic costs related to obesity. A marketing survey indicated that a staggering $10 billion is spent annually on obesity-related phenomena, such as dietary foods, medications, exercise clubs, and weight loss programs.

The ultimate health risk of obesity is, of course, a decreased life span for obese individuals. Newburgh (1942) studied mortality rates for men in the 45-to-55-year-old age range and found a 1% increase in mortality for each pound of excess weight. Similarly, Armstrong (1951) compared the mortality rates of overweight and normal-weight individuals. He found the mortality rate to be 70% higher for markedly overweight men and 42% higher for moderately overweight men. For women, the rates were 61% and 42%, respectively.

It can be concluded that obesity is one of the most widespread contemporary health problems and is associated with tremendous medical, psychological, and economic costs. The aims of this chapter are to review what is known about the etiologies, assessments, and treatments of obesity and to suggest directions for future research to improve our understanding of this psychosomatic disorder.

ETIOLOGIES OF OBESITY

Physiological Etiologies

Physiological investigations of the etiology of obesity have examined the organic processes responsible for the development and maintenance of body weight. Obesity is seen as the outcome of an alteration or malfunction in the system of regulation of body weight that leads to the excessive accumulation of adipose tissue. Research and theories regarding the roles of hereditary, neurologic and metabolic, and adipose cellularity factors as determinants of obesity will be discussed. These are, not discrete etiologies, but different physiological factors that influence regulation of body weight and interact with and influence each other. It is now known that hereditary factors can contribute to alterations in adipose cellularity in both animals and human beings. Metabolic anomalies both influence and, in turn, are influenced by characteristics of adipose tissue. Hereditary determinants, metabolic and neurologic determinants, and adipose cellularity determinants are discussed separately, in order to facilitate clarity of presentation rather than suggest that they are mutually exclusive.

Hereditary Determinants

Correlational research studies have demonstrated that obesity, especially the severe type, tends to run in families. Mayer (1957) reported finding obesity in children 80% of the time when both parents were obese, 40% of the time when only one parent was obese, and only 10% of the time when neither parent was obese. However, it is not possible to determine the relative influence of genetic and environmental factors when using this type of correlational design.

In order to gain a better understanding of the impact of hereditary and environmental factors upon body weight, Withers (1964) compared correlations of percentage overweight for parents and their biological children with correlations for parents and their foster children. The correlations in percentage overweight for parents and biological children were positive and statistically significant, while the correlations for parents and foster children were much lower and nonsignificant. These results suggest that hereditary factors play an influential role in determining obesity.

To more precisely determine the relative contributions of hereditary and environmental factors, investigators have compared within-family weight variances of pairs of monozygotic and dizygotic twins. They have also compared weight variances of monozygotic twins separated at birth and reared in different family environments. The resulting data allow a quantification of hereditary influence upon body weight through a calculation of the *heritability index* (h^2), which estimates the percentage of the variance of body weight attributable to hereditary factors. Hartz, Giefer, and Rimm (1977) reviewed four twin studies (Clark, 1956; Newman, Freeman, & Holzuiger, 1937; Osborne & DeGeorge, 1959; Shields, 1962) and computed h^2 for each study. H^2 ranged from 0.27 to 0.78 in these studies. Hartz et al. attributed this variability to small sample sizes and differences in important subject and environmental characteristics. They also criticized these studies for employing gross body weight, rather than a more adequate estimate of obesity (such as percentage overweight), as the dependent variable.

To overcome these weaknesses and provide a more accurate estimate of h^2, Hartz et al. (1977) collected data from a large sample of female members of the Take Off Pounds Sensibly (TOPS) diet club, as well as from their husbands and children. Overall, data were collected for 10,337 families with 25,554 biologically related children and for 245 families with 546 nonbiologically related children. Utilizing an analysis-of-variance technique, it was estimated that family environment accounted for 35% of the variance of obesity, while heritability accounted for only 11%. Hartz et al. concluded that "these results suggest that family environment, which consists of such things as parental example and child-rearing techniques, has an important effect on childhood obesity" (p. 193).

Family studies, which provide estimates of heritability, are valid only for the particular populations from which samples are drawn and do not provide an explanation of the mechanisms of genetic transmission. To shed light upon these mechanisms, investigators have conducted animal research in which genetic and environmental factors have been rigorously controlled. Mayer (1965, 1968) demonstrated the heritability of obesity in rodents by altering the amount of adipose tissue through selective breeding. Bray and York (1971), upon reviewing the literature regarding inheritance of obesity in rodents, described three types of established genetic transmission: *dominant inheritance, recessive inheritance,* and *polygenic inheritance*. Each of these types of inheritance leads to different biochemical or structural alterations that produce obesity. Some types of genetic transmission may have parallels in the human population. For instance, there are similarities between childhood-onset obesity in humans and recessively transmitted obesity in rodents. Bray (1975) suggested three possible abnormalities underlying this type of obesity in rodents: aberrations in adipose tissue; alterations in insulin structure, secretion, or action; and derangements in hypothalamic functioning. While animal models of obesity are of heuristic value for genetic research in human obesity, much research is required before patterns of genetic transmission and the resulting alterations can be elucidated.

Presently, several types of genetically transmitted obesity have been identified, including *Prader-Willi syndrome* and *Laurence-Moon-Biedl syndrome*. These syndromes are rare in occurrence and are the exception, rather than the rule, with human obesity. Rather than creating metabolic or endocrinological abnormalities, genetic variables may have a more pervasive influence on human obesity through the role they play in determining overall body build. Within the range of normally inherited body builds, certain builds may be associated with increased accumulations of adipose tissue.

Seltzer and Mayer (1964) examined the body builds of obese and normal female adolescents and concluded that endomorphic and mesomorphic somatotypes constitute a predisposition toward excess development of adipose tissue. This predisposition may be actualized by excess caloric intake in relation to caloric expenditure. Thus, morphological variability may be an important parameter in determining individual differences in the development of obesity.

Neurologic and Metabolic Determinants

In a year's time, the average person of normal weight consumes over 1 million calories, but there is little variation in body weight because a comparable number of calories are utilized in bodily maintenance and activity. An error of regulation of 10% in either intake or expenditure would lead to a 30-pound change in body weight within a year. It can be concluded that in normal-weight individuals, body weight is regulated with extraordinary accuracy (Stunkard & Mahoney, 1976).

The structural and biochemical components of this system of weight regulation are not completely understood at the present time. The relationship between the hypothalamus and the regulation of food intake has long been recognized, however. Lesions in the area of the ventromedial hypothalamus in experimental animals cause hyperphagia leading to obesity. While the lesioned animals do become grossly obese, they do not gain weight indefinitely but stabilize at a new, higher level (Hoebel & Teitelbaum, 1966). It appears that the ventromedial nucleus contains a satiety center, which serves as a check to keep the animal from gaining weight (Kennedy, 1957). Lesions in this area do not totally eliminate the animal's ability to regulate weight, but they do greatly elevate the set-point around which weight is regulated. In contrast, animals with lateral hypothalamic lesions lose weight rapidly. This suggests that this area contains a *feeding* center, which keeps the animals from losing weight (Powley & Keesey, 1970). Based on these findings, investigators have proposed a dual mechanism for the regulation of body weight (Nisbett, 1972). The feedback system governing food intake may be regulated by a "glucostat," a "lipostat," or an "aminostat" within the hypothalamus (Thorn & Cahill, 1977).

Patients with obesity due to hypothalamic lesions are rare. Bray (1975) identified 100 cases of hypothalamic obesity reported in the literature since 1900. Although hypothalamic lesions precipitate significant weight gain, these patients rarely weigh over 275 pounds, and no patient has ever been reported weighing over 300 pounds. Bray also found that hypothalamic obesity in man is almost uniformly associated with other symptoms (such as headache, visual impairment, and polyuria) of intracranial hypothalamic disease.

A popular conception with lay people is that obesity results from altered metabolism. It is believed that obese individuals are more efficient in digesting food and forming adipose tissue and, therefore, that they gain weight with lower caloric intake than do people of normal weight. Passmore, Strong, Swindells, and El Din (1963) found that some obese individuals gain weight in fewer calories than do nonobese individuals, thus partially supporting the notion of alterations in metabolic rates. Obesity, in fact, has been correlated with a number of metabolic anomalies involving fat and carbohydrate usage and hormonal factors (Rodin, 1977). Specifically, these anomalies include decreased glucose tolerance, hyperinsulinemia, peripheral insulin resistance, reduced growth hormones, and elevated triglyceride and blood cholesterol levels. Nevertheless, these correlations between obesity and metabolic alterations, no matter how strong, do not establish altered metabolism as the causal factor in obesity.

In a series of experiments on induced obesity, Sims and his colleagues studied subjects of normal weight who increased their body weight by 15% to

25% through overeating. As their amount of adipose tissue increased, these subjects developed metabolic alterations identical to those observed in spontaneously obese individuals (Sims, Goldman, Gluck, Horton, Kelleher, & Rowe, 1968; Sims & Horton, 1968). It has also been discovered that hyperinsulinemia and peripheral insulin resistance in spontaneously obese individuals can be reversed through caloric restriction and the resulting weight loss. Rather than causing obesity, these data imply that, in most cases, metabolic and endocrinological anomalies result from increases in adipose tissue.

Cellular Determinants

Since obesity involves the accumulation of excess body fat, it is crucial that we investigate the development, maintenance, and stability of *adipose tissue*. This tissue is composed of special body cells, or *adipocytes*, in which body fat in the form of esterified fatty acids is deposited. Two types of body fat can be distinguished: *essential* and *nonessential*. Essential body fat provides a necessary mechanism for storing energy, serves protective functions, and forms an integral part of many vital organs. Nonessential fat is not required for body maintenance and proper functioning and, in excessive quantities, is likely to be detrimental to these processes. Sex differences exist in the amount of essential body fat; these differences are related mainly to reproductive functions in females. It is estimated that, in individuals of college age, essential fat comprises 3% of total body weight in males and 13% in females (Conniff, 1978). The amount of stored body fat can be increased by enlarging the size of existing adipocytes (a process known as *hypertrophy*), by expanding the number of adipocytes (a process known as *hyerplasia*), or by a combination of these two processes (Björntorp & Sjöström, 1971). The overall quantity of body fat stored, and thus the degree of obesity, is determined by both the size and number of adipocytes.

Utilizing needle biopsies taken at several subcutaneous sites, Hirsch and Knittle (1970) discovered a positive correlation between size of fat cell and body weight in both obese and nonobese subjects, with a 40% increase in size of fat cell in the obese, as compared with the nonobese, subjects. In other words, the greater the percentage of overweight, the larger the size of the adipocytes. While enlarged adipocytes are typically found in all obese individuals, increased adipocyte number is found only in certain cases. The onset for those individuals whose obesity is conspicuously hyperplastic generally occurs during childhood. While nonobese individuals possess between 25 and 30 billion adipocytes, obese individuals may possess between two and five times that number (Hirsch & Knittle, 1970; Hirsch, Knittle, & Salans, 1966).

With the discovery of these differences in the structure of adipose tissue, investigators have attempted to elucidate normal patterns of development of adipose tissue and to identify developmental anomalies and etiological factors that produce childhood onset of hyperplastic obesity. Brook and his colleagues (Brook, 1972; Brook, Lloyd, & Wolf, 1972) utilized a cross-sectional research design to compare characteristics of adipose tissue of obese and nonobese children of various ages. On the basis of the obtained results, Brook proposed a critical period for the development of fat cells, ranging from birth to 12 months of age, which is characterized by rapid proliferation of fat cells. During this critical period, the majority of fat cells is produced, and the rate of further multiplication of fat cells, which concludes at the end of childhood, is determined. Hyperplastic obesity is seen as resulting from overnutrition during this critical period, which causes excessive multiplication of adipocytes.

In contrast to Brook's work, Knittle (1972a, 1972b) proposed different patterns of development of adipose tissue for obese and normal-weight children. Two critical periods for proliferation of fat cells in normal human development were identified. The first extends from birth to 24 months of age, and the second, from before puberty to its completion, at which point the total adult number of fat cells is established. Obese children are hypothesized to demonstrate an abnormal developmental pattern, in that fat cells continue to multiply throughout childhood and early adolescence, rather than exclusively during the critical periods.

Results contradicting both Brook et al. and Knittle were obtained by Häger, Sjöström, Arvidsson, Björntorp, and Smith (1977) from a longitudinal study that followed normal-weight infants from birth to 18 months of age. Between birth and 12 months, increases in body fat were accomplished by enlargements in cell size, with no significant increases in cell number. Proliferation in cell number began after 12 months of age, when existing cells had reached adult size. Similar results have been obtained by other investigators (Gairdner & Dauncey, 1974).

While there are disagreements regarding the development of adipose tissue, it is generally agreed that, once an individual reaches adulthood, the number of adipocytes is permanently established and remains stable, in spite of alterations in caloric intake or expenditure (Greenwood & Johnson, 1977). This stability of adipose tissue has powerful implications for individuals with childhood onset of hyperplastic obesity when they attempt to lose weight. A poorer prognosis for both weight loss and maintenance is frequently observed for individuals with childhood onset, as compared to adult onset, obesity (Weiss, 1977). While weight loss reduces the size of fat cells, the structure of adipose tissue remains unaffected, and shrunken adipocytes are easily refilled if the individual reverts to a high caloric intake in the absence of high caloric expenditure. Thus, the increased number of fat cells may provide a morphological basis for the high incidence of relapse to pretreatment weight levels that is frequently observed following various treatments of adults who had childhood onset of obesity (Rodin, 1977).

In summary, weight regulation involves a complex physiological system in which hereditary, metabolic, neurologic, and cellular factors play a role. Current research suggests, however, that only 3% to 11% of obesity cases are attributable solely to somatic factors (Hartz et al., 1977; Kaplan & Kaplan, 1957). Although physiological factors contribute to obesity, they cannot fully explain the overeating and lack of activity that are in most cases primarily responsible for obesity. To more fully understand the causes of obesity, we will next examine the psychosocial theories of obesity.

Psychosocial Etiologies

In discussing the impact of psychosocial factors in the etiology of obesity, it is necessary to distinguish between *hunger* and *appetite* (Kaplan & Kaplan, 1957). Hunger is defined as an urge to eat, based upon physiological cues signaling the depletion of somatic nutrient reserves. In contrast, appetite refers to the urge to eat, which is determined by social learning and other psychological factors. Humans eat in response to both hunger and appetite cues. Appetite may stimulate an individual to eat when no hunger signals are present or to continue eating after physiological satiety has been achieved.

Physiological etiologies of obesity, such as the *ponderostat theory*, often do not distinguish between hunger and appetite and thereby neglect the role that appetite plays in inducing overeating. The psychosocial theories presented in this chapter have in common the notion that obesity results from a derangement in appetite processes. The psychosocial theories developed to explain this derangement include psychodynamic, stimulus-bound, social-learning, and macroenvironmental etiological theories.

Energy balance is another important concept in understanding psychosocial etiologies and treatments of obestiy (Jeffrey & Katz, 1977). A positive energy balance is created when caloric intake is greater than caloric expenditure. Excess calories are stored as fat, and the individual gains weight. When caloric expenditure exceeds caloric consumption, a negative energy balance is created. This leads to consumption of stored fat and weight loss. Most of these treatments focus entirely upon restriction of caloric intake in creating a negative energy balance. Some focus primarily upon increased energy expenditure. Only the social-learning and macroenvironmental theories systematically examine both sides of energy balance and their relationship to the etiology and treatment of obesity.

Psychodynamic Theories

Although there have been numerous psychodynamic formulations, overeating and resulting obesity have traditionally been regarded as symptoms or manifestations of underlying emotional disturbance. It is theorized that obese individuals are fixated at the oral stage of psychosexual development. Frustration of needs results in regression to an oral level and eating to overcome these frustrations (Schick, 1947). Often those frustrated needs involve dependency needs, especially the "need to be loved."

Overeating serves two purposes within the psychodynamic formulation. It provides substitute gratification of an unconscious impulse, and it defends against anxiety arising from intrapsychic conflict (Kaplan & Kaplan, 1957). Overeating and consequent obesity are seen as a symbolic representation of the unconscious impulse or the dynamics of the conflict. After reviewing the literature, Kaplan and Kaplan (1957) identified 17 proposed symbolic meanings (such as penis envy and exhibitionistic impulse) for overeating of food. Kaplan and Kaplan concluded that ". . . the great number and variety [of proposed symbolic meanings] indicate that *any* emotional conflict may eventually result in the symptom of overeating; it is our conclusion that the psychodynamic factors causing obesity are non-specific" (pp. 196-197).

Psychodynamic theorizing has stimulated research concerning the relationship between psychopathology, especially anxiety and depression, and obesity. To test this psychodynamic concept, Abramson and Wunderlich (1972) subjected obese and nonobese subjects to control, interpersonal anxiety, and objective fear manipulation conditions. Following these manipulations, subjects were given a bowl of crackers to eat, under the guise of a taste test. While checks on experimental manipulations indicated their successfulness in producing anxiety and fear, obese subjects did not eat significantly more crackers than did nonobese or control subjects.

Other investigators have established a connection between anxiety and related types of arousal and increased food consumption (Atkinson & Ringuette, 1967; Leon & Chamberlain, 1973b; Weintraub & Aronson, 1969). There has been no direct experimental support, however, for the theory that the act of food consumption in itself reduces anxiety (Leon & Chamberlain, 1973a; McKenna, 1972).

Viewing overeating as a symptom of, or an attempt to alter, an underlying depression is a popular psychodynamic conceptualization. If the overeating is directly modified without resolving the underlying conflict, symptom substitution is expected to occur, producing increased depressive symptomatology. Although depressive symptoms, such as fatigue, apathy, sadness, and difficulty in concentration, are often associated with the onset of obesity and often accompany attempts to lose weight, they are not necessarily always the cause of obesity or the result of dieting. Contrary to psychodynamic predictions of increased depressive symptomatology and other emotional disturbances, Solow, Silberfarb, and Swift (1974) found that the majority of patients with intestinal bypasses experienced postsurgical decreases in depression and increases in self-esteem, ego strength, and interpersonal functioning associated with their weight loss. This evidence does not support the unidirectional conception that underlying pathology causes obesity but points to the role of obesity in contributing to depression and other emotional problems.

Stimulus-bound Theories

Other psychological characteristics of the obese individual have been investigated as possible etiological factors. In a classic sociopsychological experiment, Schachter and Singer (1962) demonstrated that subjectively perceived emotional states are significantly influenced by external situational factors. Schachter (1971a, 1971b) further hypothesized that hunger sensations are the result of cognitive labeling of physiological states and are also significantly influenced by external situational variables. Obesity results from alterations in the system of appetite regulation, in that obese individuals are more attuned to situational cues and less aware of internal physiological states than are normal-weight individuals. According to this externality, or stimulus-bound, theory of obesity, obese individuals' appetites, and thus their eating behavior, are primarily regulated by external stimuli, such as time cues, food advertisements, and the appearance and smell of food, rather than by internal physiological processes.

While a complete review of this body of experimental literature is not possible within the context of this chapter, it can be concluded that the stimulus-bound theory has been of tremendous heuristic value in stimulating a great deal of research on the eating behavior of obese and nonobese individuals. Schachter and his colleagues have investigated the roles of food-cue prominence, time awareness, food attractiveness, and taste responsiveness as external stimuli differentially influencing obese eating behavior.

After a critical examination of the stimulus-bound literature, Leon and Roth (1977) questioned whether the results of much of this research can be generalized to the eating behavior of obese individuals in their natural environments. The subject samples often do not represent the obese population as a whole, and they may differ significantly in terms of degree of obesity, age, sex, and socioeconomic status. In addition, many of the experiments involve observations of eating behavior with nuts, crackers, and cookies in artificial experimental settings. These may poorly represent situational cues that occur naturally in the environment. In terms of confirmation for the theory, Leon and Roth (1977) found many mixed and unreplicated results and concluded that "the support for Schachter's externality theory appears to be equivocal at best" (pp. 128-129).

Although the stimulus-bound theory was formulated by a social psychologist and concerns differential responsiveness beween obese and normal-weight individuals to external cues, there is an implied physiological basis for this differential responsiveness. Schachter (1971b) argued that many eating and other behaviors in obese people closely parallel those of rats with ventromedial hypothalamic lesions. Nisbett (1972) explained these parallels by suggesting that both the lesioned rat and the obese human are in a state of physiological deprivation and are genuinely hungry.

Nisbett, in elaborating the ponderostat theory of obesity, hypothesized that obesity represents proper regulation around an elevated standard of body weight rather than a malfunctioning of the system of weight regulation. This biologically determined weight standard is known as the ponderostat, and it influences food intake to maintain adipocytes at a certain size. While hyperplastic obese individuals may be obese according to height-weight charts, for them this level of body weight represents a "normal" state of affairs. Since they possess a significantly increased number of adipocytes, they are forced to reduce their fat cells to a smaller size than those of nonobese individuals in order to lose weight. It is proposed that this shrunken cell size alters hormonal or other substrate signals to the hypothalamus, resulting in perpetual hunger. This hunger stimulates eating behavior until the adipocytes return to their normal size. If the ponderostat theory is correct, it offers a pessimistic outlook for hyperplastic obese individuals who are doomed either to failure or to perpetual starvation if they maintain their weight loss.

Nisbett acknowledged that alternative theories can account for the data upon which the ponderostat theory is based and that application of the theory with obese human subjects is premature and should not deter efforts at weight reduction. Moreover, there are several weaknesses in this theory. First, the level at which the ponderostat is set cannot be independently determined but, instead, is inferred from current weight and data on onset of obesity. Second, there is a lack of clear specification of the nature of the feedback signals between adipose tissue and the hypothalamus. Third, the notion that the size of adipose cells directly influences the hypothalamus, thus stimulating hunger sensations, is largely speculative. Fourth, the ponderostat theory neglects both the role of activity levels in determining body weight and the impact of social-learning processes in influencing activity levels as well as appetite and eating behavior.

Social-Learning Theories

Social-learning theorists have also developed a psychological theory of obesity. Rather than conceptualizing obesity as the symptom of an underlying disorder, these theorists have undertaken a functional analysis of behaviors that are critical to the development and maintenance of obesity. While the etiological influence of hereditary and metabolic variables is not denied, social-learning processes are seen as playing the major etiologic role in most cases of obesity. The social-learning theory of obesity and the resulting behavioral treatments are based on the previously discussed concept of energy balance and the assumption that behaviors leading to food consumption and physical activity are learned and maintained and can be modified by social-learning principles.

Social-learning theory focuses on the acquisition and maintenance of behaviors that result from environmental factors. Classical conditioning, operant conditioning, observational learning, and human information-processing principles are included in this theory of behavior. Since our eating and physical activity habits, good or bad, are mostly acquired patterns of behavior, social-learning theory provides an excellent model for analyzing how these behaviors are acquired and maintained.

A social-learning analysis of the etiology of obesity can occur at two levels: micro and macro (Jeffrey & Lemnitzer, 1980). At a micro level, the analysis and treatment of obesity focuses upon the eating, exercise, and psychological patterns of the individual. Virtually all the behavioral and medical research reviewed in this chapter has focused on a micro analysis, that is, the treatment of individual, obese patients. This level of analysis will be examined first, followed by a presentation of the macro level of analysis.

Micro Social-Learning Analysis. Ferster, Nurnberger, and Levitt (1962) presented the first social-learning analysis of obesity. They theorized that obesity occurs because eating is reinforced by its immediate pleasurable consequences, while the negative consequences of gaining weight are delayed to the future. The development of self-control of eating behavior involves determining which variables influence eating; identifying the unwanted consequences of overeating, which creates motivation to develop self-control; and devising a program to develop self-control.

Taking up the lead provided by Ferster et al., other investigators have extended the social-learning analysis of obesity to include behavioral, mediational, and reinforcing events involved in obesity. The inquiry regarding behavior has focused on eating styles and eating rates as factors differentiating obese and lean subjects (LeBow, Goldberg, & Collins, 1977; Marston, London, Cohen, & Cooper, 1977; Stunkard & Kaplan, 1977). The importance of exercise and activity levels in influencing the energy balance and thereby determining body weight has also been stressed (Jeffrey & Katz, 1977; Stuart, 1971). Investigation of obesity-related mediational and covert events has included attitudinal body image (Leon & Chamberlain, 1973b; Stunkard & Burt, 1967; Stunkard & Mendelson, 1967), standard setting (Chapman & Jeffrey, 1978), cognitions (Mahoney & Mahoney, 1976; Nisbett & Storms, 1974), and affective states (Abramson & Stinson, 1977; Leon & Chamberlain, 1973a, 1973b; Stunkard & Rush, 1974). Examination of reinforcing events has focused on self-administered reinforcement (Jeffrey, 1974, 1977; Mahoney, 1974) and social reinforcement (Foxx, 1972; Matson, 1977).

Investigations of social-learning principles have been reported in a number of articles. Perhaps it would be helpful to illustrate clinically how these principles function in influencing the acquisition of normal-weight and obese lifestyles. There are many ways that one learns about food. Children observe and often imitate their parents' eating behavior, and they are often reinforced for engaging in the same style of eating. By the time they are 18, children will have experienced over 20,000 meals in which to observe their parents' eating and exercise habits. They learn specific attitudes about foods or eating, including misconceptions about nutrition. Members of our society learn through conditioning principles to associate food and eating with social occasions, fun, and self-gratification. Some people may learn to use food to escape from tension or boredom or to assuage hurt or depression. In the same way, attitudes and behaviors toward physical exercise are acquired. Parents may model physical inactivity and *not* reward active participation in sports. Children may learn that it requires less effort to be driven to school than to walk. They may notice their parents' or siblings' preoccupation with mechanical labor-saving devices and preference for spectator, rather than participant, sports. They may learn that school athletics are only for the sports stars, since those who do not excel are not reinforced.

While these examples illustrate how learning principles that influence the development of good or poor eating and physical activity habits are involved in the immediate home environment, these same principles are also involved at the societal level.

Macro Social-Learning Analysis. A macro analysis focuses on the total society and how it facilitates or impedes good eating habits, physical activity habits, and weight management. Such an analysis also suggests ways in which large segments of the population can come to change their eating habits and ways to treat whole classes of medical problems. In short, it seeks to expand the scope of assessment and treatment away from the single patient and toward prevention and treatment at a societal level.

A macro analysis of obesity is complex and has been discussed in detail elsewhere (Jeffrey & Lemnitzer, 1980). For purposes of this chapter, the area of television will be discussed in order to illustrate the potential of a macro analysis. Since television viewing involves observational learning, a social-learning analysis of television advertising provides an excellent model for an examination of how television commercials probably condition, in part, our eating habits.

Since World War II, the largest expenditure in the United States for public information on diet has been made by the food industry through television advertising. In 1975, about $1.15 billion was spent on advertisements for food on television, which represents about 28% of the total spending on television advertising (U.S. Senate SCNHN, 1977).

Manoff (1977) suggested that a minimum of 48% of the money spent on food advertisements on television in 1971 went for items that may be generally characterized as high in fat, saturated fat, cholesterol, sugar, salt, or alcohol. Masover and Stamler (1977) reported on a study of food advertising on four Chicago television stations. They found that almost 70% of the time was devoted to advertising foods generally high in fat, saturated fat, cholesterol, sugar, and/or salt and that only 3% of the time was devoted to fruits and vegetables.

By the time the average child enters kindergarten, he or she will have seen approximately 70,000 such commercials. The influence of television advertising of highly caloric foods is even more pronounced when we consider the amount of available nutrition information that could serve to counter the effect. Too many commercials emphasize sugar as a source of quick energy, and children may believe that sugar is the only nutrient they need.

If pronutrition announcements on television are rare and dwarfed by the number of messages about foods with little nutritional value, pronutritional messages from other sources do not fare much better. Many adults know little about nutritious eating. Primary and secondary schools rarely offer a regular curriculum on nutrition. Moreover, most teachers have had little exposure to the basic facts about good nutrition. And what children learn about food from these early sources is likely to have an impact on lifelong eating habits.

Evidence suggests that food advertising — especially advertising about foods that are low in nutrition and high in calories — abounds and that it does influence the nutrition knowledge and eating habits of the population. All the causal relationships between television advertising and eating are not known (National Science Foundation, 1977). In a methodological review of the effects of television advertising upon children's behavior, Rychtarik, Kniivila, and Jeffrey (1978) found the predominant designs to be self-report, correlational studies. On the basis of this review, they recommended that further research emphasize more experimental designs that include direct behavioral measures.

There is growing interest among researchers in conducting programmatic, experimental, and behavioral investigations into the effects of television advertising on children's eating habits. An example of this type of research is the work being conducted at the University of Montana (Jeffrey, Lemnitzer, Hess, Hickey, McLellarn, & Stroud, 1979). In two studies, children aged four and five were randomly assigned to one of three treatment groups. They were exposed to a 12-minute segment of television programming that was typical of Saturday morning. This segment was edited to contain six commercials, varied for the three experimental conditions. Group 1 saw six commercials for foods that were low in nutrition and high in calories, group 2 saw six commercials for nutritious foods, and group 3 saw six commercials for toys. Dependent measures consisted of a behavioral eating test — a tray with portions of equal size of nutritious and nonnutritious foods and beverages — and an evaluative scale on which foods and beverages from the taste test could be rated. The behavioral eating test and the food-attitude scale were administered one week before and immediately following the experimental manipulation.

Because of a complex data structure, the statistical analyses were very extensive. Briefly, increase in food consumption for group 1 suggested some preliminary support for the influence of advertising of foods that are low in nutrition. Moreover, the studies illustrated that a behavioral analysis provides an excellent methodological basis (behavioral observation) for assessing, and a theoretical basis (observational-learning theory, for providing, an empirical foundation on which to build a social policy concerning the role and regulation of children's food advertising.

In summary, personal food preferences interact with other forces in the environment and are influenced by them. People learn the patterns of their diet not only from the family and its sociocultural background but also from what is available in the marketplace and what is promoted formally through advertising and informally through general availability in schools, restaurants, supermarkets, work places, and airports. Habits of physical activity are acquired and affected in similar sociocultural ways. Clearly, additional research is needed on a macro-social analysis of obesity, since it seems to have great potential for leading to a better understanding of the etiology of obesity and for devising more effective treatment programs.

Conclusion

In summary, there have been many theoretical speculations regarding the cause of obesity, and these speculations have been very fruitful in generating research that has added to our understanding of this disorder. These empirical investigations have proceeded on many levels, from the cellular to the societal. Most theorists no longer view obesity as a unitary disorder but regard it as a complex disorder that is multiply determined by several classes of etiological factors. All the classes of etiological factors reviewed — hereditary, metabolic, cellular, psychodynamic, stimulus-bound, social-learning, and socioenvironmental — appear to contribute to this disorder. Given that obesity is a complex disorder, these classes of etiological factors will contribute, to different degrees, in the etiology of obesity in different individuals.

TREATMENTS OF OBESITY

We now turn our attention to the vast array of techniques that are currently employed in the treatment of obesity. Obesity is becoming increasingly recognized as a multifaceted problem requiring a multifaceted approach to treatment. While the focus of this chapter is on psychosomatic conceptualizations, there are several techniques deriving from a more traditional medical framework. Therefore, we will begin our review of the literature on the treatment of obesity with three contemporary medical approaches: intestinal bypass operations, therapeutic starvation, and pharmacologic treatments. Next, approaches using traditional behavioral therapy will be evaluated, followed by a review of the behavioral self-control literature. In addition, the research on self-help groups will be briefly discussed. Finally, propositions stemming from a macroenvironmental analysis for treatment of obesity will be offered.

Medical Treatments

Intestinal Bypass Operations

Intestinal bypass operations constitute an increasingly employed treatment for massive obesity. Iber and Cooper (1977) estimated that 12,000 to 20,000 of these operations have been performed in the United States. Intestinal bypass, or *jejunoileostomy*, represents a radical treatment of obesity, is based upon the rationale that massive obesity represents a substantial health risk, and is used when more conservative therapies have not been effective in helping patients to lose large amounts of weight (Bray & Benfield, 1977). In these operations, a section of the jejunum is rendered nonfunctional, and the overall absorptive capacity of the small intestine is reduced. This produces malabsorption, in which caloric intake identical to preoperative levels results in weight loss because fewer calories are absorbed. Thus, intestinal bypass operations produce a permanent iatrogenic disorder (that is, malabsorption) in order to reduce the obesity (Bray, Greenway, Barry, Benfield, Tiser, Dahms, Atkinson, & Schwartz, 1977). This iatrogenic disorder characteristically produces not only rapid, massive weight loss but a number of untold side effects as well.

The major benefit of bypass operations is that they successfully precipitate massive weight loss, a major portion of which is maintained permanently. Lanier, Younger, Scott, and Law (1969) reported a 22% to 26% weight reduction in four male patients and a 16% to 47% reduction in five female patients during a six-month postsurgical follow-up. In their experience with bypass surgery in 75 obese patients, Campbell, Hunt, Karam, and Torsham (1977) reported a mean weight loss of 45% two years after surgery. Halverson, Wise, Wazna, and Ball-inger (1978) performed jejunoileostomies on 100 obese patients and obtained a mean weight loss of approximately 40% two years after surgery. In a survey of ten hospitals performing jejunoileostomies, Iber and Cooper (1977) obtained data on 600 patients and reported that over 97% were able to lose more than 50 pounds one year after surgery.

The rate of weight loss is typically rapid during the first six months after surgery and gradually shows during the subsequent 12 months. The mean overall weight loss is about 100 pounds across several studies, with 60% lost the first year and 40% lost between two and three years after surgery. Most patients reach a steady state 24 to 36 months after the operation (Bray, 1977; Halverson et al., 1978). The average weight loss is 35% of the preoperative weight, with patients achieving a steady state of 5% to 20% above their ideal weight (Iber & Cooper, 1977). This weight loss leads to a significant reduction in obesity, because twice as much adipose tissue as lean body tissue is lost (Bray et al., 1977).

In addition to these medical benefits, positive changes in psychosocial functioning, such as increased employability and improvements in self-esteem, mood, marital and sexual relationships, and attitudinal body image, have been noted (Castelnuovo-Tedesco & Schiebel, 1976; Kalucy & Crisp, 1974; Solow et al., 1974). The psychosocial impact of jejunoileostomies is not uniformly positive, however, and psychological deterioration has been reported with some patients following surgery (Crisp, Kalucy, Pilkington, & Gazet, 1977).

There are a number of major and minor complications correlated with bypass operations. Major complications include urinary calculi, progressive liver disease, intestinal obstruction, peptic ulcer, bypass enteritis, and severe electrolyte imbalance (Bray et al., 1977). Of the Halverson et al. (1978) study's patients, 58% had at least one major complication. In addition, a number of minor complications are commonly associated with bypass surgery, including chronic diarrhea, weakness, hypokalemia, hair loss, vomiting, and malnutrition (Bray et al., 1977). These complications are so severe in some patients as to require reversal of the operation, or they will result in death. Reversal rates ranging from 4% to 19% have been reported, with liver failure and electrolyte imbalance given as the most common reasons for reversal. The most severe complication of bypass operations is surgery-related mortality. In their review of the literature covering 2,500 bypass patients, Bray and Benfield (1977) found mortality rates ranging from 0% to 6%, with a mean of 4%.

It can be concluded that jejunoileostomy constitutes an experimental procedure for the treatment of obesity. The mechanisms of weight loss, along with the complications and benefits associated with the operation, are not entirely understood at the present time. It is the only currently utilized form of treatment that is associated with a known mortality rate. Increased mortality and other complications must be weighed against the health risks arising from untreated massive obesity. The health cost-benefit ratio has not yet been sufficiently established to justify this procedure as a routine form of treatment.

Therapeutic Starvation

Therapeutic starvation involves complete restriction of caloric intake and produces rapid and often massive weight losses. This treatment is administered within a hospital setting and is usually initiated with a restricted caloric diet. Caloric intake is then totally eliminated, but fluids, vitamins, and electrolyte supplements are provided. Reportedly, a major advantage of this approach is that hunger sensations cease in the average patient after 48 to 72 hours. In contrast, patients on restricted calories frequently report hunger craving for the duration of their diets. Cessation of hunger cravings with therapeutic starvation has been attributed to elevation of ketones. During starvation, patients lose between one and two pounds per day, with losses of 50 to 150 pounds reported during hospital treatment (Swanson & Dinello, 1969).

Three types of therapeutic regimens have been reported in the literature: short-term starvation for up to 14 days, intermittent starvation alternating with restricted calorie diets, and long-term starvation for up to 120 days. Negative psychological side effects have been reported, including anxiety, depression, and even psychotic symptomatology (Rowland, 1968). Beneficial changes in psychological functioning, including increases in self-esteem, have been reported by other investigators.

Upon reviewing the literature, Stunkard and Rush (1974) concluded that length of starvation is a crucial factor in determining the existence and severity of psychopathological reactions, with short-term fasting producing fewest complications and complications increasing as fasting is extended. Low-calorie diets, however, may produce more negative psychological side effects than total fasting, because consumption stimulates, but never completely satisfies, hunger cravings. However, Rooth and Carlström (1970) found that a daily diet of 200 calories did not stimulate hunger in patients. Stunkard and Rush (1974) also concluded that patients with childhood onset of obesity are more likely to suffer untoward physical and psychological side effects than those with adulthood onset of obesity. Short-term starvation in an inpatient setting is seen as the most promising technique of starvation treatment.

An assumption underlying starvation treatments of obesity is that, if obese patients can be reduced to a more normal weight, they will be motivated by their more attractive appearance and more effective interpersonal functioning to continue restricting their caloric intake. This assumption is not supported by the available follow-up investigations of therapeutic starvation (Johnson & Drenick, 1977; Swanson & Dinello, 1969). Maintenance of weight loss is now widely regarded as the most important criterion for evaluating the success of treatment techniques, since numerous techniques can produce temporary weight losses, while few demonstrate long-term maintenance (Jeffrey, 1975; Rodin, 1977).

Lack of maintenance of weight loss following therapeutic starvation is not surprising, given that this technique does not directly influence eating or exercise habits as they occur in the natural environment. When patients terminate the fast and leave the hospital to resume the life-style that initially created or maintained their obesity, weight is rapidly regained to prestarvation levels. Because long-term efficacy has not been demonstrated, therapeutic starvation has very limited utility in treating obesity except with patients who must lose large amounts of weight rapidly for medical reasons.

Pharmacologic Treatments

Numerous pharmacologic compounds have been utilized to treat obesity. Bray and Greenway (1976) divided these compounds into the following classes: *anorexigenic drugs*, such as amphetamines, diethylpropion, mazindol, and fenfluramine, which cause a loss of appetite; *calorigenic drugs*, such a thyroid and growth hormones, which increase the rate at which calories are metabolized; agents that increase fat mobilization, especially *human chorionic gonadotrophin*; and drugs that alter levels of intestinal absorption, including *biguanides* and *hydroxycitrate*. Both the efficacy and the safety of pharmacologic approaches in treating obesity have been questioned. Many of these compounds, especially amphetamines (Edison, 1971) and thyroid compounds (Chlouverakis, 1975), have been reported to have negative medical and psychological side effects. At present, none of these pharmacologic compounds has been demonstrated as being effective in producing long-term maintenance of weight loss. While a comprehensive survey of the literature on pharmacologic treatment is beyond the scope of this chapter, interested readers should see Bray and Greenway (1976) or Chlouverakis (1975).

There have been three recent studies comparing treatments using pharmacologic approaches and those using behavioral therapy. Dahms, Molitch, Bray, Greenway, Atkinson, and Hamilton (1978) compared mazindol, diethylpropion, and placebo pills with a behavioral therapy treatment emphasizing changes in eating, exercise, and emotion-coping habits. Using absolute weight loss, percentage of initial loss, and weight-reduction index (loss that will be discussed in a later section of this chapter) as three criteria for weight change, the investigators found no significant differences in weight loss across the four treatment groups. However, the combined results for the treatment groups were significantly better than for the untreated controls. The results should be interpreted with caution because there was a very high patient attrition rate (73%), analysis of variance tests were not computed with and without patients who dropped out, and no follow-up data were reported.

A study of Ost and Götestam (1976) compared a fenfluramine treatment condition, a behavioral treatment similar to the Stuart and Davis (1972) method, and a waiting-list control. On the basis of weight-reduction indexes at post-treatment, the behavioral treatment produced significantly greater weight losses than did the fenfluramine or waiting-list control treatments, which were not significantly different. At a 12-month follow-up, the patients given behavioral treatment had maintained a greater weight loss than had patients in the other groups. These differences were no longer significant, however.

Traditional Behavioral Treatments

Stunkard and Mahoney (1976, p. 54) identified the following techniques, employed singly or in combination, as being used most frequently in behavioral research and therapy: self-monitoring of body weight and/or food intake; implicit or explicit goal setting; nutritional, exercise, and health counseling; tangible operant consequences (reward and punishment); aversion therapy; social reinforcement in the form of either therapist, group, or family support; covert conditioning and cognitive restructuring strategies; self-presented consequences (self-reward, self-punishment); and stimulus control procedures.

The application of behavioral techniques in the treatment of obesity is traced to the Ferster et al. (1962) study's conceptual analysis that emphasized stimulus control in the modification of eating behaviors. Since that time, behavioral treatments have been demonstrated as being superior to other treatment modalities in facilitating weight loss in mildly to moderately obese individuals (Abramson, 1973; Hall & Hall, 1974; Stunkard & Mahoney, 1976). Several comprehensive reviews are currently available that summarize the research literature on behavioral treatments of obesity (see Abramson, 1973, 1977; Foreyt, 1977; Jeffrey, 1976a; Leon, 1976; Stunkard & Mahoney, 1976).

Aversion Therapy

Aversion therapy in the treatment of obesity is based upon a classical conditioning paradigm. Actual food or food imagery is considered to be the conditioned stimulus and is paried with electric shock, unpleasant odors, or some other aversive event (the unconditioned stimulus). The conditioned and unconditioned stimuli are repeatedly paired, with the expectation that a conditioned aversion for highly caloric foods will develop. Upon reviewing the available literature, Frohwirth (1977) stated that the efficacy of aversive techniques has been equivocal at best and that they are time-consuming, difficult to administer, and frightening or painful for the patient. He concluded that, "considering the evidence at the present time, aversive techniques for obesity cannot be recommended for general application" (p. 74).

Covert Sensitization

Techniques of covert sensitization are also based upon an aversive conditioning paradigm. In contrast to aversion therapy, neither the conditioned stimulus (food cues) nor the unconditioned stimulus (aversive event) are physically presented. Utilizing covert sensitization, the patient imagines both the conditioned and unconditioned stimuli. It is assumed that imaginal or covert events follow the same laws as overt events (Cautela, 1972). The goal of covert sensitization is to build up avoidance responses for certain types of foods.

Despite significant differences from control conditions, the actual weight losses achieved with covert sensitization are very modest. Of the studies reporting actual weight losses, the largest is a mean loss of 11.7 pounds, while most studies average four to five pounds (Abramson, 1973). The effects of covert sensitizations are highly specific, and generalization to nontarget foods is not expected (Cautela, 1967). Relying solely upon this technique in treatment would necessitate the conditioning of many types of highly caloric foods. Abramson (1973) concluded that "it appears unlikely . . . that covert sensitization used exclusively will result in the modification of generalized patterns of inappropriate eating" (p. 48). In addition to the practical limitations, two well-designed studies (Diament & Wilson, 1975; Foreyt & Hagen, 1973) questioned the basic assumption that the effects of covert sensitization are a result of the conditioning of covert events.

Therapist Reinforcement

Techniques involving therapist reinforcement utilize operant reinforcement or punishment to facilitate weight loss. Within institutional settings, a patient's weight loss may be reinforced with tokens that are then redeemed for backup reinforcements. Dramatic weight loss has been achieved by investigators within institutional settings (Ayllon, 1963; Bernard, 1968; Moore & Crumb, 1969). There are two major limitations in the sole use of this approach. The first is that therapist reinforcement requires the therapist to assume total control over the contingencies governing eating behavior in the patient's environment. This degree of therapist control is largely unfeasible outside institutional settings. A second limitation of the use of therapist reinforcement is that changes effected within the institution have not been demonstrated to generalize to the natural environment (Abramson, 1977).

In outpatient settings, weight therapists have utilized such reinforcement techniques as contingency contracting. Patients deposit money or material possessions that are then earned back by meeting weekly goals for weight loss. If patients fail to lose weight, they forfeit the money or material possession for that week.

This technique, when utilized alone, only reinforces weight loss or punishes weight gain, and it does not systematically train patients in effective and healthy methods of losing weight. Mann (1972), using contingency contracting for weight loss, reported anecdotal information indicating that some patients resorted to extreme action, such as fasting or taking diuretics or laxatives, rather than alter basic habit patterns. Foreyt (1977) stated that "this idea, 'lose weight fast any way possible,' cannot be expected to lead to any permanent, stable weight pattern, or change in eating habits, the goal of weight loss programs" (p. 233).

Behavioral Self-Control Treatments

Self-control approaches require the individual's commitment to, and active involvement in, his or her own treatment program. A basic assumption of this treatment approach is that people possess the capacity to rearrange aspects of their external and internal environment in order to facilitate desired behavior change and maintenance. There are two general classes of self-control techniques (Jeffrey, 1977). The first class of techniques involves procedures to alter antecedent stimulus conditions of the target behavior. These include self-monitoring of food intake, physical exercise, and weight loss and self-initiated environmental rearrangement to facilitate lower food consumption and an increased level of physical activity. The second class of techniques consists of procedures to alter consequent stimulus conditions for eating, exercise, and self-management behaviors. These procedures consist of self-reinforcement for changes in eating and exercise habits, self-punishment for failure of self-management, and self-initiated social reinforcement, such as enlisting support of family and friends in efforts to lose weight.

Comparative Outcome Studies

An early comparative outcome investigation, Wollersheim's (1970, 1977) study remains one of the most thoroughly controlled studies of therapy outcome in this area. Motivated, overweight, female college students were randomly assigned to one of four experimental conditions: behavioral therapy consisting of reinforcement and stimulus-control procedures, an analog of traditional insight psychotherapy, positive expectation or social pressure to lose weight, or a no-treatment control group. Subjects in all three treatment groups lost more weight than control subjects. Comparisons between the groups indicated that the behavioral treatment was most effective in facilitating weight reduction and decreasing frequencies of reported eating behaviors. While all three treatment groups remained below their pretreatment means, they all evidenced weight gains at an eight-week follow-up. At a 16-week follow-up, however, both the social pressure and the behavioral treatment subjects reversed the trend and lost weight, while the patients given nonspecific treatment continued to gain weight.

Other comparative outcome studies have also been reported. Penick, Filion, Fox, and Stunkard (1971) utilized behavioral group therapy and contrasted it with traditional group therapy. In the behavioral group, 53% of the individuals lost more than 20 pounds, and 13% lost more than 40 pounds. Within the control group, 24% of the individuals lost more than 20 pounds, and no one lost more than 40 pounds. Hall, Hall, Hanson, and Borden (1974) compared a complex self-control group with a simple self-control group, a nonspecific treatment group, and a no-treatment control group. At posttreatment, there was no difference between the self-control groups, but both were superior to the two control groups. At a six-month follow-up, however, neither of the self-control groups was significantly better than the control groups. This contradicts Harris and Hallbauer's (1973) demonstration of successful maintenance with a self-control package.

Since self-control treatments require patients to assume responsibility for their own treatment, the active treatment ingredient might be the patients' perception of responsibility rather than any of the behavioral techniques per se. Jeffrey and Christensen (1975) examined this possibility by comparing a "will-power" treatment condition with a behavioral treatment condition and a no-treatment control. The results indicated that the behavioral treatment subjects showed greater weight loss than did the willpower or no-treatment control subjects and that losses were maintained at an 18-week follow-up. Tobias and MacDonald (1977) also obtained results indicating the superiority of a behavioral self-control treatment over a willpower treatment at both posttreatment and follow-up.

The cumulative results of these studies of comparative outcome demonstrate the general superiority of short-term self-control treatments over no-treatment controls, attention-placebo controls, traditional insight and group psychotherapy analogs and willpower treatments. Indeed, behavioral self-control treatments appear to be among the most effective nonsurgical treatments currently available for obesity.

A number of studies have compared self-control with other behavioral programs (for example, Abrahms & Allen, 1974; Bellack, Rozensky, & Schwartz, 1974; Hall, 1972, 1973; Hall, Hall, DeBoer, & O'Kulitch, 1977; Jeffrey, 1974; McReynolds, Lutz, Paulsen, & Kohrs, 1976; Romanczyk, Tracey, Wilson, & Thorpe, 1973). Overall, self-control packages appear to be as effective, or more effective, than other behavioral programs in promoting weight loss. Investigators have begun to conduct studies that analyze components typically included in self-control packages to determine which are responsible for treatment effects. If certain components are found to be more potent than others, therapists could be sure to emphasize those components in future treatment programs. On the other hand, if specific components are found to be ineffective, they could be eliminated to further improve both the efficacy and the efficiency of future treatments.

Treatment Component Studies

Two studies (Bellack, 1976; Mahoney, 1974) suggest that more complex self-control treatments are more effective than self-monitoring alone. In addition, Mahoney, Moura, and Wade (1973) evaluated the efficacy, for weight loss and habit change, of self-monitoring, self-reward, self-punishment, and self-reward plus self-punishment. At a four-month follow-up, the groups containing self-reward instructions had lost more weight than either the self-punishment or control groups.

Chapman and Jeffrey (1978) examined the role of self-standard setting as a component of the self-reinforcement process. The study employed an additive design that compared a situational-management group with a self-standard-setting group and a self-reinforcement group. The results revealed, as predicted, that the self-standard-setting subjects lost significantly more weight than did the situational-management subjects. However, the self-standard-setting group was also superior to the self-reinforcement group, which did not differ significantly from the situational-management group. These results demonstrated that the addition of self-reinforcement to enhance weight loss in fact produced short-term results inferior to those achieved by situational management. Based on questionnaire results, the authors speculated that the added systematic training in self-reinforcement increased the anxiety of the individuals to perform, and, when anxious, many of these obese individuals overate. The authors did not conclude that self-reinforcement is unimportant but that the ways typically used to teach self-reinforcement may not have beneficial effects. They speculated that self-reinforcement needs to be conceptualized and taught as part of a larger picture of personality.

On the basis of currently available, short-term component analysis and comparative outcome studies, it can be concluded that premonitoring of intake is more effective than postmonitoring (Bellack, Rozensky, & Schwartz, 1974) and that self-monitoring of caloric intake plus weight is more effective than self-monitoring of weight alone (Romanczyk et al., 1973). While self-monitoring of caloric intake has some therapeutic effects, it is, by itself, not as effective in promoting weight loss and maintenance as when it is combined with self-reinforcement and other components (Bellack, 1976; Mahoney, 1974; Romanczyk et al., 1973). At present, self-reward appears more effective than self-punishment (Mahoney et al., 1973), and self-reward for habit change appears superior to self-reward for weight loss (Mahoney, 1974). While some aspects of self-reward procedures enhance weight loss, Chapman and Jeffrey's (1978) results suggested that the self-standard setting inherent in the self-reward may be an essential component that needs more emphasis.

At the present time, there exist insufficient data to come to any final conclusions regarding the relative efficacy of various treatment components. While all the components typically included in self-control packages may not be crucial for success, more research on component analysis is needed before specific components employed in complex self-control programs are eliminated in favor of simpler programs. Until these data are forthcoming, weight therapists are well advised to continue employing complex, comprehensive self-control packages to achieve the best treatment results.

Bibliotherapy Treatments

Several research studies have investigated the role of therapist or group contact in implementation of self-control programs. If self-control principles are sufficiently outlined in written form, it is possible that bibliotherapy could be as effective as contact with a weight therapist or involvement in group therapy. Hagen (1974) determined that a bibliotherapy treatment was as effective as a self-control treatment administered through group therapy, and both were superior to a no-contact control.

Other investigators (Fernan, 1973; Hanson, Borden, Hall, & Hall, 1976; Lindstrom, Balch, & Reese, 1976; Mahoney et al., 1973; Tobias & MacDonald, 1977) have also demonstrated that subjects, with a minimum of therapist involvement, are able to lose weight using bibliotherapy materials. Long-term maintenance of weight losses achieved with bibliotherapy treatments, however, has not been reported, and it is, therefore, premature to conclude that therapist or group contact is superfluous and serves no useful function.

Currently, self-management approaches offer effective and promising methods for the treatment of obesity in outpatient settings. Until recently, there was no single source designed for use by the lay person that contained all the techniques encompassed by this approach. Instead, brief descriptions of self-management programs were scattered throughout the experimental literature. As research has accumulated, several good books have been have been written for the public on self-control approaches to weight loss (Ferguson, 1975; Jeffrey & Katz, 1977; Mahoney & Mahoney, 1976; Stuart & Davis, 1972). For example, Jeffrey and Katz (1977) presented a comprehensive, multifaceted self-management program based on the most promising research currently available. The components of this self-management package include overview of the causes of obesity; presentation of the rationale of behavioral self-management; thorough assessment of readiness to lose weight; training in self-monitoring, self-standard setting, and self-reward; description of a commonsense diet and food-exchange diet plan; discussion of caloric expenditure and a plan for physical activity; training in techniques of effective food management; techniques to gain support from family and friends; ways to handle feelings without eating;

methods to contract with a spouse or friend for weight loss; plans for long-range planning and maintenance of weight loss; and suggestions for preventing obesity in children.

Jeffrey and Katz (1977) stressed the importance of gradual weight reduction achieved through modification of self and environment. The book focuses on habit change, rather than on weight loss, and the importance of a lifelong commitment to a healthy, thin life-style.

Exercise

Available research suggests that inactivity is an important factor in creating a positive energy balance that results in obesity. Chirico and Stunkard (1960) compared daily activity levels for obese and nonobese workers and found that the obese workers walked 40% less than did the normal-weight workers. In fact, some research (Johnson, Burke, & Mayer, 1956) suggests that decreased physical expenditure may play a greater role in causing obesity than excessive caloric intake. In evaluating the relationship between activity level and weight gain, Mayer (1968) concluded that ". . . inactivity is the most important factor explaining the frequency of 'creeping' overweight in modern societies. Our bodies' regulation of food intake was just not designed for the highly mechanized sedentary conditions of modern life" (p. 82).

In spite of the acknowledgement of its importance in both the etiology and treatment of obesity, exercise has received surprisingly little investigation by behavioral researchers. Stuart (1971) added an individualized aerobic exercise program to a treatment package that involved stimulus control and nutritional counseling, but the experimental design he employed did not allow an analysis of the contribution of exercise to treatment outcome. In a later study, Harris and Hallbauer (1973) compared a self-control program for change in eating habits with a self-control program emphasizing both change in eating and exercise habits and with an attention-placebo control group. At posttreatment, subjects in all three groups had lost weight, with no significant differences between groups. A seven-month follow-up demonstrated that subjects in the self-control groups lost more weight than the attention-placebo control subjects and that the eating and exercise self-control group lost more than the eating self-control group.

Stalonas, Johnson, and Christ (1978) employed an additive design in comparing a stimulus-control treatment, a stimulus-control plus self-reinforcement treatment, and a combination treatment incorporating all three components. No significant differences in weight loss between groups were obtained at posttreatment or at a three-month follow-up. At a one-year follow-up, however, the stimulus-control group showed weight regain, while the groups with an exercise component demonstrated the best maintenance or improved weight loss.

Taken together, these results suggest that including exercise as a component in a comprehensive self-control treatment package leads to better initial loss and long-term maintenance. An added benefit is that pateints' physical and cardio-vascular conditioning is also likely to improve, and they will achieve better overall physical health. Research aimed at improving methods of retraining exercise habits would be a worthwhile direction in which to proceed in attempts to improve the overall efficacy of behavioral self-control treatment packages.

Maintenance of Weight Loss

With a disorder as refractory as obesity, merely demonstrating that a treatment technique produces weight loss is not sufficient to validate that technique clinically. Achieving weight loss to goal weight and permanent maintenance of that loss constitute the ultimate clinical criteria of effective treatment. In a review of the outcome literature through 1973, Hall and Hall (1974) found only three studies with six-month or longer follow-ups. They concluded that studies with 12-week or shorter follow-ups probably continue to find differences between experimental groups because experimental subjects have not had time to regain weight, while studies with longer follow-ups have not generally found initial differences between experimental and control groups to be significant at follow-up. In a review, Brightwell and Sloan (1977) located and reviewed 15 studies with sufficient designs and follow-up (that is, six months or longer) and found that seven of the studies revealed some degree of maintenance. Self-management treatments did not clearly demonstrate better maintenance than other behavioral treatments. Only one study (Hanson et al., 1976) reported that subjects continued to lose weight after the termination of treatment. Brightwell and Sloan concluded that, "while promising, behavior therapy has not, as yet, been clearly demonstrated to be an effective, permanent and practical treatment for obesity" (p. 898).

Realizing that the establishment of long-term maintenance is imperative for the validation of behavioral treatment approaches, investigators have attempted to identify strategies by which maintenance could be promoted. Kingsley and Wilson (1977) found booster sessions helpful, but Ashby and Wilson (1977) and Hall et al. (1974) failed to demonstrate any facilitation of maintenance. Hanson et al. (1976) investigated the strategy of gradually fading therapeutic contact by comparing a standard self-management group with high- and low-contact bibliotherapy groups. At termination, there were no significant differences between the groups, but the faded groups had continued to lose weight at a one-year follow-up, while the other groups had tended to relapse. While the results of this study are weakened by the fact that follow-up data were obtained through telephoned self-report, other studies (for example, Bellack, 1977; Carter, Rice, & DeJulio, 1977) provided results suggesting that fading of therapeutic contact enhances maintenance.

Self-Help Group Treatments

Groups involved in self-help weight reduction may constitute the most highly utilized treatment for obesity, with millions of individuals participating in a wide variety of these groups every year. In spite of their ubiquitousness, these groups have received very little systematic, experimental investigation. This may be due primarily to a lack of receptiveness to this type of investigation on the part of participating members and organizations. The two self-help organizations that have been experimentally examined are Weight Watchers and TOPS.

While Weight Watchers cannot strictly be considered a self-help group because it is commercially sponsored, it incorporates many of the procedures typically found in self-help groups. Weight Watchers is currently the largest self-help group involved in weight reduction, with over 1.5 million participating members in 1976 (Stuart, 1977). Its program consists of nutritionally balanced reducing plans as well as classes on weight reduction conducted by individuals who have successfully lost weight with the Weight Watchers program. Classes consist of lectures covering nutritional, motivational, and other issues associated with weight reduction. Recently, procedures of behavior modification (outlined in Stuart & Davis, 1972, and Stuart, 1975) were integrated into the Weight Watchers program, with the development of 18 treatment modules covering a wide range of behavioral procedures.

Stuart (1977) investigated the impact of the introduction of the behavioral procedure by comparing Weight Watchers classes in one area, which employed traditional techniques, with those in another area, which utilized the behavioral modules. Large samples of over 2,000 participants were obtained from each area, and these samples were shown to be very similar in terms of relevant demographic and weight variables. The results of the study indicated that the behavioral classes produced significantly superior results in comparison to the traditional classes. No data were presented, however, that dealt with the impact of the behavioral or traditional classes upon long-term maintenance of weight loss.

TOPS is the oldest and second largest group program for weight reduction in the country, with 350,000 members in 1972 (Stunkard, 1972). Its members belong to over 2,400 chapters in the United States, Canada, and several foreign countries. TOPS relies heavily on group identification, social support, and pressure to motivate members to lose weight. Meetings generally include songs or pledges concerning controlling emotions and eating, a ritual weigh-in, public announcement of successful losses and chastisement of gains, and didactic discussions of relevant issues.

Wagonfeld and Wolowitz (1968) compared three chapters of TOPS with a nonobese control group and found a 50% dropout rate six months after initial membership. Of those that remained beyond six months, 80% lost weight. No data on the magnitude or maintenance of weight losses were presented, however.

Stunkard (1972) studied 22 chapters of TOPS in West Philadelphia and compared the results with those from 14 groups of patients treated by medical means. The average member of TOPS was female, 45 years old, and had an initial weight of 188 pounds, which was 58% above ideal weight. These members remained in TOPS for 15 months and lost an average of 15 pounds. Across chapters, there was wide variance in weight lost, but the results were comparable or superior to losses achieved in the medically treated groups.

In the most adequately designed study to date, Levitz and Stunkard (1974) compared behavioral self-control programs, conducted by professional therapists or TOPS leaders, with a standard TOPS program within 16 TOPS chapters. During a three-month treatment program, both types of self-control groups produced greater weight loss and reduced attrition rates than did the groups following the standard TOPS program. At a 12-month follow-up, the self-control groups led by professional therapists demonstrated continued weight loss, while self-control groups led by TOPS leaders and the standard TOPS groups demonstrated a relapse to, or gain above, pretreatment mean weights.

Given the dearth of experimental data and especially long-term follow-ups, it is impossible to reach any conclusions regarding the effectiveness of the two self-help groups discussed. The studies on integration of behavioral treatment techniques with existing self-help groups are promising and deserving of future research. Existing self-help groups provide an established delivery system that may be more effective than those developed by professionals (Stuart, 1977). The possible alliance between behavioral therapists and self-help groups might provide a wider avenue for dissemination of behavioral techniques of weight control than any other means now available.

Macroenvironmental Treatments

Macroenvironmental treatments of obesity seek to make changes at a societal level and thus modify the eating and exercise habits of millions of U.S. residents. A number of such actions will be discussed here, some of which are currently being taken and some of which obviously could be taken (Jeffrey & Lemnitzer, 1980). To convey the great potential of the application of social-learning principles at the societal level, the following discussion will be presented as a series of proposals. These proposals are by no means comprehensive, nor are they without their difficulties. However, it is hoped that they will stimulate us to start thinking of behavior modification programs at the societal level of analysis and intervention.

Establish National Dietary Goals

The public is confused about what to eat to maximize health. Public policy-makers could be of considerable help in changing public awareness about food. This could be achieved through the adoption and implementation of national dietary goals, which would provide a simple guide to good eating habits and encourage a healthful selection of foods. Such goals would also facilitate government and industry decisions regarding the content of nutrition information provided to the public, the kinds of foods produced, and how foods are processed and advertised. The U.S. Department of Agriculture and the Department of Health and Human Services have at last established some general national dietary goals in 1980 that can serve as an excellent foundation for expanded goals in the coming decade.

Improve Nutrition Education Programs

We need to improve the dissemination of information about good nutrition, good eating habits, and weight control to health professionals, elementary and secondary school teachers, and the public. A number of experimental programs across the nation are attempting to achieve this. For example, the Baylor College of Medicine in Houston, funded by a five-year grant from the National Heart and Lung Institute, has been attempting to demonstrate the effectiveness of community programs on diet education for lowering plasma cholesterol and triglyceride levels in the general population (Foreyt, Scott, & Grotto, 1976). Based on the Foreyt et al. study, which suggests that a 10% reduction in serum cholesterol levels of the population would yield a 23% decrease in the incidence of heart disease, the programs use both nutrition and behavioral information. A total of 1,000 individuals are expected to participate in a three-year period. The project also works with the Texas Agricultural Extension Service of Texas A. & M. in developing monthly programs on nutrition and home economics for low-income families. Nutrition education is conducted by neighborhood aides through home visits. An estimated population of 25,000 is reached.

Improve Food Labeling

Because food is often promoted on the basis of appearance and convenience and not on the basis of nutrition and calories, clear, concise, and informative labeling of all goods is desirable, so that U.S. consumers will be able to identify and purchase nutritious, low-calorie foods. New food-labeling regulations by the Food and Drug Administration require the following information per serving: serving size, servings per container, calories, protein, carbohydrates, fat, and percentages of the U.S. Recommended Daily Allowance. It seems reasonable and simple to extend the Food and Drug Administration's labeling regulation to include *all* foods and to include the percentage of sugar in the product.

Examine the Role of Vending Machines in the Consumption of Food

An increasing part of U.S. food marketing includes the sale of food from vending machines situated in such locations as schools, parks, and sports arenas. These machines often offer a severely restricted variety of snacks — usually only those that are high in sugar, fat, and calories. A new bill, the Child Nutrition Act, signed into law in November 1977, gives authority for what can be sold in vending machines on school property to the U.S. secretary of agriculture. The Agriculture Department intends to allow only healthy, nutritious foods in vending machines of schools that receive support for the federal school-lunch program.

Investigate the Role of Advertising in the Conditioning of Our Eating Habits

As noted earlier, evidence suggests that food advertising – especially advertising of foods that are low in nutrition and high in calories – abounds and that it does influence the nutrition knowledge and eating habits of the population. We might consider regulating the type and quantity of televised food advertisements. Perhaps every time there is an advertisement for a "junk" food, an "anti-junk" commercial or one for nutritious food could be required. We might consider banning the advertisement of all junk foods on television. The Federal Trade Commission is, in fact, investigating the possible regulation of children's television commercials for such items as candy, soft drinks, and sugarcoated cereals.

Examine Tax Policies on Food Consumption

Our society has always used taxes on specific products to generate income and to reduce the purchase of those products that society has deemed unhealthy. There might also be a tax on sugar or a tax on vending machines selling junk foods in order to increase their price and thereby decrease somewhat the consumption of these foods and, as a by-product, generate tax revenue for health programs.

The same kind of approach used to improve our eating habits could also be attempted in order to increase good, and decrease poor, exercise behaviors. A number of proposals designed to meet these goals will now be discussed.

Establish National Goals of Physical Fitness

National fitness goals, serving the same functions as national dietary goals, should be established and implemented. This might involve an operational definition of *fitness* (which is the ability to perform task x in y amount of time with a heart rate of z), as well as a plan to aid citizens in reaching these goals.

Improve Programs of Physical Education

Programs of physical education similar to those proposed for nutrition education need to be increased and upgraded for health professionals, students, and the public. On the public level, we now have the President's Council on Physical Fitness and Sports, which sponsors fitness advertisements on television and several physical activity programs. The role given to this council could be expanded from that of an advisory body to one of a coordinator of greatly expanded federal and local programs encouraging physical activity.

Expand Employer-sponsored Sports Facilities and Programs

Most grade schools, high schools, and colleges provide sports facilities and programs that their students or employees are expected to use while attending school or on the job. A few governmental, medical, and corporate institutions provide employees with similar physical activity facilities and programs. Employers' efforts to maintain good health and weight control of their employees through sound physical fitness are, unfortunately, the exception rather than the rule. It is to be hoped that more institutions will develop similar programs.

In summary, these proposals are neither comprehensive nor exhaustive. Obviously, other proposals can be made, and all could be experimentally tested before deciding to implement them on a national scale. Our hope is to get scholars, educators, doctors, public policymakers, and others to start thinking about the possibilities of a macroenvironmental analysis of the causes, preventions, and treatments of obesity, cardiovascular diseases, and other medical problems at the *societal* level.

METHODOLOGICAL ISSUES IN RESEARCH AND TREATMENT OF OBESITY

Methodological issues are relevant to both research and treatment of obesity and cut across the various research and treatment orientations. In our review of methodological issues, we will discuss criteria of obesity and measurement of variables that are relevant to obesity, such as weight, body fat, eating patterns, exercise patterns, and personality variables. Finally, we will discuss some standards for evaluating the methodological adequacy of outcome studies on the treatment of obesity. A comprehensive discussion of all methodological issues that are of concern to obesity research is impossible within the space limitations of this chapter, and interested readers are directed to Hall and Hall (1974), Jeffrey (1975, 1976b), and Wilson (1978).

Criteria of Obesity

At the beginning of this chapter, we defined obesity as an excess quantity of stored body fat and went on to distinguish obesity and overweight. Since, in many research and clinical settings, body fat is not directly measured, the issue of the criterion of obesity involves specifying a point at which body weight is so far beyond normal limits that the existence of excess body fat can be inferred. This usually involves defining an ideal weight on a height-weight chart and deciding upon a percentage overweight at which the investigator is willing to define a person as obese. This practice results in making a rather arbitrary decision, often in the absence of data indicating that the chosen cutoff on the height-weight chart is actually correlated with excess body fat, as measured by more direct means.

Criteria of obesity employed in behavioral research typically range from 10% to 20% over ideal weight. These varying criteria of obesity make it difficult to directly compare results, because subjects considered obese in one study might not be considered so in another study that utilized a different criterion. Another issue concerns whether treatment results obtained from subjects 10% over ideal weight can be generalized to clinical populations with much higher percentages over ideal weight. Much of the behavioral research has been criticized because it has utilized subjects who are not sufficiently overweight to really be obese and are, therefore, not representative of clinical populations (Chlouverakis, 1975).

Bray (1978), approaching this criterion issue from a different direction, advocated employing 30% over ideal weight as the criterion for clinical obesity. Epidemiologic research has demonstrated that there is no significant increase in medical disorders for individuals under 30% over ideal weight, but, beyond this point, there is a rapid rise in disorders related to obesity with every percentage of increase over ideal weight. Bray (1978) concluded that 30% over ideal weight is a suitable criterion for obesity, because it is assuredly related to excess body fat and represents the point at which obesity significantly contributes to medical problems.

Measurement of Variables Related to Obesity

In line with the psychosomatic nature of this disorder, the variables of interest to both researchers and clinicians range from the purely somatic, including weight and body fat, to the behavioral and psychological variables of eating habits and exercise patterns. Since weight is the primary dependent variable in behavioral, medical, and other types of research concerning obesity, we will begin our discussion with this variable.

Weight

A factor that initially attracted many behavioral researchers to the study of obesity was the seeming objectivity of the dependent variable of weight. Ironically, there is still much debate about how weight data can be best presented to make the results comparable across studies. While absolute weight loss should be reported for individual subjects, it is not an adequate measure of weight loss in and of itself. It is evident that a 20-pound weight loss has much different significance for a 150-pound subject than for a 300-pound subject.

Percentage over ideal weight (current weight minus ideal weight divided by ideal weight) is a better criterion for weight loss, because it takes into account both the height and the weight loss goal, or ideal weight. Thus, the changes in percentage over ideal weight would be very different for the 150-pound subject losing 20 pounds than for the 300-pound subject losing the same amount of weight. Percentage over ideal weight, however, is still not fully adequate for comparing results across studies.

Currently, there is no widely employed, standardized improvement criterion that makes results across studies directly comparable. For instance, it is difficult to directly compare a study that reported that 53% of the patients in a behavioral therapy group lost more than 20 pounds (Penick et al., 1971) with a study that reported that a behavioral therapy group lost an average of 13 pounds (Wollersheim, 1970). Feinstein (1959) proposed a standardized improvement criterion called the weight-reduction index (RI), which is equal to the percentage of excess weight loss multiplied by relative initial obesity.

$$RI = (Wl/Ws) (Wi/Wt) \times 100$$

where Wl = weight loss, Ws = surplus weight, Wi = initial weight, and Wt = target weight.

This index takes into account weight, height, amount overweight, goal, and pounds lost. The reduction index will usually provide a value between zero (no weight loss) and 200 (a large weight loss). For example, if a subject initially weighed 250 pounds, has a target weight of 150 pounds, had a surplus weight of 100 pounds, and loses 50 pounds, then the weight-reduction index would be (50/100) (250/150) 100 = 83. If the person loses 100 pounds, the RI would be 166, and, if no weight is lost, the RI would be zero. The advantage of developing a standardized index for reporting weight loss is the convenience it offers in comparing the effectiveness of different treatments for weight reduction, regardless of their rationale or procedure.

There are several shortcomings involved in using height-weight charts as a standard for ideal weight (Jeffrey & Katz, 1977). These charts are based on a sample of insurance customers and are not necessarily representative of the entire population in terms of physical, racial, ethnic, and socioeconomic factors. Specific groups of individuals, such as athletes and minority persons, are underrepresented in current tables. Another weakness is that the norms are based on samples from the 1950s and may be outdated for today's population.

A major difficulty in using height-weight charts for either treatment or research purposes is that they require an estimation of frame size to determine the acceptable weight range. Currently, there is no quantifiable method for determining frame size, and the investigator is forced to make a subjective estimate. There is a wide range of acceptable weights across different body builds for a given height, and misestimates of frame size can result in errors. A further problem is that, after frame size has been estimated, the chart provides only a range of acceptable weight and not a precise ideal weight, which forces the investigator or clinician to arbitrarily choose a weight within that range as the "ideal" weight.

An alternative to utilizing height-weight charts in estimating ideal weight and obesity is to employ a ratio of weight relative to a specific power of height. Epidemiologic research with varied populations has demonstrated that weight divided by height squared (weight/height^2) provides the best such ratio (Thomas, McKay, & Cutlip, 1976). This ratio is known as the body mass index (BMI) and has correlations of between 0.70 and 0.80 with more direct measures of body fat, thereby providing the lowest correlations with height, independent of weight (Bray, 1978).

Thomas et al. (1976) developed a nomograph to calculate BMI that uses life-insurance data as population norms in specifying a range of acceptable weight (see Figure 7.1). This BMI nomograph provides a continuous quantitative scale of acceptable weight ranges for various heights, but it does not require an estimation of frame size to determine the acceptable range. Thomas et al. designated three sections of the acceptable range to correspond to various frame sizes, thus allowing investigators or clinicians to take skeletal structure into account in determining an ideal weight for a given patient. An advantage of the nomograph is that, for all heights, obesity is defined as the point at which the BMI is greater than 30, and this point corresponds closely with 30% overweight.

The BMI nomograph offers obvious advantages for researchers. Besides eliminating the necessity of estimating frame size, the nomograph specifies an exact BMI value for clinical obesity (that is, greater than 30) and also allows an exact specification of ideal weight. An investigator can choose a BMI within the acceptable range (for example, 23) and then determine an exact ideal-weight value for patients of differing heights. This would provide superior data for use in calculations concerning percentage over ideal weight and RI.

In spite of these advantages, the nomograph has weaknesses similar to those of the height-weight charts, because it uses insurance data in defining population norms. Therefore, the previously described problems concerning the representativeness of these norms also affect the BMI nomograph. A lack of current, representative weight norms hinders both treatment and research. Development of such norms is sorely needed and could best be accomplished by a federal government agency responsible for the quality of health care, such as the Department of Health and Human Services.

Body Fat

The literature indicates that there is an almost exclusive reliance on gross body weight, rather than indexes of body fat, as the dependent variable. While amount of body fat is the criterion of obesity, gross body weight is influenced by a number of factors besides body fat, such as the amount of body water and skeletal and muscular structure. The only direct method of determining the amount of body fat is through biopsies. Indirect measurements of the amount of body fat have been developed. For example, *densitometric analysis* compares regular weight to underwater weight in calculating the amount of lean body mass and body fat. Unfortunately, the underwater weighing equipment necessary for densitometric analysis is so expensive that it precludes wide clinical and research use.

Researchers have attempted to develop more practical assessment techniques for measuring body fat using densitometric determinations as the criteria. *Anthropometric* measurements, including body circumference and thickness of

FIGURE 7.1
Nomograph for Body Mass Index (KG/M²)

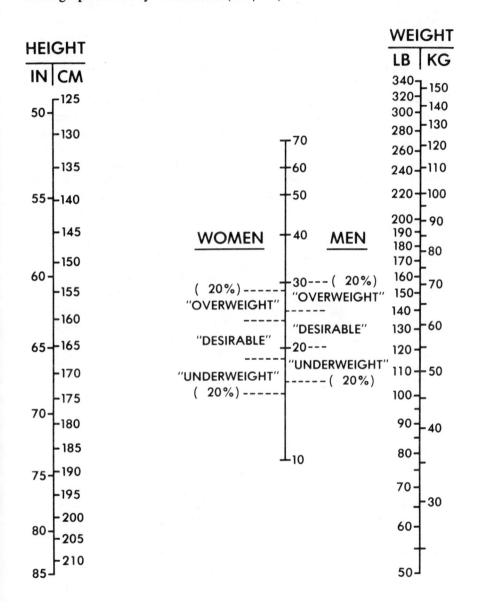

Source: Reprinted, by permission, from A. E. Thomas, D. A. McKay, and M. B. Cutlip, "Nomograph for Body Mass Index (KG/M²)" (*American Journal of Clinical Nutrition*, 1976, *29*, 302-304).

skin fold, have been employed in conjunction with regression equations to predict amount of body fat. In particular, caliper measurements of skin folds have been advocated for use in behavioral research to provide an independent assessment of body fat.

Bray (1978) evaluated the psychometric properties and clinical utility of several measurements of body circumference and caliper assessments of thickness of skin fold at several body sites. The body circumferences demonstrated greater interobserver reliability and less variability when weight remained stable than did measurements of skin fold. As reported in Bray, Greenway, Molitch, Dahms, Atkinson, and Hamilton (1978), a comparison between a regression equation utilizing four measurements of skin fold and an equation employing height and weight to predict lean body mass resulted in a correlation of 0.94. On the basis of these results, Bray et al. (1978) concluded that, "since measurement of height and weight have a smaller standard deviation than skinfolds, they would appear to be the anthropometric measurements of choice in assessing fatness rather than skinfold measurements" (p. 72).

Eating Behavior

Methods employed in measuring eating behavior have included patient self-monitoring, direct observation, and paper-and-pencil assessment. Self-monitoring of eating behavior typically involves having subjects record such information as the type, amount, and caloric value of food eaten as well as the setting, time of day, and feelings associated with eating (see Jeffrey & Katz, 1977, for a self-monitoring form). There are limitations in employing self-monitoring data as the only descriptions of eating behavior or caloric intake, since they may be biased and unreliable. Self-monitoring is a valuable therapeutic tool, however, because it increases patients' awareness of their eating behavior and provides the therapist with detailed information concerning antecedent and consequent events controlling this eating behavior. Such information is indispensable in developing a comprehensive, individualized treatment plan.

To overcome the limitations of self-monitoring data, investigators have made direct observations of eating behavior in laboratory settings. Observation of the number of crackers eaten by subjects after various experimental manipulations (Abramson & Wunderlich, 1972; Schachter, 1971a) is an example of this approach. The obtained data may be more reliable than self-monitoring data, but only to a limited degree can they be generalized to eating behavior occurring in the natural environment. This type of data also has little relevance for use in treatment planning with obese patients.

A paper-and-pencil measure that appears to have utility in obesity treatment and research is Wollersheim's Eating Patterns Questionnaire (EPQ), which was designed to assess general patterns of eating behavior. The EPQ was developed by administering a pool of items to overweight and normal-weight subjects and factor analyzing the items that discriminated between the two groups. The factor analysis yielded 44 items loading on six orthogonal factors: (1) emotional and uncontrolled overeating, (2) eating in response to interpersonal situations, (3) eating in isolation, (4) eating as a reward, (5) eating in response to evaluative situations, and (6) eating between meals. Wollersheim (1970) utilized the EPQ in her comparative outcome study and obtained significant treatment effects for the behavioral group treatment on factors 1, 3, 4, and 6. This pattern of results was subsequently replicated by Hagen (1974). While the EPQ requires further normative and validational research, it has the potential for both clinical relevance and research utility.

Levels of Physical Activity and Cardiovascular Functioning

With increasing recognition of the importance of caloric expenditure in effecting overall energy balance, investigators are beginning to seek indexes of levels of physical activity and possible improvements in cardiovascular functioning following increases in physical activity. As with eating behavior, patient self-monitoring is a practical method of obtaining data regarding physical activity levels, but it has similar research limitations. Self-monitoring of physical activity characteristically involves recording such information as type of activity, date, duration of activity, other people involved, and feelings toward the activity. Using these data, the patient or therapist can calculate the number of calories expended through various activities (see Jeffrey & Katz, 1977, for self-monitoring forms and caloric expenditure tables). The obtained information is invaluable for developing an individualized exercise plan as part of a comprehensive behavioral treatment program for obesity.

The limitations of self-report data have resulted in a search for more reliable and objective measures of physical fitness that could be easily employed as dependent variables in behavioral research. Physical performance measures that have been used are the Harvard Step Test, which assesses the length of time subjects can maintain a pace of climbing 30 steps per minute, and the sit-up test, which measures the number of sit-ups completed within a one-minute period. Simple assessments of cardiovascular functioning have included blood pressure, resting pulse rate, and recovery rate following the Harvard Step Test. These measures of physical activity can be employed in outpatient clinics. The use of more sophisticated physiological measures are encouraged for more complicated inpatient research studies.

Evaluation Issues

This section will address research issues considered important for methodologically sound studies of obesity treatment. The following is not presented as a complete discussion of all methodological issues that must be considered when completing or evaluating research in this area. Because of space limitations, some important topics (such as research designs and data analysis) cannot be covered, and the reader is referred to Jeffrey (1975, 1976b) and Wilson (1978) for a more comprehensive presentation.

Patient and Therapist Variables

It is now recognized that patient and therapist variables can greatly influence the efficacy of any treatment technique. Research suggests that the expectancy and skill of the therapist and the motivation, expectancy, and socioeconomic status of the patient are important variables affecting a wide range of therapeutic outcomes. Because of the variability in patient response to treatment, it is important to obtain and report demographic and other significant descriptive information.

Independent and Dependent Variables

If a complex package is utilized, the type of treatment techniques and the various treatment components should be clearly delineated. It is also important to describe the modality, such as individual therapy, group therapy, or bibliotherapy, and the schedule of treatment implementation. Many treatment studies involve instructing patients in the use of behavioral change techniques, which they are expected to implement in the natural environment. Weight loss is then attributed to these techniques, even though the degree to which they were actually implemented by the patient is rarely assessed (Stalonas et al., 1978).

In reporting weight data as dependent variables, the means and standard deviations for pretreatment weight, posttreatment weight, follow-up weight, and weight-reduction indexes for experimental groups should be reported. Due to individual differences, it is desirable to report individual patient data in addition to group data or, at a minimum, to note if there are "unsuccessful patients" in a "successful treatment" and to make available, upon request, the individual data. Since obesity is a multifaceted disorder, it is an unproductive research strategy to continue employing weight as the only dependent measure. Our understanding of obesity will be better advanced by employing multiple dependent measures, including such variables related to obesity as those discussed previously.

Long-Term Treatments and Follow-ups

Sustained weight loss to goal, followed by maintenance of the weight loss, is generally considered the ultimate criterion for successful treatment of obesity. This is so because many treatment approaches can demonstrate posttreatment weight loss, while few can produce long-term loss and maintenance. After reviewing the behavioral treatment literature, Hall and Hall (1974) stated that ". . . the few controlled studies including long follow-up periods . . . have generally found that the originally observed differences between experimental and control groups were no longer significant" (pp. 352-364). Clearly, there is a need to include both intermediate (for example, six months) and long-term (over one year) follow-ups in weight investigations so that the durability of the changes may be determined.

Attrition Rates

Patients dropping out prematurely from traditional treatment approaches to weight reduction have long been a problem, and a study by Harris and Bruner (1971) indicated that it is no less a problem for learning-based therapies. Since not reporting dropouts in a study can seriously affect the interpretation of the results, it seems prudent to report at least the number of patients who do not complete treatment and, whenever possible, to include the dropouts in the analyses and interpretation of the results. It also seems advisable for some studies to systematically investigate what factors contribute to patients dropping out of treatment.

Cost-Benefit Analysis

The costs of not treating a disease, in terms of human suffering, lost productivity, and money, need to be weighed against the costs and benefits of treating a disease. A cost-benefit analysis is always complex and can only be an estimate, but it would be very helpful to begin to apply these concepts to the problem of obesity. The cost of not treating obesity can begin to be estimated by the increased associated health problems of people who are obese and the money spent to treat these diseases. The human suffering involved remains an elusive variable to quantify. The benefits of treating obesity successfully can be measured, in part, by the reduced associated health problems and expenses of treating those diseases. These benefits, however, must be weighed against the success rate and expense of treating obesity. A variable that should be included in this analysis is the professional time spent in treating patients.

SUMMARY

In this chapter, we have reviewed the literature on the etiologies of obesity and discussed the variety of treatments currently used. Clearly, a major conclusion that can be drawn from the literature is that there is not a single theory or etiological factor that totally accounts for the high prevalence of obesity. However, it does appear that environmental factors account for the vast majority of the variance. The treatment literature suggests that behavioral self-control treatments and macroenvironmental treatments offer promising approaches in the treatment of obesity but that these approaches are not a panacea for the complex problem of obesity. The chapter has ended with a discussion of the methodological issues with which one must be concerned when evaluating any treatment approach. Much has been learned about the causes and treatments of obesity in the last 20 years. However, much more will need to be learned in the next 20 years — by the year 2000 — before the causes of obesity can be completely understood and totally effective treatments can be developed.

REFERENCES

Abrahms, J. L., & Allen, G. J. Comparative effectiveness of situational programming, financial pay-offs, and group pressure in weight reduction. *Behavior Therapy*, 1974, *5*, 391-400.

Abramson, E. E. A review of behavioral approaches to weight control. *Behaviour Research and Therapy*, 1973, *11*, 547-556.

Abramson, E. E. Behavioral approaches to weight control: An updated review. *Behaviour Research and Therapy*, 1977, *15*, 355-363.

Abramson, E. E., & Stinson, S. G. Boredom and eating in obese and normals. *Addictive Behavior*, 1977, *2*, 181-185.

Abramson, E. E., & Wunderlich, R. A. Anxiety, fear, and eating: A test of the psychosomatic concept of obesity. *Journal of Abnormal Psychology*, 1972, *79*, 317-321.

Armstrong, D. B. Obesity and its relation to health and disease. *Journal of the American Medical Association*, 1951, *147*, 1007-1012.

Ashbey, W. A., & Wilson, G. T. Behavior therapy for obesity: Booster sessions and long-term maintenance of weight loss. *Behaviour Research and Therapy*, 1977, *15*, 451-463.

Atkinson, R. M., & Ringuette, E. L. A survey of biographical and psychological features in extraordinary fatness. *Psychosomatic Medicine*, 1967, *29*, 121-133.

Ayllon, T. Intensive treatment of psychotic behavior by stimulus satiation and food reinforcement. *Behaviour Research and Therapy*, 1963, *1*, 53-61.

Bellack, A. S. A comparison of self-reinforcement and self-monitoring in a weight reduction program. *Behavior Therapy*, 1976, *7*, 68-75.

Bellack, A. S. Behavioral treatment for obesity: Appraisal and recommendations. In M. Hersen, R. M. Eisler, and P. M. Miller (Eds.), *Progress in behavior modification* (Vol. 4). New York: Academic, 1977.

Bellack, A. S., Rozensky, R. H., & Schwartz, J. A comparison of two forms of self-monitoring in a behavioral weight reduction program. *Behavior Therapy*, 1974, *5*, 523-530.

Bernard, J. L. Rapid treatment of gross obesity by operant techniques. *Psychological Reports*, 1968, *23*, 663-666.

Björntorp, P., & Sjöström, L. Number and size of adipose tissue fat cells in relation to metabolism in human obesity. *Metabolism*, 1961, *20*, 703-713.

Bray, G. A. The myth of diet in the management of obesity. *American Journal of Clinical Nutrition*, 1970, *23*, 1141-1148.

Bray, G. A. (Ed.). *Obesity in perspective* (Pt. 1). Washington, D.C.: U.S. Government Printing Office, 1975.

Bray, G. A. Current status of intestinal bypass surgery in the treatment of obesity. *Diabetes*, 1977, *26*, 1072-1079.

Bray, G. A. Definition, measurement, and classification of the syndromes of obesity. *International Journal of Obesity*, 1978, *2*, 99-112.

Bray, G. A., & Benfield, J. R. Intestinal bypass for obesity: A summary and perspective. *American Journal of Clinical Nutrition*, 1977, *30*, 121-127.

Bray, G. A., & Greenway, F. L. Pharmacological approaches to treating the obese patient. *Clinics in Endocrinology and Metabolism*, 1976, *5*, 455-479.

Bray, G. A., Greenway, F. L., Barry, R. E., Benfield, J. R., Tiser, R. L., Dahms, W. T., Atkinson, R. L., & Schwartz, A. A. Surgical treatment of obesity: A review of our experience and an analysis of published reports. *International Journal of Obesity*, 1977, *1*, 331-367.

Bray, G. A., Greenway, F. L., Molitch, M. E., Dahms, W. T., Atkinson, R. L., & Hamilton, K. Use of anthropometric measures to assess weight loss. *American Journal of Clinical Nutrition*, 1978, *31*, 769-773.

Bray, G. A., & York, D. A. Genetically transmitted obesity in rodents. *Physiological Reviews*, 1971, *51*, 598-646.

Brightwell, D. R., & Sloan, C. L. Long-term results of behavior therapy for obesity. *Behavior Therapy*, 1977, *8*, 898-905.

Brook, C. G. D. Evidence for a sensitive period in adipose-cell replication in man. *Lancet*, 1972, *2*, 624-627.

Brook, C. G. D., Loyd, J. K., & Wolf, O. H. Relation between age of onset of obesity and size and number of adipose cells. *British Medical Journal*, 1972, *92*, 25-27.

Bruch, H. *Eating disorders: Obesity, anorexia nervosa, and the person within.* New York: Basic Books, 1973.

Campbell, J. M., Hunt, T. K., Karam, J. H., & Torsham, P. H. Jejunoileal bypass as a treatment of morbid obesity. *Archives of Internal Medicine*, 1977, *137*, 602-610.

Carter, E. N., Rice, A. P., & DeJulio, S. Role of the therapist in the self-control of obesity. *Journal of Consulting and Clinical Psychology*, 1977, *45*, 503.

Castelnuovo-Tedesco, P., & Schiebel, D. Studies of superobesity II: Psychiatric appraisal of jejuno-ileal bypass surgery. *American Journal of Psychiatry*, 1976, *133*, 26-31.

Cautela, J. R. Covert sensitization. *Psychological Reports*, 1967, *20*, 459-468.

Cautela, J. R. The treatment of overeating by covert conditioning. *Psychotherapy: Theory, Research, and Practice*, 1972, *9*, 211-216.

Chapman, S. L., & Jeffrey, D. B. Situational management, standard setting, and self-reward in a behavior modification weight loss program. *Journal of Consulting and Clinical Psychology*, 1978, *46*, 1588-1589.

Chirico, A. M., & Stunkard, A. J. Physical activity and human obesity. *New England Journal of Medicine*, 1960, *263*, 935-940.

Chlouverakis, C. Dietary and medical treatments of obesity: An evaluative review. *Addictive Behaviors*, 1965, *1*, 3-21.

Clark, P. J. The heritability of certain anthropometric characters as ascertained from measurements of twins. *American Journal of Human Genetics*, 1956, *8*, 49-54.

Collipp, P. J. Differential diagnosis of childhood obesity. In P. J. Collipp (Ed.), *Childhood obesity*. Acton, Mass.: Publishing Sciences Group, 1975.

Conniff, J. C. G. All about body fat. *Runner*, October 1978, pp. 73-79.

Cooper, T. Diet related to killer diseases. Cited in U. S. Senate Select Committee on Nutrition and Human Need (Ed.), *Dietary Goals for the United States*. Washington, D.C.: Government Printing Office, 1977.

Crisp, A. H., Kalucy, R. S., Pilkington, T. R. E., & Gazet, J-C. Some psychosocial consequences of ileojejunal bypass surgery. *American Journal of Clinical Nutrition*, 1977, *30*, 109-119.

Dahms, W. T., Molitch, M. E., Bray, G. A., Greenway, F. L., Atkinson, R. L., & Hamilton, K. Treatments of obesity: Cost benefit assessment of behavioral therapy, placebo, and two anorectic drugs. *American Journal of Clinical Nutrition*, 1978, *31*, 774-778.

Diament, C., & Wilson, G. T. An experimental investigation of the effects of covert sensitization in an analogue eating situation. *Behavior Therapy*, 1975, *6*, 499-509.

Edison, G. R. Amphetamines: A dangerous illusion. *Annals of Internal Medicine*, 1971, *74*, 605-610.

Feinstein, A. R. The measurement of success in weight reduction: An analysis of methods and a new index. *Journal of Chronic Diseases*, 1959, *10*, 439-456.

Ferguson, J. M. *Learning to eat: Behavior modification for weight control.* Palo Alto, Calif.: Bull, 1975.

Fernan, W. *The role of experimenter contact in behavioral bibliotherapy of obesity.* Unpublished Master's thesis, Pennsylvania State University, 1973.

Ferster, C. B., Nurnberger, J. I., & Levitt, E. B. The control of eating. *Journal of Mathetics*, 1962, *1*, 87-109.

Foreyt, J. P. (Ed.). *Behavioral treatments of obesity.* New York: Pergamon, 1977.

Foreyt, J. P., & Hagen, R. L. Covert sensitization: Conditioning or suggestion? *Journal of Abnormal Psychology*, 1973, *82*, 17-23.

Foreyt, J. P., Scott, L. W., & Gotto, A. M. Diet modification in the community. In B. J. Williams, S. Martin, and J. P. Foreyt (Eds.), *Obesity: Behavioral approaches to dietary management.* New York: Bruner/Mazel, 1976.

Foxx, R. M. Social reinforcement of weight reduction: A case report on an obese retarded adolescent. *Mental Retardation*, 1972, *10*, 21-23.

Frohwirth, R. Aversive techniques in the treatment of obesity. In J. P. Foreyt (Ed.), *Behavioral treatments of obesity.* New York: Pergamon, 1977.

Gairdner, D., & Dauncey, J. The effect of diet on the development of the adipose organ. *Proceedings of the Nutritional Society*, 1974, *33*, 119.

Gordon, T., & Kannel, W. B. The effects of overweight on cardiovascular diseases. *Geriatrics*, 1973, *28*, 80-88.

Greenwood, M. R. C., & Johnson, P. R. Adipose tissue cellularity and its relationship to the development of obesity in females. *Current Concepts in Nutrition*, 1977, *5*, 119-135.

Hagen, R. L. Group therapy versus bibliotherapy in weight reduction. *Behavior Therapy*, 1974, *5*, 222-234.

Häger, A., Sjöström, L., Arvidson, B., Björntorp, P., & Smith, U. Body fat and adipose tissue cellularity in infants — a longitudinal study. *Metabolism*, 1977, *26*, 607-617.

Hall, S. M. Self-control and therapist control in the behavioral treatment of overweight women. *Behaviour Research and Therapy*, 1972, *10*, 59-68.

Hall, S. M. Behavioral treatment of obesity: A two-year follow-up. *Behaviour Research and Therapy*, 1973, *11*, 647-648.

Hall, S. M., & Hall, R. G. Outcome and methodological considerations in behavioral treatment of obesity. *Behavior Therapy*, 1974, *5*, 352-364.

Hall, S. M., Hall, R. G., DeBoer, G., & O'Kulitch, P. Self and external management compared with psychotherapy in the control of obesity. *Behaviour Research and Therapy*, 1977, *15*, 89-95.

Hall, S. M., Hall, R. G., Hanson, R. W., & Borden, B. L. Permanence of two self-managed treatments of overweight in university and community populations. *Journal of Consulting and Clinical Psychology*, 1974, *42*, 781-786.

Halverson, J. D., Wise, L., Wazna, M. T., & Ballinger, W. T. Jejunoileal bypass for morbid obesity: A critical appraisal. *American Journal of Medicine*, 1978, *64*, 461-475.

Hanson, R. W., Borden, B. L., Hall, S. M., & Hall, R. G. Use of programmed instruction in teaching self-management skills to overweight adults. *Behavior Therapy*, 1976, *7*, 366-373.

Harris, M. G., and Brunner, C. G. A comparison of self-control and a contract procedure for weight control. *Behaviour Research and Therapy*, 1971, *9*, 347-354.

Harris, M. G., & Hallbauer, E. S. Self-directed weight control through eating and exercise. *Behaviour Research and Therapy*, 1973, *11*, 523-529.

Hartz, A., Giefer, E., & Rimm, A. A. Relative importance of the effect of family environment and heredity on obesity. *Annals of Human Genetics*, 1977, *41*, 185-193.

Hirsch, J., & Knittle, J. L. Cellularity of obese and non-obese human adipose tissue. *Federal Proceedings*, 1970, *29*, 1516-1521.

Hirsch, J., Knittle, J. L., & Salans, L. B. Cell lipid content and cell number in obese and non-obese human adipose tissue. *Journal of Clinical Investigation*, 1966, *45*, 1023.

Hoebel, B. G., & Teitelbaum, P. Weight regulation in normal and hypothalamic hyperphagic rats. *Journal of Comparative and Physiological Psychology*, 1966, *61*, 189-193.

Iber, F. L., & Cooper, M. Jejunoileal bypass for the treatment of massive obesity. Prevalence, morbidity, and short- and long-term consequences. *American Journal of Clinical Nutrition*, 1977, *30*, 4-15.

Jeffrey, D. B. A comparison of the effects of external control and self-control on the modification and maintenance of weight. *Journal of Abnormal Psychology*, 1974, *83*, 404-410.

Jeffrey, D. B. Treatment evaluation issues in research on addictive behaviors. *Addictive Behaviors*, 1975, *1*, 23-36.

Jeffrey, D. B. Behavioral management of obesity. In W. E. Craighead, A. E. Kazdin, & M. J. Mahoney (Eds.), *Behavior modification: Principles, issues, and applications*. New York: Houghton Mifflin, 1976. (a)

Jeffrey, D. B. Treatment outcome issues in obesity research. In B. J. Williams, S. Martin, and J. P. Foreyt (Eds.), *Obesity: Behavioral approaches to dietary management*. New York: Bruner/Mazel, 1976. (b)

Jeffrey, D. B. Self-control approaches to the management of obesity. In J. P. Foreyt (Ed.), *Behavioral treatments of obesity*. New York: Pergamon, 1977.

Jeffrey, D. B., & Christensen, E. R. Effect of behavior therapy vs. "will power" in the management of obesity. *Journal of Psychology*, 1975, *90*, 303-311.

Jeffrey, D. B., & Katz, R. C. *Take it off and keep it off: A behavioral program for weight loss and healthy living*. New York: Prentice-Hall, 1977.

Jeffrey, D. B., & Lemnitzer, N. Diet, exercise, obesity, and related health problems: A macro-environmental analysis. In J. Ferguson and B. Taylor (Eds.), *Advances in Behavioral Medicine*. Holliswood, N.Y.: Spectrum, 1980.

Jeffrey, D. B., Lemnitzer, N. B., Hess, J. M., Hickey, J. S., McLellarn, R. W., & Stroud, J. *Children's responses to television food advertising: Experimental evidence of actual food consumption*. Paper presented at the meeting of the American Psychological Association, New York City, September 1979.

Johnson, D., & Drenick, E. J. Therapeutic fasting in morbid obesity. *Archives of Internal Medicine*, 1977, 1381-1382.

Johnson, N. L., Burke, B. S., & Mayer, J. Relative importance of inactivity and overeating in the energy balance of obese high school girls. *American Journal of Clinical Nutrition*, 1956, *4*, 37-44.

Kalucy, R. S., & Crisp, A. H. Some psychological and social implications of massive obesity. *Journal of Psychosomatic Research*, 1974, *18*, 465-473.

Kaplan, H. I., & Kaplan, H. S. The psychosomatic concept of obesity. *Journal of Nervous and Mental Disorders*, 1957, *125*, 181-201.

Kennedy, G. C. The development with age of hypothalamic restraint upon the appetite of the rat. *Journal of Endocrinology*, 1957, *16*, 9-17.

Kingsley, R. G., & Wilson, G. T. Behavior therapy for obesity: A comparative investigation of long-term efficacy. *Journal of Consulting and Clinical Psychology*, 1977, *45*, 288-298.

Knittle, J. L. Maternal diet as a factor in adipose tissue cellularity and metabolism in the young rat. *Journal of Nutrition*, 1972, *102*, 427. (a)

Knittle, J. L. Obesity in childhood: A problem in adipose tissue cellular development. *Journal of Pediatrics*, 1972, *81*, 2048. (b)

Lanier, V. C., Younger, R. K., Scott, H. W., & Law, D. H. Metabolic changes in morbidly obese men and women after massive intestinal bypass. *Surgical Forum*, 1969, *20*, 397-398.

LeBow, M. D., Goldberg, P. S., & Collins, A. Eating behavior of overweight and nonoverweight persons in the natural environment. *Journal of Consulting and Clinical Psychology*, 1977, *45*, 1204-1205.

Leon, G. R. Current directions in the treatment of obesity. *Psychological Bulletin*, 1976, *83*, 557-578.

Leon, G. R., & Chamberlain, K. Comparison of daily eating habits and emotional states of overweight persons successful or unsuccessful in maintaining a weight loss. *Journal of Consulting and Clinical Psychology*, 1973, *41*, 108-115. (a)

Leon, G. R., & Chamberlain, K. Emotional arousal, eating patterns, and body image as differential factors associated with varying success in maintaining a weight loss. *Journal of Consulting and Clinical Psychology*, 1973, *40*, 474-480. (b)

Leon, G. R., & Roth, L. Obesity: Psychological causes, correlations, and speculations. *Psychological Bulletin*, 1977, *84*, 117-139.

Levitz, L. S., & Stunkard, A. J. A therapeutic coalition of obesity: Behavior modification and patient self-help. *American Journal of Psychiatry*, 1974, *131*, 423-427.

Lindstrom, L. L., Balch, P., & Reese, S. In person versus telephone treatment for obesity. *Journal of Behavior Therapy and Experimental Psychiatry*, 1976, *7*, 367-369.

Mahoney, M. J. Self-reward and self-monitoring techniques for weight control. *Behavior Therapy*, 1974, *5*, 48-57.

Mahoney, M. J., & Mahoney, K. *Permanent weight control*. New York: Norton, 1976.

Mahoney, M. J., Moura, N., & Wade, T. The relative efficacy of self-reward, self-punishment, and self-monitoring techniques for weight loss. *Journal of Consulting and Clinical Psychology*, 1973, *40*, 404-407.

Mann, R. A. The behavior-therapeutic use of contingency contracting to control an adult behavior problem: Weight control. *Journal of Applied Behavior Analysis*, 1972, *5*, 99-109.

Manoff, R. Report to the Ninth International Congress of Nutrition. Cited in U. S. Senate Select Committee on Nutrition and Human Needs (Ed.), *Dietary Goals for the United States*. Washington, D.C.: Government Printing Office, 1977.

Marston, A. R., London, P., Cohen, N., & Cooper, L. M. In vivo observation of the eating behavior of obese and nonobese subjects. *Journal of Consulting and Clinical Psychology*, 1977, *45*, 335-336.

Masover, L., & Stamler, J. Address to the Convention of the American Public Health Association, 1976. Cited in U. S. Senate Select Committee on Nutrition and Human Needs (Ed.), *Dietary Goals for the United States*. Washington, D.C.: Government Printing Office, 1977.

Matson, J. L. Social reinforcement by the spouse in weight control: A case study. *Journal of Behavior Therapy and Experimental Psychiatry*, 1977, *8*, 327-328.

Mauro, F. J., & Feins, R. P. *Kids, food, and television: The compelling case for state action*. New York: New York State Assembly, Program and Committee Staff, 1977.

Mayer, J. Correlation between metabolism and feeding behavior and multiple etiology of obesity. *Bulletin of the New York Academy of Medicine*, 1957, *22*, 744-761.

Mayer, J. Genetic factors in obesity. *Annals of the New York Academy of Sciences*, 1965, *131*, 412-421.

Mayer, J. *Overweight: Causes, costs, and control.* Englewood Cliffs, N.J.: Prentice-Hall, 1968.

McKenna, R. J. Some effects of anxiety level and food cues on the eating behavior of obese and normal subjects: A comparison of the Schachterian and psychosomatic conceptions. *Journal of Personality and Social Psychology*, 1972, *22*, 311-319.

McReynolds, W. T., Lutz, R. N., Paulsen, B., & Kohrs, M. B. Weight loss resulting from the behavior modification procedures with nutritionists as therapists. *Behavior Therapy*, 1976, *7*, 283-291.

Monello, L. T., & Mayer, J. Obese adolescent girls: An unrecognized "minority" group? *American Journal of Clinical Nutrition*, 1963, *13*, 25.

Moore, C. H., & Crumb, B. C. Weight reduction in a chronic schizophrenic by means of operant conditioning procedures: A case study. *Behaviour Research and Therapy*, 1969, *7*, 129-131.

National Science Foundation. *Research on the effects of television advertising on children: Review and recommendations.* Washington, D.C.: Author, 1977.

Newburgh, L. H. Obesity. *Archives of Internal Medicine*, 1942, *70*, 1033-1096.

Newman, H. H., Freeman, F. N., & Holzuiger, K. J. *Twins: A study of heredity and environment.* Chicago: University of Chicago Press, 1937.

Nisbett, R. E. Hunger, obesity, and the ventromedial hypothalamus. *Psychological Review*, 1972, *79*, 433-470.

Nisbett, R. E., & Storms, M. D. Cognitive and social determinants of food intake. In H. London and R. E. Nisbett (Eds.), *Thought and feeling: Cognitive alteration of feeling states.* Chicago: Aldine, 1974,

Osborne, R. H., & DeGeorge, F. V. Stature, weight, and ponderal index. In R. H. Osborne and F. V. DeGeorge (Eds.), *Genetic basis of morphological variation: An evaluation and application of the twin study method.* Cambridge, Mass.: Harvard University Press, 1959, pp. 60-75.

Ost, L., & Götestam, K. Behavioral and pharmacological treatments for obesity: An experimental comparison. *Addictive Behaviors*, 1976, *1*, 331-338.

Passmore, R., Strong, A., Swindells, Y. E., & El Din, N. The effects of overfeeding on two fat young women. *British Journal of Nutrition,* 1963, *17*, 373.

Penick, S. G., Filion, R., Fox, S., & Stunkard, A. J. Behavior modification in the treatment of obesity. *Psychosomatic Medicine*, 1971, *33*, 49-55.

Powley, T. L., & Keesey, R. Relationships of body weight to the lateral hypo-thalamic feeding syndrome. *Journal of Comparative and Physiological Psychology*, 1970, *70*, 25-36.

Rodin, J. Bidirectional influences of emotionality, stimulus responsivity, and metabolic events in obesity. In J. Maser and M. E. P. Seligman (Eds.), *Psychopathology: Experimental models*. San Francisco: Freeman, 1977.

Romanczyk, R. G., Tracey, D. A., Wilson, G. T., & Thorpe, G. L. Behavioral techniques in the treatment of obesity: A comparative analysis. *Behaviour Research and Therapy*, 1973, *11*, 629-640.

Rooth, G., & Carlström, S. Therapeutic fasting. *Acta Medica Scandinavia*, 1970, *187*, 455-463.

Rowland, C. V. Psychotherapy of six hyperobese adults during total starvation. *Archives of General Psychiatry*, 1968, *18*, 541-548.

Rychtarik, R. G., Kniivila, C. M., & Jeffrey, D. B. *Effects of television advertising on children's behavior: A methodological review*. Paper presented at the meeting of the American Psychological Association, Toronto, September 1978.

Schachter, S. *Emotion, obesity, and crime*. New York: Academic Press, 1971. (a)

Schachter, S. Some extraordinary facts about obese humans and rats. *American Psychologist*, 1971, *26*, 129-144. (b)

Schachter, S., & Singer, J. E. Cognitive, social, and physiological determinants of emotional state. *Psychological Review*, 1962, *69*, 379-399.

Schick, A. Psychosomatic aspects of obesity. *Psychoanalytic Review*, 1947, *34*, 173-181.

Seltzer, C. C., & Mayer, J. Body build and obesity — who are the obese? *Journal of the American Medical Association*, 1964, *189*, 677-684.

Shields, J. Comparison of the separated, control, and dizygotic groups. In J. Shield (Ed.), *Monozygotic Twins. Brought up apart and brought up together*. London: University of Oxford Press, 1962.

Sims, E. A., Goldman, R. T., Gluck, C. M., Horton, E. S., Kelleher, P. C., & Rowe, D. W. Experimental obesity in man. *Transactions of the Association of American Physicians*, 1968, *81*, 153-170.

Sims, E. A. H., & Horton, E. S. Endocrine and metabolic adaptation to obesity and starvation. *American Journal of Clinical Nutrition*, 1968, *21*, 1455-1470.

Solow, C., Silberfarb, P. M., & Swift, K. Psychosocial effects of bypass surgery for severe obesity. *New England Journal of Medicine*, 1974, *290*, 300-303.

Stalonas, P. M., Johnson, W. G., & Christ, M. Behavior modification for obesity: The evaluation of exercise contingency management, and program adherence. *Journal of Consulting and Clinical Psychology*, 1978, *46*, 463-469.

Stuart, R. B. A three-dimensional program for the treatment of obesity. *Behaviour Research and Therapy*, 1971, *9*, 177-186.

Stuart, R. B. Behavioral control of overeating: A status report. In G. A. Bray (Ed.), *Obesity in perspective* (Report No. NIH 75-708). Washington, D. C.: U.S. Department of Health, Education, and Welfare, 1975.

Stuart, R. B. Self-help group approach to self-management. In R. B. Stuart (Ed.), *Behavioral self-management: Strategies, techniques, and outcomes*. New York: Bruner/Mazel, 1977.

Stuart, R. B., & Davis, B. *Slim chance in a fat world: Behavioral control of obesity*. Champaign, Ill.: Research Press, 1972.

Stunkard, A. J. The success of TOPS, a self-help group. *Postgraduate Medicine*, 1972, *51*, 143-147.

Stunkard, A. J., & Burt, V. Obesity and body image. II. Age of onset of disturbances in body image. *American Journal of Psychiatry*, 1967, *123*, 1443-1447.

Stunkard, A. J., & Kaplan, D. Eating in public places: A review of reports of the direct observation of eating behavior. *International Journal of Obesity*, 1977, *1*, 89-101.

Stunkard, A. J., & Mahoney, M. J. Behavioral treatment of the eating disorders. In H. Leitenberg (Ed.), *Handbook of behavior modification*. New York: Appleton-Century-Crofts, 1976.

Stunkard, A. J., & Mendelson, M. Obesity and the body image: Characteristics of disturbances in the body image of some obese persons. *American Journal of Psychiatry*, 1967, *1235*, 1296-1300.

Stunkard, A. J., & Rush, J. Dieting and depression reexamined. *Annals of Internal Medicine*, 1974, *81*, 526-533.

Swanson, D. W., & Dinello, F. Therapeutic starvation in the treatment of obesity. *Diseases of the Nervous System*, 1969, *30*, 669-674.

Thomas, A. E., McKay, D. A., & Cutlip, M. B. Nomograph for body mass index (KG/M^2). *American Journal of Clinical Nutrition*, 1976, *29*, 302-304.

Thorn, G. W., & Cahill, G. F. Gain in weight: Obesity. In G. W. Thorn, R. D. Adams, E. Braunwald, K. J. Isselbacher, and R. G. Petersdorf (Eds.), *Harrison's Principles of Internal Medicine*. New York: McGraw-Hill, 1977.

Tobias, L. L., & MacDonald, M. L. Internal locus of control and weight loss: An insufficient condition. *Journal of Consulting and Clinical Psychology*, 1977, *45*, 647-653.

U.S. Public Health Service. *Obesity and Health*. Washington, D.C.: U.S. Government Printing Office. (Undated monograph)

U.S. Senate Select Committee on Nutrition and Human Needs (Ed.). *Dietary Goals for the United States*. Washington, D.C.: Government Printing Office, 1977.

Wagonfeld, S., & Wolowitz, H. M. Obesity and the self-help group: A look at TOPS. *American Journal of Psychiatry*, 1968, *125*, 249-252.

Weintraub, W., & Aronson, H. Application of verbal behavior analysis to the study of psychological defense mechanisms. *Archives of General Psychiatry*, 1969, *21*, 739-744.

Weiss, A. R. Characteristics of successful weight reducers: A brief review of predictor variables. *Addictive Behavior*, 1977, *2*, 193-201.

Wilson, G. T. Methodological considerations in treatment outcome research on obesity. *Journal of Consulting and Clinical Psychology*, 1978, *46*, 687-702.

Withers, R. F. L. Problems in the genetics of human obesity. *Eugenics Review*, 1964, *56*, 81-90.

Wollersheim, J. P. Effectiveness of group therapy based upon learning principles in the treatment of overweight women. *Journal of Abnormal Psychology*, 1970, *76*, 462-474.

Wollersheim, J. P. Follow-up of behavioral group therapy for obesity. *Behavior Therapy*, 1977, *8*, 996-998.

8

ASTHMA

A. Barney Alexander

INTRODUCTION

The intent of this chapter is to describe and critically examine the role played by psychological variables in the clinical manifestations and treatment of bronchial asthma. Preceding a review of behavioral procedures in the treatment of asthma, various psychological aspects of bronchial asthma will be discussed, including a brief, yet comprehensive, synopsis of the current status of our knowledge regarding the role of psychological variables in asthma. Subsequently, behavioral strategies that have been employed in the clinical treatment of bronchial asthma will be discussed at length. Finally, the chapter will close with a summary of well-documented research results and conclusions to date as well as with some speculations and recommendations regarding future basic and applied investigation vis-a-vis behavioral intervention in asthma. Before proceeding, however, it is necessary to provide a brief summary of the medical aspects of asthma, because, as will be seen, such information is absolutely essential to an appreciation of the proper role played by behavioral factors in the understanding and treatment of bronchial asthma.

Preparation of this chapter was supported, in part, by a grant (HL07026) from the National Heart, Lung, and Blood Institute and a grant (MH30099) from the National Institute of Mental Health. The author wishes to thank Larry S. Solanch for his help on an intermediate draft of this chapter.

THE MEDICAL ASPECTS OF ASTHMA AND ITS TREATMENT

Much of the material in the following brief overview of the medical aspects of asthma was drawn from three excellent discussions (Bernstein, 1978; Reed & Townley, 1978; Siegel, Katz, & Rachelefsky, 1978), and the reader is referred to these, should more detailed background be desired.

Bronchial asthma is a syndrome characterized by episodes of obstruction to adequate air exchange in the lungs, the clinical manifestations of which include wheezing respirations, dyspnea, cough, and excessive mucus production. The changes in the bronchi and bronchioles, which cause these conditions, are mucosal edema, hypersecretion of thick mucus, and contraction of bronchial smooth muscle, all of which result in a reduction in the size of the inside diameter of the air-transporting tubes in the lung. In the case of viscid mucus production, the result can be a complete blocking of the lumen, leading to frank trapping of biologically unusable gas in the part of the lung distal to the plug. An important characteristic of asthma, as opposed to other conditions that may impair the ability of the body to transport air, is that the symptoms are reversible, either through adequate and appropriate pharmacologic means or by virtue of normal remission between attacks. This leads to a situation in which asthma sufferers may have completely normal pulmonary function in the periods, which can be as long as several months or even years, between episodes of asthma.

The most widely employed classification system is that of Rackemann (1928), in which asthma is considered to be either *extrinsic* (due to allergic reaction), *intrinsic* (nonallergic, infectious, and the like), or *mixed*. Unfortunately, most patients fall into the latter category, even though extrinsic or intrinsic factors may predominate in any particular case. Nevertheless, for most victims, the majority of asthmatic symptoms are related to allergens. While initial sensitization usually requires a very large antigen load, once sensitization has taken place, highly allergic individuals may experience symptoms following even minute exposures. Common asthmogenic allergens include tree, grass, and weed pollens; molds and fungi; animal danders and feathers; house and occupational dusts; some foods; insects, but not their stings; and some chemicals, but not in their role as irritants.

Nonallergic asthmogenic stimuli include aspirin, exercise, airway irritants, certain situations, and infections. Although not overly common, aspirin idiosyncracy can cause dangerously violent symptoms in some asthmatics. Exercise is such a ubiquitous asthmogen that exercise-induced bronchospasm has been suggested as a defining characteristic of asthma. Individual sensitivity varies from mild to severe in specific individuals but manifests a fairly tight relationship to the extent of exertion in any particular case. Usually, exercise-induced asthma reverses nonproblematically with rest and/or appropriate medication. Common airway irritants include certain chemical gases, aerosol propellants, cold air, and cough. Hyperventilation (as a situation) may cause bronchospasm, both by airway irritation and hypocapnia. Other situations, such as certain weather conditions and weather changes, can in many patients precipitate asthma idio-syncratically by means that are as yet unknown. Respiratory infections represent one of the most common asthma precipitants and are the cause of some of the most severe and prolonged episodes of asthma, often requiring hospitalization and lifesaving therapy. While it is possible, though highly uncertain, that some bacterial infections may provoke asthma, it is now known that viral infections, such as colds and influenza, are the cause of most infection-induced asthma.

The incidence of asthma in the population at large has been variously esti-mated to be anywhere from 2% to 20%, with the most realistic figure being somewhere around 5%. Of these asthma sufferers, roughly 60% are less than 17 years of age. While, as children, males are affected nearly twice as often as females, this proportion evens out in puberty. Asthma can appear at any age, but onset is most likely to occur within the first five years of life. While the mortality data (approximately two per 100,000) rank asthma among the 60 leading causes of death in the United States, the morbidity data provide real cause for concern. Among chronic diseases, asthma is one of the leading causes of loss of productive time. In children, for example, one-third of all chronic conditions and 25% of the days lost from school because of chronic illnesses are attributed to asthma. Asthma is also the third most common reason for visits to physicians due to chronic illness.

While there have been many attempts to obtain precise prognostic data, the task is, of course, a difficult one. As many as 40% of all asthmatics may show substantial or complete remission of symptoms as they grow older, especially during the early teenage years. In general, this intriguing "outgrowing" of asthma, as well as the disease's natural course and ultimate outcome, seems to relate, albeit imperfectly, to many factors. Certainly, the severity of asthma after onset relates positively to the likelihood of persistence of symptoms. Sex differences also exist. Not only are girls less likely to be afflicted than boys but the latter are slightly less likely to experience a remission of symptoms during adulthood. In regard to age of onset, poorer prognosis is associated with the appearance of symptoms either before the age of two or in adulthood. It also seems to be the case that atopic or allergic individuals manifest a greater inci-dence of more severe and persistent symptoms. In contrast, asthma in children, which seems to be due largely to respiratory infections, suggests a more favor-able prognosis.

Despite these trends and the clear expectation of partial or complete remis-sion over time for many asthmatics, the strength of these relationships is such that treatment strategy in individual cases (for example, highly conservative therapy) cannot be determined by the expectation of an ultimately favorable outcome for many sufferers. Moreover, formerly symptomatic asthma victims typically manifest lingering evidence of lung hypersensitivity and show a clear tendency to experience symptoms anew under unfavorable conditions. Finally, one note of optimism can be struck by the fact that irreversible lung damage does not seem to be significantly associated with asthma, whatever its severity or duration.

The etiology of asthma is only incompletely understood, but, in some cases, a good deal has been learned regarding the pathogenesis of asthma symptoms. Of the two broad classes of asthmogenic stimuli, *allergic* and *nonallergic*, most attention has, understandably, been focused on the former. A substantial proportion of asthma symptoms can be attributed to the antigen-antibody reaction, especially in the less severe asthmatic, whose symptoms are largely seasonal. Nevertheless, it is clear that immunological mechanisms can by no means account for all incidences of asthma.

The three most important nonimmunological pathogenic factors are *hyperirritability of the airways*, *exercise-induced bronchospasm*, and *infection-caused asthma*. The former has been extensively studied, and the existence of a vagally mediated irritant reflex, which results in bronchial constriction, has been demonstrated. Exercise asthma is less well understood, but it may involve either or both of the following: the release of chemical mediators of the kind found in the allergic response (such as histamine, and some prostaglandins) or the previously mentioned irritant reflex, which results from stimulation by insufficiently warmed air during exertion. Respiratory infections not only are potent asthma precipitants but tend to be the immediate precursors to the first appearance of asthma for the majority of individuals.

The mechanisms involved in infectious asthma are still quite speculatory. In terms of overall pathogenesis, the most comprehensive etiological theory to date is the so-called beta-adrenergic blockage proposed by Szentivanyi in 1968. According to this theory, asthmatics manifest a reduced responsiveness of the bronchodilatory beta-adrenergic receptors in the lung, leaving the lung relatively unprotected from both vagal and humoral constricting factors. Unfortunately, as appealing as this theory may be, the supporting evidence remains highly equivocal.

Precise specification of the contribution of genetic factors in allergy and asthma has been hampered by the almost complete lack of standardization of definitional, sampling, and assessment criteria. The best data on twins to date (Edfors-Lubs, 1971) suggested that familial factors may play a substantially less prominent role than had been previously assumed. In this study, a concordance rate in monozygotic twins was only 19% for asthma and 25% for all allergic disorders. Both these figures were only marginally higher than the corresponding figures for dizygotic twins. Furthermore, the results indicated only a one-in-three chance that a child will develop allergy when both parents are atopic. They also indicated that the majority of allergic children are born into families in which only one or neither parent manifested atopy.

The clinical diagnosis of asthma is based upon the history, certain laboratory tests, and, to a lesser extent, characteristic physical findings. A careful and complete history is of crucial importance. Typically, episodic dyspnea, chest tightness, wheezing, and/or cough are reported. Extensive probing for precipitants of attacks will usually reveal whether the asthma manifests a substantial allergic (extrinsic) component or is largely intrinsic. Complete information regarding the physical environment, including places frequented away from home, reactions to exercise, the periodicity of attacks, nocturnal symptoms, and so forth, is essential to both the diagnosis and the subsequent planning of treatment. A family history of allergy and/or asthma is not uncommon, although a negative family history by no means precludes a diagnosis of asthma or even allergy.

Findings during the physical examination depend greatly upon the condition of the patient at the time, namely, the presence of an active asthma episode. It must be remembered that one of the cardinal characteristics of asthma is its periodicity. Consequently, the patient may exhibit perfectly normal air exchange during periods between episodes. In some cases, especially in children, patients with histories of chronic asthma may exhibit characteristic barrel-chest deformities due to chronic hyperinflation. The eyes, ears, nose, and throat may show such classic signs of allergy as "allergic shiners" and allergic creases at the edge of the nose.

While laboratory findings are certainly of importance in the establishment of a firm diagnosis of asthma, they are particularly salient in differential diagnosis and precise specification of the nature of the disorder in the individual case. Usual laboratory procedures include complete blood counts, nasal secretion and sputum analyses (in particular, for eosinophilia indicative of allergy), chest X ray (primarily to exclude other conditions), skin tests, direct challenges of the lung, exercise challenges, and tests of pulmonary function.

Skin tests can be very useful as a way of defining those substances to which a person *might* be lung sensitive. False negatives are very rare; that is, allergic sensitivity of the bronchial tree is invariably associated with skin reactivity. The reverse, however, is not the case. The skin and other organs may exhibit allergic reactivity to an antigen that produces no effect when delivered directly to the lung. For these instances, bronchial challenges of the lung are employed.

Unlike skin tests, which may be safely carried out in an office setting, *bronchial challenges* involve significant medical risk and are usually done under more carefully controlled conditions because of the possibility of severe and/or delayed asthmatic reactions, which may require vigorous treatment. Two kinds of challenges can be used. The first involves *antigens*, such as pollen, molds, or house dust, prepared in an aerosol for inhalation. Such challenges can be indispensable when data from histories and skin tests are equivocal and/or when it is desirable to unequivocally determine the extent of bronchial reactivity to a suspected allergen, for example, as the basis for instituting immunotherapy or as a prelude to the clinical recommendation of an environmental change, which cannot be made lightly.

The second type of bronchial challenge involves similar directly inhaled challenges of the lung with *histamine* or *methacholine*, both of which cause bronchoconstrictive responses that are from 100 to 1,000 times greater in asthmatics than in nonasthmatic individuals. These tests are very useful for firmly establishing the diagnosis of reversible airways obstruction (that is, asthma), when reversibility is not clear on clinical grounds alone, and for making the longitudinal assessment of airways reactivity. For all practical purposes, results of methacholine challenge can be taken as definitive when the test is negative; that is, although there are several conditions under which the test may be positive, including asthma, a negative result precludes the diagnosis of asthma with a very high degree of certainty.

Controlled *exercise testing* can substantially aid treatment decisions and serve as a guide to activity recommendations for patients. It can further serve to clarify the diagnosis of asthma, since reversible bronchospasm following exercise is an almost universal finding in asthma.

Assessment of pulmonary function must be considered essential in the overall evaluation of the asthmatic. In particular, tests of pulmonary function can aid materially in differential diagnosis, precise specification of pathology, establishment of clinical severity, and evaluation of provocation tests and treatment effectiveness. Tests of pulmonary function include the measurement of lung volumes, pulmonary mechanics, ventilation, regional gas distribution, and arterial blood gas tensions. While many severe, chronic asthmatics manifest residual abnormalities, even when asymptomatic, testing is most revealing during periods of acute exacerbations or at differing severity levels of the chronic condition.

Of the aforementioned measures, the most useful on an ordinary basis are the *tests of ventilation*, which are based on a forced vital capacity into a spirometer, a device that measures expired volume over time. This procedure involves having the patient exhale as much air as possible into the device at maximum force following a full inhalation. From this record, a number of measures can be obtained, the most important of which are the forced expiratory volume in one second (FEV_1, the volume expired in the first second), the peak expiratory flow rate (PEFR, the highest flow rate obtainable during forced expiration), and the maximum midexpiratory flow rate (MMEF, the maximum flow rate obtained when the expired volume is between 25% and 75% of the total). FEV_1 and PEFR are highly dependent upon patient effort (that is, whether the patient blows into the device as hard as he or she can) and are sensitive primarily to large-airway obstruction.

Because the site of obstruction in asthma may be in either the large or the small airways, or both, measures that are differentially sensitive to the central (large) and peripheral (small) airways are necessary. The MMEF is relatively independent of effort and is quite sensitive to small-airway pathology. An effort-independent, large-airway measurement is more complicated than flow measures, namely, airways resistance or its reciprocal, airways conductance. This measure can be derived in several ways but is most commonly obtained from a whole body *plethysmograph*. From this large and expensive instrument are also obtained the most useful measures of lung volume, such as the functional residual capacity and residual volume, which are primarily measures of small airways.

While these measurements provide excellent information, if and when the equipment is available, the most generally useful device is the portable *PEFR meter*, such as the Wright. Because of its favorable size and cost and its ease of use, it can be employed effectively not only in the office but also at home by the patient. Furthermore, it is a device that can yield very frequent measurement of lung function. In most cases, the PEFR meter provides all the information on pulmonary function that is ever necessary for most aspects of clinical diagnosis and treatment evaluation. As the sole measure for research purposes, the effort-dependent nature and exclusive sensitivity to large airways of the PEFR may present problems. In most research contexts, other measures, such as those described previously, must be employed. Nevertheless, there are few measures of pulmonary function other than the PEFR that are as practical to obtain on a frequent, even daily basis.

Tests of regional gas distribution can be made by the closing-volume method, helium equilibration, or the technique of single-breath nitrogen washout. These are used only in specialized circumstances and need not be described further here. The same is true of the many other measurements that can be obtained from the spirogram and the flow-volume curve. They, too, become useful under less-than-ordinary conditions. Arterial oxygen and carbon dioxide tensions are not obtained routinely but often become crucial during the lifesaving clinical evaluation and treatment of very severe asthma, such as *status asthmaticus*.

Treatment of asthma always has one goal: a therapeutic approach that provides as much control of symptoms as is possible with as little therapy (mainly drugs) as is necessary, so that both the disease and its treatment interfere minimally with a productive and rewarding life-style. With few exceptions, the drugs used to treat asthma possess varying degrees of disturbing and, in some cases, dangerous side effects. As will become evident from the ensuing discussion, the hope that behavioral (that is, nonpharmacologic) intervention may significantly reduce or, in some cases, even eliminate the need for drugs in the treatment of asthma has, as yet, largely failed to materialize to any clinically significant extent. While it will also become evident that the behavioral specialist still has a vital role to play in the treatment of asthma, behavioral strategies rarely, if ever, represent the primary therapeutic modality. Behaviorists invariably find themselves working with secondary, albeit often highly important, problems *associated* with the disorder and its medical treatment. Thus, in the paragraphs that follow, the medical management of asthma will be briefly characterized, to be followed in subsequent sections by more in-depth discussion of the role of psychological variables in asthma and the behavioral strategies that, along with appropriate medical management, can be employed in the overall treatment of bronchial asthma.

As should already be evident, asthma may be manifested clinically by as little as a few mild attacks in a lifetime, or it may be a severe, life-threatening, chronic disease that responds to only the most vigorous therapy, with powerful drugs taken on a virtually continuous basis. Most asthma conditions fall somewhere in between, from seasonal asthma (requiring sustained therapy only at certain times of the year) to moderate, perennial asthma (requiring year-round therapy). A rational therapeutic regimen must be carefully tailored to each case, in accordance with diagnostic findings. The drugs available to the physician fall into three broad categories: *bronchodilators*, *corticosteroids* (whose mechanism of action is essentially unknown), and others, mainly *cromolyn sodium* (whose precise mechanism of action is also largely a matter of speculation). Also available are such methods as *immunotherapy*, the role of which will be described in turn.

For therapeutic purposes, five classes of clinical manifestation can be distinguished: mild sporadic episodes, moderate chronic asthma, severe chronic asthma, acute serious attacks (or breakthroughs, from the standpoint of chronic management), and status asthmaticus. The last represents a life-threatening medical crisis and will not be considered here, since successful management is designed to avoid this situation. Essentially, all that needs to be said is that no additional drugs are available for its treatment, but appropriate steps must often be taken to stave off, or (in the worst instances) to deal with, such consequences as respiratory failure and cardiac arrest.

The infrequent episode of *mild to moderate asthma* tends to respond well to symptomatic doses of oral or inhaled sympathomimetics. These include isoproterenol and metaproterenol (a predominantly beta$_2$ receptor agonist), which are catecholaminelike substances that produce bronchodilation by relaxation of bronchial smooth muscle. Theophylline compounds, which are bronchodilating drugs in the same general class as caffeine, can also be given orally on a symptomatic basis. In this sort of use, the drugs are usually well tolerated, with few significant side effects.

Moderate chronic asthma or extended seasonal exacerbations usually require continuous therapy. Typically, this involves daily, round-the-clock therapy (every six, eight, or twelve hours) with oral theophylline and, if necessary, oral sympathomimetics. In such cases, side effects are of much more importance — nausea, vomiting, and overstimulation of the central nervous system with the former and disturbing tremor with the latter. Particularly with theophylline, overwhelmingly the most generally useful drug in the management of chronic asthma, dosage must be titrated carefully on an individual basis, since the range between therapeutic effectiveness and toxicity is quite narrow, and drug metabolism varies widely from patient to patient.

Chronic severe asthma almost always requires regular treatment with corticosteroids, usually prednisone, *in addition to* the regimens described above. The major problem here is to avoid, as much as possible, suppression of normal hypothalamic-pituitary-adrenal axis function. Hence, prednisone therapy every other day (to allow adrenal function recovery on the day without medication) is preferred, if symptom control can be obtained. If not, daily steroid therapy must be employed.

Serious acute attacks, or breakthroughs in management, usually require parenteral therapy. Typically, this involves, in order of priority, subcutaneous epinephrine, intravenous aminophylline (theophylline), and intravenous steroids. Additionally, extended exacerbations in nonsteroid-dependent cases may require short "bursts" of steroid therapy, for possibly one or two weeks, until symptoms are brought under control. Less severe, acute attacks in chronic asthmatics may require only spot treatment with an inhaled sympathomimetic.

Other management strategies include, for example, treatment prior to expected precipitant exposure and prophylactic therapy with cromolyn sodium. The latter can, in some cases, assume an important role in the management of chronic asthma. In certain individuals, it can provide protection against exercise-induced asthma, clinical benefit in allergen-induced asthma, and steroid-sparing effects. Because it is difficult to predict in advance its therapeutic contribution in any particular case, it is usually given a therapeutic trial, because its benefits are sometimes significant. Very often, exercise-induced bronchospasm can also be successfully managed by *pretreatment* with inhaled sympathomimetics.

Other methods that can sometimes be of benefit to the asthmatic include immunotherapy (the familiar "allergy shots"), the true effectiveness of which in the treatment of asthma is still controversial. Because of the time and costs involved, some asthma specialists require that bronchial, as opposed to simply skin, reactivity be demonstrated by bronchial challenges in order to determine whether a course of immunotherapy, which usually lasts from one to three years, is worth undertaking. At the present time, however, many allergists begin immunotherapy on the basis of skin tests that are often marginal and history data alone.

The use of environmental control strategies, such as elimination diets, change of geographical location, and elimination of pets, are obvious in selected cases in which a *clear* link between stimulus and response can be demonstrated. It must be pointed out that careless recommendations in this regard can do more harm than good. Examples are almost too numerous to mention, but they include the giving up of a beloved pet; changing of many or all household articles; relocation, with family or job upheaval; expensive and unusual diets; and expensive devices for air purification. Such recommendations are all too often made without any convincing rationale or promise of success. The final method often included in descriptions of therapeutic management strategies for the asthmatic, namely, behavioral techniques of various kinds, will constitute the general focus of the body of this chapter.

Before proceeding, some special comments are in order concerning outcome assessment in applied asthma research. The problem in asthma is the varying obstruction of proper air exchange in the lung. If one is intending to effect a therapeutic impact on the basic problem in asthma itself, it is *impossible to overemphasize* the necessity of carefully and adequately measuring lung infection in the evaluation of intervention outcome. Particularly for controlled experimental purposes, reliance on patient self-report or wheezing assessment, even by stethoscopic evaluation performed by an experienced examiner, is not sufficient. If pulmonary physiological status is not directly assessed by proper pulmonary functional measurement, all manner of misleading or frankly incorrect conclusions can be reached regarding the stimuli and/or treatment procedures relating to the exacerbation or amelioration of asthma. In a strictly clinical context, erroneous and possibly dangerous treatment decisions can result when evaluation is not based, in large part, on analysis of lung function.

An example from the author's laboratory underscores this point. Some years ago, a young boy, previously trained in relaxation, was experiencing an acute exacerbation of wheezing and was brought in for symptomatic relaxation treatment prior to institution of appropriate drug therapy. Obvious obstruction of an air exchange was noted on auscultation by his physician, and dyspnea and subjective distress were reported by the boy. Following ten minutes of relaxation, the boy noted considerable subjective relief, and substantial reduction of wheezing was confirmed by his physician through clinical examination. Nevertheless, measurements of FEV_1 and MMEF had been taken before and after relaxation. FEV_1 had changed very little, and MMEF, not at all. Despite the temporary relief, this boy's lung functions continued to deteriorate, and medication was needed within a few minutes.

This example does not constitute some sort of pulmonary anomaly; rather, it is quite physiologically possible — there was some slight and short-lived degree of large- (but not small-) airway improvement. Both subjective relief and a reduction in audible wheezing can result from modest changes in large airways, while serious problems remain untouched in the crucial smaller airways. If this situation had occurred in an emergency room, a result of the patient being told to "just calm down and relax" (under the erroneous assumption that the asthma was being caused by anxiety and agitation), serious consequences could have ensued once the patient had been sent home following temporary relief from insufficient treatment. Similarly horrendous results can occur in the interpretation of data from experiments and case reports when pulmonary functions are not assessed. Thus, it is best to respectfully reserve judgment on reports of asthma experiments and therapeutic interventions if measurements of lung function are not included.

There are four basic kinds of outcome data that are relevant to assessment in asthma: measurements of pulmonary function, medication requirements, characteristics of asthma attack, and requirements for general care.

In *assessment of pulmonary function*, several important matters must be considered. Because of the constantly fluctuating nature of asthma, long-term measurement should be on a daily basis (usually morning and evening), dictating the use of such inexpensive and portable instruments as a hand-held peak-flow meter. Such measurements should be supplemented every one to four weeks by more complete functional assessment. The latter should include measures that are sensitive to the two major sites of obstruction, namely, large and small airways. *Effort-independent* measures of each site should be collected (for example, MMEF for small airways and airways resistance or its more desirable variants, such as specific airways conductance, for large airways) in addition to the more usual *effort-dependent* measures of large-airways function (such as PEFR and FEV_1). It must always be remembered that asthma is characterized by an episodic, rhythm-producing symptom remission during which pulmonary functions may be quite normal, either completely or in part.

Medication requirements represent the second most valuable tactic of outcome assessment, especially for individuals who require maintenance drugs used on a daily basis. Medications taken as needed constitute much "softer" data, because their use is usually up to the discretion of the patient. In fact, all measures of drug requirement are, to some extent, dependent upon a complex interaction between patient and physician behaviors and judgments that are difficult to specify. Since the amount and kind of medication can substantially influence lung function and its symptomatic manifestations, such as wheezing, the interpretation of drug data is always made *in relation to* such other measures as scores of daily pulmonary function or counts of asthma attack. A decrease in medication requirements, in most cases, represents a beneficial outcome only if lung function and asthma frequency have remained relatively unchanged. Similarly, otherwise noteworthy increases in lung function and/or decreases in symptom frequency may be indicative of success only when drug use has not increased. The upshot is that the reciprocal relationships between lung physiology, asthma symptomatology, and medications must always be understood and appreciated. Finally, in any case, it is best to require that the type of medication be held as constant as possible throughout the investigational period because of the great difficulties in establishing potency equivalents between different kinds of drugs.

Characteristics of *asthma attack* include frequency counts, attack duration, and severity estimates. Measurements of these characteristics rely almost exclusively on patient report, using essentially subjective criteria. It is usually impossible to bring "harder" measuring instruments to bear on these kinds of data, because one is typically interested in the events as they occur *naturally* over an extended period of time as part of the assessment of the long-term import of some therapeutic intervention. Most attempts to shore up the inherent problems with these kinds of data have met with frustration. On one occasion or another, telemetered chest sounds, very frequent clinical examinations or assessments of lung function, observer report of audible wheezing, and the like have been used at the National Asthma Center, all with little success. Measurement costs (especially in terms of the cost-benefit ratio in regard to the reliability and validity of the data obtained), lack of cooperation by subjects, roadblocks in the physical and social environment, and so forth, are examples of just some of the problems that have been encountered. If the subjective nature of the data is always kept in mind, then the measurement of characteristics of asthma attack can provide worthwhile experimental data.

The final category, requirements for *general care*, includes such things as visits to the room, hospitalizations, visits to the physician's office, phone calls to physicians, medical costs, and estimates of time lost. All these are useful when the time periods over which assessment is being made are quite long, that is, several months or years, because these are, generally, very infrequent events.

PSYCHOLOGICAL ELEMENTS

The purpose of this section is to provide a brief account of the role assumed by psychological variables in the course of asthma. For additional information on these matters, the reader is referred to two excellent reviews that facilitated the preparation of the material that follows (Knapp, Mathé, & Vachon, 1976; Purcell & Weiss, 1970).

Bronchial asthma was one of the principal focuses of early theorizing in psychosomatic medicine (Alexander, 1950; French & Alexander, 1941), which evolved as an independent specialty during the first half of this century, despite the fact that the medical profession in general continued to adhere, at the time, to the traditional view of asthma as an immunological syndrome. Psychoanalytically dominated psychiatry considered the origin or cause of asthma to be the suppression of an intense emotion, in particular, the patient's suppressed cry for his or her mother. This hypothesis regarding the etiology of bronchial asthma resulted in much misdirected theoretical, clinical, and experimental inquiry. Unfortunately, only quite recently has this conceptualization, which remained all too dominant, begun to dwindle in popularity among professionals.

The reversal of this trend was long delayed, especially since convincing empirical support for the psychoanalytic interpretation was, and remains, conspicuously absent. Specifically, no irrefutable evidence exists that demonstrates that the pathophysiology characteristic of asthma is *caused* by psychological influences. Instead, the most recent, and more empirically appropriate, viewpoint is that psychopathology may emerge during the course of asthma (just as it might as the result of coping with any chronic disease process) and that, for some asthmatics, psychological variables, such as emotional stress, fear, and anxiety, *may* occasionally play a role that is as yet unspecified in the frequency and/or severity of episodic asthma. In fact, the dissatisfaction with the traditional psychoanalytic viewpoint and its variants reached such proportions that some commentators (for example, Creer, 1978) have consequently taken the opposite theoretical stance, namely, that bronchial asthma should not be considered a psychosomatic disorder at all.

Although the current status of our knowledge concerning bronchial asthma makes it clear that psychological variables play no meaningful etiological role, another issue logically arises in its stead. Do there exist neural structures and mechanisms influenced by salient psychological events (such as emotional stress, anxiety, or anger) by means of which pulmonary function can be selectively altered? The answer to this question is apparently affirmative – but as yet only very tentatively and cautiously so! Limitations of space prohibit a lengthy discussion of possible neurologic processes. Thus, suffice it to state that the limbic system appears intimately involved in pulmonary physiology in general, with particularly influential roles assumed by the hypothalamus, sympathetic and parasympathetic divisions, and peripheral neural sites (Knapp et al., 1976).

One of the first truly experimental studies to investigate the possible role of psychological variables in asthma (Peskin, 1959, 1960) was based upon the observation that some young patients seem to experience an attenuation in the frequency and severity of asthmatic episodes, or even total remission of symptoms, after separation from their parents and siblings ("parentectomy"), although the specific reasons for such changes remain unclear. Purcell, Brady, Chai, Muser, Molk, Gordon, and Means (1969) separated asthmatic children from their families by leaving the children in the home under the care of child-care workers, while the parents lived in motels, thus controlling for changes in the physical environment. Purcell and his colleagues reported very modest amelioration of symptoms, which was statistically, but not *clinically*, significant. Despite this result, investigations specifically designed to test the hypothesis that "rejecting" or "engulfing" mothers are etiologically responsible for bronchial asthma have met with the lack of success so characteristic of attempts to experimentally verify implications derived from psychoanalytic theory.

Another implication of the psychosomatic view of asthma is that asthma consists of both organic and psychological components. Previous theoretical inquiry reflected this assumption, and, as might be expected, considerable effort has been devoted to the identificaton of a "psychosomatic subgroup" (for example, Purcell, 1963) or to postulation of an emotional-organic continuum (for example, Bloch, Jennings, Harvey, & Simpson, 1964) along which asthmatics could be conveniently classified in terms of the predominant origin of their disorder. The rationale for these approaches was empirically based, developing from evidence suggesting that asthmatic patients, and in some cases their families as well, exhibited psychopathology at levels greater than the incidence found in the general population. This finding applied only to those asthmatics whose etiology was not sufficiently accounted for by physiological mechanisms, particularly those of an allergic nature. Unfortunately, however, this line of research has *not* generated coherent empirical support for the hypothesis that, in comparison to airways of "organic" asthmatics, the respiratory tracts of purportedly "psychosomatic" or "emotional" asthmatics are characteristically hyperresponsive to psychosocial stimuli.

Apparently, the most fitting explanation for these data is that, when the clinical manifestations of the disease are primarily allergic in origin, the disorder can be both "explained" and treated in a comparatively effective and uncomplicated manner. Hence, the entire situation, in terms of disease and treatment, is less psychologically complicated for everyone involved. In contrast, when there is an absence of demonstrable allergic hypersensitivity, etiology cannot be unambiguously specified, and the syndrome is classified as "intrinsic." As noted previously, with intrinsic asthma, the significant etiological variables are largely unknown, and the patient's response to medical therapy is frequently unfavorable and problematic. As a direct consequence, intrinsic asthma engenders more intense frustration and fear, not only on the part of the patient personally, but on the part of his or her family and attending physician as well. Because of its unknown origin, and perhaps also due partly to frustrations in coping with it, intrinsic asthma is too often regarded by both laymen and medical professionals as being "all in the head" of the patient.

This misconception can lead to erratic and inconsistent therapy as well as to profound feelings of shame, embarrassment, guilt, and frustration on the part of patients and their families. Also, these patients and/or their families may sometimes report "severe" asthma attacks that, in fact, are not severe at all. Apparently, and understandably, both patients and those intimately involved with patients respond to these situations as if they were serious because of the mystery, fear, and general confusion that must necessarily surround their asthma and its treatment. Conversely, due primaily to frustration and anger, patients in this group may experience truly severe attacks, which are considered psychological in origin, that is, "all in the head."

It cannot be stressed too emphatically that coping with an inexplicable, debilitating, and life-threatening chronic disease can have devastating psychological consequences for patients and their families. Hence, it is hardly surprising that many cases of bronchial asthma are typified by the presence of pervasive psychopathology. Nevertheless, this does not constitute support for the notion that psychopathology per se plays any sort of direct or causal role in the development of the disorder.

Hindsight might make it obvious that early attempts directed at categorizing asthmatics, in terms of uniquely characteristic subgroups on emotional-organic continua, were simplistic. In any case, these research efforts have not proven capable of meaningfully answering the central question: Why should there be subgroups at all? The fundamental assumption common to all such approaches is that psychological stimuli are of definite consequence for a certain type of patient all of the time, a contention so far unsupported by incontrovertible evidence. Intuition also dictates the possibility that psychological variables might have considerable impact on the course of the syndrome for all asthmatics at some point in their lives, that is, on certain occasions and under certain conditions. Perhaps the most circumspect conclusion currently warranted is that psychological variables would be potentially important for some asthmatics some of the time, an assertion that is, unfortunately, the most complex to state operationally and thus the least subject to empirical validation.

In view of these considerations, no compelling rationale exists for assuming that the airways of atopic patients, in whom allergic mechanisms are largely responsible for bronchial asthma, are any less susceptible to psychological influences than are those of asthmatics whose etiologies are indeterminate. Given the most optimally conducive circumstances, the extent to which psychosocial variables may influence pulmonary function − if, indeed, they influence it at all − in even some asthma sufferers, is a question that remains officially open, but the prospects of finding any evidence in favor of *substantial* psychological influence over tone of airways are dim indeed.

Research has also been directed toward validating the proposition that asthmatics exhibit a characteristic, premorbid personality pattern. Although perhaps conducted far more zealously than studies designed to establish the psychopathological impact of familial stressors, this avenue of investigation has proven even less fruitful. Various investigators have reported that asthmatics are overdependent, hypersensitive, overly aggressive, and overly passive. Asthma sufferers have also been described, in comparison to "normal" individuals, as more neurotic and as possessing poorer self-concepts. These differences have vanished, however, when asthmatics are compared to patients suffering from other chronic debilitating disorders (Neuhaus, 1958). Thus, the current consensus is that asthmatics do not exhibit unique, premorbid personality patterns but, rather, that such profiles constitute merely one consequence of the prolonged struggling and coping with a life-threatening disease. Continued pursuit of a uniquely characteristic personality profile of asthmatics can only detract from investigative efforts that candidly acknowledge the critically important role of pathophysiological mechanisms in bronchial asthma.

Research investigating the psychophysiological aspects of bronchial asthma has yielded results that are more interesting than those of the psychosomatic-trait or personality-profile variety. Anecdotal clinical evidence, including patient self-reports, suggests that psychological stressors often accompany or seem to precede asthma attacks (Alexander, 1977). Consequently, several laboratory investigations have attempted to precipitate episodic attacks by exposing asthmatics to such emotionally stressful situations as anxiety-arousing films (Weiss, Lyness, Molk, & Riley, 1976), discussion or hypnotic suggestion of distressing life events (Clarke, 1970; Smith, Colebatch, & Clarke, 1970), and tape recordings of the voice of the patient's mother (Hill, 1975), among others (Knapp et al., 1976; Purcell & Weiss, 1970). Although exposure to such precipitating stimuli has occasionally been successful in altering respiratory patterns and/or has led to slightly depressed pulmonary flow rates, these experiments have consistently failed to induce genuine attacks. The results of these laboratory investigations have, in any case, been uniformly modest in the clinical sense, despite the fact that they are sometimes statistically significant. Furthermore, such effects have generally been observed in only a small number of subjects.

That continual arousal of any kind should ever serve to directly precipitate an attack of asthma presents somewhat of a paradox. The problem arises, however, from the fact that the sine qua non in the treatment of bronchial asthma has been the bronchodilatory action of beta-adrenergic drugs, which, of course, result in broad sympathetic stimulation. Thus, the question becomes:

How could emotional arousal ever result in bronchospasm at all? One possible resolution of this dilemma was proposed by Mathé and Knapp (1971), who reported the results of a series of experiments pointing to the existence of an adrenergic deficit or deficiency in asthmatics. When exposed to psychological stressors, their asthmatic sample exhibited lower levels of excreted urinary epinephrine than did healthy subjects, and the authors concluded that at least some asthmatics may produce quantities of epinephrine that are less than normal when experiencing emotional arousal. These results have not been replicated, however.

Another related avenue of psychophysiological research has addressed the question of whether bronchial asthma might constitute a vagotonic disorder (that is, a disease process that reflects generalized parasympathetic dominance), because the only innervation of the human lung appears to be vagal. Early attempts to demonstrate that such was, in fact, the case were quite unsuccessful, although interest in this issue has been revived. That the vagus is once again a major focus of psychophysiological inquiry is largely attributable to the work of Gold, Kessler, and Yu (1972). Among others, these researchers demonstrated the existence of the vagally mediated epithelial irritant receptor reflex, which can induce significant spasmodic activity in the bronchial muscles. As mentioned previously, this type of reflexive bronchospasm is now well accepted as the probable cause of mechanically induced bronchospasm in humans, as, for example, from coughing or exposure to airborne irritants. Furthermore, it is now becoming apparent that, in most instances, this mechanism is responsible for many so-called emotionally provoked asthmatic episodes. Yelling during anger, gasping when surprised, and crying or laughing when in an acute emotional state are but a few examples from everyday life that only very remotely represent "emotional" asthma.

Perhaps the most intriguing advances in understanding the role of psychological factors in regulating tone of airways have been made by investigators examining the effects of suggestion, relaxation, and placebo treatments. A number of reports in the literature (for example, Luparello, Lyons, Bleecker, & McFadden, 1968) have reliably demonstrated that inhalation of aerosolized saline can elicit bronchoconstriction similar to, but much less severe than, that induced by substances to which the subject is truly hypersensitive when the subject is persuaded that the substance in question is, in his or her particular case, a genuine allergenic agent. Even more interesting, perhaps, is that these consequent increases in airways resistance are reversible, contingent upon subsequent administration of aerosolized saline which the subject believes to be an authentic bronchodilator. Such effects are quite small, however, and can only be detected through the use of extremely sensitive instrumentation and techniques of measurement (Luparello et al., 1968). Thus, it once again becomes clear that, despite the appearance of being real, these changes in pulmonary flow are quite modest indeed! Teaching asthmatics relaxation skills may similarly lead to small, but nevertheless statistically significant, increases in pulmonary flow, an effect that will receive further attention below. Finally, Godfrey and Silverman (1973) reported that both aerosolized and intravenous premedication with placebo are capable of effecting significant inhibition of exercise-induced bronchospasm in asthmatics, not only statistically but in the clinical sense as well.

The possible control that learning or conditioning may exert on broncho-motor tone has also received considerable investigative attention from both clinical and experimental psychologists. In perhaps the first published case study dealing with psychological aspects of asthma, MacKenzie (1886) reported an anecdote describing a 32-year-old rhinitic and asthmatic woman who exhibited severe pulmonary symptoms merely at the sight of a paper rose in a glass container. Despite the fact that close to a century has passed since the publication of MacKenzie's classic article, however, this phenomenon has not been replicated under controlled conditions in the laboratory. Nevertheless, some writers (for example, Turnbull, 1962) have suggested that bronchospasmodic activity may be learned as a consequence of classical conditioning. At the present time, it would be premature to frame naturalistic antigen-induced bronchospasm or sympathomimetically mediated bronchodilation in terms of classical conditioning, and this simple conceptualization currently remains only a remote, yet provocative, possibility.

The proposition that pulmonary function may be altered as a consequence of instrumental learning or volitional control has also been recently advanced. Both Feldman (1976) and Vachon and Rich (1976) reported what appear to be very small, yet reliable, bronchodilatory effects in some asthmatics after these patients underwent biofeedback training in airways resistance. Despite the apparent therapeutic promise of such a treatment technique, implementation of training in pulmonary biofeedback necessitates complex and costly instrumentation to monitor pulmonary resistance and provide physiological feedback, virtually breath by breath. Also, these inviestigations share in the numerous difficulties affecting all other areas of biofeedback research. Well-designed and controlled psychophysiological investigations have, to date, yielded no conclusive, unambiguous evidence supporting the interpretation that autonomic regulation of visceral responses can be learned. In addition, pulmonary biofeedback research has yet to attain the levels of methodological sophistication characteristic of other areas of biofeedback research, for example, those dealing with the cariovascular system and striated musculature. It follows, therefore, that the evidence of pulmonary biofeedback reported by Feldman (1976) and Vachon and Rich (1976) must be considered with extreme caution. Insofar as the entire area of biofeedback research is, for the most part, generating increasingly discouraging scientific evidence, it would currently be premature to conjecture that either bronchospasm or bronchodilation can be operantly learned or maintained or that volitional pulmonary control is a skill that can be acquired by asthmatics, either to the detriment or benefit of this disease.

To summarize, despite much enthusiastic and dedicated effort on the part of investigators with a psychosomatic orientation, no really persuasive evidence has been produced in support of the long-held notion that psychological variables play *any* role, let alone a significant one, in the etiology of asthma. Nevertheless, it may be acknowledged that psychosocial variables may, to some degree, be capable of affecting pulmonary reactions in some individuals and, for a minority of patients, possibly the clinical course of asthma as well. Pessimistic as this assessment may be, a dispassionate appraisal can infer only that psychosocial factors exert a comparatively minor influence at best on pulmonary function and, as such, are of little practical, clinical consequence to the majority of asthmatics under most circumstances. Nor are only certain well-defined subgroups of asthma patients exclusively susceptible to the pulmonary effects of psychological stimuli. Neither, for that matter, are asthmatic people as opposed to other individuals. To be sure, the lungs of asthmatics are *hypersensitive* (that is, more reactive) when they encounter bronchoconstricting drugs (methacholine, for example) and various mechanical respiratory irritants, but the respiratory tracts of other people will also react, albeit less dramatically, to chemical or mechanical insult.

Considering the complex interaction among exogenous environmental, psychosocial, and normal and pathological physiological variables, our comprehension of bronchial asthma must become much more highly sophisticated before we are capable of more than guesswork concerning which specific psychological stimulus will influence the clinical course of asthma in any individual case at any given time. It is evident that we are faced here with a Gordian knot when we consider that past research has failed to generate any substantial evidence of either consistent similarities or differences among asthmatics vis-à-vis psychological variables.

BEHAVIORAL THERAPY

From the behavioral point of view, neurotic symptoms were considered to be conditioned anxiety responses, accompanied by maladaptive avoidance responses that were maintained by anxiety reduction. Besides the traditional interpretation of anxiety as consisting of maladaptive ideational and behavioral components, behavioral therapists viewed anxiety as also having physiological concomitants. Psychosomatic symptoms were thus conceived of as frequent and persistent anxiety responses, the effects of which became manifest, at least in part, as a hyperreaction in some biologically vulnerable target organ. What had previously been termed the phenomenon of secondary gains (compare, for example, Dollard & Miller, 1950) was presently conceptualized as maladaptive, exaggerated physiological responses instrumentally conditioned to, and maintained by, one or more of several environmental reinforcement contingencies, for example, sympathy, attention, or anxiety reduction through escape or avoidance of circumstances aversive to the patient.

The rationale underlying the clinical application of systematic desensitization in cases of psychosomatic illness was that, if the anxiety reaction could be eliminated, then the exaggerated organ reaction and the associated avoidance responses would disappear. The fundamental principle of systematic desensitization postulates that, if, under carefully controlled conditions, some behavior or set of behaviors antagonistic to, or incompatible with, anxiety (in most instances, relaxation was the behavior used) is evoked in the presence of anxiety-inducing stimuli, then the anxiety reaction can be gradually deconditioned in a deliberate and systematic manner (Wolpe, 1958). It should not be surprising that the first clinical studies focusing on the application of behavior therapy in asthma employed systematic desensitization as the treatment of choice.

Walton (1960) and Cooper (1964) reported case studies in which some form of systematic desensitization was successfully used to treat asthma. These case studies certainly represent pioneering clinical efforts; yet their value is rather limited for several reasons. First, both reports can be criticized on grounds of failure to provide either a firm medical diagnosis of asthma or any mention of a prognosis concerning its extent and severity based on reliable clinical indexes and tests of pulmonary function. Second, in each instance, the criterion index of behavioral change was subjective, consisting exclusively of patient self-reports. As discussed previously, the need for objective measures of asthma, including assessment of pulmonary function, cannot be overemphasized. In retrospect, these reports can also be criticized on heuristic grounds. Specifically, the rationale underlying therapy was that asthmatic episodes are mediated by anxiety, an assumption that is, as yet, unsupported by persuasive evidence and the validity of which is *highly* unlikely.

Moore (1965) published the first report of a controlled clinical experiment that investigated the efficacy of applying behavioral techniques in asthma treatment. In her comparison of systematic desensitization, relaxation alone, and relaxation training supplemented by suggestions of symptom remission, she predicted that the greatest clinical benefit (as shown by increases in both subjective and physiological indexes of pulmonary function) would be derived from systematic desensitization. Her hypothesis was only partially confirmed. Although differences among the three groups on subjective measures of symptomatology were not found, Moore did report a small, yet statistically significant, improvement in respiratory function in the group treated with systematic desensitization. This study is noteworthy in that it was the first report of any kind to include assessment of pulmonary function in addition to some measure of experimental control. While Moore is certainly to be commended, there is nevertheless a major problem, namely, measurement of respiratory function on only a weekly basis. Because of the highly intermittent nature of asthma, such a relatively infrequent measurement of PEFR does not permit any reliable conclusions to be drawn concerning either the immediate clinical benefits or the long-term advantages of treatment (Chai, Purcell, Brady, & Falliers, 1968).

Further research on the efficacy of systematic desensitization as a treatment for asthma was conducted most recently in the psychology laboratories of the National Asthma Center at Denver. Miklich, Renne, Creer, Alexander, Chai,

Davis, Hoffman, and Danker-Brown (1977) examined the effects of systematic desensitization, in relation to a no-treatment control group, in a large-scale, long-term investigation in which the criterion index of clinical improvement was FEV_1. This clinical outcome study represents a significant refinement over Moore's experiment, insofar as pulmonary data were collected twice daily (rather than once weekly) throughout the investigation. The subjects of the study were 26 severely asthmatic youngsters (both boys and girls, with a mean age of approximately 11 years), who were residential patients at the center. The study consisted of five distinct phases: (1) a baseline period of 16 weeks, (2) ten weeks of treatment, (3) a nine-week period of observation following treatment, (4) an interim period of 11 weeks (during which no data were collected), and, finally, (5) a follow-up phase encompassing an additional six weeks.

Subjects were assigned to the systematic desensitization (19 children) and no-treatment control (7 children) groups on an essentially random basis. The disproportionate size of the two groups was due to a selection protocol designed to assign subjects to therapists on an individual basis as both subjects and therapists became available. For example, if a subject was ready to participate in the study without a therapist being concurrently available, that particular child was assigned to the control group. All subjects were managed identically throughout the investigation, save that members of one group received treatment, whereas the remainder of the sample received none, during phase 2 of the investigation.

As mentioned above, pulmonary data were collected twice a day (except during phase 4), and, in addition, supplementary evidence concerning frequency and type of medication requirements, cumulative frequency of hospital admissions, and severity of daily symptoms was also collected. Although systematic desensitization treatment adhered to the traditional protocol (hierarchy construction and progressive relaxation training followed by desensitization proper), therapists were allowed substantial latitude in planning and administering treatment, thus enabling them to formulate a therapeutic regimen designed to meet the exact clinical requirements of each individual patient.

The outcome of the Miklich et al. investigation was, for the most part, disappointing. The sole pulmonary index on which a statistically significant difference between groups became evident was morning FEV_1. Furthermore, this difference was an extremely small one that was predominantly attributable to attentuated rates of flow in control subjects rather than to significant respiratory improvement (increased FEV_1) in those patients receiving treatment. Thus, the conclusion that systematic desensitization fails to provide lasting therapeutic effects on *pulmonary physiology* in severely asthmatic children becomes more firmly established, although whether or not such may be the case for less seriously affected children (or for adults afflicted at any level of severity) must remain an officially open issue. In view of the questionable rationale underpinning the application of systematic desensitization to bronchial asthma (namely, anxiety-mediated asthma), however, it is probably a reasonable prediction that behavioral therapy regimens based on mechanisms for the reduction of anxiety will have, at best, minimal clinical impact on pulmonary physiology in asthmatics, irrespective of age or severity of disease.

RELAXATION TRAINING AS AN ADJUNCTIVE THERAPY

Due to the prima facie therapeutic appeal of the relaxation response itself in treating asthmatics, relaxation training has also been the focus of considerable inquiry in its own right, rather than merely receiving attention as one facet of systematic desensitization treatment. Even before such reports began to appear in the psychology literature, it was common practice for physicians and other professionals involved in treating asthma patients to prescribe sitting quietly or attempting to relax at the onset of and/or during asthma episodes. Moreover, both clinicians and their patients had long anecdotally reported relaxation to be of some benefit in alleviating the wheezing that accompanies bronchospasm.

The first published study dealing exclusively with the effects of relaxation training on asthma was reported by Alexander, Miklich, and Hershkoff (1972). Alexander and his colleagues at the National Asthma Center employed a brief, progressive relaxation technique to teach 20 asthmatic children to relax. Six training sessions were required for the experimental group to learn these skills to criterion. Another independent group of children ($n = 16$), who were matched to those in the experimental group in terms of age, sex, and, as closely as possible, severity of asthma, also received six sessions in which they were merely requested to sit quietly. Their asthma ranged from moderate to very severe in intensity. PEFR was sampled just before and immediately following each session, as were the children's subjective feelings of relaxation. This investigation focused exclusively on the possible *immediate* beneficial effects of relaxation on pulmonary physiology. For this reason, a follow-up assessment of the possible long-term clinical benefits of continued practice of relaxation was not undertaken.

Subjects receiving relaxation training exhibited a statistically significant mean increase of 21.63 Liters/min in PEFR (approximately an 11% functional improvement). Children in the control group, on the other hand, displayed a mean decrease in PEFR of 6.14%. Subjective feelings of relaxation increased significantly and monotonically across sessions for those learning to relax, whereas no change was evident for control children.

Alexander (1972) replicated these results in a subsequent investigation with a new sample of 25 children comparable with those described above (Alexander et al., 1972). These 25 children were assigned to one of six training groups, each consisting of four or five children. Procedural details of the new study very closely resembled those of Alexander et al. (1972), except that subjects served as their own controls. Immediately before and after every experimental session, PEFR and "state" anxiety were assessed. In addition, all subjects completed the Spielberger Trait Anxiety Questionnaire during the first experimental session.

Procedures of data analysis resembled those employed by Alexander et al. (1972), as did certain of the results. The mean improvement in PEFR of 23.5 L/min following relaxation was virtually identical to that exhibited by the earlier experimental group. During the resting phase of the study, subjects displayed no change in PEFR. The change in pulmonary function between the two phases of the investigation was statistically significant. One enlightening result was the lack of relationship between a subject's response to resting or sitting quietly and his or her response to relaxation procedures, an outcome suggesting that purposive relaxation is not merely an extension of resting.

Furthermore, inasmuch as these two physiological states (that is, resting and relaxation) are apparently unrelated or discontinuous (that is, do not lie on a single continuum), it proved impossible to predict a given child's response to relaxation training based on his or her response to inactivity. Similarly, no relationship was evident either between the measure of trait anxiety and the relaxation response or, for any given relaxation session, between the amount of anxiety reduction and the corresponding pulmonary response. Similarly, no relationship was discovered between any given child's response to relaxation and his or her responses to questions designed to reveal which historical behavioral factors might be predictors of his or her projected differential response to relaxation.

Although it had been found in two investigations that short-term relaxation training results in an immediate increase in pulmonary function, it was necessary, nevertheless, to be cautious in drawing conclusions regarding its therapeutic properties. One important limitation common to both these relaxation studies (Alexander, 1972; Alexander et al., 1972) was that the criterion index of change in pulmonary function was PEFR, a rather variable measure of exclusively large-airways dynamics that is highly dependent in terms of motivation and effort. Its shortcomings dictated that relaxation effects be validated on the basis of more sensitive and reliable indexes of pulmonary function.

Another problem involved the duration of the relaxation effect, which was measured immediately following 20 minutes of relaxation training. To be clinically meaningful, therapeutic effects must be shown to endure for periods of time on the order of, say, at least one hour, even if the sole intent of treatment is to provide short-term or symptomatic relief. Transient increases in pulmonary physiology (that is, those lasting only during the session itself or for a very brief period thereafter) do not qualify, according to usual clinical standards.

Finally, the magnitude of the mean increases in PEFR obtained in these studies fell far short of achieving *clinical* significance. At the only modestly impaired baseline levels characteristic of the subjects studied up to this time, attainment of predicted normal function had to be demonstrated in order to be therapeutically meaningful. In both investigations reviewed above, increases in PEFR only slightly exceeded 10%.

A third, more definitive investigation (Alexander, Cropp, & Chai, 1979) attempted to deal directly with these shortcomings. The subjects were 14 experimentally naive children, similar in all respects to those employed previously by Alexander. Prior to each 20-minute laboratory session, a pretest of pulmonary function was administered, after which subjects either rested (the baseline phase, involving three sessions), learned to relax (the treatment phase, five sessions), or relaxed independently (the postexperimental assessment phase, involving three sessions). Immediately after resting or relaxing, subjects were administered the first of a series of four pulmonary postassessments. The remaining three were administered at 30-minute intervals. Thus, the total postexperimental assessment period was extended to 1.5 hours following the end of each session. The measures of pulmonary function utilized in this investigation consisted of a battery of more highly sensitive and definitive, but standard, tests of lung function. Additionally, all tests were administered by a well-trained respiratory technician, who was blind to the phase of the experiment in progress at any given time. Lastly, a variety of nonpulmonary physiological indexes were monitored continuously throughout all baseline and independent relaxation sessions.

During all resting (baseline) sessions, subjects exhibited a consistent, generally monotonic decline in pulmonary function from the presession to the fourth postsession assessment. This persistent decrement in pulmonary dynamics was due to abstention from the maintenance bronchodilator for six hours before the start of each resting session. Relaxation had an opposite effect, with the mean relaxation response manifesting itself as a statistically significant shift in pulmonary function toward recovery of pretest pulmonary status, although the magnitude of the shift was, once again, insufficient to attain *clinical* or *therapeutic* significance. Other physiological indexes provided statistically significant evidence of decreased electromyogram and heart rate during relaxation when contrasted with the resting state.

Since the first controlled experimental research conducted by Alexander and his colleagues, other investigators at the National Asthma Center have also examined the pulmonary effects of relaxation training in asthmatic children. Tal and Miklich (1976), for example, studied the short-term effects of three sessions of very brief, tape-recorded, "quasi-hypnotic" relaxation training on the pulmonary function of 60 asthmatic children. In relation to presession evaluation, FEV_1 manifested a small, but statistically significant, increase following relaxation.

Long-term influences of relaxation training on pulmonary function have also been the focus of experimental inquiry. At the National Asthma Center, Davis, Saunders, Creer, and Chai (1973) examined the effects of differential relaxation instructions on three groups ($n = 8$ in each) of asthmatic children who were similar to those participating in Alexander's original experiments. The first group received tape-recorded, progressive relaxation training; the second received an identical treatment supplemented by frontalis EMG biofeedback; and the third (control) group read various light materials and was merely instructed to try to relax. Davis et al. did not specifically detail their methodology in combining EMG biofeedback training with instruction in progressive muscular relaxation.

Analysis of both the immediate (that is, before and after), session-by-session PEFR changes and the contrast between baseline and posttreatment PEFRs failed to reveal any global intergroup differences in respiratory function. However, an a priori criterion of asthma severity was established; namely, children who were receiving corticosteroids were operationally defined as severe asthmatics, while those who were not were classified as nonsevere asthmatics. Post hoc analysis based on this severity criterion did reveal that, in general, nonseverely asthmatic children derived slightly greater immediate pulmonary benefits from both relaxation and relaxation plus feedback than they did from the control treatment. These differences did not attain significance, however, in the case of severe asthmatics. Furthermore, children receiving both progressive relaxation and biofeedback seemed to exhibit a small advantage over those who received progressive relaxation alone, although this difference fell short of statistical significance. Nevertheless, despite evidence of minor improvements in PEFR that were attributable to relaxation alone and relaxation plus feedback for nonseverely as opposed to severely asthmatic children, no differences were revealed among treatment groups between baseline and posttreatment pulmonary data. Perhaps the fact that routine pharmacotherapy was maintained throughout the investigation, irrespective of severity of asthma, accounts for this failure of differences to become manifest (compare, for example, Alexander et al., 1979), although withholding corticosteroids from severely asthmatic children for purposes of experimentation would not have been ethical.

Finally, regression analysis of the EMG data available in this study did not reveal a significant quantitative relationship between changes in PEFR and corresponding variations in frontalis EMG. Thus, although electromyographic biofeedback training *might* constitute a significant therapeutic adjunct when combined with traditional relaxation techniques, the psychophysiological source of such an advantage remains, as yet, obscure.

Results of an analogous, but more extensive, investigation were reported by Scherr, Crawford, Sergent, and Scherr (1975). Asthmatic children, summer residents at Camp Broncho Junction, participated in an eight-week experimental therapeutic program. The first week was devoted to baseline observation, whereas, during the next six weeks, the children either were administered a treatment package consisting of modified Jacobsonian relaxation and frontalis EMG biofeedback training (n = 22) or served as members of a no-treatment control group (n = 22). Not only did the experimental treatment presumably resemble that employed by Davis et al. (1973) but these authors also failed to mention procedural details regarding the combination of relaxation and biofeedback training. The final (eighth) week of the program served as a postexperimental assessment phase. Throughout the investigation, measures of PEFR were obtained thrice daily from each subject.

Although data from both control and experimental groups indicated increased levels of functioning on pulmonary as well as other dependent variables, children administered relaxation plus biofeedback training exhibited significantly greater improvement in mean PEFR (baseline as opposed to post-treatment) as well as statistically significant decreases on several ancillary medical indexes of bronchial asthma. Despite apparent benefits derived from relaxation plus biofeedback training, Scherr and his colleagues included two important interpretational caveats in reporting and discussing their findings. Lest the reader misinterpret their results, Scherr et al. specifically cautioned that, first, the special attention received by trained subjects had no counterpart in the control group, whose members received absolutely no treatment whatever beyond that routinely involved in camp attendance, and, second, compared with those in the experimental group, children in the control group were rated as more severely asthmatic by camp physicians blind to assignment of subjects to groups.

Both Davis et al. (1973) and Scherr et al. (1975) examined the tandem effects of progressive Jacobsonian relaxation and EMG biofeedback training. In a subsequent investigation, Kotses, Glaus, Crawford, Edwards, and Scherr (1976) assessed the therapeutic potential of EMG biofeedback training alone. This study at Camp Broncho Junction involved 36 youngsters (with mean age of 12 years) who were assigned randomly to one of three independent groups of subjects (n = 12 each), respectively receiving either contingent or noncontingent training in EMG biofeedback skills or no treatment (controls). Both treatments involved three 20-minute laboratory sessions each week for three weeks. The first two were exclusively devoted to acquisition of EMG biofeedback skills, and the third, to assessment of performance when feedback was withheld. All treated subjects were instructed to lower the feedback tone. By design, the experiment included the precaution of randomly yoking each noncontingent feedback subject to a child in the contingent biofeedback group. As had Scherr et al. (1975), Kotses et al. obtained measures of PEFR three times each day from each participant, although none of these data was collected immediately before and after each session.

With respect to the noncontingent biofeedback and control groups, children trained with contingent biofeedback exhibited a statistically significant mean increase in weekly PEFR. In contrast, noncontingent and control children did not differ on this measure. Additionally, analysis of electromyographic evidence pointed toward a relaxation effect (as indicated by decreased frontalis tension) derived from contingent biofeedback training, whereas children administered noncontingent biofeedback training exhibited a significant *increase* in the tension of their frontalis muscles.

The principal explanation of this polar difference in the characteristic electromyographic data of these two groups is probably artifactual, rather than of any clinical or therapeutic import, and is probably attributable to differences in the nature of the experimental tasks presented them. Noncontingent biofeedback subjects faced the virtually impossible and insoluble problem of lowering the tone in the complete absence of temporally contiguous exteroceptive information vis-à-vis performance. On the other hand, those children who had been administered contingent biofeedback training experienced a far simpler learning situation. The only systematic knowledge that members of the noncontingent group could reasonably have been expected to derive was that the information presented them (changes in the feedback tone) was entirely irrelevant to their behavior. Given such a constraint, they obviously could not comply and presumably would soon become aware that the situation was hopeless.

The likelihood of this possibility as an explanation of the Kotses et al. (1976) results was boosted immeasurably by a finding reported by Alexander, White, and Wallace (1977). These researchers demonstrated that control-group conditions like those used by Kotses et al. virtually preclude performance which subjects would otherwise be capable of without any aid whatsoever. Consequently, it is anything but surprising that children subjected to the manipulation inherent in noncontingent biofeedback training characteristically exhibit appreciably increased EMG and no increases in PEFR. Furthermore, the no-treatment group constituted an inadequate control for the contingent feedback group employed by Kotses et al. (1976), just as it had for Scherr et al. (1975).

These three investigations (Davis et al., 1973; Kotses et al., 1976; Scherr et al., 1975) focused on a substantially different facet of the application of relaxation plus biofeedback techniques than did those conducted by Alexander and his coinvestigators in Denver (Alexander, 1972; Alexander et al., 1972, 1977, 1979). In the former studies, the potential benefits of long-term practice of relaxation plus biofeedback were examined, whereas, in the latter studies, the benefits of short-term practice of these skills were investigated. In addition, Davis, Scherr, Kotses, and their collaborators were concerned with the analysis of frequent pulmonary data obtained at times other than immediately before and after each relaxation session, which was the case in the investigations conducted by Alexander and his co-workers, which were principally designed to assess the symptomatic benefits alleged to be derived from relaxation training. Davis et al. (1973) examined both the immediate and the long-term consequences of relaxation training and subsequent practice, concluding that there was no reason to assume that prolonged practice of relaxation would be of substantive clinical benefit to asthmatic children, whether severe or not. Similarly, the Alexander experiments suggested convincingly that relaxation provides no clinically useful benefit to asthmatic children.

Results of the experiments conducted at Camp Broncho Junction were similarly bereft of applied therapeutic significance. Despite statistical significance, the effects found by Kotses and Scherr were insufficient to allow any enthusiastic conclusions to be drawn regarding clinical utility of the procedures. Moreover, the latter pair of investigations was fraught with methodological artifacts and confounds (for example, the rather conspicuous lack of a suitable, attention-placebo control condition), an additional consideration prohibiting the conclusion that relaxation might be clinically beneficial to asthmatic children over a prolonged period of time (such as several weeks or even months). An outcome allowing such a conclusion failed to materialize even when an appropriate, attention-placebo control condition was included by design (compare, for example, Davis et al., 1973).

Analogously, it becomes impossible to empirically justify the supposition that training in EMG biofeedback, whether alone or as an adjunct or supplement to more traditional methods of relaxation training, is of any substantive degree of therapeutic utility in effecting desirable changes in pulmonary physiology in pediatric asthmatics. In nonpathological populations (specifically, nonasthmatic adults) as well, the existing evidence (Alexander, 1975; Alexander et al., 1977) also appears to militate against the conclusion that EMG biofeedback techniques constitute an effective behavioral technique by which to acquire general relaxation skills.

Several clinical researchers have addressed the issue of whether feedback of respiratory activity might be of therapeutic consequence in altering pulmonary function. In one such study (Kahn, Staerk, & Bonk, 1973), ten severely asthmatic children underwent a program that the authors termed *linking training*. In brief, this involved five sessions in which each child was individually taught to emit an uninterrupted response chain, or linked series, of forced vital capacity efforts (FVCs), for which the reinforcement criterion was that each successive FEV_1 be greater than the immediately preceding one. In addition to social reinforcement (verbal praise) for every correct response, each child was provided with a discriminative stimulus (red light), indicating execution of a suitable FEV_1. In a subsequent phase of the study, these children were administered ten sessions of analogous training, in which mild bronchospasm was deliberately evoked by experimental procedures that varied idiosyncratically with each child. Although significant changes were reported between baseline and follow-up on several asthma measures collected ten months after termination of training, absolutely no FEV_1 data on the linking-training procedure were offered.

Kahn et al. viewed their experimental training program as a biofeedback conditioning procedure. This is rather presumptuous, given that no real specification of the alleged conditioning procedures was provided, no data regarding whether or not conditioning even took place were offered, and none of the essential controls for an adequate learning experiment was present. Furthermore, the experiment by Kahn et al. failed to control for the generalized artifactual or confounding effects of attention. Had a suitable attention-placebo control condition been routinely included as a matter of proper experimental design, whatever results were obtained would at least have been methodologically valid, irrespective of whether or not the effect had anything to do with conditioning.

Yet, despite these perhaps glaring inadequacies in experimental conduct, Kahn (1977) reported the results of an investigation virtually identical in methodology to the previous one. In advance of any experimental manipulations, Kahn subdivided his experimental and no-treatment control subjects into reactors and nonreactors in terms of their pulmonary responses to placebo suggestions, using procedures like those of Luparello et al. (1968). Kahn maintained, once again, that instrumental conditioning of pulmonary function had occurred, although any form of supportive physiological evidence was, as before, conspicuously absent. Similarly, inadequate precautions were included to guard against the confounding artifacts of generalized special attention, duration of experimenter-subject interaction, experimenter expectation, and subject suggestibility. No differences between experimental reactors and nonreactors were found, but, despite this rather obvious evidence to the contrary, Kahn (1977) remained adamant in construing both his past and present results as indicative of the successful therapeutic application of his quite unique intervention program. This is most curious, inasmuch as the control reactor subjects in the second experiment were virtually indistinguishable, on all measures, from subjects receiving linking training.

Also militating against the conclusions drawn by Kahn from his pair of experiments are the results obtained by Danker, Miklich, Pratt, and Creer (1975). In a far more carefully designed and conducted investigation, Danker et al. detected no evidence of either immediate conditioning effects or long-term pulmonary benefits as a consequence of contingently rewarding progressively greater forced expiratory efforts. Nor did they discover improvements on any of a variety of clinical indexes regarding asthma. It thus appears that these simple reinforcement techniques, as was the case for systematic desensitization, relaxation, and biofeedback therapies, possess little or no promise as potentially therapeutic procedures for inducing clinically beneficial changes in lung functions of asthmatic children.

OTHER APPLICATIONS OF BEHAVIORAL METHODS

Clinical intervention in asthma incurs problems of other than a purely medical nature. The predominant objective in treating patients suffering from virtually any chronic disease should be effective clinical management and rehabilitation, and asthma is certainly no exception (Creer & Christian, 1976; Creer, Renne, & Christian, 1976). Problems in living that are engendered by asthma and other enduring disorders are invariably attributable to the continual battle in learning to adapt successfully to a severely constrained life-style imposed by the demands of both the disease itself and its nonmedical ramifications.

Particularly in the case of pediatric patients, although not infrequently with adults as well, such psychological ramifications typically include problems in complying with the rigors of a stringent medical regimen, maladaptive interpersonal development, developmental retardation, hyperemotionality, and various specific emotional and behavioral disturbances, to enumerate but a few. Although the predominant objective in asthma intervention has traditionally been to ameliorate pulmonary pathology, some authors have concentrated on rehabilitative psychological intervention with asthmatics in which the exclusive intent has been to modify maladaptive behaviors arising as a direct consequence of coping with asthma.

Most, if not all, strategies of behavior modification are philosophically deterministic in rationale, the central premise being that the behavior of humans is, as in the case of other species, characteristically regulated by its immediate consequences. By way of illustration, should either the *application* of a positive consequence (reward or reinforcer) or the *termination* of an undesirable, aversive event be allowed to occur contingent upon the emission of some well-specified response, then that behavior will become more highly probable in the future, given identical or even similar circumstances. A pair of related manipulations, the purpose of which is to effect an attentuated probability of response emission, involves the contingent *application* of an aversive stimulus or the *withholding* or removal of a positive, desired stimulus following the emission of a specific behavior. Together, these four basic behavioral techniques — positive reinforcement, negative reinforcement, punishment, and extinction — constitute the core of the operant behavior therapies successfully utilized in rehabilitating pediatric asthmatics. Procedures related to, or derived from, these principles, such as response cost, satiation, time-out, and counterconditioning, have proven equally effective in the behavioral clinical management of children suffering from asthma.

The literature concerned with the effective clinical application of each of these techniques in the rehabilitation and management of pediatric asthma patients has been reviewed by Creer (1978) and will only be summarized here. The experimental and clinical reports reviewed by Creer convincingly underscore the effectiveness of a variety of techniques of behavior modification in the rehabilitative treatment and management of a wide range of asthma-related maladaptive behaviors. Behaviors that have been successfully modified include the requisite skills for using equipment for inhalation therapy, malingering to avoid school, and chronic coughing.

Although the reports available in the literature have been exclusively concerned with childhood or adolescent asthmatics, there is absolutely no reason to suspect that the clinical application of these and similar behavioral procedures would be any less effective in the rehabilitative treatment of adult patients suffering from asthma. This contention is strongly supported by work in the behavioral therapy clinics at the National Asthma Center by the author and other clinical psychologists. Adult asthmatics have been successfully treated for a broad spectrum of asthma-related behavioral disorders, two notable examples of which are the reduction of asthma-related fears, or panic behavior, and the elimination of hyperventilatory activity. Indeed, it is now clear that deconditioning procedures involving traditional behavioral therapy, such as systematic desensitization, have become the treatments of choice in dealing with the problematic fears and emotional reactions so readily conditioned to the stimuli commonly associated with both an asthmatic episode and its antecedents.

Correspondingly impressive is the success deriving from the therapeutic application of principles of operant behavior modification in the rehabilitation and clinical management of pediatric asthma patients.

Of all the studies reviewed by Creer that focused on rehabilitative efforts designed to ameliorate asthma-related behavioral pathology, none either predicted or detected *any* physiological impact, whether protracted or transitory, on the asthma process per se. So convinced, in fact, were Creer and his coinvestigators by their failure to detect such changes in indexes of either asthma symptomatology or pulmonary physiology that they accepted this pattern of results as convincing evidence of the functional specificity of their strategies of behavioral intervention. Thus reflected is the growing awareness and appreciation by both applied researchers and clinicians that behavioral intervention in asthma should be framed within the entire context of rehabilitation. Furthermore, evidence is equally conclusive that strategies of behavioral intervention should generally be expected not to have any significant influence on the pathophysiological substrates of bronchial asthma or, possibly, even their daily symptomatic manifestations in respiration.

Although virtually no persuasive evidence exists in support of the assumption that emotional behaviors can directly alter pulmonary physiology to any significant degree, this should not be taken to mean that maladaptive affective behaviors cannot exert influence by more indirect routes. In fact, such is quite commonly the case with asthmatic patients. It is clinically well documented that anxious and panic reactions can drastically reduce a patient's ability to cooperate with medical personnel during pulmonary crisis intervention, cause hyperventilation, and unnecessarily generate increased physical and psychological suffering (compare, for example, Alexander, 1977; Creer, 1974; Creer & Christian, 1976; Creer et al., 1976). Through stimulus generalization, conditioned emotional responses, particularly fear, can become temporally associated with antecedent stimuli quite remote from the appearance of symptoms (for example, chest tightness or very mild wheezing), indicating the impending inception of an acute asthmatic episode. Anxiety can also become conditioned to the covert stimuli involved in imagining or anticipating the possibility of an impending bout with bronchial asthma or the presence of a known precipitant.

Procedures of behavior modification that incorporate counterconditioning or extinction (for example, systematic desensitization, emotional flooding, or implosion) should thus be as ideally suited to the elimination of asthma-related, maladaptive, conditioned fear responses as they are to the well-established treatment of fears and phobias of nonmedical origin. Although intervention employing these methods has not been a focus of controlled experimental or clinical inquiry, case reports involving the successful clinical application of these techniques to panic behavior in asthmatic children have appeared in the literature (Alexander, 1977; Creer, 1978). Neither Alexander nor Creer expected, nor did they detect, improvements in pulmonary function as a consequence of behavioral intervention. The sole clinical good was that a severely painful and aggravating side effect could be successfully eradicated.

EVALUATION AND CONCLUSIONS

Any evaluation of the scientific and clinical status of the research covered in the preceding sections — in particular, that concerned with alteration of pulmonary function — must take into account some special characteristics of the population being studied. With few exceptions, the patients have been rather young, severely and chronically asthmatic children undergoing residential treatment at highly specialized treatment centers. One characteristic of these children is that, in comparison with adults, they generally manifest reduced attention span, less interest in issues and activities that adult scientists consider important, poorer comprehension of the underlying rationales of experiments, relative inability to appreciate the potential therapeutic value of the investigations in which they are asked to participate, and problems in following often complex experimental instructions. As a result of these realities, youthful subjects may possess considerably less than optimal motivation to perform the tasks that are necessary in successful, controlled experiments. These attributes, however, must not be taken as an indictment of asthmatic children, either as children or as asthma sufferers. Indeed, they are generally quite normal attributes, largely reflective of developmental level alone. Despite the fact that we cannot fault otherwise normal youngsters who suffer from asthma because they lack enthusiasm concerning participation in our experiments, these features affect the conduct of experiments and, hence, can materially cloud the reliability and validity of any data gathered. Such factors must be taken into full account during interpretation of experimental data.

A second characteristic is that these youthful experimental subjects have, in almost all instances, been severe, chronic asthmatics, very often representative of the most severe asthmatics to be found. As pointed out in the introduction to this chapter, both children and adults with asthma of this severity have abnormalities of pulmonary function that can be very difficult to alter, even with virtually continuous therapy involving the most powerful drugs. It is, indeed, expecting a great deal to hope that psychological interventions of any sort would be capable of altering the dynamics of airways in this group of patients. Yet, this is the very population that has been the subject of study in the majority of the investigations cited.

With this warning, we can now attempt an overall evaluation of the clinical implications of the research that has been reviewed. There have been three distinct therapeutic goals to which behavioral intervention methods have been applied. The first goal is to beneficially change pulmonary function or asthma symptoms more or less directly. Relaxation, systematic desensitization specifically directed toward altering presumably asthmogenic stimulus situations, airways biofeedback, and positive reinforcement of forced expiratory efforts are examples. The second goal is to ameliorate maladaptive or uncomfortable emotional concomitants of asthma. In these cases, it should generally not be expected that pulmonary physiology will change to any therapeutically significant degree. Systematic desensitization for the reduction of anxiety or panic associated with asthma attacks is the prime example. The third goal is the therapeutic alteration of inappropriate, maladaptive, or disruptive asthma-related behaviors. Here, there should be absolutely no intent to alter asthma symptoms. Interventions involving behavior modification that are designed to alter malingering, developmental deficiencies, and manipulative or attention-getting behaviors, such as coughing, are examples.

The literature is replete with attempts to alter pulmonary physiology using behavioral methods, and with few exceptions (such as positive reinforcement of FEV_1 increase) *statistically* significant increases have resulted both with methods intended to provide immediate benefit (for example, relaxation) and with those designed to yield long-term gains (such as desensitization and daily relaxation practice). Such results, at first, appear quite encouraging, despite the methodological problems characteristic of so many of the relevant investigations. Unfortunately, however, we do not yet stand ready to recommend these methods as demonstrably useful techniques in the clinical management of asthma.

Caution in this regard is due mainly to the rather small amount of change in pulmonary function that has been evident throughout virtually all the studies, even though the changes have been statistically reliable. Initially, these findings were highly encouraging, and, sooner or later, clinically significant effects were *supposed to* emerge. It was hoped, and reasonably so, that their size could be coaxed into the therapeutic range on the basis of improved application skills, but this long-awaited event has not materialized. In the case of relaxation and airways biofeedback and probably systematic desensitization, there is now sufficient controlled experimental data to support the conclusion that these techniques reliably alter pulmonary mechanics in the desired direction in severely and chronically asthmatic children but that the amount of change obtained is of essentially no clinical benefit. In short, without notable exceptions, the young patients who have served as subjects in these many studies have entered the experiments as severely ill, chronic asthmatics and have completed their participation with absolutely no clinically significant change in their condition. Little more need be said.

Should this conclusion be taken as generally definitive for all asthma sufferers or even all childhood asthmatics? The answer must officially be no. Thus far, therapeutic effectiveness has been tested largely on inpatient populations consisting of severely ill, chronically asthmatic children. It was pointed out earlier that such a population presents a very severe (perhaps, in fact, excessively severe) test for psychological therapies intended to modify lung function. The very reliability of changes produced so far in severely asthmatic patients would seem to provide some reason to believe that individuals who experience much less severe symptoms may yet be found that are capable of benefiting from behaviorally induced alternations in lung physiology at clinically significant levels. Adequately controlled investigations of this possibility simply remain to be undertaken. For a variety of reasons, however, the author feels that the likelihood of finding results that differ from what has already been found in severely asthmatic children is very low indeed. We have seen, on the one hand, that, in virtually all cases, psychological influence on tone of airways has been very modest. There is no reason for this strong trend to be contradicted when those therapeutic procedures are applied to populations other than severely asthmatic children. On the other hand, to predict otherwise assumes a version of the subgroup hypothesis, a set of notions that has failed to find empirical support.

The second category of behavioral interventions, unlike the methods just discussed, includes those designed to effect changes in the emotional concomitants of asthma, the major example of which is anxiety or fear associated with asthma. When properly conceptualized, no assumption is made that emotional reactions can lead, in a causal sense, either to the development of asthma or even to the precipitation of attacks in already affected individuals. These emotional responses are considered to be maladaptive reactions, such as tightness or wheezing, which have become classically conditioned to asthma stimuli. These conditioned emotional responses can develop as the direct consequence of extremely frightening, life-threatening episodes, in which the fear may result from severe dyspnea and hypoxia; the anxious and fearful reactions of family members, physicians, nurses, and other medical personnel during acute attacks; and the pain associated with treatment (for example, venous and arterial punctures), among other salient aspects of a medical crisis. While there is no evidence that the emotional state directly makes lung function worse, many indirect manifestations exist to the detriment of the asthmatic condition considered as a whole. For example, they can make treating the patient difficult and can thus exacerbate and prolong the attack itself, thereby leading to increased psychological and physical discomfort for the patient, both immediately and over extended periods of time.

It is now quite generally agreed that any of the deconditioning behavioral therapies (for example, systematic desensitization or implosion) represent the treatments of choice for clinical phobias (conditioned emotional reactions) in both adults and children. Hence, fear associated with asthma (called *asthma panic*) should be eminently treatable by these behavioral therapies, and, in fact, this seems to be the case. At the National Asthma Center, numerous cases of asthma panic in youngsters, and several in adults, have been successfully treated over the past ten years or so with systematic desensitization and its variants (including in vivo desensitization and emotive imagery) and with implosion (flooding). In no case was there the intention of altering lung function. Furthermore, treatment success consisted strictly of reduced anxiety and was judged solely on such clinical criteria as subjective reports of improvement by the patient or observations by nurses, physicians, and others involved in the care of the individuals treated.

Despite the clear clinical effectiveness of the techniques, attempts to perform controlled-outcome research on the behavioral treatment of asthma fears have been frustrated. The reasons are numerous and relate to the fact that asthma panic does not yield to measurement and study in a straightforward, uncomplicated fashion. First, the behavior avoidance tests so frequently employed in experimental studies of phobias of small animals are inappropriate here. Second, subjective assessments by the patient are quite impossible when the patient may be struggling for life itself. Third, objective observational assessment (for example, by means of the commonly used checklists of fear behaviors) is also difficult to employ because of the wide range of behaviors through which asthma panic is manifested. During asthma attacks, the behavior of highly fearful patients may range from postural rigidity to extreme agitation, crying, screaming, and flailing of limbs. It may also involve active attempts to interfere with and even avoid, because of fear, such necessary, but often painful, treatment procedures as arterial punctures. Fourth, it is usually only during periods of naturally occurring, *severe* asthma attacks that panic becomes a clinical problem requiring treatment, an occasion poorly suited to controlled investigative efforts. Nevertheless, it can be confidently concluded, largely on the basis of clinical experience, that the deconditioning behavioral therapies are the treatments of choice for asthma panic. This recommendation is inferentially supported by convincing data from experiments and controlled case reports involving the successful application of these same techniques to a variety of clinical fears and anxieties that are not related to asthma.

The third category of behaviorally based treatment strategies includes those intended to alter or control behavioral excesses and/or deficits, that is, inappropriate asthma-related behaviors. These problems are only coincidentally associated with asthma per se; that is, these behavior patterns, such as malingering or poor social development, can occur in conjunction with any chronic disorder or even in the normal course of growing up and are not at all specific to asthma. Needless to say, a chronic disorder in a child can considerably increase the probability of developmental behavior difficulties, although such problems are neither insured by nor exclusive to the presence of the chronic physical disease or handicap.

It is clear from the preceding review of the applications of various techniques of behavior modification that these methods have been eminently successful when applied to common behavioral problems occurring in childhood asthmatics. But this should come as no surprise. The general effectiveness of procedures using behavior modification in the treatment of an impressively wide range of behavioral problems in children, whether in normal youngsters or in those afflicted with a chronic illness, is exceedingly well documented in the literature of applied behavior analysis. Hence, the full weight of this literature, as well as the specific successes with asthmatic youngsters, strongly supports the recommendation to apply methods of behavior modification to behavioral problems in asthmatic children. Thus, behavioral methods most certainly are among the treatments of choice for behavioral problems occurring as a result of, or in association with, asthma or any other chronic disease in children. While the available literature has dealt exclusively with childhood asthmatics, there is no reason to believe that procedures involving behavior modification should enjoy less success when appropriately applied to the asthma-related problems of adult asthma sufferers.

In summary, there has been a considerable shift in the role assigned to psychological variables in the understanding and treatment of bronchial asthma. In the past, psychological factors were thought to occupy a primary position in both the development and manifestation of asthma symptoms. It is now clear that neither of these contentions has received empirical support. It is probably no longer useful to even consider asthma a psychophysiological disorder at all, in any important sense. None of the possibilities of psychological influences in the lung, such as conditioned bronchospasm or asthma precipitated by emotion or stress, has proven valid. Correspondingly, attempts to therapeutically alter lung function through behavioral means have been disappointing, to say the least.

Clearly, a new focus is necessary. The basis for that focus can be found in the developing awareness that chronic disorders, such as asthma, have profound psychological *consequences*. While this may, at first blush, appear to signal a considerable loss of status for psychological factors, a more circumspect appraisal reveals that the new role is no less salient than the former. With this new focus, behavioral specialists would find themselves dealing with the consequences of asthma, rather than with its causes. One of those consequences, as revealed by years of experience at the National Asthma Center, is, even now, the still widely held notion that asthma is often "all in the head." The treatment of asthma requires knowledgeable, sympathetic, and sophisticated *medical* therapy and, for many victims, behavioral treatment of commensurate quality.

The fundamental rationale of behavioral intervention in asthma should be rehabilitation. The research review here points securely in this direction, as does a great deal of clinical experience. However, for some time to come, the most crucial step for behaviorists will continue to be the shedding of the misconception that psychological factors contribute to the appearance of asthma symptoms. Once free of this burdensome notion, the behavioral therapist will happily discover that demonstrably effective technologies are currently available. In the many areas in which developments are still necessary, there is no longer any need to be shackled by shopworn psychosomatic theories whose major contributions were the light shed by their own demise. In retrospect, this may not have been an ignoble fate. Much has been learned, and more remains to be discovered.

REFERENCES

Alexander, A. B. Systematic relaxation and flow rates in asthmatic children: Relationship to emotional precipitants and anxiety. *Journal of Psychosomatic Research*, 1972, *16*, 405-410.

Alexander, A. B. An experimental test of assumptions relating to the use of electromyographic biofeedback as a general relaxation training technique. *Psychophysiology*, 1975, *12*, 656-662.

Alexander, A. B. Behavioral methods in the clinical management of asthma. In W. D. Gentry and R. B. Williams (Eds.), *Behavioral approaches to medical practice*. Cambridge: Ballinger, 1977.

Alexander, A. B., Cropp, G. J. A., & Chai, H. The effects of relaxation training on pulmonary mechanics in children with asthma. *Journal of Applied Behavioral Analysis*, 1979, *12*, 27-35.

Alexander, A. B., Miklich, D. R., & Hershkoff, H. The immediate effects of systematic relaxation training on peak expiratory flow rates in asthmatic children. *Psychosomatic Medicine*, 1972, *34*, 388-394.

Alexander, A. B., White, P. D., & Wallace, H. M. Training and transfer of training effects in EMG biofeedback assisted muscular relaxation. *Psychophysiology*, 1977, *14*, 551-559.

Alexander, F. *Psychosomatic medicine*. New York: Norton, 1950.

Bernstein, I. L. Asthma in adults. In E. Middleton, C. E. Reed, & E. F. Ellis (Eds.), *Allergy: Principles and practice*. St. Louis: C. V. Mosby, 1978.

Bloch, J., Jennings, P. H., Harvey, E., & Simpson, E. Interaction between allergic potential and psychopathology in childhood asthma. *Psychosomatic Medicine*, 1964, *26*, 307-320.

Chai, H., Purcell, K., Brady, L., & Falliers, C. J. Therapeutic and investigational evaluation of asthmatic children. *Journal of Allergy*, 1968, *41*, 23-35.

Clarke, P. S. Effects of emotion and cough on airways obstructions in asthma. *Medical Journal of Australia*, 1970, *1*, 535-549.

Cooper, A. M. A case of bronchial asthma treated by behavior therapy. *Behavior Research and Therapy*, 1964, *1*, 351-356.

Creer, T. L. Biofeedback and asthma. *Advances in Asthma and Allergy*, 1974, *1*, 6-11.

Creer, T. L. Asthma: Psychological aspects and management. In E. Middleton, C. E. Reed, & E. F. Ellis (Eds.), *Allergy: Principles and practice*. St. Louis: C. V. Mosby, 1978.

Creer, T. L., & Christian, W. P. Chronically ill and handicapped children. Their management and rehabilitation. Champaign, Ill.: Research Press, 1976.

Creer, T. L., Renne, C. M., & Christian, W. P. Behavioral contributions to rehabilitation and childhood asthma. *Rehabilitation Literature*, 1976, *37*, 226-233.

Danker, P. S., Miklich, D. R., Pratt, C., & Creer. T. L. An unsuccessful attempt to instrumentally condition peak expiratory flow rates in asthmatic children. *Journal of Psychosomatic Research*, 1975, *19*, 209.

Davis, M. H., Saunders, D. R., Creer, T. L., & Chai, H. Relaxation training facilitated by biofeedback apparatus as a supplemental treatment in bronchial asthma. *Journal of Psychosomatic Research*, 1973, *17*, 121-218.

Dollard, J., & Miller, N. E. *Personality and psychotherapy*. New York: McGraw-Hill, 1950.

Edfors-Lubs, M. L. Allergy in 7000 twin pairs. *Acta Allergologica*, 1971, *26*, 249-285.

Feldman, G. M. The effect of biofeedback training on respiratory resistance of asthmatic children. *Psychosomatic Medicine*, 1976, *38*, 27-34.

French, T. M., & Alexander, F. Psychogenic factors in bronchial asthma. *Psychosomatic Medicine*, 1941, *4*, 2-94. (Monograph)

Godfrey, S., & Silverman, M. Demonstration of placebo response in asthma by means of exercise testing. *Journal of Psychosomatic Response*, 1973, *17*, 293-316.

Gold, W..M., Kessler, G. R., & Yu, D. Y. C. Role of vagus nerves in experimental asthma in allergic dogs. *Journal of Applied Physiology*, 1972, *33*, 719-725.

Hill, E. *Bronchial reactions to selected psychological stimuli and concomitant autonomic activity and asthmatic children*. Unpublished doctoral dissertation, State University of New York at Buffalo, 1975.

Kahn, A. U. Effectiveness of biofeedback and counter-conditioning in the treatment of bronchial asthma. *Journal of Psychosomatic Research*, 1977, *21*, 97-104.

Kahn, A. U., Staerk, M., & Bonk, C. Role of counter-conditioning in the treatment of asthma. *Journal of Psychosomatic Research*, 1973, *17*, 389-392.

Knapp, P. H., Mathé, A. A., & Vachon, L. Psychosomatic aspects of bronchial asthma. In E. B. Weis and M. S. Segal (Eds.), *Bronchial asthma: Its nature and management*. Boston: Little, Brown, 1976.

Kotses, H., Glaus, K. D., Crawford, P. L., Edwards, J. E., & Scherr, M. S. Operant reduction of frontalis EMG activity in the treatment of asthma in children. *Journal of Psychosomatic Research*, 1976, *20*, 453-459.

Luparello, T., Lyons, H. A., Bleecker, E. R., & McFadden, E. R., Jr. Influences of suggestion on airways reactivity in asthmatic subjects. *Psychosomatic Medicine*, 1968, *30*, 819-825.

MacKenzie, J. N. The production of the so-called "rose-cold" by means of an artificial rose, with remarks and historical notes. *American Journal of Medical Science*, 1886, *91*, 45-57.

Mathé, A. A., & Knapp, P. H. Emotional and adrenal reactions to stress in bronchial asthma. *Psychosomatic Medicine*, 1971, *33*, 323-338.

Miklich, D. R., Renne, C. M., Creer, T. L., Alexander, A. B., Chai, H., Davis, M. H., Hoffman, A., & Danker-Brown, P. The clinical utility of behavior therapy as an adjunctive treatment for asthma. *Journal of Allergy and Clinical Immunology*, 1977, *5*, 285-294.

Moore, N. Behavior therapy in bronchial asthma: A controlled study. *Journal of Psychosomatic Research*, 1965, *9*, 257-276.

Neuhaus, E. C. A personality study of asthmatic and cardiac children. *Psychosomatic Medicine*, 1958, *20*, 181-194.

Peskin, M. M. Intractable asthma of chidhood: Rehabilitation at the institutional level with a follow-up of 150 cases. *International Archives of Allergy*, 1959, *15*, 91-101.

Peskin, M. M. Management of the institutionalized child with intractable asthma. *Annals of Allergy*, 1960, *18*, 75-79.

Purcell, K. Distinctions between subgroups of asthmatic children. *Pediatrics*, 1963, *31*, 486-494.

Purcell, K., Brady, K., Chai, H., Muser, J., Molk, L., Gordon, N., & Means, J. The effect of asthma in children of experimental separation from family. *Psychosomatic Medicine*, 1969, *31*, 144-164.

Purcell, K., & Weiss, J. H. Asthma. In C. G. Costello (Ed.), *Symptoms of psychopathology*. New York: Wiley, 1970.

Rackemann, F. M. Studies in asthma: Analaysis of 213 cases in which patients were relieved for more than 2 years. *Archives of Internal Medicine*, 1928, *41*, 346-361.

Reed, C. E., & Townley, R. G. Asthma: Classification and pathogenesis. In E. Middleton, C. E. Reed, & E. F. Ellis (Eds.), *Allergy: Principles and practice*. St. Louis: C. V. Mosby, 1978.

Scherr, M. S., Crawford, P. L., Sergent, C. B., & Scherr, C. A. Effect of biofeedback techniques on chronic asthma in summer camp environment. *Annals of Allergy*, 1975, *35*, 289-295.

Siegel, S. C., Katz, R. M., & Rachelefsky, G. S. Asthma in infancy and childhood. In E. Middleton, C. E. Reed, & E. F. Ellis (Eds.), *Allergy: Principles and practice*. St. Louis: C. V. Mosby, 1978.

Smith, M. M., Colebatch, H. J. H., & Clarke, P. S. Increase and decrease in pulmonary resistance with hypnotic suggestion in asthma. *American Review of Respiratory Disease*, 1970, *102*, 236-245.

Szentivanyi, A. The beta adrenergic theory of the atopic abnormality in bronchial asthma. *Journal of Allergy*, 1968, *42*, 203-244.

Tal, A., & Miklich, D. R. Emotionally induced decreases in pulmonary flow rates in asthmatic children. *Psychosomatic Medicine*, 1976, *38*, 190-200.

Turnbull, J. W. Asthma as a learned response. *Journal of Psychosomatic Research*, 1962, *6*, 59-70.

Vachon, L., & Rich, E. S. Visceral learning in asthma. *Psychosomatic Medicine*, 1976, *38*, 122-130.

Walton, D. The application of learning theory to the treatment of a case of bronchial asthma. In H. J. Eysenck (Ed.), *Behavior therapy and the neuroses*. New York: Macmillan, 1960.

Weiss, J. H., Lyness, J., Molk, L., & Riley, J. Induced respiratory change in asthmatic children. *Journal of Psychosomatic Research*, 1976, *20*, 115-123.

Wolpe, J. *Psychotherapy by reciprocal inhibition*. Stanford: Stanford University Press, 1958.

9

ESSENTIAL HYPERTENSION:
A BEHAVIORAL PERSPECTIVE

S. Thomas Elder
Dolores J. Geoffray
Robert D. McAfee

INTRODUCTION

Historical Background

Traditionally, blood pressure (BP) has been regarded as an exclusively physiological phenomenon. In fact, the beginning of modern physiology can be traced to Harvey's (1628) landmark discovery that blood circulates throughout the body. From observations of intact mammalian heart muscle, he deduced that blood is squeezed from one chamber to the next into the pulmonary arteries and dorsal aorta through valves that open in proper sequence. When this discovery was coupled with the earlier observation of Fabricus (1603) that blood moves through the veins in only one direction because of small valves located at regular intervals along the structure, Harvey was able to argue quite forcefully that blood expelled from the heart circulates out to the periphery and back again. This was an amazingly astute observation, and, consequently, the credit for our current state of knowledge of the cardiovascular system and of the health problem of hypertension must be shared with Harvey for opening the door to a new area of investigation.

Funds for the preparation of this chapter were made available through a NHLBI grant (5 R01 HL18823-02) and by BRSG grants (RR07169-02 and RR07169-03) awarded by the Biomedical Research Support Grant Program. The authors wish to thank Charles Hill, James Hunsicker, and Marelda Parish for reading the manuscript and providing constructive criticisms and comments and Linda McMichael and Joyce Lashley for assisting with all phases of the preparation of this chapter.

The finding that blood circulated led, in turn, to other important discoveries. Among them was the observation that the pressure under which blood returns through the veins to the heart is less than the pressure under which it is propelled through the arteries to the periphery and that these parameters, in turn, are sensitive to a multitude of exteroceptive and interoceptive events. Another was the recognition that arterial pressure is not static but varies as a function of cardiac output and peripheral resistance. A third observation was that substantial elevations in BP are associated with a greater likelihood of disability, morbidity, and mortality.

It was not until the latter half of the nineteenth century that hypertension began to receive serious attention. Even then, interest was limited to post-mortem observation of hypertrophy of the kidneys, heart, and/or blood vessels. Mahomed (1877) was one of the first to attempt clinical use of crude estimates of BP in living patients and reported that increased BP could be found in some young people who were otherwise healthy, as well as in older adults prior to signs of kidney, heart, and vascular pathology. This meant that not all forms of elevated BP could be viewed as a simple product of various myocardial, pulmonary, pancreatic, and renal disease, and it paved the way for the present view that some forms of high blood pressure involve psychological processes that are subject to environmental contingencies. By the beginning of the twentieth century, hypertension was acknowledged as a serious problem of near epidemic proportions, and it soon became the focus of much epidemiologic, clinical, and experimental research.

Definition of Hypertension

Although the pathogenesis of hypertension is still not clear, some progress has been made toward understanding the problem. For example, many now agree that most cases of hypertension fall into one of two classes. On the one hand, *primary*, or *essential*, hypertension is the name given to that form of high BP that has no known physiological cause. The diagnosis is arrived at by careful exclusion of all known physiological antecedents of hypertension that are pathological, such as renal disease, Cushing's syndrome, and diabetes. *Secondary* hypertension, on the other hand, is hypertension that can be shown to be the result of physical disease.

From such a classification scheme, it is easy to presume that primary forms of hypertension are psychosomatic in origin, in contrast with secondary forms of hypertension, which are biological in nature. Such a notion does not exclude the possibility that biological antecedents to hypertension may be psychological in origin or that psychological factors that contribute to an elevation in BP may have biological referents. It simply states that instances of elevated BP can be classified on the basis of the presence or absence of immediately preceding or concurrent biological malfunctions.

If the above description is valid, control of the circulatory network should not be regarded as an exclusively involuntary system (Ranson & Clark, 1959; Winton & Bayliss, 1955). Only recently have there been experimental attempts to investigate the traditionally accepted notion of the involuntary nature of control of visceral organs, to clarify the meaning of such terms as *psychological* or *psychosomatic*, and to identify specific environmental and/or behavioral factors that contribute to the development and regulation of high blood pressure. Until recently, the doctrine that denies voluntary control of visceral effectors by the autonomic nervous system was rarely challenged. There is now an increasing amount of data, however, that suggests that BP may be brought under voluntary control and, therefore, may be subject to the established laws of learning. These behavioral considerations are the focus of the present chapter.

THEORETICAL CONSIDERATIONS

The subject of this discussion is *essential hypertension*, which has been attributed primarily to *psychological causes*. Thus, it seems appropriate to give some attention to the use of the term *psychological* within this context. Since essential hypertension is determined by the exclusion of identifiable, antecedent physiological pathology, then, perhaps, to a diagnostician, *psychological* is an adjective used to modify the noun *cause*, so that it refers to every event responsible for the development of hypertension that cannot be categorized as secondary. In short, psychological, in this context, means everything that is not biological. In this sense, the phrase is so general as to be without meaning. On the other hand, *psychological cause*, as used in mental-health circles, refers to hypothetical, underlying, elusive, psychodynamic forces that influence anatomical and physiological mechanisms, such as the cardiovasculature, under cover of the unconscious. Here, too, the term is used as a label for a host of factors and forces that remain obscure because they are not tied down, in any systematic way, to observable events. Another vague use of the term *psychological cause* refers to an array of unspecified environmental factors usually labeled as stressful and designated, a priori, as events to be avoided as much as possible. In none of the above cases, however, has the term been operationally defined. The question is, What does the term *psychology* or *psychological* mean? There is substantial agreement among behavioral scientists today that the acquisition, maintenance, and replacement of conditioned responses or response patterns take place in orderly ways and that, on the basis of the currently available data, these can be sorted into one of two models representing the basic fundamental processes, *classical* conditioning and *instrumental* (operant) conditioning. In the former case, discrete and unidirectional changes in motor and visceral behavior of relatively short duration can be brought about. In the latter instance, not only can bidirectional changes be established in motor and, perhaps, visceral responses but the topography of the behavior can be rearranged through a process called *shaping*. For this reason, the noun and adjective *psychology* and *psychological* will be put aside throughout this discussion in favor of the term *conditioning*. Moreover, the model of operant conditioning will provide the conceptual vantage point from which the current status of the problem of operant BP conditioning will be examined, since this model offers the options of bidirectional changes in behavior, and classical conditioning does not. In addition, it forms a basis from which the acquisition of some instances of hypertension may be explained, as will be illustrated in the section on etiology.

It is difficult to see how classical conditioning might be used to explain the onset or the amelioration of essential hypertension. It is much easier to postulate the etiology and therapeutic control of primary hypertension by invoking such principles as shaping, differential and partial reinforcement, and instrumental extinction.

ETIOLOGY

Since the origins of essential hypertension are not clear, there is little that can be said about the etiology of this form of high BP. There is evidence to show that such factors as diet, exercise, sodium intake, stress, and smoking are significant in the pathogenesis of essential hypertension, but these appear to be necessary, rather than sufficient, conditions. Although body weight, salt consumption, smoking, and reaction to stress are amenable to control through behavioral analysis, these matters are broad and complex and warrant consideration under separate title. They are mentioned here only because they are known to contribute to the etiology of all forms of hypertension in various ways. Instead, the following sections of the chapter will concentrate on the control of BP through the use of behavioral analysis.

In keeping with the theoretical orientation of this chapter, it is suggested that the unique history, in terms of operant conditioning, of the hypertensive individual may play a more fundamental role than has hitherto been proposed. By assuming that BP can be altered when appropriate contingencies are present, it may then be argued that, in some cases, elevations in BP may be accounted for in terms of the history of contingent reinforcement of BP of the organism.

Consider the hypothetical case of a young, normotensive journalist who, after searching diligently and with little success, finally obtains part-time employment on a neighborhood newspaper. Several weeks later, when the entire reporting staff is on assignment, the editor learns of a fast-breaking story and gives it to the inexperienced reporter for want of a better alternative. This is the break the novice has been waiting for, and he jumps at the chance to prove himself. Under conditions of sympathetic activation — vasoconstriction, release of adrenaline and noradrenaline — and all the changes that accompany these events, he races to the scene, pieces together a story, prepares a narrative, and lays it on the editor's desk just in time to get it in the next edition. The editor reads it and, in utter amazement, calls the young journalist into his office and rewards him with verbal praise, a bonus, and a promise of greater opportunities to come.

When this happens, an elaborate configuration of behavior is reinforced, including an elevation in BP that resulted originally as an unconditioned reaction and yet is now somewhat more likely to continue because of contingent reinforcement. Among the many consequences of this relationship of multiple, response-contingent feedback are, first, improved performance as a reporter and, second, an increased likelihood that elevated BP will reoccur in similar future situations as an operant response as well as a reflexive unconditioned response to neural and humoral events. Furthermore, the multitude of interoceptive as well as exteroceptive stimuli that are present become conditioned and discriminative stimuli for various components of the total response complex as they are classically and instrumentally conditioned.

The opportunities for similar response-contingent feedback to reoccur intermittently over a journalism career are enormous. After 30 years of adventitious partial reinforcement for elevations in BP, all the necessary conditions are present for our successful journalist to develop chronic hypertension as an acquired response. At that point, his situation is critical, because his hypertension is strongly resistant to extinction, and, the longer his BP remains high, the greater the prospect becomes that primary hypertension may produce pathology, such as kidney damage, which, in turn, would lead to secondary hypertension. Thus, according to this anal/sis, conditioned primary hypertension, which is theoretically reversible, may lead to secondary hypertension, which may not be reversed with equal ease.

There are many parallels to the story just recited and for that reason, it is tempting to attribute to it an empirical validity that it does not now have. On an a posteriori basis, however, it makes just enough sense to warrant experimental investigation. Harris, Gilliam, Findley, and Brady (1973) attempted, with some success, to develop an experimental animal model of operantly conditioned chronic hypertension, but their work with baboons is expensive, and ways must be found to accomplish the same experimental objectives with small laboratory animals, such as rats. If tonic increase in BP can be shaped in a rat by differentially reinforcing successive approximations to hypertensive levels, then instrumental conditioning must be added to the many other factors that play a part in the etiology of essential hypertension. There is some evidence that the bidirectional changes in the BP of normotensive subjects can be conditioned instrumentally, but these data are to be considered in a later section.

MEASUREMENT

Blood pressure can be measured *directly* or *indirectly*. Direct measurement requires invasion of the arterial tree, and, for this reason, it is used less frequently than indirect measurement, which does not require penetrating the subject's body.

Direct Methods

The direct measurement of BP can be performed in one of two ways. In the first method, one end of a catheter is inserted into a vessel, and the other is attached to an external transducer. Common practice has been to puncture the brachial arteries when direct BP measurements are done on humans (Seldinger, 1953). The abdominal aorta or other large vessels, such as the femoral and carotoid arteries, are entered when direct BP measurements are made on animals, such as rats (DiCara, Pappas, & Pointer, 1969; Still & Whitcomb, 1956), cats (Hakumaki, 1970), dogs (Anderson & Brady, 1973), monkeys (Werdegard, Johnson, & Mason, 1964), and baboons (Perez-Cruet, Plumlee, & Newton, 1966).

The second method involves the use of a small sensing device implanted within one of the larger cavities, such as the dorsal aorta or atrium of the heart. Although this method creates the prospect of monitoring BP in freely moving subjects — perhaps even in their natural environments — it is difficult to use in practice. Calibration to correct for transducer drift is a problem, as are the effects of body fluids on electrical devices. Chronic preparations can be made with both methods. However, the first of the two has been the one most frequently chosen in biobehavioral research, simply because it is less difficult to maintain patency of the system over extended periods of time.

Indirect Methods

Standard clinical practice has been to measure BP of adult humans by wrapping a cuff (13 centimeters wide and 23 centimeters long) that contains an inflatable bladder around the upper left arm, inflating the bladder rapidly until the superficial artery under the cuff has been completely occluded, placing a stethoscope at the distal margin of the cuff over the brachial artery, and detecting Korotkoff (K) sounds as the cuff is gradually deflated. These operations have been schematically illustrated in Figure 9.1. The initial, rapid inflation of the cuff is represented by a steadily increasing line, and subsequent, gradual deflation of the cuff is illustrated by the descending arm of the function. Across the horizontal time axis, the appearance and disappearance of a series of K sounds are illustrated by the inverted, U-shaped function superimposed between the boundaries of systolic blood pressure (SBP) and diastolic blood pressure (DBP). Note that SBP is defined as the level of cuff pressure at which the first sound is detected and that the level at which the last sound is heard is referred to as the DBP threshold. The first sound appears abruptly as a loud snapping noise, then becomes somewhat muffled, and gradually grows louder again.

FIGURE 9.1
A Representation of the Pressure in an Arm Cuff and the
Output of an Embedded Microphone during Cuff Deflation

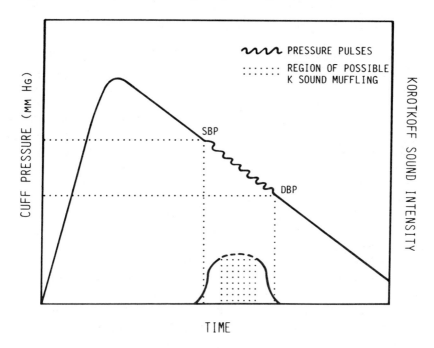

TIME

The point in time at which the last sound disappears is not always as easily identified. Thus, what is actually measured by this procedure is cuff pressure at points that are boundaries of a series of K sounds. A microphone may be substituted for the stethoscope, and the resulting signal is made audible through headphones or a speaker; but the basic procedure is the same. It was developed by Riva-Rocci (1896), has been shown to correlate fairly well with direct measures of BP (Hamilton, Woodbury, & Harper, 1936; Roberts, Smiley, & Manning, 1953; Roman, Henry, & Meehan, 1965; Woodbury, Robinow, & Hamilton, 1938), and still has wide clinical use.

Automated versions of the Riva-Rocci technique have been employed in some conditioning studies (Blanchard, Young, & Haynes, 1975; Elder & Eustis, 1975; Elder, Leftwich, & Wilkerson, 1974; Elder, Ruiz, Deabler, & Dillenkoffer, 1973; Richter-Heinrich, Knust, Muller, Schmidt, & Sprung, 1975). These devices operate on the same principle as the Riva-Rocci method, except that cuff inflation and deflation are regulated electronically and K sounds are detected through a microphone embedded in the distal margin of the occluding cuff. In this way, systolic and diastolic BP can be measured indirectly at regular intervals (usually 0.5 to 5.0 minutes) and at distances of up to eight meters from the subject, the rate of cuff inflation and deflation can be varied (usually 2.5 to

25.0 mm Hg per second), K sounds and cuff pressure can be displayed on a strip chart or recorded digitally, and binary auditory and/or visual stimuli can be generated to signal the occurrence of some previously determined criterion BP response.

As interest in the possibility of monitoring BP on a continuous basis began to grow, timely and innovative ways of measuring it were necessarily devised. One such method, developed at Harvard (Shapiro, Tursky, Gershon, & Stern, 1969; Tursky, 1974), required inflating a standard cuff until the systolic (or diastolic) pressure was reached and then recording electrocardiogram (EKG) signals and K sounds while cuff pressure was held constant at that level for a fixed number of heartbeats (usually 50 beats per minute) or a fixed interval (usually 65 seconds). In order to condition individuals to increase their systolic (or diastolic) BP, feedback was administered whenever a K sound was detected. Conditioned decreases were brought about by delivering the feedback signal (light, tone, slides) whenever a heartbeat occurred unaccompanied by an audible K sound. Shaping was carried out by gradually shifting the level of fixed pressure of the cuff in the desired direction from trial to trial. In other words, this approach is based on a procedure of threshold detection, in which BP levels are defined as the cuff pressure at which K sounds are detected 50% of the time. In order to implement these operations, it is necessary to record the R wave of the EKG signal as well as the K sounds, and this, in turn, requires the use of an on-line laboratory computer. In addition, there is the problem of rapid changes in BP threshold, such as those that occur in the case of the Valsalva maneuver, which cannot be followed by a method that requires 50 beats per minute or 65 seconds of recording in order to determine the threshold.

An alternate method, developed by Dworkin and Miller at Rockefeller University (Miller, DiCara, Solomon, Weiss, & Dworkin, 1970), involved adjusting pressure in a standard cuff every several heartbeats so as to hold the intensity of the K sounds constant. In this case, adjusted cuff pressure served as an index of moment-to-moment fluctuation in systolic (or diastolic) pressure. Subjects were trained to regulate their BP by listening to a tone that varied in pitch in proportion to changes in cuff pressure. This approach offers the advantage of following changes in BP more closely, even without the use of EKG signals. However, as does the Harvard method, this one also requires the use of an on-line computer. An additional difficulty with this approach is that, by adjusting cuff pressure in order to hold constant the upper or lower boundary intensity of the K sound, one obtains an absolute measure of BP that is always slightly below threshold value, in the former case, and slightly above it, in the latter case.

More recently, a group at the University of New Orleans (Elder, Longacre, Welsh, & McAfee, 1977) designed and constructed instrumentation and a method of usage (hereinafter referred to as the UNO system) that incorporate some features of both the Harvard and Rockefeller methods. Specifically, the operation of adjusted cuff pressure from the Rockefeller method was coupled with the Harvard procedure of detecting the lower (or upper) pressure thresholds for the detection of K sounds, but without the use of EKG signals. The system was operated by fitting the subject with the standard cuff, which contained an embedded microphone to pick up K sounds, on each arm. The cuffs were inflated alternately for 100-second intervals, during which cuff pressure was constantly readjusted by means of a logic-tracking algorithm and miniature pneumatic valves. A relatively continuous record of BP was obtained by overlapping inflation of one cuff with deflation of the other and transducing cuff pressure. The output was either displayed on a meter calibrated in mm Hg, traced with a strip chart recorder, and/or collected on-line with a laboratory computer. Conditioning was implemented by providing the subject with an auditory (or visual) feedback signal, which varied in pitch (or intensity) with cuff pressure.

Later, it became apparent that left and right cuff microphones may have differing sensitivities and outputs, possibly resulting in artifactual differences in BP measures from the left and right arms. For this reason, cuff placement had to be accurate in order to insure proper location of microphones. A newer model of the UNO device, therefore, was developed (Longacre, Elder, & McAfee, 1977) to allow tracking on the basis of pulse pressure rather than detection of K sounds. By eliminating the use of microphones used to pick up K sounds and measuring BP from both arms with the same pressure transducer, any observed left-right differences in BP may be regarded as reliable, since they cannot be attributed to differential characteristics or placement of microphones or to differences in properties of parallel transducers. Both the model using pulse pressure and that utilizing tracking of K sounds have been compared with direct, indwelling catheter measurements, and these data have been summarized in Table 9.1. Both compare well with the direct method when the subject is relatively inactive. The correlation drops when the subject grips a dynamometer or performs a Valsalva maneuver.

A photograph of the laboratory configuration of the UNO system is contained in Figure 9.2. It is relatively inexpensive, easy to operate, and portable. Indeed, the pulse pressure model, including cuffs, speaker, and air supply, was actually installed in a briefcase with the idea of home use in mind.

The use of information on finger pulse by Brener and Kleinman (1970) to measure BP represents a different approach to the problem. Their subjects were fitted with a cuff wrapped around the left index finger in such a way as to leave a portion of the dorsal surface exposed, and pulses were detected with a crystal sensor placed distally to the occluding cuff. A continuous record of SBP was obtained by raising cuff pressure approximately five mm Hg each time a pulse was detected and reducing cuff pressure three mm Hg per second in the absence of a pulse. Feedback was provided in the form of a manometer gauge and an electromagnetic counter, which operated at a rate that was proportional to cuff pressure. Advantages of this approach were that it minimized venous congestion, since the cuff was not wrapped completely around the finger,

TABLE 9.1
Pearson Coefficient of Correlation between Continuous Direct
and Indirect Measures of Diastolic Blood Pressure

| | *Subject No.* | | | |
	1	*2*	*3*	*4*
Age	46	60	36	47
Sex	M	M	F	F
Resting	.87	.98	.82	.96
Valsalva	.82	N.A.	N.A.	.52
Hand Grip	.42	.33	.58	.84
Tilt	N.A.*	.75	N.A.	.68

*N.A. = Not available.

Note: The authors wish to thank Barbara Christie, Franz Messerli, and Jose de Carvalho for assisting in the collectin of the data from which these correlations were determined.

and that it was fairly simple and inexpensive to construct and operate. One disadvantage, however, was that cuff pressure was raised in steps of five mm Hg and reduced in steps of three mm Hg. More accurate tracking might be accomplished by raising and lowering cuff pressure by smaller amounts.

Jernstedt and Newcomer (1974); Gribben, Steptoe, and Sleight (1976); and Steptoe, Smulyan, and Gribbin (1976) have described the use of pulse wave velocity (PWV) as a way of monitoring beat-by-beat changes in arterial pressure. Basically, their procedure involved determining the transit time for a given pulse wave from the most prominent component (the R component of the EKG) to the upstroke of a peripherally recorded pulse wave. Although this method does not provide absolute values of BP, Jernstedt and Newcomer reported Pearson correlation coefficients between it and arterial transmural pressure values on the order of 0.90 to 0.97, and Steptoe, Smulyan, and Gribbin obtained correlations of −0.91 to −0.98 between PWV values and BP scores determined by arterial cannulation.

Although the relationship between transit time and blood pressure is impressive, there are several features of the PWV measure that need to be considered when its use as a dependent variable in behavioral studies is contemplated. First, according to Smulyan (1978), the slope of the regressions of transit time on blood pressure varies from one subject to the next and from day to day within subjects. Second, it does not yield a measure of absolute BP but is based on the extent of relative change. Third, accurate placement of the pulse wave detector is difficult on a day-to-day basis, which is required in many types of conditioning studies, and artifacts produced by movement constitute a continuing problem. Finally, the system is expensive.

FIGURE 9.2
Photograph of Laboratory Configuration of the UNO Tracking System. Photograph shows speaker (A), wall-mounted mercury manometers used for calibration (B), tracking module (C), and external air flow meters that permit fine adjustment of air inflow during tracking mode (D).

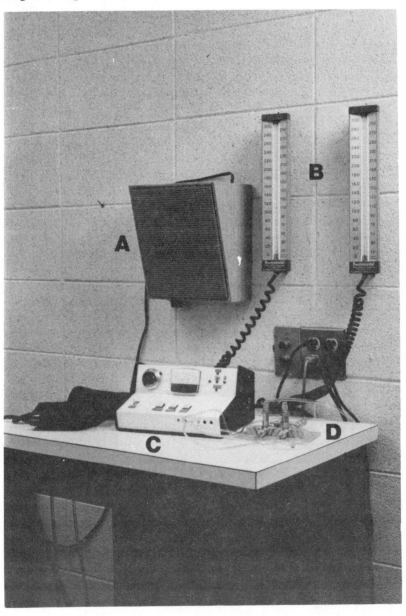

Geddes and Newberg (1977) suggested that a continuous record of changes in BP can be obtained by implementing the same principle on which Erlanger's (1904) oscillometric sphygmomanometer was based. According to them, when a partially inflated cuff is wrapped around the upper arm, pulsations are transmitted to the cuff and can be detected and recorded as oscillations in cuff pressure. If cuff pressure is set just above the point at which maximum oscillations are observed, an increase in BP is seen as an increase in pulse amplitude. If cuff pressure is set just below the point that sets up maximum oscillations, an increase in BP appears as a decrease in pulse amplitude. By recording cuff pressure and amplitude of the oscillations in cuff pressure, a continuous record of relative changes in BP is obtained.

Of somewhat more recent vintage is a device developed by Schneider (1978). This device also makes use of an occlusion cuff, microphone, air supply, and two mercury manometers. The cuff is inflated rapidly to a level above the subject's systolic threshold. It is then bled slowly until a K sound occurs. At that point, a column of mercury from one manometer in series with the cuff is locked into place, and absolute SBP can be read, even though the cuff continues to deflate. When pressure declines to some predetermined value, the cuff rapidly inflates again, and the cycle is repeated. This time, however, a column of mercury from the second manometer is locked into position when the first K sound in the descending series is located. The subject is thus able to compare the two columns. On the third inflation cycle, the first column of mercury drops and then rises in correspondence with rapid inflation of the cuff, followed by a slow reduction in pressure until the first K sound is detected. At that point, the first mercury column is again locked into place. And so the sequence is repeated, and the subject is able to compare his or her BP score with the immediately preceding one.

Although the system represents a rather unique approach, it has one possibly serious disadvantage. Repetitive rapid inflation of the occluding cuff simulates the delivery of repeated blows to the arm and underlying tissue and, depending on the state of the tissue, will sooner or later produce spasms in the skeletal musculature as well as the muscle layer of the arterial wall. The trauma inherent in the system places an early limit on the duration with which it can be used to monitor BP reliably.

Lee, Caldwell, and Lee (1977) described two versions of a tracking system that has some features in common with the UNO device. Both versions make use of an occlusion cuff, microphone for detection of K sounds, and compressed air supply, and both may be used to monitor systolic or diastolic BP. The two versions of the Lee et al. (1977) method differ in two respects. First, the inflation and deflation intervals are 45 seconds in the "fast-tracking" model and five seconds each in the "continuous" tracking system. Second, in the fast-tracking model, increments in cuff pressure occur in steps of two mm Hg when a K sound is detected, and, when K sounds fail to occur, decrements in cuff pressure of the same magnitude are made. In the continuous method, the number of

K sounds detected during a given inflation cycle of five seconds determines the initial pressure of the next inflation, and, throughout the cycle, cuff pressure is bled about three mm Hg.

Summary

For investigators or clinicians who need a method for measuring BP indirectly, there are at least nine possible choices. These are listed and described in Table 9.2. Most investigators have preferred the use of discrete training trials for reasons that are not obvious from their reports. Absolute values of BP can be obtained from five methods, and some kind of occluding cuff is necessary in all but one of them. Generally, reliability data are sparse. In fact, only two laboratories (see Table 9.2) have compared their indirect measurements with simultaneously obtained direct measurements of BP. Strong positive correlations were found in both cases, provided the subject remained relatively quiet.

Unfortunately, more complete comparison and contrast of the measurement properties of each method are not now available. In such an important problem area as conditioned BP behavior, it is desirable that a more comprehensive experimental analysis of these nine methods be made available at an early date.

ANIMAL STUDIES OF INSTRUMENTAL CONDITIONING OF BLOOD PRESSURE

In the wake of reports that galvanic skin response (Kimmel, 1967), salivation (Brown & Katz, 1967; Miller & Carmona, 1967), and heart rate (HR) (DiCara & Miller, 1968a) can be increased and/or decreased by instrumental conditioning, DiCara and Miller (1968b) trained some curarized rats to increase, and others to decrease, their SBP. First, their subjects were prepared with a catheter inserted into the lower one-third of the dorsal aorta, so that SBP could be recorded directly and continuously. Then, signaled shock escape-avoidance training was carried out by presenting a 1,000 Hertz tone, the onset of which was followed 7.5 seconds later by pulsed electric shock to the rat's tail. The shaping principle was observed by systematically adjusting the criterion BP level required to successfully postpone shock.

DiCara and Miller reported that subjects in the increase BP condition learned to raise their SBP approximately 22% and that those in the decrease BP condition learned to lower their SBP as much as 19% of their basal pressures. Since the experimental animals were compared with yoked controls, the observed changes in SBP could not be attributed to the amount and pattern of electric shock received by the two groups. Throughout the single session, HR and SBP were recorded simultaneously. When changes in SBP were correlated with changes in HR, the observed $r = 0.08$ was not significant. The observed $r = 0.39$ between HR and SBP in the case of the yoked controls also was not significant.

TABLE 9.2
Indirect Methods for Measuring Blood Pressure

Originator and/or Developer	Basic Principle	Type of Measurement	Correlation with Riva-Rocci Method	Correlation with Direct Method
Shapiro et al., 1969 Tursky, 1974	K sound detection	Continuous[a], absolute	—[b]	—
Miller et al., 1970	K sound detection	Continuous[a], absolute	—	—
Brener and Kleinman, 1970	Finger pulse	Continuous, relative	—	—
Jernstedt and Newcomer, 1974 Gribbin et al., 1976 Steptoe et al., 1976	Pulse wave velocity	Continuous, relative	—	BP $r = 0.95$
Elder et al., 1977	K sound detection	Continuous[a], absolute	DBP $r = 0.94$, SBP $r = 0.94$	DBP $r = 0.90$, SBP $r = 0.91$
Longacre et al., 1977	Pulse wave detection	Continuous, relative	—	DBP $r = 0.89$, SBP $r = 0.91$
Erlanger, 1904	Pulsatile oscillations in cuff pressure	Continuous[a], relative	—	—
Lee et al., 1977	K sound detection	Continuous, absolute	—	—
Schneider, 1978	K sound detection	Discrete, absolute	—	—

[a]A continuous record may be obtained provided the subject is fitted with a standard cuff on each arm and no time is lost in switching from one cuff to the other.
[b]No comparison was made.

Source: Compiled by the authors.

Several features of this study warrant careful consideration. DiCara and Miller reported that subjects in the increase group raised their SBP 31 mm Hg in 144 minutes of training and that those in the decrease group lowered theirs 27 mm Hg in 152 minutes of training. Thus, they succeeded in training their animals to change their SBP 19% or more within 2.5 to 3 hours of continuous training. It is important to note, however, that the baseline levels of 139 to 140 mm Hg observed here were approximately 30 mm Hg higher than those Shapiro and Milhado (1958) found in normotensive laboratory rats. Several factors may account for this elevation in the operant BP level of the curarized rat, including the kind of anesthesia used during insertion of the catheter, the curare preparation used to immobilize the animal for 2.5 hours or more, and possible strain, age, and/or sex differences between the two samples. If this particular situation is governed by the law of initial values (Wilder, 1962), the decrements in pressure observed here are easily understood, but the increments then pose a problem. If rats can raise their SBP 27 mm Hg above a baseline of 140 mm Hg in 152 minutes, where does the upper limit rest? The law of initial values dictates that only large decreases and small increases are to be expected from a spuriously elevated baseline. Perhaps curare acts to disengage mechanisms that otherwise set physiological limits on the susceptibility of visceral effectors to direct environmental influences. That sharp, large-magnitude drops and elevations in blood pressure may be constrained by somatocardiovascular interactions is, however, a matter for future experimental investigation.

To determine whether freely moving rats trained to increase or decrease SBP would perform the conditioned BP response later in the curarized state, Pappas, DiCara, and Miller (1970) used subjects prepared and trained in much the same way as those in the DiCara and Miller experiment. Rats with indwelling aortic cannulas were divided into two groups. Using a signaled shock escape-avoidance paradigm, one group was trained to raise, and the other to lower, its BP. After 200 ten-second training trials, both groups showed significant BP changes in the appropriate direction, but there was no evidence of reliable differences between the two groups in terms of HR, locomotor activity, or the amount of shock received. In fact, both groups showed a significant reduction in HR, and stabilimeter activity scores showed that both groups exhibited significant decreases in overall locomotor and gross body movements.

Retention tests and additional conditioning trials were given the next day, with the animals under curare and supported with a respirator. After 30 minutes of adaptation to the procedure, ten test trials for retention were followed by 100 additional shock-avoidance training trials. All subjects showed an increase in BP during retention. When acquisition trials were resumed, however, appropriate changes developed between the group trained to raise BP and the group trained to lower it. Thus, it appears that increases and decreases in BP can be acquired in the noncurarized as well as the curarized state. However, there was no evidence that acquired BP responses transferred from the noncurarized to the curarized condition.

Several points of interest are contained in the Pappas et al. data. First, their baseline SBP levels of 118 to 122 mm Hg observed during the free-moving training session (session 1) more nearly approached those characteristic of normotensive rats. This may have been the result of the free-training adaptation period, the fact that the subjects were free of curare, or both. That curare has some tendency to elevate BP levels was evident when Pappas et al. tested and retrained their rats in the curarized state the next day. Following injections of curare, BP rose approximately six mm Hg, thereby moving baseline more in the direction of the level of 140 mm Hg reported by DiCara and Miller. Second, interpretation of these results would have been facilitated by some important control data from a group of rats who received only shocks over sessions 1 and 2. Appropriate interpretation of data such as these requires an accurate account of the unconditioned response of BP to repetitive shock. Third, it is unfortunate that neither Pappas et al. nor DiCara and Miller saw fit to include a no-training control group. Therefore, we do not know what kind of changes in BP might take place over time in either the curarized or noncurarized states.

Unlike the procedure in the two previous studies, in which instrumental BP responses were shaped or by making shock postponement contingent upon appropriate changes in BP, that utilized by Benson, Herd, Morse, and Kelleher (1969) began with use of an unconditioned stimulus (UCS) to elicit a BP response of relatively large magnitude. This response was later maintained under discriminative stimulus control by shifting to a BP response-shock aversion contingency. Squirrel monkeys, which had been used in previous studies, were trained on signal to emit up to 30 key presses in order to terminate the warning signal and avoid an electric shock to the tail. Whenever the subject failed to produce the prerequisite number of key presses within 30 seconds of signal onset, shock was administered every 15 seconds until the animal performed the appropriate number of responses or had received a total of ten successive shocks. When stable instrumental avoidance (30 key presses within 15 to 20 seconds of onset of shock signal), accompanied by large elevations in BP (classically conditioned to onset of shock signal), was obtained, a second and alternative shock escape-avoidance contingency was added. By raising mean arterial BP five to ten mm Hg for one to four seconds, the subject illuminated a blue light (feedback signal), shock was avoided, and the shock signal terminated. Thus, the animal could avoid shock by performing an instrumental skeletal response or an instrumental BP response. Later, the key was removed, and shock could be avoided only by the occurrence of contingent elevations in arterial BP. During the final phase of the study, the schedule was reversed. In this instance, successful avoidance of shock could be accomplished only by decreases in BP.

This study deserves careful attention because of the skillful way in which an unconditioned visceral response, which accompanied execution of an instrumental motor response, was substituted later for the motor operant by transferring a shock contingency from the motor to the visceral response. Also worthy of note is the fact that, once it was apparent that elevated arterial BP could be maintained as an instrumental avoidance response, baseline levels could be restored by simply making BP reductions contingent on shock avoidance and conditioning a "decrease" response.

There are, however, some methodological problems that limit the usefulness of these data. For example, the sample size was unduly small; no control data were provided; the subjects had served in several previous experiments, thereby confounding their past conditioning histories with the independent variables; and a demonstration that the same subjects could be trained, using the same conditioning procedure, to lower their BP below baseline levels was conspicuously absent. This last point applies equally well to the studies described below, in which baboons were used as experimental subjects. Thus, the Benson et al. data may be taken as suggestive, but not conclusive, evidence of an effect.

Plumlee (1969) also used a signaled escape-avoidance paradigm. He trained four monkeys to raise their DBP by presenting a ten-second tone that terminated coincidently with electric shock to the animal's tail. Within 30 days, DBP elevations of 60 mm Hg above baseline were produced by some of the animals. These large elevations in DBP, however, were of short duration, beginning only at the onset of the warning signal and falling quickly to baseline levels when the signal ended.

In contrast, a sustained elevation of DBP of 50 to 60 mm Hg above baseline was obtained in baboons by Harris, Findley, and Brady (1971). The animals were first shaped to raise their DBP above 125 mm Hg for five seconds. Then they were shifted to a multiple schedule involving three components. First, in the presence of a white light, food was available on a fixed ratio schedule of reinforcement for lever pressing. Second, in the presence of a red light, a nine milliampere shock was delivered to the subject through a chest-band electrode whenever DBP fell below the criterion level. The third component consisted of an intermediate time phase interspersed between the white and red light. The animal could restore illumination of the white light by maintaining DBP at some criterion level. If DBP fell below this level, the red light came back on, signaling that the shock-avoidance schedule again prevailed. In general, the effect of this schedule was positive reinforcement for elevations in DBP in one condition and negative reinforcement for elevated DBP in the other.

Harris et al. (1973) also reported sustained DBP elevations of at least 30 mm Hg in baboons. This was accompanied by initial, but gradually decreasing, elevations in HR. The animals were trained with concurrent use of instrumental food reward and signaled escape-avoidance procedure. Blood pressure, systolic as well as diastolic, was measured by a catheter lodged in the femoral artery caudal to the iliac bifurcation. Whenever DBP remained above some predetermined criterion level for a minimum of ten minutes, the baboon was given five one-gram food pellets. Shock was delivered to the animal's tail whenever DBP dropped below criterion values for 30 seconds. Training was carried out for at least 40 consecutive sessions, and each session lasted 12 hours.

Using baboons and a procedure for preparation and training that was very similar to that of Harris et al. (1973), Goldstein, Harris, and Brady (1977a) went on to assess the possible effects of alpha and beta baroreceptor blocking agents on acquired hypertension. When the subjects demonstrated a DBP of 20 mm Hg difference between the average pressure during the last ten minutes immediately preceding onset of a training session and the first ten minutes of the session, stable elevated DBP was said to have developed. At that point, the effects of baroreceptor reflexes were assessed. Phentolamine or phenoxybenzamine was used to block alpha receptors, and propranolol was used to block beta receptors. Neither the alpha nor beta blocker decreased DBP significantly, although beta blockade did abolish the tachycardia that accompanied onset of the session. Combined alpha and beta blockade did reduce the conditioned increases in SBP and DBP, but the observed decrement was not large enough to cancel out the original increase in DBP and thereby restore it to baseline levels.

In a more recent study, Goldstein, Harris, and Brady (1977b), using baboons with catheters lodged in the femoral or carotid arteries, explored sensitivity changes in the baroreflex during periods of conditioned DBP elevations. Whenever a subject produced an increase in DBP, it received one gram of food and avoided shock. Whenever it failed to do so, food was withheld, and a shock of eight mA was applied to the animal's tail. Thus trained, the baboons were able to maintain significant elevations of DBP in order to obtain food and avoid shock.

All the studies in this section are similar in that direct BP measurements were employed, escape-avoidance formed all or part of the training regimen, the subjects were all rats or monkeys, and shaping was an integral part of the training program.

There were several prominent differences. For example, Miller and his associates trained their rats in one session, made avoidance of shock contingent upon changes in SBP, and conditioned up and down responses by training some animals to raise, and others to lower, their blood pressure. The other studies used squirrel monkeys or baboons, trained their subjects over days, weeks, and even months, and made a combination of shock avoidance and food reinforcement contingent upon increase in blood pressure. There are also differences among the latter group of experiments (Goldstein et al., 1977a, 1977b; Harris et al., 1973; Plumlee, 1969). Plumlee used discriminated shock avoidance (discrete trials) and produced changes in BP that were of large magnitude and short duration, while Harris et al. and Goldstein et al. used a combination of food reinforcement, escape-avoidance, and biofeedback to produce responses of equally large magnitude and relatively long duration.

Conspicuously absent from the currently available data are demonstrations that bidirectional changes in BP can be conditioned through the use of differential positive reinforcements (such as food, water, or electrical stimulation of reward sites in the brain), the use of secondary reinforcers to maintain a BP response once it has occurred, implementation of partial reinforcement to increase resistance to extinction, asymptotic levels of performance, stimulus control and stimulus generalization of acquired BP behavior, and extinction and reacquisition characteristics of instrumentally conditioned BP responses.

Before a definitive decision can be reached regarding the generality of laws of instrumental motor learning to visceral learning, including BP, data bearing on the above points must be assembled, and the gaps in the existing body of knowledge must be filled.

STUDIES WITH NORMOTENSIVE SUBJECTS

The amount of training plays a very significant part in the acquisition of motor and verbal responses and doubtless would play an important role in the acquisition of BP responses, as either a free or a discriminated operant. To emphasize this point, this section has been organized into three parts: studies with one training session, studies with two to four training sessions, and studies with five or more training sessions.

Studies with One Training Session

Some of the studies carried out to determine whether subjects can be trained to change their BP involved the use of a single training session. One of the first studies aimed at teaching human subjects to control their BP is a case in point. Shapiro et al. (1969) set out to train ten subjects to raise, and ten others to lower, their SBP. The subjects were normotensive males. All received 25, 65-second acquisition trials, with intertrial intervals lasting from 20 to 25 seconds. Whenever a K sound occurred, those in the increase group received brief (100-millisecond) exteroceptive feedback (light and tone). Whenever a K sound was not detected, subjects in the decrease group received the same feedback. Supplemental (augmented) feedback consisted of a photograph of a nude female figure displayed on a screen for five seconds after every twentieth presentation of the exteroceptive feedback stimuli. Thus, binary feedback consisting of light and tone was delivered on a continuous reinforcement schedule, and presentation of the photograph occurred on fixed-ratio 20. Comparison of the performance of the two groups showed that, in the increase group, subjects demonstrated an initial increase of small magnitude in SBP that was of short duration. Those in the decrease group eventually reduced their SBP approximately four mm Hg by the end of the single training session.

Beyond the fact that these data represent a pioneering effort, there is little that can be inferred from them. The absence of a control group, the failure of the increase group to sustain an elevation in SBP until the end of the training session, and the use of confounded reinforcements and reinforcement schedules make it difficult to conclude that the experiment was successful. That the decrease group lowered its SBP four mm Hg in one session is not particularly impressive, since a reduction of this magnitude may be attributed to passive relaxation on the part of the subject or may have developed as a result of adaptation or habituation to the apparatus and procedure.

From recordings of HR made simultaneously with SBP, Shapiro et al. observed a decline in HR for both the increase and decrease groups over the course of the session. This prompted Shapiro, Tursky, and Schwartz (1970) to investigate whether or not subjects might learn to raise or lower their BP without simultaneously raising or lowering their HR. In their study, 20 male subjects were distributed randomly over four cells of a two-by-two design, in which increases and decreases in HR were compared with increases and decreases in SBP. Respiration, HR, and SBP were recorded simultaneously from all subjects over a single series of acquisition trials. Light and tone feedback followed every correct response, and the photograph of a nude female was presented on a fixed-ratio 20 schedule in keeping with the procedure of Shapiro et al. (1969).

Evidence for SBP conditioning was equivocal, but, when the performance scores of a few subjects who showed some evidence of conditioning were grouped with a set of similar scores from the Shapiro et al. (1969) study, they yielded evidence for conditioned SBP effects without corresponding changes in HR. No corresponding changes in respiration were observed. Combining the best performance data from two experiments, however, is not the most convincing way to demonstrate an effect, particularly when the two experiments were carried out for the purpose of establishing defining operations. If, perhaps, the subjects in either study had been given more training, the data in each case might have stood alone, and the results would have been more compelling.

As a sequel to the Shapiro et al. (1970) experiment, Shapiro, Schwartz, and Tursky (1972) trained ten male subjects to raise, and ten others to lower, their DBP. The apparatus and procedure used in this experiment were essentially the same as in the two preceding studies, except that phasic changes in HR and DBP were observed using a procedure developed by Schwartz, Shapiro, and Tursky (1971). The entire experiment took place over a single session and consisted of five baseline trials; five acquisition trials, during which a partial reinforcement schedule of 50% was in effect; and 35 trials, during which the type and availability of feedback were in keeping with the acquisition procedure of the earlier Shapiro et al. (1969, 1970) studies. The session ended with ten trials, during which feedback was withdrawn, and half the subjects were instructed to maintain voluntary control of their DBP, while the other half were told that the experiment was over and they were simply to relax and stay quiet while the experimenter made additional DBP measurements.

It is important to note that, during acquisition, subjects were paid in proportion to their DBP performance, thereby adding an additional factor of feedback reinforcement to the light and tone and slide forms of feedback already present. More important is the fact that, although light and tone and slide forms of feedback were removed during the last ten trials (apparent extinction), proportional feedback in the form of monetary reward was not. Thus, since one of many forms of feedback employed in this experiment was present during the last phase of the experiment, it was inappropriate to refer to that phase as extinction. What really happened was that the experimentally available forms of feedback (light and tone, slides, money) were reduced from four to one (money) during the so-called extinction phase. Moreover, the fact that the voluntary control group was able to maintain the acquired BP response, when instructed to do so, says more about the role of verbal stimuli as controlling agents of conditioned BP response (discriminative stimuli) than it does about extinction.

The results of this study suggest that relatively small, but apparent, changes in the predicted directions did occur. It was also observed that subjects in the voluntary control group were able to maintain their performance over the last ten trials, whereas the other (rest group) could not. Analysis of the HR and respiration data revealed that, whenever reinforcement of an appropriate DBP change coincided with a change in HR, an apparently patterned effect emerged. More specifically, changes in DBP and HR were positively correlated, but the correlations failed to satisfy even minimal standards of statistical reliability.

One aim of this study was to provide some data on BP response extinction, and that was an important undertaking. However, this experiment suffers from some of the same shortcomings as did the earlier experiments by this group. It is difficult to draw conclusions when the type and schedules of feedback have been confounded, when there are no control data, and when subjects continue to be reinforced with money during tests for extinction.

The suggestion that BP can be raised and lowered by instrumental conditioning, without accompanying changes in HR, led Schwartz (1972) to investigate still further the interrelationship between these two variables. Using essentially the same apparatus and experimental strategy as Shapiro and his associates, Schwartz factorially compared increases and decreases in SBP with increases and decreases in HR. His sample consisted of 40 subjects, who received five adaptation trials, five random reinforcement, and 35 acquisition trials. Statistical treatment of his data disclosed that the subjects could learn to raise or lower SBP and HR together or independently and that they were better able to change HR and SBP in the same direction than they were able to change them in opposite directions.

To determine whether or not similar patterns or specific effects between DBP and HR could be found, Schwartz, Shapiro, and Tursky (1972), according to Schwartz (1974), repeated the Schwartz experiment with two alterations. First, they substituted DBP for SBP as one of the dependent variables, and, second, they added an additional group of subjects who received random reinforcement over the 35 acquisition trials. It was again observed that subjects were able to increase or decrease DBP and HR together. However, in contrast with the results of the earlier experiment, they found little evidence that subjects could change DBP and HR in opposite directions. Thus, it appears that SBP-HR and

DBP-HR patterns can be conditioned quite easily and that SBP-HR divergences are conditioned with difficulty. Schwartz found no evidence that DBP and HR can be conditioned in opposing directions.

Hnatiow (1971) used 80 male subjects in an experiment in which some subjects were required to control their HR and others were trained to control their SBP. The dependent variables were HR, respiratory rate (RR), and SBP. Proportional feedback consisted of a visual display driven by the subjects' HR or SBP, with mean HR or SBP reflected by the position of one black pointer and variability of HR or SBP performance indicated by the position of two red ones. Those subjects assigned the task of controlling their SBP showed significant decreases in mean SBP from no-feedback to feedback conditions, but subjects in the control group did not. Some, but not all, were able to reduce SBP variability.

Schneider (1978) reported reductions in SBP that were conditioned through the use of the system of rapid absolute feedback developed by him, as described earlier in this chapter. In his study, 12 male and 12 female subjects were assigned to one of three groups: no-feedback control, low-frequency feedback, and high-frequency feedback. Subjects in the low-frequency condition received visual feedback from a mercury manometer at two-minute intervals, and subjects in the high-frequency condition were allowed to view the manometer scale every 12 seconds. The dependent variable was SBP, and training was carried out for 15 minutes. Data analysis showed that the group given high-frequency feedback exhibited a reliable reduction in SBP when compared with either the group given low-frequency feedback or the control group. The latter groups were not significantly different from one another.

The most striking feature of these data is that a significant reduction occurred after 15 minutes of training. Were it not for the fact that repetitive operation of rapid absolute feedback may be traumatic to the arterial wall, it would have been interesting to know the outcome of additional training. There are other characteristics of this experiment that cloud the usefulness of these data, including the fact that the subjects in the three treatment groups received differential instructions and the fact that the instructions and feedback were confounded.

Studies with Two to Four Training Sessions

Studies using two to four training sessions may be further divided into two groups. The first group consists of several studies from different laboratories in which subjects were tested for either two or three sessions and SBP was the dependent variable. The second group is composed of a series of studies by Steptoe and his colleagues in England in which subjects were given four sessions and the dependent variable was PWV.

One of the first studies in which more than one training session was used was reported in 1970 by Brener and Kleinman. In this experiment, SBP was determined with the finger-pulse method (as described earlier), and HR was recorded as a concomitant dependent measure. Proportional exteroceptive feedback was provided in two forms: a manometer gauge, which fluctuated in response to changes in finger-cuff pressure, and an electronic counter, which operated at a rate proportional to finger-cuff pressure. One of the two groups of subjects was trained to decrease SBP, and the other served as a control. It is important to note that rather detailed instructions regarding the nature of the experiment and expected outcome were given to the subjects in both groups. In the first of two training sessions, the feedback group lowered its SBP a statistically significant amount by the end of 20 trials, but the control group did not. Both groups displayed a reduction in SBP during the second session, but the experimental group was able to reduce SBP significantly more than was the control. The observed differences in HR between the two groups were not statistically significant.

In addition to providing supplemental evidence that human subjects can be trained to lower their SBP, this experiment clearly established the need for the observation of behavioral changes in BP over more than one session. For example, the performance curve of the experimental (feedback) group described a gradual decrease in SBP over trials during session 1, while the performance of the control group remained relatively stable. In session 2, the experimental group began at a level somewhat lower than the initial baseline and gradually decreased SBP from trial to trial, a pattern that is commensurate with what one might expect from the data on motor learning. The control subjects also displayed a reduction, although not as great as that of the feedback group. Consideration of the change in performance of control and experimental subjects over trials and sessions is central to the whole question of instrumental visceral learning. If BP is subject to instrumental conditioning, changes in performance from session to session should be examined and quantified. Unfortunately, these experimenters did not include an increase group. Had they found homologous increases in SBP over trials and sessions, the conclusion that their data demonstrated that learning had taken place would have been on much firmer ground.

One of the surprising features of the early studies, which were aimed at illustrating that human subjects could be taught to control their BP, is that some investigators were quite arbitrary in selecting SBP or DBP as the specific response to be trained. But, in fact, do subjects learn best with feedback contingent upon SBP or DBP? There is only one study in the literature dealing with this important question.

To determine whether feedback contingent upon SBP or DBP produces the most rapid learning, Elder et al. (1974) tested 32 volunteer subjects in a design in which feedback contingent upon SBP and that contingent upon DBP were compared directly. The first session was used to determine baseline levels, after which training was carried out over three consecutive daily sessions. Systolic and diastolic BP were measured every two minutes, using an electronic version of the Riva-Rocci method. Independent groups of subjects were assigned to treatment conditions, so that determination of significant increases and decreases in BP required a comparison between subjects. At each session, 20 trials were administered, and each trial was followed by binary feedback in the form of a brief green light, indicating correct responses, or a brief red light, signifying incorrect responses. In terms of SBP performance, neither condition produced an effect, but, when DBP scores were examined, the DBP contingency was found to be effective.

More specifically, the data showed that subjects in the increase and decrease groups began with approximately the same baseline values and gradually changed their DBP with training, so that their respective performance curves diverged. A similar, but somewhat less dramatic, effect began to emerge in the SBP data on the second day of acquisition. Thus, in terms of the rapidity with which evidence of acquisition appears, the diastolic feedback condition was most effective.

These data were directed at a rather important question, and they provided only a partial answer. They left several other related issues unresolved. For example, would the SBP contingent feedback condition have worked as well or better if more training trials had been given? Or, to what extent can SBP and DBP be uncoupled, or changed in corresponding directions?

Two somewhat similar studies were carried out and reported by Fey and Lindholm. In the first one (1975), the effect of visual binary feedback on SBP was assessed by comparing the performance of four groups of subjects: a no-feedback (control) condition, random (noncontingent) feedback, feedback for increasing SBP, and feedback for decreasing SBP. In the second study (1978), the relative effects of progressive muscular relaxation followed by biofeedback were assessed by comparing progressive relaxation followed by biofeedback training, progressive relaxation followed by sessions during which SBP was simply monitored, and relaxation training in the presence of white noise followed by biofeedback training. In both experiments, BP was measured with a variation of the constant-cuff method developed at Harvard, and feedback consisted of a light bulb located behind a translucent screen that could be programmed to flash, on one hand, only when K sounds were detected or, on the other hand, only when K sounds could not be heard.

From the first study, Fey and Lindholm found that subjects in the feedback group were successful in lowering their SBP but that there was no evidence that they acquired an increase response. Random feedback and the control (no-feedback) conditions had no observable effect. From the second study, they made several discoveries. First, all the groups displayed a reduction in SBP at the end of session 1, as a result of relaxation training. Second, biofeedback training following relaxation training led to further reductions in SBP. Third, the group that received white noise during relaxation training was the only group that failed to show a decrease during a follow-up session one week after training. Finally, DBP and HR decreased in all three groups.

These data are difficult to reconcile with the studies by Shapiro, Schwartz, and their associates and with the data of Brener and Kleinman, which showed that increases as well as decreases could be conditioned. Since Fey and Lindholm used only a flash of light as an incentive, there is a real possibility that their subjects were trained under insufficient drive-incentive conditions. Alternatively, perhaps the fact that they used only one form of exteroceptive feedback, while the other investigators used several forms (augmented feedback), accounts for this difference. In the absence of a sufficient incentive, it is not surprising that their subjects were unable to produce increases in BP; they may have been nothing more than passive participants. On the other hand, the task with which their subjects were confronted may have been one that can be performed only by highly motivated subjects who become active participants in the experiment. While there are, as yet, no data clarifying the role of factors of incentive and motivation in BP conditioning, there is no reason to doubt that such factors are crucial in the acquisition of visceral, as well as motor, learning.

Shannon, Goldman, and Lee (1978) trained four groups of subjects under conditions of proportional feedback at 75-second intervals, relatively continuous proportional feedback, a form of continuous binary feedback, and no feedback. SBP was the principal dependent variable. DBP, HR, RR, and respiration volume (RV) were recorded concomitantly. SBP was measured using the control system devised by Lee, Caldwell, and Lee (1977). In the case of the first two groups, the system was operated in a semitracking mode. In the case of the third group, a mode using discrete trials and constant-cuff pressure was used. Group 1 received feedback that was administered intermittently. Group 2 received feedback continuously, with the use of a strip-chart recording placed directly in front of the subject. Group 3 was provided with binary feedback in the form of a light flash whenever a K sound did not accompany the R wave of the heart cycle.

From their data, Shannon et al. reported that continuous binary feedback was most useful in producing SBP control and that DBP often increased within sessions, even when SBP decreased. No consistent covariance between SBP and other physiological responses was observed, even though, at times, some of these variables were influenced by the instructions.

Steptoe and his associates executed a series of studies in which subjects were trained to raise or lower their PWV over four training sessions. In one of the first experiments, Steptoe and Johnston (1976a) observed the PWV and HR performance of ten subjects over four sessions. In two sessions, the subjects were trained to raise their BP, and, in the other two, they were trained to lower it. Proportional feedback was provided in the form of a display of a cathode-ray tube (CRT) and monetary reward. When trial scores were compared with the initial (session 1) baseline value, it was observed that BP and HR remained at the baseline value during the increase training session and dropped significantly during the decrease session. When the scores of BP and HR trials were evaluated against a running baseline (by expressing each trial score as a percentage of the measure obtained during the preceding intertrial interval), all subjects exhibited decreases in PWV over all four sessions.

In a second study (Steptoe & Johnston, 1976b), a group of subjects receiving instructions but no feedback was compared with a group that received both. When the data were analyzed by comparing performance during acquisition trials with initial baseline values, both groups showed decreases in BP, but only the group receiving instructions plus feedback exhibited an increase.

Since subjects in the Steptoe and Johnston studies were supplied with detailed instructions, thereby confounding feedback with instructions, Steptoe (1976) performed a direct comparison of feedback and instructions. In this study, 40 subjects were divided into four groups with instructions to raise BP, instructions to lower BP, instructions to raise BP plus feedback, or instructions to lower BP plus feedback. Again, feedback consisted of a visual display, which was varied over sessions 3 and 4 to promote interest on the part of the subject, and monetary reward. When feedback effects were assessed in terms of changes from the initial baseline (session 1), all four groups showed changes in the appropriate direction, with the group receiving instructions plus feedback showing the greatest effect.

Following much the same procedure, Steptoe (1977) instructed one group to lower BP, and a second group received instructions plus feedback to lower BP. After training, they were exposed to a simple reaction time (RT) task to determine whether they could maintain acquired BP reductions under a slight environmental load. The subjects who were trained with instructions plus feedback were slightly more successful in maintaining acquired reductions while performing the RT task than were those who received instructions only.

More recently, Steptoe (1978) compared instructions plus relaxation and instructions plus feedback under resting and under the conditions of an auditory RT task. Both groups were equally successful in lowering BP in the resting condition. However, only the group receiving instructions plus feedback was able to maintain the decrease BP response while performing the RT task. In a companion experiment described in the same report, it was observed that subjects in the group receiving instructions plus feedback were better able to overcome more rapidly the initially disruptive influence of performing an arithmetic task than could those assigned to the relaxation conditions.

Several points must be remembered when evaluating the data from this series of experiments. For example, the effects of visual and monetary biofeedback were confounded with the effects of instructions; the observed increases and decreases in PWV occurred within, but not between, sessions, raising a question as to the kind of learning taking place; and the data suffer from the inherent defects of PWV as a dependent measure. On the positive side, the questions Steptoe and his colleagues raised are fundamental ones, and the data they have assembled indicate that feedback plus instructions leads to the acquisition of a specific BP response that can be executed even when the subject is performing motor and cognitive tasks.

Studies with Five or More Training Sessions

Although there are several methodological differences among the studies to be considered here, they have in common the following characteristics: subjects were observed over five or more sessions, and increases and decreases in BP were demonstrated as between-subjects or within-subjects effects. Both of these points should be borne in mind when considering the placebo effect as an alternative interpretation to instrumental conditioning for the data considered in this section. Multiple training sessions do not entirely rule out the possibility of a placebo effect, but they make it more difficult to account for the data in such terms. Although more attention will be given later to this possibility, it is appropriate here to also point out that the placebo interpretation of the data is less tenable when subjects learn to raise and lower BP under the same training conditions.

An experiment that represents an attempt to take cognizance of these two points (Elder, Welsh, Longacre, & McAfee, 1977) was carried out to compare a free-operant format with the format of discrete-trials training necessitated by use of mechanical or electronic versions of the Riva-Rocci procedure. Development of the UNO system paved the way for treatment of the BP response as a free operant. Until that time, investigators tended to use one of two methods: manual or electronic versions of the Riva-Rocci method or tracking procedures, such as those developed at Harvard and Rockefeller Universities. In both instances, BP was measured over discrete trials of relatively short duration, and they were separated by intertrial intervals of varying lengths.

Once a method was available for measuring BP continuously, one of the first questions to be raised was, How do continuous measurement and feedback of BP response compare with discrete BP response feedback training? The experiment by Elder, Welsh, Longacre, and McAfee (1977) was designed to answer this question. In addition, the study was designed to compare the instrumental conditioning procedure with one in which subjects received only instructions from the experimenter and a control condition in which the subjects were simply allowed to relax (passive relaxation). Because instructions given alone, without feedback, have been shown to have an effect on some forms of motor behavior (for example, Baron, Kaufman, & Stauber, 1969), electroencephalogram (EEG) activity (Beatty, 1972), and PWV (Steptoe, 1976), assessment of their potential effect on DBP responses was considered an important issue.

A further objective of the study was to examine the possibility that discrete and/or free-operant BP responses, produced by instrumental conditioning or as instrumental sets, could be brought under the control of an exteroceptive discriminative stimulus. The importance of this question is based upon two considerations. First, if BP can, in fact, be treated as a free-operant response, then it must be subject to control by a discriminative stimulus, as are motor responses. Second, if conditioning is to be viewed as a potentially therapeutic procedure, it becomes necessary to determine to what extent acquired BP behavior generalizes or remains attached to spatially and temporally contiguous stimuli present during acquisition.

To satisfy the several purposes of this study, a two-by-three design was used, in which two conditioning formats (free operant and discrete trials) were factorially compared with three strategies: instrumental conditioning, instructional set, and control. There were 24 subjects who were assigned to the six groups. Exposure to the assigned procedures was repeated until all subjects exhibited an increase and decrease in DBP of 10% to 15% for two consecutive training sessions or until they had completed a total of ten successive training sessions.

The results were unequivocal. Although both control groups (free operant and discrete trials) exhibited observable reductions in DBP, approximately 5% to 6% of baseline, the group under free-operant instrumental conditioning learned to raise and lower its DBP 10% to 15% of baseline in five sessions. Training of the other five groups was discontinued after ten sessions, when they failed to reach the criterion of bidirectional changes of 10% to 15% in DBP. The performance of each individual subject in the group under free-operant instrumental conditioning is illustrated in Figure 9.3. Note that all subjects learned to

FIGURE 9.3
Comparison of Individual Subjects' Mean Diastolic Blood Pressure. Expressed as Percent of Basal over Training Sessions, Test Sessions, and Follow-up for the IC-FO Condition Only. Both *up* and *down* responses are included.

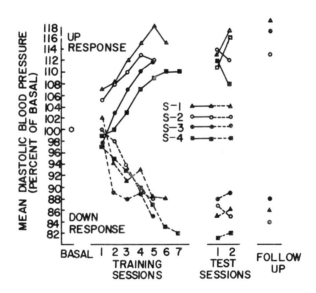

Source: Reprinted by permission, from S. T. Elder, D. M. Welsh, A. Longacre, Jr., and R. McAfee, "Acquisition, Discriminative Stimulus Control, and Retention of Increases/Decreases in Blood Pressure of Normotensive Human Subjects" (*Journal of Applied Behavior Analysis*, 1977, *10*, 381-390).

change their DBP in either the up or down direction. Also worthy of note is the performance of subjects during test and follow-up sessions. Since increase and decrease training had taken place in the presence of discriminative stimuli (distinctive room illumination), test and follow-up sessions were carried out, during which the discriminative stimuli were present but feedback was not. The data in Figure 9.3 show that the bidirectional response was retained through the three-week follow-up test and that room illumination had become discriminative stimulus for elevations and reductions in DBP.

Because these data were obtained with a novel procedure, Elder, Verzwyvelt, and McAfee (1978) attempted to replicate and extend the study. Their apparatus was the same as that employed by Elder, Welsh, Longacre, and McAfee (1977), but their method was different, in that their subjects were trained to raise DBP on one day and lower DBP on another day, rather than being required to practice both on the same day. Subjects were trained for 30 minutes each day for 14 consecutive training sessions. The data showed that their ability to elevate and reduce their DBP improved each day, until they reached a criterion change of 10% to 15% of baseline. Thus, with respect to the prediction of bidirectional changes in DBP of relatively large magnitude, the previous experiment was successfully replicated.

A second purpose of the Elder et al. (1978) study was to examine the possibility that subjects could acquire bidirectional control of their DBP in the presence of muscle tension. This was considered an important issue for two reasons. First, the study dealt with the theoretical question of cardiovascular-somatomotor interactions and the extent to which skeletal responses operate as potential mediators of voluntary visceral behavior. Second, in the light of evidence that blood pressure can be reduced through the use of progressive relaxation, the study focused on the question of the comparative effectiveness of deep muscle relaxation and conditioned control of blood pressure as methods of controlling hypertension. The advantage of the use of relaxation to control high blood pressure is that relaxation requires little or no complex and expensive equipment. The adoption of relaxation as a treatment procedure is limited, however, because a hypertensive patient cannot be expected to maintain a state of deep muscle relaxation for very long. On the other hand, if subjects can be conditioned to change their BP, even in the presence of muscle tension, the suitability of instrumental conditioning as a therapeutic procedure would be enhanced. Such a demonstration would indicate that control of blood pressure can be acquired and maintained, even when the individual is in an active (non-relaxed) state. Although the results of this study were not astonishing, they did indicate that subjects can acquire a decrease DBP response when some of the somatic musculature is in use as well as when they are sitting quietly in a chair with nothing else to do but practice lowering their DBP.

Goldman and Lee (1978), using the method of BP tracking described by Lee et al. (1977), performed an experiment in which three groups of subjects were used to compare SBP feedback, SBP, RR, and RV feedback, and SBP feedback coupled with frontalis electromyogram (EMG) feedback training. Subjects were given five training sessions of five trials each, and SBP training was always in the decrease direction with respect to baseline. Their data indicated that subjects in the first two groups learned to lower their SBP, with subjects in the SBP, RR, and RV feedback condition performing most efficiently. Frontalis EMG feedback had no demonstrable effect.

These data are important because they identify an advantage of conditioning patterned reductions in responses (for example, SBP, RR, and RV) over conditioning a single response. Nevertheless, the results must be interpreted with caution for three reasons. First, subjects were given specific instructions to "lower" or "not lower" their SBP at regular points during each session, thereby confounding instructions with feedback. Second, the superior performance of the SBP, RR, and RV feedback group may have been the result of concomitant cardiovascular and respiratory contingent feedback, as Goldman and Lee suggested, or the superior performance may have been due to RR and RV feedback alone. Third, the group receiving frontalis EMG feedback failed to display a discernible reduction in BP, although previously many investigators have successfully observed such an effect (for example, Benson, 1975; Jacobson, 1938). In spite of the methodological difficulties, the idea of coupling BP and respiration to bring about quick and substantial reductions in BP is an important contribution, and the data derived from it form a useful base for further experimental effort.

The last study to be considered in this section was carried out by Elder, Gamble, McAfee, and Van Veen (1979). Its purpose was threefold: to replicate the production of bidirectional DBP responses within subjects, which was reported by Elder, Welsh, Longacre, and McAfee (1977) and Elder et al. (1978); to confirm whether HR and RR changes accompany DBP response development over several sessions, as Schwartz (1974) and Schwartz et al. (1972) found with only one training session; and to determine whether male and female subjects acquire the bidirectional response at different rates. (Consideration of the latter factor was occasioned by the report from Elder and Eustis, 1975, that female hypertensives learned to lower their DBP slightly faster than did hypertensive males and by the failure of Fey and Lindholm, 1975, to find evidence of a sex differential.) In the Elder et al. (1979) study, 16 subjects were given one baseline and eight consecutive training sessions, each of which lasted one hour. DBP measurement and conditioning conformed closely to the procedure used in the two previous experiments. When the acquisition scores were analyzed, they revealed that subjects were able to acquire a bidirectional response, thereby confirming earlier reports. Analysis of the HR and RR data disclosed no consistent relationship or pattern, as had been reported earlier, and comparison of male and female BP performance failed to yield evidence of reliable sex differences.

Summary

The first point to be emphasized is that reductions in BP occurred in every study considered above. Although most of the experimental designs included provisions for the acquisition of increase and decrease responses, as indicated in Table 9.3, reliable increase responses were not observed in some cases. Whether the observed decrements can be best accounted for in terms of relaxation, feedback, or a combination of the two is not known. It is clear that subjects did learn to lower their BP, sometimes in one session. The fact that subjects were told to sit back and relax creates the possibility that passive relaxation may have interacted with the consequences of exteroceptive feedback. The evidence that deep muscle relaxation leads to decrements in BP is unequivocal (Silver & Blanchard, 1978). It is now time to sort out the independent effects of passive relaxation and exteroceptive feedback whenever the production of decrease BP responses is undertaken.

A second point about the studies discussed above is the curious fact that only a few investigators were able to produce increases in BP. Differences in method of measuring BP (see Table 9.2); type, number, and schedule of feedback; and variations in the magnitude of drive-incentive variables are the most suspect contributors to this inconsistency. As stated earlier, demonstration of bidirectional changes in BP between subjects and, more importantly, within subjects provides the most dramatic evidence that observed changes in BP reflect bona fide learning (conditioning) processes. Therefore, it is essential, at this point, to identify the variables that play the most central role in the acquisition of bidirectional BP responses. Until this is done, any suggestion that instrumental conditioning might be used in the treatment of essential hypertension is premature.

Related to this argument is the very interesting finding that subjects who have been systematically trained to lower their BP can continue to perform the decrease BP responses simultaneously with the induction of muscle tension or performance of a mental arithmetic task.

Finally, it is disappointing that there are so few studies aimed at isolating those variables that facilitate acquisition of BP behavior. The fact that there exists a set of data dealing with motor and verbal learning from which a number of principles have been extracted makes determination of the generality of these principles to visceral learning a matter of urgent theoretical concern. Few investigators, however, have focused on isolating the fundamental principles of visceral learning. This has created a serious gap in the existing body of data. If the acquisition of BP control is to be understood, and if explanation and prediction are to be the end product, much more attention must be focused on extracting the factors that regulate its acquisition and extinction.

It should also be noted that feedback contingent upon BP led to changes in BP, unaccompanied by changes in, for example, HR and RR. In other words, the

TABLE 9.3
Summary of Studies with Normotensives

Authors	Sex of Subject	Number of Sessions	Direction of BP Change	Control	Concomitant Dependent Measures
Shapiro et al., 1969	M	1	U D	—	HR – No correlation RR – No correlation
Brener and Kleinman, 1970	*	2	— D	No FB	HR – No correlation
Shapiro et al., 1970	M	1	U D	—	HR – No correlation RR – No correlation
Hnatiow, 1971	M	1	— D	Yoked	HR – No correlation RR – No correlation
Shapiro et al., 1972	M	1	U D	—	HR – No correlation RR – No correlation
Schwartz, 1972	M	1	U D	—	HR – No correlation RR – No correlation
Elder et al., 1974	M&F	4	U D	No FB	None
Fey and Lindholm, 1975	M&F	3	U D	Noncontingent FB	HR – Uncertain
Steptoe and Johnston, 1976a	M&F	4	U D	—	IBI* – Gross relationship RR – Gross Relationship
Steptoe and Johnston, 1976b	M&F	4	U D	(Instructions)	IBI* – Some correlation RR – Some correlation
Steptoe, 1976	M&F	4	U D	(Instructions)	IBI* – No correlation RR – No correlation
Elder, Welsh, Longacre, and McAfee, 1977	M&F	5-10	U D	No FB	None
Schneider, 1978	M&F	1	— D	No FB	None

Steptoe, 1977	*	4	–	D	– (Instructions)	IBI* – Uncertain
						RR – No correlation
						None
Elder et al., 1978	M&F	14	U	D	No FB	HR – No correlation
Fey and Lindholm, 1978	M&F	2	–	D	No FB	RR – 0.83-0.99
Goldman and Lee, 1978	F	5	–	D	–	EMG – No correlation
Shannon et al., 1978	*	3	–	D	No FB	HR – Uncertain
						RR – Uncertain
Steptoe, 1978	M&F	4	–	D	– (Instructions)	IBI* – Uncertain
						RR – No correlation
Elder et al., 1979	M&F	8	U	D	No FB	HR – No correlation
						RR – No correlation

*Interbeat interval

Source: Compiled by the authors.

effect of feedback training appears to be specific. When patterned effects are desired, feedback must be made contingent on correlated changes in all responses that are incorporated in the behavioral complex. This was illustrated by Schwartz (1974) and Goldman and Lee (1978). In either case (single-response feedback or multiple-response feedback), it appears the responses that are learned are those that come under the influence of an environmental contingency.

STUDIES WITH HYPERTENSIVE SUBJECTS

The first report that essential hypertension can be managed by operant conditioning with performance-contingent feedback came from Miller's laboratory (Miller et al., 1970). A female patient learned to lower her BP, eventually reducing it as much as 30 mm Hg. Shortly thereafter, Benson, Shapiro, Tursky, and Schwartz (1971) reported successfully training five of seven patients with essential hypertension to lower their systolic pressure as much as 16 to 34 mm Hg. Blood pressure was measured and conditioned using the Harvard method.

This study also represented a pioneering effort on the part of Shapiro and his associates. Unfortunately, there are few inferences that can be drawn from the data. In the absence of control data, and in view of the fact that the hypertensive subjects were given rather extensive instruction, the observed reductions in SBP cannot be attributed to augmented feedback. Without any control data, these results are particularly vulnerable to a placebo interpretation. An additional problem centers on the fact that all but two of the subjects were maintained on antihypertensive medication, thereby confounding drug with behavioral treatments.

The first experiment in which a control group was included was carried out at the Veterans Administration Hospital in New Orleans by investigators at the University of New Orleans. With the use of an automated version of the Riva-Rocci technique, Elder et al. (1973) employed 18 hospitalized patients with essential hypertension, who were distributed over three groups. The first was a control (no-feedback) group. The second was an experimental group in which a response-contingent exteroceptive signal was given to the patient whenever a reduction in DBP occurred. In the third group, verbal approval was paired with exteroceptive feedback. All patients received 20 training trials per session at the rate of two sessions per day for four consecutive days.

Although trends in the expected direction occurred in the SBP data, the most significant outcome emerged from the DBP scores. Significant reductions in pressure were observed in sessions 7 and 8 among subjects in the second group and as early as session 3 among subjects in the third group. Thus, both feedback groups succeeded in reducing their DBP, but the group receiving feedback plus verbal approval showed the most dramatic decrease.

Blanchard and Young (1973) have rightfully criticized this experiment because the subjects in the various groups received slightly different instructions on the first day of training. It is virtually impossible to conduct experiments with human subjects without giving the subjects some instructions, but it is highly desirable that ways be found to design experiments so as to avoid the use of differential instructions. In a later review of some of the data on this topic, Blanchard (1979) criticized this study because only one baseline session was used. Actually, the data on the control group showed that control SBP and DBP means remained relatively stable over all eight sessions. That a gradually declining baseline may account for the decrement in BP observed in the experimental group is an argument that cannot be justified from these data.

There are other points that Blanchard and Young did not emphasize. First, the subjects were highly motivated, having been hospitalized because of hypertension, and, therefore, were eager to get their blood pressure under control so they could return home. Second, since the subjects were hospitalized through diagnostic workups, this increased the accuracy of the diagnosis of essential hypertension. Third, all subjects in this experiment were confined to bed rest between sessions during the entire course of the experiment. This latter point may be a more important factor than one might suspect, since it means that interpolated activity, with its possibly damaging inhibitory influences, was controlled during the intersession intervals. Both motivation and interpolated tasks are factors that have a profound influence on motor and verbal learning, and there is no reason, at this point, to believe that they do not have an equally great effect on acquired visceral behavior. Certainly, they are factors to be considered in future investigations of this problem.

In the next experiment (Elder & Eustis, 1975), essential hypertensives that were outpatients were used as subjects. The two aims were to train volunteer outpatients to reduce their systolic and diastolic BP through the use of instrumental conditioning and to assess the long-term consequences of such treatment, with a view toward establishing a feasible procedure that could be carried out in the home or in the clinic on a routine basis. The apparatus and training procedure were very similar to those used in the Elder et al. (1973) experiment. Some of the patients were given distributed training trials. In other cases, the training sessions followed one another on consecutive days. Both groups received a total of ten training sessions.

Comparison of the two groups, in terms of SBP and DBP, revealed that only the massed practice group was successful to a small, but significant, degree. Only two of the 22 subjects showed relatively large decrease responses, perhaps because most of the subjects were on antihypertensive medication, which may have interfered with learning. In addition, motivation to actively acquire self-control of BP was relatively mild, since no changes in their work, social schedules, and life-styles were required.

Using an approach somewhat similar to the Elder and Eustis procedure, Blanchard, Young, and Haynes (1975) trained four patients to lower their SBP nine to 15 mm Hg over four to nine sessions. Feedback was supplied by transmitting to the subject, over a closed-circuit television system, a graphic display of trial-by-trial variations. Control measurements were obtained by allowing the subject to view selected television programs during part of each session.

In a study similar to the Elder et al. (1973) experiment, Richter-Heinrich et al. (1975) produced positive results. Instead of using a visual feedback signal and/or verbal praise as feedback, Richter-Heinrich et al. showed their hospitalized subjects slides of landscapes. Rather than make feedback contingent on appropriate changes in DBP, feedback contingent on changes in SBP was employed. A yoked feedback, instead of a no-feedback, condition constituted the control group. Although both groups (feedback and yoked control) demonstrated reductions in SBP, the feedback subjects were significantly more successful at the task than were their yoked counterparts. Analysis of concomitant DBP and HR data failed to show systematic differences between the groups within or between sessions.

Despite the fact that this study suffers from the weaknesses of yoked designs, as Church (1964) pointed out, there are other features that make it worthy of note. As in the Elder et al. (1973) experiment, the subjects were hospitalized, which may account for the large reductions in BP. Second, the experimental subjects displayed a gradual and systematic reduction in performance within and between sessions. This conforms with the negatively decelerating change in performance one might ordinarily expect when acquisition of an instrumental, decrease BP response develops over a series of discrete training trials. In contrast, the yoked controls exhibited an initial reduction in BP during session 1, after which SBP stabilized. The reduction displayed by the group under contingent feedback was far greater.

In a study that extended the Benson et al. (1971) data considerably, Kristt and Engel (1975) selected five essential hypertensives and placed them in a three-phase training and test regime. The duration of phase 1 was seven weeks, during which subjects recorded their own SBP and DBP four times a day at home and reported the results by mail. During phase 2, which lasted three weeks, the subjects were conditioned to raise and/or lower their SBP using the Harvard method. Phase 3 lasted three months, and, during that time, subjects once again recorded their BP at home and reported the results by mail.

Upon completion of phase 1, the subjects were hospitalized for the duration of phase 2, at which time training occurred. During the first week of this phase, subjects were conditioned to raise SBP; during the second week, they learned to lower SBP; and during the third week, they practiced both raising and lowering SBP during each session. A typical session consisted of 30 trials, and sessions took place at the rate of 14 per week for a total of 42 sessions. The subjects were supplied with detailed instructions. A green light was illuminated to signal increase training, a red one to indicate decrease training, and a yellow lamp to show that the subjects' SBP performance was in the appropriate direction.

In addition, the patients were taught both to use the Riva-Rocci method to measure BP and to practice lowering SBP by holding pressure in the cuff constant at the systolic threshold long enough for the K sound to disappear. Then they lowered cuff pressure slowly, until the first K sound was detected again, in order to determine the magnitude of the decrement just produced. Following discharge, the patients practiced this maneuver four to 30 times a day and reported the results by mail.

All five patients demonstrated an increase response that averaged 15% and a decrease response that averaged 11% of baseline. HR, RR, EMG, and EEG were recorded at regular intervals throughout training, but none of these measures changed in a corresponding or systematic way. Home training led to additional BP reductions in some cases. Posttraining follow-up data collected at one- and three-month intervals indicated that subjects were able to sustain the decrement in BP they had acquired while in the hospital. Although some control data would have helped considerably in the interpretation of these results, they certainly suggest that BP conditioning has therapeutic value. Because the patients were observed over a long period of time, interpretation of this outcome as a placebo phenomenon is much less reasonable.

The Kristt and Engel data are encouraging, and, when coupled with the results of Elder et al. (1973) and Richter-Heinrich et al. (1975), they indicate that hospitalized patients (for undetermined reasons) perform better than nonhospitalized hypertensive patients, that many training sessions are far better than a few, and that, in at least some cases, generalization or transfer of the conditioned decrease response from the hospital (original) environment to the nonhospitalized (different) environment does occur.

Surwit, Shapiro, and Good (1978) used three groups of hypertensive patients, with eight in each group. One group was trained to lower their BP using feedback contingent upon SBP, one group was trained to reduce tension in the forearm and frontalis muscles using feedback contingent upon EMG, and one group was trained to meditate and relax using the Benson (1975) method. All patients received two baseline sessions, eight training sessions, and posttraining follow-up sessions at intervals of six weeks and one year. SBP was monitored and conditioned using the Harvard method, and respiration and HR were recorded as concomitant dependent variables.

The results were equivocal. None of the three groups exhibited reduction in BP greater than those observed during baseline. Perhaps this experiment might have been more successful if the subjects had had a greater incentive to learn.

The studies with hypertensive subjects can be characterized, in general, as poor. Basic weaknesses in the designs include inadequate controls in some cases and no controls in others, confounding of instructional with feedback effects, and failure to rule out placebo effects.

In an earlier review of clinical uses of biofeedback, Blanchard and Young (1974) were critical of the studies on hypertension (to the date of their review) because only one led to clinically significant results.* Since then, there have

---

*These authors have proposed a change of at least 20% as a minimum criterion for clincial significance. Although this seems to be rather severe and arbitrary, there is at least one report that conditioned decreases in the order of 20% to 30% do occur (Elder et al., 1973).

been at least two more: Richter-Heinrich et al. (1975), and Kristt and Engel (1975). In each case, training was carried out within a hospital setting. As suggested earlier, hospitalization per se might not have been as important as changes in motivation and in the control of potentially disruptive interpolated activities, which hospitalization facilitated. In addition, learning was achieved in a systematic way over multiple training sessions, throughout which progressive changes in BP were observed. Actually, it is no surprise that performance was seen to improve with rewarded practice.

SOME UNSETTLED ISSUES

It is clear that progress in identifying and quantitating the factors that contribute to the acquisition and extinction of BP behavior has been impeded by several methodological and/or conceptual issues as well as by significant and conspicuous gaps in the currently available data. Because the methodological and conceptual problems are matters that cannot be ignored in the interpretation of the current data and the design of future experiments, some direct, albeit brief, attention will be given to them here. Areas in which there are data shortages have been summarized in previous sections.

Placebo Effects

There can be little doubt that, in certain circumstances, powerful placebo effects can be introduced experimentally and clinically. When present, these effects confound the influence of independent variables under examination. They often arise inadvertently, and care must be exercised to rule them out or to assess their impact so that they can be controlled or removed by subtraction. Shapiro (1960) narrated some of the history and described some of the problems encountered in dealing with the placebo effect in research and treatment situations, and the reader is referred to that article.

If the effect of feedback on BP performance is to be isolated from the contaminating influence of placebo, the use of designs in which bidirectional changes in performance and groups under noncontingent feedback control are used must become common practice, particularly among those working with human subjects. To do so makes the experimental task more complex, requires the use of more control groups, and increases the cost of conducting this line of research, but the importance of the issue requires that these things be done. Cohen, Graham, Fotopoulos, and Cook (1977) described the use of a doubleblind procedure for administering contingent or noncontingent EEG/EMG feedback training to opium addicts, and their work provides a model that some may find useful in studies of conditioned BP. Similar comparison of groups receiving contingent and noncontingent BP feedback must be included in future studies along with the production of bidirectional changes in BP if the potential, contaminating effect of placebo is to be removed or ruled out.

Response Specificity

The problem of response specificity may be approached from at least three directions. First, there is the question of whether or not a response acquired and performed in the laboratory or clinic will tend to reoccur in other situations. Second, response specificity may be seen as the tendency for forms of behavior other than the BP response to change in correspondence with progressive changes observed in the primary dependent variables. Third, there is the question of whether or not conditioned SBP changes generalize to DBP, and vice versa.

When the first two sides of the issue are examined within the context of BP conditioning, the bulk of the evidence indicates that the consequences of feedback bears directly upon the response to which it was linked, with little or no spread of the effect to collateral response systems. Not yet available is direct evidence that bears on the generalization of the BP responses to other than the original situation in which it was conditioned. From the Elder, Welsh, Longacre and McAfee (1977) data, which showed discriminative-stimulus control of BP, one could invoke the principle of stimulus generalization and predict at least some decrement in the BP response either when it occurs in a subsequent, similar situation or when it fails to occur in a situation that is altogether different. First, however, the characteristics of stimulus generalization of BP must be known. If it is found that sharp decrements in stimulus generalization occur, ways of enhancing generalization to new and different situations must be found before the clinical efficacy of conditioned BP becomes clear.

It should also be noted that Schwartz (1974) asserted that DBP-contingent feedback is not governed by the specificity principle, in that HR covaries with it. He based his case on some correlations between DBP and HR that were reported by Shapiro et al. (1972) and on the results of an unpublished paper summarized by Schwartz (1974). Neither of these two sets of data can be given serious consideration, however, since, in the first case, none of the correlations was statistically significant and, in the latter, only a sketchy report of the study was published (Schwartz, 1974). When Elder et al. (1979) correlated DBP and HR on a subject-by-subject and session-by-session basis, they found the correlations between DBP and HR to vary in direction and magnitude between subjects and even between sessions for the same subject. Thus, in terms of the first two sides of the specificity question, conditioned DBP seems to be quite specific.

The third side to the specificity issue, and one that has been almost entirely ignored, has to do with the generalization of conditioned SBP changes to DBP, and vice versa. The data of Elder et al. (1974) suggested that some generalizations from DBP to SBP occurred, but the effect was small and began to take place 24 hours after evidence of conditioning emerged in their DBP data. Much more data is needed however, before any firm inferences regarding this side of the specificity issue can be made.

Related to the issue of specificity versus generalization is response transfer, that is, the effects that prior motor and visceral learning have on acquisition of a

BP response and the effect that learning a BP response in the laboratory has on learning it in a new situation. Once again, however, there is a conspicuous lack of data bearing on this subject. Careful analysis of potential positive and negative transfer characteristics between visceral effectors, such as BP, HR, and/or RR, and between visceral and motor responses, such as BP and piano playing, will undoubtedly have some influence on the future success of conditioning as a way of training hypertensives to control their BP routinely.

Relaxation

By now, there is little dispute over the observation by Jacobson in 1938 that deep muscle relaxation is often as effective as feedback in reducing BP, and, since biofeedback requires rather elaborate and sometimes expensive equipment, while relaxation does not, it has been argued that relaxation may be the best behavioral alternative to the treatment of hypertension at this point.

There is another side to this issue, however, that has to do with the question of what happens to hypertensive patients who have learned to lower their BP through relaxation and who then return to work or enter otherwise demanding situations. When Steptoe (1977) compared subjects trained with feedback with those who received instructions only during an RT task, he found both were able to maintain the previously acquired decrements in BP. However, when he compared feedback-trained and relaxation-trained groups (1978) during performance of RT and a mental arithmetic task, those in the group trained with feedback were able to maintain previously acquired BP reductions, while those trained with relaxation were not. Moreover, Elder et al. (1978) found that subjects were able to produce decrease DBP responses simultaneously with the induction of masseter muscle tension. It is unfortunate that Steptoe (1977) did not report data on reaction time and mental arithmetic performance; the comparability or lack thereof between the instructed and feedback-trained groups on these tasks is crucial to an understanding of the outcome of his experiment.

The Steptoe (1978) and Elder et al. (1978) data point to what may be an important distinction between relaxation and feedback as models for reducing BP. Apparently, both relaxation and feedback lead to significant reductions in BP, but only BP feedback training equipped the subjects to produce or maintain the decrease BP response under cognitive and/or motor work loads.

Instructional Set

One advantage of an animal preparation in studies of BP is that difficulties produced by the necessity of giving the subjects some form of instruction are easily avoided. In studies of human subjects, some instructions must be given, and there are times when the main effect of instructions may account for, or interact with, effects that one might otherwise attribute to the independent variables.

The studies with human subjects considered here may be divided into several categories: those in which the same explicit instructions were given to all subjects in all groups, those in which different explicit instructions were given to the subjects in the various treatment conditions, experiments in which the instructions were given only on the first day of training, experiments in which the instructions were repeated to the subjects at the beginning of each session, and those studies in which instructions were presented to the subjects but were not reported.

Elder, Welsh, Longacre and McAfee (1977) included an instructional-set control group in their experiment and found no evidence for an instructional BP set. In contrast, Steptoe and Johnston (1976b) and Steptoe (1976) repeated the instructions to their subjects at the beginning of each daily session. Is it necessary to repeat instructions in order to have an observable effect on BP? Do they affect PWV and DBP differentially? These and other questions regarding possible interaction effects of instructions with feedback contingent on BP cannot be answered from the data at hand. As do the matters of BP response transfer, extinction, and the like, they await the collection of additional data.

CONCLUSION

In spite of the long-standing bias in favor of the idea that autonomic effectors are exclusively under involuntary control and, therefore, are immune to contingent environmental events, and in spite of a number of methodological issues that cloud interpretation of many of the data considered here, the preponderance of the evidence assembled to date supports the tentative conclusion that blood pressure is, at least to some degree, under voluntary control and can be instrumentally conditioned. Even after ten years of research on the problem, however, little more than this can be said because of significant weaknesses and conspicuous omissions in the existing body of data.

Perhaps, during the next decade, the use of tighter experimental designs, larger numbers of training sessions, and more stringent controls will produce cleaner data, from which a more definitive position can be reached on the therapeutic value of instrumental conditioning in the control of blood pressure. In addition, the basic question of the voluntary versus involuntary nature of the autonomic nervous system — along with the related issue of whether or not visceral behavior can be shaped, maintained by primary and/or secondary reinforcers administered under a variety of schedules, and extinguished — is central to the broader theoretical question of one-process versus two-process learning.

REFERENCES

Anderson, D. E., & Brady, J. V. Prolonged preavoidance upon blood pressure and heart rate in the dog. *Psychosomatic Medicine*, 1973, *35*, 4-12.

Baron, A., Kaufman, A., & Stauber, K. A. Effects of instructions and reinforcement-feedback on human operant behavior maintained by fixed-interval reinforcement. *Journal of the Experimental Analysis of Behavior*, 1969, *12*, 701-712.

Beatty, J. Similar effects on feedback signals and instructional information on EEG activity. *Physiological Behavior*, 1972, *9*, 151-154.

Benson, H. *Relaxation response.* New York: Morrow, 1975.

Benson, H., Herd, J. A., Morse, W. H., & Kelleher, R. T. Behavioral induction of arterial hypertension and its reversal. *American Journal of Physiology*, 1969, *217*, 30-34.

Benson, H., Shapiro, D., Tursky, B., & Schwartz, G. E. Decreased systolic blood pressure through operant conditioning techniques in patients with essential hypertension. *Science*, 1971, *173*, 740-742.

Blanchard, E. B. Biofeedback and the modification of cardiovascular dysfunctions. In R. J. Gatchel & K. P. Price (Eds.), *Clinical appliction of biofeedback: Appraisal and status*. New York: Pergamon Press, 1979.

Blanchard, E. B., & Young, L. D. Self-control of cardiac functioning: A promise as yet unfulfilled. *Psychological Bulletin*, 1973, *79*, 145-163.

Blanchard, E. B., & Young, L. D. Clinical applications of biofeedback training. *Archives of General Psychiatry*, 1974, *30*, 573-589.

Blanchard, E. B., Young, L. D., & Haynes, M. R. A simple feedback system for the treatment of elevated blood pressure. *Behavior Therapy*, 1975, *6*, 241-245.

Brener, J., & Kleinman, R. A. Learned control of decreases in systolic blood pressure. *Nature*, 1970, *226*, 1063-1064.

Brown, C. C., & Katz, R. A. Operant salivary conditioning in man. *Psychophysiology*, 1967, *4*, 156-160.

Church, R. M. Systematic effect of random error in the yoked control design. *Psychological Bulletin*, 1964, *62*, 122-131.

Cohen, H. D., Graham, C., Fotopoulos, S. S., & Cook, M. R. A double-blind methodology for biofeedback research. *Psychophysiology*, 1977, *14*, 603-608.

DiCara, L. V., & Miller, N. E. Changes in heart rate instrumentally learned by curarized rats as avoidance responses. *Journal of Comparative and Physiological Psychology*, 1968, *65*, 8-11. (a)

DiCara, L. V., & Miller, N. E. Instrumental learning of systolic blood pressure responses by curarized rats: Dissociation of cardiac and vascular changes. *Psychosomatic Medicine*, 1968, *30*, 489-494. (b)

DiCara, L. V., Pappas, B. A., & Pointer, F. A technique for chronic recordings of systemic arterial blood pressure in the unrestrained rat. *Behavior Research Methods and Instrumentation*, 1969, *1*, 221-223.

Elder, S. T., & Eustis, N. K. Instrumental blood pressure conditioning in outpatient hypertensives. *Behavior Research and Therapy*, 1975, *13*, 185-188.

Elder, S. T., Gamble, E. H., McAfee, R. D., & Van Veen, W. J. Conditioned diastolic blood pressure. *Physiology and Behavior*, 1979, *23*, 875-880.

Elder, S. T., Leftwich, D. A., & Wilkerson, L. A. The role of systolic- versus diastolic-contingent feedback in blood pressure conditioning. *Psychological Record*, 1974, *24*, 171-176.

Elder, S. T., Longacre, A., Jr., Welsh, D. M., & McAfee, R. D. Apparatus and procedure for training subjects to control their blood pressure. *Psychophysiology*, 1977, *14*, 68-72.

Elder, S. T., Ruiz, Z. R., Deabler, H. L., & Dillenkoffer, R. L. Instrumental conditioning of diastolic blood pressure in essential hypertensive patients. *Journal of Applied Behavior Analysis*, 1973, *6*, 377-382.

Elder, S. T., Verzwyvelt, E. A., & McAfee, R. D. Conditioned diastolic blood pressure as a function of induced masseter muscle tension. *Psychophysiology*, 1978, *15*, 422-428.

Elder, S. T., Welsh, D. M., Longacre, A., Jr., & McAfee, R. Acquisition, discriminative stimulus control, and retention of increases/decreases in blood pressure of normotensive human subjects. *Journal of Applied Behavior Analysis*, 1977, *10*, 381-390.

Erlanger, J. An experimental study of blood pressure and of pulse pressure in man. *Johns Hopkins Hospital Reports*, 1904, *12*, 53-110.

Fabricus, H. *De venarum ostiolis*. Padusa: L. Pasquatus, 1603.

Fey, S., & Lindholm, E. Systolic blood pressure and heart rate changes during three sessions involving biofeedback or no feedback. *Psychophysiology*, 1975, *12*, 513-519.

Fey, S., & Lindholm, E. Biofeedback and progressive relaxation: Effects on systolic and diastolic blood pressure and heart rate. *Psychophysiology*, 1978, *15*, 239-247.

Goldman, M. S., & Lee, R. M. Operant conditioning of blood pressure: Effects of mediators. *Psychophysiology*, 1978, *15*, 531-537.

Goldstein, D. S., Harris, A. H., & Brady, J. V. Sympathetic adrenergic blockade effects upon operantly conditioned blood pressure elevations in baboons. *Biofeedback and Self-Regulation*, 1977, *2*, 93-105. (a)

Goldstein, D. S., Harris, A. H., & Brady, J. V. Baroreflex sensitivity during operant blood pressure conditioning. *Biofeedback and Self-Regulation*, 1977, *2*, 127-138. (b)

Gribbin, B., Steptoe, A., & Sleight, P. Pulse wave velocity as a measure of blood pressure change. *Psychophysiology*, 1976, *13*, 86-90.

Hakumaki, M. O. K. Function of the left atrial receptors. *Acta Physiologica Scandinavica*, 1970 (Suppl. 144), pp. 1-54.

Hamilton, W. F., Woodbury, R. A., & Harper, H. T., Jr. Physiologic relationships between intrathoracic, intraspinal, and arterial pressures. *American Medical Association Journal*, 1936, *107*, 835.

Harris, A. H., Findley, J. D., & Brady, J. V. Instrumental conditioning of blood pressure elevations in the baboon. *Conditional Reflex*, 1971, *6*, 215-226.

Harris, A. H., Gilliam, W. J., Findley, J. D., & Brady, J. V. Instrumental conditioning of large magnitude, daily, 12-hour blood pressure elevations in the baboon. *Science*, 1973, *182*, 175-177.

Harvey, W. *Exercitatio de motu cordis et sanguinis en animalibus.* Frankfort: W. Fitzer, 1628.

Hnatiow, M. Learned control of heart rate and blood pressure. *Perceptual and Motor Skills*, 1971, *33*, 219-226.

Jacobson, E. *Progressive relaxation.* Chicago: University of Chicago Press, 1938.

Jernstedt, G. C., & Newcomer, J. P. Blood pressure and pulse wave velocity measurement for operant conditioning of autonomic responding. *Behavior Research Methods and Instrumentation*, 1974, *6*, 393-397.

Kimmel, H. D. Instrumental conditioning of autonomically mediated behavior. *Psychological Bulletin*, 1967, *67*, 337-345.

Kristt, D. A., & Engel, B. T. Learned control of blood pressure in patients with high blood pressure. *Circulation*, 1975, *51*, 370-378.

Lee, R. M., Caldwell, J. R., & Lee, J. A. Blood pressure tracking systems and their application to biofeedback. *Biofeedback and Self-Regulation*, 1977, *2*, 435-447.

Longacre, A., Jr., Elder, S. T., & McAfee, R. D. A blood pressure monitor/ conditioner. Reprinted from the *Proceedings of the IEEE Southeast Conference*, 1977, pp. 371-374.

Mahomed, F. On sphygmographic evidence of arterio-capillary fibroses. *Pathological Society Transactions*, 1877, *28*, 394-397.

Miller, N. E., & Carmona, A. Modification of a visceral response, salivation in thirsty dogs, by instrumental training with water reward. *Journal of Comparative and Physiological Psychology*, 1967, *63*, 1-6.

Miller, N. E., DiCara, L. V., Solomon, H., Weiss, J. M., & Dworkin, B. Learned modifications of autonomic functions: A review and some new data. *Circulation Research*, 1970, *27* (Suppl. 1), 3-11.

Pappas, B. A., DiCara, L. V., & Miller, N. E. Learning of blood pressure responses in the noncurarized rat: Transfer to the curarized state. *Physiology and Behavior*, 1970, *5*, 1029-1032.

Perez-Cruet, J., Plumlee, L., & Newton, J. E. Chronic basal blood pressure in unanesthetized dogs using the ring-catheter technique. *Proceedings of the Symposium for Biomedical Engineering*, 1966, *1*, 383-386.

Plumlee, L. A. Operant conditioning of increases in blood pressure. *Psychophysiology*, 1969, *6*, 283-290.

Ranson, S. W., & Clark, S. L. *The anatomy of the nervous system*. Philadelphia: Saunders, 1959.

Richter-Heinrich, E., Knust, U., Muller, W., Schmidt, K. H., & Sprung, H. Psychophysiological investigations in essential hypertension. *Journal of Psychosomatic Research*, 1975, *19*, 251-258.

Riva-Rocci, S. Uno nuovo sfignomanometro. *Gazzetta Medica Torino*, 1896, *47*, 981-1001.

Roberts, L. N., Smiley, R. A., & Manning, G. W. A comparison of direct and indirect blood pressure determinations. *Circulation*, 1953, *8*, 232-242.

Roman, J., Henry, J. P., & Meehan, J. P. Validity of flight blood pressure data. *Aerospace Medicine*, 1965, *36*, 436-441.

Schneider, J. A. Rapid absolute blood pressure feedback: Introducing a new method of providing blood pressure feedback. *Biofeedback and Self-Regulation*, 1978, *3*, 213. (Abstract)

Schwartz, G. Voluntary control of human cardiovascular integration and differentiation through feedback and reward. *Science*, 1972, *175*, 90-93.

Schwartz, G. E. Toward a theory of voluntary control of response patterns in the cardiovascular system. In P. A. Obrist, A. H. Black, J. Brener, & L. V. DiCara (Eds.), *Cardiovascular psychophysiology*. Chicago: Aldine, 1974.

Schwartz, G. E., Shapiro, D., & Tursky, B. Learned control of cardiovascular integration in man through operant conditioning. *Psychosomatic Medicine*, 1971, *33*, 57-62.

Schwartz, G., Shapiro, D., & Tursky, B. Self control of patterns of human diastolic blood pressure and heart rate through feedback and reward. *Psychophysiology*, 1972, *9*, 270.

Seldinger, S. I. Catheter replacement of the needle in percutaneous arteriography. *Acta Radiologica*, 1953, *39*, 368-375.

Shannon, B., Goldman, M., & Lee, R. Biofeedback training of blood pressure: A comparison of three feedback techniques. *Psychophysiology*, 1978, *15*, 53-59.

Shapiro, A. Contribution to a history of the placebo effect. *Behavior Science*, 1960, *5*, 109-135.

Shapiro, A., & Milhado, J. Observations on blood pressure and other physiologic and biochemical mechanisms in rats with behavioral disturbances. *Psychosomatic Medicine*, 1958, *20*, 303-313.

Shapiro, D., Schwartz, G. E., & Tursky, B. Control of diastolic blood pressure in man by feedback and reinforcement. *Psychophysiology*, 1972, *9*, 296-304.

Shapiro, D., Tursky, B., Gershon, E., & Stern, M. Effects of feedback and reinforcement on the control of human systolic blood pressure. *Science*, 1969, *163*, 588-590.

Shapiro, D., Tursky, B., & Schwartz, G. E. Differentiation of heart rate and systolic blood pressure in man by operant conditioning. *Psychosomatic Medicine*, 1970, *32*, 417-423.

Silver, B. V., Blanchard, E. B. Biofeedback and relaxation training in the treatment of psychophysiological disorders: Or are the machines really necessary? *Journal of Behavioral Medicine*, 1978, *1*, 217-239.

Smulyan, H. *Pulse wave velocity as an index of systolic arterial pressure*. Paper presented at the meeting of the American Psychological Association, Toronto, 1978.

Steptoe, A. Blood pressure control: A comparison of feedback and instructions using pulse wave velocity measurements. *Psychophysiology*, 1976, *13*, 528-535.

Steptoe, A. Voluntary blood pressure reductions measured with pulse transit time: Training conditions and reactions to mental work. *Psychophysiology*, 1977, *14*, 492-498.

Steptoe, A. The regulation of blood pressure reactions to taxing conditions using pulse transit time feedback and relaxation. *Psychophysiology*, 1978, *15*, 429-438.

Steptoe, A., & Johnston, D. The control of blood pressure using pulse-wave velocity feedback. *Journal of Psychosomatic Research*, 1976, *20*, 417-424. (a)

Steptoe, A., & Johnston, D. The control of blood pressure with instructions and pulse-wave velocity feedback. *European Journal of Behavioral Analysis and Modification*, 1976, *3*, 147-154. (b)

Steptoe, A., Smulyan, H., & Gribbin, B. Pulse wave velocity and blood pressure change: Calibration and applications. *Psychophysiology*, 1976, *13*, 488-493.

Still, J. W., & Whitcomb, E. R. Technique for permanent long-term intubation of rat aorta. *Journal of Laboratory and Clinical Medicine*, 1956, *48*, 152-154.

Surwit, R., Shapiro, D., & Good, M. Comparison of cardiovascular biofeedback, neuromuscular biofeedback, and meditation in the treatment of borderline essential hypertension. *Journal of Consulting and Clinical Psychology*, 1978, *46*, 252-263.

Tursky, B. The indirect recording of human blood pressure. In P. A. Obrist, A. H. Black, J. Brener, & L. V. DiCara (Eds.), *Cardiovascular psychophysiology*. Chicago: Aldine, 1974.

Werdegard, D., Johnson, D. B., & Mason, J. W. A technique for continuous measurement of arterial blood pressure in unanesthetized monkeys. *Journal of Applied Physiology*, 1964, *19*, 519-521.

Wilder, J. Basimetric approach (law of initial values) applied to biological rhythms. *Annals of the New York Academy of Science*, 1962, *98*, 1211-1220.

Winton, F. R., & Bayliss, L. E. *Human physiology* (4th ed.). Boston: Little, Brown, 1955.

Woodbury, R. A., Robinow, M., & Hamilton, W. F. Blood pressure studies on infants. *American Journal of Physiology*, 1938, *122*, 472.

10

CARDIAC ARRHYTHMIAS
AND SUDDEN DEATH

Benjamin H. Natelson

INTRODUCTION

In a typical year, nearly a half million Americans awake feeling fine, but sometime over the course of the day, they suddenly collapse and die (American Heart Association, 1974; Carveth, 1974). This phenomenon accounts for 25% of all deaths and is the leading cause of mortality in the twenty-to-sixty-four-year-old age group (De Silva & Lown, 1978). The social and personal significance of sudden death is easily imagined. The victim, usually a man, at the height of his economic and intellectual potential, is suddenly stricken dead. This is a common occurrence in America, and the problems of adjustment for the widow and children are great. Additionally, the loss to society of such a person is enormous, because the ten to fifteen years in which he could contribute his expertise to his business or profession is lost. The purpose of this chapter is, first, to review what is known medically about this syndrome of "sudden death" and, then, to review the research done with humans and animals on its causes.

There have been a number of autopsy studies of victims of sudden death (see Weinberg, 1978, for a review). The majority of the cases are male (60-85%), with a mean age of fifty-eight years. A history of prior cardiac symptoms is usually, but not always, found. When autopsies are performed on these victims, coronary artery disease in the form of *arteriosclerotic thrombotic plaques* is seen very frequently (Friedman, Manwaring, Rosenman, Donlon, Ortega, &

Preparation of this chapter was supported by a Veterans Administration Career Development Award. The experiments reported here were funded by grants from the American Heart Association-New Jersey Affiliate and from the Foundation of the College of Medicine and Dentistry of New Jersey.

Grube, 1973; Liberthson, Nagel, Hirshman, Nussenfield, Blackbourne, & Davis, 1974). In over 90% of cases, there is greater than 75% narrowing of at least one coronary artery; moreover, three-vessel disease is found in about half the hearts. A similar frequency of old *myocardial infarction* (MI) (heart attack), is found. Acute *intracoronary thrombi* (i.e., blood clots), indicative of very recent myocardial infarction, are seen in less than half the cases. Thus, the majority of cases do not appear to be associated with recent thrombosis or infarction. Moreover, of interest and importance is the fact that the hearts and cardiac vessels of 10% of sudden death victims seem totally normal.

These pathological findings plus the rapidity of collapse often seen in sudden death victims point to *ventricular arrhythmia* as the terminal event. Recent data collected from mobile rescue units have confirmed this hypothesis (Liberthson et al., 1974; Pantridge & Geddes, 1967). Prior to the establishment of these units, it was estimated that 50% of people having a heart attack died before reaching hospital. To combat this, *cardiopulmonary resuscitation* has been taught throughout the U.S. (for review, see American Heart Association, 1974), and suitably trained personnel, who have been taught to treat any cardiac arrhythmias they may find, are swiftly transported to the sick person's side.

Indeed, what is usually found is *ventricular fibrillation* (VF) — an electrocardiographic (EKG) diagnosis consonant with chaotic ventricular activity that does not effectively pump blood throughout the body and thus quickly produces collapse and then death. Moreover, when patients are resuscitated from ventricular fibrillation, less than half ever meet diagnostic criteria for myocardial infarction. Thus, there appear to be two groups of patients who develop VF. The majority sustain VF without myocardial necrosis; in general, their prognosis is poor, with a two-year mortality of 47%. The second group is composed of patients who develop VF shortly after acute MI; following resuscitation, the prognosis of these patients is the same as for those suffering similar infarctions not complicated by VF (Weinberg, 1978). For both groups, therefore, the nearly fatal event can be viewed as an electrical accident which can be reversed by the appropriate treatment and, once reversed, is unlikely to recur (Lown, Verrier, & Rabinowitz, 1977).

A prospective, epidemiologic study (Kannel, Doyle, McNamara, Quickerton, & Gordon, 1975) was done to delineate those factors, seen at an initial physical examination of people clinically free of coronary artery disease, which put them at risk for sudden death. Factors associated with high risk include hypertension, cigarette smoking, obesity, and elevated serum cholesterol. An even more striking *risk factor* is the presence of *ventricular premature contractions* (VPC) (Vismara, Zakanddin, Foerster, Amsterdam, & Mason, 1977). These abnormal, ventricular ectopic beats occur only rarely in young people; their incidence increases with age, but they are still uncommon in the asymptomatic person (Raftery & Cashman, 1976). Their incidence correlates with the presence of organic heart disease (Chiang, Perlman, Ostrander, & Epstein, 1959).

In another study, in which electrical activity of the heart was recorded for six hours in middle-aged men undergoing a number of physical and mental stress tests designed to simulate normal activities, Hinkle, Carver, and Stevens (1969) found VPCs and complex ventricular arrhythmias in 62% of the recordings. After long-term follow-up, these workers noted that the chance of sudden death in people with the arrhythmias was ten times greater than in people initially showing no ventricular arrhythmias.

The data from these two studies strongly suggest that ventricular ectopic beats are not normal but, instead, reflect underlying heart disease. Since a routine EKG can miss ectopy, long-term monitoring (for up to twenty-four hours) is needed for diagnosis of ventricular aberrant beats (Vismara et al., 1977). A strong correlation also exists in middle-aged people between sudden death and repetitive ventricular responses to a ventricular pacing stimulus, delivered via transvenous electrodes (Greene, Reid, & Schaeffer, 1978): people with normal cardiac activity never showed repetitive ventricular responses while the majority of people with recurrent symptomatic ventricular tachycardia or previous MI frequently did show it and had a significantly greater chance of succumbing to sudden death than those who did not.

In addition to ventricular irritability, another electrocardiographic finding is associated with a significantly increased chance of sudden death in middle-aged men. This is *sustained slow heart rates*, that is, mean heart rates that do not rise during a day's activity and do not increase, as is normal, during sighing, coughing, or straining (Hinkle, Carver, & Plakun, 1972). This EKG pattern was found to not necessarily be accompanied by VPCs, and, yet, it was found, prospectively, to correlate strikingly with sudden cardiac death.

In summary, sudden death, apparently attributable to cardiac dysfunction, is a leading cause of mortality among adults in the twenty-to-sixty-four-year-old age group. A number of researchers have investigated cardiac events associated with the sudden death syndrome. Pathological findings at autopsies include the presence of coronary artery disease, narrowing of coronary arteries, indices of old myocardial infarction, and acute intracoronary thrombi. Death is preceded by some potentially reversible cardiac arrhythmia. Factors found to be predictive of the sudden death syndrome include hypertension, cigarette smoking, obesity, elevated serum cholesterol, ventricular premature contractions, ventricular arrhythmias during stress testing, repetitive ventricular responses to a ventricular pacing stimulus, and sustained slow heart rates.

MEASUREMENT

By the all-or-nothing nature of the process, measuring the frequency of sudden death is simple. What becomes harder to measure is some other variable which correlates strongly with the occurrence of sudden death. The previous section of this chapter touched on some of those variables, and they will be discussed more fully here.

For human studies, the technique is primarily epidemiologic. People are examined by a physician and undergo a battery of lab tests including resting electrocardiogram, stress electrocardiogram (done while the person is jogging on a treadmill) and plasma cholesterol. People are blocked by the results of these tests and the presence of absence of other factors such as cigarette smoking, hypertension, or diabetes, and are then followed medically over time. Frequencies of sudden death or myocardial infarction are tallied, and between-group comparisons made.

Another useful technique for identifying the person prone to the sudden death syndrome is to use a system of monitoring the electrocardiogram in the ambulatory subject. The classic way of doing this is to use a *Holter monitor*. This is a miniaturized, battery-operated, analog tape recorder which can be carried by the subject. A Holter tape can store at least twenty-four hours of sequential cardiac electrical activity. These tapes can later be read by trained personnel, using a computer which scans the entire tape in twelve minutes. The new generation Holter computers are programed to automatically count VPCs. Good baseline data exist for people of different ages doing their normal daily activities, but, as yet, such data do not exist for people undergoing moderate psychologial or physical stress. Obviously, Holter monitors can be used in the study of animals, or, more simply, if the time of study is brief enough, EKGs can be directly recorded on paper.

Stress testing has been used increasingly more often in the last five years as an aid to identifying patients at risk for sudden death. In such a procedure, the patient, wearing EKG electrodes, jogs on a treadmill to the point at which his heart rate reaches a predetermined value. The electrocardiogram is then examined for signs of *cardiac ischemia* (localized hypoxia due to obstructed circulation) or arrhythmias. A major controversy currently exists regarding its efficacy in identifying people at risk (Epstein, 1978; Morris & McHenry, 1978). The major criticism against its use is that it is not cost-effective (Epstein, 1978), since it can at best identify the 3.5% of the male population at risk of sudden death but cannot pick from this group the 0.3% who will die that year. The other problem about the method is that it is not clear what represents a normal response to the stress test. VPCs have been reported to occur in normal men (Beard & Owen, 1973) but their frequency has been noted to increase with age (McHenry, Fisch, Jordan, & Corya, 1972). Diagnosis of cardiac disease thus becomes a relative thing, based on seeing larger numbers and more serious arrhythmic episodes (Lown, Calvert, Armington, & Ryan, 1975; McHenry et al., 1972). It must be emphasized that the idea that VPCs can occur in "normal" exercising men is open to debate. Another, equally credible interpretation is that an element of heart disease does exist in those asymptomatic men who develop VPCs during a stress test. This analysis is strengthened by autopsy data on American fatalities in the Korean war (Enos & Holmes, 1953). Surprising amounts of coronary arteriosclerosis were found in the hearts of soldiers in the second and third decades of life. Thus, it may be possible that the stress test does dichotomize the well from the marginally to substantially affected. To test this idea will require a large series of stress tests of "normal" people, beginning from the first decade of life. Developing EKG norms for people of all ages subjected to physical and mental stress should be a high priority for people interested in this area.

Finally, recent work (Moss, DeCamilla, & Davis, 1977) was directed at identifying those patients who have already sustained a myocardial infarction and later succumb to sudden death. As with the overall group of sudden death victims, recent coronary thrombosis was relatively rare, and acute myocardial infarction was seen in only one-third of the patients (Friedman et al., 1973). Importantly, use of digitalis and diuretic and antiarrhythmic agents was significantly greater in this group during the week before death than in a group of survivors. Although this may merely mean the nonsurvivors had more myocardial and electrical dysfunction, it is also possible that these agents, alone or in combination, may contribute to an unfavorable outcome.

Another technique which employs ventricular pacing has been used to study ventricular arrhythmogenesis. In such a technique, a pacing wire is threaded through a surface vein and is implanted in the right ventricle. The heart is paced by this electrode at a constant rate, so that changes in autonomic nervous activity do not affect cardiac rate. Then, shortly after a paced beat, one to three extra pulses are delivered. The current of the final test pulse is varied until a spontaneous, nonpaced, ventricular extrasystole is seen. Matta, Verrier, and Lown (1976) showed in animals that the amount of current needed to produce these *repetitive extrasystoles* (RE) correlates highly with the amount of current needed to produce ventricular fibrillation; thus, these workers felt that they were testing the system responsible for VF by determining the current needed to produce RE. Their reason for developing this technique was to make it applicable to humans, as in the work by Greene et al. (1978). Another reason lies with the fact that studying frank onset of ventricular arrhythmias in large animals is very expensive, because the arrhythmia is fatal unless it is rapidly reversed by transthoracic defibrillation, a process which, itself, could affect the structural integrity of the heart. Recently, however, Lawler, Botticelli, and Lown (1976) indicated that repeated production of REs by exogenous shock can produce cardiac damage.

In summary, efforts at measuring cardiac arrhythmias and sudden death have focused on medical identification of cardiac abnormalities and epidemiologic procedures. Medical assessment has included stress electrocardiograms, the Holter monitor to record the electrocardiograms of ambulatory subjects, the study of patients who have already experienced a myocardial infarction, and ventricular pacing to study ventricular arrhythmogenesis. There are strengths and weaknesses of each method, but data derived from these assessment efforts are facilitating the identification of etiological factors and the development of intervention strategies.

ETIOLOGY

Current Theoretical Conceptualizations

The first theoretical concept is concerned with susceptibility to psycho-somatic disease in general. The author's major notion is that lethal disease, for instance, cardiac arrhythmias or peptic ulcers, does not occur commonly in people or animals subjected to stress — no matter how massive — unless they are also somehow predisposed to developing that particular illness. Evidence from the general psychosomatic literature in support of this construct will be considered here; in the next section will be an in-depth review of how aptly this construct pertains to the role of psychosomatic factors in the production of the sudden death syndrome.

The notion of predisposition was most strongly made by Weiner, Thaler, Reiser, and Mirsky (1957) in their classic study, which identified army draftees who were at risk either for having peptic ulcers at the start of basic training or for developing them by its end. These authors used *blood pepsinogen*, which correlates roughly with acid secretory capacity, to delimit two groups of subjects: the 10% with the highest values and the 10% with the lowest, referred to, respectively, as hypersecretors and hyposecretors. Based on psychological interviews, Weiner et al. selected ten draftees who they thought were at risk for having or getting ulcers. Importantly, seven of these men actually had or did develop ulcers by the end of basic training and nine of these men were from the hypersecretor group. Thus, when ulcers developed, they did so in the predis-posed group.

The author's own efforts to replicate the famous "executive" monkey experiment strengthened my view that potentially lethal disease did not occur in normal subjects. Natelson, DuBois, and Sodetz (1977) used a multiple stress procedure on a group of monkeys. The animals' stomach and proximal duodenum were directly viewed bi-weekly by a flexible fiberoptic endoscope. Lesions developed in seven of the eight monkeys studied and a correlation was found to exist between lesion frequency and the psychological demands of the schedule. Regardless of the continuation and escalation of stress, however, lesions healed and remained relatively superficial. Frank deep ulcers were never seen.

There is additional evidence that severe stress in the otherwise healthy individual is not necessarily pathogenetic. Such evidence can be found from reports of concentration camp inmates, some of whom actually attained better health when removed from their jobs and thrust into camps during World War II (Wolf & Goodell, 1968). Similarly, Hinkle, Kane, Christenson and Wolff

(1959) prospectively studied the health patterns of several groups of refugees from the Hungarian Revolution of 1956. Despite this upheaval, the people reported an improvement in their general health and well-being, in most instances. Based on several decades of prospective studies correlating life stresses with disease onset, Hinkle (1974) recently came to the following conclusion: Assuming a relatively constant physical environment, "exposure to culture change, social change and change in interpersonal relations may lead to a significant change in health if (a) a person has pre-existing illness or susceptibility to illness, and (b) he perceives the change as important to him" (pp. 7-44). Thus, as Rabkin and Struening (1976) conclude, "exposure to stressors alone is almost never a sufficient explanation for the onset of illness in ordinary human experience" (p. 1018).

As noted above, arteriosclerosis is thought to be the major pathological factor responsible for sudden death and VF is thought to be the cardiac mechanism responsible for this event. It is important to realize at this point that this conclusion is more inferential than factual. Let us look at VF first: When a resuscitation team arrives to treat someone who has collapsed, they find ventricular tachyarrhythmias (VT) 73% of the time; the remainder are bradyarrhythmias (Liberthson et al., 1974). Because of this, some investigators have focused primarily on understanding the mechanism of ventricular fibrillation. This assumes, however, that ventricular fibrillation was precipiated by ventricular irritability in the form of the runs of VPCs that characterize VT. It is a well-known clinical fact, however, that bradyarrhythmias can degenerate into ventricular fibrillation. Thus, it is possible that many of the patients found to be fibrillating at the time of resuscitation actually had bradyarrhythmias first. If this alternative inference is at least possible, it means that scientists cannot focus all their attention on etiological factors that increase cardiac automaticity, such as activation of the sympathetic nervous system. Indeed, since a constant, slow heart rate in a middle-aged man is a risk factor for sudden death (Hinkle et al., 1972), and since cardiac arrest following the most destructive myocardial infarctions is frequently due to asystole or the cessation of heart beats (Robinson, Sloman, Mathew, & Goble, 1965), a role of the parasympathetic nervous system in producing the sudden death syndrome must be considered.

The other question relates to what pathological state produces the electrical event that suddenly causes collapse and death. Histologic diagnostic analysis results in different opinions as to the etiological factor. It is commonly agreed that about half of all patients are found, at autopsy, to have pathological evidence of very recent myocardial infarction. Assuming this incidence figure is reliable, an important question is to determine when these infarctions occurred. Scott and Briggs (1972) addressed their attention to this issue and report myocardial infarcts from six hours to one week old in 47% of cases. These data mean one of two things: either the patient did not feel any chest pain associated with his myocardial infarction (so-called "*silent infarction*") or he misinterpreted or ignored the symptoms that he did feel.

Two inferences can be drawn from this report. First, it may be possible through medical education to reduce the number of people dying suddenly of acute myocardial infarction. This could be done by teaching the public that the probability of sudden death following a heart attack is greatest in the first hours after the attack and that anybody over forty years old who has serious chest pain should see a doctor with dispatch. The other inference about which a great deal of disagreement exists is that a much greater percentage of sudden death may be due to myocardial infarction, which produces sudden death so quickly that inadequate time transpires for histologic changes to develop in the myocardium.

Lie and Titus (1975) have been interested in developing techniques that histologically date the time of infarction. In general, diagnosis of myocardial ischemia or infarction can be done with reliability six hours after the infarction. Lie and Titus developed histologic signs of acute myocardial ischemia – that is, *myofibrillar degeneration, sinuous fibers*, and *fuchsinophilic staining* – that develop less than six hours after experimental infarction. They found at least one of these histologic criteria in the hearts of 81% of sudden death victims and all three criteria in 52%. The interpretation of these findings, however, is open to different interpretations. Lie and Titus believed this means that acute myocardial infarction is responsible for many cases of sudden death, while another interpretation (Weinberg, 1978) is that these changes are secondary to the ischemia produced by the terminal cardiac arrhythmia.

Definition of who is a sudden death victim may also affect what is found on autopsy. Thus, in contrast to data reported above on patients dying within a day of the onset of symptoms is the work of Friedman et al. (1973). These workers divided their cases into those people collapsing within a minute of symptom onset and those collapsing within minutes to twenty-four hours after the onset of symptoms. What was common across the groups was the presence of severe, chronic, occlusive, coronary artery disease. Acute infarction and acute thromboses were rare in the first group and relatively common in the second group. This finding, plus the different prognoses in those suffering acute infarction when compared to those not having evidence of this (Weinberg, 1978) does not support the notion that acute MI is responsible for sudden death. Further pathologic investigation of this question using multivariate data analysis would go a long way toward resolving this question.

Regardless of whether infarction is a very common cause of sudden death or a not-too-common cause, another major unknown producing different conceptualizations of etiology revolves around the intracardiac pathology. The frequency of acute intracoronary thrombi in sudden death victims varies from 5%, seen in those collapsing immediately after symptom onset (Friedman et al., 1973), to 47%, seen in those collapsing within an hour after symptom onset (Scott & Briggs, 1972). Regardless of which figure is believed, the frequency of acute thrombotic disease is usually less than that of acute myocardial infarction. From this, one can infer that frank infarction need not always be preceded by acute thrombosis and/or that thrombosis need not necessarily cause infarction (Chandler, Chapman, Eckardt, Roberts, Schwartz, Sinapius, Spain, Ness, &

Simon, 1974). The other possibility is that some mechanism could produce cardiac ischemia severe enough to cause arrhythmia but not severe enough to cause frank infarction.

Schwartz and Gerrity (1975) suggested a number of other pathological states which could produce myocardial ischemia. Efforts to find disease in the small vessels of the heart and in the cardiac conducting systems have been unsuccessful (Lie & Titus, 1975). The experimental work of Jorgensen, Rowsell, Hovig, Glynn, and Mustard (1967), however, makes it clear that *platelet thrombi* within tiny vessels deep in the heart can produce areas of focal cardiac ischemia and infarction; when the small vessels were examined at autopsy, platelet aggregates were found only occasionally within the microcirculation. Thus, any mechanism producing microthrombi could produce enough ischemia to produce an arrhythmia without leaving evidence of its presence. Recently, spasm of the coronary arteries has been implicated as a cause of MI (Maseri, L'Abbate, Baroldi, Chierchia, Marzilli, Ballestra, Severi, Parodi, Biagini, Distante, & Resola, 1978). What triggers this spasm is unknown but autonomic nervous activation or platelet-related vasospasm have been suggested (Braunwald, 1978).

Next, focus should be directed to the pathological state seen in the hearts of 85-90% of patients dying suddenly: *chronic arterisclerotic heart disease.* Coincident with this pathological finding is the fact that an equal frequency of patients with known heart diseases, who die suddenly at some time subsequent to being studied, are found to have moderate to severe impairment of myocardial function many months prior to demise (Margolis, Hirshfeld, McNeer, Starmer, Rosati, Peter, Behar, & Kong, 1975). Whether or not similar changes exist in the hearts of asymptomatic people who die suddenly is, of course, not known. If such changes do exist one might imagine that changes in cardiac output could produce areas of myocardial ischemia, which could trigger off arrhythmias.

Finally, some attention must be directed to the 10-15% of victims who have no evidence of cardiac disease. Obviously, several viewpoints can be used to speculate about what is wrong with these people. One is that they have some form of cardiac disease, such as *cardiomyopathy*, whose pathology occurs at the submicroscopic level. Another view is that such people are dramatically sensitive to changes in autonomic neural activity and that these changes could produce ischemia, either directly or via the release of adrenal epinephrine (Lown et al., 1977). The resolution of these different theoretical conceptualizations will require new data based on new anatomical diagnostic techniques.

Empirical Research

Physiological

Because of the nature of the sudden death syndrome, there is an obvious dearth of data on cardiac physiological function in human victims of the syndrome. Myerburg, Sung, Conde, Mallon, and Castellanos (1977), however, collected some electrophysiologic data on patients resuscitated from unexpected cardiac arrest outside the hospital. Of the ten patients studied, four had collapsed with VF and six with VT. None had evidence of acute MI but five of the six VT patients had ventricular aneurysms (localized dilation which functions poorly, if at all, due to structural defects). Since the autopsy studies reviewed in previous sections did not reveal aneurysms, it is possible that these represented histologically normal areas that functioned abnormally. Using programed pacing with the extra ventricular stimulus method, these authors produced, in five of the six VT patients, a VT similar to the one that had originally produced their collapse. In contrast, no ventricular arrhythmias occurred in the VF patients. The authors concluded that in patients with aneurysm, in contrast to those with VF the electrophysiological defect underlying VT is persistent; thus, they inferred that the disturbance underlying unexpected VF may be transient.

In another study prospectively studying cardiac function in preselected patients who had had angiographically documented coronary artery disease for up to four years, Margolis et al. (1975) found a strikingly increased prevalence of such abnormalities as three-vessel arteriosclerotic disease, localized areas of ventricular dyssynergy, diffusely abnormal ventricular contraction, moderate to severe degrees of mitral regurgitation, a widened arteriovenous O_2 difference across the heart, a decreased cardiac index, and an increased left ventricular end-diastolic pressure in patients dying suddenly. Only one of the twenty-nine victims had mild coronary artery disease and normal ventricular function.

The result of this severe arteriosclerotic disease, therefore, is ventricular dysfunction, which can produce areas of focal ischemia if blood flow demands are suddenly changed, as can occur with emotional excitement or physical stress. Importantly, Friedman et al. (1973) found that, of their twenty-seven cases of abrupt collapse and death, fourteen occurred during or directly after severe or moderate physical activity. These findings were confirmed and extended to include acute emotional tension by Lown et al. (1975).

Before turning specifically to how ischemic foci in the myocardium can trigger arrhythmias, let us first examine the data relevant to the electrophysiological mechanisms involved in cardiac arrhythmias. Perhaps because ventricular fibrillation is the most common arrhythmia seen in patients who have suddenly collapsed, most of the arrhythmia research is directed toward understanding the pathogenesis of VF. Pathogenesis may be divided into three general categories: disorders of *impulse formation* (*automaticity*), disorders of *impulse condition* (*reentry*), or combinations of both (Bigger, 1973). Automaticity refers to the ability of a cell or group of cells to spontaneously generate action potentials by a net intracellular accumulation of positive charges which reduce the membrane potential toward zero (Zipes, 1975). If the membrane potential reaches threshold potential, excitation occurs. Reentry involves (1) the unidirectional block of conduction at some site, (2) the propagation over an alternate route at a velocity slow enough to allow delayed excitation of the tissue beyond the block, and (3) the reexcitation of the tissue proximal to the block (Zipes, 1975).

Any normal heart can be made to fibrillate if a single induction shock is delivered to it at a particular time in the cardiac cycle. The capacity to fibrillate, therefore, is normal and relates to the fact that various segments of the ventricle have electrophysiological properties such as action potential duration and rate of rise, conduction velocity, refractoriness, and excitability which are not uniform (Zipes, 1975). Classically, if the single shock is delivered a few milliseconds before the peak of the T wave (that is, the long latency upward wave on the EKG, indicative of ventricular repolarization), VF usually occurs. This is the case because stimulation at this time encounters some cells fully repolarized, others partially repolarized and still others absolutely refractory. Conduction becomes fractionated and is likely to result in areas of slowed conduction and block, creating the necessary requirements for reentry. Matta et al. (1976) recently explored the electrophysiology of this phenomenon. In twenty-nine of thirty-two dogs, these workers found that the occurrence of a repetitive extrasystole (RE) following a ventricular exogenous stimulus prophesied the development of VF; the two dogs not showing this relation were found to have heart worms. They additionally noted a .83 correlation between the amount of current needed to produce an RE and that required to produce VF. Because of this, and because the nadir for RE occurred at the same time as the vulnerable period threshold for VF, the authors inferred that RE and VF are due to a common mechanism.

If an exogenous electrical impulse can produce fibrillation, one would expect that an endogenous one, such as a VPC, can do the same. This is, indeed, a well-known phenomenon: VPCs occurring on top of the T wave (the so-called *R on T phenomenon*) have been shown to elicit VF and are thought to be especially dangerous (Lown et al., 1975). The probability of the occurrence of VF also relates to the size of the ischemic or infarcted portion of the heart (Wit & Bigger, 1975). Small bits of normal ventricle are unable to sustain fibrillatory behavior, probably because the electrophysiological characteristics of these bits are so homogeneous. In addition, large areas of cardiac ischemia can maximize the probability of reentry, because conduction through some fibers would probably approach normal, while that through others might be severely slowed (Wit & Bigger, 1975). In some cases of focal ischemia, reentry may be triggered merely by heart rate increases or decreases, indicative of changes in autonomic activity (Kerzner, Wolf, Kosowsky, & Lown, 1973; Zipes, 1975). Ischemia itself, acidosis, digitalis toxicity, and hypothermia can also decrease the ventricular fibrillation threshold (Zipes, 1975).

It is conceivable that VPCs initiate VF, not by a reentrant mechanism, but by their triggering automatic focal discharges. Such triggerable foci have been demonstrated following aconitine and digitalis administration and in calcium-dependent preparation (Zipes, 1975). It is important to realize that automaticity is a normal occurrence in all cardiac cells (Katzung, 1978), but that it can be increased in focal areas within the myocardium by such a drug as digitalis or by changes in autonomic activity.

How digitalis produces cardiac arrhythmias is a controversial subject in clinical pharmacology. Originally, it was thought that the drug merely acted locally upon the heart to produce its major toxic side effects of cardiac arrhythmias (Moe & Farah, 1975). Subsequent research has demonstrated, however, that arrhythmias begin early because of activation of the autonomic nervous system (Levitt, Cagin, Somberg, & Kleid, 1976). Gillis, Raines, Sohn, Levitt, and Standaert (1972) showed this most clearly by demonstrating firing in preganglionic sympathetic and parasympathetic fibers, which just precedes the onset of arrhythmia; they also showed that arrhythmias can be retarded by ablating the autonomic input to the heart.

Hashimoto, Kimura, & Kubota (1973) contributed greatly to the understanding of the interaction between digitalis, the heart, and the autonomic nervous system. These authors elegantly used an in vitro preparation of sino-atrial node and papillary muscle, which was perfused by blood from a donor dog receiving an infusion of ouabain. In two groups, donor dogs anesthetized with morphine and urethane and donor dogs subjected to spinal cord section, arrhythmic contraction of the isolated muscle occurred simultaneously with the appearance of ventricular arrhythmias in the donor dog. In contrast, a dissociation was noted in those groups in which the donor dogs were subjected either to adrenalectomy or to spinal cord destruction: as the ouabain was infused, contractility in the in vitro papillary muscle increased, while automaticity decreased markedly; finally, the donor animal died of cardiac arrhythmia while the in vitro preparation did not show any change in automaticity. The authors also reported that the dose required to produce ventricular arrhythmia in the donor dog was increased somewhat by adrenalectomy, spinal cord section, or spinal cord destruction. These findings suggest that digitalis triggers a spinal cord reflex that releases epinephrine from the adrenal gland, and that it is epinephrine and perhaps some other as yet unidentified plasma substance(s) which produce the changes in cardiac automaticity which are usually attributed to digitalis.

The fact that alterations in autonomic activity can affect cardiac automaticity should suggest to the reader that stimulation of both central and peripheral neural sites can produce ventricular arrhythmias. This is, indeed, the case, and a review of this literature reveals dozens of papers in which brain stimulation produces arrhythmias (see Mauck & Hochman, 1967). Stimulation throughout the limbic brain, that is, the rhinencephalon, diencephalon, and mesencephalon, produce these arrhythmias. Their pathogenesis is dependent on when they begin, in relation to the onset and offset of brain stimulation. Knowledge is most complete about the mechanism of ventricular arrhythmias stemming from hypothalamic stimulation. Stimulation of posterior hypothalamic sites produces a progressive narrowing of the P-R interval, until the P wave disappears, and a nodal rhythm is seen. Evans and Gillis (1974) showed that this is due to intense sympathetic stimulation: they recorded hyperactivity from the sympathetics at the time of the arrhythmia, were able to block it with injection of sympatholytics (that is, beta blockers) but not with anticholinergics, and were able to mimic it by direct stimulation of peripheral sympathetic nerves. D'Agrosa (1977) corroborated the fact that stimulation of peripheral sympathetics can produce arrhythmias, both junctional and ventricular in origin. Importantly, Gillis, Pearle, and Hoekman (1974) were unable to prevent these arrhythmias after adrenergic and/or cholinergic blockade. This finding indicates that these arrhythmias are not the result of norepinephrine or acetylcholine release at the neuromyocardial junction.

In other experiments, Verrier, Calvert, and Lown (1975) demonstrated that the electrical threshold for VF was significantly reduced by posterior hypothalamic stimulation. This effect was not due merely to rate increases, because similar decreases in these thresholds were found in dogs with surgically produced heart block. Beta-adrenergic blockade prevented this decrease while vagotomy and adrenalectomy were without effect. Approaching this problem from the other side, Rabinowitz and Lown (1978) increased central serotoninergic stores by injection of precursor and enzyme blockers, a treatment that had been shown to diminish sympathetic activity (Baum & Shropshire, 1975). This treatment produced significant increases in the threshold of the ventricle for repetitive extrasystoles after exogenous stimulation.

When the stimulating electrode was moved more rostrally to the region of the ventromedian nucleus, arrhythmias did not develop during stimulation but did so after the stimulus current was turned off (Evans & Gillis, 1978). During stimulation, heart rate and blood pressure increased; following cessation of stimulation, heart rate fell, and nodal or ventricular beats were seen. That this was due to a reflex cholinergic mechanism was proven by the fact that anticholinergics blocked it. If the stimulus-bound hypertension was prevented either by hemorrhage, ganglion blocking sympatholytics, or spinal cord section, so, too, was the arrhythmia.

Cardiac arrhythmias also follow nonspecific but severe head trauma (Evans, Alter, Shatsky, & Gunby, 1976). Following temporoparietal head impact, cardiac arrhythmias and hypotension developed in a group of rhesus monkeys. The arrhythmias included nodal rhythm, atrioventricular (AV) dissociation, and multifocal nodal and ventricular rhythms. That these arrhythmias were due to intense vagal stimulation was proven by the fact that atropine blocked their development, while alpha and beta blockers were without effect.

When the heart is made ischemic, the propensity of brain or sympathetic nerve stimulation to produce arrhythmias is increased (Corr & Gillis, 1978; Lown & Verrier, 1976; Lown et al., 1977). Thus, where no arrhythmia regularly develops following hypothalamic stimulation, it does if stimulation is done after coronary artery occlusion. Conversely the incidence of VF after occlusion of a coronary artery is lessened by pharmacologic adrenergic blockade. Complicating the analysis, however, is the work of Kerzner et al. (1973), who showed that vagal stimulation in the ischemic heart also precipitates VT.

In summary, data exist to suggest that sudden death victims have ventricular dysfunction, which can trigger ventricular arrhythmias in the face of an episode of transient ischemia to the heart. The mechanism of arrhythmogenesis relates either to reentry or to automaticity. The probability of seeing arrhythmias is increased if digitalis, a common cardiac tonic, is being taken. Although the mechanism for this effect is not clear, it probably involves the activation of some central neural reflex. Other experiments have shown that direct activation of brain or peripheral nerves can produce cardiac arrhythmias.

Psychological

This section will first consider the human data relating psychological factors to the production of cardiac arrhythmias and sudden death and then will review the animal studies.

Human. Frequently, medical knowledge advances in a rather stereotyped way. A physician notes an interesting association in a patient and publishes this as a case report. When a number of these exist in the literature, someone writes a review and makes some inferences. Then, epidemiologic studies are done, first retrospectively and then prospectively. Finally, if it is consonant with good ethics, laboratory experiments are done to prove a cause-and-effect relationship. This outline has been closely followed in demonstrating the role of psychological factors in the production of sudden death and cardiac arrhythmias.

Case reports make up the first bit of evidence for the role of psychosomatic factors in the production of the sudden death syndrome. The first of these was biblical. St. Luke noted that when Ananias was charged by Peter, "You have not lied to man but to God, " Ananias fell down dead (Acts 5:1-2). In modern times, attention was focused on this phenomenon by Cannon's early paper on voodoo death (1942). In that paper Cannon reviewed the anthropologic literature for instances of otherwise normal people dying inexplicably after being hexed or after violating some taboo. Other anecdotal descriptions exist (Yawger, 1936).

Some of the earliest reports can be faulted, in that their authors merely inferred that arrhythmia onset was caused by emotional stress. Thus, Benedict and Evans (1952) believed that their patient's second degree heart block was related to his psychological state, because episodes could occasionally be precipitated by discussing emotionally arousing subjects. Others have attributed arrhythmias to anxiety states without adequately documenting the correlation (Marmon & Kent, 1958; Rahe & Christ, 1966; Silverman & Goodman, 1951). Similarly, other case reports have noted a correlation between either chronic anxiety (Goodfriend & Wolpert, 1976) or acute emotional arousal (Jarvinen, 1955; Levine, 1963) and sudden death.

Based on these data, a number of retrospective analyses have been done. Foremost among these is that of Engel (1971), who reviewed the emotional precedents of sudden death in 170 victims. He purposely skewed his distribution to only those newspaper reports which contained clear reference to a precipitating life situation. The events that were correlated with sudden death usually evoked intense emotional arousal of either a happy or sad nature. Other factors which Engel factored out as important correlates were the victim's perception that he could no longer control his environment and/or his feeling that he was giving up and no longer cared about the situation. In another retrospective study of twenty-five men suddenly succumbing, Greene, Goldstein, and Moss (1972) reported data suggesting that the majority of the men had been depressed for a variable length of time before death. Death then occurred in a setting of acute arousal, engendered by increased work and activity or by circumstances precipitating reactions of anxiety or anger; frequently, these related to loved ones leaving home. Unfortunately, a study such as this one is open to all the criticisms of retrospective testing, in that the interviewers could unconsciously prompt the subjects or sway their answers. The other caveat is that even with such a retrospective analysis, the relation is not always there: in the study of Greene et al., an association between death and emotional arousal was found in only 50% of the study group.

A number of investigators have documented that arrhythmias can be either precipitated or strikingly increased by perturbing the patient's emotional state. Wolf (1969) noted that, of seventeen patients on a cardiac care unit (CCU) at a time when another patient had a cardiac arrest, thirteen reacted with anxiety, depression or morbid dreams, and all thirteen had either an increased number of VPCs, VT, blood pressure elevation, hyperventilation, respiratory difficulties, angina, cardiac arrest, or death. Lown et al. (1975) noted that, of fifteen people experiencing unexpected cardiac arrest, five died immediately after stress, three while engaged in competitive sports, and two while under acute emotional tension.

Stevenson, Duncan, Wolf, Ripley, and Wolff (1949) brought into the laboratory a group of twelve unselected patients with histories of cardiac arrhythmias. The patients' ages ranged from thirty to seventy-four, and most of them had some history of organic cardiac disease. After attaching EKG leads, the investigators discussed the patients' life situations or tried to precipitate anxiety. Concurrent with these manipulations, they found that ventricular extrasystoles either developed or increased strikingly in frequency. Lown et al. (1977) were able to show a similar relation in a number of post-MI patients who had been free of arrhythmias prior to the emotionally disturbing interview.

In other work, Lown and DeSilva (1978) documented this relationship further. These workers studied nineteen patients with spontaneous ventricular arrhythmias; four of the subjects had no cardiac abnormality demonstrable by cardiac catheterization and coronary angiography, while the remainder had documented cardiac disease. Subjects were stressed by having to perform mental arithmetic, read from colored cards and recount emotionally charged experiences. Such stresses produced a significant increase in VPC frequency in eleven of the nineteen people, and one developed paroxysms of VT. Elicitation of vagal or sympathetic autonomic reflexes failed to induce significant arrhythmias in thirteen of fourteen subjects tested.

Several cases have evaluated people with recurrent, severe ventricular arrhythmias and hearts that showed no evidence of disease. In the first of these, Harvey and Levine (1952) showed that acute anxiety could precipitate runs of VT. In another, Lown, Temte, Reich, Gaughan, Regestein, and Hai (1976) thoroughly evaluated a thirty-nine-year-old man with a history of recurrent VF. After being subjected to the most up-to-date tests for cardiac disease, no reason for these arrhythmic episodes could be found. The authors demonstrated that VPC frequency could be increased either by visits from the psychiatrist or by submitting the subject to psychosocial stresses. Based on his apparently normal heart and a careful psychiatric evaluation, the authors concluded retrospectively that his emotional state might have been the cause of his arrhythmias. Of interest was the fact that this man had frequent VPCs during REM sleep, at the very time he later recalled having had emotionally laden dreams. In contrast with this was the earlier report of this group (Lown, Tykocinski, Garfein, & Brooks, 1973) of fifty-four patients who were not acutely ill and who slept in their own homes. Among twenty-two patients, sleep was associated with a 50% or greater reduction in the incidence of VPCs. In thirteen others, VPC frequency decreased 25-50% during sleep. Based on this work, Lown et al. (1976) inferred that central nervous system activation of a cognitive type could produce lethal arrhythmias in people without organic heart disease.

Taggart, Gibbons, and Somerville (1969) have prospectively tested, in the natural environment, the notion that stress can produce arrhythmias. They recorded EKGs in experienced drivers accustomed to busy city traffic while driving their own cars along familiar routes. Both normal people and those with coronary artery disease showed heart rate increases. Importantly, arrhythmias developed only in the diseased subgroup. Five of twenty-four developed multiple VPCs; additionally, two drivers with coronary disease experienced anginal pain, and two developed left ventricular failure. In a follow-up study, Taggart, Carruthers, and Somerville (1973) recorded EKGs in a group of twenty-three apparently normal subjects, aged twenty-one to fifty-eight, and in seven subjects with cardiac disease, aged forty-two to fifty-eight, while they spoke to an audience. Ectopic beats at a rate of more than 6/min were recorded in six of the normal group; the beats were prolific and multifocal in two. Five of the seven cardiac patients had multiple and often multifocal VPCs. Concurrently with the rapid rate induced by the public speaking exercise, plasma norepinephrine levels increased significantly.

The mechanism for these emotionally related arrhythmias has been speculated upon. First, it is important to review how cognitive factors may affect heart rate and produce arrhythmias. It is common knowledge that heart rate increases in the expectation of an important occurrence. Conversely, in people with hyperactive parasympathetic nervous systems, striking bradycardias can be produced. For example, one man was reported who has the ability to slow his heart to the stopping point on volition (McClure, 1959). Similarly, cases have been reported of emotional stimuli producing such a marked vasovagal response that Adams-Stokes attacks with cardiac arrest occur (Meinhardt & Robinson, 1962; Schlesinger, Barzilay, Stryjer, & Almog, 1977). Thus, mechanisms exist for major heart rate changes in either direction. Lown and DeSilva (1978) suggested that because rates usually increase, sympathetic activation is primarily responsible. This notion is supported by the observation of Taggart et al. (1973), who found that arrhythmias produced by speaking before an audience can be aborted by treatment with a beta-adrenergic blocker. Inconsistent with this finding, however, is the observation of Lown and DeSilva (1978) that reflex stimulation of either pure parasympathetic or pure sympathetic activity did not increase arrhythmia frequency in patients while mental stress did.

Wolf (1967) suggested that metabolic products from ischemic myocardium may activate a primitive reflex, known as the diving reflex, in a misguided attempt to conserve oxygen. This reflex is seen preponderantly in diving mammals, but it also occurs in man. Following face immersion in cold water, bradycardia, decreased peripheral blood flow producing a rise in blood pressure, and lactic acidosis develop. The bradycardia can be so intense in a normal man accustomed to face immersion that a frank nodal rhythm can develop (Kawakami, Natelson, & DuBois, 1967).

In his review of emotional causes of sudden death, Dimsdale (1977) suggested that both vagal and sympathetic activation are requisite. Engel (1971) came to the same speculation, based on his finding that "giving up" is a prominent premonitory finding in people with emotional correlates of sudden death. Unfortunately, the nature of the syndrome allows speculation but does not produce empirical facts.

Based on the general notion that certain environmental factors or personality characteristics might affect the probability of sudden death, a number of important epidemiologic studies have been done. One of the most interesting is that of Parkes, Benjamin, and Fitzgerald (1969). These authors hypothesized that the intense grief sustained by the death of a spouse could affect mortality. In Engel's (1971) study, death of a loved one was shown to precede death in 42% of all the cases of sudden death with psychological precedent. Parkes et al. followed the life course of 4,486 widowers over fifty-five years of age for a nine-year period since the death of their spouses in 1957. About 5% of these men died in the six months after their wife's death — a figure which is 40% above the expected rate for married men of that age. Thereafter, the mortality rate fell gradually to that expected. The greatest increase in mortality in that first 6-month period was found to be due to cardiac disease. Rahe, Romo, Bennett and Siltanen (1974), in a retrospective study, compared the life events preceding the sudden death of 226 Finns to the life events preceding a non-lethal MI in 279 other Finnish subjects. By necessity, Rahe et al. interviewed the victims' spouses; with the group of survivors, they interviewed the patients themselves as well as their spouses. When life events, as reported by an MI survivor and his or her spouse, were scored and then compared, significant correlations were usually found, but these correlations never exceeded a Spearman rank coefficient of .74, thus indicating substantial differences between survivors and spouses in recall of past events. With this bias in mind, the authors found significant increases in disruptions of routine family life in both groups in the six months prior to either death or MI. The subjects who had suddenly died had the greatest score for changes in lifestyle in the preceding six-month period. A few life events were reported more often by the spouses of cardiac-death subjects than by MI survivors; these were related to problems at home, at work, with their family, or with their personal or interpersonal life. Thus, no single area of life stress differentiated the two groups.

An interesting study was also recently done by Theorell and Rahe (1975), who examined the careful clinical records of Dr. Stewart Wolfe's outpatient clinic and selected the charts of thirty-six people who had had an MI, half of whom had ultimately died of their disease, and half of whom had survived over a six-year period. All patients came to clinic regularly, and the clinic physician made extensive notes about the patient's life situation at the time of his clinic visit. Theorell and Rahe prepared the charts so there was no indication of who died and who survived, and, then they scored each chart for magnitude of disruption of lifestyle over six-month intervals. The patients who died showed a significant build-up of disruptive events in their lives which peaked in the year before the fatal incident; such fluctuations in lifestyle disruptions were not seen in the survivor group. In their discussion, the authors review the possibilities as to whether the disruptions caused the lethal event or were merely the index of a more severe cardiac disease. Wolf (1969) did an important pilot study on a group of patients who had sustained myocardial infarction and a group of case-matched controls. Based on a psychological assessment for depression, Wolf chose ten people who he thought would succumb to recurrent MI. All ten were among twenty-two of the patient group who died during the four-year follow-up; eight of these people succumbed to sudden death, and the others died of suicide. This important pilot project bears repeating.

The final work relates to epidemiologic studies, the purpose of which is to identify psychological/environmental risk factors that predict sudden death. Jenkins (1976) extensively reviewed the psychosocioeconomic predictors for coronary disease, and his review should be consulted for those interested in this broader question. Correlates for sudden death are fewer. One relates to personality type. Glass (1977) defines this type A behavior pattern as one consisting of such predispositions as competitive achievement, striving, a sense of time urgency, and hostility — all of which can be elicited and observed in the presence of appropriate environmental circumstances. Friedman et al. (1973) noted an increased incidence of this personality type in people dying immediately or several hours after the onset of cardiac symptoms. A newly described risk factor relates to level of education over a three-year study period. Weinblatt, Ruberman, Goldberg, Frank, Shapiro, and Chaudbary (1978) noted that men with ventricular ectopic beats and less than eight years of formal education had over three times the risk of sudden death as found among better educated men with the same arrhythmia.

To summarize, psychological/environmental factors have been correlated in a causative way with cardiac arrhythmias. This relation occurs most clearly and most commonly in people with obvious cardiac disease.

Animal. In this section, will first be a review of experiments in which purportedly normal animals, when psychologically stressed, either become the victims of sudden death or develop a cardiac arrhythmia. Von Holst (1972) noted that when two male tree shrews are placed together, a brief battle will occur after which the defeated shrew lies quietly but alertly. If the dominant animal is not then removed, it will continue to attack the defeated shrew but will render little physical damage. Soon after, the defeated animal will begin breathing irregularly, then stop breathing, and die. A similar syndrome has been reported in wild Norway rats, but not in albino rats, when a newcomer male is placed into an established colony (Barnett, 1955). Similar instances of sudden death in zoo animals have been reported to rarely follow similar, seemingly mild, environmental perturbations (Christian & Ratcliffe, 1952).

Richter (1957) was the first to systematically study sudden death when he noted that this syndrome occurred in wild rats subjected to swimming stress. For these animals, especially after he had trimmed their whiskers, Richter found that, a striking bradycardia leading to asystole frequently occurred when the rat dived to the bottom of the swimming jar. When rats were given prior experience in the swimming jar, this lethal effect was prevented. Pretreatment with atropine also prevented the bradycardia and its lethal consequences.

Subsequent work has replicated and extended these findings to the laboratory albino rat (Binik, Theriault, & Shustack, 1977; Lynch & Katcher, 1974). These workers showed that the probability of survival in the water stress was diminished if the rats were repeatedly handled by humans before the stress. They reasoned that the handled animals were less fearful and explored their environment more than the unhandled controls. In the course of exploration, the handled animals dived and, in the course of doing this repeatedly, became anxoic and died. Death in this instance probably related, however, to elicitation of the diving reflex, a primitive oxygen-conserving reflex seen most prominently in diving mammals (Wolf, 1964). Thus, although normal, the rats in this particular stress situation were subject to a phenomenon which sensitized them so that stress did not merely produce trivial changes in cardiac rate but actually caused asystole with loss of consciousness and death.

In another study (Johansson, Jonsson, Lannek, Blomgren, Lindberg, & Poupa, 1974), alert pigs were rendered immobile by an injection of succinylcholine, a systemic, skeletal-muscle-paralyzing agent, and were subjected to occasional electric shock to the hind leg for the next fifteen to twenty minutes. Muscle relaxation was achieved without producing respiratory distress, and blood gas concentrations remained normal. Two pigs died suddenly during the experimental stress period. EKG recordings in these animals revealed profound sinus bradycardia, terminating in ventricular standstill; prior to death, one of these animals demonstrated VF on the EKG. The most frequent arrhythmia seen was VT; it occurred in one animal prior to its being shocked and in fourteen other pigs at some time during the shock period. Autopsy evaluation of the hearts of the pigs that died suddenly during the experiment revealed multiple hemorrhages throughout the heart as well as pale areas in the papillary muscles of the left ventricle. The authors noted that similar pathology had been produced in dogs by infusion of high doses of catecholamines.

Corley and his associates recorded EKGs in monkeys performing shock avoidance (Corley, Mauck, & Shiel, 1975; Corley, Shiel, Mauck, & Greenhoot, 1973) and in yoked control monkeys which could not perform an operant to affect shock delivery (1975). The authors reported that the paradigm produced progressive bradycardia leading to idioventricular rhythm, ventricular arrest, and death in some of the subjects in both groups.

Because Gascon (1977) mentioned that acute restraint stress could produce ventricular arrhythmias in otherwise normal rats, Natelson and Cagin (1979) decided to study this phenomenon in greater depth. Using Holter monitors, they recorded continuous EKGs from adult male guinea pigs, wearing a harness attached to a communtator, which allowed them to freely walk about an experimental chamber. About a week later, they recorded the EKG for another 24 hour period during which time the animals were restrained by snaring their paws with leather loops and holding their body still with a leather flap attached to the restraint board. The data are in Table 10.1. Three of the guinea pigs did show at least one VPC during their control sessions. For animals 6 and 7, these occurred minutes after being put into the chamber and thus may relate to the mild stress inherent in the novelty of the situation and in being handled by humans. During the restraint period, significantly more episodes of arrhythmias were seen, and, in addition, significantly more abnormal beats were recorded. Importantly, the severity of the arrhythmias was worse in the restrained state than in the free-ranging state: couplets of VPCs and VT developed in four of the seven animals. There were no fatalities, however.

A major contribution to the notion that cardiac arrhythmias may be a psychosomatic process comes from Lown's research. This scientist has used the exogenous ventricular stimulation technique to look at thresholds for repetitive ventricular response, which he believes is an index of VF (Matta et al., 1976), during control periods and during psychological perturbation. Lown's group's first experiment was the neatest (Lown, Verrier, & Corbalan, 1973). Dogs were placed in a Pavlov sling, in which they were given an unsignaled shock to the chest. Following several such sessions, the amount of current needed to

TABLE 10.1
Arrhythmias

Guinea Pig	Free-Ranging			Restrained		
	Number of Episodes	Abnormality Seen*	Number of Abnormal Beats	Number of Episodes	Abnormality Seen*	Number of Abnormal Beats
1	0	none	0	11	S, C, VT	148
2	0	none	0	1	VT	3
3	0	none	0	2	VT	23
4	0	none	0	1	S	1
5	1	S	1	9	S, C	24
6	1	S	6	2	S	5
7	2	S	5	6	S	8

*S = single VPC
C = couplet of VPCs
VT = three or more consecutive VPCs

Source: Compiled by the author.

produce a repetitive ventricular response dropped from 43 mA, found in the dogs in an environment designed to minimize discomfort and disturbance to the animal, to 14 mA, for those animals in the sling during a whole day, during which no shock was delivered.

Data during the development of the conditioned fear response would have been useful in assessing this report but were, unfortunately, not provided. The authors inferred the mechanism was due to sympathetic activation, due to the facts that the animals' heart rates increased 33% and that they all showed a somatic tremor during the period in the sling. Although no dog died, the authors concluded that psychological factors can predispose to electrical instability of the heart. DeSilva and Lown (1978) replicated this experiment and have noted that the threshold for RE quickly fell from 32 to 18 mA when dogs were moved from a nonstress environment to a Pavlov sling where shock had been delivered on previous days; the decrease attained statistical significance ten minutes after the move. Interestingly, this effect did not lessen on the fourth extinction trial. When dogs were given an injection of morphine, the threshold for RE was increased in the stress environment. The mechanism of morphine's action is not a simple one; that it is not merely a protective effect due to its vagotonic action was proven by the fact that atropinization did not reduce the current for RE to the original low level but produced only a partial lowering.

In other experiments, Matta, Lawler, and Lown (1976) reported currents necessary for an RE in dogs during their initial experience with signaled shock avoidance. Even on the first day, threshold for RE fell 50% (from 40 mA); this decrease could be blocked by a beta-adrenergic blocking agent. Since sessions were only twenty minutes long, however, these data merely indicate the animals' responses to electric shock and tell us little about the role of psychological factors in producing this change. The seemingly clear interpretation of their elegant early work (Lown et al., 1973) is complicated by a recent experiment on dogs given ten ninety-minute sessions, during which they could escape a signal for shock as well as prevent shock delivery, by emitting an operant response whenever the signal was turned on. Lawler et al. (1976) used lower intensity current to try to elicit the RE because of the possibility that local burns of the heart would be produced with high currents. They elicited REs in nearly one-fourth of all determinations, but these developed as frequently during preavoidance periods as during periods of performing active avoidance. Determining the threshold for RE for a group of control dogs who were allowed equal experience in the apparatus but who never experienced shock would help clarify the meaning of these data; the fall in current required to produce an RE could be related to physical factors, to confinement in the apparatus, or to the psychological contingencies related to it.

To summarize, experiments in this section indicate that severe stress can produce cardiac arrhythmias and, rarely, sudden death in normal animals. The cleanest example is Von Holst's (1972) work with the tree shrew. The next is that of Johansson et al. (1974), which is complicated by the fact that the immobile pigs were physically stressed by shock. Despite this, their work suggests the pig as an important animal for those interested in psychosomatic heart disease. The work of Natelson and Cagin (1979) and of Lown, Verrier, and Corbalan (1973) strongly supports the idea that lethal arrhythmias are not the rule in stressed, "normal," laboratory animals. If, however, their hearts are sensitized, as was the case in the swimming stress studies, sudden death occurs commonly. Thus, the next section will look at those studies in which animals with a predisposition to arrhythmias are stressed.

Only a few such experiments have been done. Corbalan, Verrier, and Lown (1974) trained dogs to know that, when they were placed in a Pavlov sling, a particular signal would be followed by a transthoracic shock. Myocardial infarctions were then produced by occluding a balloon catheter, which had previously been placed around the left anterior descending coronary artery. The dogs were allowed to recuperate from the spontaneous ventricular ectopic activity that followed the MI and were then placed in the Pavlov sling. Seven of the eight dogs showed either VPCs or VT in association with the signal that had previously been paired with shock. VT developed in two distinct patterns; in four dogs, a persistent sinus tachycardia developed; the VT that developed in these dogs was irregular and slower than the basal sinus rhythm. Another two dogs exhibited VPCs with an R on T phenomenon, as well as showing multifocal beats. Thus, these latter animals had the most dangerous arrhythmias. The arrhythmic response to psychological stress waned over a period of three days despite persistence of somatic tremor and other behavioral indices of stress. Since arrhythmias could not be induced thereafter, it seems that frank arrhythmogenesis required a substratum of electrical instability of the myocardium, Skinner, Lie, and Entman (1975) have done a similar experiment in pigs surgically prepared to allow reversible myocardial ischemia. These animals with ischemic hearts ubiquitously showed VF shortly after their first experience at being restrained; when they were restrained during prior adaptation periods, VF either did not occur or occurred long after the occlusion. This effect was not due merely to cardiac rate increases, because the latency to VF remained high in nonstressed pigs, whose hearts were exogenously paced at the same rates displayed by the restrained group. Of interest and some surprise to those postulating a sympathetic mechanism for this arrhythmia (Lown et al., 1977) was the fact that beta-adrenergic blockade was actually deleterious: it did not prevent the early development of VF in nonadapted animals, and, in fact, it hastened it.

Because of his belief that potentially lethal psychosomatic disease rarely occurs in animals with no predisposition to disease, Natelson decided to look at the production of cardiac arrhythmias in laboratory animals that were predisposed to developing arrhythmias because of prior treatment with digitalis. The model he developed seemed heuristically important, not only because it could be used to show how psychological factors could produce disease, but also because digitalis is the fourth most commonly prescribed drug in America, and it is a drug with a very narrow range between therapeutic efficacy and the potentially lethal side effect of cardiac arrhythmias (Moe & Farah, 1975). Efforts in the past to define why certain individuals develop digitalis toxicity while taking a standard dose of the medication had centered on changes in the internal milieu, that is, in the concentration of ions and hormones in the blood (Smith, 1975). Even after taking such factors into account, however, there was no obvious reason why many patients should become digitalis toxic, and, in fact, measurement of serum levels of the drug was not a terribly good predictor of who would become toxic in the future. Because a review by this author indicated that digitalis produced its toxic arrhythmias by activating the autonomic nervous system, Natelson reasoned that psychological stress could act additively or synergistically to produce this toxic side effect earlier.

To test this notion, Natelson, Cagin, Donner, and Hamilton (1978) placed two groups of guinea pigs into a restraint chamber, which allowed EKG recording without substantial artifact. One group of pigs was subjected to the periodic onset of a sixty-second signal, which was often, but not always, followed by an electric shock to the rump. The other group was subjected to the same paradigm, except shock was never delivered. On Fridays, the pigs were given an intraperitoneal injection of ouabain, a fast-acting cardiac glycoside, and then, seventy-five minutes later, they were put into their chambers. As on training days, the signal was periodically delivered but, different from previously, shock never was. EKGs were recorded for the minute prior to, and the minute during, the signal.

Natelson et al., reported that the shock-exposed group developed significantly more arrhythmias during the signal period than before it, while the control group did not show this differential effect. In addition to this difference in arrhythmogenesis, the shock-exposed group was found to display significantly more abnormal beats per arrhythmic episode than the nonshocked controls. Also, the majority of the arrhythmias in the shock-exposed group developed early in the session, while those in the nonshocked group developed late in the session, at a time when the drug would be expected to be at its peak concentration within the blood and, thus, most likely to produce toxicity.

The arrhythmias that developed during the signal for the shock-exposed group were varied and striking: first-degree A-V block, Wenckebach phenomenon, sinus arrest, junctional tachycardia, ventricular escape beats, VPCs, VT, and idioventricular bradycardia. Because many of these are bradyarrhythmias, and because they were often preceded by a mild to moderate bradycardia, Natelson et al. postulated a vagal mechanism for their pathogenesis. These data indicate that the signal alone, for the group for which the signal predicted shock, could precipitate potentially fatal cardiac arrhythmias in animals that were in normal sinus rhythm prior to the onset of the signal. Thus, the arrhythmias elicited by the signal were psychosomatic in origin. One problem with this model, however, was that the nonshocked control animals developed arrhythmias, even though they did not reliably occur in association with the signal.

Based on this, Natelson, Hoffman, and Cagin (1980) reasoned that, perhaps, the stress of being placed in restraint was so great as to lessen the effect of prior training in a signaled shock paradigm. To test this notion, they decided to assess the effect of restraint stress on the LD_{50} of ouabain. Adult male guinea pigs were given six days to adapt to laboratory conditions. They were then picked up and injected intraperitoneally with a previously determined dose of ouabain. They were returned to their home cages for forty-five minutes and then were picked up again and placed into one of three treatment groups: back into their home cages after food and water had been removed, into restraint on a board prepared to limit mobility by snares around the paws and a leather flap over the body, or into a novel cage (to control for the novelty inherent in the last condition). No differential effect of treatment was found at either low or high dose, but at the intermediary dose of 175 mcg/kg, a difference was found: there was a significantly higher death rate among restrained pigs than home cage or novel cage control pigs. Thus, this experiment corroborated their earlier findings that acute psychological stress, and not mere novelty, sensitizes an animal to the arrhythmogenic potential of digitalis. In other experiments, Natelson et al. (1980) learned that repeatedly subjecting the animal to restraint stress shifted the lethal dose the other way. The drug did not consistently produce its lethal consequences at either 175 or 200 mcg/kg but did so at the very high dose of 225 mcg/kg. This experiment indicates that repeated presentation of a stressor can protect the organism from visceral perturbations and is thus empirical data supporting the value of psychiatric confrontation therapies.

In summary, these experiments showed that potentially lethal cardiac arrhythmias can be elicited if an animal with a predisposition to such a problem is stressed.

Integration of Physiological and Psychological Factors

The main issue bridging physiology and psychology relates to the arrhythmic mechanism responsible for the sudden death syndrome. The bulk of work has been directed toward understanding the mechanisms of ventricular fibrillation, perhaps because this is the terminal arrhythmia seen so often at the scene of a cardiac collapse. Because of this body of work, some (e.g., Lown et al., 1977) have stressed the idea that sympathetic hyperactivity is responsible for the arrhythmias that develop in the stressed person or animal. The evidence for this leap is not overly compelling, however. First, vagal stimulation is known to precipitate VF in the presence of infarcted myocardium (Pantridge, 1978). Next, arrhythmias other than VF are seen at the time of collapse. In addition, it is not clear whether the VF seen is the result of an earlier tachyarrhythmia, such as VT, or of an earlier bradyarrhythmia, such as idioventricular conduction. Supporting this is the report of Matta, Lawler, and Lown (1976), who showed that two dogs with experimental MIs had the most serious arrhythmias, when stressed, if a bradycardia, rather than a tachycardia, developed. Also bringing into question the idea that stress-induced VF is primarily due to sympathetic hyperactivity is the finding of Skinner et al. (1975) that beta-adrenergic blockade does not prevent the development of VF in stressed pigs with experimental cardiac ischemia. Finally, when sudden death occurs either in stressed "normal" animals (see previous section), or spontaneously (Branch, Robertson, Beckett, Waldo, & James, 1977), bradyarrhythmias leading to cardiac standstill have been found; VF has not. In Engel's (1978) recent retrospective review of psychosomatic factors and sudden death, he cautioned against the view that arrhythmias relate merely to sympathetic activation. This review has come to the same conclusion. Thus, before mechanistic conclusions can be made, more experiments will have to be done.

What about when digitalis is being taken? Based on the pattern of arrhythmias that developed in the guinea pigs during a signal for shock, one can speculate that parasympathetic influences may be important. It is well known that producing a bradycardia in a digitalized subject can uncover ventricular irritability (Vassalle, Greenspan, & Hoffman, 1963). What is thought to happen is that during a prolonged interbeat (R-R) interval, the ventricle fires on its own, due to the effect of digitalis on cardiac automaticity. This uncovering of digitalis toxicity can occur when a human subject on the drug voluntarily decreases his heart rate by biofeedback (Bleecker & Engel, 1973). Some arrhythmias were seen, however, which were preceded by only a small bradycardia, thus suggesting that vagal hyperactivity may not be the whole answer. Of course, the work of Gillis's group (1972) suggests that digitalis toxicity occurs in the anesthetized animal because of concurrent activation of both sympathetic and parasympathetic nerves. Because stress also activates both systems, one might expect the mechanism for psychosomatic digitalis toxicity to involve both divisions of the autonomic nervous system.

Current Status of Conceptualization, Trends, Recent Advances

Our ability to further our understanding of how psychosomatic factors play a role in the genesis of the sudden death syndrome requires suitable animal models. These seem to currently exist. Lown's group has focused its attention on producing changes in ventricular automaticity in normal dogs during stress. They chose RE, rather than VF, as their end point, because they felt that the production of VF could injure the heart; however, Lawler et al. (1976) make it clear that even repeated testing for RE can produce burns of the myocardium. There are two apparent difficulties with this model: first, it assumes that the sudden death syndrome relates to VF; second, frank arrhythmias never develop in the normal dog when stressed.

Obviously, understanding the mechanisms for VF will be important for cardiology, but, for the reasons reviewed in the last section, it might not be that germane for understanding the reasons for sudden death. Thus, efforts to deal with the problem should not be limited to studies of just VF. This becomes a special problem if a frank arrhythmia does not actually develop in the stressed animal, but only electrical changes in cardiac responsivity are seen. Despite the intense stress of restraint, guinea pigs of Natelson and Cagin (1979) never developed fatal arrhythmias, although runs of VT did develop. Because of this finding, and because of the earlier observation that gastric disease healed in monkeys despite the continuation of stress (Natelson, Dubois, & Sodetz, 1977), Natelson and his colleagues decided to use a model in which the animal had a predisposition to arrhythmias. Digitalis was chosen as the predisposing agent, rather than myocardial infarction, which had been used by others, because the drug can be repeatedly administered and, at toxic doses, consistently produces increased automaticity, while MI does so for only a few days after its production. Also, digitalis ingestion is a risk factor for sudden death (Moss et al., 1977). Conceptually, it was felt that more would eventually be learned if cardiac arrhythmias could be reliably produced by psychological factors. Since this can be done in the animal with a predisposition to arrhythmias, the next move is to analyze how the fatal event is produced. This approach should also be used after experimental MI. Another alternative would be to use pug dogs, a species known to suffer sudden death due to cardiac standstill with no apparent elicitor (Branch et al., 1977).

Since it has been demonstrated that stimulation of both central and peripheral neural sites can produce arrhythmias, however, it is feasible for a person with a totally normal heart to have stress-induced arrhythmias. The question that evolves is whether the 15% of sudden death victims with no obvious pathology truly do or do not have intracardiac pathology. James, Frogatt, and Marshall (1967) studied the hearts of athletes who suddenly died, and found subtle abnormalities in their cardiac conductive tissue. Prior to this careful study, these hearts would have been called "normal." Thus, the ability to determine if an organ is normal is a relative one and depends on the state of the art and the care with which it is applied.

TREATMENT

The acknowledged treatment for cardiac arrhythmias is pharmacologic. When the problem is frequent VPCs, beta-adrenergic blockade is used; when the problem is A-V dissociation and severe bradyarrhythmias, atropine or isoproterenol is used. If the bradyarrhythmia is so severe as to cause loss of consciousness and seizures (due to poor cerebral circulation), control of ventricular rate must be achieved by the physician. This is done by threading a pacing wire into the ventricle and stimulating a controlled ventricular rhythm by a battery-operated pacemaker. Battery development has been so great that changes are no longer necessary more often than every two years. If the arrhythmia that is detected is

VF, coordinated cardiac contraction can be restored only by shocking across the heart itself. This process, known as *defibrillation*, produces a discharge of all cardiac cells that are not in the refractory period, and a normal pacemaker can then trigger orderly ventricular contraction. This procedure can be applied by trained personnel at the scene of a cardiac collapse (American Heart Association, 1974).

Physiological

The treatment of cardiac arrhythmias is beyond the scope of this chapter. Interested readers should consult any standard textbook of medicine or cardiology. The only way that the sudden death of previously asymptomatic people can be prevented is either by early identification, which is an enormously expensive proposition, because it is so hard to do, or by education. The primary purpose of the latter is to instruct the lay population about the major risk factors − smoking, blood pressure, and overweight − and to try to convince them to control these. The other purpose of education is to make the public aware of the symptoms of a heart attack, so they will seek medical attention promptly.

By definition, prophylactic treatment is limited to those people who have already sustained a myocardial infarction. A recent, double-blind study (Wilhelmsson, Vedin, Wilhelmsen, Tibblin, & Werko, 1974) has shown that treatment of postinfarct patients with a beta blocking drug lessened the probability of sudden death. Similar, beneficial results have been reported to follow coronary artery bypass surgery with ventricular aneurysmectomy (Ricks, Winkle, Shumway, & Harrison, 1977).

Psychological

Voukydis and Forwand (1977) reported that, in twenty-two patients with serious ventricular arrhythmias in whom conventional medical therapy was ineffective, arrhythmia frequency decreased after they learned to perform the relaxation response. This effect was seen during the first session and remained decreased, by Holter monitoring, over the eleven-week follow-up period, during which the patients continued to perform the relaxation response.

Benson (1977) defined the relaxation response as a set of integrated physiological changes that are elicited when a subject assumes a relaxed position, often with closed eyes, within a quiet environment, and then engages in repetitive mental action while passively ignoring distracting thoughts. The physiological changes are thought to relate to decreased sympathetic tone and thus are consistent with the notion that sympathetic hyperactivity is responsible for the arrhythmias causing sudden death.

In striking contrast are the data of Weiss and Engel (1971), who showed that VPC frequency can be diminished, in some patients, by biofeedback training, producing either cardiac slowing or acceleration. This study is important in two respects: first, it opens up the possibility that behavioral techniques can be used in conjunction with pharmacologic agents in the suppression of ventricular ectopic sites, and second, it strongly suggests that the mechanism for VPCs is not due purely to sympathetic activation. Both points are reemphasized by the recent report of Pickering and Miller (1977) who replicated the earlier work and again showed that biofeedback can lessen VPCs by causing a tachycardia.

Trends and Recent Advances

Because of the clear-cut data showing the effect of brain activation on arrhythmogenesis following experimental myocardial infarction or digitalis toxicity, some attention has been directed toward exploring the antiarrhythmic action of pharmacologic agents whose parimary site of action is thought to be the brain rather than the heart. Thus, Gillis, Thirodeaux, and Barr (1974) showed that chlordiazepoxide treatment will reduce arrhythmia frequency in animals predisposed to cardiac arrhythmias. Similarly, Evans and Gillis (1975) were able to block the arrhythmias usually produced by the combination of ouabain infusion and brain stimulation by pretreatment with diphenylhydantoin.

The realization that environmental factors can play a role in the development of arrhythmias in the predisposed individual has already caused experimental pharmacologists searching for antiarrhythmic drugs to shift their focus from drugs whose primary site of action is the heart to others whose site of action is the brain. This is an important break with tradition and should be productive in the development of new drugs effective against hard-to-control cardiac arrhythmias. Another major break in classical medical thinking occurred when behavioral techniques were shown to be another effective therapeutic modality to lessen arrhythmia frequency. The place of these techniques in the physician's therapeutic armamentarium requires further elucidation but seems assured.

CONCLUSIONS AND SUGGESTIONS FOR FUTURE RESEARCH

A major advance is the realization that sudden death and severe cardiac arrhythmias are very rare in man or animal unless the organism is predisposed to such arrhythmias. One can infer this fact from the human literature, in which case reports of sudden death or severe arrhythmia in the purportedly normal person are very few. Conversely, in people with prior history of heart disease with ventricular ectopic foci and taking digitalis, frequency of arrhythmias and sudden death is high. This means that psychosocial risk factors, such as stress, type A personality, or poor education, are not risk factors until a person has an element of organic heart disease. Thus, the author believes that future research should primarily use existing animal models, in which psychological factors produce frank arrhythmogenesis and/or death. From these, hopefully, will come data about etiology and pathogenesis which will be pertinent to the human condition of sudden death. This would be invaluable, since the nature of the sudden death syndrome in man does not allow for prospective study. The recent finding of Maseri et al. (1978) in humans that coronary vasospasm can produce MI may be the mechanistic link between environmental perturbation, brain activation, arrhythmogenesis, and sudden death.

The prospective epidemiologic research of Rahe and his colleagues (Rahe et al., 1974) is the best we have showing that stress can actually produce a cardiac death. Wolf (1969) reported pilot data from the ideal sort of experiment needed to make definite the point that environmental perturbations can produce lethal consequences. Such a prospective experiment will wed the talents of cardiologists, psychologists, and biostatisticians. A large company with its own internal medical staffing should be approached; this has been done in the past with branches of AT&T. A group of people from forty-five to fifty-five years of age should be selected for careful medical evaluation, which would consist of a careful medical workup, with attention paid to the presence of the previously defined risk factors. Based on this, a high risk and a low risk group could be delineated. These patients would then be followed over time medically, socially, and psychologically. The purpose would be to track the relation between affective events in the patients' lives and the development of severe arrhythmias or sudden death. By designing the study in such a way, one would maximize the probability of finding a relation since a group predisposed to these problems would be studied prospectively.

Although anecdotes have existed for millenia that psychological/environmental perturbations are related to sudden death, it is only in the past five years that hard data have accumulated to support this idea. Thus, the brain must be the transducer of such perturbations. The effect of these ideas on the medical practitioner and clinical pharmacologist is, as yet, small. As more data are collected, however, and this sophisticated audience becomes educated to these facts, we can expect to see changes in how a doctor practices medicine, which will relate to the growing importance of this area of behavioral medicine.

REFERENCES

American Heart Association. Standards for cardiopulmonary resuscitation (CPR) and emergency cardiac care (ECC). *Journal of the American Medical Association*, 1974, *227* (Suppl.), 837-868.

Barnett, S. A. Physiological effects of "social stress" in wild rats. I: The adrenal cortex. *Journal of Psychosomatic Research*, 1955, *3*, 1-11.

Baum, T., & Shropshire, A. T. Inhibition of efferent sympathetic nerve activity by 5-hydroxytryptophan and centrally administered 5-hydroxytryptamine. *Neuropharmacology*, 1975, *14*, 227-233.

Beard, E. F., & Owen, C. A. Cardiac arrhythmias during exercise testing in healthy men. *Aerospace Medicine*, 1973, *44*, 286-289.

Benedict, R. B., & Evans, J. M. Second-degree heart block and Wenckebach phenomenon associated with anxiety. *American Heart Journal*, 1952, *43*, 626-633.

Benson, H. Systemic hypertension and the relaxation response. *New England Journal of Medicine*, 1977, *296*, 1152-1156.

Bigger, J. T., Jr. Electrical properties of cardiac muscle and possible causes of cardiac arrhythmias. In L. S. Dreifus & W. Likoff (Eds.), *Cardiac arrhythmias*. New York: Grune & Stratton, 1973.

Binik, Y. U., Theriault, G., & Schustack, B. Sudden death in the laboratory rat: Cardiac function, sensory and experiential factors in swimming deaths. *Psychosomatic Medicine*, 1977, *39*, 82-92.

Bleecker, E. R., & Engel, B. T. Learned control of ventricular rate in patients with atrial fibrillation. *Psychosomatic Medicine*, 1973, *35*, 161-175.

Branch, C. E., Robertson, B. T., Beckett, S. D., Waldo, A. L., & James, T. N. An animal model of spontaneous syncope and sudden death. *Journal of Laboratory and Clinical Medicine*, 1977, *90*, 592-603.

Braunwald, E. Coronary spasm and acute myocardial infarction – New possibility for treatment prevention. *New England Journal of Medicine*, 1978, *299*, 1301-1303.

Cannon, W. B. "Voodoo" death. *American Anthropologist*, 1942, *44*, 169-181.

Carveth, S. Standards for cardiopulmonary resuscitation and emergency cardiac care. *Journal of the American Medical Association*, 1974, *227*, 796-797.

Chandler, B., Chapman, I., Eckardt, C. R., Roberts, W. C., Schwartz, W. C., Sinapius, D., Spain, D. M., Ness, P. M., & Simon, T. L. Coronary thrombosis in myocardial infarction: Report of a workshop on the role of coronary thrombosis in the pathogenesis of acute myocardial infarction. *American Journal of Cardiology*, 1974, *34*, 823-833.

Chiang, B. N., Perlman, L. V., Ostrander, L. O., & Epstein, F. H. Relationship of premature systoles to coronary heart disease and sudden death in the Tecumseh Epidemiologic Study. *Annals of Internal Medicine*, 1959, *70*, 1159-1166.

Christian, J. D., & Ratcliffe, H. L. Shock disease in captive wild animals. *American Journal of Pathology*, 1952, *28*, 725-737.

Corbalan, R., Verrier, R., & Lown, B. Psychological stress and ventricular arrhythmias during myocardial infarction in the conscious dog. *American Journal of Cardiology*, 1974, *34*, 692-696.

Corley, K. C., Mauck, H. P., & Shiel, F. O. Cardiac responses associated with "yoked-chair" shock avoidance in squirrel monkeys. *Psychophysiology*, 1975, *12*, 439-444.

Corley, K. C., Shiel, F. O., Mauck, H. P., & Greenhoot, J. Electrocardiographic and cardiac morphological changes associated with environmental stress in squirrel monkeys. *Psychosomatic Medicine*, 1973, *35*, 361-364.

Corr, P. B., & Gillis, R. A. Autonomic neural influences on the dysrhythmias resulting from myocardial infarction. *Circulation Research*, 1978, *43*, 1-9.

D'Agrosa, L. S. Cardiac arrhythmias of sympathetic origin in the dog. *American Journal of Physiology*, 1977, *233*, H535-H540.

DeSilva, H., & Lown, B. Ventricular premature beats, stress, and sudden deaths. *Psychosomatics*, 1978, *19*, 649-661.

Dimsdale, J. E. Emotional causes of sudden death. *American Journal of Psychiatry*, 1977, *134*, 1361-1366.

Engel, G. L. Sudden and rapid death during psychological stress: Folklore or folk wisdom? *Annals of Internal Medicine*, 1971, *74*, 771-782.

Engel, G. L. Psychologic stress, vasodepressor (vasovagal syncope), and sudden death. *Annals of Internal Medicine*, 1978, *989*, 403-412.

Enos, W., & Holmes, R. Coronary disease among United States soldiers killed in action in Korea. *Journal of the American Medical Association*, 1953, *152*, 1090-1093.

Epstein, S. E. Value and limitations of the electrocardiographic response to exercise in the assessment of patients with coronary artery disease. *American Journal of Cardiology*, 1978, *942*, 667-674.

Evans, D. E., Alter, W. A., Shatsky, S. A., & Gunby, E. N. Cardiac arrhythmias resulting from experimental head injury. *Journal of Neurosurgery*, 1976, *45*, 609-616.

Evans, D. E., & Gillis, R. A. Effect of diphenylhydantoin and lidocaine on cardiac arrhythmias induced by hypothalamic stimulation. *Journal of Pharmacology and Experimental Therapeutics*, 1974, *191*, 506-517.

Evans, D. E., & Gillis, R. A. Effect of ouabain and its interaction with diphenyl-hydantoin on cardiac arrhythmias induced by hypothalamic stimulation. *Journal of Pharmacology and Experimental Therapeutics*, 1975, *195*, 577-586.

Evans, D. E., & Gillis, R. A. Reflex mechanisms involved in cardiac arrhythmias induced by hypothalamic stimulation. *American Journal of Physiology*, 1978, *234*, H199-H209.

Friedman, M., Manwaring, J. H., Rosenman, R. H., Donlon, G., Ortega, P., & Grube, S. M. Instantaneous and sudden death: Clinical and pathological differentiation in coronary artery disease. *Journal of the American Medical Association*, 1973, *225*, 1319-1328.

Gascon, A. L. Effect of acute stress and ouabain administration on adrenal catecholamine content and cardiac function of rats pretreated with diazepam. *Canadian Journal of Physiology and Pharmacology*, 1977, *55*, 65-71.

Gillis, R. A., Pearle, D. L., & Hoekman, T. Failure of beta-adrenergic receptor blockade to prevent arrhythmias induced by sympathetic nerve stimulation. *Science*, 1974, *185*, 70-72.

Gillis, R. A., Raines, A., Sohn, Y. J., Levitt, B., & Standaert, F. G. Neuroexcitatory effects of digitalis and their role in the development of cardiac arrhythmias. *Journal of Pharmachology and Experimental Therapeutics*, 1972, *183*, 154-168.

Gillis, R. A., Thirodeaux, H., & Barr, L. Antiarrhythmic properties of chlordiazepoxide. *Circulation*, 1974, *49*, 272-282.

Glass, D. C. Stress, behavior pattern, and coronary disease. *American Scientist*, 1977, *65*, 177-187.

Goodfriend, M., & Wolpert, E. A. Death from fright: Report of a case and literature review. *Psychosomatic Medicine*, 1976, *38*, 348-356.

Greene, H. L., Reid, P. R., & Schaeffer, A. H. The repetitive ventricular response in man: A predictor of sudden death. *New England Journal of Medicine*, 1978, *299*, 729-734.

Greene, W. A., Goldstein, S., & Moss, A. J. Psychosocial aspects of sudden death. *Archives of Internal Medicine*, 1972, *129*, 725-731.

Harvey, W. P., & Levine, S. A. Paroxysmal ventricular tachycardia due to fright. *Journal of the American Medical Association*, 1952, *150*, 479-480.

Hashimoto, K., Kimura, T., & Kubota, K. Study of the therapeutic and toxic effects of ouabain by simultaneous observations on the excised and blood-perfused sino-atrial node and papillary muscle preparations and the in situ heart of dogs. *Journal of Pharmacology and Experimental Therapeutics*, 1973, *186*, 463-471.

Hinkle, L. E. The effect of exposure to culture change, social change, and changes in interpersonal relationships on health. In B. S. Dohrenwend & B. P. Dohrenwend (Eds.), *Stressful life events*. New York: Wiley, 1974.

Hinkle, L. E., Carver, S. T., & Plakun, A. Slow heart rates and increased risk of cardiac death in middle-aged men. *Archives of Internal Medicine*, 1972, *129*, 732-748.

Hinkle, L. E., Carver, S. T., & Stevens, M. The frequency of asymptomatic disturbances of cardiac rhythm and conduction in middle-aged man. *American Journal of Cardiology*, 1969, *24*, 629-650.

Hinkle, L. E., Kane, F. D., Christenson, W. N., & Wolff, H. G. Hungarian refugees: Life experiences and features influencing participation in the revolution and subsequent flight. *American Journal of Psychiatry*, 1959, *116*, 16-19.

James, T. N., Frogatt, P., & Marshall, T. Sudden death in young athletes. *Annals of Internal Medicine*, 1967, *67*, 1013-1021.

Jarvinen, K. A. J. Can ward rounds be a danger to patients with myocardial infarction? *British Medical Journal*, 1955, *91*, 318-320.

Jenkins, C. D. Psychologic and social risk factors for coronary disease. *New England Journal of Medicine*, 1976, *294*, 987-994; 1033-1038.

Johansson, G., Jonsson, L., Lannek, N., Blomgren, L., Lindberg, P., & Poupa, O. Severe stress-cardiopathy in pigs. *American Heart Journal*, 1974, *87*, 451-457.

Jorgensen, L., Rowsell, H. C., Hovig, T., Glynn, M. F., & Mustard, J. F. Adenosine diphosphate-induced platelet aggregation and myocardial infarction in swine. *Laboratory Investigation*, 1967, *17*, 616-643.

Kannel, W. E., Doyle, J. T., McNamara, P. M., Quickerton, P., & Gordon, T. Precursors of sudden coronary deaths. *Circulation*, 1975, *51*, 606-613.

Katzung, B. G. Automaticity in cardiac cells. *Life Sciences*, 1978, *923*, 1309-1316.

Kawakami, Y., Natelson, B., & Dubois, A. Cardiovascular effects of face immersion and factors affecting diving reflex in man. *Journal of Applied Physiology*, 1967, *23*, 964-970.

Kerzner, J., Wolf, M., Kosowsky, B. D., & Lown, B. Ventricular ectopic rhythms following vagal stimulation in dogs with acute myocardial infarction. *Circulation*, 1973, *47*, 44-50.

Lawler, J. E., Botticelli, L. J., & Lown, B. Changes in cardiac refractory period during signalled shock avoidance in dogs. *Psychophysiology*, 1976, *13*, 373-377.

Levine, S. A. Benign atrial fibrillation of forty years' duration with sudden death from emotion. *Annals of Internal Medicine*, 1963, *58*, 681-684.

Levitt, B., Cagin, N. A., Somberg, J. C., & Kleid, J. J. Neural basis for the genesis and control of digitalis arrhythmias. *Cardiology (Basel)*, 1976, *61*, 50-60.

Liberthson, R. R., Nagel, E. L., Hirshman, J. C., Nussenfield, S. R., Blackbourne, B. D., & Davis, J. H. Pathophysiologic observations in prehospital ventricular fibrillation and sudden cardiac death. *Circulation*, 1974, *949*, 790-798.

Lie, J. T., & Titus, J. L. Pathology of the myocardium and the conduction system in sudden coronary death. *Circulation*, 1975, *51-52* (Suppl. III), 41-52.

Lown, B., Calvert, A. F., Armington, R., & Ryan, M. Monitoring for serious arrhythmias and high risk of sudden death. *Circulation*, 1975, *51-52* (Suppl. III), 189-197.

Lown, B., & DeSilva, R. A. Roles of psychologic stress and autonomic nervous system changes in provocation of ventricular premature complexes. *American Journal of Cardiology*, 1978, *941*, 979-985.

Lown, B., Temte, J. V., Reich, P., Gaughan, C., Regestein, Q., & Hai, H. Basis for recurring ventricular fibrillation in the absence of coronary heart disease and its management. *New England Journal of Medicine*, 1976, *294*, 623-629.

Lown, B., Tykocinski, M., Garfein, A., & Brooks, P. Sleep and ventricular premature beats. *Circulation*, 1973, *48*, 691-701.

Lown, B., & Verrier, R. L. Neural activity and ventricular fibrillation. *New England Journal of Medicine*, 1976, *294*, 1165-1170.

Lown, B., Verrier, R. L., & Corbalan, R. Psychologic stress and threshold for a repetitive ventricular response. *Science*, 1973, *182*, 834-836.

Lown, B., Verrier, R. L., & Rabinowitz, S. H. Neural and psychologic mechanisms and the problem of sudden death. *American Journal of Cardiology*, 1977, *39*, 890-902.

Lynch, J. J., & Katcher, A. H. Human handling and sudden death in laboratory rats. *Journal of Nervous and Mental Diseases*, 1974, *159*, 362-365.

Margolis, J. R., Hirshfeld, J. W., McNeer, J. F., Starmer, C. F., Rosati, R. A., Peter, R. H., Behar, V. S., & Kong, Y. Sudden death due to coronary artery disease: A clinical, hemodynamic, and angiographic profile. *Circulation*, 1975, *51-52* (Suppl. III), 180-188.

Marmon, J., & Kent, M. J. Paroxysmal ventricular tachycardia. *California Medicine*, 1958, *88*, 325-329.

Maseri, A., L'Abbate, A., Baroldi, G., Chierchia, S., Marzilli, M., Ballestra, A. M., Severi, S., Parodi, O., Biagini, A., Distante, A., & Resola, A. Coronary vasospasm as a possible cause of myocardial infarction. *New England Journal of Medicine*, 1978, *299*, 1271-1277.

Matta, R. J., Lawler, J. E., & Lown, B. Ventricular electrical instability in the conscious dog. Effects of psychologic stress and beta-adrenergic blockade. *American Journal of Cardiology*, 1976, *38*, 594-598.

Matta, R. J., Verrier, R. L., & Lown, B. Repetitive extrasystole as an index of vulnerability to ventricular fibrillation. *American Journal of Physiology*, 1976, *230*, 1469-1473.

Mauck, H. P., Jr., & Hockman, C. H. Central nervous system mechanisms mediating cardiac rate and rhythm. *American Heart Journal*, 1967, *74*, 96-109.

McClure, C. M. Cardiac arrest through volition. *California Medicine*, 1959, *90*, 440-441.

McHenry, P. L., Fisch, C., Jordan, J. W., & Corya, B. R. Cardiac arrhythmias observed during maximal treadmill exercise testing in clinically normal men. *American Journal of Cardiology*, 1972, *29*, 331-336.

Meinhardt, K., & Robinson, H. A. Stokes-Adams syndrome precipitated by emotional stress. *Psychosomatic Medicine*, 1962, *24*, 325-330.

Moe, G. K., & Farah, A. E. Digitalis and allied cardiac glycosides. In L. S. Goodman & A. Gilman (Eds.), *The pharmacological basis of therapeutics*. New York: Macmillan, 1975.

Morris, S. N., & McHenry, P. L. Role of exercise stress testing in healthy subjects and patients with coronary heart disease. *American Journal of Cardiology*, 1978, *42*, 659-666.

Moss, A. J., DeCamilla, J., & Davis, H. Cardiac death in the first 6 months after myocardial infarction: Potential for mortality reduction in the early post hospital period. *American Journal of Cardiology*, 1977, *39*, 816-820.

Myerburg, R. J., Sung, R. J., Conde, C., Mallon, S. M., & Castellanos, A. Intracardiac electrophysiologic studies in patients resuscitated from unexpected cardiac arrest outside the hospital. *American Journal of Cardiology*, 1977, *39*, 275.

Natelson, B. H., & Cagin, N. A. Stress-induced ventricular arrhythmias. *Psychosomatic Medicine*, 1979, *41*, 259-262.

Natelson, B. H., Cagin, N. A., Donner, K., & Hamilton, B. E. Psychosomatic digitalis-toxic arrhythmias in guinea pigs. *Life Sciences*, 1978, *22*, 2245-2250.

Natelson, B. H., Dubois, A., & Sodetz, F. J. Effect of multiple stress procedures on monkey gastro-duodenal mucosa, serum gastrin and hydrogen ion kinetics. *American Journal of Digestive Diseases*, 1977, *22*, 888-897.

Natelson, B. H., Hoffman, S. L., & Cagin, N. A. A role for environmental factors in the production of digitalis toxicity. *Pharmacology, Biochemistry, and Behavior*, 1980, *12*, 235-237.

Pantridge, J. F. Autonomic disturbance at the onset of acute myocardial infarction. In P. J. Schwartz, A. M. Brown, A. Milliani, & A. Zanchetti (Eds.), *Neural mechanisms in cardiac arrhythmias*. New York: Raven Press, 1978.

Pantridge, J. F., & Geddes, J. S. A mobile intensive care unit in the management of myocardial infarctions. *Lancet*, 1967, *2*, 271-273.

Parkes, C. M., Benjamin, B., & Fitzgerald, R. G. Broken heart: A statistical study of increased mortality among widowers. *British Medical Journal*, 1969, *1*, 740-743.

Pickering, T. G., & Miller, N. E. Learned voluntary control of heart rate and rhythm in two subjects with premature ventricular contractions. *British Heart Journal*, 1977, *939*, 152-159.

Rabinowitz, S. H., & Lown, B. Central neurochemical factors related to seritonin metabolism and cardiac ventricular vulnerability for repetitive electrical activity. *American Journal of Cardiology*, 1978, *41*, 516-522.

Rabkin, J. G., & Struening, E. L. Life events, stress and illness. *Science*, 1976, *194*, 1013-1020.

Raftery, E. B., & Cashman, P. M. M. Long-term recording of the electrocardiogram in a normal population. *Postgraduate Medical Journal*, 1976, *52*, 32-37.

Rahe, R. H., Romo, M., Bennett, L., & Siltanen, P. Recent life changes, myocardial infarction, and abrupt coronary death. *Archives of Internal Medicine*, 1974, *133*, 221-228.

Rahe, R. H., Jr., & Christ, A. E. An unusual cardiac (ventricular) arrhythmia in a child: Psychiatric and psychophysiologic aspects. *Psychosomatic Medicine*, 1966, *28*, 181-188.

Richter, C. P. On the phenomenon of sudden death in animals and man. *Psychosomatic Medicine*, 1957, *3*, 192-198.

Ricks, W. B., Winkle, R. A., Shumway, N. E., & Harrison, D. C. Surgical management of life-threatening ventricular arrhythmias in patients with coronary artery disease. *Circulation*, 1977, *56*, 38-42.

Robinson, J. S., Sloman, G., Mathew, T. H., & Goble, A. S. Survival after resuscitation from cardiac arrest in acute myocardial infarction. *American Heart Journal*, 1965, 740-747.

Schlesinger, Z., Barzilay, J., Stryjer, D., & Almog, C. H. Life-threatening "vagal reaction" to emotional stimuli. *Israel Journal of Medical Sciences*, 1977, *13*, 59-61.

Schwartz, C. J., & Gerrity, R. G. Anatomical pathology of sudden unexpected cardiac death. *Circulation*, 1975, *51-52* (Suppl. III), 18-26.

Scott, R. F., & Briggs, T. S. Pathologic findings in pre-hospital deaths due to coronary atherosclerosis. *American Journal of Cardiology*, 1972, *29*, 782-787.

Silverman, J. J., & Goodman, R. Extraordinary alteration of the P-R interval in neurocirculatory asthenia. *American Heart Journal*, 1951, *41*, 155-159.

Skinner, J. E., Lie, J. T., & Entman, M. C. Modification of ventricular fibrillation latency following coronary artery occlusion in the conscious pig. *Circulation*, 1975, *51*, 656-663.

Smith, T. W. Digitalis toxicity: Epidemiology and clinical use of serum concentration measurements. *American Journal of Medicine*, 1975, *58*, 470-476.

Stevenson, I. P., Duncan, C. H., Wolf, S., Ripley, H. S., & Wolff, H. G. Life situations, emotions and extra systoles. *Psychosomatic Medicine*, 1949, *11*, 257-272.

Taggart, P., Carruthers, M., & Somerville, W. Electrocardiogram, plasma catecholamines and lipids, and their modification by oxprenolol when speaking before an audience. *Lancet*, 1973, *2*, 341-346.

Taggart, P., Gibbons, D., & Somerville, W. Some effects of motor-car driving on the normal and abnormal heart. *British Medical Journal*, 1969, *4*, 130-134.

Theorell, T., & Rahe, R. H. Life change events, ballistocardiography and coronary death. *Journal of Human Stress*, 1975, *1*, 18-24.

Vassalle, M., Greenspan, K., & Hoffman, B. F. Analysis of arrhythmias induced by ouabain in dogs. *Circulation Research*, 1963, *13*, 132-148.

Verrier, R. L., Calvert, A., & Lown, B. Effect of posterior hypothalamic stimulation on ventricular fibrillation threshold. *American Journal of Physiology*, 1975, *228*, 923-927.

Vismara, L. A., Zakanddin, V., Foerster, J. M., Amsterdam, E. A., & Mason, D. T. Identification of sudden death risk factors in acute and chronic coronary artery disease. *American Journal of Cardiology*, 1977, *39*, 821-828.

Von Holst, D. Renal failure as a cause of death in *Tupara belageri* exposed to persistent social stress. *Journal of Comparative Physiology*, 1972, *78*, 236-273.

Voukydis, P. C., & Forwand, S. A. The effect of elicitation of the relaxation response in patients with intractable ventricular arrhythmias. *Circulation*, 1977, *55-56* (Suppl. III), 157.

Weinberg, M. Sudden cardiac death. *Yale Journal of Biology and Medicine*, 1978, *51*, 207-217.

Weinblatt, E., Ruberman, W., Goldberg, J. D., Frank, C. W., Shapiro, S., & Chaudbary, B. S. Relation of education to sudden death after myocardial infarction. *New England Journal of Medicine*, 1978, *299*, 60-65.

Weiner, H., Thaler, M., Reiser, M. F., & Mirsky, I. A. Etiology of duodenal ulcer. I. Relation of specific psychological characteristics to rate of gastric secretion (serum pepsinogen). *Psychosomatic Medicine*, 1957, *19*, 1-10.

Weiss, T., & Engel, B. T. Operant conditioning of heart rate in patients with premature ventricular contractions. *Psychosomatic Medicine*, 1971, *33*, 301-321.

Wilhelmsson, C., Vedin, J. A., Wilhelmsen, L., Tibblin, G., & Werko, L. Reduction of sudden death after myocardial infarction by treatment with alprenolol. *Lancet*, 1974, *2*, 1157-1160.

Wit, A. L., & Bigger, J. T., Jr. Possible electrophysiological mechanisms for lethal arrhythmias accompanying myocardial ischemia and infarction. *Circulation*, 1975, *51-52* (Suppl. III), 96-115.

Wolf, S. Bradycardia of the dive reflex – Possible mechanism of sudden death. *Transactions of the American Clinical and Climatological Association*, 1964, *76*, 192-200.

Wolf, S. The bradycardia of the dive reflex – A possible mechanism for sudden death. *Conditional Reflex*, 1967, *2*, 88-95.

Wolf, S. Psychosocial forces in myocardial infarction and sudden death. *Circulation*, 1969, *39-40* (Suppl. IV), 74-83.

Wolf, S., & Goodell, H. *Harold G. Wolff's stress and disease.* Springfield, Ill.: Charles C. Thomas, 1968.

Yawger, N. S. Emotions as a cause of rapid and sudden death. *Archives of Neurology and Psychiatry*, 1936, *36*, 875-879.

Zipes, D. P. Electrophysiological mechanisms involved in ventricular fibrillation. *Circulation*, 1975, *51-52* (Suppl. III), 120-130.

11

MUSCLE-CONTRACTION HEADACHE: A PSYCHOPHYSIOLOGICAL PERSPECTIVE OF ETIOLOGY AND TREATMENT

Stephen N. Haynes

INTRODUCTION

Muscle-contraction headache is, perhaps, one of the most common psycho-somatic disorders, with incidence estimates in the general population varying between 20% and 60% (Ad Hoc Committee on Classification of Headache, 1962; Friedman, Von Storch, & Merritt, 1954; Harrison, 1970; McGehee, 1968) and with higher incidence estimates for some specific populations. Cassidy (1957) reported that 36% of medically sick individuals and 25% of healthy controls complained of headache. Harper and Steger (1978) estimated that 65% of the general population suffers from periodic headache, 31% have two or more head-aches per month, and 1% have daily headaches. Kashiwagi, McClure, and Wetzel (1972) reported that 28.1% of medical school patients had headache as their primary complaint. In a sample of 4,634 individuals reported by Ogden (1952), 65% reported periodically suffering from headache, 48% reported at least one headache per month, and daily headaches were reported by 1%. Ziegler, Hassanein, and Couch (1977) noted that 70% of women and 50% of men in a nonclinic population reported having had a disabling headache. Although most of these studies failed to differentiate muscle-contraction from migraine and other types of headache, it is evident that muscle-contraction headache comprises the majority of headache cases in these samples. The high incidence of muscle-contraction headache can also be inferred from the millions of dollars spent yearly in advertising and consuming over-the-counter headache pain medication.

Preparation of this chapter was supported, in part, by a Research Grant (NIH-1-R01-NS/GM-14739-01) from the National Institute of Mental Health.

Muscle-contraction headache is usually characterized as an aching, a tightness around the neck or head, or a tight band surrounding the head. Localization of the pain may vary but is most frequently in the back of the neck and in the frontal and occipital regions of the head. The pain is most frequently nonthrobbing and bilateral. The duration may vary between a half hour and several days, and the intensity between mild and debilitatingly painful.

The importance of muscle-contraction headache as a psychosomatic disorder stems not only from its high incidence but from the personal distress accompanying painful headache, the social consequences, such as interruption in occupational, recreational, or social activities, and the vast amounts of time and money spent yearly in seeking remedies (Bakal, 1975).

Muscle-contraction headache has been conceptualized as a psychophysiological disorder, because its occurrence and intensity have been assumed to covary with environmental events, particularly stressful events, and with various personality of psychiatric constellations. Although the relationship between environmental and psychological factors and muscle-contraction headache has not been firmly established, it has been assumed that some individuals react to stress with elevated levels of autonomically mediated physiological arousal and sustained contraction of the muscles of the head and neck, which may lead to muscle-contraction headache. It has also been assumed (Lachman, 1972) that operant/environmental factors may affect muscle-contraction headache activity.

This chapter will review research and current issues concerning these etiological assumptions and medical and nonmedical treatments of muscle-contraction headache. Topics include diagnosis, muscle contraction etiology, vascular etiology, the role of other physical and nonphysical etiological factors, personality and behavioral correlates, and medical and nonmedical interventions.

DIAGNOSIS

Symptom Heterogeneity

Diagnosing muscle-contraction headache and differentiating it from other headache types has been problematic from both clinical and research perspectives. As noted by Philips (1977), muscle-contraction headache is most frequently diagnosed by the *exclusion* of symptoms indicative of other headache types. The absence of auras, nausea, vomiting, intense throbbing, and unilaterality, for example, would suggest that the headache is not of vascular origin (migraine), and the absence of a relationship between headache symptoms and climate changes, colds, allergy problems, or nasal discharge helps differentiate muscle-contraction from sinus headache. Other than localization, there are few positive indicators to suggest that a particular headache pain syndrome can be classified as muscle-contraction headache. Diagnosis by symptom exclusion, although currently necessary, is likely to have an adverse effect on the reliability of the diagnostic procedures.

Compounding the difficulties of diagnosing muscle-contraction headache by symptom exclusion is the fact that the symptoms accompanying other headaches demonstrate between- and within-subject variability. For example, typically less than one-third of migraine headache patients report an aura preceding a headache, and migraine headaches can sometimes be bilateral and occur without feelings of nausea. In addition, individuals with apparent migraine headaches report an aura on some occasions but not on others. Similarly, the location of some sinus headaches in the frontal region increases the difficulty in differentiating them from muscle-contraction headache. To further complicate diagnostic efforts, many individuals report having some headaches with muscle-contraction symptomatology, some with migraine symptomatology, and others of mixed symptomatology.

In a 1972 study, Ziegler, Hassanein, and Hassanein addressed the issue of the validity of traditionally identified symptom clusters in headache subjects. Although the study focused primarily on migraine headache, the results have implications for headache diagnosis in general. The authors administered a twenty-seven-item headache symptom questionnaire to 289 headache subjects, who were free of organic problems. Factor analysis of the individual items resulted in seven factors; the authors noted that no single factor consisted of all the symptoms traditionally assumed to be associated with migraine headache. Ziegler et al. also reported that subjects demonstrated inconsistent symptom patterns, and they suggested that, because of the heterogeneity of symptom clusters, researchers should use subjects who are homogeneous in symptomatology.

Diagnostic Procedures

The methods of diagnosing muscle-contraction headache in the published clinical and research reports invariably consist of interviews, and sometimes questionnaires, focusing on self-reported symptomatology (Chesney & Shelton, 1976). Reliability of the diagnoses is almost never assessed — a particularly striking deficit in view of the unreliability of headache symptom clusters, the difficulty in identifying specific headache types, and the heterogeneous symptoms usually reported by any one subject.

Because of the difficulty in relying on self-reported symptoms as the basis for diagnosis, researchers have recently used physiological or psychophysiological diagnostic procedures to supplement self-report measures. For example, the use of the electroencephalogram (EEG) was recommended by Masland (1978) to rule out organic etiological factors in headache cases. Sargent, Green and Walter (1973) used EEG along with chest x-ray, urinalysis, and a complete physical in their pretreatment diagnostic efforts with migraine and muscle-contraction headache subjects. As with self-report methods, however, physiological diagnostic procedures are used primarily to exclude other possible causes for the head pain and are not used as positive indices of muscle-contraction headache.

Assuming a significant relationship between frontal and neck electromyogram (EMG) and muscle-contraction headache, several authors have used EMG recordings of headache subjects, at rest or during stress, to help determine if headaches are muscle-contraction in origin (Epstein, Abel, Collins, Parker, & Cinciripini, 1978; Peck & Kraft, 1977; Philips, 1977). In the study by Epstein et al., muscle-contraction headache subjects were selected on the basis of frontal EMG levels; subjects whose mean integrated frontal EMG levels were at least 10 uV during a headache period and whose frequency and self-reported symptoms met other criteria were selected for the study. Peck and Kraft took ten one-second samples from several muscle sites (trapezius, cervical, paraspinalis, masseter, and frontal) prior to biofeedback training. Although not used to discriminate muscle-contraction from other headache types, the data was used to select the site from which biofeedback was provided. Similar procedures were used by Philips, who assessed differential EMG levels of the temporal and frontal muscle groups to select the target muscle for biofeedback training.

Although a promising addition to the technology of headache diagnosis, psychophysiological approaches are based upon untested assumptions about etiological factors or physiological correlates of muscle-contraction headache. Use of frontal EMG as a diagnostic criterion, for example, is based on the assumption that elevated frontal EMG levels can be used to discriminate muscle-contraction from other types of headache cases. As noted in subsequent sections of this chapter, however, several studies have noted that frontal EMG levels of muscle-contraction headache subjects are not always greater than those of no-headache controls or subjects with migraine headaches (Bakal & Kaganov, 1977; Martin & Mathews, 1978). It would be premature, therefore, to emphasize the discriminative power of EMG levels in identifying headache type.

Summary

In summary, there are currently no satisfactory criteria for differentiating muscle-contraction from other types of headaches. Diagnostic difficulties are attributable to heterogeneous symptom clusters accompanying various headache types and within-subject variance in reported symptoms. Similarly, there is currently no physiological or psychophysiological procedure which has been shown to reliably and validly discriminate among headache types. Muscle-contraction headaches tend to be diagnosed on the basis of exclusion of symptoms indicative of other headache types, and the criteria used for this diagnosis tend to vary across studies. The implications of these diagnostic difficulties are quite clear: variance among studies in methods and criteria for diagnosis is likely to be associated with conflicting and inconsistent research findings attributable to heterogeneous subject groups.

In considering issues and problems in the research and clinical literature dealing with the diagnosis of muscle-contraction headache, several suggestions can be offered: (1) the specific diagnostic criteria and procedures used should be clearly spelled out, (2) estimates of the interrater reliability of diagnoses should be ascertained, (3) subject groups with homogeneous symptoms should be employed in research, and (4) diagnostic procedures should include self-report and psychophysiological measures, but care should be exercised in their interpretation and in the weighted value placed on each.

ETIOLOGY

Muscle-contraction headache has been hypothesized to be a function of numerous etiological factors. The most frequently hypothesized causative factor is sustained contraction of the muscles of the head and neck, but cephalic vasomotor factors, stress, lower pain thresholds, social/operant factors, and other organic factors have also been hypothesized to influence the occurrence, duration, and/or intensity of muscle-contraction headache (Bakal, 1975; Beaty & Haynes, 1979; Dalessio, 1972). This section will review and discuss the research concerning the etiology of muscle-contraction headache.

Elevated Muscle Tension in the Head and Neck

Elevated muscle tension levels about the head and neck is, perhaps, the most commonly hypothesized etiological factor in muscle-contraction headache, which is usually assumed to be due to *sustained* tension (Bakal, 1975; Beaty & Haynes, 1979; Martin, 1972). Within this model, headache pain is assumed to be a function of pain receptors in the contracted muscles or of pain associated with decreased regional blood flow or edemic responses during muscle contraction.

If muscle tension contributes to muscle-contraction headache, several empirical predictions can be made.

1.   Resting head and/or neck EMG levels would be expected to be higher for muscle-contraction headache subjects than for no-headache subjects.

2.   The EMG response to stress of headache subjects would be expected to be greater than that of no-headache subjects.

3.   Experimental manipulations of cephalic and neck EMG levels would be expected to be associated with commensurate modifications in headache pain level.

4.   A positive and significant correlation between EMG levels in the head and neck areas and headache pain would be expected.

5.   EMG levels would be expected to be elevated during headache, as opposed to no-headache, periods.

6.   Site specificity would be expected: muscle tension levels at the headache site would be expected to be higher than at a no-headache site.

The published research relevant to each of these predictions will be considered in subsequent sections, following an overview of pain mechanisms.

Muscle Contraction Pain Mechanisms

The mechanisms by which muscle contraction may be associated with pain have been outlined in two papers by Dalessio (1974, 1978) and are summarized below. The muscle tension-pain interactions presented are general but are applicable to muscle-contraction headache.

1. Muscle spasm is most frequently initiated by a multisynaptic withdrawal reflex. Nerve impulses stimulated by local pathological processes are transmitted to the spinal cord and ventral roots and, through efferent nerves, to the neuromuscular junction, initiating muscle movement.

2. The initial stimulus is also conducted up the spinal cord to thalamic and central levels through polysynaptic spinal pathways and the leminiscal system. Pain awareness occurs at this level.

3. Impulses traverse the reticulospinal system from the brain and activate the gamma efferent neurons, causing muscle contraction.

4. The discharge of the efferent peripheral nerve is augmented when the contracting muscle spindle evokes a monosynaptic stimulus, which travels directly to the ventral horn.

Dalessio (1974) noted: "If the gamma efferent system continues to fire, because of cortical influences or local systemic disease, the muscle spindle remains tight and the muscle contracts continually until the contraction itself becomes painful. Hence arises the cycle of pain, spasm, anxiety, or muscle-contraction headache" (p. 57).

EMG Levels of Headache and No-Headache Subjects

Several studies have examined the cephalic and/or neck EMG levels of subjects with muscle-contraction headache, no headache, or headache other than muscle-contraction. These studies have been based on assumptions that elevated muscle tension levels in the head and neck area is the primary cause of muscle-contraction headache.

Malmo and Shagass (1949), in one of the earlier studies on the relationship between muscle tension levels and head pain, compared "head pain" patients with patients suffering from cardiovascular disorders, on the basis of their muscle tension responses to thermal pain stimuli (focused light from a five hundred-watt projection lamp). Although the thermal pain did not produce any reports of headache, patients with a history of head pain, compared with control subjects, demonstrated significantly higher neck EMG levels during thermal stimulation. In an extension of this methodology, Malmo, Wallerstein, and

Shagass (1953) monitored forehead EMG, neck EMG, forearm extensor EMG, forearm flexor EMG, heart rate, and blood pressure of headache-prone psychiatric patients, non-headache-prone psychiatric patients, and nonpatient controls while they were receiving painful thermal stimulation. Headache-prone patients showed increased EMG levels to thermal stimulation but only at the sight of their reported pain. Such differences were not found in the no-headache groups, and there were no significant between-group differences in blood pressure or heart rate.

Tunis and Wolff (1954) compared the EMG levels of muscle-contraction headache subjects during headache and during headache-free periods with no-headache controls. Although no statistical analyses were employed, the authors reported the headache subjects had a dramatic increase in EMG levels during headache periods compared with no-headache periods. In addition, no differences were noted between the no-headache group and the muscle-contraction headache group during a no-headache state.

Poziak-Patweica (1976) monitored cervical and temporalis EMG levels during relaxation in subjects manifesting a variety of headache types. The author noted sustained muscular contraction in 46% of the twenty muscle-contraction headache subjects but in none of the controls. EMG levels of the muscle-contraction headache group were less than those of the migraine group.

Bakal and Kaganov (1977) monitored forehead and neck EMG levels of subjects with muscle-contraction headache, migraine headache, or no headache. Headache subjects were monitored during both headache and headache-free periods. Forehead EMG levels were found to be significantly higher for migraine patients than for either muscle-contraction headache patients or no-headache controls. There was no significant difference between muscle-contraction headache patients and no-headache controls in frontal EMG measures, but muscle-contraction headache patients demonstrated significantly greater neck EMG levels. There were no significant differences in EMG levels between headache and headache-free periods for either headache group.

In a more recent study, Martin and Mathews (1978) compared the frontal and neck EMG levels of headache and no-headache subjects during four phases: (1) ten-minute instructions to relax, (2) a thermal stressor (light focused on forehead), (3) administration of twenty-four problems from an IQ test, and (4) instructions to relax. There were no overall significant differences between groups, but there was a significant group-by-phase interaction, reflecting the finding that the headache group, compared with the no-headache control group, evidenced higher EMG levels during rest periods but lower EMG levels during the stressors.

Similar results to those of Martin and Mathews were reported by Vaughn, Pall, and Haynes (1977). In their study, subjects with either a high frequency or a low frequency of muscle-contraction headaches were exposed to rest, stress (mental arithmetic), and recovery conditions. Compared with low-frequency headache subjects, high-frequency headache subjects were found to have higher resting frontal EMG levels during rest conditions but lower frontal EMG levels during stress conditions.

Frontal, temporalis, neck, and trapezius EMG levels of subjects with muscle-contraction headache, migraine headache, headache of mixed symptomatology, and no headache (controls) were monitored in a study by Philips (1978). Over a four-minute rest period, only measures of frontal EMG resulted in significant between-group differences. Migraine subjects demonstrated the greatest frontal EMG levels, followed by subjects with mixed symptomatology, muscle-contraction headache subjects, and then no-headache control subjects.

Acosta, Jamamoto, and Wilcox (1978) monitored frontal EMG levels of schizophrenic, neurotic, and muscle-contraction headache patients during ten weekly sessions of EMG feedback and found no significant differences between groups in mean EMG levels.

In summary, between-group comparisons of subjects with muscle contraction headache, migraine headache, and no headache have yielded inconsistent results. Most, but not all, studies found that the EMG levels, particularly from the frontal area, of muscle-contraction headache subjects are greater than those of no-headache controls but less than those of migraine headache subjects. While such findings provide partial support for the hypothesized muscle contraction etiology of muscle-contraction headache, they do not explore the possibility that elevated EMG levels are a result, rather than a cause, of head pain. This assumption would account for the frequent finding that migraine subjects, compared with muscle-contraction headache subjects, generally report higher headache pain levels and demonstrate higher EMG levels.

EMG Response to Stress

Several studies have evaluated the EMG responses of muscle-contraction headache subjects and no-headache control subjects exposed to stressors. In the previously cited studies by Malmo and Shagass (1949), Malmo et al. (1953), Martin and Mathews (1978), and Vaughn et al. (1977), muscle-contraction headache subjects and no-headache controls were exposed to various types of stressors. In the two studies by Malmo, headache subjects demonstrated greater EMG responses to painful stimuli, while in the studies by Martin and Mathews and Vaughn et al., the mean response to stress was less in muscle-contraction headache subjects than in no-headache comparison subjects. Although they were important early studies in the field, the studies by Malmo should be interpreted more cautiously, because the headache groups were composed of subjects with a variety of headache types; therefore, inferences about the etiology of muscle-contraction headache are more difficult to draw from these studies.

The results of the studies by Martin and Mathews and Vaughn et al. suggest that, based on measures of frontal EMG, muscle-contraction headache subjects are not more responsive to brief stressors than no-headache subjects. While somewhat surprising, it should be noted that this finding is not inconsistent with the hypothesis that muscle-contraction headache is a function of *sustained* contraction of the muscles of the head and neck; longer duration laboratory stressors may be necessary to adequately test this hypothesis, and this study is currently being conducted in the author's laboratory.

The Effect of Experimental Manipulation of EMG on Headaches

The causal relationship between head and neck muscle contraction and muscle-contraction headache may also be assessed through the manipulation of muscle tension at these sites and the observation of concomitant changes in head pain. If the hypothesized causative role of muscle contraction in muscle-contraction headache is valid, increases in head and neck EMG levels should be associated with increases in reported head pain, and decreases in EMG levels from those sites should be associated with decreases in reported head pain.

Strongly supporting the etiological role of frontal EMG in muscle-contraction headache are those studies which have attempted to directly reduce frontal EMG levels through frontal EMG feedback (Budzynski, Stoyva, Adler, & Mullaney, 1973; Chesney & Shelton, 1976; Cox, Freundlich, & Meyer, 1975; Epstein & Abel, 1977; Epstein et al., 1978; Feuerstein, Adams, & Beiman, 1976; Haynes, Griffin, Mooney, & Parise, 1975; Hutchings & Reinking, 1976; Kondo & Canter, 1977; Martin & Mathews, 1978; Peck & Kraft, 1977; Philips, 1977; Raskin, Johnson, & Rondestvedt, 1973; Reeves, 1976; Whatmore & Kohli, 1974; Wickramasekera, 1972, 1973). As noted in the review by Beaty and Haynes (1979), the published studies using frontal EMG feedback in the treatment of muscle-contraction headache have consistently found that frontal EMG feedback is associated with a significant reduction in self-reported muscle-contraction headache frequency, intensity, and/or duration.

While these data provide strong support for the hypothesized etiological functions of elevated muscle tension, a closer examination of the data suggests a more cautious interpretation. For example, Chesney & Shelton found that frontal EMG feedback, by itself, was not an effective intervention modality with muscle-contraction headache. Epstein and Abel noted that for only one out of six subjects was there a significant relationship between frontal EMG levels and headache reports. Feuerstein et al. noted that, although frontal EMG feedback (along with cephalic vasomotor feedback) was associated with a reduction in headache activity, the relationship between EMG feedback and EMG changes was inconsistent. Haynes, Griffin, Mooney, and Parise noted significant individual differences among headache subjects in the association between EMG levels and headache reports. For some subjects, there was a close correspondence between headache activity and frontal EMG levels; for others, the association was small and insignificant. Martin and Mathews and Philips noted that there was no significant relationship between EMG levels during frontal EMG feedback and headache frequency, although the biofeedback intervention was associated with significant reductions in headache activity.

Additional data on the relationship between EMG modifications and headache activity was provided by Epstein et al. (1978). They exposed six muscle-contraction headache subjects to sixteen sessions of EMG feedback, using music as a contingency. Each session involved a twenty-minute phase, in which subjects practiced maintaining their decreased EMG levels. There was a significant correlation (.47, .48) between EMG levels and headache reports for only two subjects. Correlations for the other subjects ranged from -.14 to .18. In a second experiment with two muscle-contraction headache subjects, the authors provided feedback to increase and decrease frontal EMG levels, while head pain reports were taken. The correlations between EMG level and head pain reports were varied and difficult to interpret. For subject 1, the correlations were -.36 during adaptation, -.43 during baseline, .80 during increase training, .44 during decrease training, and .11 overall. Correlations for subject 2 were similar. Overall, the results from these experiments suggest that reports of muscle-contraction headache are relatively independent of frontal EMG levels for most subjects.

In summary, the results of several studies have suggested that experimental manipulation of frontal EMG levels is associated with analogous modifications in self-reported headache activity; other studies have noted that the two variables do not evidence a significant degree of covariation. In all studies, significant individual differences were noted, with some subjects evidencing a strong correlation between head pain and frontal EMG levels, and other subjects demonstrating an insignificant or inverse relationship between these variables. Furthermore, as noted by Beaty and Haynes (1979), reductions in headache activity accompanying frontal EMG feedback support the hypothesized etiological function of cephalic muscle tension only if it has been demonstrated that frontal EMG levels were actually modified and that there were *corresponding* changes in headache activity. Unfortunately, many studies did not demonstrate that frontal EMG levels were effectively modified, and etiological inferences must be drawn with caution.

The Relationship between Muscle Tension Levels and Headache Intensity and Occurrence

Several researchers have compared frontal EMG levels of muscle-contraction headache subjects during headache and no-headache periods. Although alternative explanations are difficult to rule out, higher EMG levels during headache periods than during no-headache periods would be consistent with the hypothesized muscle contraction etiology of muscle-contraction headache. Bakal and Kaganov (1977) found no significant differences in frontal EMG when comparing headache and headache-free periods in muscle-contraction headache subjects. Significant differences in frontal EMG level between headache and headache-free periods, however, were reported in studies by Dixon and Dickel (1967), Haynes, Griffin, Mooney, & Parise (1975), Sainsbury and Gibson (1954), and Tunis and Wolff (1954). Martin and Mathews (1978) reported no significant differences in forehead or neck EMG level as a function of whether measures were taken during headache or headache-free periods.

The studies cited above compared EMG levels between headache and headache-free conditions. Another methodological approach is to assess the linear relationship between frontal and neck EMG level and headache intensity: a correlational rather than an analysis-of-variance approach would be facilitated by scaling headache intensity and correlating it with EMG level. Several studies have evaluated this relationship and have reported a range of correlation coefficients from negative and insignificant to positive and significant (Dixon & Dickel, 1967; Jacobs & Felton, 1969; Lader & Mathews, 1971; Malmo & Shagass, 1949; Shedivy & Kleinman, 1977).

Although not specifically aimed at muscle-contraction headache, Alexander (1975) monitored EMG levels from several sites along with self-reports of tension and found low correlations between these two variables. Cox et al. (1975) reported a correlation coefficient of .42 between headache activity and frontal EMG. Budzynski, Stoyva, Adler, and Mullaney (1973) reported a much higher correlation (.90) between frontal EMG level and headache intensity. As noted previously, correlations for individual subjects in the study by Epstein et al. (1978) ranged from -.14 to .48 in their first experiment and between -.43 and .80 in their second experiment, involving biofeedback training for two subjects.

Harper and Steger (1978) exposed muscle-contraction headache subjects to two experimental sessions (interview, MMPI, symptom checklist) and monitored frontal EMG levels and subjective ratings of head pain. The authors found no statistically significant relationship between EMG and head pain ratings, although EMG was correlated with other dependent measures, such as depression and anxiety.

In summary, published studies of the association between head and neck EMG and measures of headache pain in muscle-contraction headache subjects have, in some cases, confirmed, and in other cases, not confirmed, the hypothesized etiological role of muscle contraction. In some studies, but not others, and for some subjects, but not others, a significant positive relationship between these two variables has been found. These inconsistent findings may result from variability in methodology and subject selection across studies or from subject variance in the etiological role of muscle-contraction headache. These methodological factors will be considered in further detail in the following section.

Summary of the Etiological Role of Muscle Contraction in Muscle-Contraction Headache

We have reviewed a variety of experimental approaches and studies which test the hypothesis that muscle-contraction headache is a result of elevated tension in the muscles of the head and neck. Mixed findings have resulted from comparing EMG levels of headache and no-headache subjects, analyzing frontal and neck EMG responses to stress, assessing the effects of experimental manipulations of frontal and neck EMG levels on headache activity, and assessing the linear relationship between EMG levels and headache activity in muscle-contraction headache subjects. The results of many of the studies are consistent with the hypothesized muscle contraction etiology of muscle-contraction headache, but the results of others failed to support this hypothesis. Furthermore, between-subject differences were noted in the apparent etiological role of muscle tension; significant positive correlations between EMG level and headache activity were noted for some headache subjects, but low or negative correlations were demonstrated for others.

As noted by Bakal (1975), Bakal and Kagnov (1977), Beaty and Haynes (1979), Epstein et al. (1978), Harper and Steger (1978), Lader and Mathews (1971), and Ziegler (1978), the results from these studies suggest that muscle-contraction alone is insufficient to account for the occurrence or intensity of muscle-contraction headache. One concept that is important when considering etiological factors is *explained variance*, or the proportion of the variance in headache occurrences or intensity that can be explained by knowledge of an hypothesized etiological factor, such as frontal or neck EMG level. Although not formally assessed in any of the studies cited above, explained variance (R^2) can be estimated, from inspection of correlation coefficients and F ratios, to be generally less than .30, suggesting that, in most studies, less than 30% of the variance in headache frequency, duration, or intensity can be accounted for by reference to muscle tension levels. It does appear, however, that for some subjects, or under some conditions, muscle tension plays a significant etiological role. Before considering additional etiological factors, some methodological parameters of the studies cited and their influence upon derived estimates of explained variance will be considered.

One potential source of variance between studies is differences in subject populations, or *population heterogeneity*. As mentioned in the section on diagnosis, very few studies have reported explicit diagnostic criteria, and those that have frequently differ in the diagnostic criteria they have used. The result of these methodological differences is that subject samples across studies may not be similar, and differences in the apparent role of muscle tension in headache may reflect differences in populations sampled.

Studies have also varied in the severity of headaches reported by the subjects, with some studies (such as Vaughn et al., 1977) using nonclinical subjects with mild cases of headache, and other studies (for example, Malmo & Shagass, 1949) using subjects from clinical populations with more severe headaches. It is possible that the significance of an etiological factor varies with the severity of a headache.

Between-subject differences in the relationship between EMG level and headache intensity may also be a function of the muscle site monitored and of headache location. If muscle-contraction headache were caused by *localized* sustained muscle contractions, frontal EMG levels would be significantly associated with headache occurrence or intensity only for subjects with muscle-contraction headaches in the frontal region. Unfortunately, the specificity or generality of the muscle contraction response in muscle-contraction headache has not been ascertained.

The findings of individual differences in the apparent role of muscle-contraction headache and of multiple determinants for muscle-contraction headache have implications for diagnostic and therapeutic efforts with this pain disorder. As noted in the earlier section on diagnosis, caution should be exercised in utilizing neck and head EMG levels as a screening criterion. There is no evidence that such a procedure has reliable discriminative validity. These findings also suggest that frontal EMG feedback is likely to be an efficacious therapeutic modality only for muscle-contraction headache subjects in whom headaches can be attributed to contraction of the frontal musculature.

Vascular Etiological Factors

Another prominent theory of the etiology of muscle-contraction headache is that it is a function of vasoconstriction or ischemia (Friedman, 1964b; Wolff, 1963) or vasodilation (Onel, Friedman, & Grossman, 1961) in affected muscle sites. Evidence relevant to these theories has come from several studies which have compared cephalic vasomotor behavior of muscle-contraction headache and no-headache subjects, evaluated muscle-contraction headache subjects' cephalic vasomotor response to stress, evaluated the effects of experimental manipulations of cephalic vasomotor behavior on muscle-contraction headache, and evaluated the association (linear relationship) between cephalic vasomotor behavior and reports of muscle-contraction headache.

In a study comparing extracranial vasomotor responses of muscle-contraction headache and no-headache subjects, Tunis and Wolff (1954) examined the extracranial pulse amplitude (temporal artery) of muscle-contraction headache subjects during headache and headache-free states and of no-headache control subjects. Although the study presents difficulties because blood volume pulse amplitudes were treated as absolute rather than relative measures (Haynes, 1978; Haynes & Wilson, 1979), the authors suggested, from their inspection of 254 series of pulse wave records (twenty-six subjects), that lower pulse wave amplitudes, which are indicative of vasoconstriction, were more evident for the muscle-contraction headache than for the no-headache subjects. Pulse wave amplitude measures were also lower during headache than headache-free periods.

Ostfeld, Reis, and Wolff (1957) published a series of seven experiments which further supported the hypothesized vasoconstriction etiology of muscle-contraction headache. The authors studied bulbar conjunctival ischemia of headache and no-headache subjects, during rest and stress, in response to vasoconstrictor and vasodilator substances and to ganglion blocking agents. The series of experiments is too complex to describe here in detail, but it may be summarized as follows:

1. There was an increase in bulbar conjunctival ischemia in no-headache medical students as they approached final examinations. This finding was consistent with hypothesized extracranial vasoconstriction associated with external stressors.

2. Examination of muscle-contraction headache subjects before, during, and after headaches suggested that increased arteriole vasomotor constriction and spasm and localization of the ischemia were associated with localization of the headache. There was a close correspondence between headache duration and ischemia duration.

3. Administration of a vasoconstrictor substance (intravenous levarterenol) was associated with an increase in the severity of headache symptoms in ten of twelve headache subjects but in none of the no-headache subjects. The authors, however, noted significant individual differences in sensitivity to this vasoconstrictive substance.

4. Increased vasodilation, associated with administration of amyl nitrite, was associated with a decrease in the intensity of the headaches. Headache symptoms returned when inhalation of amyl nitrate ceased.

5. The operation of neurogenic factors was investigated by the administration of a ganglion blocking agent during a muscle-contraction headache; no effect on local ischemia or on reported head pain was noted.

6. The humoral component of bulbar conjunctival ischemia was investigated by the administration of oral cortisone doses on thirteen occasions to three male patients; ischemia was noted only at large doses and was not associated with reports of headache pain.

Although the research by Ostfeld et al. (1957) was very ambitious and helped illuminate the etiological role of local ischemia in muscle-contraction headache, it should be emphasized that many of the manipulations used by these authors (such as inhalation of amyl nitrite and administration of ganglion blocking agents) have systemic effects, and alternative explanations for the results of these experiments can readily be offered. The significant individual differences in subjects' responses to these manipulations should also be noted; although the results of the group data support the hypothesized etiological role of localized ischemia, they leave a substantial proportion of the variance in headache occurrence still unaccounted for.

Wolff (1963) reported a series of studies involving a variety of methodologies to study vasomotor responses associated with headache. Head pain was induced by various methods, such as noxious stimuli to the head, spinal fluid drainage, and histamine injections. In addition to noting that these results support the hypothesized muscle contraction etiology of muscle-contraction headache,

Wolff also noted that noxious stimulation was associated with cephalic vaso-constriction and that ischemia could enhance the pain response associated with sustained muscle contraction. Although using a small number of subjects, Wolff noted that reductions of head pain were associated with the administration of vasodilators and that increases in head pain were associated with the administration of vasoconstrictors. These results are consistent with those of Friedman and Merritt (1959), who observed that cranial artery pressure pulse waves were markedly diminished during a headache, a finding indicative of increased vaso-constriction.

Indirect support for the etiological role of vasoconstriction in headache comes from a study by Feuerstein et al. (1976). Although there were inferential difficulties, because their single subject had combined muscle-contraction and migraine headaches, the authors found that cephalic vasomotor feedback, along with EMG feedback, was associated with reduced frequency of vasomotor spasms and reduced frequency, duration, and intensity of headaches.

Bakal and Kaganov (1977) compared subjects with muscle-contraction head-ache, migraine headache, or no headaches on measures of pulse wave velocity (an indirect measure of vascular constriction and dilation) in the superficial temporal arteries. Headache subjects were evaluated during a headache and a headache-free period. There were no significant differences for headache subjects as a function of whether they had a headache or were headache free. Vasocon-striction to noise stimuli was noted for both headache groups, but the opposite effect, vasodilation, was observed for the no-headache controls.

Results contrary to those of the previously cited studies were reported by Onel et al. (1961). These authors used radioactive sodium to monitor capillary flow rate; flow rates were estimated by introducing radioactive sodium chloride into tissues and then observing the rate at which it was removed from the tissues. This procedure was used seventy-one times with a large group of muscle-contrac-tion headache subjects and with no-headache control subjects. Each subject rested for ten to fifteen minutes, an anesthesia was administered, and radioactive sodium chloride was introduced into the splenius capitis muscle. A Geiger-Müller body counter was placed over the injection site, and readings were begun after five minutes and continued for twenty to twenty-five minutes. Fifty measures were taken during no-headache states and sixteen during headache states.

Significantly faster clearance rates (indicating vasodilation) were found during headache states than during no-headache states and during headache states than in no-headache control subjects. There were no differences in sodium clear-ance rate between headache subjects during a no-headache state and no-headache subjects. The authors interpreted these findings as being inconsistent with the hypothesis that muscle-contraction headache is associated with muscle ischemia.

Results implicating vasodilation as an etiological factor were also reported by Martin and Mathews (1978). These authors administered a vasodilator sub-stance (amyl nitrite) or a placebo to subjects during a muscle-contraction headache. The placebo had no effect on reported headache pain, but the amyl nitrite was associated with increases in head pain in 48% of the cases and no change in 43% of the cases. These results suggest that muscle-contraction headache may be a function of vasodilation rather than vasoconstriction.

In summary, except for studies by Martin and Mathews (1978) and Onel et al. (1961), the results of most studies have been consistent with the hypothesis that vasoconstriction and ischemia may be contributing factors in muscle-contraction headache. A variety of experimental methodologies have been employed, including the comparison of pulse wave velocities and photoplethysmography responses of muscle-contraction headache and no-headache subjects, the assessment of the vasomotor responses of headache and no-headache subjects to stress, and the assessment of the effects of cephalic vascular modifications on head pain. Several authors have suggested that localized vasoconstriction may exacerbate pain associated with muscle contraction by diminishing the blood supply to muscles which may already be experiencing an oxygen deficit and symptoms of muscle fatigue. It should be emphasized, therefore, that the hypothesized etiological role of vasomotor responses is not necessarily an alternative to the muscle-contraction hypothesis; both may be elements of the same etiological factor.

Differences in outcome between the studies are difficult to account for but are possibly attributable to methodological differences, such as those noted in the section concerning muscle-contraction etiology. Differences in results may also be a function of variance in diagnostic criteria, measurement methodology, or other nonspecific factors, such as demand or experimenter bias.

Additional Etiological Factors

Other etiological factors have been postulated to account for the frequency, duration, and/or intensity of muscle-contraction headache. As noted by Fordyce (1976, 1978) and Lachman (1972), establishing the etiology of pain disorders, such as muscle-contraction headache, was complicated by the fact that their assessments were dependent on self-report. *Verbal report* of headache is under the control of many factors, such as demand aspects in the assessment situation or social-operant factors operating in the individual's environment, in addition to the occurrence of pain. If we assume that the occurrence of muscle-contraction headache is controlled by the degree of sustained contraction of the cephalic musculature, variance would still be introduced in assessing the EMG-headache relationship, because the *report* of its occurrence and intensity would be influenced by factors in addition to EMG level.

As suggested by Fordyce (Fordyce, 1976, 1978; Fordyce, Fowler, & DeLateur, 1966; Fordyce, Fowler, Lehmann, & DeLateur, 1968; Fordyce, Fowler, Lehmann, DeLateur, Sand, & Trieschmann, 1973), headache reports can have strong effects on the subject's social environment and can be under the control of environmental contingencies. Reports of headache pain may be associated with avoidance of an unpleasant activity, such as doing housework or attending a class, empathic and sympathetic communication from significant others, or other forms of externally delivered reinforcers. It should be noted, however, that while the operant control over verbal and psychophysiological behavior has been frequently demonstrated, there is no evidence to substantiate the hypothesis that such factors account for a significant proportion of the variance in muscle-contraction headache or in its report. Longitudinal studies of high-frequency and low-frequency headache subjects, with concomitant measurement of possible operant consequences for "headache behavior," are needed to clarify the etiological role of social/operant factors.

Most theorists (among them, Bakal, 1975; Friedman, 1964b; Kiritz & Moos, 1974; Mitchell & White, 1976; Ziegler, 1978) have also suggested that *stress* is an important factor in muscle-contraction headache etiology. As indicated in other chapters of this book, there is a vast amount of research suggesting that environmental stressors, both in the laboratory and in the natural environment, have significant physiological effects. In addition, many of the studies previously cited have documented the occurrence of increased EMG levels and vasomotor responses to stressors; these findings suggest that stress can initiate or exacerbate a headache because of its physiological effects. As in the case of operant etiological factors, there has been little empirical research on the role of naturally occurring stressors in causing headache. Additional research is needed on other parameters, such as the duration of stress necessary to elicit a headache, the types of stressors which may be associated with muscle-contraction headache, and individual differences in response to stress.

Martin and Mathews (1978) suggested that differential *pain thresholds* may be a factor in accounting for individual differences in headache behavior. Physiological and anatomical factors, such as *endorfinic concentration, synaptic transmission* trigger levels, or complexity of nerve branching, may vary among subjects and affect their perception of a stimulus as painful. Bond (1976) previously noted individual differences in pain behavior and suggested that differences may be related to concentration of endorfin (endogenous morphine-like substances affecting synaptic transmissions). Similarly, psychological and environmental factors, such as previous experience with painful stimuli and the environmental consequences accompanying pain reports, may affect apparent pain sensitivity. The role of pain sensitivity is currently being investigated in the author's laboratory, by monitoring pain responses of headache and no-headache subjects to an inflated occlusion cuff placed around the arm.

Behavioral and Personality Correlates

A number of authors (Bond, 1976; Martin, 1966; Philips, 1976; Sternbach, Wolf, Murphy, & Akeson, 1973) have suggested that muscle-contraction headache is a secondary symptom or covariate of personality disorders or types.

Within this model, headache may be viewed as a consequence or covariate of psychological stress, as a symptom of psychiatric disturbance, as an expression of intrapsychic conflict, or as an element in a general personality constellation or dimension. The mechanism by which these conflicts, disturbances, or personality dimensions lead to muscle-contraction headache, however, has not been specified.

Several authors (Cassidy, 1957; Dalessio, 1963, 1968; Diamond, 1964; Diamond & Baltes, 1971; Kashiwagi et al., 1972; Kudrow, 1976) have reported that muscle-contraction headache is frequently associated with depression. Support for this hypothesis comes from studies assessing the correlation between these two variables and from studies which have monitored headache activity before, during, and following antidepressant therapy. Kudrow, for example, suggested that antidepressant medication, such as amitriptyline (a tricyclic), may be useful in the treatment of depressed subjects with muscle-contraction headache. Dalessio (1968) also noted that self-reported pain from headache frequently diminishes following the administration of antidepressant medication.

Diamond and Baltes, noting that muscle-contraction headache is frequently associated with depression, also evaluated the efficacy of administrating tricyclic compounds (amitriptyline) to depressed patients and monitoring the effect of these medications on headache activity. In a double-blind study, ninety patients who complained of headache and either depression or anxiety were randomly assigned to one of three treatment groups: (1) amitriptyline, 25 mg, (2) amitriptyline, 10 mg, or (3) placebo. Each patient took two tablets at bedtime and then gradually increased dosages but never exceeded six per day. Each patient was assessed four times during the study, and seven measures were taken in addition to headache activity. Although the authors did not report the type of statistics used, and the drop-out rate was quite high (twenty-seven patients did not complete the four-week program), the authors found that 10 mg of amitriptyline was associated with the greatest reduction in headache activity.

A high correlation between the occurrence of headache and depression has been reported by several authors. Diamond (1964) noted that 84% of depressed patients also report frequent headaches. Cassidy (1957), in a study of one hundred manic-depressives, fifty medically sick control subjects, and fifty healthy controls, found that 49% of the manic-depressive patients, but only 36% of the medically sick controls and 25% of healthy controls, complained of frequent or intense headaches. In a study of 473 patients at a medical school, Kashiwagi et al. (1972) noted that 28.1% had headache as their chief complaint and that there was a strong association between the occurrence of depression (unipolar affective disorder) and muscle-contraction headache. The authors noted, however, that muscle-contraction headache was the most frequent headache type in those subjects with no psychiatric disturbance.

Other authors have suggested that headache, in general, and muscle-contraction headache, in particular, are associated with general psychiatric and personality syndromes. For example, Dalessio (1974) noted that headache may be indicative of, or a symptom of, general psychiatric disturbance. Diamond (1969) suggested that headache may be a form of "body language" used by the patient to express personal and interpersonal conflicts and that it may be a symptom of "psychogenic overlay." Friedman (1964a, 1972) hypothesized that headache is usually associated with psychological problems or emotional factors or is a function of repressed psychosexual conflicts. An association between muscle-contraction headache and anxiety denial, neurosis, poorly controlled anger, compulsiveness, and sexual problems was noted by Martin (1972) in twenty of seventy headache patients. In other reports, Martin (Martin, 1966, 1978; Martin, Rome, & Swenson, 1967) also suggested that muscle-contraction headache is associated with personality problems, poorly repressed hostility, unresolved dependency needs, or psychosexual conflicts. Similar correlations between muscle-contraction headache and personality factors were suggested by Ziegler (1978). He also noted that considerable methodological difficulties and differences in outcome are apparent in the studies on psychological etiology but that such factors as psychological tension, reactions to stress, and poorly controlled hostile impulses may be implicated.

An association between headache, in general, or, specifically, muscle-contraction headache, and general psychiatric disturbance has been noted by several other authors. Harrison (1975) reviewed a number of studies assessing psychological factors in headache and noted that, although inconsistencies were evident in the results of these studies, they tended to indicate a profile for headache subjects of hypochondriasis, hysteria, and depression. Howarth (1965) administered the Maudsley Personality Inventory to muscle-contraction headache and no-headache subjects and found no significant differences between the two groups on introversion-extroversion, but he found that headache subjects scored significantly higher on the neuroticism scale. Howarth noted that, although there was a significant association between headache and neuroticism, subjects along a continuum of neuroticism experienced headaches. Negative findings were reported by Davis, Wetzel, and Kashiwagi (1976), who found no significant correlation between measures of the California Personality Index and headache type.

Philips (1976) administered the Maudsley Personality Inventory to thirty-nine migraine and twenty-four muscle-contraction headache patients and found no significant differences between the two groups. When compared with a no-headache control group, however, the muscle-contraction headache group scored higher on measures of "neuroticism." Philips went on to point out that assumptions that subjects with muscle-contraction headache are more neurotic than no-headache controls may be a result of sampling bias, in that physicians and researchers are likely to have contact with the more neurotic headache subjects.

In a study outlined previously, Harper & Steger (1978) exposed thirty-three headache patients to two sessions of interviews and questionnaires (MMPI, Cornell Medical Index, symptom checklist). They found significant correlations between headache ratings and measures of hypochondriasis (.47), depression (.34), hysteria (.43), total number of complaints on the Cornell Medical Index (.50), number of nervous system complaints (.47), and illness frequency (.37).

In summary, although significant methodological difficulties are present in all the studies which have addressed the issue of personality or psychiatric correlates of muscle-contraction headache, numerous studies using a variety of methodologies have reported significant relationships between headache activity and various indices of psychological disturbance. Methodological problems which reduce the confidence that can be placed in these results include sampling biases associated with subjects being primarily medical referrals, insufficient specification of diagnostic criteria, and lack of controls for a number of non-specific factors, such as experimental demand effects or experimenter bias. One serious hinderance to the interpretation of these studies is that many of them evaluated "headache" subjects without performing separate analyses on subjects with muscle-contraction headache, specifically. Regardless of the methodological limitations, it may be useful to assume the validity of these results and consider factors which may account for such a relationship.

One error commonly made by researchers evaluating psychological factors associated with headache is their assumption of causative functions from an association between psychological factors and muscle-contraction headache. For example, a common interpretation of studies on depression and headache is that muscle-contraction headache can be caused by, or is a symptom of, depression. Although such an assumption is also consistent with the results of studies which have demonstrated a reduction in headache activity accompanying successful treatment of depression, causative inferences are unwarranted at this time. Dalessio (1974, 1978), for exzmple, noted that antidepressant medication can affect central responses to pain stimuli and, sometimes, have muscle-tension-reducing properties; these effects, rather than the antidepressant effects, may account for the reported reduction in headaches that accompanies antidepressant medication.

There is, however, sufficient reason to predict that muscle-contraction headache will be found to be associated with a variety of psychological disturbances. As indicated in previous sections, muscle-contraction headache is apparently a function of such factors as sustained muscle tension, operant consequences of pain reports, and environmental stress. These factors have also been associated with a variety of psychological disturbances. Several studies, for example, have noted elevated EMG levels in depressed versus nondepressed individuals, and, certainly, environmental stress plays a crucial role in a wide variety of psychological disturbances. Therefore, an association between muscle-contraction headache and other classes of behavior problems is not surprising. Perhaps a more fruitful direction for research would be the identification of factors contributing to the individual variation or covariation between these factors. Some depressed individuals manifest muscle-contraction headaches, while others do not; similarly, some individuals with muscle-contraction headaches score higher than no-headache control subjects on measures of psychological disturbance, but others do not.

In summary, a variety of studies have been conducted on the association between muscle-contraction headache and personality type and psychiatric disturbance. While results of the studies have not been entirely consistent, and serious methodological flaws are evident, there is some suggestion that an association between these variables may exist. Such a relationship would not be surprising, however, when the hypothesized causative factors of each are considered. Particular care should be exercised in ascribing causative functions to the psychological factors, and continued research on the association between these variables is needed.

Summary

A variety of factors with potential etiological significance for muscle-contraction headache have been discussed in the previous sections. There is some evidence to support the hypothesized etiological functions of muscle contraction, vasoconstriction, vasodilation, operant/environmental factors, differential pain sensitivity, stress, and psychological and psychiatric factors. Perhaps one of the most valid inferences that can be drawn from this literature review is the importance of multiple determinants and individual differences in etiology. It is apparent that no single factor can account for substantially all the variance in the occurrence of muscle-contraction headache, which, like all behavior disorders, is probably a function of multiple causative factors. It can also be assumed that the relative contribution of these factors probably varies among and within individuals.

In addition to the methodological problems which diminish confidence in obtained results — diagnostic inadequacies, sampling and subject biases, insufficient attention to individual differences — the self-report nature of muscle-contraction headache presents particular difficulties. Muscle-contraction headache can only be inferred from verbal report, and, as numerous authors have noted, verbal report can be influenced by factors other than the occurrence of the target behavior (muscle-contraction headache). The second major methodological problem stems from the fact that the reliability of diagnostic procedures cannot be assumed, because it has been inadequately reported. Therefore, considerable heterogeneity is likely to exist among subjects between studies and within any one study. This certainly impedes interpretation of results and minimizes their generalizability.

TREATMENT

The two most frequently reported treatment approaches for muscle-contraction headache are medical interventions, through analgesics, and, more recently, psychophysiological intervention, involving biofeedback or relaxation training. The first approach is aimed at interrupting the muscle contraction-pain perception-muscle contraction circle. Analgesics or other medical interventions, such as sedatives or anesthetics, although they have some muscle-relaxing qualities, operate primarily by minimizing pain sensations. Biofeedback and relaxation training are assumed to function by enhancing muscle relaxation responses, although vascular responses and modification in pain perception may also accompany these interventions. The subsequent sections will consider these interventions more closely, along with other behavioral interventions.

Medical Interventions

One of the most widely used interventions with muscle-contraction headache is analgesics (Borges & Zavaleta, 1976; Friedman, 1964a; Harrison, 1970; McGehee, 1968), and one of the most widely used analgesics is aspirin (Dalessio, 1974, 1978). Dalessio (1974) noted that analgesics, as well as anesthetics, serve to inhibit the multiple synaptic network transmitting afferent pain impulses. By altering psychological perception of pain, analgesics (and also sedatives, some tranquilizers, and antidepressants) serve to reduce muscle tension levels at the headache site. Except for the application of local analgesics, most analgesics operate centrally, by modifying the subject's perception of pain. Local analgesics affect the pain response by blocking nerve impulses.

General anesthetics involve primarily central factors, in which complete muscle relaxation is obtained, and the cortical reaction to pain is at its minimum. During general anesthesia, cortical reactions to pain are inhibited, although afferent pain impulses continue to be transmitted (Dalessio, 1974, 1978). Friedman (1964a) noted that centrally acting tranquilizers are also sometimes prescribed for the treatment of headache, although side effects associated with these medications suggest caution in their use.

Both Weber (1973) and Ziegler (1978) have cautioned about the excessive use of analgesics and have suggested that they are, perhaps, the most overused medications. Ziegler noted that exceeding optimal dosage does not add to analgesic effects, but continued excessive usage can be associated with habituation and renal damage. Ziegler also recommended the use of mild sedatives for muscle-contraction headache patients who are anxious.

Weber reported a study on the effects of diazepam (a drug with both anxiety- and muscle-tension-reducing qualities) on muscle-contraction headache. Weber had noted that analgesics, such as acetylsalicylic acid (ASA), aspirin, or propoxyphene, do not have antianxiety effects and that diazepam might be more congruent with etiological conceptualizations about muscle-contraction headache. Nineteen muscle-contraction headache subjects, who had never used diazepam, stopped all other medications and were given either 10-15 mg of diazepam or a placebo for three weeks; then they were switched to the other condition. Most subjects were evaluated at three and seven weeks after completion of the treatment program. Although there were some obvious design, measurement, and statistical problems, Weber noted that of the nineteen patients, twelve reported being "greatly improved," four were "mildly improved," and three had "no change" with the diazepam. Eighteen subjects reported "no difference" between the placebo and medication conditions.

As noted in a previous section, several authors have recommended the use of antidepressant medication in the treatment of muscle-contraction headache (Dalessio, 1974, 1978; Diamond, 1964; Diamond & Baltes, 1971; Kudrow, 1976). This approach is based on the assumption that depression functions as an etiological factor with muscle-contraction headache. As Dalessio (1974, 1978) noted, however, beneficial effects derived from antidepressant medication may also be attributed to its central effects on pain perception or inherent, muscle relaxation properties.

Behavioral Intervention: Biofeedback and Relaxation Training

Behaviorally oriented treatment methods are based on the assumption that individuals react to stress with elevated physiological arousal and sustained contraction of the muscles of the head and neck. Another assumption underlying behavioral interventions is that muscle-contraction headache may be under the control of environmental contingencies. These contingencies, such as social attention or avoidance of unpleasant activities, may be particularly important, because the disorder is defined by self-report rather than by physiological dysfunction. Although social learning approaches have been employed (Daniels, 1973; Fowler, 1975), behavioral interventions are more frequently aimed at decreasing general physiological arousal and, specifically, decreasing muscle tension in the head and neck region. Although currently a prevalent method of treating muscle-contraction headache, the application of behavioral intervention methods is a recent innovation. In Bakal's (1975) review, only five, nonmedical treatment studies were noted.

The most frequent intervention procedures have been frontal EMG feedback and relaxation instructions, although contingency management and cognitive approaches have also been used. Although the majority of studies have utilized uncontrolled, case study formats, the outcomes of published reports are consistent in indicating that a variety of behavioral interventions can effectively reduce muscle-contraction headache activity. Inferences that behavioral intervention procedures are effective in treating muscle-contraction headache must be constrained, however, when methodological issues in the published studies are delineated.

As noted by Mitchell and White (1976), most of the behavioral interventions have been directed at the last element in the chain leading to a headache, that is, the muscle tension response to stress. Only in studies by Daniels (1973),

Fowler (1975), Epstein and Abel (1977), Mitchell and White (1976), Reeves (1976), and Whatmore and Kohli (1974) was there an attempt to modify the source of stress. It is notable that the majority of reports are single- or multiple-case studies. Only studies by Cox et al. (1975), Haynes, Griffin, Mooney, and Parise, (1975), Budzynski et al. (1973), Chesney and Shelton (1976), Hutchings and Reinking (1976), and Philips (1977) included control groups. Other investigators (Budzynski et al., 1973; Epstein, Herson, & Hamphill, 1974; Mitchell & White, 1976) utilized designs involving some degree of intrasubject control.

Intervention Strategies of Controlled Group Studies

Beaty and Haynes (1979) reviewed behaviorally oriented treatment approaches, and some of the material presented in the following sections draws on that review. One of the early controlled studies was conducted by Budzynski et al. (1973). They had subjects self-monitor headache activity for a two-week baseline period and then, for sixteen weeks, provided them with twice-weekly training sessions of either frontal EMG feedback, pseudofeedback (false-feedback tone), or no feedback. Significantly lower frontal EMG levels were associated with the experimental group, both during the last two weeks of training and at a three-month follow-up. Four of the six patients in the experimental group reported significant declines in headache activity; only one of the six in the pseudofeedback group, and no one in the no-treatment control group, reported such a decline. Improvement was maintained at a three-month follow-up. The experimental group reported a dramatic decrease in medication use, but only a slight decrease was reported by those in the control conditions. After a three-month follow-up, subjects from the pseudofeedback and no-feedback control groups were given frontal EMG feedback. Of the eight subjects who received the training, six demonstrated significant declines in their reported headache activity.

Haynes, Griffin, Mooney, and Parise (1975) exposed muscle-contraction headache subjects to six, twice-weekly training sessions of either frontal EMG feedback, relaxation instructions, or self-relaxation, following a two-week, self-monitoring baseline period. EMG feedback and the relaxation training instructions were equally effective in reducing headache activity, and both were significantly more effective than the self-relaxation control. A five-to-seven-month follow-up suggested that the improvement was maintained.

A study similar in design to that of Haynes, Griffin, Mooney, and Parise (1975) was reported by Cox et al. (1975). Following two weeks of baseline self-monitoring, muscle-contraction headache patients were given either frontal EMG feedback, progressive relaxation, or a medication placebo. Both experimental groups were trained in cue-controlled relaxation (Russell & Sipich, 1973) and were instructed to practice at home. The frontal EMG feedback and relaxation instructions groups demonstrated significantly greater reductions in reported headache activity and medication usage than did the control group.

A four-month follow-up suggested that improvements in the experimental groups were maintained.

Similar results were reported by Hutchings and Reinking (1976). These investigators compared frontal EMG feedback, verbal relaxation instructions, and a combination of the two, across ten sessions. All three interventions were associated with significant reductions in self-reported headache activity; there were no significant differences between groups. Reduction of headache activity occurred earlier for the groups receiving frontal EMG feedback.

Chesney & Shelton (1976) compared the treatment efficacy of frontal EMG feedback, relaxation instructions, a combination of the two, and a no-treatment control group. Subjects were seen for three to five sessions during a two-week period. The greatest reductions in headache frequency were associated with the combined relaxation instructions-EMG biofeedback condition, although each procedure, independently, was also effective in reducing headache frequency. A lack of follow-up, however, inhibits confidence in the results.

Philips (1977) exposed fifteen muscle-contraction or mixed muscle-contraction-migraine headache subjects to twelve sessions of either EMG feedback or false feedback. Subjects in the feedback group heard variable frequency clicks along with verbal praise following successful training trials; subjects in the false-feedback group heard recording of clicks and verbal praise. The target muscle group (frontal or temporalis) for EMG feedback was selected on the basis of degree of reactivity in prior assessment. Although there was no significant between-group difference in headache frequency, subjects in the EMG feedback group demonstrated significantly greater reductions in headache intensity following treatment as well as at follow-up (six to eight weeks), and they reported significantly less medication intake at follow-up.

Martin and Mathews (1978) divided twenty-four muscle-contraction headache subjects into two groups and provided one group with progressive relaxation training and the other with EMG feedback (both forehead and neck EMG feedback) for fourteen sessions; no control group was included. Significant reductions in headache activity across groups were noted, although these reductions were not correlated with EMG reductions. There was no significant difference between the two groups in headache activity at follow-up.

Beaty and Haynes (1979), in their review of controlled group outcome studies, summarized the results as follows: (1) intervention packages involving relaxation instructions or EMG feedback from the frontal region have been more effective than no-treatment or placebo treatment in reducing muscle-contraction headache activity; (2) improvements tend to be maintained at three-to-twelve-month follow-up, and (3) there has been no statistically significant difference in effectiveness between relaxation instructions and frontal EMG feedback in reducing muscle-contraction headache activity. The comparative effectiveness of a treatment package combining biofeedback and relaxation instructions has not been sufficiently investigated to warrant tentative conclusions.

Case Studies

A number of reports involving the treatment of one or several cases have appeared in the literature to further support the apparent efficacy of frontal EMG feedback or relaxation treatment of muscle-contraction headache. These studies vary in the degree of within-subject control procedures incorporated in the design, but they generally report positive results consistent with those of the controlled group studies. For example, in a report by Epstein et al. (1978), frontal EMG feedback with a music contingency was used with six muscle-contraction headache patients for sixteen sessions; in a second experiment, two additional subjects also received frontal EMG feedback for increases and decreases in muscle tension levels. In both experiments, overall decreases in muscle-contraction headache activity was noted. Acosta, Jamamoto, and Wilcox (1978) exposed five subjects with muscle-contraction headache to ten weekly EMG feedback sessions at an outpatient clinic. Significant effects were noted following treatment sessions, and these effects were not related to IQ, education, social class, or motivation. Epstein, Hersen, and Hamphill (1974) exposed one muscle-contraction headache subject to sequential sessions of no-feedback self-monitoring, six sessions of frontal EMG feedback, a baseline period, and four sessions of EMG feedback and home relaxation practice. The active intervention phases were associated with decreases in headache intensity and levels. Additional studies have reported the successful implementation of EMG feedback and/or relaxation training (Feuerstein et al., 1976; Fichtler & Zimmerman, 1973; Jacobson, 1938; Peck & Kraft, 1977; Raskin et al., 1973; Tasto & Hinkle, 1973; Warner & Lance, 1975; Whatmore & Kohli, 1974; Wickramasekera, 1972, 1973).

Active Components of Treatment Packages

Those studies cited above used treatment packages composed of a combination of frontal EMG feedback, relaxation instructions, verbal feedback, home practice, and nonspecific components, such as therapist contact, patient expectancies, and experimental demand factors. Identification of the active components in a treatment package is important, because it has implications for the etiology of muscle-contraction headache and for improvements in the efficiency of the intervention program. Identification of an important component in a treatment package may suggest hypotheses concerning causative factors or may support already existing hypotheses. Similarly, deleting inactive components from the intervention program can facilitate the efficiency and reduce the cost of the intervention program.

Home practice has been indicated as an important determinant of therapeutic success in case studies by Budzynski et al. (1973), Epstein et al. (1974), Fichtler and Zimmerman (1973), Tasto and Hinkle (1973), and Warner and Lance (1975). But its contribution has not been empirically investigated. Nonspecific treatment factors may also be contributing components. Although all the controlled group and controlled single-case studies found that the behavioral intervention packages were more effective than no-treatment or placebo treatment procedures in reducing self-report measures of headache activity, the credibility of the placebo procedures was not assessed. As Borkovec and Nau (1972) suggested, placebo intervention must be viewed by subjects with a level of credibility equal to that of the experimental treatment method, if these factors are to be validly assessed.

Credibility is particularly suspect when false-feedback procedures are used as a control. Because of the sensitivity of the feedback modality to small changes in EMG level, and because of subjects' tendencies to "experiment" with the feedback tone, it might soon become apparent to the subjects that the tone is not related to their behavior. In this case, the credibility of the control procedure and its utility in the evaluation of nonspecific treatment factors is compromised.

That nonspecific factors may account for some of the effects was supported in a study by Epstein and Abel (1977), which included in each training session a phase to assess the degree to which subjects could control their frontal EMG. It was noted that voluntary control of frontal EMG was only transitory, even though indices of headache activity were significantly reduced as a function of the biofeedback program. This finding suggests that reductions in headache activity cannot be attributed to control of frontal muscle tension.

Another possible contributing component is the reactive effects of self-monitoring (Johnson & White, 1971; Kanfer, 1970). That self-monitoring alone is insufficient to account for the effectiveness of the treatment packages, however, is suggested by the studies in which subjects who only self-monitored (control groups) demonstrated significantly less reduction in self-reported headache activity than did the experimental groups who self-monitored and were treated.

The contribution of other intervention variables also remains to be assessed. These include therapist contact, demand factors inherent in the treatment program, and subject expectancies prior to beginning the program. Most of these factors apply to all intervention studies and have been discussed in greater detail by Bordin (1974), Kerlinger (1973), and Korchin (1976).

As noted by Beaty & Haynes (1979), there is moderately strong evidence that intervention packages involving frontal EMG feedback and/or relaxation instructions can effect a beneficial change in self-reported muscle-contraction headache. These packages, however, involve a complex set of interrelated components, which have not been independently assessed. In addition to the primary treatment components, factors which may contribute to the overall effectiveness of the packages include home practice, reactive effects of self-monitoring, experimental demand factors, subject expectancy, and therapist contact.

Measurement Issues

Measurement of headache activity has consisted of daily or hourly self-reports of frequency, intensity, duration, and/or arithmetic transformation of these measures. Because self-report measures may be more sensitive to response bias or demand factors (Haynes, 1978; Kanfer & Phillips, 1970), criterion-related validity assessment utilizing other outcome measures is desirable. Criterion-related validation is difficult, however, because headache is a self-reported disorder without externally observable manifestations. Although the monitoring of medication intake can be used as a concurrent validity measure, it is also a self-report variable. In view of the unavailability of other validation measures, monitoring by participant observers, such as spouses or parents of the subjects, headache verbal reports might provide an additional measure of intervention effects.

As noted by Beaty and Haynes (1979), the use of psychophysical scaling techniques might contribute to the understanding of muscle-contraction headache etiology. Training headache subjects to rate pain levels on a scale prior to beginning self-monitoring might increase the between-subjects comparability of headache data. Standardization of self-monitoring procedures is also desirable, but it is impossible, at this time, to identify which methods would be most valid and sensitive.

Reporting EMG levels from the frontal or other muscle groups during sessions provides data on the covariation between frontal EMG levels and muscle-contraction headache activity. Some studies have not reported this, which makes it more difficult to assess individual differences in frontal EMG level of muscle-contraction headache subjects, covariation between frontal EMG level and headache activity, and the mediational role of muscle relaxation in reducing muscle-contraction headache activity.

Physiological measures, other than frontal EMG, have been infrequently reported. Philips (1977) monitored frontal EMG for some subjects and temporalis EMG for others but did not report data separately. In view of the finding that frontal EMG feedback is not more effective in reducing headache activity than is general relaxation instructions, monitoring additional physiological variables may help determine whether intervention effects are a function of specific reductions in EMG level in the head and neck region or of generalized decreases in autonomically mediated arousal.

Periodic follow-up is also necessary to assess maintenance of treatment effects. Although arbitrary, a postintervention follow-up of at least three to six months is desirable (Beaty & Haynes, 1979). Periodic follow-up may also help ascertain the need for, and timing of, "booster" sessions. Although attrition has been a problem, and some recidivism has been noted, follow-up assessment has suggested that reductions in headache activity can be maintained from four to twelve months.

Most of the studies have analyzed the dependent measures by analysis-of-variance procedures or have not used statistical procedures at all. Because self-report of headache is a repeated measure, time series analyses (Gottman, McFall, & Barnett, 1969) might be applicable. Time series analysis is particularly useful with controlled, single-subject designs; it takes into consideration the serial dependency of the data, while analyzing means, slope, variability, and changes in level between phases. With time series analyses, it is possible to assess whether changes observed during one phase are significantly different from what would be predicted from a projection of the slope in the previous phase.

Subject Variables and Individual Differences

The studies cited above differ in the extent to which they provided a description of subjects and diagnostic procedures. The need for assessment of individual differences in topography, rate, physiological covariates, and etiology of muscle-contraction headache has already been noted (Beaty & Haynes, 1979). The need to evaluate individual differences emphasizes the importance of including in published reports a detailed description of target populations, selection procedures, and diagnostic procedures.

The construct validity of behavioral intervention with muscle-contraction headache depends on establishing the identity of the target populations. Variables used to diagnose headache type should be reported to establish that the type of headache being treated is muscle-contraction. Valid diagnosis is particularly important because of the diversity of headache symptoms, types, and causes. As noted earlier in this chapter, the origin of headaches may be vascular, neurologic, or due to sinus congestion, or headaches may be a secondary covariate of other disorders. The assessment of interrater reliability (agreement between two diagnosticians) would aid in establishing the validity of diagnostic procedures.

Description of subject variables is also necessary to assess the influence of expectancy or demand factors. Borkovec (1973) and Nicolis and Silvestri (1967) have suggested that subjects with moderate or low levels of behavioral disturbance are more strongly influenced by experimental demand variables than are those with severe behavioral disturbance. If this hypothesis is valid, subjects with low or moderate levels of muscle-contraction headache activity would be more responsive to nonspecific factors in the intervention programs, such as contact with a therapist or pretreatment expectancies, than would those with higher levels. Because some studies used subjects with relatively moderate levels of headache activity, without assessing placebo or control credibility, the possibility of significant placebo effects is further indicated.

Cost Efficiency

Issues of cost efficiency are relevant when two or more intervention procedures have been shown to be effective. In the treatment of muscle-contraction headache, several studies have found frontal EMG feedback and various forms of relaxation instructions to be approximately equal in effectiveness. Relaxation instructions may be the treatment modality of choice because of (1) less cost for equipment, (2) greater ease of application in the laboratory, (3) reduced danger to the subject, and (4) greater ease of application to the natural environment.

In addition to cost efficiency, relaxation instruction and EMG feedback may also differ in side effects and applicability across populations and headache types.

For example, one behavioral intervention method may have the side effect (that is, an effect other than on the main target behavior) of increasing overall feelings of relaxation or ability to sleep, it may be more suitable for adolescents or children with headaches, or it may be more effective with frequent, as opposed to infrequent but intense, headaches. These are important considerations in selecting an intervention procedure, and the assessment of these factors will require further study.

Other Behavioral Interventions

Several studies have used behavioral intervention procedures, other than biofeedback and relaxation instructions, in the treatment of muscle-contraction headache. Generally, these interventions have been aimed at modifying the source of environmental stress or the individual's cognitive or physiological response to stress. Daniels (1973) used covert modeling and systematic desensitization to treat one case of muscle-contraction headache. Fowler (1975) used a series of operant procedures (social reinforcement for diminished pain reports, medication contingencies, completion of tasks) in the treatment of a muscle-contraction headache subject. In a case study by Mitchell and White (1976), relaxation training was used in conjunction with self-monitoring and self-management training. Pinpointing antecedent situations and teaching cognitive coping skills were used, along with frontal EMG training, in a single-case study by Reeves (1976). Although all these studies reported successful reduction in headache activity, all were relatively uncontrolled case studies, and the efficacy of these behavioral interventions remains undemonstrated. The author could locate no published controlled group outcome study which used interventions other than frontal EMG feedback and/or relaxation instructions.

Summary

The application of behavioral intervention procedures is based on the assumption that muscle-contraction headache is a psychophysiological disorder, the frequency, intensity, and/or duration of which covaries with environmental events. Intervention procedures most frequently have involved EMG feedback from the frontal region or relaxation instructions, although other behavioral interventions have also been used.

Although valid inferences are difficult to draw from case studies, results from the controlled group studies suggest that treatment packages involving EMG feedback from the frontal region and/or relaxation instructions may be effective in reducing headache activity. Such components as placebo factors, client expectancies, experimental demand factors, home practice, and self-monitoring may account for some of the intervention effects but have not been studied experimentally. The need to assess the credibility of the placebo treatment procedures has been stressed.

Physiological data can be particularly helpful in the assessment of individual differences in etiology and in response to treatment and in the evaluation of the role of muscle relaxation in the observed treatment effects; some studies have, and others have not, reported physiological data from treatment sessions. The need for standardized measures, minimal durations of baseline recording and follow-up, and the potential for use of psychophysical scaling procedures was discussed. Future statistical analyses might include time-series analyses as well as traditional statistics appropriate for factorial designs.

In view of the finding by some researchers that EMG feedback and relaxation instructions may be approximately equal in effectiveness, relaxation instructions may be the treatment modality of choice. Other factors — particularly side effects — must be considered, however, in the evaluation of an intervention package.

REFERENCES

Acosta, F. X., Jamamoto, J., & Wilcox, S. A. Application of electromyographic biofeedback to the relaxation training of schizophrenic, neurotic and tension headache patients. *Journal of Consulting and Clinical Psychology*, 1978, *46*, 275-281.

Ad Hoc Committee on Classification of Headache. *Journal of the American Medical Association*, 1962, *179*, 717-718.

Alexander, A. B. An experimental test of assumptions relating to the use of electromyographic biofeedback as a general relaxation training technique. *Psychophysiology*, 1975, *12*, 656-662.

Bakal, D. A. Headache: A biopsychological perspective. *Psychological Bulletin*, 1975, *82*, 369-382.

Bakal, D. A., & Kaganov, J. A. Muscle contraction and migraine headache: Psychophysiologic comparison. *Headache*, 1977, *17*, 208-215.

Beaty, E. T., & Haynes, S. N. Behavioral intervention with muscle-contraction headache: A review. *Psychosomatic Medicine*, 1979, in press.

Bond, M. R. The relation of pain to the Eysenck Personality Inventory, Cornell Medical Index, and Whiteley Index of Hypochondriasis. *British Journal of Psychiatry*, 1976, *128*, 280-289.

Bordin, E. S. *Research strategies in psychotherapy*. New York: Wiley, 1974.

Borges, J. S., & Zavaleta, C. Study of a new analgesic compound in the treatment of tension headache. *Journal of Internal Medicine Research*, 1976, *4*, 74-78.

Borkovec, T. The role of expectancy and physiological feedback in fear research: A review with special reference to subject characteristics. *Behavior Therapy*, 1973, *4*, 491-505.

Borkovec, T., & Nau, S. Credibility of analogue therapy rationales. *Journal of Behavior Therapy and Experimental Psychiatry*, 1972, *3*, 257-260.

Budzynski, T. H., Stoyva, J. M., Adler, C. S., & Mullaney, D. J. EMG biofeedback and tension headache: A controlled outcome study. *Psychosomatic Medicine*, 1973, *35*, 474-496.

Cassidy, W. L. Clinical observations in manic-depressive disease. A quantitative study of 100 manic-depressive patients and 50 medically sick controls. *Journal of the American Medical Association*, 1957, *164*, 1535-1546.

Chesney, M. A., & Shelton, J. L. A comparison of muscle relaxation and electromyograph biofeedback treatments for muscle contraction headache. *Journal of Behavior Therapy and Experimental Psychiatry*, 1976, *7*, 221-225.

Cox, D. J., Freundlich, A., & Meyer, R. G. Differential effectiveness of electromyograph feedback, verbal relaxation instructions and medication placebo with tension headaches. *Journal of Consulting and Clinical Psychology*, 1975, *43*, 892-898.

Dalessio, D. J. Recent experimental studies on headache. *Neurology*, 1963, *13*, 7-11.

Dalessio, D. J. Some reflections on the etiologic role of depression in head pain. *Headache*, 1968, *8*, 28-31.

Dalessio, D. J. *Wolff's headache and other headpain* (3rd ed.). New York: Oxford University Press, 1972.

Dalessio, D. J. Mechanisms and biochemistry of headache. *Postgraduate Medicine*, 1974, *56*, 55-62.

Dalessio, D. J. Mechanisms of headache. *Medical Clinics of North America*, 1978, *62*, 429-442.

Daniels, L. Treatment of urticaria and severe headache by behavior therapy. *Psychosomatics*, 1973, *14*, 347-351.

Davis, R. A., Wetzel, R. D., & Kashiwagi, M. D. Personality, depression and headache. *Headache*, 1976, *16*, 246-251.

Diamond, S. Depression headaches. *Headache*, 1964, *4*, 255-260.

Diamond, S. Psychosomatic aspects of headaches. *Illinois Medical Journal*, 1969, *135*, 153-156.

Diamond, S., & Baltes, B. J. Chronic tension headache treated with amitriptyline — A double blind study. *Headache*, 1971, *11*, 110-116.

Dixon, H. H., & Dickel, H. A. Tension headache. *Northwest Medicine*, 1967, *66*, 817-820.

Epstein, L. H., & Abel, G. G. An analysis of biofeedback training effects for tension headache patients. *Behavior Therapy*, 1977, *8*, 37-47.

Epstein, L. H., Abel, G. G., Collins, F., Parker, L., & Cinciripini, P. M. The relationship between frontalis muscle activity and self-reports of headache pain. *Behavior Research and Therapy*, 1978, *16*, 153-160.

Epstein, L. H., Hersen, M., & Hamphill, D. P. Contingent music and antitension exercises in the treatment of a chronic tension headache patient. *Journal of Behavior Therapy and Experimental Psychiatry*, 1974, *5*, 59-63.

Feuerstein, M., Adams, H. E., & Beiman, I. Cephalic vasomotor electromyographic feedback in the treatment of combined muscle contraction and migraine headaches in a geriatric case. *Headache*, 1976, *16*, 232-237.

Fichtler, H., & Zimmerman, R. R. Changes in reported pain from tension headaches. *Perceptual and Motor Skills*, 1973, *36*, 712.

Fordyce, W., Fowler, R., & DeLateur, B. An application of behavior modification technique to a problem of chronic pain. *Behavior Research and Therapy*, 1966, *6*, 105-107.

Fordyce, W., Fowler, R., Lehmann, J., & DeLateur, B. Some implications of learning in problems of chronic pain. *Journal of Chronic Diseases*, 1968, *21*, 179-190.

Fordyce, W., Fowler, R., Lehmann, J., DeLateur, B., Sand, P., & Trieschmann, R. Teatment of chronic pain by operant condition. *Archives of Physical Medicine and Rehabilitation*, 1973, *54*, 399-408.

Fordyce, W. *Behavioral methods for chronic pain and illness*. St. Louis: C. V. Mosby, 1976.

Fordyce, W. *Behavioral methods for chronic pain and illness*. St. Louis: C. V. Mosby, 1978.

Fowler, R. Operant therapy for headache. *Headache*, 1975, *15*, 63-68.

Friedman, A. P. Migraine and tension headaches: A clinical study of 2000 cases. *Neurology*, 1964, *14*, 773-789. (a)

Friedman, A. P. Reflection on the problem of headache. *Journal of the American Medical Association*, 1964, *190*, 121-123. (b)

Friedman, A. P. Current concepts in the diagnosis and treatment of chronic recurring headaches. *Medical Clinics of North America*, 1972, *56*, 1257-1271. (a)

Friedman, A. P. Treatment of headache. *International Journal of Neurology*, 1972, *9*, 11-22. (b)

Friedman, A. P., & Merritt, H. H. *Headache: Diagnosis and treatment.* Philadelphia: F. A. Davis, 1959.

Friedman, A. P., Von Storch, J. C., & Merritt, H. H. Migraine and tension headache: A clinical study of two thousand cases. *Neurology*, 1954, *4*, 773-779.

Gottman, J. M., McFall, R. M., & Barnett, J. T. Design and analysis of research using time series. *Psychological Bulletin*, 1969, *72*, 299-306.

Harper, R. G., & Steger, J. C. Psychological correlates of frontalis EMG and pain in tension headache. *Headache*, 1978, *18*, 215-218.

Harrison, R. H. Psychological testing in headache. A review. *Headache*, 1975, *13*, 177-185.

Harrison, T. F. *Principles of internal medicine* (6th ed.). New York: McGraw-Hill, 1970.

Haynes, S. N. *Principles of behavioral assessment.* New York: Gardner Press, 1978.

Haynes, S. N., Griffin, P., Mooney, D., & Parise, M. Electromyographic biofeedback and relaxation instructions in the treatment of muscle contraction headache. *Behavior Therapy*, 1975, *6*, 672-678.

Haynes, S. N., & Wilson, C. C. *Recent advances in behavioral assessment.* San Francisco: Jossey-Bass, 1979.

Howarth, E. Headache, personality and stress. *British Journal of Psychiatry*, 1965, *111*, 1193-1197.

Hutchings, D. V., & Reinking, R. H. Tension headaches: What form of therapy is most effective? *Biofeedback and Self Regulation*, 1976, *1*, 183-190.

Jacobs, A., & Felton, G. S. Visual feedback of myoelectric output to facilitate muscle relaxation in normal persons and patients with neck injuries. *Archives of Physical Medicine and Rehabilitation*, 1969, *50*, 34-39.

Jacobson, E. *Progressive Relaxation*. Chicago: University of Chicago Press, 1938.

Johnson, S. M., & White, G. Self-observation as an agent of behavioral change. *Behavior Therapy*, 1971, *2*, 488-497.

Kanfer, F. H. Self-monitoring: Methodological limitations and clinical applications. *Journal of Consulting and Clinical Psychology*, 1970, *35*, 148-152.

Kanfer, F. H., & Phillips, J. S. *Learning foundations of behavior therapy*. New York: Wiley, 1970.

Kashiwagi, T., McClure, J. N., Jr., & Wetzel, R. D. Headache and psychiatric disorders. *Diseases of the Nervous System*, 1972, *33*, 659-663.

Kerlinger, F. N. *Foundations of behavioral research* (2nd ed.). New York: Holt, Rinehart & Winston, 1973.

Kiritz, S., & Moos, R. H. Physiological effects of social environments. *Psychosomatic Medicine*, 1974, *36*, 96-115.

Kondo, C., & Canter, A. True and false electromyographic feedback: Effect on tension headache. *Journal of Abnormal Psychology*, 1977, *86*, 93-95.

Korchin, S. J. *Modern clinical psychology: Principles of intervention in the clinic and community*. New York: Basic Books, 1976.

Kudrow, L. Tension headache. In *Pathogenesis and treatment of headache*. New York: Spectrum, 1976.

Lachman, S. *Psychosomatic disorders: A behavioristic interpretation*. New York: Wiley, 1972.

Lader, M. H., & Mathews, A. M. Electromyographic studies of tension. *Journal of Psychosomatic Research*, 1971, *15*, 479-486.

Malmo, R., & Shagass, C. Physiologic study of symptom mechanisms in psychiatric patients under stress. *Psychosomatic Medicine*, 1949, *11*, 25-29.

Malmo, R. B., Wallerstein, H., & Shagass, C. Headache proneness and mechanisms of motor conflict in psychiatric patients. *Journal of Personality*, 1953, *22*, 163-187.

Martin, M. J. Tension headache: A psychiatric study. *Headache*, 1966, *6*, 47-54.

Martin, M. J. Muscle-contraction headache. *Psychosomatics*, 1972, *13*, 16-19.

Martin, M. J. Psychogenic factors in headache. *Medical Clinics of North America*, 1978, *62*, 559-570.

Martin, M. J., Rome, H. P., & Swenson, W. M. Muscular contraction: A psychiatric review. In A. P. Friedman (Ed.), *Research and clinical studies on headache*. New York: Karger, Basel, 1967.

Martin, P. R., & Mathews, A. M. Tension headaches: Psychophysiological investigation and treatment. *Journal of Psychosomatic Research*, 1978, in press.

Masland, W. S. Electroencephalography and electromyography in the diagnosis of headache. *Medical Clinics of North America*, 1978, *62*, 571-584.

McGehee, A. *The principles and practice of medicine* (17th ed.). New York: Appleton-Century-Crofts, 1968.

Mitchell, K. R., & White, R. G. Self-management of tension headaches: A case study. *Journal of Behavior Therapy and Experimental Psychiatry*, 1976, *7*, 387-389.

Nicolis, F., & Silvestri, L. Hypnotic activity of placebo in relation to severity of insomnia: A quantitative evaluation. *Clinical Pharmacology and Therapeutics*, 1967, *8*, 841-848.

Ogden, H. D. Headache studies. Statistical data. I. Procedure and sample distribution. *Journal of Allergy*, 1952, *23*, 58-75.

Onel, Y., Friedman, A. P., & Grossman, J. Muscle blood flow studies in muscle contraction headaches. *Neurology*, 1961, *11*, 935-939.

Ostfeld, A. M., Reis, D. J., & Wolff, H. G. Studies on headache: Bulbar conjunctival ischemia and muscle-contraction headache. *Archives of Neurology and Psychiatry*, 1957, *77*, 113-119.

Peck, C. L., & Kraft, G. H. Electromyographic biofeedback for pain related to muscle tension. A study of tension headache, back and jaw pain. *Archives of Surgery*, 1977, *112*, 889-895.

Philips, C. Headache and personality. *Journal of Psychosomatic Research*, 1976, *20*, 535-542.

Philips, C. The modification of tension headache pain using EMG biofeedback. *Behavior Research and Therapy*, 1977, *15*, 119-129.

Philips, C. Tension headache: Theoretical problems. *Behavior Research and Therapy*, 1978, *16*, 249-261.

Poziak-Patweica, E. "Cephalic" spasm of head and neck muscles. *Headache*, 1976, *14*, 261-269.

Raskin, M., Johnson, G., & Rondestvedt, J. Chronic anxiety treated by feedback induced muscle relaxation. *Archives of General Psychiatry*, 1973, *28*, 263-267.

Reeves, J. L. EMG-biofeedback reduction of tension headache: A cognitive skills-training approach. *Biofeedback and Self Regulation*, 1976, *1*, 217-225.

Russell, R., & Sipich, J. Cue-controlled relaxation in the treatment of test anxiety. *Journal of Behavior Therapy and Experimental Psychiatry*, 1973, *4*, 47-49.

Sainsbury, P., & Gibson, J. Symptoms of anxiety and tension and the accompanying physiological changes in the muscular system. *Journal of Neurology, Neurosurgery and Psychiatry*, 1954, *17*, 216-224.

Sargent, J. D., Green, E. E., & Walter, E. D. Preliminary report on the use of autogenic feedback training in the treatment of migraine and tension headaches. *Psychosomatic Medicine*, 1973, *35*, 129-135.

Shedivy, D. I., & Kleinman, K. M. Lack of correlation between frontalis EMG and either neck EMG or verbal ratings of tension. *Psychophysiology*, 1977, *14*, 182-186.

Sternbach, R. A., Wolf, S. R., Murphy, R. W., & Akeson, W. H. Traits of pain patients: The low back "loser." *Psychosomatics*, 1973, *14*, 226-229.

Sternbach, R. A. *Pain patients*. New York: Academic Press, 1974.

Tasto, D. L., & Hinkle, J. E. Muscle relaxation treatment for tension headaches. *Behavior Research and Therapy*, 1973, *11*, 347-349.

Tunis, M., & Wolff, H. Studies on headache. *Archives of Neurology and Psychiatry*, 1954, *71*, 425-434.

Vaughn, R., Pall, M. L., & Haynes, S. N. Frontalis EMG response to stress in subjects with frequent muscle-contraction headaches. *Headache*, 1977, *16*, 313-317.

Warner, G., & Lance, J. Relaxation therapy in migraine and chronic tension headache. *Medical Journal of Australia*, 1975, *1*, 298-301.

Weber, M. B. The treatment of muscle-contraction headaches with diazepam. *Current Therapy Research*, 1973, *15*, 210-216.

Whatmore, G., & Kohli, D. *The pathophysiology and treatment of functional disorders*. New York: Grune & Stratton, 1974.

Wickramasekera, I. Electromyographic feedback training and tension headache: Preliminary observations. *American Journal of Clinical Hypnosis*, 1972, *15*, 83-85.

Wickramasekera, I. The application of verbal instructions and EMG feedback training to the management of tension headache — Preliminary observation. *Headache*, 1973, *13*, 74-76.

Wolff, J. G. *Headache and other head pain*. New York: Oxford University Press, 1963.

Ziegler, D. K. Tension headache. *Medical Clinics of North America*, 1978, *62*, 495-505.

Ziegler, D. K., Hassanein, R. S., & Couch, J. R. Characteristics of life headache histories in a nonclinic population. *Neurology*, 1977, *27*, 265-270.

Ziegler, D. K., Hassanein, R., & Hassanein, K. Headache syndromes suggested by factor analysis of symptom variables in a headache prone population. *Journal of Chronic Diseases*, 1972, *25*, 335-365.

12

THE PARAMETERS, ETIOLOGY, AND TREATMENT OF MIGRAINE HEADACHES

Ellie T. Sturgis
Henry E. Adams
Phillip J. Brantley

INTRODUCTION

Chronic head pain is considered, by many individuals, to be the most common medical complaint experienced by the modern American. Until recently, headache phenomena were largely ignored, by both the medical and the psychological professions. Physicians were not interested in headaches, because they saw them as resulting from emotional and psychological difficulties, whereas psychologists viewed them as primarily physiological-biochemical in nature and, thus, as a problem for the medical profession. In recent years, however, interest in headache as a biopsychological phenomenon and disorder has increased in both disciplines (Adams, Feuerstein, & Fowler, 1980; Bakal, 1975). The purposes of this chapter will be to review the relevant characteristics of headaches labeled as migraine, to address issues in the assessment of this disorder, to review relevant biological and psychological theories of migraine, and to evaluate the efficacy of current treatment approaches.

DEFINING CHARACTERISTICS AND SYMPTOMS

The classification system used to describe headaches was developed by the Ad Hoc Committee on the Classification of Headache (AHCCH) (1962). The committee described four categories of headache which had psychological components: the *vascular headache*, the *muscle-contraction headache*, the *combined migraine-muscle contraction headache*, and the *psychogenic, conversion*, or *hypochondriacal headache*. This chapter will be limited to coverage of migraine and combined migraine-muscle-contraction headaches. The tension or muscle-contraction headache is discussed in Chapter 11.

When diagnosing headaches, it is important to remember that individuals frequently experience more than one type of chronic, recurring head pain. Consequently, the possibility of several types of cephalalgia in the same individual should be evaluated. Vascular headaches of the *migraine* type are frequently unilateral, rapid in onset, and associated with anorexia, nausea, vomiting, and decreased tolerance for light and sound (phonophobia and photophobia), and they may be preceded by sharply defined, transient sensorimotor prodromes. Vascular headaches may be further subdivided into:

classic migraines — 10% of migraine population, presence of prodromal symptoms, usually unilateral, mean duration 6-8 hr

common migraines — 85% of migraine population, absence of prodromal symptoms, more frequently bilateral, typically longer in duration

cluster migraines or *histamine headaches* — 4% of population, absence of prodromes, unilateral, occurring for a period of 2-3 months and followed by an extended headache-free period

hemiplegic migraines — moderate, unilateral pain accompanied by extra-ocular muscular palsy involving the third cranial nerve

lower half headaches — localized in lower half of face, atypical facial neuralgia, spenapalatine ganglion neuralgia, and vidian neuralgia.

The lower half and hemiplegic migraines are rare phenomena, occurring in less than 1% of the migraine population (AHCCH, 1962). The majority of studies in the headache literature do not differentiate between migraine variants; thus, a distinction between migraine types will not be made in this paper. The most salient features of migraine headache are noted in Whitty and Hockaday's (1968) definition. They identified migraines as recurring, throbbing headaches associated with at least two of the following features: unilateral headache, nausea and/or vomiting, visual or sensory aura, cyclical vomiting in childhood, and a family history of migraine.

It is hypothesized that the following physiological events occur during a migraine headache. During the preheadache period, there is an increased lability in the *temporal artery*, followed by vasoconstriction, which may or may not be subjectively experienced or labeled as prodromal in nature (O'Brien, 1971, 1973). A rebound dilation phase involving the internal and external cranial arteries follows the constriction phase and is associated with the onset of headache (Dalessio, 1972). This phase is characterized by a subjective experience of throbbing and severe pain. In the latter part of the headache period, edema of the vasculature occurs, causing abnormally large increases in the amount of fluid in the intercellular tissue space. This *edema* is accompanied by increased rigidity of the blood vessels. A steady, aching pain, tenderness of the scalp, nausea, vomiting, dryness of the mouth, sweating, and chills may distinguish the second phase (Dalessio, 1972). The postheadache phase is marked by pain from sustained muscle contraction of the scalp and neck, which is accompanied by deep, aching pain (Friedman, 1973).

Combined migraine-muscle-contraction headaches are defined as the occurrence of migraine and muscle-contraction headache in the same subject. Clinical observation appears to indicate these headaches may or may not be independent, depending on the subject. This issue, however, is clouded by the fact that migraines are usually associated with increased muscle contraction activity (Dalessio, 1972), although the individual can experience a tension headache without accompanying migraine characteristics. The muscle-contraction headache is characterized by feelings of tightness, constriction, and/or pressure. Tension headaches differ widely in intensity, duration, and frequency. The headache appears to result from sustained electromyographic (EMG) activity in the cephalic and neck musculature, but this basic assumption has recently been questioned (Epstein, 1976). Additional information concerning the relationship between EMG activity and the psychological perception of pain is needed. The pain of a muscle-contraction headache is usually bilateral, occipital, frontal, or facial in distribution. A common description of the pain sensation is that it feels as if the individual were wearing a very tight headband or hat. The headaches are usually nonpulsatile and range from several hours to several days in duration.

Incidence

It has been estimated that at least 70% of the population of the United States have experienced some type of headache problem in their lives (Ogden, 1952; Zeigler, Hassanein, & Hassanein, 1972). The National Migraine Foundation has estimated that almost twelve million Americans experience variants of migraine (Adams et al., 1980). Estimates of incidence vary from study to study. Bakal (1975) reported the incidence to vary from 3% to 12% of the population, while three epidemiologic studies in the United Kingdom reported a range from 23% to 29% in females and 15% to 20% in males. Reasons for such differences are unclear.

Sex differences in the incidence of migraine have been a topic of investigation for several years. Selby and Lance (1960) reported 60% more female migraine sufferers than male. Friedman, von Storch, and Merritt (1954) and Walker (1959) found similar results. A recent study by Zeigler et al., (1972), however, found very little difference in the incidence of migraines across sexes when a questionnaire was given to nonclinic subjects. Waters and O'Connor (1975) replicated Zeigler et al.'s findings and suggested that further research on this issue is needed. It may be that more females than males come to a clinic requesting assistance for headache. It is also interesting to note that the higher incidence of migraines in females is not present in children before puberty (Zeigler, 1976).

The age at which headaches begin to occur is helpful in the determination of headache type. Headaches beginning in childhood and adolescence are frequently migraine in nature. The mean age of onset is twenty years, although migraines are relatively common at ten years of age and have been reported as early as eighteen months (Selby & Lance, 1960). After the age of thirty, the probability of developing vascular headaches is greatly decreased (Adams et al., 1980).

The frequency of headache in the majority of migraine cases varies from one to four episodes per month (Selby & Lance, 1960). It has been found that when the individual experiences more than ten headaches per month, tension headaches are also likely to be present; however, the client may have difficulty differentiating the two pain types (Selby & Lance, 1960). The duration of pain ranges from four to twenty-four hours. Severity is commonly associated with the presence of prodromal symptoms, the unilateral/bilateral distribution of pain, and the presence of nausea (Adams et al., 1980).

Disease Progression and Severity

Little information has been reported on the course of the migraine phenomenon. Once the individual begins to experience migraines, the frequency increases for a period, then often becomes relatively stable. Certain environmental events, such as the intake of dietary products which include tyramine, monosodium glutamate, sodium nitrite, and alcohol, the presence of certain emotional states, exposure to glare and/or flickering lights, and changes in hormonal levels – any of these may precipitate attacks, but this varies between individuals. The migraine episode itself causes no structural damage, but in rare cases, the side effects of medications taken for migraines may cause cardiovascular damage (Medina & Diamond, 1976). In some individuals, headaches may decrease or disappear following puberty or menopause. At present, we do not understand the course of this disorder, especially the differential pattern found among migraine sufferers (Dalessio, 1972).

Social and Personal Significance

In many individuals, the migraine headache interferes with their lives to a considerable degree. Many migraineurs are forced to retreat to a darkened, quiet bedroom for a day or so, each time an attack is experienced. Such a disability may easily contribute to difficulties within the family or on the job, problems concerning financial matters, and possible difficulties of depression or other related emotional states. Thus, the seriousness of the disorder is seen primarily as the consequence of the inability of the individual to deal effectively with the demands of life during the frequent headache episodes. Further, addiction may occur if frequent injections of narcotics are required.

ASSESSMENT

With any headache symptom, a thorough assessment of the problem is extremely important. A diagnosis of migraine headache involves the elimination of alternative physical and psychological explanations for head pain. This process is best accomplished by requiring an adequate physical examination, conducting a complete interview of the nature and history of the head pain as well as of other psychological problems, performing a psychophysiological assessment, and having the individual self-monitor pain behavior.

Medical Assessment

The medical diagnosis of migraine headache is made on the basis of behavioral symptoms and negative findings on a series of medical tests. Ryan and Ryan (1978) provided a detailed guide for the diagnosis of head pain. These physicians consider the interview to be the most valuable diagnostic tool available to the physician who is attempting to diagnose and classify headaches. Of particular relevance are the site, source, character, frequency, and duration of the head pain and the symptoms occurring with the headache attack. The most pathognomonic associated symptoms are drowsiness, personality changes, aphasia, convulsions, vertigo, memory distortions, nystagmus, ataxia, and papilledema. None of these symptoms is characteristic of the migraine; thus, the presence of any of them indicates that further medical investigation is necessary.

Following the interview designed to assess the nature of the presenting problem, a general physical examination, including an eye, ear, nose, and throat examination, laboratory tests, and a neurological evaluation, is indicated. If any abnormalities are noted, subsequent evaluation should be made by the appropriate specialist.

The most likely difficulties in making the differential diagnosis are confusion of the migraine with other types of head pain. Differentiation from the histamine or cluster headache is made on the basis of the history and the characteristics of the head pain, which is intense, boring, and burning in quality. The migraine can be distinguished from the allergic or sinus headache by the presence of allergic rhinitis in the latter. Head pain resulting from cerebral tumors is diagnosed by results of the electroencephalogram (EEG), computerized axial tomography (CT scan), the pneumoencephalogram, and the gammaencephalogram. Glaucoma is differentiated from the migraine on the basis of increased intraocular pressure, which most likely occurs after the age of forty. The berry aneurysm may be detected by using the arteriogram. An intracranial angioma is evaluated on the basis of abnormal physical signs observed during the nervous system evaluation. Finally, the posttraumatic headache is differentiated from the migraine on the basis of a history of head trauma. Further discussion of these procedures and head conditions is found in Ryan and Ryan's text (1978).

Contact with a patient's physician regarding the use of medication during psychological treatment is also important. Psychological interventions rarely provide immediate relief from migraine; therefore, medications should not be abruptly discontinued. Prescribed medications typically produce little interference with psychological treatment. Possible exceptions include oversedation from high doses of tranquilizers and pain medications and continuous use of vasoconstrictive drugs, which tend to attenuate the acquisition of self-regulation of cephalic vasoconstriction and vasodilation.

Once psychological intervention of the headache is initiated, a careful record of symptoms and results should be maintained. Should unusual and unexpected results be obtained that do not fit into the formulation of the case, consultation with the referring physician is recommended. Intermittent correspondence between physician and therapist during treatment may also prove beneficial in terms of promoting consistency in the modification of concurrent psychological problems involving a patient's inappropriate emotional response to chronic pain, misuse of medication, and needless restrictions in activities (Fordyce, Fowler, Lehmann, Dellateur, Sand, & Trieschmann, 1973).

The Initial Interview

The clinical interview remains a major component of any type of psychological assessment. Interview information obtained from migraine patients aids the therapist in making a correct diagnosis, targeting psychological adjuncts of migraine, establishing rapport, and tailoring a systematic treatment plan. Interviews are typically conducted during the initial visit. A period of 1-1½ hours is usually required, although the interview time can be shortened through the use of questionnaires. Critical areas to be assessed include a detailed history of head pain, a family history of headache or other chronic pain, a detailed medical history of head pain, a detailed medical history that includes types of treatment received along with various medications tried, a comprehensive assessment of the nature of the pain, the environmenatal factors involved, the degree of interference with daily activities, the related psychological disturbances, and an evaluation of the reasons for seeking treatment. Information obtained from the interview enables the therapist to confirm more accurately a diagnosis of migraine. Often the term *migraine* is used loosely by the public and, occasionally, by physicians to imply the severity of pain. It is important to determine whether the pain mechanism is of a vascular or a musculoskeletal origin. Such a discrimination can often be made by exploring areas of symptomatology characteristic of headache.

Family History

Assumptions that migraine may be determined, in part, by genetic factors, although tentative at best, demand attention because of the high concordance among relatives in the occurrence of migraines (Lance & Anthony, 1966; Selby

& Lance, 1960). Patient reports of family history of migraine should be verified, if possible. Questioning similar to that used to assess the patient's head pain can be used in an abbreviated form. Of interest is the amount of patient contact with other migraineurs, his/her reaction and the reaction of the family members to the patient's pain behavior, and the patient's thoughts and beliefs about the relationship between heredity and the migraine. Theory and research findings in social learning have suggested that pain behavior can be learned through the modeling process (Craig & Lowery, 1969; Craig & Weiss, 1971). A reliable difference in the incidence of a positive family history, however, does exist between migraine and muscle-contraction headache cases (Adams et al., 1980).

Nature of Head Pain

Interview data should include a complete description of head pain. Location of specific pain sites in the head should be noted. Diagrams of pain sites are often helpful for recording purposes. Migraineurs typically report initial pain in the temporal areas. Pain may be unilateral or bilateral, or it may vary with each incident. The quality of migraine pain is described as initially pulsating and then becoming more of a dull ache during the latter stages of the headache. Pain later extends throughout the areas of the head and neck. Such a pattern helps differentiate migraine from muscle-contraction headaches, which are usually characterized by a nonpulsating pain, typically bilateral, and occipital, frontal, facial, or "headband"-like in distribution (Friedman, 1973).

Frequency and duration of head pain also provide diagnostic clues. Migraine attacks often range from one to four per month, although many people report frequencies of ten or more (Selby & Lance, 1960). Duration typically ranges between four and twenty-four hours. Severity of pain should also be assessed, possibly by establishing a graded numerical scale which corresponds to different levels of subjective pain, degree of disability, or amount of medication required for pain relief. For example, one end of the scale might represent a barely noticeable pain, with the other end representing the worst pain ever experienced or pain necessitating a visit to the hospital. This procedure allows for individual, standardized ratings from which average severity and representative patterns of severity across time may be obtained.

The question of whether the patient can detect the onset of head pain in advance is very important. Such symptoms as sharply defined, transient visual or auditory changes, increased activity level, polyuria, hypersensitivity to light, sound, or odors, stiffness in the neck, or menstrual changes are characteristic of the classic migraine. These phenomena may occur minutes or even hours before the onset of the actual pain. The symptoms are reported by approximately 10% of migraineurs and are very rarely reported with muscle-contraction headaches.

Questions should also assess associated symptoms accompanying head pain. Nausea and vomiting is experienced by approximately 50% of migraineurs during their headaches but by only 10% of those having muscle-contraction headaches (Adams et al., 1980). Other common symptoms include cramps, dizziness, nasal congestion or dryness, photophobia, phonophobia, swelling of the ears and the eyes, sweating, flushing, blanching, throat irritations, chills, loss of appetite, general body swelling, and visual disturbances.

Care should be taken to assess whether the patient can differentiate types of headaches. It is not uncommon for patients to experience both migraine and muscle-contraction headaches. Complete details should be obtained concerning frequency, duration, intensity, quality of pain, and other parameters of *all* types of head pain experienced.

Precipitating Factors

Although specific cause-and-effect relationships have not been established between environmental factors and migraines, this information can be valuable for diagnostic and treatment purposes. Patients should be asked if they can name any specific emotions, substances, or activities that trigger their migraines. The muscle-contraction headache is commonly presumed to be precipitated by tension or stress, while the vascular headache is associated with a variety of factors. Various emotions and stress have been implicated as etiological factors of migraines. Of interest, however, is the fact that migraineurs often report headaches to occur after stressful periods are over and during relaxed periods, such as weekends and vacations. Migraineurs also report that certain foods, such as chocolate, cheese, and citrus fruits, are associated with the onset of migraines. Alcohol, particularly red wine, has also been implicated. Other associated factors include menstruation, fatigue, and mood changes (Adams et al., 1980).

Response to Pain

Behaviors the patient exhibits to relieve the head pain provide valuable information concerning the nature and mechanism of the pain. It is often valuable to have the patient describe in detail what he or she does when a headache occurs. Migraineurs typically follow ritualistic patterns regarding medication use, cognitive coping precedures, and pain control activities. Significant areas for assessment include the types, order, amount, and schedule of medication intake. Aspirin and minor pain medication usually provide little relief from the migraine. The patient's emotional response to migraine is of primary importance, as are the reactions of significant others to the patient's pain behavior. Extreme emotional upset is important, since it tends to increase the subject's perceptions of pain and possibly prolong the headache duration (Fordyce, 1976).

Family reactions to the migraineur's pain must be carefully assessed in terms of the degree of sympathy, consideration, and support for coping with the pain. Does the client attempt to continue activities or does he or she immediately go to bed or contact a physician? Noticing the medications and activities which provide maximal relief can help differentiate vascular head pain from other types of headache. Relevant questions include: Does holding the head in a specific position help? What are the effects of applying hot or cold compresses? Does manual pressure on the temporal area help? What are the effects of eating, drinking, or having a bowel movement? From this information, the therapist may provide assistance in helping the patient plan effective coping strategies for chronic head pain or determine if pain behavior is being maintained by social reinforcement.

Degree of Interference

Motivation for psychological treatment of migraines is greatly affected by the degree of interference with the patient's life. Individuals who have fewer than one migraine headache per month, or who have headaches of a mild to moderate severity, may present significant treatment compliance problems. Psychological treatments require work on the part of a patient, and unless the migraines interfere substantially, the treatment may prove to be more troublesome than the migraines. Patients with infrequent migraines may respond well to pharmacologic intervention without the high risk of severe side effects. Infrequent and irregular migraines also present problems in terms of evaluating success of treatment, because their low rate necessitates prolonged baseline and follow-up periods.

Psychophysiological Assessment

An assessment technique that is being used increasingly more often is psychophysiological evaluation. Such a procedure typically involves multichannel recordings of multiple physiological systems, along with recording of reactivity to stress. A major criticism of many biofeedback studies is their failure to assess adequately the baseline levels of autonomic activity. Baseline levels of physiological activity are important for diagnostic purposes and for evaluation of treatment efficacy. These records are critical for evaluating biofeedback intervention, in spite of the fact that baseline levels are affected by characteristics of the situation, the state of the individual, and various aspects of the psychophysiological assessment. A psychophysiological assessment is often conducted during the initial visit, following the interview, if the patient is adequately relaxed. The recordings thus provide representative measures of the relaxed state. It should be emphasized that the following suggestions have not been adequately verified by research evidence.

The physiological response systems typically monitored with potential migraine patients include electromyography (EMG), *skin temperature* (TEMP), and the *cephalic vasomotor response*, or *blood volume pulse* (BVP). The EMG levels are usually monitored from frontalis and/or trapezius muscle groups, while temperature measures are recorded at the fingers and/or the forehead. The BVP recordings are taken from temporal sites of the head; they can be taken from both temples for comparative purposes, although, frequently, a single recording is made on the temple where pain is most often noted.

The EMG recordings are useful in determining the degree to which muscle activity may affect total head pain. Many patients report two distinct types of pain: muscle contraction and migraine. Other patients report that migraine attacks are preceded by muscle-contraction headaches. High-level EMG readings from the cephalic or neck musculature may indicate a need to decrease muscle activity as an adjunct or prerequisite to migraine treatment.

Currently, assessment of baseline levels of hand temperature or BVP provides little specific information concerning parameters of migraine activity. Migraineurs do, however, tend to have higher amplitude and more variable BVP activity than nonmigraineurs. Further research is required before baseline levels of BVP and TEMP of migraineurs can be used as diagnostic devices.

Self-Monitoring

Self-monitoring represents a popular assessment tool for recording and analyzing behavior. Such a procedure requires an individual to record the occurrence of a targeted behavior as well as its antecedents and consequences. Self-monitoring prior to treatment allows for the establishment of baseline frequencies of the specified behavior and the explanation of functional relationships among the targeted behavior patterns and the environmental and internal antecedents and consequences of the behavior. Continued self-recording during treatment is also helpful in comparing baseline data to changes occurring during treatments.

Self-recording of headache activity is extremely important in the assessment and treatment of migraine. Apart from the benefits of providing data on migraine activity and related events, the procedure can be indicative of patient motivation and/or cooperation and thus provide a prediction of success in treatment. It seems reasonable to assume that patients who fail to comply with self-monitoring requirements are likely to neglect other essential treatment requirements.

Adequate self-monitoring for migraineurs includes a detailed description of location, intensity, and quality of head pain (pulsatile or nonpulsatile), frequency per unit of time, and duration. Since these data are subjective reports and may be somewhat ambiguous, it is also helpful to utilize behavioral indices. Although they represent indirect measures, such behaviors as amount of time in bed, amount of time off from work, and the number of hospital visits aid in obtaining consistent labeling of pain intensity. A particularly good indicator of migraine activity is the medication taken, both type and quantity. A method for equating various medications for comparison purposes was devised by Fordyce et al. (1973).

Self-monitoring can be accomplished in several ways, depending upon the demands of the situation and the creativity of the therapist. One may choose to have the client keep a behavioral diary, with narrative accounts of headache activity. An advantage of this approach is that it involves little preparation time or expense for the therapist. It does require substantial effort on the part of the client, however, and often produces data that are nonspecific and inconsistent in terms of behavioral definitions and reported pain behavior.

A more systematic approach involves the use of structured record forms. Not only do they provide consistent recordings, they also require less effort for the patient, thus increasing the probability of compliance. Well-designed record forms also communicate the therapist's view of the importance of accurate and consistent self-monitoring, which has also been shown to increase the probability of compliance (Ciminero, Nelson, & Lipinski, 1977). A possible format might involve daily checks for the following information:

1. *Type of headache.* The patient should distinguish vascular and muscular head pain and should be well informed of diagnostic criteria for making this distinction.

2. *Intensity of headache.* A numerical scale with well-defined extremes may be used. For example, a rating of one may represent barely noticeable pain, while a rating of four may represent pain subjectively perceived as most severe.

3. *Associated symptoms.* A list of frequently reported symptoms, such as nausea, vomiting, and photophobia, might be included, or the patient could simply list symptoms.

4. *Degree of disability.* A numerical rating scale, with correspondence to specific pain-related behaviors, may be used. Behaviors might range from no interference with daily activities to the requirement of medical assistance.

5. *Duration of headache.* Duration is conveniently expressed in terms of hours. If both migraine and muscle-contraction headaches are present, separate listings of durations should be included. Duration can be listed in terms of total hours or, better, the actual time of day the headache is noted and when it terminates.

6. *Medication use.* Types and quantity of medications taken are listed. Having the patient record the time of intake also provides information on such factors as the patient's tendency to rely on medication, misuses of medication, drug reactions, and similar information.

7. *Presence of prodromes.* The patient may be asked to list or check off the presence of warning signals, such as visual changes, numbness, and similar sensations.

Other targets for self-monitoring involve ratings or description of general mood states, distressing events, cognitive responses to pain, or physical location and cognitions at the onset of pain. No matter what events one chooses to monitor, it is of extreme importance that the client fully understand the discriminations required. To insure the procedure is understood, the therapist may wish to role play the self-monitoring procedure and have the patient practice. Periodic checks and retraining are also advised. Without such preventative techniques, much time and expense may be wasted, along with valuable information.

When done properly, self-monitoring provides the therapist with sensitive data sources, which often detect subtle changes in headache activity, which would go undetected with less systematic and precise methods. Besides its usefulness as an assessment procedure, self-monitoring has been shown to possess reactive effects on targeted behaviors, although its effectiveness for reduction of migraine is doubtful (Mitchell & White, 1977). In addition, self-monitoring tends to attenuate behaviors perceived as negative or unwanted (Broden, Hall, & Mitts, 1971). This fact has implications for detection of inappropriate pain response, medication use, and similar problems.

CURRENT THEORETICAL CONCEPTUALIZATIONS OF ETIOLOGY

The variables considered of primary importance in the etiology of the migraine are biological and psychological in nature. The biological theories include vascular and chemical theories, while the psychological theories include conceptualizations of emotional specificity, personality types and predispositions, and the impact of environmental stimuli. While no single theory has been able to explain why certain individuals develop migraines and others do not, or even why headaches develop in certain situations and not in others, the more recent integration of biological and psychological theories may prove to be more accurate and of more heuristic value than were earlier, more circumscribed theories.

Biological Theories

Numerous studies have suggested that the intra- and extracranial carotid arteries play a critical role in the development of the migraine headache (Kaneko, Shiraishi, Inaoka, Furukawa, & Sekiyama, 1978; Lance, 1973; O'Brien, 1971, 1973; Skinhøj, 1973). Classically, the prodromal phase has been viewed as the result of vasoconstriction of the internal and external carotid arteries caused by sympathetic nervous system action. Unilateral prodromes were hypothesized to result from localized cranial vasoconstriction. Since the common migraine has no associated prodrome it was hypothesized that vasoconstriction was not associated with these headaches. O'Brien (1971), however, observed a bilateral decrease of about 20% in the blood flow to both cerebral hemispheres during the prodromal phase. In a later study of common headache sufferers, O'Brien (1973) observed vasoconstriction in individuals having no history of prodromal symptoms. Both findings cause one to question the validity of the hypotheses which suggest that localized and specific blood flow decrements alone account for the unilateral and prodromal symptoms of the classic migraine. It has been hypothesized that the constriction effects an *ischemia* (oxygen deficiency) in the tissues of the cranial area. The ischemia then induces a rebound dilation of the cranial arteries in an attempt to bring oxygen-rich blood to the ischemic cranial tissues (O'Brien, 1973). It is during this vasodilatory phase that the severe head pain occurs (Dalessio, 1972).

The involvement of the cranial arteries in the migraine was first investigated by Graham and Wolff (1938). *Ergotamine tartrate*, a vasoconstrictive substance, was administered to subjects during the headache phase. Extracranial vasomotor activity was recorded from the temporal and occipital arteries. Ergotamine injections effected a 16-84% decrease in the magnitude of the pulse amplitude. Decreases in pulse amplitudes corresponded with decreases in headache activity. Finally, the vasodilation was observed to be specific to the hemisphere experiencing head pain.

Tunis and Wolff (1952) compared the pulse wave amplitudes of migraineurs, in headache and headache-free states, with those of normal subjects. Each measured component in the migraine group was of greater magnitude and was more variable than in the control group. Recordings during the headache state were of larger amplitude and variability than were similar measures during the nonheadache state. Migraineurs showed even greater variability during the eighteen-to-seventy-two-hour period prior to the onset of head pain.

All the cranial arteries have been found to be pain sensitive. Distention of the arterial walls via mechanical stimulation results in well-localized, aching pain, which lasts as long as the walls are distended. By rhythmically distending and collapsing the arterial walls, a pain of a throbbing quality, similar to migraine pain, has been produced. Injections of procaine hydrochloride near the temporal artery produced immediate anesthesia of the surrounding area, implicating the involvement of the sensory nerve supply traveling along the arteries (Ray & Wolff, 1945). To date, although the intracranial and extracranial arteries are clearly involved in the migraine headache, the manner in which they are involved in the etiology of the headache remains unclear.

Because of the involvement of the vasculature in the pathogenesis of migraine, it is not surprising that a current focus of research involves the control of the arteries by vasoneuroactive chemicals (Dalessio, 1972, 1976; Diamond, Dalessio, Graham, & Medina, 1975). Serotonin, histamine, neurokinin, and several other humoral substances have been hypothesized to play a key role in the etiology of headache. There is ample evidence that vasodilation alone does not invariably lead to headache. Prolonged exercise, such as jogging, tennis, or football, and such experiences as soaking in a hot tub or sauna all lead to cranial vasodilation. Headache under such conditions, however, is rare. The manifestation of vascular head pain is related to vasodilation, which is also associated with a local sterile inflammatory reaction.

Changes in *blood plasma serotonin* levels have been correlated with vasomotor changes and accompanying headache. Serotonin is an endogenous vasoconstrictive chemical. Sicuteri (1972) hypothesized that migraineurs have a biochemical deficit which leads to a release of excess serotonin into the blood plasma following certain stimuli. This excess serotonin then induces cerebral vasoconstriction. A subsequent depletion of the increased platelet serotonin levels decreases arterial tonus, a process resulting in passive distention of the arterial walls (Fanchamps, 1974). Controversy exists concerning the specific role of serotonin upon intra- and extracranial circulation. Spira, Mylecharane, and Lance (1976) found intracarotid infusions of serotonin produced dose-dependent decreases in internal and external carotid flow, increased vascular resistance, and no changes in systemic blood pressure of CO_2 expiration levels. Animal studies showed decreased blood flow in the internal and external carotid arteries following intracranial injections of serotonin (Welch, Hashi, & Meyer, 1973; Welch, Spira, Knowles, & Lance, 1974).

In two studies of migraine clients, serotonin injections exerted little effect upon the internal carotid artery but produced vasoconstriction of the external carotid (Lance, Anthony, & Gonsky, 1967). Dexter and Riley (1975) showed that plasma serotonin levels decrease at the onset of migraine pain. While elevated levels of serotonin result in vasoconstriction, consistent reductions of platelet serotonin (60-80%) have been reported during the headache phase (Curran, Hinterberger, & Lance, 1976). Dalessio (1976) found increased plasma levels of serotonin in the vasoconstrictive state and increased concentrations of 5-hydroxyindoleacetic acid, a major metabolite of serotonin, during the vaso-dilation and headache states.

Another biochemical implicated in the pathogenesis of the migraine is *histamine*. Histamine is a vasodilatory substance which has been implicated, most definitively, in the cluster or histamine headache (Dalessio, 1976; Sjaastad, 1975). Anthony and Lance (1975), as well as Sjaastad, found an increased concentration of urinary histamine during a migraine attack, compared with other times. It is possible that the dilatory effect of histamine is enough to potentiate the pathological dilation of already labile arteries.

The final chemical implicated in the migraine headache is *neurokinin*, a polypeptide found to accumulate around the arterial surfaces in patients with migraines. Dalessio (1972) reported an experiment in which subjects were injected with "blister fluid" when the cranial artery was dilated. In test trials administered in a double-blind fashion, all subjects developed unilateral, pulsating headache on the side injected with blister fluid when the cranial artery was dilated. In test trials administered in a double-blind fashion, all subjects developed unilateral, pulsating headaches on the side injected with the blister fluid rather than on the side injected with saline control. In two further studies, fluid was aspriated from the headache area and the corresponding area of the opposite hemisphere. The experimental and control aspirates were injected into corresponding and reversed forearms in a single-blind fashion. The side injected with the fluid from the headache site consistently caused a 10-15% greater decrease in pain threshold than did the control injection site.

Biochemical assays have determined that the pain-producing fluids are neurokinin and *protease*, a neurokinin-producing enzyme. Neurokinin is a very powerful vasodilator. Both neurokinin and protease have been implicated in vasomotor control. The pain of vascular headaches of the migraine type is presently viewed as the result of the combined effects of arterial dilation and the action of pain-threshold-lowering substances accumulating in the blood vessels and perivascular tissue (Dalessio, 1972).

Other chemical theories, which are less well developed, but which seem implicated in the migraine syndrome, are the hormonal and amine theories. The *hormonal theory* is poorly developed at present, possibly due to the difficulty involved in the quantification and assay of hormones and the difficulty in manipulating one hormone at a time. The hormone theory has two principal components. One component assumes that migraines result from varying seizure thresholds of the *hypothalamus*. This concept is similar to one theory concerning the mechanism of epilepsy, in which hormonal changes produce varying seizure thresholds of the cortex (Pearce, 1975). This hormonal conception of migraines would partially explain the variability of the attack.

A second component of the hormonal theory concerns the hormones *estrogen* and *progesterone*. Migraines often change in frequency and duration during pregnancy, as well as at the beginning and termination of the menstrual cycle. The intake of oral contraceptives also affects the nature of the migraine headache. It is unclear whether the substances themselves or disturbances related to their presence contribute to the development of the migraine. This area, however, remains a target for further investigation (Diamond et al., 1975; Kudrow, 1976; Spira et al., 1976).

The *amine theory* is related to the serotonin theory, for the amines most directly implicated include serotonin (5-hydroxytryptamine), its metabolite, 5-hydroxyindoleacetic acid (5HIAA), dopamine, norepinephrine, and monoamine oxidase. All these substances have been found to be important in controlling blood vessel reactivity and may therefore assume a pathogenic role in the production of migraine attacks (Appenzeller, 1976).

Since biochemical substances are intricately involved in the cranial vasomotor response, it is likely that both the vascular and biochemical theories are involved in the explanation of the migraine response. If this is the case, it becomes more important to identify the internal and external precipitants which trigger the abnormal humoral and vasomotor responses.

Psychological Theories

The personality theories of migraine headache have stressed two approaches, both of which have yielded disappointing results. The first approach is the *emotional specificity theory*, which assumes that specific emotional patterns elicit very specific types of physiological response patterns. Continued emotional overstimulation resulting from chronic arousal contributes to the development of an overreactive and, eventually, dysfunctional organ system (Alexander, 1950). Such an approach would indicate that migraineurs have difficulties in some specific emotional response, which then causes, or at least contributes to, the development of the dysfunction in the cerebral vascular and muscular system.

Studies to date have not been able to isolate the specific, dysfunctional, migraine-causing emotion (Henryk-Gutt & Rees, 1973). Harrison (1975), however, found that the majority of the studies implicated unexpressed anger as the critical dysfunctional emotion. If the theory is accurate, then unexpressed anger should specifically affect the cephalic vasomotor system. The majority of the research concerning anger and other emotions, however, indicate the activation of numerous physiological responses, with no specific patterns for any emotion (Greenfield & Sternbach, 1972). On the other hand, recent work by Schwartz (1975), involving depressives and normals, demonstrated differential physiological response patterns associated with various emotions. The appropriateness of an emotional specificity theory in the etiology of migraines requires additional data assessing the patterning of cephalic artery reactivity and other autonomic responses to emotions (Adams et al., 1980).

The second approach, which has received much attention, is the delineation of the *personality characteristics* of migraineurs. Goodell (1975) provided a description of the typical "migraine personality."

> The elaboration of a pattern of meticulous perfectionism for dealing with feelings of insecurity begins early in childhood. The individual with migraine aims to gain approval by doing *more than* and better than his fellows through application and hard work and to gain security by holding to a stable environment and a given system of excellent performance, even at high cost of energy. This brings increasing responsibility and admiration, but gains little love, and greater resentment at the pace he feels obligated to maintain. Then the tension associated with repeated frustration, sustained resentment, and growing anxiety is often followed by prostrating fatigue, the setting in which the migraine occurs (p. 159).

Information concerning the migraine personality has been derived primarily from clinical interview. More controlled work has compared migraineurs with nonheadache and other type of headache controls, on the basis of responses on the Rorschach test, the Minnesota Multiphasic Personality Inventory, the Cornell Medical Index, the Symptom Checklist 90-R, the Wechsler Adult Intelligence Scale, the Buss-Durkee Scale of Hostile Attitudes, and the Eysenck Personality Inventory (Harrison, 1975). One problem with the majority of these studies is that they have involved only clinical cases, introducing potential subject error caused by the difference in clients who seek help for headaches and those who do not. Harrison (1975) concluded that migraineurs do not differ from normals or from headache controls on intelligence, and results on the other measures are inconclusive and contradictory.

Even if it were possible to find trait characteristics which differentiate migraineurs from other groups, it would be difficult to determine whether the personality and life-style led to the head pain or the head pain led to differences in personality and life-style. It may be that it is more appropriate to view the personality characteristics as extraclassificatory attributes of the migraine rather than as defining characteristics themselves (Zigler & Phillips, 1961). If it is, indeed, an aberrant vascular system which leads to the migraine, specific personality styles may interact differentially with the vasculature to effect different migraine patterns. There is increasing interest in the assessment of the interaction of situations and personality characteristics in the prediction of behavior (Bem & Allen, 1974; Bem & Funder, 1978). Such an approach to the investigation of precipitants of migraine head pain appears to have merit.

Integration of Physiological and Psychological Theories

Wolff was the initial proponent of the psychobiological approach to migraine headache (Dalessio, 1972). He proposed a genetic predisposition to the development of migraines. The cephalic vasomotor system of the individual was hypothesized to be vulnerable to the effects of stress, becoming dysfunctional, and resulting in vascular headaches, following sufficient amounts of stress. He also agreed with many investigators and proposed that the majority of migraine sufferers have certain attitudes and personality characteristics. A recent self-monitoring study demonstrated that "environmental stress" precipitated 54% of the migraine episodes, lending support for the *psychological stress theory* (Henryk-Gutt & Rees, 1973); however, 46% of the episodes were not identified as resulting from stress. It does appear that the vasculature of the migraineur is more labile and reactive than other organ systems. The relationship between various eliciting stimuli (physical or psychological) and reactivity of the BVP remains confusing, however, and requires further investigation.

An area of psychophysiological research of possible value to the investigation of migraine phenomena is the *response specificity theory* (Lacey & Lacey, 1958). This theory assumes that human physiological systems are organized in an orderly and hierarchical fashion, such that one system is more reactive to physical and psychological stimuli than are other systems. These patterns of autonomic reactivity vary among individuals. In this framework, it would be hypothesized that the migraineur exhibits greatest autonomic reactivity in the vasomotor system, particularly the temporal arteries; constriction and dilation of the temporal arteries by some type of conditioning or shaping procedure causes the arteries to become hyper- and hyporesponsive to a variety of internal and external cues. There is currently no evidence for a response specificity theory of migraines, although an investigation of this possibility is currently in progress (Sturgis, 1979).

The specificity of the autonomic response pattern may result from environmental conditioning, genetic factors, or an interaction of both. The implication of this theory is that the headache may result from a number of diverse internal or external stimuli, but the overall pattern of reactivity would be similar across individuals, while the precipitants of the reactivity would be specific to the individual. The migraine headache may result not only from stress, but also from exposure to novel stimuli. The migraine response appears similar to the orienting response and the defensive response, in that both have characteristics of vaso-constriction and/or vasodilation (Hare, 1972; Sokolov, 1963). The orienting response typically leads to dilation in the cephalic vasculature, coupled with constriction in the digital areas. The defensive reaction encompasses vasocon-striction of both areas. A recent study suggested these responses are atypical in migraine subjects (Cohen, 1978). Further research relating the response to novel or stressful stimuli and determining the nature of triggering stimuli would be useful. Analysis of situation, by person and by physiological response inter-actions, seems to be the appropriate way in which to gain information concern-ing the nature of the migraine response.

Current Status of Research

Interest in the mechanisms of head pain decreased in the 1960s but increased during the 1970s, as more interdisciplinary work is being conducted. Although there is some evidence that aids in our understanding of the process of the migraine phenomenon, more recent studies have posed problems in achieving such understanding. For example, Bakal and Kaganov (1977) found evidence that migraineurs have higher levels of EMG activity than do muscle-contraction individuals. Sovak, Kunzel, Sternbach, & Dalessio (1976) found evidence of both vasoconstriction and vasodilation in the first, constrictive phase and have hypothesized that some individuals are constrictors, while others are dilators. They also provided evidence creating difficulties with Wolff's conceptu-alization of the external arteries being more directly involved with the headache phenomenon. Thus, it appears that replication of many of the classic studies in headache is needed.

Another problem, which needs careful consideration, is the assessment of migraines. The definition of a migraine headache varies significantly across studies, and this variability makes it very difficult to determine the population examined. Careful reporting of the headache description, frequency, duration, intensity, response to medication, and physiological data obtained during the headache and nonheadache state would be helpful. It also appears important to teach the client to discriminate different types of head pain which might be experienced, so he or she can provide the therapist with relevant information.

An encouraging trend is the increasing acceptance of the notion that basic research and applied research are necessary for understanding migraines. The advent of the single-case design has made it possible to test models of headache as well as investigate relevant treatment procedures (Sturgis, Tollison, & Adams, 1978). At present, it appears that an interdisciplinary or systems approach to the response mechanisms involved in migraines will lead to more valid models of the etiology of chronic migraines.

MODIFICATION OF MIGRAINE

Analogous to the biological and psychological theories of migraine etiology, most treatment approaches to the modification of migraine activity are either medical or psychological in nature. A recent review of treatment efficacy has indicated that the migraine literature is plagued with problems of inadequate definitions, poor designs, and unreliable indices of improvement. Because of the difficulty in assessing outcome, the effectiveness of most treatment techniques is questionable (Adams et al., 1980).

Medical Interventions

Several drugs are used in migraine treatment. The categories of drugs include those designed to cause vasoconstriction, those that inhibit serotonin action, adrenergic blocking agents which prevent vasodilation by acting on the blood vessel receptors, and drugs designed to prevent the depletion of vasoactive amines (Adams et al., 1980). Vasoactive drugs (that is, ergot compounds) are used to provide symptomatic relief by initiating vasoconstriction and interrupting the migraine cycle. Other drugs are used because of the prophylactic characteristics which inhibit serotonin action.

Friedman and Merritt (1957) presented data questioning the efficacy of drug intervention. A total of 2,511 migraineurs were investigated. Forty-six percent of those taking active medications and 25% of those taking placebo medication demonstrated symptomatic relief. Ergot plus caffeine, a vasoconstrictor, was most effective (83% relief). Similar data were presented for 1,644 migraineurs receiving prophylactic treatment. Fifty-four percent of the patients using active medications and 50% of those receiving placebo medications showed some improvement. There are a number of contraindications and serious side effects associated with chronic usage of such drugs as the ergot compounds ("AMA Drug Evaluation," 1972; Medina & Diamond, 1976).

Sedatives and tranquilizers have been used in the treatment of migraine in an attempt to lower the state of arousal of the autonomic nervous system. In general, the efficacy of this approach has not been well documented (Adams et al., 1980).

Additional medical approaches to the management of migraine include surgery, acupressure, and mild electrical stimulation. The surgical procedures employed include trigeminal tractotomy, which attempts to eliminate pain by sectioning the sensory roots of the trigeminal nerve (Olivercrona, 1947); carotidectomy (Lance et al., 1967), which involves the removal of the carotid artery to eliminate vasodilation; and cryosurgery on the cranial branches of the carotid

(Cook, 1973). Each of these procedures has severe side effects, including permanent facial analgesia, paralysis, visual disturbances, and loss of olfactory sensations.

Mild electrical stimulation for long durations was used by Howeler, de Munnick, and Boertien (1973) in the treatment of migraines. Fifty-four percent of the individuals showed some improvement, much of which was only slight. Thus, one concludes that there are no nondrug treatment procedures which have been demonstrated to be effective and practical in the treatment of migraine.

Psychological Interventions

Attempts to modify migraine headaches can be directed toward several levels of activity. The migraine headache cycle includes a minimum of three levels of activity, which are depicted in Figure 12.1. The first level of headache activity includes both internal and external *eliciting stimuli*. The nature of the stimuli which lead to headaches is ambiguous, as discussed in an earlier section. Potential external stimuli which are related to migraine activity include glare, flickering lights, noise, and the intake of food or drinks containing tyramine, sodium nitrite, and monosodium glutamate. Internal stimuli include emotional

FIGURE 12.1
Migraine Response and Intervention Levels

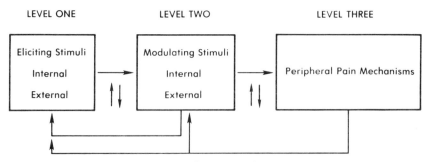

Feedback Mechanisms of Therapies

states, reactions to fatigue and stress, and changes in serotonin, hormonal, and histamine activity.

The second level of headache activity includes *modulating variables*, defined as states of the organism or the environment which amplify or attenuate the input from the eliciting stimuli. As is the case with the eliciting stimuli, the modulating variables may be either internal or external in nature. Internal modulating variables refer to the state of the organism at the time of stimulation. Genetic vasomotor predisposition and the level of vasomotor and overall arousal of the individual are important internal modulating variables, while the environmental stressors and support systems are important external modulating variables.

The final level of the headache cycle concerns the states of the *peripheral pain mechanisms*, which are directly related to the headache. For the migraine phenomenon, the state of vasodilation of the artery and the degree of humoral inflammation surrounding the arterial wall are the relevant pain mechanisms. The role of electromyographic involvement in the migraine phenomenon is currently unknown.

The various psychological interventions may be viewed as intervening at different levels in the migraine cycle. A discussion of the various treatments and the level at which the intervention is hypothesized to be effective follows.

Eliciting Stimuli

Treatments directed at external eliciting stimuli are lacking in the psychological literature. Self-monitoring of headache activity may be helpful in the identification of such stimuli. Once these variables are identified, self-control procedures, which lead to avoidance of the external stimuli, appear warranted.

Treatments directed toward internal eliciting stimuli have been more thoroughly studied. The most commonly-used treatment procedures include procedures designed to alter the emotional state of the organism (that is, insight psychotherapy, assertiveness training, and desensitization) and procedures designed to modify the life-style of the individual. In a controlled single-case study, Lambley (1976) investigated the effects of assertiveness training and dynamic psychotherapy (level 1 interventions) on headache activity. Assertiveness training was accompanied by a 59% decrease in headache frequency, while the addition of psychotherapy was accompanied by a further decrease of 29%. At five months, the individual was headache free; at nine months, however, she reported an occasional headache.

Modulating Variables

No studies to date have systematically examined the effects of modification of the external stressors or support systems, which are level 2 variables. A number of studies, however, have examined the role of internal modulating variables, especially the role of autonomic overarousal of the organism, in the migraine phenomenon. Techniques which have been used to lower the level of autonomic overreactivity include hypnosis (Anderson, Basker, & Dalton, 1976; Graham, 1975; Kroger, 1963), autogenic training (Luthe & Schultz, 1970), occipital EEG biofeedback (Gannon & Sternbach, 1971), relaxation (Blanchard, Theobald, Williamson, Silver, & Brown, 1978; Hay & Madders, 1973; Lutker, 1971), thermal feedback (Blanchard et al., 1978; Johnson & Turin, 1975; Mullinix, Norton, Hack, & Fishman, 1978; Sargent, Walters, & Green, 1973; Turin & Johnson, 1976), and EMG biofeedback (Bild & Adams, 1980; Feuerstein, Adams, & Beiman, 1976; Sturgis et al., 1978).

A representative study of each treatment technique will be discussed in this section. Anderson et al. (1976) conducted a controlled group outcome study involving forty-seven patients, which compared the effects of hypnotherapy and a placebo medication. Subjects in the hypnotherapy group received a minimum of six sessions. Headache frequency for the experimental group evidenced an 89% decline, while the control group demonstrated a 9% decrease. At a one-year follow-up, 43% of the subjects in the hypnosis group were asymptomatic, while only 12% of the placebo group were headache free.

Autogenic training was used in the treatment of migraines by Luthe and Schultz (1970). These investigators reported use of the technique in two anecdotal case studies. The autogenic process involved self-relaxation and self-instructions memorized and recited by the client to achieve general relaxation and feelings of warmth in the extremities. Baseline data for the subject were not provided, but the client was asymptomatic at the end of treatment and remained symptom free at a three-year follow-up.

Relaxation training has been used as a treatment method or adjunct treatment procedure for a number of clients. Blanchard et al. (1978) presented a controlled group outcome study comparing Jacobsonian relaxation training, temperature biofeedback, and a waiting list control group. Thirty patients completed the six-week treatment project. Individuals in the two treatment groups were seen twice a week for twelve sessions. Temperature biofeedback for hand-warming was combined with autogenic training. This procedure is theoretically associated with decreased sympathetic activity, digital vasodilation, and cephalic vasoconstriction. In the relaxation procedure, clients were trained to lower overall tension through a muscle tension-release cycle involving sixteen muscle groups. Instructions and suggestions of looseness, heaviness, and warmth were interposed between exercises. For both treatment groups, the individuals were encouraged to practice the procedures at home twice a day.

Results indicated that both treatment procedures effected a significant improvement in headache activity relative to the waiting list group. At the termination of treatment, the relaxation group appeared superior to the temperature biofeedback group; at three month follow-up, however, there was no difference between groups.

Temperature biofeedback has been studied by a number of investigators. Turin and Johnson (1976) employed a multiple baseline design in assessing the question of expectancy effects in temperature feedback. Three of seven subjects were initially trained to lower rather than raise hand temperature. Subjects were allowed to devise their own means for temperature change. Temperature feedback directed at hand cooling failed to reduce migraine attacks. One individual actually reported an increase in migraine activity. Seven subjects were then taught to increase hand temperature during six to fourteen weeks of sessions held twice a week. All subjects demonstrated substantial improvement in headache activity following training.

Three recent studies question the basis for thermal feedback. Mullinix et al. (1978) employed skin temperature biofeedback in the treatment of eleven migraineurs. All subjects were told that the effectiveness of temperature biofeedback was being investigated; they were also told that some patients would receive altered feedback at times. The experimental group received true auditory feedback, while the control group received a similar signal independent of skin temperature changes and controlled by the investigator. Results showed that the experimental group increased digital skin temperature significantly more than the control group. Both groups, however, showed similar improvement in headache activity, thus implicating a nonphysiological effect in the amelioration of migraine head pain.

Werbach and Sandweiss (1978) employed biofeedback-assisted relaxation training with thirty-seven migraine patients. Frontalis EMG measures, digital skin temperature, and skin conductance measures were taken, and analog biofeedback was continuously provided by utilizing signals derived from one of the three targeted variables. Selection of the variable for feedback was made during each session and was typically the variable with the highest activation level. Other relaxation procedures, such as progressive muscle relaxation, meditative mantras, and autogenic phrases were used. Results indicated that 73% of the subjects were rated as improved following treatment. No significant correlation, however, was found between temperature gain scores across sessions and treatment outcome. Again, results indicate that the ability to warm the hands is not related to changes in migraine activity.

Sovak, Kunzel, Sternbach, and Dalessio (1976) investigated the relationships between superficial temporal, supraorbital, and digital blood volume pulse during volitional and externally caused increases in hand temperature. Five normal and ten migraine clients were tested. All subjects were taught autogenic relaxation and were given temperature feedback. All but two migraineurs mastered the techniques. Both normals and improved migraineurs demonstrated decreases in supraorbital responses with volitional hand temperature increases. The superficial temporal artery showed vasoconstriction for only the normal subjects and not the migraineurs. There was a tendency toward bradycardia in normals and improved migraineurs, while the unimproved migraineurs evidenced no change in heart rate. With digital heat applied, all normal subjects demonstrated increased pulse volume in the supraorbital and temporal arterial beds; the degree and direction of the response varied for the migraineurs. Using Doppler ultrasonography, the investigators found that in normals, volitionally induced increases in finger pulse volume coincided with decreased blood flow in the supraorbital and temporal arteries. The skin temperature changes, however, were found to occur after a substantial lag period. Thus, the authors concluded that skin temperature is an inaccurate indicator of skin perfusion. The information given to the patient is considerably delayed and of questionable efficiency in learning the volitional vasodilation.

The use of electromyographic feedback in the treatment of migraine headache has shown mixed results. Feuerstein and Adams (1977) and Sturgis et al. (1978) found EMG biofeedback to be ineffective in reducing migraine headache activity but effective in reducing muscle-contraction headache activity. Bild and Adams (1980), however, found the procedure to be more effective than self-monitoring in reducing migraine activity. The EMG biofeedback was inferior to procedures used to alter the state of the vascular tonus, that is, the peripheral pain mechanism (level 3 intervention).

Two studies have compared interventions involving level 1 and level 2 treatments. Mitchell and Mitchell (1971) compared interventions at levels 1 and 2 to an intervention at level 2 alone. One group received a combination of muscle relaxation training (level 2), desensitization (level 1), and assertiveness training (level 1), while a second group received only muscle relaxation training. Their results showed significantly higher ratings of headache relief in the more comprehensive program. The authors concluded that, although treatment designed to modify the overreactivity of the individual is useful, it provides only limited effectiveness. Mitchell and Mitchell asserted that effective treatment should involve examination, isolation, and intervention at earlier stages in the migraine cycle.

A subsequent study by Mitchell and White (1977) demonstrated the usefulness of behavioral self-monitoring of headache activity, progressive muscle relaxation (level 2), and self-desensitization (level 1). A second group received additional self-management training (assertiveness training, thought stopping, and rational thinking) (level 1). Greater reductions of headache activity were noted in the more comprehensive program.

In recent years several studies have investigated the effectiveness of treatment targeting the peripheral pain mechanisms of migraine headaches (level 3). These treatments attempt to modify or recondition the cephalic cardiovascular overreactivity implicated as the pain mechanism of the migraine (Dalessio, 1972). The procedure attempts to attenuate sympathetic nervous system activity, thus decreasing the blood flow to the cephalic arteries. The blood volume pulse training involves monitoring and feedback of cephalic blood volume pulse, an index of vasoconstriction and/or vasodilation.

Biofeedback treatment of migraines using BVP feedback was first demonstrated by Friar and Beatty (1976). One group received training in vasoconstriction of extracranial arteries, while a control group was given feedback for vasoconstriction of digital arteries. At the completion of eight sessions, all subjects were given a session designed to assess the ability to voluntarily control cephalic vasomotor activity without feedback. All subjects trained in cephalic vasoconstriction demonstrated voluntary control, while those trained in digital vasoconstriction failed to demonstrate cephalic vasoconstriction. Comparisons of pre- and postheadache records showed the group trained in cephalic vaso-constriction was significantly improved, while stable rates of migraine activity were observed in the digital controls.

Sturgis et al. (1978) investigated the effectiveness of BVP and EMG bio-feedback in two subjects with combined migraine-muscle-contraction headaches. A multiple baseline design across subjects and responses indicated that control of the physiological responses was specific to the type of feedback given. The headache activity was also feedback specific, with decreases in migraine head-ache associated with BVP feedback and decreases in muscle-contraction headache associated with EMG feedback. Similar results have been found by Bild and Adams (1980); Feuerstein and Adams (1977), and Feuerstein et al. (1977).

Treatment Summary

Pharmacologic treatment for the elimination of migraines has been demon-strated to be moderately effective, while prophylactic treatment seems less effective. While the efficiency of controlling migraines with drug treatment is well documented, this form of treatment is undesirable, or, in rare cases, danger-ous for some individuals. Psychological interventions have received increasing attention, and the few controlled studies have yielded encouraging results. Treatments may be directed at the eliciting stimuli, the moderating variables, and/or the peripheral pain mechanisms. To date, no particular level of inter-vention has been found to be maximally effective. Thorough, three-channel assessment and multiple baseline treatment strategies will be helpful in the determination of which treatment(s) is/are most effective with which particu-lar patients.

CONCLUSIONS

There are several critical problems existent in the literature on the migraine phenomenon. The classification criteria are ambiguous; thus, investigators are faced with a muddled state of affairs when attempting to interpret the literature. Until one can reliably classify phenomena, the proposed mechanisms of head pain cannot be determined. Collaborative, interdisciplinary research investi-gating the nature of pain precipitants and moderating factors, as well as their internal and external consequences, should help to clarify important issues concerning migraine. We are faced with a number of isolated facts concerning headache. Careful, controlled, systematic research is needed if these facts are to become valuable in the understanding and treatment of this disorder.

REFERENCES

Adams, H. E., Feuerstein, M., & Fowler, J. L. The migraine headache: A review of parameters, theories, and interventions. *Psychological Bulletin*, 1980, *87*, 217-237.

Ad Hoc Committee on the Classification of Headache. Classification of headache. *Neurology*, 1962, *12*, 378-380.

Alexander, F. *Psychosomatic medicine*. New York: Norton, 1950.

AMA drug evaluation. Chicago: American Medical Association, 1971.

Anderson, J. A. D., Basker, M. A., & Dalton, R. Migraine and hypnotherapy. *International Journal of Clinical and Experimental Hypnosis*, 1976, *23*, 48-58.

Anthony, M., & Lance, J. W. The role of serotonin in migraine. In J. Pearce (Ed.), *Modern topics in migraine*. London: Heineman, 1975.

Appenzeller, O. Monoamines, headache, and behavior. In O. Appenzeller (Ed.), *Pathogenesis and treatment of headache*. New York: Spectrum, 1976.

Bakal, D. A. Headache: A biopsychological perspective. *Psychological Bulletin*, 1975, *82*, 369-383.

Bakal, D. A., & Kaganov, I. A. Muscle contraction and migraine headache: Psychophysiologic comparison. *Headache*, 1977, *17*, 208-215.

Bem, D. J., & Allen, A. On predicting some of the people some of the time: The search for cross-situational consistencies in behavior. *Psychological Review*, 1974, *81*, 506-520.

Bem, D. J., & Funder, D. C. Predicting more of the people more of the time: Assessing the personality of situations. *Psychological Review*, 1978, *85*, 485-501.

Bild, R., & Adams, H. E. Modification of migraine headaches by cephalic blood volume pulse and EMG biofeedback. *Journal of Consulting and Clinical Psychology*, 1980, *48*, 51-57.

Blanchard, E. B., Theobald, D. E., Williamson, D. A., Silver, B. V., & Brown, D. A. Temperature biofeedback in the treatment of migraine headaches. *Archives of General Psychiatry*, 1978, *35*, 581-588.

Broden, M., Hall, R. V., & Mitts, B. The effect of self-recording on the classroom behavior of two eighth-grade students. *Journal of Applied Behavior Analysis*, 1971, *4*, 191-199.

Ciminero, A. R., Nelson, R. O., & Lipinski, D. P. Self-monitoring procedures. In A. R. Ciminero, K. S. Calhoun, & H. E. Adams (Eds.), *Handbook of behavioral assessment*. New York: Wiley-Interscience, 1977.

Cohen, M. J. Psychophysiological studies of headache: Is there similarity between migraine and muscle contraction headaches? *Headache*, 1978, *18*, 188-196.

Cook, N. Cryosurgery of migraine. *Headache*, 1973, *12*, 143-150.

Craig, K. D., & Lowery, J. H. Heart rate components of conditioned vicarious autonomic responses. *Journal of Personality and Social Psychology*, 1969, *11*, 381-387.

Craig, K. D., & Weiss, S. M. Vicarious influences on pain-threshold determinations. *Journal of Personality and Social Psychology*, 1971, *19*, 53-59.

Curran, D. A., Hinterberger, H., & Lance, J. W. Methysergide. In A. P. Friedman (Ed.), *Research and clinical studies in headache: An international review* (Vol. 1). New York: Karger, 1976.

Dalessio, D. J. *Wolff's headache and other head pain*. New York: Oxford University Press, 1972.

Dalessio, D. J. Disorders of immune mechanisms and headache. In O. Appenzeller (Ed.), *Pathogenesis and treatment of headache*. New York: Spectrum, 1976.

Dexter, J., & Riley, T. Studies in nocturnal migraine. *Headache*, 1975, *15*, 51-62.

Diamond, S., Dalessio, D. J., Graham, J. R., & Medina, J. L. (Eds.). *Vasoactive substances relevant to migraine*. Springfield, Ill.: Charles C. Thomas, 1975.

Epstein, L. H. Psychophysiological measurement in assessment. In M. Hersen & A. S. Bellack (Eds.), *Behavioral assessment: A practical handbook*. Oxford: Pergamon Press, 1976.

Fanchamps, A. The role of humoral mediators in migraine headache. *Canadian Journal of Neurological Sciences*, 1974, *1*, 189-195.

Feuerstein, M., & Adams, H. E. Cephalic vasomotor feedback in the modification of migraine headache. *Biofeedback and Self-Regulation*, 1977, *2*, 241-253.

Feuerstein, M., Adams, H. E., & Beiman, I. Cephalic vasomotor and electromyographic feedback in the treatment of combined muscle contraction and migraine headaches in a geriatric case. *Headache*, 1976, *16*, 232-237.

Fordyce, W. *Behavioral methods for chronic pain and illness.* St. Louis: C. V. Mosby, 1976.

Fordyce, W. E., Fowler, R., Lehmann, J., Dellateur, B., Sand, P., & Trieschmann, R. Operant conditioning in the treatment of chronic clinical pain. *Archives of Physical Medicine and Rehabilitation,* 1973, *954,* 399-408.

Friar, L. R., & Beatty, J. Migraine: Management by trained control of vasocon-striction. *Journal of Consulting and Clinical Psychology,* 1976, *44,* 46-53.

Friedman, A. P. *Chronic recurring headache: A multimedia learning system.* East Hanover, N. J.: Sandoz Pharmaceuticals, 1973.

Friedman, A. P., & Merritt, H. H. Treatment of headache. *Journal of the American Medical Association,* 1957, *163,* 1111-1117.

Friedman, A. P., von Storch, T. J. C., & Merritt, H. H. Migraine and tension headaches: A clinical study of two thousand cases. *Neurology,* 1954, *4,* 773-778.

Gannon, L., & Sternbach, R. A. Alpha enhancement as a treatment for pain: A case study. *Journal of Behavior Therapy and Experimental Psychiatry,* 1971, *2,* 209-213.

Goodell, H. Evolution of the concept of neurokinin in migraine headache. In S. Diamond, D. J. Dalessio, J. R. Graham, & J. L. Medina (Eds.), *Vaso-active substances relevant to migraine.* Springfield, Ill.: Charles C. Thomas, 1975.

Graham, J. R., & Wolff, H. G. Mechanism of migraine headache and action of ergotamine tartrate. *Archives of Neurology and Psychiatry,* 1938, *38,* 737-739.

Graham, W. F. Hypnotic treatment for migraine headaches. *International Journal of Clinical and Experimental Hypnosis,* 1975, *23,* 165-171.

Greenfield, N. W., & Sternbach, R. A. (Eds.). *Handbook of psychophysiology.* New York: Holt, Rinehart & Winston, 1972.

Hare, R. D. Cardiovascular components of orienting and defensive responses. *Psychophysiology,* 1972, *9,* 606-614.

Harrison, R. H. Psychological testing in headache: A review. *Headache,* 1975, *15,* 177-185.

Hay, K. M., & Madders, J. Methods of management of fatigue and tension. In J. N. Cumings (Ed.), *Background to migraine: Fifth migraine symposium.* New York: Springer-Verlag, 1973.

Henryk-Gutt, R., & Rees, W. L. Psychological aspects of migraine. *Journal of Psychosomatic Research*, 1973, *17*, 141-153.

Howeler, M., de Munnick, D., & Boertien, A. H. The effects of mild electro-stimulation on migraine and tension headache. *International Mental Health Research Newsletter*, 1973, *15*, 11-13.

Johnson, W. G., & Turin, A. Biofeedback treatment of migraine headache: A systematic case study. *Behavior Therapy*, 1975, *6*, 394-397.

Kaneko, A., Shiraishi, J., Inaoka, H., Furukawa, T., & Sekiyama, M. Intra- and extracerebral hemodynamics of migraineous headache. In R. Greene (Ed.), *Current concepts in migraine research*. New York: Raven Press, 1978.

Kroger, W. S. Hypnotherapeutic management of headache. *Headache*, 1963, *3*, 50-62.

Kudrow, L. Hormones, pregnancy, and migraine. In O. Appenzeller (Ed.), *Pathogenesis and treatment in headache*. New York: Spectrum, 1976.

Lacey, J. I., & Lacey, B. C. Verification and extension of the principle of autonomic response-stereotypy. *American Journal of Psychology*, 1958, *71*, 51-73.

Lambley, P. The use of assertive training and psychodynamic insight in the treatment of migraine headache: A case study. *The Journal of Nervous and Mental Disease*, 1976, *163*, 61-64.

Lance, J. W. *The mechanism and management of headache*. London: Butterworth, 1973.

Lance, J. W., & Anthony, M. Some clinical aspects of migraine: A prospective survey of 500 patients. *Archives of Neurology*, 1966, *915*, 356-361.

Lance, J. W., Anthony, M., & Gonski, A. Serotonin, the carotid body, and cranial vessels in migraine. *Archives of Neurology*, 1967, *16*, 553-558.

Luthe, W., & Schultz, J. H. *Autogenic therapy: Research and theory* (Vol. IV). New York: Grune & Stratton, 1970.

Lutker, E. R. Treatment of migraine headache by conditioned relaxation: A case study. *Behavior Therapy*, 1971, *2*, 592-593.

Medina, J. L., & Diamond, S. Drug dependency in patients with chronic headache. *Headache*, 1977, *17*, 12-14.

Mitchell, D. R., & Mitchell, D. M. Migraine: An exploratory treatment application of programmed behaviour therapy techniques. *Journal of Psychosomatic Research*, 1971, *15*, 137-157.

Mitchell, K. R., & White, R. G. Behavioral self-management: An application to the problem of migraine headaches. *Behavior Therapy*, 1977, *98*, 213-221.

Mullinix, J. M., Norton, B. M., Hack, S., & Fishman, M. A. Skin temperature biofeedback and migraine. *Headache*, 1978, *17*, 242-244.

O'Brien, M. D. Cerebral blood flow changes in the migraine headache. *Headache*, 1971, *10*, 139-143.

O'Brien, M. D. The haemodynamics of migraine: A review. *Headache*, 1973, *12*, 160-162.

Ogden, H. D. Headache studies: Statistical data. *Journal of Allergy*, 1952, *23*, 58-75.

Olivercrona, H. Notes on the surgical treatment of migraine. *Acta Medica Scandinavica*, 1947, *196* (Suppl.), 229-238.

Pearce, J. (Ed.). *Modern topics in migraine*. London: Heineman, 1975.

Ray, B. S., & Wolff, H. G. Studies on pain. "Spread of pain": Evidence on the site of spread within the neuroaxis of effects of painful stimulation. *Archives of Neurology and Psychiatry*, 1945, *53*, 257.

Ryan, R. E., & Ryan, R. E. *Headache and head pain: Diagnosis and treatment*. St. Louis: C. V. Mosby, 1978.

Sargent, J. D., Walters, E. D., & Green, E. E. Psychosomatic self-regulation of migraine headaches. *Seminars in Psychiatry*, 1973, *5*, 415-423.

Schwartz, G. E. Biofeedback, self-regulation, and the patterning of physiological processes. *American Scientist*, 1975, *63*, 314-324.

Selby, G., & Lance, J. W. Observations of 500 cases of migraine and allied vascular headache. *Journal of Neurology, Neurosurgery, and Psychiatry*, 1960, *23*, 230-232.

Sicuteri, F. Headache as possible expression of deficiency of brain 5-hydroxytryptamine (central denervation supersensitivity). *Headache*, 1972, *12*, 69-72.

Sjaastad, O. Is histamine of significance in the pathogenesis of headache. In S. Diamond, D. J. Dalessio, J. R. Graham, & J. L. Medina (Eds.), *Vasoactive substances relevant to migraine*. Springfield, Ill.: Charles C. Thomas, 1975.

Skinhøj, E. Hemodynamic studies within the brain during migraine. *Archives of Neurology*, 1973, *29*, 95-98.

Sokolov, E. N. *Perception and the conditioned reflex.* New York: Macmillan, 1963.

Sovak, M., Kunzel, M., Sternbach, R. A., & Dalessio, D. J. Is volitional manipulation of hemodynamics a valid rationale for biofeedback therapy of migraine. *Headache*, 1976, *17*, 197-202.

Spira, P. J., Mylecharane, E. J., & Lance, J. W. The effects of humoral agents and antimigraine drugs on the cranial circulation of the monkey. *Research and Clinical Studies on Headache*, 1976, *4*, 37-75.

Sturgis, E. T. *Lability and reactivity in the headache response.* Unpublished manuscript, University of Georgia, 1979.

Sturgis, E. T., Tollison, C. D., & Adams, H. E. Modification of combined migraine-muscle-contraction headaches using BVP and EMG feedback. *Journal of Applied Behavior Analysis*, 1978, *911*, 215-233.

Tunis, M. M., & Wolff, H. G. Analysis of cranial artery pulse waves in patients with vascular headache of the migraine type. *American Journal of Medical Sciences*, 1952, *224*, 565-568.

Turin, A., & Johnson, W. G. Biofeedback therapy for migraine headaches. *Archives of General Psychiatry*, 1976, *33*, 517-519.

Walker, C. H. Migraine and its relationship to hypertension. *British Medical Journal*, 1959, *2*, 1430-1433.

Waters, W. E., & O'Connor, P. J. Prevalence of migraine. *Journal of Neurology, Neurosurgery, and Psychiatry*, 1975, *38*, 613-616.

Welch, E. M. A., Hashi, K., & Meyer, J. S. Cerebrovascular response to intracarotid injection of serotonin before and after middle cerebral artery occlusion. *Journal of Neurology, Neurosurgery, and Psychiatry*, 1973, *36*, 724-735.

Welch, K. M. A., Spira, P. J., Knowles, L., & Lance, J. W. Simultaneous measurement of internal and external carotid blood flow in the monkey. *Neurology*, 1974, *24*, 450-452.

Werbach, M. R., & Sandweiss, J. H. Peripheral temperatures of migraineurs undergoing relaxation training. *Headache*, 1978, *18*, 211-214.

Whitty, C. W. M., & Hockaday, J. M. Migraine: A follow-up study of 92 patients. *British Medical Journal*, 1968, *91*, 735-736.

Zeigler, D. K. Epidemiology and genetics of migraine. In O. Appenzeller (Ed.), *Pathogenesis and treatment of headache.* New York: Spectrum, 1976.

Zeigler, D. K., Hassanein, R., & Hassanein, K. Headache syndromes suggested by factor analysis of symptom variables in a headache prone population. *Journal of Chronic Disease*, 1972, *25*, 353-363.

Zigler, E., & Phillips, L. Psychiatric diagnosis: A critique. *Journal of Abnormal and Social Psychology*, 1961, *63*, 607-618.

NAME INDEX

SUBJECT INDEX